DRAMA
for Students

for DRAMA Students

Presenting Analysis, Context and Criticism on Commonly Studied Dramas

Volume 2

David Galens, Lynn Spampinato, Editors

Barbara Dubb, Farmington/Farmington Hills School District, Michigan, Advisor

Marie Slotnick, English Department Chair, Center Line High School, Center Line, Michigan, Advisor

GALE

DETROIT • LONDON

STAFF

David Galens and Lynn M. Spampinato, *Editors*

Thomas Allbaugh, Craig Bentley, Terry Browne, Christopher Busiel, Stephen Coy, L. M. Domina, John Fiero, Carol L. Hamilton, Erika Kreger, Jennifer Lewin, Sheri Metzger, Daniel Moran, Terry Nienhuis, Bonnie Russell, Arnold Schmidt, William Wiles, Joanne Woolway, *Contributing Writers*

Elizabeth Cranston, Kathleen J. Edgar, Joshua Kondek, Marie Lazzari, Tom Ligotti, Marie Napierkowski, Scot Peacock, Mary Ruby, Diane Telgen, Patti Tippett, Kathleen Wilson, Pam Zuber, *Contributing Editors*

Pamela Wilwerth Aue, *Managing Editor*

Jeffery Chapman, *Programmer/Analyst*

Victoria B. Cariappa, *Research Team Manager*
Michele P. LaMeau, Andy Guy Malonis, Barb McNeil, Gary Oudersluys, Maureen Richards, *Research Specialists*
Julia C. Daniel, Tamara C. Nott, Tracie A. Richardson, Cheryl L. Warnock, *Research Associates*

Susan M. Trosky, *Permissions Manager*
Kimberly F. Smilay, *Permissions Specialist*
Sarah Chesney, *Permissions Associate*
Steve Cusack, Kelly A. Quin, *Permissions Assistants*

Mary Beth Trimper, *Production Director*
Evi Seoud, *Assistant Production Manager*
Shanna Heilveil, *Production Assistant*

Randy Bassett, *Image Database Supervisor*
Mikal Ansari, Robert Duncan, *Imaging Specialists*
Pamela A. Reed, *Photography Coordinator*

Cynthia Baldwin, *Product Design Manager*
Cover design: Michelle DiMercurio, *Art Director*
Page design: Pamela A. E. Galbreath, *Senior Art Director*

∞™ This book is printed on acid-free paper that meets the minimum requirements of American National Standard for Information Sciences—Permanence Paper for Printed Library Materials, ANSI Z39.48-1984.
ISBN 0-7876-1684-2
ISSN applied for and pending
Printed in the United States of America
10 9 8 7 6 5 4 3 2

Table of Contents

The Study of Drama

We study drama in order to learn what meaning others have made of life, to comprehend what it takes to produce a work of art, and to glean some understanding of ourselves. Drama produces in a separate, aesthetic world, a moment of being for the audience to experience, while maintaining the detachment of a reflective observer.

Drama is a representational art, a visible and audible narrative presenting virtual, fictional characters within a virtual, fictional universe. Dramatic realizations may pretend to approximate reality or else stubbornly defy, distort, and deform reality into an artistic statement. From this separate universe that is obviously not "real life" we expect a valid reflection upon reality, yet drama never is mistaken for reality—the methods of theater are integral to its form and meaning. Theater is art, and art's appeal lies in its ability both to approximate life and to depart from it. By presenting its distorted version of life to our consciousness, art gives us a new perspective and appreciation of reality. Although, to some extent, all aesthetic experiences perform this service, theater does it most effectively by creating a separate, cohesive universe that freely acknowledges its status as an art form.

And what is the purpose of the aesthetic universe of drama? The potential answers to such a question are nearly as many and varied as there are plays written, performed, and enjoyed. Dramatic texts can be problems posed, answers asserted, or moments portrayed. Dramas (tragedies as well as comedies) may serve strictly "to ease the anguish of a torturing hour" (as stated in William Shakespeare's *A Midsummer Night's Dream*)—to divert and entertain—or aspire to move the viewer to action with social issues. Whether to entertain or to instruct, affirm or influence, pacify or shock, dramatic art wraps us in the spell of its imaginary world for the length of the work and then dispenses us back to the real world, entertained, purged, as Aristotle said, of pity and fear, and edified—or at least weary enough to sleep peacefully.

It is commonly thought that theater, being an art of performance, must be experienced—that is, seen—in order to be appreciated fully. However, to view a production of a dramatic text is to be limited to a single interpretation of that text—all other interpretations are for the moment closed off, inaccessible. In the process of producing a play, the director, stage designer, and performers interpret and transform the script into a work of art that always departs in some measure from the author's original conception. Novelist and critic Umberto Eco, in his *The Role of the Reader: Explorations in the Semiotics of Texts,* explained, "In short, we can say that every performance offers us a complete and satisfying version of the work, but at the same time makes it incomplete for us, because it cannot simultaneously give all the other artistic solutions which the work may admit."

Thus Laurence Olivier's coldly formal and neurotic film presentation of Shakespeare's *Hamlet* (in which he played the title character as well as directed) shows marked differences from subsequent adaptations. While Olivier's Hamlet is clearly entangled in a Freudian relationship with his mother, Gertrude, he would be incapable of shushing her with the impassioned kiss that Mel Gibson's mercurial Hamlet (in director Franco Zeffirelli's 1990 film) does. Although each of the performances rings true to Shakespeare's text, each is also a mutually exclusive work of art. Also important to consider are the time periods in which each of these films were produced: Olivier made his film in 1948, a time in which overt references to sexuality (especially incest) were frowned upon. Gibson and Zeffirelli made their film in a culture more relaxed and comfortable with these issues. Just as actors and directors can influence the presentation of drama, so too can the time period of the production affect what the audience will see.

A play script is an open text from which an infinity of specific realizations may be derived. Dramatic scripts that are more open to interpretive creativity (such as those of Ntozake Shange and Tomson Highway) actually require the creative improvisation of the production troupe in order to complete the text. Even the most prescriptive scripts (those of Neil Simon, Lillian Hellman, and Robert Bolt, for example), can never fully control the actualization of live performance, and circumstantial events, including the attitude and receptivity of the audience, make every performance a unique event. Thus, while it is important to view a production of a dramatic piece, if one wants to understand a drama fully it is equally important to read the original dramatic text.

The reader of a dramatic text or script is not limited by either the specific interpretation of a given production or by the unstoppable action of a moving spectacle. The reader of a dramatic text may discover the nuances of the play's language, structure, and events at their own pace. Yet studied alone, the author's blueprint for artistic production does not tell the whole story of a play's life and significance. One also needs to assess the play's critical reviews to discover how it resonated to cultural themes at the time of its debut and how the shifting tides of cultural interest have revised its interpretation and impact on audiences. And to do this, one needs to know a little about the culture of the times which produced the play as well as the author who penned it.

Drama for Students supplies this material in a useful compendium for the student of dramatic theater. Covering a range of dramatic works that span from the fifth century B.C. to the 1990s, this book focuses on significant theatrical works whose themes and form transcend the uncertainty of dramatic fads. These are plays that have proven to be both memorable and teachable. *Drama for Students* seeks to enhance appreciation of these dramatic texts by providing scholarly materials written with the secondary and college/university student in mind. It provides for each play a concise summary of the plot and characters as well as a detailed explanation of its themes and techniques. In addition, background material on the historical context of the play, its critical reception, and the author's life help the student to understand the work's position in the chronicle of dramatic history. For each play entry a new work of scholarly criticism is also included, as well as segments of other significant critical works for handy reference. A thorough bibliography provides a starting point for further research.

These inaugural two volumes offer comprehensive educational resources for students of drama. *Drama for Students* is a vital book for dramatic interpretation and a valuable addition to any reference library.

Source: Eco, Umberto, *The Role of the Reader: Explorations in the Semiotics of Texts,* Indiana University Press, 1979.

Carole L. Hamilton
Author and Instructor of English
Cary Academy
Cary, North Carolina

Introduction

Purpose of Drama for Students

The purpose of *Drama for Students* (*DfS*) is to provide readers with a guide to understanding, enjoying, and studying dramas by giving them easy access to information about the work. Part of Gale's "For Students" literature line, *DfS* is specifically designed to meet the curricular needs of high school and undergraduate college students and their teachers, as well as the interests of general readers and researchers considering specific plays. While each volume contains entries on "classic" dramas frequently studied in classrooms, there are also entries containing hard-to-find information on contemporary plays, including works by multicultural, international, and women playwrights.

The information covered in each entry includes an introduction to the play and the work's author; a plot summary, to help readers unravel and understand the events in a drama; descriptions of important characters, including explanation of a given character's role in the drama as well as discussion about that character's relationship to other characters in the play; analysis of important themes in the drama; and an explanation of important literary techniques and movements as they are demonstrated in the play.

In addition to this material, which helps the readers analyze the play itself, students are also provided with important information on the literary and historical background informing each work.

This includes a historical context essay, a box comparing the time or place the drama was written to modern Western culture, a critical overview essay, and excerpts from critical essays on the play. A unique feature of *DfS* is a specially commissioned overview essay on each drama by an academic expert, targeted toward the student reader.

To further aid the student in studying and enjoying each play, information on media adaptations is provided, as well as reading suggestions for works of fiction and nonfiction on similar themes and topics. Classroom aids include ideas for research papers and lists of critical sources that provide additional material on each drama.

Selection Criteria

The titles for each volume of *DfS* were selected by surveying numerous sources on teaching literature and analyzing course curricula for various school districts. Some of the sources surveyed included: literature anthologies; *Reading Lists for College-Bound Students: The Books Most Recommended by America's Top Colleges;* textbooks on teaching dramas; a College Board survey of plays commonly studied in high schools; a National Council of Teachers of English (NCTE) survey of plays commonly studied in high schools; St. James Press's *International Dictionary of Theatre;* and Arthur Applebee's 1993 study *Literature in the Secondary School: Studies of Curriculum and Instruction in the United States.*

Input was also solicited from our expert advisory board (both experienced educators specializing in English), as well as educators from various areas. From these discussions, it was determined that each volume should have a mix of ''classic'' dramas (those works commonly taught in literature classes) and contemporary dramas for which information is often hard to find. Because of the interest in expanding the canon of literature, an emphasis was also placed on including works by international, multicultural, and women playwrights. Our advisory board members—current high school teachers—helped pare down the list for each volume. If a work was not selected for the present volume, it was often noted as a possibility for a future volume. As always, the editor welcomes suggestions for titles to be included in future volumes.

How Each Entry Is Organized

Each entry, or chapter, in *DfS* focuses on one play. Each entry heading lists the full name of the play, the author's name, and the date of the play's first production or publication. The following elements are contained in each entry:

- **Introduction:** a brief overview of the drama which provides information about its first appearance, its literary standing, any controversies surrounding the work, and major conflicts or themes within the work.

- **Author Biography:** this section includes basic facts about the author's life, and focuses on events and times in the author's life that inspired the drama in question.

- **Plot Summary:** a description of the major events in the play, with interpretation of how these events help articulate the play's themes. Subheads demarcate the plays' various acts or scenes.

- **Characters:** an alphabetical listing of major characters in the play. Each character name is followed by a brief to an extensive description of the character's role in the plays, as well as discussion of the character's actions, relationships, and possible motivation.

Characters are listed alphabetically by last name. If a character is unnamed—for instance, the Stage Manager in *Our Town*—the character is listed as ''The Stage Manager'' and alphabetized as ''Stage Manager.'' If a character's first name is the only one given, the name will appear alphabetically by the name.

Variant names are also included for each character. Thus, the nickname ''Babe'' would head the listing for a character in *Crimes of the Heart,* but below that listing would be her less-mentioned married name ''Rebecca Botrelle.''

- **Themes:** a thorough overview of how the major topics, themes, and issues are addressed within the play. Each theme discussed appears in a separate subhead, and is easily accessed through the boldface entries in the Subject/Theme Index.

- **Style:** this section addresses important style elements of the drama, such as setting, point of view, and narration; important literary devices used, such as imagery, foreshadowing, symbolism; and, if applicable, genres to which the work might have belonged, such as Gothicism or Romanticism. Literary terms are explained within the entry, but can also be found in the Glossary.

- **Historical and Cultural Context:** This section outlines the social, political, and cultural climate *in which the author lived and the play was created.* This section may include descriptions of related historical events, pertinent aspects of daily life in the culture, and the artistic and literary sensibilities of the time in which the work was written. If the play is a historical work, information regarding the time in which the play is set is also included. Each section is broken down with helpful subheads.

- **Critical Overview:** this section provides background on the critical reputation of the play, including bannings or any other public controversies surrounding the work. For older plays, this section includes a history of how the drama was first received and how perceptions of it may have changed over the years; for more recent plays, direct quotes from early reviews may also be included.

- **For Further Study:** an alphabetical list of other critical sources which may prove useful for the student. Includes full bibliographical information and a brief annotation.

- **Sources:** an alphabetical list of critical material quoted in the entry, with full bibliographical information.

- **Criticism:** an essay commissioned by *DfS* which specifically deals with the play and is written specifically for the student audience, as well as excerpts from previously published criticism on the work.

In addition, each entry contains the following highlighted sections, set separate from the main text:

- **Media Adaptations:** a list of important film and television adaptations of the play, including source information. The list may also include such variations on the work as audio recordings, musical adaptations, and other stage interpretations.

- **Compare and Contrast Box:** an "at-a-glance" comparison of the cultural and historical differences between the author's time and culture and late twentieth-century Western culture. This box includes pertinent parallels between the major scientific, political, and cultural movements of the time or place the drama was written, the time or place the play was set (if a historical work), and modern Western culture. Works written after the mid-1970s may not have this box.

- **What Do I Read Next?:** a list of works that might complement the featured play or serve as a contrast to it. This includes works by the same author and others, works of fiction and nonfiction, and works from various genres, cultures, and eras.

- **Study Questions:** a list of potential study questions or research topics dealing with the play. This section includes questions related to other disciplines the student may be studying, such as American history, world history, science, math, government, business, geography, economics, psychology, etc.

Other Features

DfS includes "The Study of Drama," a foreword by Carole Hamilton, an educator and author who specializes in dramatic works. This essay examines the basis for drama in societies and what drives people to study such work. Hamilton also discusses how *Drama for Students* can help teachers show students how to enrich their own reading/viewing experiences.

A Cumulative Author/Title Index lists the authors and titles covered in each volume of the *DfS* series.

A Cumulative Nationality/Ethnicity Index breaks down the authors and titles covered in each volume of the *DfS* series by nationality and ethnicity.

A Subject/Theme Index, specific to each volume, provides easy reference for users who may be studying a particular subject or theme rather than a single work. Significant subjects from events to broad themes are included, and the entries pointing to the specific theme discussions in each entry are indicated in **boldface**.

Each entry has several illustrations, including photos of the author, stills from stage productions, and stills from film adaptations.

Citing Drama for Students

When writing papers, students who quote directly from any volume of *Drama for Students* may use the following general forms. These examples are based on MLA style; teachers may request that students adhere to a different style, so the following examples may be adapted as needed.

When citing text from *DfS* that is not attributed to a particular author (i.e., the Themes, Style, Historical Context sections, etc.), the following format should be used in the bibliography section:

"Our Town," *Drama for Students*. Ed. David Galens and Lynn Spampinato. Vol. 1. Detroit: Gale, 1997. 8–9.

When quoting the specially commissioned essay from *DfS* (usually the first piece under the "Criticism" subhead), the following format should be used:

Fiero, John. Essay on "Twilight: Los Angeles, 1992." *Drama for Students*. Ed. David Galens and Lynn Spampinato. Vol. 1. Detroit: Gale, 1997. 8–9.

When quoting a journal or newspaper essay that is reprinted in a volume of *DfS*, the following form may be used:

Rich, Frank. "Theatre: A Mamet Play, 'Glengarry Glen Ross'." *New York Theatre Critics' Review* Vol. 45, No. 4 (March 5, 1984), 5–7; excerpted and reprinted in *Drama for Students*, Vol. 1, ed. David Galens and Lynn Spampinato (Detroit: Gale, 1997), pp. 61–64.

When quoting material reprinted from a book that appears in a volume of *DfS*, the following form may be used:

Kerr, Walter. "The Miracle Worker," in *The Theatre in Spite of Itself* (Simon & Schuster, 1963, 255–57; excerpted and reprinted in *Drama for Students*, Vol. 1, ed. Dave Galens and Lynn Spampinato (Detroit: Gale, 1997), pp. 59–61.

We Welcome Your Suggestions

The editor of *Drama for Students* welcomes your comments and ideas. Readers who wish to suggest dramas to appear in future volumes, or who have other suggestions, are cordially invited to contact the editor. You may contact the editor via E-mail at: **david_galens@gale.com**. Or write to the editor at:

David Galens, *Drama for Students*
Gale Research
835 Penobscot Bldg.
645 Griswold St.
Detroit, MI 48226-4094

Literary Chronology

c. 496 B.C.: Sophocles born in Colonus, Greece, c. 496 B.C.

c. 480 B.C.: Euripides born in Athens, Greece, c. 480 B.C.

442 B.C.: *Antigone* is written as the last work in Sophocles's "Theban Trilogy."

431 B.C.: *Medea* debuts at the Great Dionysia, a festival in Athens, 431 B.C.

430 B.C.: *Oedipus the King,* the second play in Sophocles's Theban Trilogy, is produced at the Great Dionysia of 430 B.C.

c. 406 B.C.: Euripides dies an expatriot in Macedonia, c. 406 B.C.

c. 406 B.C.: Sophocles dies in Athens, Greece, c. 406 B.C.

1564: Christopher Marlowe is born in Canterbury, England, in February of 1564.

1593: Marlowe is killed by a dining companion during a tavern fight, May 30, 1593, in Deptford, England; there is considerable speculation as to whether the murder was a random act or an assassination.

1594: An early version of Marlowe's *Dr. Faustus* is posthumously produced by a theatrical troupe known as the Earl of Nottingham's Men.

1728: The son of a minister, Oliver Goldsmith is born November 10, 1728, in Ballymahon, Ireland.

1773: Goldsmith's *She Stoops to Conquer* debuts in England in 1773.

1774: Goldsmith dies on April 4, 1774, in London, England; he is buried in Temple Church in London, with a monument erected to him in Westminster Abbey.

1828: Henrik Ibsen born March 20, 1828, to Knud and Marichen (Altenburg) Ibsen, in Skien, Norway.

1856: George Bernard Shaw is born on July 26, 1856, to George Carr and Lucinda Elizabeth (Gurly) Shaw, in Dublin, Ireland.

1860: Anton Chekhov is born on January 16, 1860, to Pavel Yegorovitch and Yevgeniya Yakovlevna (Morozov) Chekhov in Taganrog, Russia.

1868: Edmond Rostand is born on April 1, 1868, in Marseilles, France, to Eugene Rostand and his wife.

1879: *A Doll's House* published on December 4, 1879 and first performed in Copenhagen, Denmark, on December 21, 1879.

1888: Eugene O'Neill is born on October 16, 1888, to James and Mary Ellen (Quinlan) O'Neill, in New York City.

1889: George S. Kaufman is born November 16, 1889, to Joseph S. and Nettie Schamberg (Myers) Kaufman, in Pittsburgh, Pennsylvania.

1890: Agatha Christie is born on September 15, 1890, to Frederick Alvah and Clarissa Miller, in Torquay, Devon, England.

1895: Oscar Hammerstein is born on July 12, 1895, to William and Alica Vivian (Nimmo) Hammerstein, in New York City.

1897: Thornton Wilder is born on April 17, 1897, to Amos Parker and Isabella Thornton (Niven) Wilder, in Madison, Wisconsin.

1897: Rostand's *Cyrano de Bergerac* is first produced at the Porte Saint-Martin Theater in Paris, France, on December 28, 1897.

1900: *The Cherry Orchard,* under its original Russian title of *Vishnyovy Sad: Komediya v chetyryokh deystriyakh,* is first produced in Moscow, Russia, at the Moscow Art Theater on January 17, 1900.

1902: Richard Rodgers is born on June 28, 1902, to William Abraham and Mamie (Levy) Rodgers, in New York City.

1904: Chekhov dies of tuberculosis July 2, 1904, in Badenweiler, Germany; he is buried in Moscow, Russia.

1904: Moss Hart is born on October 24, 1904, to Barnett and Lillian (Solomon) Hart in New York City.

1906: Ibsen dies from complications resulting from a series of strokes on May 23, 1906, in Oslo, Norway.

1906: Samuel Beckett is born on April 13, 1906, to William Frank and Mary Jones (Roe) Beckett, in Foxrock, Dublin, Ireland.

1906: Lillian Hellman is born on June 20, 1906, to Max Bernard and Julia (Newhouse) Hellman, in New Orleans, Louisiana.

1911: Tennessee Williams is born on March 26, 1911, to Cornelius Coffin and Edwina (Dakin) Williams, in Columbus, Mississippi.

1914: William Gibson is born on November 13, 1914, to George Irving and Florence (Dore) Gibson, in New York City.

1914: *Pygmalion* is first produced in London, England, at His Majesty's Theatre, April 11, 1914.

1915: Arthur Miller is born on October 17, 1915, to Isidore and Augusta (Barnett) Miller, in New York City.

1915: Jerome Lawrence is born on July 14, 1915, to Samuel and Sarah (Rogen) Lawrence, in Cleveland, Ohio.

1918: Rostand dies on December 2 (one source says December 22), 1918, in Paris, France.

1918: Robert E. Lee is born on October 15, 1918, to Claire Melvin and Elvira (Taft) Lee, in Elyria, Ohio.

1920: Alice Childress is born on October 12, 1920, in Charleston, South Carolina.

1924: Robert Bolt is born on August 15, 1924, to Ralph and Leah (Binnion) Bolt, in Sale, Manchester, England.

1925: Gore Vidal is born on October 3, 1925, to Eugene Luther and Nina (Gore) Vidal, at the U.S. Military Academy, West Point, New York.

1927: Neil Simon is born on July 4, 1927, to Irving and Mamie Simon, in Bronx, New York.

1928: Edward Albee is born on March 12, 1928, probably in Virginia; adopted by Reed A. and Frances (Cotter) Albee.

1930: Lorraine Hansberry is born on May 19, 1930, to Carl Augustus and Nannie (Perry) Hansberry, in Chicago, Illinois.

1936: Eugene O'Neill awarded the Nobel Prize in literature; he is only the second American to receive this honor.

1936: *You Can't Take it with You* is first produced on Broadway at the Booth Theatre, December 14, 1936.

1936: Hart and Kaufman are awarded the Pulitzer for their comedy.

1937: Tom Stoppard is born on July 3, 1937, to Eugene Straussler and Martha Stoppard, in Zlin, Czechoslovakia.

1938: *Our Town* is first produced in Princeton, New Jersey, on January 22, 1938; produced in New York City at the Henry Miller Theatre, February 4, 1938.

1939: Wilder's play receives the Pulitzer Prize despite initially mixed reviews of the drama.

1939: *The Little Foxes* is first produced in New York City at the National Theatre on February 15, 1939.

1944: *The Glass Menagerie* is first produced in Chicago, Illinois, in 1944; the play is produced on Broadway the following year.

1947: Williams's play is first published in 1947; the play has productions staged in both Boston and New York.

1947: Marsha Norman born on September 21, 1947, to Billie Lee and Bertha Mae (Conley) Williams, in Louisville, Kentucky.

1947: David Mamet born on November 30, 1947, to Bernard Morris and Lenore June (Silver) Mamet, in Chicago, Illinois.

1948: Williams's play is awarded the Pulitzer for drama in addition to winning the New York Drama Critics Circle Award.

1948: Ntozake Shange born on October 18, 1948, to Paul T. and Eloise Williams, in Trenton, New Jersey.

1949: *Death of a Salesman* first produced on Broadway at the Morosco Theatre, February 10, 1949.

1949: Miller's play receives the prestigious Pulitzer as well as the New York Drama Critics Circle Award for best play of the year.

1950: Shaw dies November 2, 1950, in Ayot Saint Lawrence, Hertfordshire, England.

1950: Anna Deveare Smith is born on September 18, 1950, to Deveare Young and Anna (Young) Smith, in Baltimore, Maryland.

1951: Rodgers and Hammerstein's *The King and I* makes its debut on Broadway in 1951.

1951: Tomson Highway born on December 6, 1951 (some sources say 1952), in Northwest Manitoba, Canada.

1952: Beginning its record-breaking run, *The Mousetrap* is first produced on the West End of England, at the Ambassadors' Theatre, November 25, 1952; produced Off-Broadway at the Maidman Playhouse in 1960.

1952: Beth Henley born on May 8, 1952, to Charles Boyce and Elizabeth Josephine (Becker) Henley, in Jackson, Mississippi.

1953: *Waiting for Godot* is first produced in Paris, France, at Theatre de Babylone, January 5, 1953.

1953: O'Neill dies of pneumonia on November 27, 1953, in Boston, Massachusetts; he is buried December 2, 1953, in Forest Hills Cemetery, Boston.

1954: *A Man for All Seasons* is first broadcast as a radio play by the British Broadcasting Corporation (BBC) in 1954; a televised adaptation airs on BBC-TV in 1957; a full-length play is produced in London in 1960 and in New York the following year.

1955: *Inherit the Wind* is first produced on Broadway at the National Theatre (now the Nederlander Theatre, also formerly the Billy Rose Theatre), April 21, 1955.

1955: *A Visit to a Small Planet* is produced as a radio play; an expanded edition has its first Broadway production at the Booth Theater on February 7, 1957; the play is adapted by Edmund Beloin and Henry Garson as a film starring Jerry Lewis in 1960.

1956: Following O'Neill's instructions that the play not be produced until after his death, *Long Day's Journey into Night* is first produced in Stockholm, Sweden, at the Kungliga Dramatiska Teatern, February 10, 1956; the play is produced on Broadway at the Helen Hayes Theatre, November 7, 1956.

1956: Following a posthumous production in Sweden, the first published edition of O'Neill's play receives the Pulitzer.

1957: *The Miracle Worker* debuts as a television play produced by the Columbia Broadcasting System (CBS) for the anthology series *Playhouse 90* in 1957; the play is rewritten for the stage and produced on Broadway at the Playhouse Theatre, October 19, 1959; it is adapted for film and produced by United Artists in 1962; the play comes full circle with another television adaptation by the National Broadcasting Company (NBC) in 1979.

1959: Hansberry becomes the first black female playwright to have her work produced on Broadway when *A Raisin in the Sun* debuts in 1959. She later becomes the first black playwright to win the New York Drama Critics Circle Award; she is also the youngest playwright to receive this honor.

1959: *Zoo Story* is produced for the first time in Berlin, Germany, on September 28, 1959, at the Schiller Theatre Werkstatt; the play debuted off-

Broadway at the Provincetown Playhouse on January 14, 1960.

1960: Hammerstein dies on August 23, 1960, in Doylestown, Pennsylvania.

1961: Hart dies on December 20, 1961, in Palm Springs, California.

1961: Kaufman dies following a heart attack, June 2, 1961, in New York City.

1965: Hansberry dies of cancer on January 12, 1965, in New York City. She is buried in Beth El Cemetery.

1965: *The Odd Couple* debuts on Broadway in March of 1965.

1966: Childress's *Wedding Band* receives its first production in 1966; due to concerns about the play's interracial themes, a production is not mounted on Broadway until 1972.

1966: *Rosencrantz and Guildenstern Are Dead* is first produced as an amateur production in Edinburgh, Scotland, in 1966; it has subsequent productions in London and New York in 1967.

1975: Shange's *for colored girls . . .* is first produced in New York City at Studio Rivbea, July 7, 1975; it is later produced Off-Broadway at the Anspacher Public Theatre in 1976; it is produced on Broadway at the Booth Theatre, September 15, 1976.

1975: Wilder dies of a heart attack, December 7, 1975, in Hamden, Connecticut.

1976: Christie dies January 12, 1976, in Wallingford, England.

1979: Rodgers dies on December 30, 1979, in Manhattan, New York.

1979: *Crimes of the Heart* is first produced in Louisville, Kentucky, at the Actors' Theatre of Louisville, February 18, 1979; produced on Broadway at the John Golden Theatre, November 4, 1981.

1981: Henley is awarded the Pulitzer Prize in drama for her first play.

1982: Norman's *'night, Mother* is first produced at the American Repertory Theatre, Cambridge,

Massachusetts, in 1982; it is later produced on Broadway at the Golden Theatre in 1983.

1983: *Glengarry, Glen Ross* is first presented at the Cottlesloe Theatre of the Royal National Theatre, in London, England, on September 21, 1983; the play's American premier takes place at the Goodman Theatre in Chicago, Illinois, on February 6, 1984; with one cast change, the production then transfers to Broadway's Golden Theatre on March 5, 1984.

1983: Norman wins the Pulitzer for drama just two years after her southern colleague Beth Henley.

1983: Williams chokes to death on February 24, 1983, in his suite at Hotel Elysee in New York City; he is buried in St. Louis, Missouri.

1984: Mamet's play about business and greed, *Glengarry Glen Ross,* is awarded the Pulitzer for drama.

1984: Hellman dies of cardiac arrest on June 30, 1984, in Martha's Vineyard, Massachusetts.

1986: *The Rez Sisters* is first produced at the National Canadian Centre in Toronto, Ontario, in 1986.

1986: Highway's play wins both the Dora Mavor Award and is runner-up for the Floyd F. Chalmers Award for outstanding Canadian play of 1986.

1989: Beckett dies of respiratory failure, December 22, 1989, in Paris, France.

1993: Following the Los Angeles riots that inspired the work, *Twilight: Los Angeles, 1992* begins its premier run on May 23, 1993, in Los Angeles, California, at the Center Theatre Group/Mark Taper Forum.

1993: Smith's play garners several major awards, including an Obie Award, Drama Desk Award, Outer Critics Circle Award.

1994: Childress dies of cancer, August 14, 1994, in Queens, New York.

1995: Bolt dies on February 20, 1995, in Hampshire, England.

Acknowledgments

The editors wish to thank the copyright holders of the excerpted criticism included in this volume and the permissions managers of many book and magazine publishing companies for assisting us in securing reproduction rights. We are also grateful to the staffs of the Detroit Public Library, the Library of Congress, the University of Detroit Mercy Library, Wayne State University Purdy/Kresge Library Complex, and the University of Michigan Libraries for making their resources available to us. Following is a list of the copyright holders who have granted us permission to reproduce material in this volume of *DFS*. Every effort has been made to trace copyright, but if omissions have been made, please let us know.

COPYRIGHTED EXCERPTS IN *DFS*, VOLUME 2, WERE REPRODUCED FROM THE FOLLOWING PERIODICALS:

Books in Canada, v. 18, March, 1989 for "No Wings Yet" by Carol Bolt. Reprinted by permission of the author.—*The Chesterton Review,* v. 19, May, 1993 for "Adam, Eve, and Agatha Christie: Detective Stories As Post-Darwinian Myths of Original Sin," by John Wren-Lewis. Reproduced by permission of the author.—*Commentary,* v. 27, June, 1959 for "Thoughts on 'A Raisin in the Sun'" by Gerald Weales. Copyright © 1959 by the American Jewish Committee. Copyright renewed © 1987 by Gerald Weales. All rights reserved. Reprinted by permission of the publisher and the author.—*The Commonweal,* v. LXIII, March 16, 1956. Copyright © 1956 Commonweal Publishing Co., Inc. Reprinted by permission of Commonweal Foundation.—*Drama,* Spring, 1974 for "Quite a Nice Run" by Eric Shorter. Reproduced by permission.—*Educational Theatre Journal,* v. 29, May, 1977 for review of "for colored girls who have considered suicide/when the rainbow is enuf," by Lynn F. Miller. Copyright © 1977. Reproduced by permission of The Johns Hopkins University Press.—*English Journal,* v. 57, January, 1968 for "In Defense of Albee" by Carolyn E. Johnson. Copyright © 1968 by the National Council of Teachers of English. Reproduced by permission of the publisher and the author.—*Films in Review,* v. 11, August/September, 1970. Reproduced by permission.—*Maclean's,* v. 100, October, 1987. Copyright © 1987 by Maclean's Magazine. Reprinted by permission of the publisher.—*The Nation,* v. 222, May 1, 1976; v. 236, May, 1983. Copyright © 1976, 1983 The Nation magazine/The Nation Company, Inc. Both reproduced by permission of the publisher.—*The New Republic,* v. 210, May, 1994. Copyright © 1994 The New Republic, Inc. Reproduced by permission of *The New Republic.* November, 1959 Copyright © 1959 The New Republic, Inc. Renewed 1987 by *The New Republic.* Reproduced by permission of *The New Republic.*—*Newsweek,* v. CIII, April 9, 1984. Reproduced by permission.—*The New York Herald Tribune,* March, 1965. Copyright © 1965 by the New York Times Company. All rights reserved. Reproduced by permission.—*New*

York Theatre Critics' Reviews, v. XXXXV, March 5, 1984. Copyright © 1984 by The New York Times Company. Reproduced by permission.—*New York Times Magazine,* September, 1958. Copyright © 1958 by the New York Times Company. All rights reserved. Reproduced by permission.—*New York,* v. 14, January 12, 1981. Reproduced by permission.—*The New Yorker,* May, 1993 for a review of ''A Raisin in the Sun'' by Kenneth Tynan. Reproduced by permission of the Literary Estate of the author.—*The New Yorker,* v. 32, February, 1957. © 1957 by The New Yorker Magazine, Inc. Reprinted by permission of the publisher.—*The New York Times,* May, 1955; March 1965; November 5, 1981. Copyright © 1955, 1965, 1981 by the New York Times Company. All rights reserved. All reproduced by permission.—*The Nation,* November 13, 1972. Copyright 1972 The Nation magazine/ The Nation Company, Inc. Reprinted by permission of the publisher.—*Virginia Quarterly Review,* v. 71, Autumn, 1995. Reproduced by permission.

COPYRIGHTED EXCERPTS IN *DFS,* VOLUME 2, WERE REPRODUCED FROM THE FOLLOWING BOOKS:

Atkinson, Brooks. From *Onstage: Selected Theater Reviews from The New York Times, 1920-1970.* Edited by Bernard Beckerman and Howard Siegman. Arno Press, 1973. Copyright © 1973 by the New York Times Company. Reproduced by permission of The New York Times Company.—Barnes, Clive. From *Onstage: Selected Theater Reviews from The New York Times, 1920-1970.* Edited by Bernard Beckerman and Howard Siegman. Arno Press, 1973. Copyright © 1973 by the New York Times Company. Reproduced by permission of The New York Times Company.—Browder, Sally. ''I Thought You Were Mine: Marsha Norman's 'night, Mother,'' in *Mother Puzzles: Daughters and Mothers in Contemporary American Literature.* Edited by Mickey Pearlman. Greenwood Press, 1989. Copyright © 1989 by Mickey Pearlman. All Rights Reserved. Reproduced by permission.—Hayman, Ronald. From *Contemporary Playwrights: Samuel Beckett.* Heinemann Educational Books, 1968. Copyright © 1968 by Ronald Hayman. Reproduced by permission of the Peters, Fraser & Dunlop Group Ltd.—Kerr, Walter. From *The Theater in Spite of Itself.* Simon & Schuster, 1963. Copyright © 1963 by Walter Kerr, renewed 1991. All rights reserved. Reproduced by permission.—Taubman, Howard. From *Onstage: Selected Theater Reviews from The New York Times, 1920-1970.* Edited by Bernard Beckerman and Howard

Siegman. Arno Press, 1973. Copyright © 1973 by the New York Times Company. Reproduced by permission of The New York Times Company.—Tynan, Kenneth. From *Right and Left: Plays, Films, People, Places, and Events.* Atheneum, 1967. Copyright © 1960 by Kenneth Tynan. All rights reserved. Reproduced by permission of the Literary Estate of Kenneth Tynan.—Wiley, Catherine. ''Whose Name, Whose Protection: Reading Alice Childress's The Wedding Band,'' from *Modern American Drama: The Female Canon.* Edited by June Schlueter. Associated University Presses, 1990. Copyright © 1990 by Associated University Presses. Reprinted by permission of the publisher.

PHOTOGRAPHS AND ILLUSTRATIONS APPEARING IN *DFS,* VOLUME 2, WERE RECEIVED FROM THE FOLLOWING SOURCES:

Henley, Beth, photograph. AP/Wide World Photos. Reproduced by permission.—Movie still from *Crimes of the Heart,* by Beth Henley. De Laurentiis Entertainment Group. Courtesy of The Kobal Collection. Reproduced by permission.—Shange, Ntozake, photograph. AP/Wide World Photos. Reproduced by permission.—Production still for *for colored girls who have considered suicide/when the rainbow is enuf* by Ntozake Shange. Martha Swope. Reproduced by permission.—Mamet, David, photograph. AP/Wide World Photos. Reproduced by permission.—Book cover of *Glengarry Glen Ross,* by David Mamet. Grove/ Atlantic, Inc. Reproduced by permission.—Production still for *Glengarry Glen Ross,* by David Mamet. Donald Cooper, London. Reproduced by permission.—*Playbill* from the April 21, 1955 premiere at the National Theatre for *Inherit The Wind,* by Jerome Lawrence and Robert E. Lee. *Playbill* (r) is a registered trademark of Playbill Incorporated, NYC. All rights reserved. Reproduced by permission.—*Playbill* from the Royale Theatre production of, *Inherit The Wind,* by Jerome Lawrence and Robert E. Lee. *Playbill* (r) is a registered trademark of Playbill Incorporated, NYC. All rights reserved. Reproduced by permission.—O'Neill, Eugene, photograph by Carl Van Vechten. The Library of Congress.—Production still for *Long Day's Journey into Night,* by Eugene O'Neill. The Raymond Mander & Joe Mitchenson Theatre Collection. Reproduced by permission.—Bolt, Robert, photograph. AP/Wide World Photos. Reproduced by permission.—Movie still for *A Man For All Seasons,* by Robert Bolt. Archive Photos. Reproduced by permission.—Gibson, William, photograph. Archive Photos, Inc. Reproduced by permission.—Movie production still for *The Miracle Worker,* by William Gibson. Archive Photos. Reproduced by permission.—Production still for *The Miracle Worker,* by William Gibson. Archive Photos. Reproduced by permission.—Christie, Agatha, photograph. AP/Wide World Photos. Reproduced by permission.—Promotional bill for *The Mousetrap* by Agatha Christie. Mousetrap Productions Limited. Reproduced by permission.—Norman, Marsha, photograph. AP/Wide World Photos. Reproduced by permission.—Movie still for *'night, Mother,* by Marsha Norman. Archive Photos/ Universal Studies. Reproduced by permission.—Simon, Neil, photograph. AP/Wide World Photos. Reproduced by permission.—Two movie stills from *The Odd Couple* by Neil Simon. Archive Photos, Inc. Reproduced by permission.—Hansberry, Lorraine, photograph. Corbis-Bettman. Reproduced by permission.—Movie still for *A Raisin in the Sun* by Lorraine Hansberry. Archive Photos, Inc. Reproduced by permission.—Stoppard, Tom, photograph. AP/Wide World Photos. Reproduced by permission.—Production still for *Rosencrantz and Guildenstern Are Dead* by Tom

Stoppard. Donald Cooper, London. Reproduced by permission.—*Playbill* from the Cort Theatre production of, *Twilight: Los Angeles, 1992,* by Anna Deavere Smith. *Playbill* (r) is a registered trademark of Playbill Incorporated, NYC. All rights reserved. Reproduced by permission.—Vidal, Gore, photograph. AP/Wide World Photos. Reproduced by permission.—An illustration by Paul Anderson for *Visit to a Small Planet* by Gore Vidal. Reproduced by permission by Paul Anderson.—Beckett, Samuel, photograph. Archive Photos, Inc. Reproduced by permission.—Production still for *Waiting for Godot* by Samuel Beckett. The Raymond Mander & Joe Mitchenson Theatre Collection. Reproduced by permission.—Childress, Alice, photograph by Jerry Bauer. Copyright © Jerry Bauer. Reproduced by permission.—A photograph by Mark Avery of *Wedding Band* by Alice Childress. Milwaukee Repertory Theater. Reproduced by permission.—Albee, Edward, photograph. Archive Photos, Inc. Reproduced by permission.—Photograph by Hank Kranzler of *The Zoo Story* by Edward Albee. American Conservatory Theater, San Francisco. Reproduced by permission.

Crimes of the Heart

BETH HENLEY
1979

Beth Henley completed *Crimes of the Heart,* her tragic comedy about three sisters surviving crisis after crisis in a small Mississippi town, in 1978. She submitted it to several regional theatres for consideration without success. Unknown to her, however, a friend had entered it in the well-known Great American Play Contest of the Actors' Theatre of Louisville. The play was chosen as co-winner for 1977-78 and performed in February, 1979, at the company's annual festival of New American Plays. The production was extremely well-received, and the play was picked up by numerous regional theatres for their 1979-81 seasons.

At the end of 1980, *Crimes of the Heart* was produced off-Broadway at the Manhattan Theatre Club for a limited, sold-out, engagement of thirty-two performances. By the time the play transferred to Broadway in November, 1981, *Crimes of the Heart* had received the prestigious Pulitzer Prize. Henley was the first woman to win the Pulitzer for Drama in twenty-three years, and her play was the first ever to win before opening on Broadway. *Crimes of the Heart* went on to garner the New York Drama Critics Circle Award for Best New American Play, a Gugenheim Award, and a Tony nomination. The tremendously successful Broadway production ran for 535 performances, spawning regional productions in London, Chicago, Washington, Atlanta, Los Angeles, Dallas, and Houston. The success of the play—and especially the prestige of the Pulitzer award—assured Henley's place among the

elite of the American theatre for years to come. As Henley herself put it, with typically wry humor, "winning the Pulitzer Prize means I'll never have to work in a dog-food factory again" (Haller 44).

Often compared to the work of other "Southern Gothic" writers like Eudora Welty and Flannery O'Connor, Henley's play is widely appreciated for its compassionate look at good country people whose lives have gone wrong. Henley explores the pain of life by piling up tragedies on her characters in a manner some critics have found excessive, but she does so with a dark and penetrating sense of humor which audiences—as the play's success has demonstrated—found to be a fresh perspective in the American theatre.

AUTHOR BIOGRAPHY

Beth Henley was born May 8, 1952, in Jackson, Mississippi, the daughter of an attorney and a community theatre actress. Her southern heritage has played a large role in the setting and themes of her writing, as well as the critical response she has received—she is often categorized as a writer of the "Southern Gothic" tradition. As an undergraduate at Southern Methodist University (SMU) in Dallas, Texas, Henley studied acting and this training has remained important to her since her transition to playwriting. Directors and fellow playwrights have observed that Henley "approaches a play from the point of view of theater, not literature" and that "as an actress, she then knows how to make her works stageworthy" (Haller).

She wrote her first play, a one-act titled *Am I Blue,* to fulfill a playwriting class assignment. When it was produced at SMU her senior year, she modestly used the pseudonym Amy Peach. The play has an adolescent perspective—two insecure and lonely teenagers meet in a squalid section of New Orleans—but audiences and critics (who reviewed the play when it was revived in 1981) found in it many of the themes, and much of the promise, of Henley's later work. Henley undertook graduate study at the University of Illinois, where she taught acting and voice technique. By this time, however, she was growing more interested in writing, primarily out of a frustration at the lack of good contemporary roles for southern women.

Henley completed *Crimes of the Heart* in 1978 and submitted it for production consideration, with-

out success, to several regional theatres. The play was eventually produced in the Actors' Theatre of Louisville's 1979 Festival of New Plays. The successful production in this prestigious festival led to several regional productions, an off-Broadway production at the Manhattan Theatre Club, and a Pulitzer Prize for Drama, unprecedented for a play which had not yet opened on Broadway. When it did, in November, 1981, the play was a smash success, playing for 535 performances and spawning many other successful regional productions. When *Crimes of the Heart* was made into a film in 1986 it received mixed reviews, but Henley did receive an Academy Award nomination for her screenplay adaptation.

With the prestige of the Pulitzer Prize and all the acclaim afforded *Crimes of the Heart*—her first full-length play—Henley was catapulted to success in the contemporary American theatre. The attention paid to her also, however, put extreme pressure on her to succeed at that level. As Henley said of the Pulitzer: "Later on they make you pay for it" (Betsko and Koenig 215). Many critics have been hard on Henley's later plays, finding none of them equal to the creativity of *Crimes of the Heart.* Her second full-length play, *The Miss Firecracker Contest* was, however, predominantly well-received. Similarly a dark comedy about a small Mississippi town, the play was completed in 1980, and premiered in several regional productions in 1981-82 before opening at the Manhattan Theatre Club in 1984. It played off-Broadway for a total of 244 performances, moving to larger quarters in the process. *The Miss Firecracker Contest* was adapted into a film in 1988, starring Holly Hunter.

In October, 1982, *The Wake of Jamey Foster,* Henley's third full-length play, closed on Broadway after only twelve performances. Henley felt that this commercial flop (not uncommon under the severe financial pressures of Broadway production) was "part of the cost of winning" the Pulitzer Prize (Betsko and Koenig 215). Her next play, *The Debutante Ball,* was better received, and throughout the last decade Henley has remained a productive and successful writer for Broadway, the regional theatres, and film. Her major projects include the plays *The Lucky Spot, Abundance,* and *Control Freaks.* She also wrote the screenplay for *Nobody's Fool* (as well as screen adaptations of her own plays) and collaborated with Budge Threlkeld on the Public Broadcasting System's *Survival Guides* and with David Byrne and Stephen Tobolowsky on the screenplay for Byrne's 1986 film *True Stories.*

PLOT SUMMARY

The entire action of the play takes place in the kitchen of the MaGrath sisters' house in Hazlehurst, Mississippi

Act I

The action opens on Lenny McGrath trying to stick a birthday candle into a cookie. Her cousin, Chick, arrives, upset about news in the paper (the content of which is not yet revealed to the audience). She wonders how she's "gonna continue holding my head up high in this community." She and Lenny discuss going to pick up Lenny's sister Babe. Chick expresses displeasure with other facets of the MaGraths' family, as she gives Lenny a birthday present—a box of candy. Doc Porter, an old boyfriend of the other McGrath sister, Meg, arrives, and Chick leaves to pick up Babe. Lenny is upset at Doc's news that Billy Boy, an old childhood horse of Lenny's, was struck by lightning and killed. Doc leaves to pick up his son at the dentist.

Lenny receives a phone call with news about "Zackery" (who we learn later is Babe's husband), who is hospitalized with serious injuries. Meg arrives, and as she and Lenny talk, it is revealed that Babe has shot her husband and is being held in jail. There is an awkwardness between the two sisters as they discuss their grandfather; Lenny has been caring for him (sleeping on a cot in the kitchen to be near his room), and he has recently been hospitalized after a stroke. Lenny learns that Meg's singing career, the reason she had moved to California, is not going well—as is evidenced by her return to Hazelhurst.

Chick returns to the house, accompanying Babe. Chick shows obvious displeasure for Meg, and for Babe, who "doesn't understand how serious the situation is." Lenny and Chick run out after a phone call from a neighbor having an emergency. Meg and Babe, left alone together, discuss why it was that their mother committed suicide, hanging herself along with the family cat. Babe also begins revealing to her sister more about shooting her husband. The sisters also discuss Lenny, whose self-consciousness over her shrunken ovary, they feel, has prevented her from pursuing relationships with men, in particular a Charlie from Memphis who Lenny dated briefly. Noticing the box of candy, Meg and Babe realize they've forgotten Lenny's birthday. They plan to order her a cake, as Babe's lawyer

Beth Henley

Barnette arrives at the house. Babe hides from him at first, as Meg and Barnette, who remembers her singing days in Biloxi, become reacquainted.

Barnette reveals that he's taken Babe's case partly because he has a personal vendetta against Zackery, Babe's husband. Barnette also reveals that medical records suggest Zackery had abused Meg leading up to the shooting. Barnette leaves and Babe reappears, confronted by Meg with the medical information. Babe admits she's protecting someone: Willie Jay, a fifteen year-old African American boy with whom Babe had been having an affair. The shooting, Babe says, was a result of her anger after Zackery threatened Willie Jay and pushed him down the porch steps. As the act ends, Babe agrees to cooperate with Barnette for the benefit of her case, and the two sisters plan a belated birthday celebration for Lenny.

Act II

Evening of the same day. Barnette is interviewing Babe about the case. Babe says after the shooting her mouth was "just as dry as a bone" so she went to the kitchen and made a pitcher of lemonade. She is afraid that this detail is "gonna look kinda bad." Zackery calls, threatening that he has evidence damaging to Babe. Barnette leaves to meet him at the hospital, after answering Babe's question about the nature of his personal vendetta against Zack: "the major thing he did was to ruin my father's life."

Lenny enters, fuming; Meg, apparently, lied "shamelessly" to their grandfather about her career in show business. Old jealousies resurface; Lenny asks Babe about Meg: "why should Old Grandmama let her sew twelve golden jingle bells on her petticoats and us only three?" Babe and Lenny discuss the hurricane which wiped out Biloxi, when Doc's leg was severely injured after his roof caved in. Many people have the perception, apparently, that Meg, refusing to evacuate, "baited Doc into staying there with her."

Meg enters, with a bottle of bourbon from which she has already been drinking. An apology for her lying to grandpa is quickly forthcoming, but she says "I just wasn't going to sit there and look at him all miserable and sick and sad!" The three sisters look through an old photo album. Enjoying one another's company at last, they decide to play cards, when Doc phones and is invited over by Meg. Lenny begins criticizing Meg, who counters by asking Lenny about Charlie; Lenny gets angry at Babe for having revealed this secret to Meg. Meg continues to push the point, and Lenny runs upstairs, sobbing. Babe follows, to comfort her.

At this less than opportune moment, Doc arrives. He and Meg drink together, and talk about the hurricane and hard times. Meg reveals to Doc that she "went insane" in L.A. and ended up in the psychiatric ward of the country hospital. The two decide to go off together and continue to drink; there is an obvious attraction, but Doc is careful to say they're "just gonna look at the moon" and not get in over their heads. There is a knock at the back door, and Babe comes downstairs to admit Barnette. He has bad news for Babe: Zackery's sister, suspicious of Babe, had hired a detective, who produced compromising photographs of Babe with Willie Jay. Babe is devastated, and as a final blow to close the act, Lenny comes downstairs to report that the hospital has called with news that their grandfather has suffered another stroke.

Act III

The following morning. Babe enters and lies down on Lenny's cot. Lenny enters, also weary. Chick's voice is heard almost immediately; her questions reveal that grandpa is in a coma and will

likely not live. Chick and Lenny divide between them a list of people they must "notify about Old Granddaddy's predicament." Chick goes off with obvious displeasure with the sisters. Lenny and Babe ruminate about when Meg might be coming home.

Meg actually returns a moment later, exuberant. Exhausted by their traumatic night, Lenny and Babe break down in hysterical laughter telling Meg the news about their grandfather. As the three sisters talk, Meg and Babe convince Lenny to call her man Charlie and restart their relationship. With her confidence up, Lenny goes upstairs to make the call. Babe shows Meg the envelope of incriminating photographs.

Barnette arrives; he states that he's been able to dig up enough scandal about Zackery to force him to settle the case out of court. In order to keep the photos of Babe and Willie Jay secret, however, he will not be able to expose Zackery openly, which had been his original hope and intention. Willie Jay, meanwhile, will be sent North to live in safety. Barnette leaves; so does Meg, to pick up Lenny's late birthday cake.

Lenny comes downstairs, frustrated at having been too self-conscious to call Charlie. Chick arrives a moment later, calling Meg a "low-class tramp" for going off with Doc. Lenny confronts Chick and tells her to leave; she does, but continues to curses the family as Lenny chases her out the door. Zackery calls, informing Babe he's going to have her committed to a mental institution. She defies him to do so and hangs up the phone, but she is clearly disturbed by the threat. Lenny re-enters, elated at her triumph over Chick, and decides to make another try at calling Charlie. Babe takes rope from a drawer and goes upstairs.

Lenny makes the call; it goes well, and she makes a date with him for that evening. Wanting to tell someone, she runs out back to find Babe. There is a thud from upstairs; Babe comes down with a broken piece of rope around her neck. She makes another attempt to commit suicide, on-stage, by sticking her head in the oven. Meg finds her there and pulls her out. Babe, feeling enlightened, says she knows why their mother killed the cat along with herself; not because she hated it but because she loved it and "was afraid of dying all alone." Meg comforts Babe by convincing her Zackery won't be able to make good on his threat. Lenny returns and is surprised by her sisters with a late birthday celebration. Despite the many troubles hanging over them, the play ends with the MaGrath sisters smiling and laughing together for a moment, in "a magical, golden, sparkling glimmer."

CHARACTERS

Babe

Babe is the youngest MaGrath sister. At the start of the play, she has shot her husband, Zackery, a powerful and wealthy lawyer. At first, the only explanation she gives for the act is the defiant statement: "I didn't like his looks! I just didn't like his stinking looks!" Eventually, she reveals that the shooting was the result of her anger at Zackery's cruel treatment both of her and of Willie Jay, a fifteen year-old African American boy with whom Babe had been carrying on an affair.

Babe makes two attempts to kill herself late in the play. After being rescued by Meg, Babe appears enlightened and at peace with her mother's suicide. Babe says she understands why their mother hanged the family cat along with herself; not because she hated it but because she loved it and "was afraid of dying all alone."

Becky

See Babe

Rebecca Botrelle

See Babe

Chick Boyle

The sisters' first cousin, who is twenty-nine years old. She is a very demanding relative, extremely concerned about the community's opinion of her. When news is published of Babe's shooting of Zackery, Chick's primary concern is how she's "gonna continue holding my head up high in this community." Chick is critical of all aspects of the MaGrath's family and is always bringing up past tragedies such as the mother's suicide. Chick is especially hard on Meg, whom she finds undisciplined and calls a "low-class tramp," and on Babe, who "doesn't understand how serious the situation is" after shooting Zackery. Chick seems to feel closest to Lenny, and is genuinely surprised to be

ushered out of the house for her comments about Lenny's sisters.

Barnette Lloyd

Barnette is Babe's lawyer. An ambitious, talented attorney, Barnette views Babe's case as a chance to exact his personal revenge on Zackery. "The major thing he did," Barnette says, "was to ruin my father's life." Barnette also seems to have a strong attraction to Babe, whom he remembers distinctly from a chance meeting at a Christmas bazaar. Barnette is prevented from taking on Zackery in open court by the desire to protect Babe's affair with Willie Jay from public exposure. He is willing to make this sacrifice for Babe, and the play ends with some hope that his efforts will be rewarded.

Lenny MaGrath

Lenny, at the age of thirty, is the oldest MaGrath sister. Her sisters have forgotten her birthday, only compounding her sense of rejection. Lenny is frustrated after years of carrying heavy burdens of responsibility; most recently, she has been caring for Old Granddaddy, sleeping on a cot in the kitchen to be near him. Lenny loves her sisters but is also jealous of them, especially Meg, whom she feels received preferential treatment during their upbringing. Meg has also been surrounded by men all her life, while Lenny has feared rejection from the opposite sex and become withdrawn as a result. She fears continuing the one romantic relationship, with a Charlie Hill from Memphis, which has gone well for her in recent years.

While almost continuously pushed beyond the point of frustration, Lenny nevertheless has a close bond of loyalty with her sisters. Chick is constantly criticizing the family (culminating in her calling Meg a "low-class tramp"); when Lenny is finally pushed to the point that she turns on her cousin, chasing her out of the house with a broom, this is an important turning point in the play. It demonstrates the ultimate strength of family bonds—and their social value—in Henley's play.

Meg MaGrath

Meg is the middle sister at twenty-seven years of age. As an eleven year-old child, Meg discovered the body of their mother (and that of the family cat) following her suicide. This traumatic experience provoked Meg to test her strength by confronting morbidity wherever she could find it, including

MEDIA ADAPTATIONS

- *Crimes of the Heart* was adapted as a film in 1986, directed by Bruce Beresford and starring Diane Keaton, Jessica Lange, Sissy Spacek, and Sam Shepard. The film adds as fully-realized characters several people who are only discussed in the play: Old Granddaddy, Zackery and Willie Jay. The film received decidedly mixed reviews but also garnered three Academy Award nomi-

nations, for Henley's screenplay and for the acting of Spacek and Tess Harper, who played the catty Chick.

- In a rare example of reverse adaptation from drama to fiction, Claudia Reilly published in 1986 a novel, *Crimes of the Heart,* based on Henley's play.

---

poring over medical photographs of disease-ridden victims and staring at March of Dimes posters of crippled children. At the beginning of the play Meg returns to Mississippi from Los Angeles, where her singing career has stalled and where, she later tells Doc, she had a nervous breakdown and ended up in the psychiatric ward of the county hospital.

The other MaGrath sisters share a perception that Meg has always received preferential treatment in life. When Lenny ponders "why should Old Grandmama let her sew twelve golden jingle bells on her petticoats and us only three?" this is not a minor issue for her and Babe. The two sisters feel on some level that this special treatment has led Meg to act irresponsibly—as when she abandoned Doc, for whatever reason, after he was severely injured in the hurricane. Lenny is angry with Meg for lying to Old Granddaddy in the hospital about her career, but Meg states "I just wasn't going to sit there and look at him all miserable and sick and sad!" Both Babe and Lenny are concerned when Meg disappears with Doc her first night back in Mississippi. Both sisters, however—especially Lenny—are also protective of Meg, especially from the attacks of their cousin Chick.

Rebecca MaGrath
See Babe

Doc Porter
Doc is Meg's old boyfriend. He is still known affectionately as "Doc" although his plans for a

medical career stalled and eventually died after he was severely injured in Hurricane Camille—his love for Meg (and her promise to marry him) prompted him to stay behind with her while the rest of the town evacuated the storm's path. Many people now have the perception (as Meg and Lenny discuss) that Meg "baited Doc into staying there with her." Doc, who now has his own wife and children, nevertheless remains close to the MaGrath family. Although Meg abandoned him when she left for California, Doc remains fond of her, and Meg is extremely happy to have his friendship upon her return from California.

THEMES

Absurdity
Much like the playwrights of the Theatre of the Absurd, Henley dramatizes a vision of a disordered universe in which characters are isolated from one another and are incapable of meaningful action. With the constant frustration of their dreams and hopes, Henley's characters could easily find their lives completely meaningless and absurd (and indeed, each of the MaGrath sisters has been on the brink of giving up entirely). At the end of *Crimes of the Heart,* at least, the sisters have found a kind of unity in the face of adversity. While Lenny's vision, "something about the three of us smiling and laughing together," in no way can resolve the many

TOPICS FOR FURTHER STUDY

- Research the destructive effects of Hurricane "Camille," which in 1969 traveled 1,800 kilometers along a broad arc from Louisiana to Virginia. Why do you think Henley chose to set *Crimes of the Heart* in the shadow, as it were, of this Hurricane? What does Camille represent for each of the major characters and thematically to the play as a whole?

- Consider Babe's legal position at the end of the play. What do you think is likely to happen to her? Draw from your understanding of Barnette's case against Zackery and Zackery's case against Babe. From your own perspective, how do you think Babe will change as a result of this event and what do you feel her future should rightly be?

- Contrast Lenny's and Meg's life strategies: how do they each view responsibility, career, family, romance? How spontaneous—or not—is each one? What are the strongest bonds between the sisters, and what are their sources of conflict?

- Research the prestige of the Pulitzer Prizes and the history of the Pulitzer for Drama—you might begin with Thomas P. Adler's book *Mirror on the Stage: The Pulitzer Plays as an Approach to American Drama.* When Henley won the Pulitzer for Drama in 1981, who was the last woman who had won the prize, twenty-three years earlier? Why did winning the Pulitzer draw so much attention to Henley, as it did to Marsha Norman two years later, when she won with her play *'Night, Mother?*

conflicts that have unfolded in the course of the play, it does endow their lives with a collective sense of hope, where before each had felt acutely the absurdity, and often the hopelessness, of life.

Death

Reminders of death are everywhere in *Crimes of the Heart:* the sisters are haunted by the memory of their mother's suicide; Babe has shot and seriously wounded her husband; Lenny learns that her beloved childhood horse has been struck by lightning and killed; Old Granddaddy has a second stroke and is apparently near death; Babe attempts suicide twice near the end of the play. Perhaps even stronger than these reminders of physical death, however, are the images of emotional or spiritual death in the play. Lenny, for example, has rejected Charlie, her only suitor in recent years, because she feels worthless and fears rejection herself. Meg, meanwhile, has experienced a psychotic episode in Los Angeles and has prevented herself from loving anyone in order to avoid feeling vulnerable. Significant transitions occur near the end of the play, individual "rebirths" which preface the significant

rebirth of a sense of unity among the sisters: Lenny gains the courage to call her suitor, and finds him receptive; Meg, in the course of spending a night out with Doc, is surprised to learn that she "could care about someone," and sings "all night long" out of joy; and finally, Babe has a moment of enlightenment in which she understands that their mother hanged the family cat along with herself because "she was afraid of dying all alone." This revelation allows her to put to rest finally the painful memory of the mother's suicide, and paves the way for the moment of sisterly love at the conclusion of the play.

Good and Evil

Henley challenges the audience's sense of good and evil by making them like characters who have committed crimes of passion. "I thought I'd like to write about somebody who shoots somebody else just for being mean," Henley said in *Saturday Review.* "Then I got intrigued with the idea of the audience's not finding fault with her character, finding sympathy for her." While Babe's case constitutes the primary exploration of good and evil in the play, the conflict between Meg and her sisters is another example of Henley presenting a number of perspectives on a character's actions in order to complicate her audience's notions of good and bad behavior. Lenny and Babe find many of Meg's actions (abandoning Doc after his accident, lying to Granddaddy about her career in Hollywood) to be dishonest and selfish, but the sisters eventually learn to understand Meg's motivations and to forgive her. Through this process, Henley suggests the sheer complexity of human psychology and behavior—that often, actions cannot be easily labeled ''good'' or ''evil'' in a strict sense.

Limitations and Opportunities

Virtually all the characters, to some extent, have throughout their lives been limited in their choices, experiencing a severe lack of opportunity. Lenny, in particular, resents having had to take upon herself so much responsibility for the family (especially for Old Granddaddy). Much of Babe's difficulty in her marriage to Zackery, meanwhile, seems to have grown out the fact that she did not choose him but was pressured by her grandfather into marrying the successful lawyer. Meg, however, at least to Lenny and Babe, appears to have had endless opportunity. Lenny wonders at one point: ''Why, do you remember how Meg always got to wear twelve jingle bells on her petticoats, while we were only allowed to wear three apiece? Why?!'' Lenny is clearly fixating on a minor issue from childhood, but one she feels is representative of the preferential treatment Meg received. The bells are, she says to Meg later, a ''specific example of how you always got what you wanted!'' Meg, however, has learned a hard lesson in Hollywood about opportunity and success. Old Granddaddy has always told her: ''With your talent, all you need is exposure. Then you can make your own breaks!'' Contrary to this somewhat simplistic optimism, however, Meg's difficulty sustaining a singing career suggests that opportunity is actually quite rare, and not necessarily directly connected to talent or one's will to succeed.

Public vs. Private Life

When Babe reveals to Meg her affair with Willie Jay, she admits that she's ''so worried about his getting public exposure.'' This is a necessary concern for public opinion, as Willie Jay might physically be in danger as a result of such exposure. Chick, meanwhile, has what Henley characterizes as an unhealthy concern for public perception — she cares much more about what the rest of the town

thinks of her than she does about any of her cousins. Immediately upon her entrance at the beginning of the play, Chick focuses not so much upon Babe's shooting of Zackery, but rather on how the event will affect her, personally: ''How I'm gonna continue holding my head up high in this community, I do not know.'' Similarly, in criticizing Meg for abandoning Doc, Chick thinks primarily of her own public stature: ''Well, his mother was going to keep *me* out of the Ladies' Social League because of it.'' Near the end of the play, Lenny becomes infuriated over Chick calling Meg ''a low-class tramp,'' and chases her cousin out of the house. This moment of family solidarity is a significant turning point, in which Lenny clearly indicates that the private, family unity the three sisters are able to achieve by the end of the play is far more important than the public perception of the family within the town.

Violence and Cruelty

Accompanying the exploration of good and evil in *Crimes of the Heart* are its insights into violence and cruelty. While Babe has ostensibly committed the most violent act in the play by shooting Zackery in the stomach, the audience is persuaded to side with her in the face of the violence wrought by Zackery upon both Babe (domestic violence stemming, as Babe says, from him ''hating me, 'cause I couldn't laugh at his jokes''), and, in a jealous rage, on Willie Jay. There occur other, less prominent acts of cruelty in the course of the play, as well as numerous ones the audience learns about through exposition (such as Meg's abandonment of Doc following his injury). In the end, Henley encourages the audience to take a less absolute view of what constitutes cruelty, to understand some of the underlying reasons behind the actions of her characters, and to join in the sense of forgiveness and acceptance which dominates the conclusion of *Crimes of the Heart.*

STYLE

Set in the small southern town of Hazlehurst, Mississippi, *Crimes of the Heart* centers on three sisters who converge at the house of their grandfather after the youngest, Babe, has shot her husband following years of abuse. The other sisters have their own difficulties—Meg's Hollywood singing career is a bust, and Lenny (the eldest) is frustrated and lonely after years of bearing familial responsibility (most recently, she has been sleeping on a cot in the kitchen in order to care for the sisters' ailing grandfather). Over the course of two days, the sisters endure a number of conflicts, both between themselves and with other characters. In the end, however, they manage to come together in a moment of unity and joy despite their difficulties.

Beth Henley is most often praised, especially regarding *Crimes of the Heart,* for the creative blending of different theatrical styles and moods which gives her plays a unique perspective on small-town life in the South. Her multi-faceted approach to dramatic writing is underscored by the rather eclectic group of playwrights Henley once listed for an interviewer as being her major influences: Anton Chekhov, William Shakespeare, Eugene O'Neill, Tennessee Williams, Samuel Beckett, David Mamet, Henrik Ibsen, Lillian Hellman, and Carson McCullers. In particular, Henley's treatment of the tragic and grotesque with humor startled audiences and critics (who were either pleasantly surprised, or unpleasantly shocked). While this macabre humor is often associated with the Southern Gothic movement in literature, Henley's dramatic technique is difficult to qualify as being strongly of one theatrical bent or another. For example, *Crimes of the Heart* has many of the characteristics of a naturalistic work of the ''well-made play'' tradition: a small cast, a single set, a three-act structure, an initial conflict which is complicated in the second act and resolved in the third. As Scott Haller observed in *Saturday Review,* however, Henley's purpose is not the resurrection of this tradition but the ''ransacking'' of it. ''In effect,'' he wrote, ''she has mated the conventions of the naturalistic play with the unconventional protagonists of absurdist comedy. It is this unlikely dramatic alliance, plus her vivid Southern vernacular, that supplies Henley's idiosyncratic voice.''

The rapid accumulation of tragedies in Henley's dramatic world thus appears too absurd to be real, yet too tangibly real to be absurd, and therein lies the playwright's originality. Many critics have joined Haller in finding in Henley's work elements of the Theatre of the Absurd, which presented a vision of a disordered universe in which characters are isolated from one another and are incapable of meaningful action. There is, however, much more specificity to the plot and lives of the characters in *Crimes of the Heart* than there is, for example, in a

play by absurdists like Beckett or Eugene Ionesco. Nevertheless, Henley shares with these playwrights, and others of the Absurd, a need to express the dark humor inherent in the struggle to create meaning out of life.

Henley's macabre sense of humor has resulted in frequent comparisons to Southern Gothic writers such as Flannery O'Connor and Eudora Welty. Providing a theatrical rationale for much of what appears to be impossibly eccentric behavior on the part of Henley's characters; in the *New York Times,* Walter Kerr wrote: ''We do understand the groundrules of matter-of-fact Southern grotesquerie, and we know that they're by no means altogether artificial. People do such things and, having done them, react in surprising ways.'' Although Henley once stated that when she began writing plays she was not familiar with O'Connor, and that she ''didn't consciously'' say that she ''was going to be like Southern Gothic or grotesque,'' she has since read widely among the work of O'Connor and others, and agrees the connections are there. Of her eccentric brand of humor Henley, quoted in *Mississippi Writers Talking,* suspected that ''I guess maybe that's just inbred in the South. You hear people tell stories, and somehow they are always more vivid and violent than the stories people tell out in Los Angeles.''

While *Crimes of the Heart* does have a tightly-structured plot, with a central and several tangential conflicts, Henley's real emphasis, as Nancy Hargrove suggested in the *Southern Quarterly,* is ''on character rather than on action.'' Jon Jory, the director of the original Louisville production, observes that what so impressed him initially about Henley's play was her ''immensely sensitive and complex view of relationships. . . . And the comedy didn't come from one character but from between the characters. That's very unusual for a young writer'' (Haller 42). The nature of Henley's dramatic conclusion in *Crimes of the Heart* goes hand-in-hand with her primary focus upon characterization, and her significant break with the tradition of the ''well-made play.'' While the plot moves to a noticeable resolution, with the sisters experiencing a moment of unity they have not thus far experienced in the play, Henley leaves all of the major conflicts primarily unresolved. Stanley Kauffmann wrote in the *Saturday Review* assessment of the Broadway production that ''Crimes moves to no real resolution, but this is part of its power. It presents a condition that, in minuscule, implies much about the state of the world, as well as the state of Mississippi, and about human chaos; it says, "Resolution is not my business. Ludicrously horrifying honesty is."

Because of the distinctive balance that Henley strikes—between comedy and tragedy, character and plot, conflict and resolution—the playwright whose technique Henley's most resembles may be Chekhov (although her sense of humor is decidedly more macabre and expressed in more explicit ways). Henley has said of Chekhov's influence upon her that she appreciates how "he doesn't judge people as much as just shows them in the comic and tragic parts of people. Everything's done with such ease, but it hits so deep," as she stated in *Mississippi Writers Talking.* About a production of Chekhov's *The Cherry Orchard* which particularly moved her, Henley commented in *The Playwright's Art: Conversations with Contemporary American Dramatists* that "It was just absolutely a revelation about how alive life can be and how complicated and beautiful and horrible; to deny either of those is such a loss."

HISTORICAL CONTEXT

Crimes of the Heart, according to Henley's stage directions, takes place "[i]n the fall, five years after Hurricane Camille." This would set the play in 1974, in the midst of significant upheavals in American society. Henley's characters, however, seem largely unmoved by the events of the outside world, caught up as they are in the pain and disappointment of their personal lives.

Vietnam

The war continued in 1974, setting off a civil war in Cambodia as well. U.S. combat troops had been removed from Vietnam in 1973, although American support of anti-Communist forces in the South of the country continued. Perhaps more important to the American social fabric, the many rifts caused by our involvement in the war in Vietnam were slow to heal. Students and others who had protested against the war remained largely disillusioned about the foreign interests of the U.S. government, and society as a whole remained traumatized by U.S. casualties and the devastation wrought by the war, which had been widely broadcast by the media; the Vietnam War was often referred to as the "living room war" due to the unprecedented level of television coverage.

Watergate

Perhaps the most significant event in American society in 1974 was the unprecedented resignation of President Richard Nixon, over accusations of his granting approval for the June 17, 1972, burglary of Democratic National Committee offices at the Watergate complex in Washington, D.C. By the end of 1973, a Harris poll suggested that people believed, by a margin of 73 to 21 percent, that the president's credibility had been damaged beyond repair. Like public opinion over Vietnam, Watergate was an important symbol both of stark divisions in American society and a growing disillusionment with the integrity of our leaders. Less than two years after being re-elected in a forty-nine-state landslide and after declaring repeatedly that he would never resign under pressure, Nixon was faced with certain impeachment by Congress. Giving in to the inevitable, he resigned his office in disgrace on August 9.

World Crises: Food, Energy, Inflation

1974 was an especially trying year for the developing world, as massive famine swept through Asia, South America, and especially Africa, on the heels of drought and several major natural disasters. As they watched this tragedy unfold, citizens of industrialized nations of the West were experiencing social instability of another kind. In the fall of 1973, Arab members of the Organization of Petroleum Exporting Countries (OPEC) leveled an embargo on exports to the Netherlands and the U.S. The United States, with its unparalleled dependency on fuel (in 1974, the nation had six percent of the world's population but consumed thirty-three percent of the world's energy), experienced a severe economic crisis. U.S. economic output for the first quarter of 1974 dropped $10-20 billion, and 500,000 American workers lost their jobs. The U.S. government blamed the Arabs for the crisis, but American public opinion also held U.S. companies responsible for manipulating prices and supplies to corporate advantage. Related to the energy crisis and other factors, the West experienced an inflation crisis as well; annual double-digit inflation became a reality for the first time for most industrial nations.

Civil Rights

On the twenty-year anniversary of the historic Supreme Court decision on school integration, fierce battles were still being fought on the issue, garnering national attention. The conflict centered mostly on issues of school busing, as the site of conflict largely shifted from the South to the cities of the

North. In Boston, for example, police had to accompany buses transporting black children to white schools. Meanwhile, baseball player Hank Aaron's breaking of Babe Ruth's career home-run title in 1974 was a significant and uplifting achievement, but its painful post-script—the numerous death threats Aaron received from racists who did not feel it was proper for a black athlete to earn such a title—suggests that bigoted ideas of race in America were, sadly, slow to change.

Growing out of its roots in the 1960s, the movement to define and defend the civil rights of women also continued. 1974 marked a midpoint in the campaign to ratify the Equal Rights Amendment (ERA), which declared: "Equality of rights under the law shall not be denied or abridged by the United States or by any State on account of sex." The amendment was originally passed by the Senate in March, 1972, and by the end of 1974, thirty-one states had ratified it, with a total of thirty-eight needed. Support for the ERA (which eventually failed) was regionally divided: while every state in the Northeast had ratified the amendment by this time, for example, it had been already defeated in Georgia, Florida, and Louisiana. Legislative action was stalled, meanwhile, in many other southern states, including North and South Carolina, Alabama, Mississippi, and Arkansas.

In *Crimes of the Heart,* the characters seem untouched by these prominent events on the national scene. The absence of any prominent historical context to the play may reflect Henley's perspective on national politics: she has described herself as a political cynic with a "moratorium on watching the news since Reagan's been president," as she described herself in *Interviews with Contemporary Women Playwrights.* It may also be a reflection of Henley's perspective on small-town life in the South, where, she feels, people more commonly come together to talk about their own lives and tell stories rather than watch television or discuss the national events being covered in the media. The South of *Crimes of the Heart,* meanwhile, seems largely unaffected by the civil rights movement, large-scale economic development, or other factors of what has often been called an era of unprecedented change in the South.

Regarding the issue of race, for example, consider Babe's affair with Willie Jay, a fifteen-year-old African American youth: while the revelation of it would compromise any case Babe might have against her husband for domestic violence, it presents a greater threat to Willie Jay himself. Because the threat of possible retribution by Zachary or other citizens of the town, Willie Jay has no option but to leave "incognito on the midnight bus—heading North." Henley has made an important observation about race relations in Mississippi, in response to a question actually about recent trends in "color-blind" casting in the theatre. Henley stated in *The Playwright's Art: Conversations with Contemporary American Dramatists* that "it depends on how specific you're being about the character's background as to whether that's an issue." In a play like *Crimes of the Heart,* "if you're writing about a specific time or place ... then obviously race is important because there is a segregated bigoted thing going on."

CRITICAL OVERVIEW

Beth Henley did not initially have success finding a theatre willing to produce *Crimes of the Heart,* until the play's acceptance by the Actors' Theatre of Louisville. From that point onward, however, the public and critical reception was overwhelmingly positive. Few playwrights achieve such popular success, especially for their first full-length play: a Pulitzer Prize, a Broadway run of more than five hundred performances, a New York Drama Critics Award for best play, a one million dollar Hollywood contract for the screen rights. John Simon's tone is representative of many of the early reviews: writing in the *New York Times* of the off-Broadway production he stated that *Crimes of the Heart* "restores one's faith in our theatre." Simon was, however, wary of being too hopeful about Henley's future success, expressing the fear "that this clearly autobiographical play may be stocked with the riches of youthful memories that many playwrights cannot duplicate in subsequent works."

Reviews of the play on Broadway were also predominantly enthusiastic. Stanley Kauffmann, writing in the *Saturday Review,* found fault with the production itself but found Henley's play powerfully moving. "The play has to fight its way through the opening half hour or so of this production before it lets the author establish what she is getting at— that, under this molasses meandering, there is madness, stark madness." While Kauffmann did identify some perceived faults in Henley's technique, he stated that overall, "she has struck a rich, if not inexhaustible, dramatic lode.'' Similarly, Richard Corliss, writing in *Time* magazine, emphasized that Henley's play, with its comedic view of the tragic and grotesque, is deceptively simple: ''By the end of the evening, caricatures have been fleshed into characters, jokes into down-home truths, domestic atrocities into strategies for staying alive.''

Not all the Broadway reviews, however, were positive. Walter Kerr of the *New York Times* felt that Henley had simply gone too far in her attempts to wring humor out of the tragic, falling into ''a beginner's habit of never letting well enough alone, of taking a perfectly genuine bit of observation and doubling and tripling it until it's compounded itself into parody.'' Throughout the evening, Kerr recalled, ''I also found myself, rather too often and in spite of everything, disbelieving—simply and flatly disbelieving.'' In making his criticism, however, Kerr observed that ''this is scarcely the prevailing opinion'' on Henley's play. Michael Feingold of the *Village Voice,* meanwhile, was far more vitriolic, stating that the play ''gives the impression of gossiping about its characters rather than presenting them . . . never at any point coming close to the truth of their lives.'' Feingold's opinion, that the ''tinny effect of *Crimes of the Heart* is happily mitigated, in the current production, by Melvin Bernhardt's staging'' and by the ''magical performances'' of the cast, is thus diametrically opposed to Kauffmann, who praised the play but criticized the production.

Given Henley's virtually unprecedented success as a young, first-time playwright, and the gap of twenty-three years since another woman had won the Pulitzer Prize for Drama, one of the concerns of critics was to place Henley in the context of other women writing for the stage in the early 1980s. Mel Gussow did so famously in his article ''Women Playwrights: New Voices in the Theatre'' in the *New York Times Sunday Magazine,* in which he discussed Henley, Marsha Norman, Wendy Wasserstein, Wendy Kesselman, Jane Martin, Emily Mann, and other influential female playwrights. While Gussow's article marked an important transition in the contemporary American theatre, it has been widely rebutted, found by many to be ''more notable for its omissions than its conclusions'' according to Billy J. Harbin in the *Southern Quarterly.* In particular, critics have been interested in comparing Henley to Norman, another southern woman who won the Pulitzer for Drama (for her play *'night, Mother).* Gussow wrote that among the numerous women finding success as playwrights ''the most dissimilar may be Marsha Norman and

Beth Henley.'' Lisa J. McDonnell picked up this theme several years later in an issue of the *Southern Quarterly,* agreeing that there are important differences between the two playwrights, but exploring them in much more depth than Gussow was able to do in his article. At the same time, however, McDonnell observed many important similarities, including ''their remarkable gift for storytelling, their use of family drama as a framework, their sensitive delineation of character and relationships, their employment of bizarre Gothic humor and their use of the southern vernacular to demonstrate the poetic lyricism of the commonplace.''

The failure of Henley's play *The Wake of Jamey Foster* on Broadway, and the mixed success of her later plays, would seem to lend some credence to John Simon's fear that Henley might never again be able to match the success of *Crimes of the Heart.* While many journalistic critics have been especially hard on Henley's later work, she remains an important figure in the contemporary American theatre. The many published interviews of Henley suggests that she attempts not to take negative reviews to heart: in *The Playwright's Art: Conversations with Contemporary American Dramatists,* she observed with humor that ''H. L. Mencken said that asking a playwright what he thinks of critics is like asking a lamppost what he thinks of a dog.'' *Crimes of the Heart,* meanwhile, has passed into the canon of great American plays, proven by the work of literary critics to be rich and complex enough to support a variety of analytical interpretations. Writing in the *Southern Quarterly,* Nancy Hargrove, for example, examined Henley's vision of human experience in several of her plays, finding it ''essentially a tragicomic one, revealing . . . the duality of the universe which inflicts pain and suffering on man but occasionally allows a moment of joy or grace.''

Billy Harbin, writing in the *Southern Quarterly,* placed Henley's work in the context of different waves of feminism since the 1960s, exploring the importance of family relationships in her plays. While the family is often portrayed by Henley as simply another source of pain, Harbin felt that *Crimes of the Heart* differs from her other plays in that a ''faith in the human spirit . . . can be glimpsed through the sisters' remarkable endurance of suffering and their eventual move toward familial trust and unity.'' Henley's later characters, according to Harbin, ''possess little potential for change,'' limiting Henley's ''success in finding fresh explorations of [her] ideas.'' With this nuanced view, Harbin nevertheless conforms to the prevailing critical view that Henley has yet to match either the dramatic complexity or the theatrical success of *Crimes of the Heart.* Lou Thompson, in the *Southern Quarterly,* similarly found a sense of unity at the end of the *Crimes of the Heart* but traced its development from of the dominant imagery of food in the play. While the characters eat compulsively throughout, foraging in an attempt ''to fill the void in the spirit—a hunger of the heart mistaken for hunger of the stomach,'' the sisters share Lenny's birthday cake at the end of the play ''to celebrate their new lives.''

CRITICISM

Christopher Busiel

Busiel holds a Ph.D. in English from the University of Texas. In this essay he discusses Henley's dramatic technique.

While *Crimes of the Heart* does have a tightly-structured plot, with a central and several tangential conflicts, Henley's real emphasis, as Nancy Hargrove suggested in *Southern Quarterly,* is ''on character rather than on action.'' Her characters are basically good people who make bad choices, who act out of desperation because of the overwhelming sense of isolation, rejection, and loneliness in their lives. Speaking of Babe in particular, Henley said in *Saturday Review:* ''I thought I'd like to write about somebody who shoots somebody else just for being mean. Then I got intrigued with the idea of the audience's not finding fault with her character, finding sympathy for her.'' This basic premise is at the center of Henley's theatrical method, which challenges the audience to like characters their morals might tell them not to like. ''I like to write characters who do horrible things,'' Henley said in *Interviews with Contemporary Women Playwrights,* "but whom you can still like . . . because of their human needs and struggles. . . . I try to understand that ugliness is in everybody. I'm constantly in awe that we still seek love and kindness even though we are filled with dark, bloody, primitive urges and desires.'' Henley's drama effectively illustrates the intimate connection between these two seemingly disparate aspects of human nature. Henley achieves a complex perspective in her writing primarily by encouraging her audience to laugh, along with the characters, at the tragic and grotesque aspects of life.

Tragic events treated with humor abound in *Crimes of the Heart,* powerful reminders of the intention behind Henley's technique. For example, when Babe finally reveals the details of her shooting of Zackery, the audience is no doubt struck by her matter-of-fact recounting of events: ''Well, after I shot him, I put the gun down on the piano bench, and then I went out in the kitchen and made up a pitcher of lemonade.'' While Babe's story lends humor to the present moment in the play (a scene between Babe and her lawyer, Barnette), we can appreciate the human trauma behind her actions. Writing in the *New York Times,* Walter Kerr identified in Henley's play ''the ground-rules of matter-of-fact Southern grotesquerie,'' which is ''by no means altogether artificial. People do such things and, having done them, react in surprising ways.''

As the scene continues, however, Henley may perhaps push her point too far; Babe's actions begin to seem implausible except in the context of Henley's dramatic need to achieve humor. Babe recounts: ''Then I called out to Zackery. I said, 'Zackery, I've made some lemonade. Can you use a glass?' . . . He was looking up at me trying to speak words. I said 'What? . . . Lemonade? . . . You don't want it? Would you like a Coke instead?' Then I got the idea—he was telling me to call on the phone for medical help.'' In a realistic context the audience understands that Babe is still in shock, not thinking clearly. At the same time, however, it is difficult not to find her unbelievably dense—or, from a dramatic perspective, becoming more of a caricature to serve Henley's comedic ends than a fully-realized, human character. Moments like this are seized upon by Henley's harshest critics; Kerr, for example, wrote that *Crimes of the Heart* suffers from her ''beginner's habit of never letting well enough alone, of taking a perfectly genuine bit of observation and doubling and tripling it until it's compounded itself into parody.'' Even Kerr admitted, however, that despite moments of seeming excess, ''*Crimes of the Heart* is clearly the work of a gifted writer.''

Most other critics, meanwhile, have been more enthusiastic in their praise of Henley's technique. Far from finding in *Crimes of the Heart* a kind of parody, they have elucidated how *real* Henley's characters seem. Hargrove offered one possible explanation for this phenomenon, finding that one of ''the real strengths of Henley's work is her use of realistic details from everyday life, particularly in the actions of the characters. These details reinforce the idea that ordinary life is like this, a series of small defeats happening to ordinary people in ordinary family relationships. Her characters unobtru-

WHAT DO I READ NEXT?

- *The Miss Firecracker Contest* (New York: Dramatists Play Service, 1985). Henley's most successful play next to *Crimes of the Heart*. Also set in a small Mississippi town (Brookhaven), it follows the trials and tribulations of Carnelle Scott, a twenty-four-year-old woman with a bad reputation in town who seeks to redeem herself by winning the title of Miss Firecracker for the Fourth of July celebration. With a cast full of very odd characters who, like Carnelle, seek some kind of redemption from their lives, the play probes the grotesque even more so than *Crimes of the Heart*. While some critics have suggested that Henley merely reworks the same ideas from play to play, others have found *The Miss Firecracker Contest* a fresh, original expression of Henley's unique view of life in small southern towns. The play was adapted into a film in 1989, starring Holly Hunter.

- Marsha Norman: *'night, Mother*. Henley and Marsha Norman are often compared and/or contrasted to one another because they each won a Pulitzer Prize for Drama in the early 1980s. Reading this play helps highlight the similarities and differences between the two playwrights.

- Flannery O'Connor: *Collected Works* (New York: Library of America, 1988) and *The Complete Stories* (New York: Farrar, Straus and Giroux, 1971). Reading some of the work of this legendary writer of the "Southern Gothic" tradition, you can judge for yourself the validity of the connections numerous critics have drawn between her work and Henley's plays.

- Carol S. Manning, editor, *The Female Tradition in Southern Literature* (Urbana, IL: University of Illinois Press, 1993). A collection of essays both on specific writers, and on topics such as "Southern Ladies and the Southern Literary Renaissance" and "Spiritual Daughters of the Black American South." Containing extensive analysis of Eudora Welty and Flannery O'Connor, two writers of "Southern Gothic" fiction to whom Henley is often compared, the volume is also is quite useful in placing Henley within a historical continuum of southern women writers, and examining common threads of experience with other writers from whom she differs in other ways.

- John B. Boles, editor, *Dixie Dateline: a Journalistic Portrait of the Contemporary South* (Houston: Rice University Press, 1983). A collection of eleven essays by eminent journalists, presenting a variety of perspectives on the South, its culture, its history, and its future.

---

sively but constantly are doing the mundane things that go on in daily life.''

The roots of our modern theatre in ancient Greece established a strict divide between comedy and tragedy (treating them as separate and distinct genres); more than two thousand years later, reactions to Henley's technique suggest the powerful legacy of this separation. Audiences and critics were either pleasantly surprised by *Crimes of the Heart*—finding the dramatic interweaving of the tragic and comedic refreshingly original—or, less frequently, were shocked by what appeared to be Henley's flippant perspective on life's difficulties.

The scene in which the sisters learn that Old Granddaddy has suffered a second stroke in the hospital, and is near death, is another powerful example of Henley's strategy of treating the tragic with humor. Meg, feeling guilty for having lied to her grandfather about her singing career, is resolved to return to the hospital and tell him the truth: "He's just gonna have to take me like I am. And if he can't take it, if it sends him into a coma, that's just too damn bad.''

Struck by the absurdity of this comment (for Meg, unlike Lenny and Babe, does not yet know that her grandfather already *is* in a coma), Meg's

A scene from the 1986 film adaptation, starring Jessica Lange, Sissy Spacek, and Diane Keaton

sisters break into hysterical laughter. The resulting scene depicts them swinging violently from one emotional extreme to the other. "I'm sorry," Lenny says, momentarily gaining control. "It's—it's not funny. It's sad. It's very sad. We've been up all night long." When Meg asks if Granddaddy is expected to live, however, Babe's response "They don't think so" sends the sisters, inexplicably, into another peal of laughter. While on the surface, the laughter (both that of Lenny and Babe, and that generated among the audience) seems shockingly flippant, the moment is devastatingly human. The audience sees the deepest emotions of characters who have been pushed to the brink, and with no place else to go, can only laugh at life's misfortunes.

While the mistakes her characters have made are the source of both the conflict and the humor of *Crimes of the Heart,* Henley nevertheless treats these characters with great sympathy. Jon Jory, who directed the first production of *Crimes of the heart* in Louisville, observed in the *Saturday Review* that "most American playwrights want to expose human beings. Beth Henley embraces them." With the possible exception of Chick, whose exaggerated concern for what is "proper" provides a foil to Lenny and her sisters, Henley's characters seem

tangibly human despite the bizarre circumstances in which the audience sees them. "Like Flannery O'Connor," Scott Haller wrote in the *Saturday Review,* "Henley creates ridiculous characters but doesn't ridicule them. Like Lanford Wilson, she examines ordinary people with extraordinary compassion." While in later plays Henley was to write even more exaggerated characters who border on caricatures, *Crimes of the Heart* remains a very balanced play in this respect. Jory noted that what struck him about the play initially was this sense of balance: "the comedy didn't come from one character but from between the characters. That's very unusual for a young writer."

While humor permeates *Crimes of the Heart,* it is often a hysterical humor, as in the scene where Meg is informed of her grandfather's impending death. Just as Lou Thompson has observed in the *Southern Quarterly* that the characters eat compulsively throughout the play, a "predominant metaphor for . . . pathological withdrawal," so the laughter in the play is equally compulsive, more often an expression of pain than true happiness. By the conclusion of *Crimes of the Heart,* however, hysterical laughter has been supplanted by an almost serene sense of joy—however mild or fleeting.

Lenny expresses a vision of the three sisters "smiling and laughing together . . . it wasn't forever; it wasn't for every minute. Just this one moment and we were all laughing." In addition to drawing strength from one another, finding a unity that they had previously lacked, the sisters appear finally to have overcome much of their pain (and this despite the fact that many of the play's conflicts are left unresolved). They have perhaps found an absolution which Henley, tellingly, has described as a process of writing itself. "Writing always helps me not to feel so angry," she stated in *Interviews with Contemporary Women Playwrights.* "I've written about ghastly, black feelings and thoughts that I've had. The hope is that if you can pin down these emotions and express them accurately, you will somehow be absolved."

Source: Christopher Busiel, in an essay for *Drama for Students,* Gale, 1997.

Frank Rich

In the following favorable review of Crimes of the Heart, *Rich comments on Henley's ability to draw her audience into the lives and surroundings of her characters. Rich argues that Henley "builds from a foundation of wacky but consistent logic until she's constructed a funhouse of perfect-pitch language and ever-accelerating misfortune."*

Rich is an American drama critic.

Beth Henley's *Crimes of the Heart* ends with its three heroines—the MaGrath sisters of Hazelhurst, Miss.—helping themselves to brick-sized hunks of a chocolate birthday cake. The cake, a "super deluxe" extravaganza from the local bakery, is as big as the kitchen table, and the sisters laugh their heads off as they dig in. The scene is the perfect capper for an evening of antic laughter—yet it's by no means the sum of *Crimes of the Heart.* While this play overflows with infectious high spirits, it is also, unmistakably, the tale of a very troubled family. Such is Miss Henley's prodigious talent that she can serve us pain as though it were a piece of cake.

Prodigious, to say the least. This is Miss Henley's first play. Originally produced at Louisville's Actors Theater, it won the Pulitzer Prize and New York Drama Critics Circle Award after its New York production last winter at the Manhattan Theater Club. Last night that production arrived, springier than ever, at the Golden, and it's not likely to stray from Broadway soon. Melvin Bernhardt, the director, has fulfilled Miss Henley's comedy by casting

young actors whose future looks every bit as exciting as the playwright's.

Crimes is set "five years after Hurricane Camille" in the MaGrath family kitchen, a sunny garden of linoleum and translucent, flowered wallpaper designed by John Lee Beatty. The action unfolds during what the youngest sister, 24-year-old Babe (Mia Dillon), calls "a bad day." Babe knows whereof she speaks: She's out on bail, having just shot her husband in the stomach. And Babe's not the only one with problems. Her 27-year-old sister Meg (Mary Beth Hurt), a would-be singing star, has retreated from Hollywood by way of a psychiatric ward. Lenny (Lizbeth Mackay), the eldest MaGrath, is facing her 30th birthday with a "shrunken ovary" and no romantic prospects. As if this weren't enough, Old Granddaddy, the family patriarch, is in the hospital with "blood vessels popping in his brain."

A *comedy,* you ask? Most certainly—and let's not forget about the local lady with the "tumor on her bladder," about the neighbor with the "crushed leg," about the sudden death by lightning of Lenny's pet horse, Billy Boy. Miss Henley redeems these sorrows, and more, by mining a pure vein of Southern Gothic humor worthy of Eudora Welty and Flannery O'Connor. The playwright gets her laughs not because she tells sick jokes, but because she refuses to tell jokes at all. Her characters always stick to the unvarnished truth, at any price, never holding back a single gory detail. And the truth—when captured like lightning in a bottle—is far funnier than any invented wisecracks.

Why did Babe shoot her husband? Because, she says, "I didn't like his looks." Why, after firing the gun, did she make a pitcher of lemonade before calling an ambulance? Because she was thirsty. Why did she carry on with a 15-year-old black boy during the months before her crime? "I was so lonely," explains Miss Dillon, "and he was *goooood.*" Why has Babe's lawyer, a young, sheepish Ole Miss grad (Peter MacNicol), taken on such a seemingly hopeless case? Because Babe won his heart when she sold him poundcake at a long-ago church bazaar—and because he believes in "personal vendettas."

You see Miss Henley's technique. She builds from a foundation of wacky but consistent logic until she's constructed a funhouse of perfect-pitch language and ever-accelerating misfortune. By Act III, we're so at home in the crazy geography of the MaGraths' lives that we're laughing at the slightest prick of blood. At that point Miss Henley starts kindling comic eruptions on the most unlikely lines— ''Old Granddaddy's in a coma!''—without even trying. That's what can happen when a playwright creates a world and lets the audience inhabit it.

We're not laughing *at* the characters, of course, but with them. We all have bad days, when we contemplate—or are victims of—irrational crimes of the heart. In this play, Miss Henley shows how comedy at its best can heighten reality to illuminate the landscape of existence in all its mean absurdity. But the heightening is not achieved at the price of credibility. The MaGraths come by their suffering naturally: It's been their legacy since childhood, when their father vanished and their mother hanged herself—and her pet cat—in the cellar. *Crimes of the Heart* is finally the story of how its young characters escape the past to seize the future. ''We've got to figure out a way to get through these bad days here,'' says Meg. That can't happen for any of us until the corpses of a childhood are truly laid to rest. . . .

Source: Frank Rich, ''Beth Henley's *Crimes of the Heart*'' in the *New York Times,* November 5, 1981.

John Simon

In the following review, Simon applauds Crimes of the Heart, asserting that the play ''bursts with energy, merriment, sagacity, and, best of all, a generosity toward people and life that many good writers achieve only in their most mature offerings, if at all.''

Simon is a Yugoslavian-born American film and drama critic.

From time to time a play comes along that restores one's faith in our theater, that justifies endless evenings spent, like some unfortunate Beckett character, chin-deep in trash. This time it is the Manhattan Theatre Club's *Crimes of the Heart,* by Beth Henley, a new playwright of charm, warmth, style, unpretentiousness, and authentically individual vision.

We are dealing here with the reunion in Hazlehurst, Mississippi, of the three MaGrath sisters (note that even in her names Miss Henley always hits the right ludicrous note). Lenny, the eldest, is a patient Christian sufferer: monstrously accident-prone, shuttling between gentle hopefulness and slightly comic hysteria, a martyr to her sexual insecurity and a grandfather who takes most

> HENLEY BUILDS FROM A FOUNDATION OF WACKY BUT CONSISTENT LOGIC UNTIL SHE'S CONSTRUCTED A FUNHOUSE OF PERFECT-PITCH LANGUAGE AND EVER-ACCELERATING MISFORTUNE"

of her energies and an unconscionable time dying. Babe Botrelle, the youngest and zaniest sister, has just shot her husband in the stomach because, as she puts it, she didn't like the way he looked. Babe (who would like to be a saxophonist) is in serious trouble: She needs the best lawyer in town, but that happens to be the husband she shot. Meg, the middle sister, has had a modest singing career that culminated in Biloxi. In Los Angeles, where she now lives, she has been reduced to a menial job. She is moody and promiscuous, and has ruined, before leaving home, the chances of ''Doc'' Porter to go to medical school. She made him spend a night with her in a house that lay in the path of Hurricane Camille; the roof collapsed, leaving Doc with a bad leg and, soon thereafter, no Meg.

The time of the play is ''Five years after Hurricane Camille,'' but in Hazlehurst there are always disasters, be they ever so humble. Today, for instance, it is Lenny's thirtieth birthday, and everyone has forgotten it, except pushy and obnoxious Cousin Chick, who has brought a crummy present. God certainly forgot, because he has allowed Lenny's beloved old horse to be struck dead by lightning the night before, even though there was hardly a storm. Crazy things happen in Hazlehurst: Pa MaGrath ran out on his family; Ma MaGrath hanged her cat and then hanged herself next to it, thus earning nationwide publicity. Babe rates only local headlines. She will be defended by an eager recent graduate of Ole Miss Law School whose name is Barnette Lloyd. (Names have a way of being transsexual in Hazlehurst.) Barnette harbors an epic grudge against the crooked and beastly Botrelle as well as a nascent love for Babe. But enough of this plot-recounting— though, God knows, there is so much plot here that I can't begin to give it away. And all of it is demented, funny, and, unbelievable as this may sound, totally believable.

> THE THREE SISTERS ARE WONDERFUL CREATIONS: LENNY OUT OF CHEKHOV, BABE OUT OF FLANNERY O'CONNOR, AND MEG OUT OF TENNESSEE WILLIAMS IN ONE OF HIS MORE BENIGN MOODS"

The three sisters are wonderful creations: Lenny out of Chekhov, Babe out of Flannery O'Connor, and Meg out of Tennessee Williams in one of his more benign moods. But ''out of'' must not be taken to mean imitation; it is just a legitimate literary genealogy. Ultimately, the sisters belong only to Miss Henley and to themselves. Their lives are lavish with incident, their idiosyncrasies insidiously compelling, their mutual loyalty and help (though often frazzled) able to nudge heartbreak toward heart-lift. And the subsidiary characters are just as good—even those whom we only hear about or from (on the phone), such as the shot husband, his shocked sister, and a sexually active fifteen-year-old black.

Miss Henley is marvelous at exposition, cogently interspersing it with action, and making it just as lively and suspenseful as the actual happenings. Her dialogue is equally fine: always in character (though Babe may once or twice become too benighted), always furthering our understanding while sharpening our curiosity, always doing something to make us laugh, get lumps in the throat, care. The jokes are juicy but never gratuitous, seeming to stem from the characters rather than from the author, and seldom lacking implications of a wider sort. Thus when Meg finds Babe outlandishly trying to commit suicide because, among other things, she thinks she will be committed, Meg shouts: ''You're just as perfectly sane as anyone walking the streets of Hazlehurst, Mississippi.'' On one level, this is an absurd lie; on another, higher level, an absurd truth. It is also a touching expression of sisterly solidarity, while deriving its true funniness from the context. Miss Henley plays, juggles, conjures with context—Hazlehurst, the South, the world.

The play is in three fully packed, old-fashioned acts, each able to top its predecessor, none repetitious, dragging, predictable. But the author's most precious gift is the ability to balance characters between heady poetry and stalwart prose, between grotesque heightening and compelling recognizability—between absurdism and naturalism. If she errs in any way, it is in slightly artificial resolutions, whether happy or sad. . . .

I have only one fear—that this clearly autobiographical play may be stocked with the riches of youthful memories that many playwrights cannot duplicate in subsequent works. I hope this is not the case with Beth Henley; be that as it may, *Crimes of the Heart* bursts with energy, merriment, sagacity, and, best of all, a generosity toward people and life that many good writers achieve only in their most mature offerings, if at all.

Source: John Simon, ''Sisterhood is Beautiful'' in *New York,* Vol. 14, No. 2, January 12, 1981, pp. 42,44.

FURTHER READING

Beaufort, John. ''A Play that Proves There's No Explaining Awards'' in the *Christian Science Monitor,* November 9, 1981, p. 20.
  A very brief review with a strongly negative opinion of *Crimes of the Heart* that is rare in assessments of Henley's play. Completely dismissing its value, Beaufort wrote that *Crimes of the Heart* is ''a perversely antic stage piece that is part eccentric characterization, part Southern fried Gothic comedy, part soap opera, and part patchwork plotting.''

Berkvist, Robert. ''Act I: The Pulitzer, Act II: Broadway'' in the *New York Times,* October 25, 1981, p. D4.
  An article published a week before *Crimes of the Heart*'s Broadway opening, containing much of the same biographical information found in more detail in later sources. Berkvist focused on the novelty of a playwright having such success with her first full-length play, and summarizes the positive reception of the play in Louisville and in its Off-Broadway run at the Manhattan Theatre Club. The article does contain some of Henley's strongest comments on the state of the American theatre, particularly Broadway.

Betsko, Kathleen, and Rachel Koenig. ''Beth Henley'' in *Interviews with Contemporary Women Playwrights,* Beach Tree Book, 1987, pp. 211-22.
  An interview conducted as Henley was completing her play *The Debutante Ball.* Henley discussed her writing and revision process, how she responds to rehearsals and opening nights, her relationship with her own family (fragments of which turn up in all of her plays), and the different levels of opportunity for women and men in the contemporary theatre.

Corliss, Richard. "I Go with What I'm Feeling" in *Time*, February 8, 1982, p. 80.

A brief article published during the successful Broadway run of *Crimes of the Heart* to introduce Henley to a national audience. Corliss stated concisely and cleverly the complexities of Henley's work. "Sugar and spice and every known vice," the article begins; "that's what Beth Henley's plays are made of." Corliss observed that Henley's plays are "deceptively simple. . . . By the end of the evening, caricatures have been fleshed into characters, jokes into down-home truths, domestic atrocities into strategies for staying alive." Henley is quoted in the article stating that "I'm like a child when I write, taking chances, never thinking in terms of logic or reviews. I just go with what I'm feeling." The article documents a moment of new-found success for the young playwright, facing choices about the direction her career will take her.

Feingold, Michael. "Dry Roll" in the *Village Voice*, November 18-24, 1981, p. 104.

Perhaps the most negative and vitriolic assessment of *Crimes of the Heart* in print. (The title refers to the musical *Merrily We Roll Along*, which Feingold also discussed in the review.) Feingold finds the play completely disingenuous, even insulting. He wrote that it "gives the impression of gossiping about its characters rather than presenting them . . . never at any point coming close to the truth of their lives." Feingold gave some credit to Henley's "voice" as a playwright, "both individual and skillful," but overall found the play "hollow," something to be overcome by the "magical performances" of the cast.

Gussow, Mel. "Women Playwrights: New Voices in the Theatre" in the *New York Times Sunday Magazine*, May 1, 1983, p. 22.

Discusses Henley along with numerous other contemporary women playwrights, in an article written on the occasion of Marsha Norman winning the 1983 Pulitzer Prize for Drama. Gussow traced a history of successful women playwrights, including Lillian Hellman in a modern American context, but noted that "not until recently has there been anything approaching a movement." Among the many underlying forces which paved the way for this movement, Gussow mentioned the Actors' Theater of Louisville, where Henley's *Crimes of the Heart* premiered.

Haller, Scott. "Her First Play, Her First Pulitzer Prize" in the *Saturday Review*, November, 1981, p. 40.

Introducing Henley to the public, this brief article was published just prior to *Crimes of the Heart* opening on Broadway. Haller marveled at the success achieved by a young "29-year-old who had never before written a full-length play." Based on an interview with the playwright, the article is primarily biographical, suggesting how being raised in the South provides Henley both with material and a vernacular speech. This theatrical dialect, combined with Henley's "unlikely dramatic alliance" between "the conventions of the naturalistic play" and "the unconventional protagonists of absurdist comedy" gives Henley what

Haller called her "idiosyncratic voice," which audiences have found so refreshing.

Harbin, Billy J. "Familial Bonds in the Plays of Beth Henley" in the *Southern Quarterly*, Vol. 25, no. 3, 1987, pp. 80-94.

Harbin begins by placing Henley's work in the context of different waves of feminism since the 1960s.

Hargrove, Nancy D. "The Tragicomic Vision of Beth Henley's Drama" in the *Southern Quarterly*, Vol. 22, no. 4, 1984, pp. 80-94.

Hargrove examines Henley's first three full-length plays, exploring (as the title suggests) the powerful mixture of tragedy and comedy within each.

Heilpern, John. "Great Acting, Pity about the Play" in the London *Times*, December 5, 1981, p. 11.

A review of three Broadway productions, with brief comments on *Crimes of the Heart*. "I regret," Heilpern wrote, "it left me mostly cold." It is interesting to consider whether, as Heilpern mused, he found the play bizarre and unsatisfying because as a British critic he suffered from "a serious culture gap." Instead of a complex, illuminating play (as so many American critics found (*Crimes of the Heart*), Heilpern saw only "unbelievable 'characters' whose lives were a mere farce. I could see only Southern 'types', like a cartoon."

Jones, John Griffin. "Beth Henley" in *Mississippi Writers Talking*, University Press of Mississippi, 1982, pp. 169-90.

A rare interview conducted *before* Henley won the Pulitzer Prize for *Crimes of the Heart*. As such, it focuses on many biographical details from Henley's life, which had not yet received a great deal of public attention.

Kauffmann, Stanley. "Two Cheers for Two Plays" in the *Saturday Review*, Vol. 9, no. 1, 1982, pp. 54-55.

A review of the Broadway production of *Crimes of the Heart*. Kauffmann praised the play but says its success "is, to some extent, a victory over this production." Kauffmann identified some faults in the play (such as the amount of action which occurs offstage and is reported) but overall his review is full of praise.

Kerr, Walter. "Offbeat—but a Beat Too Far" in the *New York Times*, November 15, 1981, p. D3.

In this review of the Broadway production of *Crimes of the Heart*, Kerr's perspective on the play is a mixed one. He offers many examples to support his opinion. Kerr is insightful about the delicate balance Henley strikes in her play—between humor and tragedy, between the hurtful actions of some the characters and the positive impressions of them the audience is nevertheless expected to maintain.

McDonnell, Lisa J. "Diverse Similitude: Beth Henley and Marsha Norman" in the *Southern Quarterly*, Vol. 25, no. 3, 1987, pp. 95-104.

A comparison and contrasting of the techniques of southern playwrights Henley and Norman, who won the Pulitzer Prize for Drama within two years of one another. The playwrights share "their remarkable gift for storytelling, their use of family drama as a framework, their sensitive delineation of character and relationships, their employment of bizarre Gothic humor and their use of the southern vernacular to demonstrate the poetic lyricism of the commonplace.'' Despite the similarities between them (which do go far beyond being southern women playwrights who have won the Pulitzer), McDonnell concluded that ''they have already, relatively early in their playwriting careers, set themselves on paths that are likely to become increasingly divergent.''

Oliva, Judy Lee. ''Beth Henley'' in *Contemporary Dramatists,* 5th edition, St. James Press, 1993. 290-91.

A more recent assessment which includes Henley's play *Abundance,* an epic play spanning 25 years in the lives of two pioneer women in the nineteenth century. Oliva examined what she calls a ''unifying factor'' in Henley's plays: ''women who seek to define themselves outside of their relationships with men and beyond their family environment.'' In Oliva's assessment, ''it is Henley's characters who provide unique contributions to the dramaturgy.'' As important to Henley's plays as the characters are the stories they tell, ''especially those stories in which female characters can turn to other female characters for help.''

Simon, John. ''Sisterhood is Beautiful'' in the *New York Times,* January 12, 1981, pp. 42-44.

A glowing review of the off-Broadway production of *Crimes of the Heart,* which ''restores one's faith in our theatre.''

Thompson, Lou. ''Feeding the Hungry Heart: Food in Beth Henley's *Crimes of the Heart*'' in the *Southern Quarterly,* Vol. 30, nos. 2-3, 1992, pp. 99-102.

Drawing from Nancy Hargrove's observation in an earlier article that eating and drinking are, in Henley's plays, ''among the few pleasures in life, or, in certain cases, among the few consolations *for* life,'' Thompson explored in more detail the pervasive imagery of food throughout *Crimes of the Heart.*

Willer-Moul, Cynthia. ''Beth Henley'' in *The Playwright's Art: Conversations with Contemporary American Dramatists,* Rutgers University Press, 1995, pp. 102-22.

A much more recent source, this interview covers a wider range of Henley's works, but still contains detailed discussion of *Crimes of the Heart.* Henley talks extensively about her writing process, from fundamental ideas to notes and outlines, the beginnings of dialogue, revisions, and finally rehearsals and the production itself.

for colored girls who have considered suicide/when the rainbow is enuf

NTOZAKE SHANGE

1975

for colored girls who have considered suicide/when the rainbow is enuf is a choreopoem, a poem (really a series of 20 separate poems) choreographed to music. Although a printed text cannot convey the full impact of a performance of *for colored girls. . . ,* Shange's stage directions provide a sense of the interrelationships among the performers and of their gestures and dance movements.

The play begins and ends with the lady in brown. The other six performers represent the colors of the rainbow: the ladies in red, orange, yellow, green, blue, and purple. The various repercussions of "bein alive & bein a woman & bein colored is a metaphysical dilemma" are explored through the words, gestures, dance, and music of the seven ladies, who improvise as they shift in and out of different roles. In the 1970s, when Ntozake Shange herself performed in *for colored girls. . . ,* she continually revised and refined the poems and the movements in her search to express a female black identity. Improvisation is central to her celebration of the uniqueness of the black female body and language, and it participates in the play's theme of movement as a means to combat the stasis of the subjugation. In studying this play in its textual, static format one should, therefore, keep in mind the improvisational character of actual performance and realize that stasis is the opposite of what Shange wanted for this play. In fact, in her preface she announces to readers that while they listen, she herself is already "on the other side of the rainbow"

with "other work to do." She has moved on, as she expects her readers to do as well.

AUTHOR BIOGRAPHY

Born Paulette Williams on October 18, 1948, Shange, at the age of twenty-three, adopted the Zulu name Ntozake (pronounced "en-toe-zak-ee" and meaning "she who comes with her own things") Shange (pronounced "shon-gay" and meaning "who walks like a lion") as a name more appropriate to her poetic talents. She felt that her Anglo-Saxon last name was associated with slavery and her given name was a feminized version of the male name Paul. Shange once stated in an interview that she changed her name to disassociate herself from the history of a culture that championed slavery.

Shange grew up in an affluent family and read voraciously in English, French, and Spanish (the latter with the aid of dictionaries). She also associated with jazz greats Josephine Baker, Chuck Berry, Miles Davis, Dizzie Gillespie, and Charlie Parker, who were friends of her parents. She led a privileged existence, but she felt overprotected and not an active part of the Civil Rights movement taking place around her, though racism affected her daily school life in St. Louis during the family's five-year stay in that city. She explained, in an interview with Jacqueline Trescott in the *Washington Post,* that "nobody was expecting me to do anything because I was colored and I was also female, which was not very easy to deal with." After graduating from Barnard with honors, she moved to Harlem and became closely acquainted with the plight of impoverished black women in the city. The anger she felt as a result of the victimization she witnessed and experienced was expressed in the poem "Beau Willie" (later to be adapted as "a nite with beau willie brown" in *for colored girls who have considered suicide/when the rainbow is enuf*), which she wrote while listening to the screams of a woman being beaten by her husband, who laughed as he hit her. Shange experienced more unhappiness while briefly married to a law student, and attempted suicide a number of times. Still undecided on a career, she earned her Master of Arts degree in American studies at the University of Southern California, Los Angeles, in 1973 and began teaching classes at various colleges in Northern California.

One night while driving home after teaching an evening class and feeling especially depressed, Shange saw a huge rainbow over the city of Oakland, California, and realized that women have a right to survive, because as she asserted in a 1976 *New York Times* interview, they "have as much right and as much purpose for being here as air and mountains do." In that same interview, Shange explained that she realized that the rainbow is "the possibility to start all over again with the power and beauty of ourselves." Her experience inspired the title of *for colored girls . . . ,* composed of twenty poems she wrote over a period of years and read in women's bars in San Francisco during the summer of 1974. She later took her choreographed poems to New York. After two years of off-Broadway performances and with the help of a New York director, Shange combined her poems and formed them into a production that ran for 747 performances on Broadway. Shange continues to write drama, fiction, and poetry, but *for colored girls . . .* remains her biggest commercial and critical success. She has indicated that she would prefer to be known for more than this work. She would rather be known for her current non-commercial work, including her bilingual work with Latin American working people's theater, her association with the Feminist Art Institute, and her construction of installation art.

PLOT SUMMARY

dark phrases

The play opens with seven women dressed in the colors of the rainbow plus brown, running onto the stage from various directions and then freezing in place. The spotlight picks out the lady in brown, who comes to life and performs the poem "dark phrases," which speaks of the trials of a young black girl growing into womanhood in America. The other six women chime in—after the lady in brown says "let her be born"—as being from "outside Chicago," "outside Detroit," "outside Houston," and so on. The melancholy mood shifts to a playful rendition of "mama's little baby loves shortnin" and dance ("let your backbone slip") and a game of freeze tag, which is interrupted by the next poem.

graduation nite

A theme of male assault combined with longing for male companionship is introduced, as the lady in yellow narrates, with some pride, how she lost her virginity in the back seat of a car. The other ladies variously express their agreement with or disgust over her joy in the discovery of sex.

now i love somebody more than

Their discussion slides into this next poem, narrated by the lady in blue, who says she has Puerto Rican blood. Speaking some Spanish she describes her love of music and dancing and of the men who make music. The rest of the ladies softly join in saying "te am mas que" ("I love you more than").

no assistance

The lady in red interrupts to tell that in spite of rebuffed love she continues to "debase herself for the love of another." But she ends in strength when she says "this note is attached to a plant/i've been waterin' since the day i met you/you may water it/yr damn self." The lady in orange responds with a throwback to her desire for love and joy ("i wanna sing make you dance"). The rest of the ladies join in with "we gotta dance to keep from cryin," "we gotta dance to keep from dyin."

i'm a poet who

The dancing culminates in an declaration of pride in expression summed up by the lines, "hold yr head like it was a ruby sapphire/i'm a poet who writes in english/come to share worlds with you."

latent rapists

A sudden change of light causes the ladies to "react as if they had been struck in the face," and they collaborate on a poem describing the shock of date rape for those who expected violence to come from a stranger, "a man wit obvious problems," and not a friend. "The nature of rape has changed" and now a woman may find violence instead of the companionship she seeks.

abortion cycle #1

Again the lighting announces a slap to the face, as the lady in blue describes her experience with an abortion as "steel rods" inside, and no one comes to comfort her because in her shame, she had told no one. She exits.

sechita

The lady in purple narrates the uneasy queenage of a beautiful biracial stage star, Sechita, who nightly dances the role of an Egyptian goddess of love in

Ntozake Shange in 1976

a tawdry Creole carnival while men try to throw gold coins between her legs. As the lady in purple narrates, the lady in green dances the life of Sechita. At the end both exit and the lady in brown appears.

toussaint

The lady in brown now relates how at age eight, while reading in the adult library, she discovered Toussaint L'Ouverture, the admired hero of the Haitian French Revolution of the late 18th century. Toussaint becomes her ideal imaginary black male companion until she meets Toussaint Jones, who also claims to "take no stuff from no white folks," and who has the advantage of being in the here and now. She accepts him as a replacement for Toussaint L'Ouverture.

one

The lady in red narrates her story of a sequined butterfly and rose-adorned prostitute who plays her role perfectly, a hot, "deliberate coquette." She uses mens' desires to get what she wants, and she hopes to wound them in return, on behalf of other women "camoflagin despair &/stretchmarks." Before dawn, she bathes and throws the man out, writes the episode into her diary, and then cries herself to sleep.

A scene from the 1976 Broadway production

i used to live in the world

The lady in blue next describes the telescoping of her world down to a stifling six blocks in Harlem, where, if she is ''nice'' or a ''reglar beauty,'' she runs the risk of being molested by a black man in the dark. The four ladies freeze and then move into place for the next poem.

pyramid

The lady in purple describes a three-way female friendship that is ''like a pyramid'' with ''one laugh'' and ''one music.'' They all fall in love with one man, who chooses one of them. The others fend off his attempts to betray her with them, honoring their friendship over their need for a man. Finally, the chosen one finds the rose she'd given to him on her friend's desk. The two discover him with yet another woman, and so the three ladies join together for support and love. Sharp music interrupts them and the ladies dance away ''as if catching a disease from the lady next to her,'' and then they freeze.

no more loves poems #1, #2, #3, and #4

The four poems which follow are spoken by the ladies in orange, purple, blue, and yellow, respec-

tively. #1 laments the plight of the ''colored girl an evil woman a bitch or a nag'' who ends up ''in the bottom of [some man's] shoe.'' #2 asks to be accepted just as she is, ''no longer symmetrical & impervious to pain.'' #3 asks why black women (''we'') don't go ahead and ''be white then/& make everythin dry & abstract wit no rhythm'' but she realizes that she can't think her way out of wanting love even if she cannot find someone worthy to love. #4 announces that ''bein alive & bein a woman & bein colored is a metaphysical/dilemma.'' All seven ladies join in a chorus of ''my love is too delicate [alternately: beautiful; sanctified; etc.] to have thrown back in my face.'' This leads to a celebratory dance and chant.

somebody almost walked off wid alla my stuff

The lady in green testifies that someone has robbed her of her memories and her things that make her who she is—everything except her poems and dance.

sorry

The ladies chime in, scorning the variations on ''i'm sorry'' that men have told them.

a nite with beau willie brown

The refrain ''there was no air'' punctuates this wrenching poem in which beau willie brown tries to force crystal to say she'll marry him by holding their two children out of the fifth-floor window; when she can only whisper her affirmative answer, he drops the children.

a laying on of hands

All of the ladies join in declaiming the power of ''a laying on of hands,'' not a man or even a mother's hug, to heal them through their own holiness. The lady in red announces that she found god in herself and ''loved her fiercely.'' The play ends with the lady in brown, who repeats the opening lines with the verb in present tense: ''& this is for colored girls who have considered/suicide/but are movin to the ends of their own/rainbows.''

CHARACTERS

lady in blue

The lady in blue in ''now i love somebody more than'' says she is racially mixed (her daddy thought he was puerto rican), she speaks a little Spanish, and she loves to dance ''mamba bomba merengue.'' She ran away at age sixteen to meet willie colon at a dance marathon, and when he didn't show up, she realized she loved him more than music. The lady in blue also relates the poem ''abortion cycle #1'' which portrays a young woman undergoing the brutality of abortion alone because ''nobody knew.'' Her third piece, ''i used to live in the world,'' describes the claustrophobia-inducing prison space of ''six blocks'' of Harlem, where a pretty girl risks being raped. Partway through the poem the lady in blue becomes a stalking man following the lady in orange. Finally she narrates ''sorry,'' a poem that expresses feeling fed up with men's meaningless apologies.

lady in brown

The performers in *for colored girls. . .* are not unique characters but take on various black female identities in the separate poems. However, the lady in brown begins and ends the play, and, being clothed in the one color not present in a rainbow, she stands out among the others. The lady in brown participates in a few of the poems and relates the

MEDIA ADAPTATIONS

- *for colored girls who have considered suicide/ when the rainbow is enuf* was produced on June 14, 1983, by Public Broadcasting Service's *American Playhouse,* starring Patti LaBelle as the lady in brown, with music arranged by Baikida Carroll. LaBelle brings a decidedly gospel rendering of the music to the play. Shange discusses the adaptation process in *TV Guide,* February 20, 1982, pp. 14-15.

- The original sound recording of the Broadway production of *for colored girls who have considered suicide/when the rainbow is enuf* was recorded by Buddah Records, catalog number BDS 95007-OC, 1976.

- Offended by the negative image of black males they saw in Shange's work, a group of prison inmates created a parody entitled *For Colored Guys Who Have Gone beyond Suicide and Found No Rainbow: A Choreopoem/Drama.* The authors are James Able, Harrison Bennet, Harry McClelland, John Mingo, Roland Roberston, and Baari Shabazz; all male prisoners who constituted the Writers Club at the Maryland House of Correction for Men in Jessup, Maryland, 1986. The inmates' play borders on misogyny in its allegation that the problems faced by black men result from the inability of black women to sympathize with the men's struggle to survive in a racist sociopolitical system.

poem ''toussaint.'' Because she is dressed in brown, she may represent the black female ''everywoman.''

lady in green

The lady in green dances the poem ''sechita'' while the lady in purple narrates it. Sechita psychologically turns the tables on her situation and rises above the dirty carnival of Natchez, Mississippi, by making her face ''immobile,'' ''like neferetiti'' and becoming an Egyptian goddess ''conjurin the spirit'' of the men who throw coins between her legs instead of allowing herself to be possessed by them. She also relates the angry poem "somebody almost walked off wid alla my stuff," in which a woman realizes that by fastening her attention on a man, she allowed herself to be left "danglin on a string of personal carelessness" and she wants back her "calloused feet & quik language" and her "whimsical kiss"; her "stuff."

lady in orange

The lady in orange plays the stalked woman in "i used to live in the world." In another poem she defines herself as someone other than a "colored girl an evil woman a bitch a nag" only to discover that doing so leaves her no identity at all. She laments over "bein sorry & colored at the same time/it's so redundant in the modern world."

lady in purple

The lady in purple begins as one of the anonymous group of women, then steps forward to tell the story of Sechita (danced by the lady in green) and later tells of a trio of friends courted by one man in "pyramid." In "no more love poems #2" she says "lemme love you just like i am/a colored girl/i'm finally bein' real/no longer symmetrical and impervious to pain," marking a move toward acceptance of black female identity as it is and not as an unachievable ideal.

lady in red

The lady in red narrates the poem "one" about "the passion flower of southwest los angeles," a "hot" woman, "a deliberate coquette" who allows men to love and bed her, then evicts them before dawn, writes about the adventure in her diary, and cries herself to sleep. She also narrates the painful story of Crystal in "a nite with beau willie brown," whose two children Willie drops out of a fifth-floor window when she whispers too quietly that she will, after all, marry him.

lady in yellow

The lady in yellow relates the poem "graduation nite" and in another poem says "bein alive & bein a woman & bein colored is a metaphysical; dilemma / i havent conquered yet," a statement that sums up the central problem of the choreopoem. Like the other performers, lady in yellow is not a fully developed character but one voice of many in the collective experience of black women portrayed by Shange.

THEMES

Identity

"When I die, I will not be guilty," Shange proclaimed in an interview with Claudia Tate in *Black Women Writers at Work*, "of having left a generation of girls behind thinking that anyone can tend to their emotional health other than themselves." Shange has expressed a desire to make *for colored girls . . . ,* a play that explores the pain and promise of "bein alive & bein a woman & bein colored," available—on library and school bookshelves or given as a gift—to young women coming of age in America. This play is to supplement the widely available information on contraception with "emotional information," the kind of information Shange says did not get as a child, even though she grew up in an affluent, loving home. This work, like her other pieces, is meant to dispel the myths and lies that little girls hear and to replace them with something they can really use. "I want them to know that they are not alone and that we adult women thought and continue to think about them," Shange told Tate. *for colored girls . . .* is an exploration, beginning with the made metaphor of including a lady in brown among those dressed in colors of the rainbow, of the concept of a "colored girl" as "a girl of many colors." Facets of the black woman from gender- and socially oppressed victim to triumphant spell weaver and self-actualized person combine to portray a rainbow of possible selves that celebrate the black female identity.

Alienation and Loneliness

Throughout the poems of *for colored girls . . .* runs a persistent pattern of frustrated desire for male companionship and love. The inability to find a man suitable, meaning honorable and attentive, enough to return the love that these women have to offer causes a kind of inner death; the women "have died in a real way" by no longer knowing how to or what it means to love fully. They try various modes of defense, adopting the equally self-destructive masks of arrogance, revenge, and self-sufficiency. When each of these stances are ultimately debunked, the ladies are left alone with their pain and vulnerability. Reaching this point of self-honesty, the lady in purple announces, "i'm finally bein/real/no longer symmetrical and impervious to pain." After its debut in 1976, the essence of Shange's portrayal of black male-female relationships was promptly and ironically interpreted as other than it was intended by a group of male critics who accused Shange of sexism, even of man-hating. The journal *Black Scholar* carried a heated debate about the social responsibility of the play, a series of editorials that later came to be called "The Black Sexism Debate," in which Shange's conception of the black female's role in gender conflicts was obscured. The poignant irony of this misunderstanding lies in its pepetuation of a rift between black men and women, exacerbated by some participants' preoccupation with which party is the most oppressed. Thus, the ladies of *for colored girls . . .* more than ever represented the blighted and lonely status of black women in America in the 1970s.

Race and Racism

Throughout *for colored girls . . .* Shange uses the term "colored" (which she preferred because of its connotation of many-hued, rather than "black" or "African American," which she considers "artificial") as an adjective for women, not men. This is a story of the experience of "colored girls," not black people, black men, or women in general. The lot of colored girls in Shange's play is circumscribed by race, such that a girl who grew up thinking she "lived in the world" discovers her imprisonment in "six blocks" of Harlem. Her plight is further confined by sexism. In fact, sexism is Shange's predominant concern, and the theme of racism in *for colored girls . . .* is subsumed under the context of black male-female relationships. Shange, who grew up during the height of the Civil Rights Movement and of the feminist movement, outlines how in the 1970s black female identity is affected by both social oppression and the domination of black men. The effect of her play was to cause "both [the white feminist and the predominantly male black power] movements to question their exclusion of African-American women, to question their own complicity in racism and sexism," according to Karen Cronacher in *The International Dictionary of Theatre, Volume 1: Plays.*

STYLE

Choreopoem

for colored girls who have considered suicide/ when the rainbow is enuf is a choreopoem, a poem (really a series of 20 separate poems) choreographed to music. The performers dance the poems as well as narrate the lines. These are not poems set to

TOPICS FOR FURTHER STUDY

- Describe the relationship between movement and arrest or stasis in this choreopoem.

- What is the feminist ideology that informs this poem? How has feminist ideology changed since Shange wrote this play?

- Who is the intended audience of *for colored girls . . .?*

- Why does Shange spell words as she does? What is the role of language in the black female identity as she defines it? What factors contribute to or frustrate this identity?

music with accompanying dance steps, but an integration of movement, gesture, and music that together comprise the choreopoem. Improvisation is central to the choreopoem, allowing the performer to adjust the performance to her own mood and that of the audience. Shange invented this medium as a way to produce a new space for the expression of black culture, a medium that would not be judged by the stifling conventions of European and American theater because it defies definition.

Symbolism

As the title of the choreopoem implies, the rainbow is a predominant symbol in the play, one consciously applied to the ladies' costumes, which are the colors of the rainbow, plus brown. The presence of brown in the rainbow of colors symbolizes black identity within the rainbow of existence. The rainbow itself signifies the multiplicity of experience and the many facets of identity. "The rainbow is a fabulous symbol for me," Shange explained in a quote from an article by Mark Ribowsky that appeared in *Sepia* magazine, "If you see only one color, it's not beautiful. If you see them all, it is. A colored girl, by my definition, is a girl of many colors. But she can only see her overall beauty if she can see all the colors of herself. To do that, she has to look deep inside her. And when she looks inside herself, she will find . . . love and beauty."

Monologue

The twenty poems of *for colored girls . . .* were written and read at women's bars in San Francisco long before Shange decided to weave them together into a formal dramatic production. Thus, each poem exists and stands on its own, often narrated in monologue (a dramatic sketch performed by one actor) by one of the ladies, while the other performers look on, encourage, or enact the story. The collection of monologues narrated by different performers (not characters per se because they take on different roles) gives a sense of multiple perspectives, of fragmentation. However, each fragment amplifies the others such that they are unified by a common theme, the rendering of black female identity.

Leitmotif

Leitmotif is defined as music that signifies an idea, person, or situation. Musical motifs run throughout the play. Besides the music and dance that are integral to the choreopoems, music and musical terms are used as metaphors to describe the condition of ''colored girls,'' which moves from disharmony to wholeness in the course of the play. In the opening poem, words and phrases such as ''half-notes,'' ''without rhythm,'' ''no tune,'' ''the melody-less-ness of her dance'' evoke an image of clumsy discord for young black women who have been denied their girlhood. But by the end of the play, all of the ladies dance and chant together in harmony and evidently have found a rhythm that expresses their identity fully. Music also lures women dangerously toward men, as when a virgin, pretending sexual prowess while dancing to the Dells' ''Stay,'' later loses her virginity to her one of dance partners; it is also a refuge against men, as the lady in purple implies when she says ''music waz my ol man.'' Sometimes it allows women to transcend reality for a time but but only temporarily. Sechita finds a source of power in music, using dance to ''conjure'' the cracker men in the audience of a tawdry carnival. Ultimately, music becomes part of the harmony of the black female identity.

HISTORICAL CONTEXT

The 1970s: Counterculture Gives Way to Skeptical Indifference

In the 1970s ongoing protest against the war in Vietnam finally resulted in a massive withdrawal of American troops, culminating in the Fall of Saigon in 1975. The war had cost America billions of dollars, 56,000 U.S. lives, and the credibility of the U.S. military. It would have cost President Nixon his credibility, had he not already sullied himself with Watergate, a cover-up that failed as one by one his minions, fearing prosecution, exposed Nixon's extensive and illegal system for spying on the Democratic party. Confidence in the government hit an all-time low and inflation instigated a pervasive sense of pessimism about the future. Young people sought refuge in the sudden abundance of discotheques, where they gyrated to formulaic and repetitive tunes that required little thought or imagination; other forms of escapism prevailed.

The Civil Rights Movement Collides with the Feminist Movement

While the Civil Rights Movement contained an inner conflict between militant Black Panthers and Malcolm X and the passive resistance promoted by Martin Luther King, Jr., the feminist movement was a virtual study in contrasts. Barbie doll sales hit the first of many sales peaks in 1963, just when women were proclaiming their right not to be measured by an unhealthy physical ideal. Twiggy, a skinny model weighing no more than 95 pounds, exemplified the new antifeminine figure. At the same time that the popularity of hotpants and topless bathing suits contributed to revealing female fashions, women expressed resentment at being viewed as sex objects. Miniskirt hemlines shot up and then dropped to maxi ankle-length in 1972, around the same time that many women expressed a preference to be addressed as Ms. instead of Mrs. or Miss. Pantsuits replaced the requisite skirt at many workplaces. The first black Barbie doll hit the market in 1968, the same year that Shirley Chisolm became the first black female member of the House of Representatives. During this period of sexual upheaval women's lib consisted of sexual freedom bordering on licentiousness (made possible by the widespread availability of the birth control pill in the early 1960s) oddly coupled with the suppression of sexuality as a marker of female identity. Divorce rates began a climb that did not slow for several decades as women became economically and socially self-sufficient.

Unfortunately, neither the Civil Rights Movement nor the Women's Liberation movement made a viable place for black women. This situation would change, partly as a result of Shange's play. African Americans, no longer referred to as colored people, sought to amend their identity by embracing

COMPARE
&
CONTRAST

- **1970s:** During the Civil Rights Movement era of the 1950s, 1960s, and 1970s, African Americans sought freedom to vote, work, and obtain an education equal to white Americans. Women, almost exclusively white women, began the women's liberation movement in the 1960s. But both groups excluded black women, who had even more difficulty than black men in finding an equitable place in society.

  Today: Louis Farrakhan's 1995 Million Man March in Washington, D.C. acknowledged that black men must step up to greater responsibility in the black American family, providing the respect to black women for which the women of Shange's play hoped.

- **1970s:** Opportunities for black women were limited by societal restraints and a culture that was slow to accept them in arenas such as business, politics, and the arts. Following Lorraine Hansberry's bow on Broadway, it was nearly twenty years before Shange, the second black woman playwright on Broadway, made her debut.

  Today: While black Americans in general, and particularly black women, still have a great ways to go in attaining equality in American society, many have made significant inroads, thanks in great part to the pioneering spirit of women like Shange, poet Maya Angelou, and politicians such as Barbara Jordan. Playwrights such as Anna Deveare Smith owe a great deal to Shange's innovations, both socially and dramatically.

---

their African heritage. Alex Haley's 1976 epic, *Roots,* played a large role in the popularity of African heritage and raised many African Americans' awareness of their own genealogies. Lorraine Hansberry's 1959 play, *A Raisin in the Sun* had tangentially alluded to potential difficulties for African American relations with Africans, specifically for black women. In the play, Beneatha Younger cuts her hair in an afro style, dons African dress, and plays African music, but she refuses to marry her African suitor and relocate to Africa, preferring the more obstacle-ridden course of pursuing a career as a doctor in racist America. Her plight remains unresolved at the end of the play. By the 1970s, black female identity was still largely subsumed beneath black identity and female identity. For Shange to proclaim in 1976 that black women were oppressed was not news but to declare that they were oppressed by black males (in addition to white society as a whole) was a revelation. Shange showed that black women existed on the bottommost rung of the social hierarchy. The budding women's movement crossed paths with the growing civil rights movement to reveal that black women were doubly oppressed.

The expression of rage in *for colored girls . . . ,* directed primarily at black males, caused a stir in 1976. The journal *Black Scholar* ran a series of debates on black sexism. Robert Staples voiced the sense of shock felt by some black men that black women would turn against their racial brothers, and black women accused Staples and others who expressed similar opinions of ignoring the ways in which black males did in fact oppress their racial sisters. It is a debate that lost its intensity over the next ten years as black women found strength in their racial and gender identity. Ultimately black women rose in social status so that by the 1990s black men stood on the bottom of the social hierarchy, a situation that prompted the Million Man March on Washington D.C., an event organized by Louis Farrakhan in 1995.

Theater

Drama in the 1960s was a forum for challenging convention, for experimenting with new styles. The stage musical *Hair* in 1967 introduced nudity, shocking language, and celebration of the hippie lifestyle, an aesthetic that valued personal expressions of uniqueness and freedom over more main-stream, middle-class values, and shocked the nation on its wildly controversial road tour. In 1969 *Oh, Calcutta,* a series of erotic sketches, made *Hair* look tame in comparison. In 1971 *Godspell* and *Jesus Christ Superstar* committed what many felt was a sacrilege, namely conflating religion with Broadway spectacle, to huge success. However, rising inflation in the 1970s slowed the impetus of experimental theater. One of the few notable works produced besides *for colored girls . . .* was *The Wiz,* a version of *The Wizard of Oz* in which the characters are black and the settings are urban. The play began a run of over 1,000 performances in 1975. By this time such novelties as audience interaction, open staging, unconventional costuming, and revolutionary content had become theatrical stock-in-trade. Musicals no longer consisted of the blithe romance of a Rodgers and Hammerstein production; now audiences expected to be shocked and challenged as a form of entertainment. In black theater Imamu Amiri Baraka (also known as LeRoi Jones) broke with tradition by producing works centered on racial confrontation. Shange adopted his radical use of slashes, lower case letters, phonetic spelling and dialect as well as his militant program of making theater a center for consciousness-raising for black rights and for building the black community. Baraka expressed the belief that theatre was more effective at reaching a wider black audience than were other media, Shange (the second black female playwright to have her work produced on Broadway, the first being Lorraine Hansberry) proved that theatre could be just as effective at reaching white audiences.

CRITICAL OVERVIEW

Taking *for colored girls who have considered suicide/when the rainbow is enuf* to New York City in 1976 entailed polishing the act for a more demanding, theater-sophisticated audience than the appreciative and supportive mostly female audiences in the cafes and women's bars of San Francisco. Shange, just twenty-seven at the time, relied on theater director Oz Scott to transform the twenty separate poems into a unified and cohesive play, sharpening the theatrical elements along the way. The predominantly black audiences of the Joseph Papp Anspacher Theater production reacted with obvious pride and exhilaration. Alan Rich's review for *New York* magazine treated the play as an anomaly, "respectable plays by blacks being a

comparatively new phenomenon.'' Clive Barnes, who in 1982 would include Shange's choreopoem in the 8th edition of *Best American Plays,* expressed appreciation in his 1976 *New York Times* review for the fact that, rather than make him "feel guilty at being white and male" the play made him "proud . . . with the joyous discovery that a white man can have black sisters.'' But not all of the reviews were so positive. Theater critic John Simon did not share the sense of euphoria, snidely asking in his *New Leader* review: "Is this poetry? Drama? Or simply tripe? Would it have been staged if written by a white?''

Literary critic Neal Lester, writing in 1995, suggested that Simon's inability to appreciate Shange's innovative work stemmed from a need for a new critical language that would assess the choreopoem on "its own cultural and aesthetic terms.'' The concept of a play in which the plot proceeds through music and dance was not without precedent; *West Side Story* (1957) was not so much a musical, a drama with music added, but a ballet or opera with dialogue added. Broadway had just experienced a transformation of theatrical conventions in the form of long-running hits, *Hair* (1967), *Godspell* and *Jesus Christ Superstar* (both 1971), and *A Chorus Line* (1975), that took for granted the integration of music and action. However, even in these landmark works, poetry, music, and improvisational dance had never before been fused together with such force and integrity as Shange accomplished, and the new critical language required to discuss the "choreopoem" on its own terms would be a while longer in coming.

Reviews of the Broadway debut of *for colored girls . . .* were mixed. Theater critic Jessica Harris applauded the play for being the first popular success by a female black playwright who, rather than proffer the expected stereotypes, portrayed the black female condition truthfully. But negative reactions came from African American men, who focused on the negative portrayal of black males. Their voices were included in a series of essays in *Black Scholar* later to be known collectively as the Black Sexism Debate. From an outsider's perspective it looks like a turf battle over which group was more oppressed. Robert Staples, quoted in an *African American Review* article by Lester, saw in the play "a collective appetite for black male blood" and complained that the characters portray circumstances far from his own personal experience. Furthermore, Staples interpreted the "laying on of hands" conclusion of the play as a dangerous move toward narcissism. He chided Shange for failing to explain how black men suffer in self-respect at the hands of black women. According to Lester, also author of *Ntozake Shange: A Critical Study of the Plays,* "Staples's comments are typical of the partriarchy's reversing the roles of victim and perpetrator." Shange herself replied to Staples and other contributors in the form of two poems, "is not so gd to be born a girl" and "otherwise I would think it odd to have rape prevention month." In all, the Black Sexism Debate filled forty-eight pages of the May-June 1979 edition of the journal. It was followed by a spate of assertions in *Black American Literature Forum, Black Scholar,* and elsewhere that Shange demonstrated compassion and integrity in her ruthlessly honest portrayal of a few black males in *for colored girls . . . ,* that her intent was not to malign black males but to paint reality as it was for African Americans of both genders.

As the black sexism debate lost its fury, later critics found new ways to discuss the choreopoem. One way looks at the ideology expressed in it— Sandra Richards in 1983 explored the conflict experienced by characters who "ricochet from a devastating social reality wherein they are totally vulnerable to an ecstatic spirituality wherein they are identical with an eternal, natural power." Another focuses on the performance aspect of the choreopoem; John Timpane in 1989 argued that the improvisational character and collage structure of the performance and even the creative orthography of the script work to undermine audience expectations for closure and tidy structure. This resistant dramatic structure thus serves to create new possibilities for the identity of those it celebrates; according to Timpane, "it is used to challenge preconceived notions, show unexpected connections, and call forth the richness and dynamism of existence." Tejumolo Olaniyan in 1995 focused upon the play's use of language. Quoting Shange as asserting "After all I didn't mean whatever you can ignore. I mean what you have to struggle with," Olaniyan aligned the playwright with French linguistic philosopher Jean-Francois Lyotard, who says that language joins in the oppression of a victim by making it impossible to express the crime. Shange has asserted that her predicament has led her to "attack deform n maim the language that i was taught to hate myself in." Olaniyan explored the way in which Shange's improvisational use of language succeeds in molding a language that can both express the crime and reconstitute the victim.

Shange and numerous critics have noted that the era for which she constructed *for colored girls . . .* was unique in history, short-lived, and that the play no longer fits the social reality of some black women, although many still find themselves trapped in similar situations. However, the timeless power of the piece continues to command audience attention through its improvisational dance and its fusion of unique language, structure, and meaning.

CRITICISM

Carole L. Hamilton

Hamilton, an instructor of English at Cary Academy, discusses Shange's departures from conventional drama.

Shange has asserted that the form of the conventional play is too restrictive; in her introductory essay to *three pieces,* which was quoted in *Ntozake Shange: A Critical Study of the Plays,* she called it "a truly european framework for european psychology" which cannot serve as a medium in which to express black culture, psychology, and sensibility. In that same essay, she explained that because she views American theater as "overwhelmingly shallow . . . stilted, and imitative," she insists upon calling herself a "poet or writer" rather than a playwright. Indeed, *for colored girls who have considered suicide/when the rainbow is enuf* has more in common with poetry, music, and dance than with traditional theater scripts, but it is certainly good theater—good dramatic theater—as well. In a departure from conventional theater, she jettisons characters and plot, instead presenting transient performer/characters who portray an apartment house of stories. Within each apartment, each episodic poem, lives a black girl, trying to escape the confines of an oppressive society. Yet even though Shange has done away with plot, there is a progression within the poems that explores the "metaphysical dilemma" of "bein alive & bein a woman & bein colored." The play ends with a sense of closure as though the dilemma has been accepted or understood and fully expressed, and, if not resolved, on the way to a solution. Typical of Shange's style, she coins a new term for her dramatic work— "choreopoem," a choreographed poem. Her poems are not just accompanied by music and dance, but "danced poems" in which dance, movements, and gestures express as much meaning as do the words of the poem.

WHAT DO I READ NEXT?

- Maya Angelou's poem ''Phenomenal Woman'' in the collection *Chicken Soup for a Woman's Soul* celebrates the spiritual and physical aspects of black female identity.

- Nikki Giovanni's poem ''Ego Tripping (There May Be a Reason Why)'' (1970) in *The Norton Anthology of Modern Poetry*, edited by Richard Ellman and Robert O'Clair, is another celebration of black female identity.

- A book of seven poems describing seven ''common'' women in *The Common Woman* by Judy Grahn (1970) served as a model for Shange's *for colored girls who have considered suicide/when the rainbow is enuf*

- Mary Daly's polemical text, *Gyn/Econlogy: The Metaethics of Radical Feminism*, Beacon, 1978 (Boston), underlies Shange's form of feminism, in which she attempts to redefine femaleness through creation of a new, more affirming, language.

- The chapter called ''Beauty and Ethnicity'' in Robin Lakoff's work *Face Value: The Politics of Beauty*, Routledge and Kegan Paul, 1984, discusses the social stereotypes and implications of black female beauty and her *Language and Woman's Place*, Octagon, 1976, discusses how standard English reflects and encourages the lower social status of women.

- Lorraine Hansberry's play, *A Raisin in the Sun*, while not exclusively devoted to sexism, realistically portrays the different expectations and limitations that face black men and women in Chicago in the 1960s.

- Imamu Amiri Baraka's 1972 essay ''Black Revolutionary' Poets Should Also be Playwrights'' in *Black World*, Vol. 21, April, 1972, pp. 4-6, explains his strategy of militant black theater to raise consciousness about racism.

Movement and innovation are key themes in *for colored girls . . .* and are important concepts in all of Shange's work. She sees herself as creating a new place where her ''voices'' (her characters as well as her thoughts), ''can be heard, where they can move around, they can dance or they can hear music that they want to hear,'' as she explained in an interview with Angela Davis in 1989. In removing the structure of the conventional play and focusing on her invented medium of choreopoem, which she alone does best, Shange withdraws her work from the range of sniping (white, male) critics. She finds this an exhilarating place to be and has described it as being ''at war with and making love to the world at the same time,'' as quoted in *Ntozake Shange: A Critical Study of the Plays.*

Dance carries differing meanings within *for colored girls. . . .* Sometimes transcendent moments of joy in movement and dance are halted by harsh reality. The poem ''latent rapists'' interrupts celebratory dancing at the end of ''i'm a poet who'' with a sudden change of light that causes the ladies ''to react as if they had been struck in the face.'' They stop dancing and withdraw into themselves. This arrest of movement announces the topic of date rape, a situation in which trust is betrayed by overpowering domination and violence. Domination, whether by physical force such as in rape or through the social strictures of living in a white-dominated world, imposes a stultifying order over these women.

Dancing and movement also makes the women vulnerable. To dance is to participate in life to the fullest degree and yet a young girl may pay a terrible price for a night of celebrating joy in dance and sexual awakening, as described in ''abortion cycle #1.'' The young girl who danced with complete abandonment suddenly finds herself on a hospital gurney, alone and strapped down for an emotionally and physically torturous procedure. There is no escaping, however, the urge to dance and be completely alive. In "no more love poem #3" the lady in purple realizes that she doesn't want to "dance wit ghosts," that the only way to live is to interact with men and pay the consequences. The lady in yellow regrets her "dependency on other livin beins for love" because she knows that her love will only be "thrown back on [her] face." Nevertheless, the ladies continue to long for male relationships. That the men in this play—with the possible exception of Toussaint Jones—never live up to women's expectations of them has been interpreted by some as an invective against black males. Shange sees this perspective as limited and limiting because it once again takes the focus off of women and places it on men.

In an earlier poem, Sechita, a tawdry carnival dancer, tries to evade the vulnerability of dancing by adopting a mask. She "made her face immobile/ she made her face like nefertiti" as a defense against the whoops of the drunken men of the carnival audience. Then Sechita uses the very dance meant to display her like a piece of merchandise to turn the tables on her audience so that rather than being the object of their lewd gazes, she becomes an Egyptian goddess performing a rite, "the conjurin of men," holding them in thrall. Through her performance she improvises a place of honor where none existed before, a commendable effort.

However, even the triumph of Sechita, kicking out her leg in vicious command, is a kind of failure because ultimately, she is alone. She is like the "passion flower" who, with a different kind of mask, lures men to her bed in order to reject them before dawn, succeeding at punishing them for having the arrogance to want her but still crying herself to sleep after recording her exploits in her diary. Thus, the immobility of the mask is itself stultifying and serves only to remind a young black woman that she cannot "survive on intimacy & tomorrow" if she has no one with whom to share it. It does no good to adopt a false stance because the stance itself prevents intimacy. Even though intimacy may bring pain, it is better to risk being vulnerable, to be "real/no longer symmetrical & impervious to pain" and possibly find love and fulfillment.

Unfortunately, some young black women are victimized by the kind of intimacy that socially wounded black men offer. In "a nite with beau willie brown," Crystal holds too tightly to her children, and her act of immobility destroys them and her. She too finds it impossible to engage in a mutually responsive and responsible dance with a black man. Throughout the poem, movement vies with stasis and neither Crystal nor Willie is capable of reading the signs around them or from each other. If they could, perhaps they might move beyond their psychologically-impaired marriage. Willie, a Vietnam War veteran, keeps getting placed into in remedial reading classes and cannot secure a good job. He is depicted as "an ol frozen bundle of chicken" sweating in his bed. When Crystal gets pregnant a second time, he beats her. She combats his violent behavior by getting a court order denying him access to his children. When he comes to visit her, apparently wanting to prove himself a good husband and father at last, Crystal is too mired up in the pain of their past to move toward him. She holds her children tight to her, so that getting possession of them becomes his sole objective. They fight each other with forms of entrapment, the weapon that society has used upon them. The refrain "there waz no air" weaves through the poem, suggesting a universal suffocation. In response to Willie's demand for public acceptance of him, Crystal can only whisper in his oppressive presence. Her voice fails her because, metaphorically speaking, she has no "voice" in her relationship or in her world. Because her lackluster response fails to satisfy Willie, he drops the children out of the fifth-story window. If Crystal had been allowed to have a voice, she might have stopped Willie; if she been able to improvise, she might have risen above their past, allowing him to respond in kind. But there "waz no air."

Movement is a means to escape stasis or imprisonment. According to critic Olaniyan: "In the hands of the dominated but rebellious poet, the slippery, unfixable forms, music and dance, become instruments for breaking down and reaching beyond the claustrophobic dominated space." Harlem is a closing tunnel, a six-block universe, where a girl has to turn up the music loud until "there is no me but dance." The dancer escapes the fetters of an uncivil society, albeit only briefly. Transcendence is merely a form of escapism, a temporary respite during which one manages to ignore reality for a time. But movement can also serve as a means of creating and maintaining a strong sense of self. Once she overcame the misperception that the black female body is not ideal, Shange discovered that dance can meld body and soul into a more harmonious unit. As Shange explains in the preface to *for colored girls who have considered suicide/when the rainbow is enuf:* "With the acceptance of the ethnicity of my thighs & backside, came a clearer understanding of my voice as a woman & as a poet. The freedom to move in space, to demand of my own sweat a perfection that could continually be approached, though never known, was poem to me, my body & mind ellipsing, probably for the first time in my life." The improvisational movement and dance of *for colored girls . . .* transcends limiting reality and leads to the unlimited realm of creativity and self-actualization.

The lasting qualities of Shange's work lie in the production of a new vision of self—black female self. Improvisational performance and dance participate in this production, as do gesture and language. For in language, too, Shange practices improvisation. She is quoted in *Ntozake Shange: A Critical Study of the Plays* as asserting: "I like the idea that letters dance, not just that words dance, of course, the words also dance." To make words and letters dance, Shange eliminates capitalization and punctuation and spells phonetically. More than dialect, her language is new one, a fusion of poetry and vernacular. The lady in green refers to it as her "quik language." Quik language is witty, creative, incisive—oral poetry invented on the spot and for the moment only, in phrases like "push your leg to the moon with me." This new language refuses to be bound by conventional orthography. Even when Shange needs punctuation to indicate a pause, she invents her own, inserting virgules (/), normally reserved for marking off poetic feet, as short stops. In her introductory essay to *three pieces,* Shange explained her unconventional use of language: "i haveta fix my tools to/my needs," she said "i have to take it apart to the bone/so that the malignancies/fall/away leaving us space to literally create our own image." The convergence of quik language with "quik feet" and music "like smack" brings into being the "felt architecture" that Shange likes to create. In this emotional environment, a colored girl can experience what Flannery O'Connor termed "moments of being," flashes of self-actualization in a world that makes such moments precious indeed. Shange explains her emphasis on improvisation in her manifesto entitled "takin a solo/a poetic possibility/a poetic imperative." Weaving her own poetic theory among snippets of poems by Ishmael Reed, Leroi Jones, Victor Hernandez Cruz, and others, she proclaims, "i am giving you a moment/like something that isnt coming back." For the audience, trying to comprehend the specta-

cle, her moments may prove puzzling. Shange clearly articulated her motive in an interview with Claudia Tate: "I can't let you get away with thinking you know what I mean. I didn't mean whatever you can ignore. I mean what you have to struggle with." Struggling with what she means is a fruitful exercise in mental improvisation. Just as inserting the color brown into the rainbow presents a potential new definition of "colored girls," Shange's work also succeeds in redefining the rest of the world as well.

Source: Carole L. Hamilton, in an essay for *Drama for Students,* Gale, 1997.

Lynn F. Miller

In the following review, Miller explores the structure and style of for colored girls*. . . . She credits both Ntozake Shange and director Oz Scott with creating a stirring poetic enactment of a black girl's initiation into womanhood.*

Miller is an educator and critic who has worked extensively with women in the visual and performing arts.

Joseph Papp has developed a system for moving talented new playwrights, directors, and actors from workshop beginnings through Off-Broadway productions to Broadway. *For Colored Girls* has successfully followed the Papp program: from its beginnings as a workshop production at the Henry Street Settlement Playhouse, to an Off-Broadway production at the Public, and on to the Booth.

For Colored Girls has a wider appeal than its title suggests; it is not for black women only, although the experiences culled and given life on the Booth stage are directly related to the lives of many black women. Ming Cho Lee's huge red paper peony up center, placed in front of the deep purple backdrop, is the only scenic element; it is all that is needed, standing as it does for the unified heart, brain, gut, womb, and center of being not only of the "colored girls" in the title but of all women. The purity, incisiveness, and truth of the writing reaches into the red flower at the center of all women; universal truths, drawn in detail, spill out in well-controlled poem-monologues from the actresses on stage directly into the emotional receivers in the guts of the audience. It is the directness of the emotional communication that electrifies the audience.

By means of his arrangement of Ntozake Shange's autobiographical poetry pieces, each an investigation into a particular aspect of private

black womanhood, the director, Oz Scott, has created a form resonant of a rite of passage. The passage
is from girlhood and innocence, through adolescence and the beginnings of self-discovery, into
adult suffering through love, and finally to self-
acceptance. The action of the piece—finding and
accepting oneself—has been created by structuring
the poems into a pattern as sensitive as flowers
arranged by an Ikebana artist.

While not a traditional play, *For Colored Girls*
is essentially theatrical, rooted in rite, ceremony,
and mythology. The characters experience deep
conflicts, and a resolution is achieved. In structure
the work is musical, resembling jazz riffs, once
improvisationally emerging directly from street experience, now structured like Ellington's music into
notations that record and codify joyfulness, melancholy, or a sense of tragic despair. With choreogra-
phy by Paula Moss (also one of the actresses), the
poems insist on being danced as well as acted.

Judy Dearing's costumes confirm the importance of movement in the piece; they are really
dance costumes that free the actresses' bodies for
any movement. The most superb moments are in the
poem ''Sechita'' evoking African goddesses of the
distant past through the recreation of a cabaret
dancer in New Orleans. The poem is expertly spok-
en by Rise Collins and danced by Paula Moss.

There are elements of comedy, tragedy, and
biting satire in the production. The most vividly
tragic piece, ''Nite with Beau Willie Brown,'' produces near-hysterical laughter culminating in tears.
A crazed black war veteran beats his abused lover
with a highchair in which their baby still sits, an
unfamiliar, savage image, offbeat and almost surre-
al, as are many of the images in this piece.

Ntozake Shange has served up slices of her
world. For some people this reality is intolerable,
requiring the defense of laughter. Even for Shange,
reality is too much sometimes. In ''I Used to Live in
the World (But then I Moved to Harlem),'' the poet
lashes out with bitterness at the shrunken existence
in such a constricted universe.

Rites of initiation traditionally culminate in a
vision of the godhead. *For Colored Girls,* structured
as an initiation rite into full adult womanhood—
passing through the stages of life in concretely
remembered specific experiences—culminates in
the joyous affirmation of the beauty and integrity of
the black woman's self. It is a rousing yet delicate,

> WHILE NOT A TRADITIONAL
> PLAY, *FOR COLORED GIRLS* IS
> ESSENTIALLY THEATRICAL, ROOTED
> IN RITE, CEREMONY, AND
> MYTHOLOGY"

strongly felt spiritual dedicated to the earthy reality of the great goddess/mother/source-of-all-
life, sincerely perceived by Shange to be a woman,
probably a black woman. (pp. 262–63)

Source: Lynn F. Miller, in a review of *for colored girls who
have considered suicide/when the rainbow is enuf,* in *Educational Theatre Journal,* Vol. 29, No. 2, May, 1977, pp.
262–63.

Harold Clurman

*In the following excerpt, Clurman offers a
positive review of* for colored girls *... declaring:
"There is no black (or white) sentimentality here,
no glamorizing of Harlem or any other ghetto
existence; there is the eloquence of moral and
sensory awareness couched in language powerful
in common speech and a vocabulary both precise
and soulfully felt."*

*Highly regarded as a director, author, and
longtime drama critic for the* Nation, *Clurman was
an important contributor to the development of the
modern American theater.*

I hope a way may be devised to arrange a national
tour to a presentation I recently saw at the Henry
Street Settlement's New Federal Theatre (on Grand
Street) in cooperation with Joseph Papp's Public
Theatre: it was for me a signal event.

It is called *For Colored Girls Who Have Considered Suicide/When the Rainbow is Enuf. . . .* Its
author, St. Louis-born Ntozake Shange, is a young
woman who appeared as one of its performers and is
now an artist-in-residence of the New Jersey
State Council on the Arts. She calls her piece a
''choreopoem''—poems in verse and prose to be
voiced singly, in pairs or in unison by four actresses
and three women dancers, with occasional accom-

> ❝ THERE IS NO BLACK (OR WHITE) SENTIMENTALITY HERE, NO GLAMORIZING OF HARLEM OR ANY OTHER GHETTO EXISTENCE; THERE IS THE ELOQUENCE OF MORAL AND SENSORY AWARENESS COUCHED IN LANGUAGE POWERFUL IN COMMON SPEECH AND A VOCABULARY BOTH PRECISE AND SOULFULLY FELT"

panying music. The women hail from various parts of the country.

Because the text is composed of a series of poems of decided literary worth, I first thought that the performance would have greater impact if they were recited so that no word was lost through movement. But as the evening went on (and on examining the script) I realized that my first impression was mistaken. The faces and bodies as well as the voices of the actresses give the occasion its special force. Much credit for the success of the event is also due to its director, Oz Scott, who saw the "play" in the material.

In a number of respects this work is unique. Its stress is on the experience of black women—their passionate outcry, as women, within the black community. There is no bad-mouthing the whites: feelings on that score are summed up in the humorously scornful lines addressed to a black man which begin: "ever since I realized there was someone callt a colored girl, a evil woman, a bitch or a nag, I been tryin' not to be that and leave bitterness in somebody elses cup. . . . I finally bein real no longer symmetrical and inervious to pain . . . so why don't we be white then and make everythin' dry and abstract wid no rhythm and no reelin' for sheer sensual pleasure. . . ." The woman who utters these words, like all the others, speaks not so much in apology or explanation of her black condition but in essential human protest against her black lover whose connection with her is the ordinary (white or black) callousness toward women. Thus she asserts "I've lost it/touch with reality/I know who's doin'

it. . . . I should be unsure, if I'm still alive. . . . I survive on intimacy and to-morrow. . . . But bein' alive and bein' a woman and bein' colored is a metaphysical dilemma."

This gives only a pitifully partial notion of the pain and power, as well as the acrid wit—"so redundant in the modern world"—which much of the writing communicates. The thematic emphasis is constantly directed at the stupid crudity and downright brutality of their own men, which, whatever the causes, wound and very nearly destroy their women. These women have been driven to the very limits of their endurance (or "rainbow") and are desperately tired of hearing their men snivel that they're "sorry." Part of the joy in the performance lay in the ecstatic response of the women in the audience!

There is no black (or white) sentimentality here, no glamorizing of Harlem or any other ghetto existence; there is the eloquence of moral and sensory awareness couched in language powerful in common speech and a vocabulary both precise and soulfully felt. . . .

Source: Harold Clurman, in a review of *for colored girls who have considered suicide/when the rainbow is enuf,* in the *Nation,* Vol. 222, no. 17, May 1, 1976, pp. 541–42.

FURTHER READING

Baraka, Imamu Amiri. "Black 'Revolutionary' Poets Should Also Be Playwrights." *Black World,* April, 1972, pp. 4-7.
  A manifesto for black playwrights to use the theater as a platform for demanding social change.

Brown-Guillory, Elizabeth. *Their Place on the Stage: Black Women Playwrights in America,* Greenwood Press, 1988.
  A treatise on the influence of black female playwrights with part of one chapter devoted to Shange.

SOURCES

Barnes, Clive. "Ntozake Shange's *For Colored Girls* Opens at Papp's Anspacher Theater." *New York Times,* June 2, 1976, p. 44.

Cronacher, Karen. "*for colored girls who have considered suicide/when the rainbow is enuf* by Ntozake Shange." in *International Dictionary of Theatre-1: Plays,* pp. 258-60, St. James, 1992.

Davis, Angela. "Ntozake Shange Interview with Angela Davis." Videotape, American Poetry Archives, The Poetry Center, San Francisco State University, May 5, 1989.

Flower, Sandra Hollin. "Colored Girls: Textbook for the Eighties" in *Black American Literature Forum* Vol. 15 (1981), p. 52.

Harris, Jessica. "*for colored girls* . . . from Ntozake to Broadway" in *New York Amsterdam News/Arts and Entertainment,* October 9, 1976, p. D11.

Hooks, Bell. *Talking Back: Thinking Feminist, Thinking Black,* South End (Boston), 1989.

Lester, Neal A. "Shange's Men: *for colored girls* . . . Revisited, and Movement Beyond" in *African American Review* Vol. 26, no. 2, 1992.

Lester, Neal A. *Ntozake Shange: A Critical Study of the Plays* Garland Publishing, 1995.

New York Times, June 16, 1976.

Olaniyan, Tejumola. "Ntozake Shange: The Vengeance of Difference, or The Gender of Black Cultural Identity" in *Scars of Conquest, Masks of Resistance: The Invention of Cultural Identities in African, African-American, and Caribbean Drama,* Oxford University Press, 1995.

Ribowsky, Mark. "A Poetess Scores a Hit with Play on 'What's Wrong with Black Men'" in *Sepia,* December 25, 1976, p. 46.

Rich, Alan. "Theater: For Audiences of any color when 'Rex' is not enuf" in *New York,* June 14, 1976, p. 62.

Richards, Sandra L. "Conflicting Impulses in the Plays of Ntozake Shange" in *Black American Literature Forum,* Vol. 17, no. 2, Summer, 1983, pp. 73-78.

Simon, John. "Stage: 'Enuf' is Not Enough" in *New Leader* Vol. 59, July 5, 1976.

Smith, Yvonne. "Ntozake Shange: A 'Colored Girl' Considers Success" in *Essence,* February, 1982, p. 12.

Tate, Claudia P. "Ntozake Shange" in *Black Women Writers at Work,* Continuum, 1983, pp. 149-174.

Timpane, John. "'The Poetry of a Moment': Politics and the Open Forum in the Drama of Ntozake Shange" in *Studies in American Drama, 1945-Present,* Vol 4, 1989, pp. 91-101.

Trescott, Jaqueline. "Ntozake Shange: Searching for Respect and Identity" in *Washington Post,* June 29, 1976, p. B5.

Glengarry Glen Ross

DAVID MAMET

1983

David Mamet's *Glengarry Glen Ross* was first presented at the small Cottlesloe Theatre of the Royal National Theatre, in London, England, on September 21, 1983. The critics gave the play strongly positive reviews and the production played to sold-out audiences. It was later awarded the Society of West End Theatres Award (similar to the American "Tony" Award) as best new play. The American premier of *Glengarry Glen Ross* took place at Chicago's Goodman Theatre on February 6, 1984; with one cast change, the production then transferred to Broadway's Golden Theatre on March 25. With very few exceptions, the New York critics recognized the play as brilliant in itself and a major advance for Mamet as a playwright. Nevertheless, ticket sales were slow and the play lost money for two weeks. After it was awarded the Pulitzer Prize, sales increased significantly. It ultimately ran for 378 performances, closing on February 17, 1985.

Many critics in both England and America pointed out that, for all its use of "four-letter words," *Glengarry Glen Ross* is a morality play. They noted that the work is an abrasive attack on American business and culture and a withering depiction of the men whose lives and values are twisted by a world in which they must lie, cheat, and even steal in order to survive. Virtually all of the critics commented extensively on Mamet's use of language, not only to create tension and define character, but also as a sort of musical poetry: "hot jazz and wounding blues," as Frank Rich, critic for

the *New York Times* put it. Even those few critics who were lukewarm about the play as a whole appreciated the distinctive, powerful language. Critics also appreciated the savage, scalding comedy of the play.

The influences of playwrights Samuel Beckett and Harold Pinter on Mamet has been pointed out by numerous critics, and Mamet has said that he has also been influenced by Lanford Wilson, Eugene Ionesco, Bertolt Brecht, and Anton Chekhov. He has also acknowledged the influence of Thorstein Veblen's *Theory of the Leisure Class.* A strong nonliterary influence has been his study of the Stanislavsky system (named for the famed director of the Moscow Art Theatre, Konstantin Stanislavsky) of actor training as interpreted and taught by Sanford Meisner and Lee Strasberg at the Actors Studio.

AUTHOR BIOGRAPHY

David Mamet was born in Chicago, Illinois, on November 30, 1947. His father was a labor lawyer and his mother a schoolteacher. After his parents' divorce in 1958, Mamet lived with his mother and sister. He played football, wrestled, and was a voracious reader. In 1963, he moved to North Chicago to live with his father and attend the private Francis Parker school where he first took drama classes and played the lead in a musical. He also worked backstage at Hull House theatre and at the famous improvisational Second City Company.

Mamet studied literature and drama at Goddard College in Vermont, where he received a B.A. degree in 1969. His first short play, *Camel,* was written to fulfill his thesis requirement. During his time at Goddard, he spent a year "in the field" at the Neighborhood Playhouse School of the Theatre in New York City, where he studied the Stanislavsky system of acting under the direction of Sanford Meisner. During his college years Mamet's summer jobs included work as an actor and "specialty dancer" with several theatres. Following his graduation in 1969, he worked in Montreal with a company based on the campus of McGill University. He then returned to Chicago where he worked as a cab driver and, for almost a year, in the office of a "dubious" real estate firm. The latter experience is clearly evident in *Glengarry Glen Ross.* In 1970, Mamet taught acting at Marlboro College in Vermont, where he wrote *Lifeboat,* based on his experiences with one summer job. The following two years, he

David Mamet

taught at Goddard and, while there, presented the first versions of *Duck Variations* and *Sexual Perversity in Chicago. Duck Variations* was subsequently presented in Chicago in the fall of 1972, marking the first production of a play by Mamet in his hometown. In the fall of 1973, Mamet moved back to Chicago. *Sexual Perversity in Chicago* was presented by the Organic Theatre Company in the summer of 1974, drew large audiences, and was awarded the prestigious Joseph Jefferson Award. In 1975 he completed *American Buffalo* and that work was presented by the Goodman Theatre with critical and popular success. On January 23, 1976, *American Buffalo,* with a new cast, opened at St. Clement's theatre in New York City, receiving generally positive notices. Mamet moved to New York the next month. That summer *Sexual Perversity in Chicago* and *Duck Variations* opened at the Off-Broadway Cherry Lane Theatre, where they would enjoy a long run; in February 1977, *American Buffalo* opened on Broadway and was awarded the New York Drama Critics' Circle Award.

Mamet's career flourished throughout the 1980s and 1990s, with such notable works as *Edmund* (1982), *Glengarry Glen Ross* (1983), *Speed-the-Plow* (1988), and *Oleanna* (1992). He also ventured into film during this period, writing the scripts for

The Postman Always Rings Twice (1981), *The Verdict* (1982)—which won an Academy Award nomination—*The Untouchables* (1987), and *Hoffa* (1992). His success as a screenwriter led to opportunities as a director, including the films *House of Games* (1988), *Homicide* (1991), and *Oleanna* (1995), all of which he also wrote.

PLOT SUMMARY

Act I

Glengarry Glen Ross has a daring structure with two very different forms for the two acts. Act One is broken up into three scenes, each set in a different booth in a Chinese restaurant in Chicago; while not clearly stated, all of the action may be occurring simultaneously. Through these scenes we come to know the jargon of the real estate sales world: "lead" is a sales prospect; the "board" is a chart of sales closings; "sit" is a face-to-face meeting with a prospect; "closing" is getting the customer's signature on a contract and a check. We also learn, bit by bit, that there is a sales contest on and that the winner of the first prize will receive a Cadillac, second prize a set of steak knives—all the rest of the salesmen will be fired.

In the first scene, Shelly Levene, once a top salesman but now, in his fifties, down on his luck, is begging Williamson, the real estate office manager, for "A-list" leads. Levene has not closed a sale in months—but he is convinced that one good lead will restore his confidence and put him back on track. As the salesman becomes more desperate, Williams offers to sell him the leads for $50 each—and a percentage of any commissions Levene might earn. Levene agrees to the offer but doesn't have the cash.

In the second scene, David Moss and the hopeless George Aaranow, both men in their fifties, commiserate about the difficulties of closing a sale, especially without the good leads—and the good leads go only to those who close sales. Moss suggests that if they could steal the leads from their office a competitor would be willing to buy them. When Aaranow asks if Moss is suggesting a burglary, Moss acts as if the thought had never occurred to him. However, he eventually not only suggests a burglary but insists that Aaranow must carry it out

and that Aaranow is already involved as an "accessory" before the fact "because you listened."

In the third scene, Richard Roma, the office's star salesman, is talking with a man named Jim Lingk. Roma delivers a virtual monologue that seems to be about sex, loneliness, and the vagaries and insecurities of life. His tone is intimate and conversational, indicating that Lingk is an old friend of his. At the end, however, his tone changes and it is revealed that he has been lulling Lingk into a sales pitch with his casual demeanor.

Act II

Act II plays out the forces set in motion in the previous act with a more conventional structure. It is also much more comic than the first act. The act opens in the ransacked real estate office the next morning. A police detective, Baylen, is there to investigate the burglary and one by one the salesmen are called into Williamson's office to talk to the detective. Roma arrives and demands to know if his contract for the sale of land to Lingk the previous night had been filed or stolen. Williamson waffles but eventually says that it was filed before the burglary. The sale will put Roma "over the top" and win him the Cadillac. Aaranow is nervous about being questioned and Roma advises, "tell the truth, George. Always tell the truth. It's the easiest thing to remember." Levene enters and says he has just sold eight parcels (properties). As he is discussing the closing, Moss comes out of the office highly insulted by Baylen's accusatory treatment. The tension leads to savage, and very funny, confrontations with Roma and Levene. After Moss stalks out, Levene continues crowing about his success with Roma flattering and egging him on. Williamson comes in and Levene boasts about his sale. He attacks the office manager, telling him he has no "balls" and belittling him for having never been out on a sit. Roma spots Lingk coming into the building and smells trouble. He and Levene quickly go into an improvised scene with Levene playing a rich investor. Lingk is there because his wife insisted he cancel the contract. Roma stalls him saying that he has to get Levene to the airport. He further states that he has a prior obligation and that he will talk to Lingk on the following Monday. Lingk says that he has to cancel before that—his wife has called the Attorney General's office and the contract cannot go into effect for three business days after the check has been cashed. Roma claims that the check hasn't been cashed and that it won't be

A scene from Glengarry Glen Ross*'s first production in London, 1983*

cashed until after he has talked to Lingk the following Monday. Aaranow bursts into the middle of this scene complaining about how he was treated by Baylen. Williamson, trying to be helpful, tells Lingk that his check has already been cashed. Lingk leaves after apologizing profoundly to Roma for having to back out of the deal. Roma screams at Williamson for ruining his deal. Seething, he goes into the office for his interrogation with the detective. Levene picks up where Roma left off, attacking Williamson for scuttling his friend's sale. In his anger, Levene lets slip that he knew the contract had not in fact gone to the bank. Williamson realizes that the only way Levene could have known this information was if he had been in the office the night before, which he states. Williamson now knows that it was Levene who broke into the office and stole the leads. Adding insult to the broken salesman's injury, he also points out that Levene's sale was worthless— the people he closed were well-known eccentrics who had no money. When Roma comes back, Williamson enters his office to talk with Baylen. Roma says he wants to form a partnership with Levene. When Levene goes in to talk with Baylen, Roma tells Williamson that his "partnership" with Levene means that Roma gets all of his own commission and half of Levene's. The play ends with Aaranow saying that he hates his job and Roma

leaving for the Chinese restaurant to hunt for more prospects.

CHARACTERS

George Aaranow

George Aaranow is a fairly stupid salesman in his fifties who seems to be sucked into Moss's scheme to steal the leads and sell them to a competitor. In Act II, Aaranow displays the only loyalty shown in the play: he keeps his mouth shut about Moss.

Baylen

Baylen is a police detective in his early forties. He is in the ransacked office in Act II to investigate the burglary and, although we never see him in direct questioning, he is rough enough to outrage even the tough salesmen.

Shelly Levene

Shelly Levene is a man in his fifties, formerly a hot salesman and now down on his luck. He needs a sale to survive. In Act I, scene 1, Levene pleads with his office manager, Williamson, for good leads and

MEDIA ADAPTATIONS

- *Glengarry Glen Ross* was adapted as a film by David Mamet, directed by James Foley, and starring Jack Lemmon, Al Pacino, Ed Harris, Alec Baldwin, Alan Arkin, Kevin Spacey, Jonathan Pryce, Bruce Altman, and Jude Ciccolella; distributed by LIVE Entertainment, Movies Unlimited, Baker & Taylor Video.

agrees to bribe him but doesn't have the necessary cash. Levene is so strapped for cash that he even has to worry about having enough to buy gas. He is the only character about whom we learn anything of his outside life: he lives in a resident hotel, he has a daughter, and the daughter is apparently dependent on him and perhaps is even in a hospital. When we see him in Act II, he enters the ransacked office crowing about having just closed a sale for eight parcels. He tells a detailed story of how he forced the buyers, two old people with little money, to close. In his new-found glory, he also berates Williamson for not being a man, for not knowing how to sell. In his excitement, he lets slip the fact that he knew that Williamson had not turned in Roma's contract for the Lingk sale the night before and Williamson perceives that Levene could know that only if he had been in the office. He knows that Levene did the burglary and, in spite of pleading by Levene, turns him in to the police.

James Lingk

James Lingk is a customer to whom Roma sells a parcel of land. Lingk's wife sends him back to cancel the deal, thus leading to an impromptu improvisational scene between Roma and Levene and a blown deal because of Williamson's intrusion. Even after he knows that Roma lied to him, Lingk apologizes for breaking the deal.

The Machine

See Shelly Levene

Dave Moss

Dave Moss is a bitter man in his fifties who sets up a deal to sell the stolen leads to a competing firm headed by Jerry Graff. In Act I, scene 2, he seems to have trapped George Aaranow, a fellow salesman, into doing the actual burglary. In Act II we see an outraged Moss after he has been interrogated by the police. He says that no one should be treated that way and decides to leave for the day. Later, in an attempt to save himself, Levene tells Williamson that it was Moss who set up the burglary.

Richard Roma

Richard Roma, in his early forties, is the "star" salesman of the office. In Act I, scene 3, he seems to be talking to a friend but it turns out that he is merely softening up a stranger, Jim Lingk, for a sales pitch. In Act II we learn that he did close the deal but sees the deal fall through due to the ignorant intrusion of Williamson. Near the end of the play Roma seems to want to team up with Levene but even that apparent show of unity is just another scam.

John Williamson

John Williamson, a man in his early forties, is the office manager and is in charge of giving the "leads" to the salesmen. This gives him great power. He gives the best leads to those who have the best sales records, and the only way to sell is to have the best leads. In Act I he agrees to give top leads to Levene if Levene pays him fifty dollars per lead and twenty percent of his commissions. In Act II, Williamson is with the police detective, Baylen, questioning the salesmen. Williamson does intrude into the scene being played out by Roma and Levene in an attempt to keep Lingk from cancelling his contract and, in his ignorance, manages to spoil the deal. Both Roma and Levene attack him verbally and Levene lets slip the clue that allows Williamson to expose Levene as the burglar.

THEMES

The plot of *Glengarry Glen Ross* is simple: in Act I in three brief two-person scenes set in a Chinese restaurant we meet the principal characters and learn that they are under extreme pressure to sell apparently worthless land in Florida and that to succeed in this they need good sales "leads," which

TOPICS FOR FURTHER STUDY

- Read *The Death of a Salesman* by Arthur Miller and compare the view of selling in that play with that in *Glengarry Glen Ross*. Is Willy Loman anything like the salesmen in *Glengarry Glen Ross*?

- Investigate consumer protection laws in your state. Do you think they are needed to protect the consumer, or do they just provide more red tape for the businessperson?

- Explore environmental problems caused by overdevelopment in Florida, Arizona, or Southern California.

- How much does the name of a product reflect what that product actually is rather than what the producer would like us to think it is?

- Are there limits on capitalism now? If so, what are they? Should there be more or fewer?

---

are under the control of the reptilian office manager, Williamson. Act II begins the next morning; the office has been ransacked and the leads stolen. The act ends with the apprehension of Levene, one of the salesmen, as the thief.

Duty and Responsibility

The major theme of *Glengarry Glen Ross* is business and, by extension, capitalism. Mamet never discusses, neither to praise nor to condemn, the workings of business; he shows the quintessential paradigm of business, the salesman, striving to survive by his wits in the system and how it damages and drains his better humanity. In the published play, Mamet includes a quote of the "Practical Sales Maxim: 'Always Be Closing.'" Everything is business, even personal relationships.

American Dream

The American dream that we can "get ahead" through honest hard work is undermined by the fact that, for these salesmen at least, the only measure of success is material and the only way to succeed is to sell. They are selling land—probably worthless land—to people who dream that buying that land will somehow provide the big score, the chance to make large profits when they resell it. It is interesting to note that no one mentions building on or settling on the land; it is always referred to as an investment opportunity. Moreover, the salesmen will say anything and promise anything to "close."

Alienation and Loneliness

Certainly all of the characters suffer alienation both from nature and other people. They are apparently unfamiliar with the land they sell and refer to it as "crap." It is just a commodity. They are also alienated from their customers, whom they despise, and from each other. They do have a unity in despising what they know is an unfair system, but whenever it seems that friendship is involved—whether with one another or with a customer—we soon learn that it is just another scam, another preparation for "closing." For example, Moss seems to commiserate with Aaranow but is really setting him up to do a burglary for him; Roma seems to be having a heartfelt conversation with Lingk, and it even appears to the audience that they are old friends; but, we find that he is just disarming a stranger when he produces a sales pamphlet; Roma suggests that he and Levene work as partners only to betray him almost immediately afterwards.

Language

Language will be discussed in some detail under "style," but it should be noted here that language is also a major theme in *Glengarry Glen Ross*. Language as a means of communication has been subverted. Nothing that is said is necessarily true even when it seems to be in support of friendship or to express a philosophy of life. Language is used by these people solely as a tool to manipulate potential customers and each other.

Deception

Deception is at work on every level. We see lying and fantasy as a way of thinking and operating: certainly there seems to be little truth to anything anyone says to anybody. The most explicit example is in Act II when Lingk comes to the office to cancel his contract. Roma and Levene put on an elaborate improvised show for him in which Levene pretends to be an important executive with American Express who is a large investor in the land Roma is trying to sell. Throughout the play, the characters immediately turn to deception when they are in a tight corner—which is most of the time.

Success and Failure

Success and failure are very easily measured in the closed world of *Glengarry Glenn Ross* and by extension in the larger world of American capitalism. To succeed is to get money; to fail is not to get money. Again, it is not only the salesmen who measure success materially: their customers also think that if they buy the land they will sell it at a huge profit and eventually get something for nothing. Also, if these people do not make sales their whole sense of self is destroyed. For the salesman, selling is not just a job but a persona; it is who and what they are.

Morals and Morality

There is no mention of morals or morality or even business ethics in *Glengarry Glen Ross.* Morality and ethics are not part of the operating procedure. In Roma's pseudo-philosophical discourse to Lingk, he says that he does ''that today which seem to me correct today.'' While Roma purports to accept that there may be an absolute morality, he says, ''And then what?'' It is the very absence of morality which gradually dawns on the audience and frames the entire play. These people operate in a vicious jungle in which only the strong survive and nothing else matters.

Conscience

Similarly, not one of the characters is troubled by conscience. Conscience does not seem to exist as a part of anyone's makeup. Again, it is Roma who mentions the concept in Act I, scene 3: ''You think that you're a thief? So What? You get befuddled by a middle-class morality . . . ? Get shut of it. Shut it out. You cheated on your wife . . .? You did it, live with it. (Pause) You fuck little girls, so be it?''

Sexism

Glengarry Glen Ross depicts a world of men and men's relationships. Selling is the sign of manhood. Roma and Levene both tell Williamson that he is not a man because he has never actively made sales. There are only two females who are even mentioned in the play: Lingk's wife and Levene's daughter. Lingk's wife has forced Lingk to confront Roma and cancel his contract. Roma commiserates with him and, seemingly at least, wants to talk to him man-to-man about his problems. Lingk does cancel the contract with apologies for having ''betrayed'' Roma. Levene's daughter, for whom he has provided an education, is apparently ill. This barely-mentioned daughter seems to provide the only glimpse of human warmth in this group of men.

Anger and Hatred

In that world of vicious competition devoid of morality or friendship, all the characters seem to operate out of anger and hatred: they are angry at Williamson for not producing better leads; they are angry with each other because the success of one means the failure of another. They are caught in an unfair system and they know it. Finally, at the end of the play, Aaranow states openly what all, with the possible exception of Roma, feel: ''Oh, God, I hate this job.''

STYLE

Plot

The structure of *Glengarry Glen Ross* is unusual. Act I consists of three brief scenes, each scene a duologue. Through these scenes we learn the jargon of the real estate sales world, come to know the characters involved, and are introduced to the possiblity of a burglary of the sales office by two of the salesmen. Act II has a more conventional structure and is similar to that of a mystery play in which the perpetration of the crime is sought and caught. However, it would be a mistake to think that the interest of *Glengarry Glen Ross* is sustained by the plot. The main action is contained in the language and takes place through the shifting relationships and stories of the characters.

Action

Mamet is very clear about what is important in his plays. In one of his essays in *Writing in Restaurants* he points out that it is not the theme of the play to which we respond, but the action. In another essay in the same book he points out that "good drama has no stage directions. It is the interaction of the characters' objectives expressed solely by what they say to each other—not by what the author says about them." There is very little description even of the set in *Glengarry Glen Ross* and no directions for character action. Character is habitual action, and the author shows us what the characters do. It is all contained in the dialogue. There is no nonessential prose.

Language

In *Writing in Restaurants* Mamet says, "Technique is knowledge of how to translate incohate desire into clear action—into action capable of communicating itself to the audience." The Characters in *Glengarry Glen Ross* are created by the language they use and, for the salesmen, at least, their livelihoods depend on their use of language. This language is not used to communicate truth but rather to hide truth, to manipulate others, savagely attack each other, and to tell stories that celebrate victory—as Levine does when telling how he closed a deal for eight parcels of land. It is no mistake that the salesmen far outshine the office manager Williamson, the customer Lingk, and the police detective Baylen (although through the reactions of Aaranow and Moss we know that Baylen also uses language powerfully when he is in charge of the interrogation off stage in Williamson's office.) Language is ammunition in the primal battles for power and survival.

It is widely agreed that Mamet has an exact ear for male dialogue (Robert Cushman, an English critic, says, "Nobody alive writes better American"). However, his language is not naturalistic, not an exact copy of how people really speak; it is very carefully structured. The speech patterns, repetitions, interruptions, hesitations, great outbursts of savage obscenities, and scatologocal bombs becomes a sort of poetry. Remember, stage dialogue is not written to be read but rather to be heard. Mamet's dialogue becomes musical. As Jack Shepard, the actor who played Roma in the first production, put it, "The rhythms are slick, fast, syncopated, like a drum solo." We hear and feel the power of the music and sense the fear, panic, and desolation beneath it. The rhythm and the action are the same; the salesmen use their arias or duets to impress and control their audience, whether that audience is a potential customer or a colleague, or the theatre audience. And the theatre audience can get caught in these stories just as the characters on stage can. Levene's story in Act II of the closing, his cutting away of nonessential words, the masterful uses of pauses in the storytelling, and the story itself (he tells of sitting silently for twenty-two minutes by the kitchen clock), and the solemn toast that took place after they signed draws the audience into the world of Levene. Roma's speech to Lingk in Act I makes little logical sense, but it is masterful. Roma spins a tale filled with allusions to common bonds of sexuality, guilt, acceptance of oneself and of life, and builds a sense of male comradeship. He gives no pause in his double and triple talk except to allow Lingk to agree with him. Roma plays on Lingk's obvious need for male friendship. He uses language to fascinate and then, like a cobra, strikes with the sales presentation.

Dramatic Irony

Glengarry Glen Ross is a very funny play in spite of its dark moral vision of a corrupt and demoralizing system. Part of the reason we are able to respond positively to the play is Mamet's use of dramatic irony. Dramatic irony means that the audience knows more than some or all of the characters. Mamet assumes that we will feel superior to the characters on stage, that we know we live in a better world and behave in a better manner than they. This allows us to feel superior. We also sense, and this too figures into the dramatic irony, that Mamet likes and even admires his characters. In spite of their venality, greed, immorality, lack of loyalty, and vicious lies, he sees them as victims of the system in which they are forced to strive. It is the system that forces them to use their considerable talents to achieve unworthy ends. The characters are quick-witted, brilliantly audacious, and display the sort of tenacity common to all great comic characters. Perhaps the ultimate irony is that, to some extent, we do admire these characters and so recognize ourselves in them.

HISTORICAL CONTEXT

Business

While most people may not be familiar with the inner workings of a high pressure real estate sales office, the world surrounding *Glengarry Glen Ross* in 1983, the year the play was completed and first performed, certainly made that world seem not only plausible but almost inevitable. The 1980s in American business were a time of corporate takeovers, both friendly and unfriendly, in which those engineering those takeovers reaped personal rewards in the tens of millions of dollars. Frequently, those takeovers were funded by high-yield "junk bonds," first proposed by Drexel Burnham Lambert executive Michael R. Milkin. Assets of the target company were pledged to repay the principal of the junk bonds, which yielded thirteen to thirty percent.

Former Japanese prime minister Kakuei Tonaka was convicted in Tokyo District Court October 12 of having accepted a $2.2 million bribe from Lockheed Corporation to use his influence to persuade All Nipon Airways to use Lockheed Tristar jets.

Politics

Social Security legislation was signed by President Reagan which delayed cost-of-living increases in payments and increased payroll deductions.

President Reagan told an evangelical group at Orlando, Florida, on March 8 that the Soviet Union was "an evil empire," and was "the focus of evil in the modern world." On March 23, President Reagan had proposed his "Strategic Defense Initiative," a high-tech shield of satellites that would use lasers to shoot down incoming enemy missiles. Senator Ted Kennedy dubbed the program "Star Wars," and few scientists believed the program to be possible despite its projected staggering costs.

On October 25, three thousand U.S. Marines, accompanied by three hundred military personnel from Caribbean nations, invaded the island nation of Grenada to topple "political thugs" who had taken over the government in a coup on October 12, and who seemed to be creating a new bastion for communism in the Caribbean.

November 2, President Reagan signed legislation to create a holiday in January to celebrate the birthday of Martin Luther King, a holiday which will be ignored by financial markets and most business firms.

Environment

Secretary of the Interior James G. Watt, who had fought to open federal lands to private exploitation including oil drilling, resigned October 9. He had caused outrage by lightheartedly declaring that his coal advisory commission was a well-balanced mix: "I have a black, a woman, two Jews, and a cripple."

In the Soviet Union, commercial fishing ceased in the Aral Sea. The draining of water from the inland sea's two source rivers in a massive project to irrigate surrounding desert had shrunk the sea by one third, doubled its salinity, and created an ecological disaster as winds blew chemically contaminated dust and salt from the sea bottom onto surrounding fields, poisoning water supplies and even mothers' milk

Communications

In December, Chicago motorists began talking on cellular telephones in their cars, available at $3,000 plus $150 per month for service. The telephones quickly became not only handy business tools but highly desirable status symbols.

Miscellaneous

Cabbage Patch dolls became black market items as stores ran out of supplies.

CRITICAL OVERVIEW

The initial critical reactions in London to *Glengarry Glen Ross* were overwhelmingly, but not unanimously, positive. Robert Cushman in the *Observer* called it "the best play in London." He was especially taken with Mamet's use of language and mentioned his "fantastic ear for emphasis and repetition and the interrupting of people who weren't saying anything anyway. Nobody alive writes better American." He went on to say, "Here at last, carving characters and conflicts out of language, is a play with real muscle: here, after all the pieces we have half-heartedly approved because they mention 'important' issues as if mentioning were the same as dealing with. *Glengarry Glen Ross* mentions nothing, but in its depiction of a driven, consciousless world it implies a great deal."

Michael Billington in the *Guardian* talked of Mamet's brilliant use of language to depict character and attitudes and praised both the play and the production. Milton Shulman in the *Standard* praised the play and said, "There is a glib, breathtaking momentum in the speech rhythms that Mamet has devised for this pathetic flotsam." Clive Hirschhorn in the *Sunday Express* was not enthusiastic about the first act, but called the second act "a dazzler." Michael Coveny in the *Financial Times* was enthusiastic and said, "The text bubbles like a poisoned froth." Giles Gordon in the *Spectator* called the play "something of a let-down," and went on to say of the production that the "actors give the performances they always give."

In New York, the plaudits were even greater. The most important critic, Frank Rich of the *New York Times,* gave a rave review of the play and said, "This may well be the most accomplished play its author has yet given us. As Mr. Mamet's command of dialogue has now reached its most dazzling pitch, so has his mastery of theatrical form." Howard Kissel in the influential *Women's Wear Daily* was very positive and mentioned that, in spite of the lack of physical movement in the first act (which he likened to "some arcane Oriental puppet theatre"), the mood was not static: "intense animation comes from Mamet's brilliant dialogue, the vulgar sounds one hears on any street corner shaped into a jarring, mesmerizing music."

The headline above Clive Barnes's *New York Post* review read, "Mamet's 'Glengarry:' A Play To See and Cherish." Barnes called it "Mamet's most considerable play to date." He said that Mamet's language was able to "transform the recognizable into the essential," and that "the characters and situations have never looked more special." Jack Kroll in *Newsweek* said, "Mamet seems to get more original as his career develops," and called him, "The Aristophanes of the inarticulate." He went on to say, "He is that rarity, a pure writer." Dennis Cunningham of WCBS said, "I could simply rave to the heavens," and called *Glengarry Glen Ross* a "theatrical event, altogether extraordinary, an astonishing, exhilarating experience . . . and that rarest of Broadway achievements, a major American play by a major American playwright." Douglas Watt of the *Daily News* found the play dull and said, "To elevate it to the status of a bitter comment on the American dream would amount to cosmic foolishness. It is what it is, a slice of life."

Glengarry Glen Ross continues to receive serious critical attention. The first book-length study of Mamet was C. W. E. Bigsby's *David Mamet,* published in 1985, which studies Mamet's works from the beginning through *Glengarry Glen Ross.* Bigsby sees Mamet as a major writer whose concern has been with "dramatizing the inner life of the individual and of the nation." Dennis Carroll's book-length study, *David Mamet,* published in 1987, assesses Mamet at "Mid-Career," and deals with the plays in thematic categories. Carroll also considers Mamet's place in the larger context of drama and theatre and points out that, while each major play is open to many different interpretations, "This is

the mark of any major artist whose special qualities nag at the sensibilities, but who cannot be too easily pigeonholed or defined. His achievements already stamp him as a major American playwright of his generation, whose work has both the vividness and the power to cross national boundaries."

A brilliant major study by Anne Dean, *David Mamet: Language as Dramatic Action,* focuses on Mamet's celebrated use of language and Mamet as a dramatic poet. There have been many critical essays dealing with *Glengarry Glen Ross,* some of the best collected in *David Mamet: A Casebook,* edited by Leslie Kane. Mamet and *Glengarry Glen Ross* have also become the subjects of numerous masters theses and doctoral dissertations.

CRITICISM

Terry Browne

Browne is an instructor at the State University of New York who specializes in drama. In this essay he discusses morality and characterization in Mamet's play.

There is no doubt that David Mamet is a major writer and perhaps the preeminent American playwright of his generation. As Dennis Carroll pointed out in *David Mamet,* Mamet is the only American playwright to emerge from the 1970s who has managed to establish a significant international reputation. His plays have appealed to a large and wide range of audience.

Glengarry Glen Ross met with success not only in London and New York, but had a long United States national tour and quickly received major productions in Tel Aviv, Israel; Johannesburg, South Africa; Dublin, Ireland; Marseilles, France; Genoa, Italy; Sydney, Australia; Helsinki, Finland; and Tokyo, Japan. Moreover, Mamet had had major successes before *Glengarry Glen Ross* and has continued to write excitingly and successfully for the theatre in addition to his steady output of scripts for movies and his career as a film director. Furthermore, as Carroll pointed out, Mamet has created a body of work rich in complex variations on his themes rather than merely repeating himself obsessively.

He has written plays focusing on relationships between men and women, parents and children,

WHAT DO I READ NEXT?

- *American Buffalo,* Mamet's 1975 play about three low-life men plotting to steal a rare coin, gives another slant on Mamet's view of American business.

- *Speed-the-Plow* is Mamet's 1987 "Hollywood play" produced in New York with Joe Mantegna, Ron Silver, and Madonna.

- *Oleanna,* Mamet's 1992 play, deals with teaching and the power of "political correctness" to utterly destroy a college professor.

- *The Death of a Salesman* is Arthur Miller's 1947 classic play about a salesman and distorted values in America.

- *Writing in Restaurants,* a book of essays by Mamet, gives a good look at his philosophy of writing and his view of contemporary America.

- *A Whore's Profession,* 1996, is Mamet's most recent book of essays about working as a writer.

- The entry on David Mamet by Patricia Lewis and Terry Browne in *Dictionary of Literary Biography,* Volume 7: *Twentieth-Century American Dramatists,* published in 1981 by Gale, gives a good overview of Mamet's early works.

---

sexual politics, communion, redemption, the power of language and the debasement of language, the passing on of knowledge and tradition, to mention only some major themes. He has also written books of essays, childrens' plays, radio plays, and television scripts. While *Glengarry Glen Ross* contains many layers of thematic concern, it is usually grouped with *American Buffalo* and *Speed-the-Plow* as major plays that focus primarily on business and capitalism. In *American Buffalo* the characters are small-time thieves who consider themselves to be businessmen. *Speed-the-Plow* focuses on Hollywood , where the *product* is films and the focus is on raw power and making money.

There is no doubt that Mamet is a moral writer who seeks to make the audience aware of what he sees as the spiritual vacuum in present-day America (and, judging from the broad range of productions, in other countries as well). We are pressured to succeed, to make more money, to buy more things that we don't need. We don't take the time to regenerate our spirit. We do not accept responsibility for what happens to ourselves but rather operate on received values without questioning whether they are good or even aimed at making us happy. People full of energy and talent spend themselves seeking empty rewards. Mamet says in his book of essays *Writing in Restaurants,* "Our civilization is convulsed and dying, and it has not yet gotten the message. It is sinking, but it has not sunk into complete barbarity, and I often think that nuclear war exists for no other reason than to spare us that indignity."

In another essay, Mamet says that "the essential task of the drama (as of the fairy tale) is to offer a solution to a problem which in nonsusceptible to reason. To be effective, the drama must induce us to suspend our rational judgment, and to follow the *internal* logic of the piece so that our *pleasure* (our "cure") is the release at the end of the story." We suspend reason in order to gain deep insights. The purpose of theatre is not to teach a lesson or to provide a neat "moral;" the purpose of theatre is to provide us with a communal experience which we then ponder, as we do all forceful experiences in our lives. Mamet does not *preach* his themes at us; his themes are played out. He does not describe his characters; he puts them into action. Mamet has said that the job of the dramatist is to translate the imperfectly formed desire of the characters into clear action that is capable of communicating itself to the audience.

In drama, just as in life, we judge people by what they do, by their actions. Aristotle, the ancient Greek philosopher, rightly said that character is just habitual action. The dramatist must show us what the character does rather than have him described by either himself or others. In his studies of the Stanislavksy system of acting with Sanford Meisner at the Neighborhood Playhouse School of Theatre, Mamet came to appreciate that the actor is always pursuing the character's objectives, trying *at each moment* to achieve what the character wants. This action, which is always present in well written dialogue, is known as the "subtext." It is by discovering the character's objectives and *how* the character would go about trying to win those objectives, and then doing those things—the actions—that the actor and the character become one and the same. It is not a psychotic experience for the actor; it is mental focus. Moreover, by focusing on winning those objectives the actor is freed from extraneous considerations. The actor performs the actions, and the "meaning" of the play is in those actions. It is precisely his mastery and *economy* of action in dialogue which impresses audiences and makes plays by Mamet challenging and exciting for actors.

Joe Mantegna, who has acted in several Mamet plays and films and played Roma in the first U.S. production of *Glengarry Glen Ross,* said in an interview with Leslie Kane in her *David Mamet: A Casebook,* "The great thing about David is the way he can say so much with so little . . . everything else seems so over-written. There are certainly other writers who have that capability, such as Shakespeare and Pinter. As much is said between the lines as with the lines." He also pointed out that because the writing is so concise and full of meaning, the actor must be precise in his choice of how each line is delivered. Mamet says that the actor does not need to *characterize,* he simply needs to find the correct action and then do it. From seeing those actions, the audience will draw its own conclusions about the character. Mantegna says, "You don't have to worry about dropping little clues or hints that will help the audience figure this out later. No, you just play the moment as real as you can."

Mamet has long been fascinated with language. His father would often stop conversation at the dinner table until David or his sister Lyn could find the exact word to express their meaning. In *Writing in Restaurants* he remembers that "our schoolyard code of honor recognized words as magical and powerful unto themselves," and that "The School-boy Universe was not corrupted by the written

word, and was ruled by the power of sounds." It is that "power of sounds" which the characters in *Glengarry Glen Ross* use to achieve their objectives. As Jack Shepard, the Roma in the original London production, described it to Anne Deane in *David Mamet: Language as Dramatic Action,* "The rhythms are slick, fast, syncopated like a drum solo." Frank Rich, the critic for the *New York Times,* talked of the dialogue in musical terms: "In the jagged riffs of coarse, monosyllabic words, we hear and feel both the exhilaration and sweaty desperation of the huckster's calling." In the interview with Dean, Shepard recalled the great tension of the rehearsal period: "There is just so much to remember at any one time in Mamet's works . . . Mamet knows exactly what he wants . . . he is very fast, very dynamic." The language has the feeling of improvisation with speeches overlapping, people interrupting each other, thoughts unfinished. It sounds like ordinary street talk or natural speech, but it has been painstakingly and specifically created to have an impact. It is crafted for the actor to use as *action.* This fact is especially important for the actors in *Glengarry Glen Ross* because the characters use language and storytelling to survive and to celebrate survival. The characters themselves are actors. This is most obvious during the improvised performance with which Roma and Levene attempt to steer Lingk away from his intention to cancel his contract, with Levene playing the vice president of American Express who is a major client and friend of Roma. Roma gives Levene only a few cues on how to proceed, and Levene enters the role. Another obvious instance occurs when Williamson tells Roma that Murray, one of the partners in the firm, will take care of re-closing Roma's sales himself: "he'll be the *president,* just come *in* from out of *town.*" Playing roles is natural for these people, and they change roles to suit their purposes in any given circumstances.

Levene is a master at this. In Act I he pleads with Williamson in an attempt to get good leads. He is submissive, repeats Williamson's name, John, is careful not be critical of him, strives to appear confident, uses delaying tactics to prevent Williamson from turning him down. At the same time, Mamet has incorporated the rhythms of desperation into Levene's speech. In Act II, when Levene tells the story of his sale, his enthusiasm and pride are unbounded and infectious. He carefully draws the scene, gives us enough detail without getting tedious, uses fluid phrasing to pull us along, and holds us in suspense as he recalls sitting silently at the kitchen table with the old couple for *"twenty-two minutes* by the kitchen *clock"* until "they wilted all at once. No *gesture* . . . nothing. Like together. They, I swear to God, they both kind of *imperceptibly slumped.*" After this climax to the story, Levene provides a denouement as he quietly recalls having a small drink to solemnize the occasion: "Little shot glasses. A pattern in 'em. And we toast. In silence. (Pause.)" The story winds down gently and all are quiet in appreciation. The viewer may find reprehensible the fact that Levene has sold worthless land to old people who cannot afford it, but his story pulls us in and and we admire his performance nevertheless. The audience sees Levene the actor as masterful storyteller, and they also "see" Levene in a scene which he writes and in which he is the star actor. The viewer sees Levene selling himself.

Mamet based the characters in *Glengarry Glen Ross* to some extent on the men with whom he had worked for a year in a dubious real estate office in Chicago. He admired their ability to live by their wits and their dynamic addiction to what they did. He found them amazing. That does not mean that he approves of what they do. As he points out in *Writing in Restaurants,* "The desire to manipulate, to treat one's colleagues as servants, reveals a deep sense of personal worthlessness: as if one's personal thoughts, choices, and insights could not bear reflection, let alone a reasoned mutual examination." Behind all the foul-mouthed manipulation and boasting are people who are empty or nearly empty of humane values. They victimize others, but they are victims themselves of a system which offers no rewards but money and punishes failure by taking away the means of earning a living.

The mass media has created an audience who expect everything to be neatly summed up and easily spelled out for them, including laugh-tracks to tell them when to laugh and somber music to tell them when to be sad. They want simple answers, lessons. Then they will know what to say about the play, if they feel the need to say anything at all, and can go on the next diversion. But that is not the job of theatre and David Mamet does not do that for us. *Glengarry Glen Ross* is character-centered and the characters are expressed through fast-paced action. The audience is given an exceptional and disturbing experience. Later, when we think about that experience, there are plenty of clues to the deeper meanings in the play for those who are attuned. The experience becomes our experience to ponder.

Source: Terry Browne, in an essay for *Drama for Students,* Gale, 1997.

Jack Kroll

In the following excerpt, Kroll offers a mixed review of Glengarry Glen Ross, *asserting that in "trying to wed the uncompromising vision of moral primitivism in [his earlier play]* American Buffalo *with a more accessible, even commercial appeal," Mamet introduces "elements of relatively conventional plotting and farce that occasionally wobble; the resolution of the real-estate-office rip-off doesn't quite ring true." Nevertheless, Kroll declares that "in all other respects Mamet is better than ever."*

"It's contacts, Ben, contacts!" says Willy Loman. "Give me the leads!" exhorts Shelly (The Machine) Levene in David Mamet's dazzling new play, *Glengarry Glen Ross.* Willy dies the death of a salesman; Shelly says, "I was born for a salesman," but then suffers a fate that's a kind of grotesque counterpart to the ignominious end of Willy. Mamet's play is a funny and frightening descent into the Plutonic world of sleazy hucksters who peddle dubious real estate with deceptively poetic names like Glengarry Highlands and Glen Ross Farms.

Mamet's salesmen have created a lingo of their own, a semantic skullduggery that can fake out a prospective buyer with non sequiturs, triple-talk and a parody of philosophical wisdom that's breathtaking in its jackhammer effrontery. The first act of *Glengarry Glen Ross* consists of three colloquies in a murky Chinese restaurant as the salesmen spar and jockey with their fink of a boss (J. T. Walsh), with a befuddled client and with each other. The second act takes place in their sales office, which has been broken into and burglarized; a detective is on scene, and this squall of criminality blows open the hidden frustrations and ferocities of these jacketed jackals.

Mamet's pitchmen sandbag their gullible customers and slash away in cutthroat competition with each other, trying to win the "sales contests" their bosses use to drive them on, rewarding the winners with Cadillacs and the losers with threats of dismissal. Their code is pathetically macho; yet they have their own mystique, a perverse chivalry of chiselers. One of them recounts with almost mystic ecstasy how he nailed a deal with a pair of customers. "They signed, Ricky," he says. "It was great. It was like they wilted all at once. No gesture. . . nothing. Like together. They, I swear to God, they both kind of imperceptibly slumped. They signed. It was all so solemn."

Mamet seems to get more original as his career develops. His antiphonal exchanges, which dwindle to single words or even fragments of words and then explode into a crossfire of scatological buckshot, make him the Aristophanes of the inarticulate. He makes the filthiest male-to-male dialogue pop with the comic timing of Jack Benny or pile up into a profane poetry that becomes the music of desperation. In *Glengarry Glen Ross* Mamet appears to be trying to wed the uncompromising vision of moral primitivism in *American Buffalo* with a more accessible, even commercial appeal. The move is a good one, but it costs him something. His second act introduces elements of relatively conventional plotting and farce that occasionally wobble; the resolution of the real-estate-office ripoff doesn't quite ring true.

But in all other respects Mamet is better than ever. He's that rarity, a pure writer, and the synthesis he appears to be making, with echoes from voices as diverse as Beckett, Pinter and Hemingway, is unique and exciting. . . .

Source: Jack Kroll, "Mamet's Jackals in Jackets," in *Newsweek,* Vol. CIII, No. 15, April 9, 1984, p. 109.

MAMET'S PITCHMEN SANDBAG THEIR GULLIBLE CUSTOMERS AND SLASH AWAY IN CUTTHROAT COMPETITION WITH EACH OTHER"

Frank Rich

In the following review, which originally appeared in the New York Times *on March 26, 1984, Rich offers praise for* Glengarry Glen Ross, *applauding Mamet's ability to make "all-American music—hot jazz and wounding blues—out of his salesmen's scatological native lingo," and asserting that* Glengarry Glen Ross *"may well be the most accomplished play its author has yet given us."*

Rich is an American editor and performing arts critic.

The only mellifluous words in David Mamet's new play are those of its title—*Glengarry Glen Ross*. In this scalding comedy about small-time, cutthroat real-estate salesmen, most of the language is abrasive—even by the standards of the author's *American Buffalo*. If the characters aren't barking out the harshest four-letter expletives, then they're speaking in the clammy jargon of a trade in which "leads," "closings" and "the board" (a sales chart) are the holiest of imperatives. There's only one speech in which we hear about such intimacies as sex and loneliness—and that speech, to our shock, proves to be a prefabricated sales pitch.

Yet the strange—and wonderful—thing about the play at the Golden is Mr. Mamet's ability to turn almost every word inside out. The playwright makes all-American music—hot jazz and wounding blues—out of his salesman's scatological native lingo. In the jagged riffs of coarse, monosyllabic words, we hear and feel both the exhilaration and sweaty desperation of the huckster's calling. At the same time, Mr. Mamet makes his work's musical title into an ugly symbol of all that is hollow and vicious in the way of life his characters gallantly endure. The salesmen—middle-class bloodbrothers of the penny-ante Chicago hustlers of *American*

> ❝ IN THE JAGGED RIFFS OF COARSE, MONOSYLLABIC WORDS, WE HEAR AND FEEL BOTH THE EXHILARATION AND SWEATY DESPERATION OF THE HUCKSTER'S CALLING ❞

Buffalo—are trying to unload worthless tracts of Florida land to gullible victims. It's the cruelest cut of all that that real estate is packaged into developments with names like ''Glengarry Highlands'' and ''Glen Ross Farms.''

Mr. Mamet's talent for burying layers of meaning into simple, precisely distilled, idiomatic language—a talent that can only be compared to Harold Pinter's—is not the sum of *Glengarry Glen Ross.* This may well be the most accomplished play its author has yet given us. As Mr. Mamet's command of dialogue has now reached its most dazzling pitch, so has his mastery of theatrical form. Beneath the raucous, seemingly inane surface of *Glengarry* one finds not only feelings but a detective story with a surprise ending. And there's another clandestine story, too, bubbling just underneath the main plot: Only as the curtain falls do we realize that one of the salesmen, brilliantly played by Robert Prosky, has traveled through an anguished personal history almost as complex as Willy Loman's.

So assured and uncompromising is Mr. Mamet's style that one must enter his play's hermetically sealed world completely—or risk getting lost. Taken at face value, the actual events, like the vocabulary, are minimal; the ferocious humor and drama are often to be found in the pauses or along the shadowy periphery of the center-stage action. But should this work fail to win the large public it deserves—a fate that has befallen other Mamet plays in their first Broadway outings—that won't be entirely because of its idiosyncratic form. *Glengarry* which was initially produced at London's National Theater last fall, is being seen here in a second production, from Chicago's Goodman Theater. Mr. Prosky's contribution aside, this solid but uninspired staging isn't always up to the crackling tension of the script.

In the half-hour-long first act, that tension is particularly Pinteresque. We watch three successive two-character confrontations that introduce the salesmen as they conduct business in the Chinese restaurant that serves as their hangout and unofficial office. The dialogue's unfinished sentences often sound like code; one whole scene turns on the colloquial distinction the characters draw between the phrases ''speaking about'' and ''talking about.''

But these duologues in fact dramatize primal duels for domination, power and survival, and, as we penetrate the argot, we learn the Darwinian rules of the salesmen's game. Those who sell the most ''units'' receive a Cadillac as a bonus; those who hit ''bad streaks'' are denied access to management's list of ''premiere leads'' (appointments with likely customers). Worse, this entreprenurial system is as corrupt as it is heartless. The losing salesmen can still get leads by offering kickbacks to the mercurial young manager (J. T. Walsh) who administers the business for its unseen owners.

When the characters leave the dark restaurant for the brighter setting of the firm's office in Act II, Mr. Mamet's tone lightens somewhat as well. The office has been ransacked by burglars, and a detective (Jack Wallace) arrives to investigate. Even as the salesmen undergo questioning, they frantically settle fratricidal rivalries and attempt to bamboozle a pathetic, tearful customer (Lane Smith) who has arrived to demand a refund. As written (though not always as staged), Act II is farce in Chicago's ''Front Page'' tradition—albeit of a blacker contemporary sort. While we laugh at the comic cops-and-robbers hijinks, we also witness the unravelling of several lives.

The play's director is Gregory Mosher, Mr. Mamet's long-time Chicago collaborator. Mr. Mosher's work is often capable, but sometimes he italicizes Mr. Mamet's linguistic stylization: Whenever the actors self-consciously indicate the exact location of the text's hidden jokes and meanings, they cease being salesmen engaged in do-or-die warfare. This is not to say that the actors are inept—they're good. But, as we've seen with other Mamet works, it takes a special cast, not merely an adequate one, to deliver the full force of a play in which even the word ''and'' can set off a theatrical detonation.

The actors do succeed, as they must, at earning our sympathy. Mr. Mamet admires the courage of these salesmen, who are just as victimized as their clients; the only villain is Mr. Walsh's manager—a cool deskman who has never had to live by his wits on the front lines of selling. Among the others, there's particular heroism in Mike Nussbaum, whose frightened eyes convey a lifetime of blasted dreams, and in Joe Mantegna, as the company's youngest, most dapper go-getter. When Mr. Mantegna suffers a critical reversal, he bravely rises from defeat to retighten his tie, consult his appointments book and march back to the Chinese restaurant in search of new prey.

Mr. Prosky, beefy and white-haired, is a discarded old-timer: in the opening scene, he is reduced to begging for leads from his impassive boss. Somewhat later, however, he scores a "great sale" and expands in countenance to rekindle his old confidence: Mr. Prosky becomes a regal, cigar-waving pontificator, recounting the crude ritual of a contract closing as if it were a grand religious rite.

Still, this rehabilitation is short-lived, and soon Mr. Prosky is trying to bribe his way back into his employer's favor. As we watch the bills spill from his pockets on to a desk, we at last see greenery that both befits and mocks the verdant words of the play's title. But there's no color in the salesman's pasty, dumbstruck face—just the abject terror of a life in which all words are finally nothing because it's only money that really talks.

Source: Frank Rich, "Theatre: A Mamet Play, *Glengarry Glen Ross*" in *New York Theatre Critics' Reviews,* Vol. XXXXV, no. 4, March 5, 1984.

FURTHER READING

Bigsby, C. W. E. *David Mamet,* Methuen, 1985, p. 15.
    The first book-length study of Mamet covers from the beginning through *Glengarry Glen Ross.* An excellent introduction to the approaches and themes of Mamet.

Carroll, Dennis. *David Mamet,* MacMillan, 1987, p. 155.
    An excellent assessment of Mamet at mid-career, from the beginnings through *Glengarry Glen Ross* approached by thematic groupings.

Dean, Anne. *David Mamet: Language as Dramatic Action,* Associated University Presses, 1990, pp. 96-197.
    A brilliant analysis of Mamet's use of language, approached overall and play-by-play. There are also useful insights into themes and the rehearsal process taken from interviews by the author.

Gordon, Clive. Review of *Glengarry Glen Ross* in the *Spectator,* September 27, 1983.
    A remarkably unperceptive and arrogant review of the London production.

Kane, Leslie. Interview with Joe Mantegna, in her *David Mamet: A Casebook,* Garland, 1992, pp. 254-55, 259.
    A fascinating look into the work of a fine actor in approaching and rehearsing a character. There are other essays in the *Casebook* that are helpful, notably "Power Plays: David Mamet's Theatre of Manipulation" by Henry I. Schvey; and "Comedy and Humor in the Plays of David Mamet" by Christopher C. Hudgins.

Mamet, David. *Writing in Restaurants,* Penguin, 1986, pp. 3, 6, 13, 14, 20, 32, 116, 124-25.
    A broad range of essays that are very useful in understanding of Mamet's view of theatre, tradition, technique, and life in general.

Rich, Frank. Review of *Glengarry Glen Ross* in the *New York Times,* March 26, 1984.
    A long, rich, and insightful review of the New York production.

SOURCES

Barnes, Clive. Review of *Glengarry Glen Ross* in the *New York Post,* March 26, 1984.

Billington, Michael. Review of *Glengarry Glen Ross* in *Guardian,* September 25, 1983.

Coveney, Michael. Review of *Glengarry Glen Ross* in *Financial Times,* September 22, 1983.

Cushman, Robert. Review of *Glengarry Glen Ross* in *Observer,* September 25, 1983.

Hirschhorn, Clive. Review of *Glengarry Glen Ross* in *Sunday Express,* September 25, 1983.

Kissel, Howard. Review of *Glengarry Glen Ross* in *Womens Wear Daily,* March 26, 1984.

Kroll, Jack. Review of *Glengarry Glen Ross* in *Newsweek,* April 9, 1984.

Shulman, Milton. Review of *Glengarry Glen Ross* in the *Standard,* September 22, 1983.

Watt, Douglas. Review of *Glengarry Glen Ross* in the *Daily News,* March 26, 1984.

Inherit the Wind

JEROME LAWRENCE AND
ROBERT E. LEE

1955

In the blistering hot summer of 1925, two nationally-known legal minds, Clarence Darrow and William Jennings Bryan, battled in a tiny courtroom in Dayton, Tennessee, and, for a time, captured the attention of the world. The issue? A state law that forbid the teaching of evolution and a local teacher's violation of that law. The official name of this encounter was Tennessee vs. John Thomas Scopes, but it became known the world over as the Scopes "Monkey Trial."

Thirty years later, in 1955, playwrights Jerome Lawrence and Robert E. Lee published their dramatized version of the events of the summer of 1925. In a brief note at the beginning of the play, the playwrights admit that the Scopes Monkey Trial was clearly the inspiration for their work. But, the authors emphasize "*Inherit the Wind* is not history" and that the "collision of Bryan and Darrow at Dayton was dramatic, but . . . not drama."

Bringing history to life through drama involves a risk that the central issues will be seen as "of the past" and of no relevance to the present. *Inherit the Wind*, however, has thrived for over three decades, suggesting an attraction for theater-goers far greater than that of a quaint look at America's past. As people search for meaning in an increasingly complex world, the different belief systems that attempt to provide some kind of understanding can, and do, come into conflict. Whether these systems wear such labels as religion, science, or politics, the

struggles that exist within and between them is reflective of a cultural conflict that has yet to be, and may never be, resolved. *Inherit the Wind* then, is far more than the story of twelve exciting days in a Tennessee courtroom; it is a narrative of a nation and its people as they struggle to come to grips with the forces of change.

AUTHOR BIOGRAPHY

From the 1940s until Lee's death in 1994, Jerome Lawrence and Robert E. Lee were a writing and publishing team. Together they wrote some 39 plays, including 14 Broadway productions. During World War II, Lawrence and Lee co-founded the Armed Forces Radio Services, which provided entertainment and news to thousands of troops.

Jerome Lawrence (original name, Jerome L. Schwartz) was born in Cleveland, Ohio, on July 14, 1915, the son of a printer and a poet. He earned a B.A. from Ohio State University in 1937. Although he spent the bulk of his career as both a writer and publisher teamed with Lee, Lawrence also wrote the biography *Actor: The Life and Times of Paul Muni* independent of Lee.

Robert E(dwin) Lee was born in Elyria, Ohio, on October 15, 1918. His father was an engineer and his mother a teacher. He studied at several different colleges and universities but never earned a formal degree. Lee died in 1994 after a long struggle with cancer.

Several of the pair's plays were adapted for film, most notably *Inherit the Wind, The Night Thoreau Spent in Jail, Mame,* and another courtroom story, *First Monday in October.* With *Inherit the Wind,* the Lawrence and Lee team won best play honors at the New York Drama Critics Poll and the Tony Awards (formally known as the Antionette Perry Awards) in 1955. The play also won the British Drama Critics Award in 1960. The pair would win a Tony Award nomination in 1966 for *Mame* and the Emmy Award for best comedy/ drama special for a 1988 television presentation of *Inherit the Wind.*

In an interview with Nina Couch in *Studies in American Drama, 1945-Present,* Lawrence related: "Almost if not all of our plays show the theme of the dignity of every individual mind and that mind's life-long battle against limitation and censorship." The Lawrence and Lee collection is maintained at

A playbill from the National Theatre performance.

the Lincoln Center Library for the Performing Arts in New York City.

PLOT SUMMARY

Act One, Scene I

Inherit The Wind opens just after dawn on a July day that "promises to be a scorcher." The story centers around a schoolteacher who is on trial for teaching evolution—the theory that man evolved from lower primates such as monkeys—in his classroom, a violation of Tennessee's Butler Law. The lines are already drawn in this sleepy Southern town of Hillsboro, Tennessee. Creationism or evolution? Religion or science? The local minister's daughter, a young teacher named Rachel, visits her imprisoned colleague, Bert Cates, at the local jail. The Baltimore *Herald* newspaper has sent E. K. Hornbeck, the country's most famous columnist, to cover the trial, along with the nation's most famous trial lawyer, Henry Drummond to defend Bert. The town is abuzz with the impending arrival of the prosecution's lawyer, three-time Presidential candidate and self-proclaimed Bible expert Matthew Harrison Brady. It is clear from the "READ YOUR

BIBLE'' banner strung across Main Street and the frequent singing of hymns that many of the townspeople are creationists—the religious belief that man was created, fully-evolved, by God— and are against Bert.

Hornbeck, cynical and condescending, supports the merits of Evolution while mocking the views of Creationism. When Brady arrives by special train, the townspeople fawn over him, name him an honorary Colonel in the state militia, and feed him a hearty dinner. Both Brady and the town express surprise and concern when they learn that Henry Drummond will represent the defense. And, when Drummond enters at the end of the scene, he is greeted by Hornbeck with the words, ''Hello, Devil. Welcome to Hell.''

Act One, Scene II

At the jury selection phase of the trial a few days later, Brady and Tom Davenport, the local District Attorney, trade barbs with Drummond over several potential jurors. The air in the courtroom is more like a circus than a legal proceeding, with numerous spectators and reporters crowding the room. After court adjourns for the day, Rachel begs Bert to stop fighting. Bert wavers, and Drummond agrees to settle the case with Brady if Bert honestly believes he committed a crime ''against the citizens of this state and the minds of their children.'' Bert decides to see things through, leaving Rachel shaken and confused. Drummond is satisfied that he is on the right side.

Act Two, Scene I

That same evening, Rachel's father Reverend Brown leads a bible meeting. With the nationally known orator, Brady, seated near him on the platform, Brown launches into a ''hellfire and brimstone'' speech denouncing Bert and the evil that he has taught. When Rachel attempts to defend Bert, Brown calls for divine retribution against his own daughter. Brady intervenes, advising the overzealous Reverend with the Biblical quotation from *Proverbs* that provides the play's title: ''He that troubleth his own house shall inherit the wind.'' After the meeting disperses, Brady and Drummond—once good friends and colleagues—speak briefly. Brady asks why their relationship has drifted apart. Drummond responds that maybe it is Brady who has moved away by standing still. This rebuke stuns Brady, literally knocking him off balance as he exits, leaving Drummond alone on stage.

Act Two, Scene II

The trial is in full swing. Howard, a student from Bert's class, is on the witness stand. Brady skillfully manipulates Howard's testimony to favor the prosecution, ending his examination with an impassioned and overtly biased speech against the ''evil-lutionsts.'' Drummond's cross-examination shows the whole point of the defense—Howard, or anyone else, has the right to listen to new ideas and the right to think about what those new ideas mean. Later, Rachel is called to testify. Brady questions Rachel about Bert's faith in God and then manipulates her into repeating Bert's observation that God created Man in His own image, and Man returned the favor. Realizing that everything she says makes Bert appear even more guilty, Rachel breaks down in tears and leaves the witness stand before Drummond can cross-examine her. Brady rests the prosecution's case. Drummond begins the defense by calling three prominent scientists to the stand, but the court rules that their possible testimony is irrelevant to this particular case.

Drummond appears to have no witnesses to testify for the defense. He seizes on the idea that if the court refuses to allow testimony on science or Charles Darwin (the scientist whose work supports the evolution theory), it should allow testimony on the Bible. He calls Brady to the stand as an expert on the Bible, over the objections of D.A. Davenport. At first, Brady fends off Drummond's questions about Biblical events with pious platitudes. As Drummond continues, however, Brady is forced to admit that the first day of creation was ''not necessarily a twenty-four hour day.'' When Drummond gets Brady to admit that he believes God speaks to him, telling him what is right and wrong, the prosecutor's credibility is destroyed. He is left on the stand, ignored, reciting scripture, as the court adjourns for the day.

Act Three

Bert and Drummond discuss the possible outcome of the trial. Drummond tells Bert about a toy rocking horse he received as a childhood birthday present from his parents. The horse, which he named Golden Dancer, was beautiful, yet when he tried to actually ride the horse, it broke in two. This, Drummond asserts, illustrates that many things are not what they appear to be, that a beautiful, strong-looking toy horse may in fact be cheap and weak— just as an age-old belief may in fact be false. Back in court, the jury returns a verdict of guilty and the judge fines Bert $100. Brady objects, claiming that the penalty is too lenient. Drummond shocks the court by declaring that he will appeal to the state Supreme Court—and would do so even if the fine were a single dollar. Vexed at not winning a more decisive victory, Brady tries to have his views read into the record, but he is rebuffed by the judge, ignored by the people in the court, and cut-off by a radio broadcaster. Brady suddenly collapses and is rushed from the courtroom, leaving Bert, Drummond, and Rachel to discuss the case. When the judge returns to announce that Brady has died, Hornbeck cynically attacks Brady and his views. Drummond turns on him angrily, denouncing Hornbeck's attitude as self-serving and without compassion. Hornbeck leaves, confused, and Bert and Rachel make plans to depart together on the afternoon train. Drummond picks up Rachel's copy of Darwin's *The Origin of Species*—a sort of bible to evolutionists—which she has forgotten, but Bert and Rachel are out of earshot. Drummond spots the court's Bible on the judge's bench, weighs them against each other in his hands, slaps the two volumes together, and jams them into his briefcase side by side. He walks out of the courtroom and across the town square.

CHARACTERS

Matthew Harrison Brady

Matthew Harrison Brady has run for the Presidency of the United States three times—all unsuccessfully. But, that does not detract from his power as an orator and a politician. His experience with national politics has made him enjoy being in the spotlight, especially hearing the sound of his own voice and the adulation of an audience of devoted followers. Despite his losses in three national elections, Brady remains popular among the rural citizenry because of his staunchly conservative and fundamentalist interpretation of the Bible. Although it is never expressly stated, there is a suggestion that Brady will use the publicity of this trial to launch a fourth run for the country's highest office.

Sarah Brady

Although she is Brady's wife, she seems more like his mother. She is constantly looking out for his welfare, reminding him not to overeat, to watch his activity level, to take a nap, and to be careful of the "treacherous" night breezes. She gathers him into her arms and comforts him after his humiliation at the hands of Drummond at the end of Act II.

Rachel Brown

Rachel Brown is, like her accused boyfriend, Bert, a schoolteacher. She is also the daughter of the fiery Reverend Brown, a staunch defender of creationism. Rachel is squarely in the middle of the central argument of the play. If she sides with Bert because she loves him, she abandons her father and her religious faith. If she sides with her father's beliefs, she deserts the man she loves. A kind and gentle person who would rather give in than fight, Rachel must confront her own beliefs and doubts and discover what is most important in her life.

Reverend Jeremiah Brown

Reverend Brown is the voice of unyielding fundamentalism. If Bert is the representation of freedom of thought, Brown is his opposite. He believes that everything in the Bible is true "as written" and that anything that calls that truth into question is blasphemy. When Rachel protests his damnation of Bert during an impassioned sermon in Act II, Reverend Brown's religious fervor provokes him to curse his own daughter.

Bert Cates

Bert Cates is a quiet, reserved schoolteacher. Even though he disagrees with the Reverend Brown's view of religion, Bert taught evolution because he thought that it was unjust to keep new ideas from people simply because they might be in conflict with someone's religious views. He is not a rabble-rouser. In fact, he does not like all the hoopla his case has stirred up and nearly admits defeat so that he can return his life to normal.

Henry Drummond

The attorney for the defense, Henry Drummond, has defended some of the most notorious criminals in America. His courtroom demeanor—passionate, charming, and witty—seems at odds with the quiet and reserved behavior we see in private. He sees the law as a vehicle to search for the truth. He has the heart of an idealist but knows full well the reality of the law. His purpose in coming to Hillsboro is not to represent a schoolteacher who has broken a law but

MEDIA ADAPTATIONS

- *Inherit the Wind* became a film in 1960. Produced and directed by Stanley Kramer, this version is available from CBS/Fox Video. It stars Spencer Tracy as Henry Drummond, Frederic March as Matthew Harrison Brady, and Gene Kelly as the acerbic E. K. Hornbeck.

- In 1965, the *Hallmark Hall of Fame* and George Schaefer produced a television movie version of *Inherit the Wind*. It starred Melvyn Douglas as Drummond and Ed Begley, Sr. as Brady. (Douglas had replaced Paul Muni during the play's original run on Broadway.)

- A different television production of *Inherit the Wind* surfaced in March, 1988. This version starred Jason Robards in the role of Henry Drummond, Kirk Douglas as Matthew Harrison Brady, and Darren McGavin as Hornbeck.

to defend the rights of an individual to think and reason without interference from the government.

E. K. Hornbeck

A cynical big-city reporter, Hornbeck enjoys lampooning the simple life of Hillsboro as well as their skeptical view of evolution. He takes particular pleasure in skewering Brady and his ideas. He views himself as the sole possesor of the "real" truth and scoffs at any and all who don't see the world as he does. As an element in the play itself, Hornbeck represents the "intellectual elite," while, at the same time, he serves as the comic relief.

THEMES

Individual vs. Machine

Jerome Lawrence said in an interview with Nina Couch that "almost if not all of our plays share the theme of the dignity of every individual mind." The machine in this case is a combination of government and traditional thought, which are allied in *Inherit the Wind* to serve as adversaries against the right to think freely and exchange—or teach—those thoughts. In the exchange with Brady on the witness stand, Drummond asks the witness if he believes a sponge thinks and if a man has the same

privileges that a sponge does. When Brady responds in the affirmative, Drummond raises his voice for the first time and roars that his client "wishes to be accorded the same privileges as a sponge. He wishes to think." Drummond explores this idea further when he offers the supposition that "an un-Brady thought might still be holy." Drummond further illustrates his belief in the dignity of the individual mind after Brady's death when he asserts to Hornbeck that Brady had just as much right to his strict religious views as that the reporter does to his liberal ideals.

God and Religion

The idea of separation of church and state is as old as the American Republic itself, and it continues to be a source of controversy to this day. The central question of the play asks if the government, as represented by the city of Hillsboro and the laws of the state of Tennessee, should make decisions regarding what people can believe. Should one particular way of looking at the world be preferred over another? The question about the authority of the Bible also raises concerns: which translation or edition should be adopted as the "official" version of events? Drummond comments that the Bible is a good book—but not the only resource with which to view the world. God and religion are not the antagonists in *Inherit the Wind,* however, but merely provide the raw materials that people like Brady and Reverend Brown will use to combat Bert's

TOPICS FOR FURTHER STUDY

- Investigate the current debate between creationists and evolutionists. The World Wide Web and the Index to a major newspaper, such as the *New York Times,* can provide a number of specific instances of this discussion.

- Research instances of censorship in schools. What types of material have different groups tried to remove from public school classrooms over the past five years? Discuss why an attempt to ban materials might be successful in one community but unsuccessful in another. The events in Kanawha County, West Virginia, during the late 1960s can provide some interesting parallels to the climate surrounding the fictional Hillsboro.

- Read further about the lives and careers of the historical people around whom *Inherit the Wind* revolves—Clarence Darrow, William Jennings Bryan, and H. L. Mencken. Compare and contrast the historical and dramatic personalities.

- Investigate the American Civil Liberties Union (ACLU). What is the mission of this organization and how effective is it in carrying out that mission? List some famous trials in which the ACLU played a pivotal role.

teaching of evolution. Like many lessons in blind faith, the play illustrates how unyielding devotion to a set of beliefs can lead a person to refute even the most obvious of truths. The play's optimism lies with Rachel and Bert, who, it is suggested, will find a balance between religion and science in their life together.

Custom and Tradition

In 1925, the world was changing. Radio was beginning to replace the newspaper as a source of information. This, along with the widespread implementation of the telephone, provided a means for quickly relaying facts from one point to another. Technologies such as these brought new thought processes to once-isolated rural towns, new ways of seeing and interpreting the world. There were enormous social changes taking place as well. Women had recently earned the right to vote, and many blacks were planting the seeds that would flower into the civil rights movement of the 1960s. To many people accustomed to a set way of life, these new developments presented a threat. One approach to dealing with this rapid change was to ignore it and retreat into their old, comfortable ways. When new modes of thinking threatened to change these traditions, people became uncomfortable, rejecting the

''new'' simply because it was not familiar. Not only did Bert's teaching of evolution represent a new way of thinking, to many it attacked the most sacred of all traditions, religion and thus their very way of life. Whereas many of the townfolk are fearful of this change, people like Brady and the Reverend resent it because it threatens their prosperity and power—the more people blindly believe, the easier they are to manipulate. Drummond's comment that maybe Brady had moved away by standing still illustrates how the prosecutor has profited from encouraging a stagnation of thought.

Appearances and Reality

When Drummond tells the story of Golden Dancer, he outlines the characteristics of appearances and reality. A toy-store rocking horse, Golden Dancer's bright red mane, blue eyes, and golden color with purple spots dazzled the young Drummond. His parents worked extra and surprised him with the horse as a birthday present, and, when the excited boy jumped on the horse to ride, it broke in two. There was no substance to the object of Drummond's desire, only ''spit and sealing wax.'' Drummond wants Cates, and by extension the audience of the play, to look closely at the arguments of people like Brady and Reverend Brown. They may have no more substance than Golden Dancer.

STYLE

In their Playwrights' Note, Lawrence and Lee state that *Inherit the Wind* is not history and that the play has a life of its own. While recognizing the historical Scopes Trial and the extensive newspaper coverage it received at the time, the authors raise the idea that the issues of the conflict between Clarence Darrow and William Jennings Bryan "have acquired new meaning in the . . . years since they clashed at the Rhea County Courthouse." The ambiguity of the stage directions for the play's time period ("Not too long ago.") allows for the ideas generated by the characters, rather than the facts generated by scores of reporters, to assume center stage.

Image and Irony

The stage directions call for the courtroom to be in the foreground. This is appropriate as the site of the drama's action. The directions also call for the town to be "visible always, looming there, as much on trial as the individual defendant." This "image" of the town on trial presents the central irony of the play: Bert Cates is on trial for his forward thinking, while the town of Hillsboro is on trial for its backward thinking.

Extended Metaphor

At the beginning of Act III, before the jury returns with the verdict, Drummond muses aloud about Golden Dancer. As a child, Drummond had seen a brightly colored rocking horse in a store window, and his parents, through extra work and sacrifice, bought the toy for the young Drummond as a birthday present. When he jumped on it to start to ride, the horse broke apart. "The wood was rotten, the whole thing was put together with spit and sealing wax! All shine and no substance." This brief monologue suggests why Drummond takes on "unpopular" cases. "If something is a lie," Drummond tells Cates, "show it up for what it really is!" By illustrating this point with a story rather than by simply having Drummond make a blanket statement, the playwrights direct the viewer/reader's attention to the idea behind the action.

Symbolism

Throughout the play, Lawrence and Lee present a variety of symbols for consideration. Much of the verbal symbolism comes from Hornbeck's cynical perspective. He refers to Brady as "A man who wears a cathedral for a cloak/A church spire for a hat" and as a "Yesterday Messiah," referring to Brady's religious position on the issue of evolution. Hornbeck's snide comments on Hillsboro as the "buckle on the Bible Belt" and "Heavenly Hillsboro" paint the town in a backward, unfavorable light. His allusion to the Biblical creation story, where he tells Rachel he is not the serpent and the apple he has just bitten does not come from the Tree of Knowledge, again focuses attention on the central argument of the play.

Artistic License

Here are some instances where Lee and Lawrence modified history so that *Inherit the Wind* would stand separate from the historical trial. (The names of the historical characters are used in this list for convenience.)

1. The trial originated, not in Dayton, Tennessee, but in the New York City offices of the American Civil Liberties Union. It was this organization that ran an announcement in Tennessee newspapers, offering to pay the expenses of any teacher willing to test the New Tennessee anti-evolution law.

2. When a group of Dayton leaders decided to take advantage of this offer, their main reason was not so much defense of religion as it was economics. They saw the trial as a great means of publicity that would attract business and industry to Dayton.

3. Others responsible for the trial were the media who worked hard to persuade Bryan and Darrow to participate in the trial.

4. John T. Scopes was not a martyr for academic freedom. He volunteered to help test the law, even though he could not remember ever teaching evolution and had only briefly substituted in biology. He was never jailed, nor did he ever take the witness stand in the trial. The people of Dayton liked him, and he cooperated with them in making a test case of the trial.

5. William Jennings Bryan was not out to get Scopes. Bryan though the Tennessee law a poor one because it involved fining an educator. He offered to pay Scopes's fine if he needed the money.

6. Bryan was familiar with Darwin's works, and he was not against teaching evolution—if it were presented as a theory, and if other major options, such as creationism, were taught as well.

7. The trial record discloses that Bryan handled himself well, and, when put on the stand unexpectedly by Darrow, defined terms carefully, stuck to the facts, made distinctions between literal and figurative language when interpreting the Bible, and questioned the reliability of scientific evidence when it contradicted the Bible. Some scientific experts at the trial referred to such "evidence" as the Piltdown man (now dismissed as a hoax).

8. Scopes dated some girls in Dayton, but did not have a steady girlfriend.

9. The defense's scientific experts did not testify at the trial because their testimony was irrelevant to the central question of whether a law had been broken, because Darrow refused to let Bryan cross-examine the experts, and because Darrow did not call on them to testify. But, twelve scientists and theologians were allowed to make statements as part of the record presented by the defense.

10. Instead of Bryan's being mothered by his wife, he took care of her because she was an invalid.

11. The people of Dayton in general, and fundamentalist Christians in particular, were not the ignorant, frenzied, uncouth persons the play portrays them as being.

12. Scopes was found guilty partly by the request of his defense lawyer, Darrow, in the hope that the case could be taken to a higher court.

13. Bryan did not have a fit while delivering his last speech and die in the courtroom. In the five days following the trial, Bryan wrote a 15,000-word speech he had hoped to give at the trial before the proceedings were cut short. He inspected sites for a school the people of Dayton were interested in building, traveled several hundred miles to deliver speeches in various cities and speak to crowds totaling 50,000, was hit by a car, consulted with doctors about his diabetic condition, and conferred with printers about his last message. On Sunday, July 26, Bryan drove from Chattanooga to Dayton, participated in a church service, and died quietly in his sleep that afternoon.

These differences between the actual events of the Scopes Trial and those depicted in *Inherit the Wind* illustrate the ways in which facts can be manipulated in a drama to serve the intent of the writer(s). Lawrence and Lee wished to deliver a strong message that the real facts of the case presented but did not clearly define. The playwrights took liberties with many characters, creating broader personalities that distinctly represented each side of the issue. Likewise, many portions of the real trial were mediocre and uneventful. Through careful pacing and well-constructed conflict situations, Lawrence and Lee took the real events and created an often gripping courtroom drama that provokes thought. Often referred to as "artistic license," this is a common technique in dramatic representations of actual events.

HISTORICAL CONTEXT

After the upheaval and tension caused by World War I, a mood of collective nostalgia took hold in America. The culture heard calls to rid itself of "enemies" and to return to the simplicity and normalcy of the prewar society. In the mid-1920s, the enemy became embodied in Charles Darwin and the theory of evolution. The Fundamentalists sought to eradicate such thoughts from society, beginning with the schools. They were influential in several southern states, passing laws that prohibited the teaching of evolution in the classroom. Modernists, those who supported the study of Darwin and opposed a literal interpretation of the Bible, became increasingly wary of what they perceived as attacks on their constitutional rights. Their response was to look for ways to test these laws.

In the mid-1950s when *Inherit the Wind* was written and first produced, the country experienced a tension between the seemingly prosperous post-World War II society and a wave of anti-Communist hysteria that, led by Wisconsin Senator Joseph McCarthy, swept the nation. McCarthy's fervor for rooting Communists out of American society took the form of a set of hearings on "Un-American Activities." These "hearings" identified numerous Americans—often incorrectly—as Communist. Many lives were ruined because their beliefs ran counter to the majority. Another American playwright, Arthur Miller, used the Salem witch trials as a setting for his play, *The Crucible,* to explore the societal conflicts raised by McCarthy's "witch hunt." Lawrence and Lee, in trying to make sense of this climate of anxiety and attacks on intellectual freedom, found their nearest parallel in the Scopes Monkey Trial of thirty years prior. Because the play is a dramatization and not a history lesson, the authors can focus on a conflict in the culture that is not bound by a particular time and place, a conflict that was as current in 1955 as it was in 1925.

Beginning in the 1950s and continuing through the 1960s, the modernists transformed into progressives who sought a variety of political and social reforms that were part of a process of finding "truth." The civil rights movement expanded to include not only blacks, but women, students, and other groups who considered themselves "oppressed." On the other side of the society, however, were those fundamentalists who believed that, in society's progress forward, much that was of value was being lost. The heightened debate over evolution and creationism intensified this apprehension as well as a longing for the perceived stability of the past.

COMPARE
&
CONTRAST

- **1920s/1930s:** After World War I, the country seemed to change. Idealism was replaced by cynicism. Some authors began to question both authority and tradition. Moral codes changed along with hemlines and language. The sense of connection to the past appeared to be deteriorating.

  1950s/1960s: After World War II, the country did change. Women who worked in the factories during the war were reluctant to return to their traditional pre-war domestic roles. Men who had seen the horrors of battle wanted to return to the way things were before they left. The technology that was to be for the benefit and improvement of humankind destroyed cities and ushered in a sense of helplessness and disorientation.

  Today: With the collapse of the Berlin Wall and the end of the Cold War, relative peace reigns. However, uncertainty about the future still holds people in its grasp. Authority and tradition are still under attack, and moral codes, or lack of them, occupy the interest of many.

  1920s/1930s: The Scopes Monkey Trial raised issues about what should be taught in public school classrooms. Several states, including Tennessee, passed laws proscribing the presentation of certain topics, such as the origin of humans, and how they could or could not be presented to their schoolchildren.

  1950s/1960s: The issue of what should be taught in public schools extended to individual books. The issue of human origins remained a hot topic but was gradually replaced by issues concerning sexuality (specifically sex education in the classroom) as a topic of debate and discussion.

  Today: Special interest groups, each with its own agenda, regularly attack school textbooks and curricula. The issue of sexuality has been broadened to include homosexuality, and the debate between those who favor creation theory and those who favor evolutionary theory rages on. Several states have introduced legislation that requires creation theory to be taught alongside evolution. The Tennessee Senate considered a bill that would allow school boards to fire teachers who taught evolution as fact. The billed failed to become law by only seven votes.

  1920s/1930s: The newspaper was the primary source of information about the world at large. Radio began to make inroads, but more people turned to radio for entertainment than for news. Extensive newspaper coverage of not only the Scopes Trial but other courtroom dramas such as the Fatty Arbuckle trial, Sacco and Vanzetti, Leopold and Loeb, and, later, the Lindbergh baby kidnapping trial, captured the imagination of the nation.

  1950s/1960s: The Cold War brought fear and anxiety to new heights. The advent of television as the medium to bring news into America's homes began with the broadcasts of hearings chaired by Wisconsin Senator Joseph McCarthy that purported to seek out Communists in the government of the United States.

  Today: The nation watches the murder trial of sports star O.J. Simpson from opening arguments to the verdict either as it happens or through nightly updates on the local and national news. Cable channels devoted exclusively to live broadcasts of trials can be received by many American households.

CRITICAL OVERVIEW

During the 1950s, America was in the process of settling in after the tumultuous years of World War II. But, beneath an air of prosperity and comfort, social tension existed. Lawrence and Lee sought to make some kind of sense of the climate of anxiety and fear fed by McCarthyism and anti-Communist sentiment. They found a parallel in the Scopes Monkey Trial of 1925. The story of *Inherit the Wind* is a dramatization, not a history lesson, as the playwrights make clear in their foreword to the play. It is a story about conflict in American culture.

Despite the play's overwhelming popularity, *Inherit the Wind*'s historical accuracy became an issue almost from the start. Those connected with the play itself (producers, directors, and other theater personnel) saw the Scopes Trial as a dramatic piece of history that could be made more dramatic by bringing it to the stage. Quoted on the University of Virginia's website, *American Studies,* Merle Debuskey, a promotional man behind the play, described the link between drama and factual events as "a vibrant, pulsating, slam-bang production, acclaimed by the critics as entertainment first and history by incidence." Another public relations firm, Daniel E. Lewitt Associates, called the play "living drama rather than a period piece" and said that *Inherit the Wind* has significance to students because it illuminates a fragment of America's scholastic past [and] espouses important ideas dramatically."

On the other side of the issue, some had problems with *Inherit the Wind* as a history lesson for two reasons. First, there are significant discrepancies between the courtroom events of the play and the actual trial records. Even though Lawrence and Lee opened the play with a disclaimer, many viewed the play as a learning tool.

The other problem with using *Inherit the Wind* as historical documentation is the bias against the South that permeates the drama. The character of E. K. Hornbeck consistently refers to the South in less than flattering terms. Hornbeck longs to return to the North and escape the stultifying society of Hillsboro. Additionally, the play seems to suggest that the Scopes Monkey Trial is a southern failure and a sign of stagnation and ignorance. Drummond responds to Brady when asked why the two have moved so far apart: "Perhaps it is you who have moved away—by standing still." The Southerners, on the other hand, see Drummond and Hornbeck as

intruders from the North. Drummond is referred to as "the gentleman from Chicago," a term not of respect but of scorn and derision.

In spite of these problems, Lawrence and Lee position themselves firmly in support of freedom of thought and tolerance. Through Drummond, the playwrights try to establish a way for a culture or society to survive with its members holding differing beliefs. They support the importance of conflict and disagreement within a society, as well the idea that each position has its own merits and validity.

Whitney Bolton, in a *Morning Telegraph* review, said: "This is a play which, in the pleasant tasting icing of excellent theatre, gets across to its audience the core of value beneath the icing: there is no more holy concept that the right of a man to think. . . . What is of importance is that from that musty little town . . . came a note of hope; that men could think of themselves without censure or impoundment and that . . . the accused made it easier, even though by only a fractional amount, for the next accused thinker to take his stand for it."

In a review published in the *Christian Science Monitor,* John Beaufort wrote that "Drummond's [defense of Brady] is an indictment of all dogma—whether springing from blind ignorance or blind intellectualism."

CRITICISM

William P. Wiles

Wiles is an educator with more than twenty years of experience. In this essay he examines Lawrence and Lee's play as a historical work as well as a piece of thought-provoking theater.

There is a saying that comes from the Bible which states: "You shall know the truth and the truth shall set you free." Therein lies the problem of *Inherit the Wind*. Which version of the truth is it that one should know—the version of *Genesis* championed by Brady and his followers or the version of Charles Darwin's *The Origin of Species?* Is the answer to that question an either/or proposition? Or, as Drummond suggests by clamping the two books together at the close of the play, is there a way for the two different views of humankind's roots to exist side-be-side?

The early years of the twentieth century brought many sweeping technological changes that those

WHAT DO I READ NEXT?

- *To Kill A Mockingbird*, Harper Lee's 1960 novel about justice in a small southern town during the Depression. Of particular interest for reader of *Inherit the Wind* are the courtroom scenes, as well as the attitudes of the townspeople.

- *The Night Thoreau Spent in Jail*, Lawrence and Lee's 1970 drama that focuses on the right of another individual to think.

- John T. Scopes, the historical person behind the *Inherit the Wind*'s Bert Cates, published an auto-biography in 1967 (written with James Presley) titled, *Center of the Storm*.

- L. Sprague deCamp wrote an account of the events of that hot July, 1925, in *The Great Monkey Trial* published by Doubleday in 1968.

- Irving Stone's riveting biography, *Clarence Darrow for the Defense*, Doubleday, 1941, provides a compelling portrait of the best-known lawyer of the early part of the twentieth century.

---

near the end of the same century take for granted. In Act II, Drummond outlines some of those changes in his examination of Brady as an expert on the Bible: "Gentlemen, progress has never been a bargain. You've got to pay for it. Sometimes I think there is a man behind a counter who says, All right, you can have a telephone; but you'll have to give up privacy, the charm of distance. Madam, you may vote; but at a price; you lost the right to retreat behind a powder puff or a petticoat. Mister, you may conquer the air; but the birds will lose their wonder, and the clouds will smell of gasoline." It is in the middle of these changes that the case of Bert Cates is argued, not only before a small-town southern judge but before the entire world. It is the changes themselves, especially those improvements in communication, that make this trial such a spectacle. Enhancements in telegraph and telephone transmission allowed reporters to send their stories quickly and efficiently to their editors back home and onto the front pages of the next edition. Radio had evolved to permit live, on-site broadcasting of the story as it happened. To many people, these changes all seemed to be happening at once, and many of them felt overwhelmed. Add to that anxiety an element that shakes their belief system and a trial of the century erupts.

The central issue in the struggle between Drummond and Brady and the forces each repre-sents is the meaning of "truth." Brady and his followers steadfastly believe there is "only one great Truth in the world"—the Bible as it is written in the King James version. Drummond, on the other hand, argues the position that, because humans have been given the power to think and question, there exists the possibility of another version of truth, a Bert Cates version or a Charles Darwin version, for example.

Truth in *Inherit the Wind* is often equated with right and everything else is equated with wrong. Throughout the play, Brady insists there is only ONE right way. But, under fierce questioning from Drummond, that way appears to be Brady's way. When Brady equates himself with God's personal messenger

Drummond: Oh. God speaks to you.

Brady: Yes.

Drummond: He tells you exactly what's right and what's wrong?

Brady: Yes.

Drummond: And you act accordingly?

Brady: Yes.

It can be seen that it is Brady's own vanity that translates into a "positive knowledge of Right and Wrong."

Drummond, on the other hand, constantly assails this attitude to make his point. In an early exchange with Brady, Drummond presents the notion that "*Truth* has meaning—as a direction. But one of the peculiar imbecilities of our time is the grid of morality we have placed on human behavior: so that every act of man must be measured against an arbitrary latitude of right and longitude of wrong—in exact minutes, seconds, and degrees." He also argues that "the Bible is a book. A good book. But it's not the only book." Drummond continually asks the question "what if?" Can there be a way of looking at the world that is different from Brady's version? "What if . . . an un-Brady thought might still be holy?" That is the key question of the entire play.

In addition to questions about truth and right, *Inherit the Wind* presents a struggle between urban and rural societies, as well as between the cities of the industrialized North and towns of the agrarian (farm-based economy) South. The E. K. Hornbeck character, modeled after Baltimore newspaperman and noted literary critic H. L. Mencken, speaks about the people and town of Hillsboro in condescending and pejorative tones. Referring to Hillsboro as "Heavenly" and the "buckle on the Bible Belt," Hornbeck reveals an attitude that the trial and its attending hoopla is a sign of the region's ignorance and stagnation. His cynical commentary indicates that he hates the suffocating society of Hillsboro and desperately wants to return to the "big city." (As he tells a woman who offers him a "nice clean place to stay": "I had a nice clean place to stay, madame /And I left it to come here.") It is not only the Northerners who harbor attitudes toward others. The Southerners, particularly represented by Tom Davenport, the attorney assisting Brady, regard Drummond and the North in general as "intruders." Davenport's constant references to Drummond as "the gentleman from Chicago" in a voice laced with utter scorn reveal an unwillingness to look beyond a label to the actual human being across the room. Drummond recognizes this antagonism between North and South, urban and rural, in the play's most comical moment. When Drummond removes his suit coat revealing wide, bright purple suspenders (often called "galluses"), Brady asks with "affable sarcasm" (as the stage directions indicate) if this is the latest fashion in "the great metropolitan city of Chicago?" Drummond responds that he bought these at a general store in Brady's own hometown—"Weeping Water, Nebraska."

A playbill from the Royale Theatre performance

This blending of urban and rural symbols makes it difficult to cast Drummond as a complete enemy of the South and its rural inhabitants.

From all these conflicts, which sides do Lawrence and Lee—and their play—support? None. The play does not take sides. Instead, amid the polarization and heightened tension, Lawrence and Lee use the drama to argue in favor of tolerance and freedom of thought and belief, for some form of mutual respect. Society must search for ways to survive despite different beliefs of its individual members. The importance of conflict and the value of each argument must be recognized. When he slaps Bert's copy of Darwin and the judge's Bible together and jams them into his briefcase side by side, Drummond shows that there is no single right or wrong way of looking at the world, only different perspectives.

Source: William P. Wiles, in an essay for *Drama for Students,* Gale, 1997.

Films in Review

The following excerpt from a brief review of the 1960 film adaptation of Inherit the Wind *empha-*

❝APART FROM HISTORICAL
INTEREST, IT WAS EASY TO DRAW
A CONTEMPORARY PARALLEL WITH
THE LATENT FORCES OF
MCCARTHYISM STANDING IN FOR
THE BIGOTED FUNDAMENTALISTS"

sizes the real-life events upon which the drama is based.

Although Stanley Kramer, who produced as well as directed this film version of a Broadway play about the 1925 trial of John Thomas Scopes in Dayton, Tenn., for teaching Darwin's theory of human evolution, doesn't use the names of the real-life characters, his publicity for the picture stresses the fact that the film *is* about the so-called "Monkey Trial."

Therefore, and for the benefit of all who are too young to remember that bizarre occurrence, I would like to point out that Kramer's film departs from truth on two fundamentally important points. First, Scopes was not arrested in the course of persecution by bigots but as the result of *volunteering* to make a test case of a newly enacted Tennessee statute forbidding the teaching of evolution in Tennessee-supported institutions. Second, Clarence Darrow, Arthur Garfield Hayes and Dudley Field Malone volunteered to defend Scopes for the same publicity-chasing reasons that inspired William Jennings Bryan to volunteer to aid the prosecution. . . .

Some of the most interesting occurrences at the trial have not been used, and one of them is badly muffed (Bryan, knowing the press of the entire country would make a fool of him for saying it, nevertheless declared, with a bravado that was not without nobility, that he believed Jonah could have swallowed the whale if God had wanted him to). A sub-plot involving a minister, anachronistically wearing a clerical collar, and his daughter, is clumsy and unnecessary. The Scopes character is almost as much of a forgotten man in *Inherit the Wind* as the real-life Scopes was at the actual trial. . . .

Source: "Hors D'Oeuvre" in *Films in Review,* Vol. 11, no. 7, August/September, 1970, p. 427.

John Gillett

In the following review, Gillett offers a mixed assessment of the film version of Inherit the Wind.

It was clearly only a matter of time before some enterprising producer turned his attention to Tennessee's famous "Monkey Trial" of 1925, when Clarence Darrow defended a schoolteacher accused of teaching Darwinism against the hell-fire attack of the noted attorney and presidential candidate, William Jennings Bryan. Its theatrical potentialities were clearly demonstrated in the play written around the trial by Jerome Lawrence and Robert E. Lee. And, apart from historical interest, it was easy to draw a contemporary parallel, with the latent forces of McCarthyism standing in for the bigoted fundamentalists of thirty-five years ago.

Stanley Kramer's *Inherit the Wind* takes full advantage of all these conflicts and adds some of its own. Its best scenes conjure up an atmosphere of passionate polemics, of stubborn convictions and old-fashioned loyalties. At its worst, it reveals Kramer's main limitations as a director: a weakness for caricature and a certain banality in the handling of emotional relationships. But this is not a stylist's film. Rather, it provides a field-day for two of Hollywood's great veterans—Spencer Tracy (as the film's Darrow) and Fredric March (Bryan). Dominating the central court-room scenes, they provide the film with its real excitements—a battle between two elderly giants who, at their most intense, look strangely like their Mr. Hydes of many years ago.

If Tracy can be said to win on points, this may be due to the fact that March has been slightly over-directed. This kind of flamboyancy can be made to work on the stage, but a close-up view inevitably emphasises the essential theatricality of the writing; and Kramer's own handling has its inflationary aspects. Yet the fascination remains. Both actors have marvellous timing, they weave and attack like experienced boxers, and even their mannerisms (which are all on display here) are made to play their full part. Curiously, perhaps, the power of these two performances contributes a little to the feeling that the exploitable nature of the material attracted Kramer at least as much as its undertones of contemporary meaning. Sympathies are more or less equitably distributed; and although there is plenty of excitement and passion in it, the film's very enclosure somehow makes it difficult to reach out into life itself.

Source: John Gillett, in a review of *Inherit the Wind,* in *Sight and Sound,* Vol. 29, no. 3, Summer, 1960, p. 147.

FURTHER READING

Cornelius, R. M. "William Jennings Bryan, The Scopes Trial, and *Inherit the Wind,*" http://www.concentric.net/~paulvon/wjbinfo.html], 1996.
A World Wide Web site written by an English professor from William Jennings Bryan College in Dayton, Tennessee. Provides a resource for the discrepancies between the actual Scopes Trial and the proceeding depicted in the play.

Hanlon, Kathy. *Inherit the Wind Currcilum Unit,* Center for Learning, Brown Publishers, 1990.
A curriculum unit for the play with excerpts from: *Natural History* by Stephen Jay Gould, 1981; *Center of the Storm* by John T. Scopes and James Presley, Holt Reinhart and Winston, 1967; *A Treasury of Great Reporting* edited by Richard Morris and Louis

L. Snyder, Simon and Schuster, 1949; and *Thru the Bible with J. Vernon McGee* by J. Vernon McGee, Volume III, Thomas Nelson, Inc.

McCabe, Lyndsey. "Inherit the Wind" on the University of Virginia's *American Studies* website, http://xroads.virginia.edu/~UG97/inherit/intro.html, April, 1996.
A World Wide Web Site that presents a chronological layout with links to relevant reviews, contemporary news events, and other background information. Some photos from the 1960 and 1965 film versions.

SOURCES

Bolton, Whitney. Review of *Inherit the Wind* in the *Morning Telegraph,* April, 1955.

Beaufort, John. Review of *Inherit the Wind* in the *Christian Science Monitor,* April, 1955.

Couch, Nina. *Studies in American Drama, 1945-Present.*

Long Day's Journey into Night

EUGENE O'NEILL

1956

Although Eugene O'Neill had completed *Long Day's Journey into Night* by 1941, it was not produced until 1956, three years after his death. He had originally stipulated that it was not to be produced or published until twenty-five years after he died. However, before his death he gave verbal permission to the Royal Dramatic Theatre to stage it in Stockholm, Sweden, a country that had accorded him a special loyalty throughout his career.

The Stockholm production, which opened on February 10, 1956, was very successful and prompted wide interest in the play. Nine months later, on November 7, the play opened to mixed but mostly favorable reviews at the Helen Hayes Theatre in New York. Featured in the cast were Frederic March as James Tyrone, Florence Eldridge as Mary, Jason Robards, Jr. as Jamie, Bradford Dilman as Edmund, and Katherine Ross as Cathleen. Jose Quintero both produced and directed the play.

Carlotta O'Neill, the playwright's widow, saw to the play's publication in the same year. In 1955 she had copyrighted the work as an unpublished play, and in the following year she asked Random House publish it. The editors declined, even though they held a sealed copy of the script that O'Neill had originally deposited with them. Mrs. O'Neill then offered the publication rights to the Yale Library, which arranged its release through the Yale University Press with the provision that the play royalties would be used to endow the Eugene O'Neill Memo-

rial Fund at the Yale School of Drama. The published work met with great critical acclaim and won for O'Neill a fourth Pulitzer Prize.

AUTHOR BIOGRAPHY

It was because *Long Day's Journey into Night* was so transparently autobiographical that Eugene O'Neill forbade the play's production and publication during his lifetime. The main characters are thinly veiled portraits of his father, James, his mother, Ella, his brother, Jamie, and himself.

James Gladstone O'Neill was born on October 6, 1888, in a Broadway hotel, son to the popular actor, James O'Neill, and Ella Quinlan. He was raised in the world of theater, and, as a result, in his boyhood and teen years he traveled all over America.

At eighteen, O'Neill entered Princeton but was expelled for a drunken prank and ''general hell-raising.'' Thereafter he drifted. He served briefly as a business firm clerk, tried his hand at gold prospecting in Central America, and finally signed on a ship as an ordinary seaman in the Atlantic trade routes. After three years of wandering, he returned to New York, supporting himself with odd jobs and living on that city's squalid waterfront. In 1912, the year in which *Long Day's Journey into Night* is set, O'Neill broke off his three-year marriage to Kathleen Jenkins. In that same year, ill with tuberculosis and haunted by his ''rebellious dissipations,'' he reached a personal low point and even attempted suicide.

While in a sanatorium recovering from tuberculosis, O'Neill studied the master dramatists of the world and set out to become a playwright. Dissatisfied with his early efforts in the form, he enrolled at Harvard to study the craft, becoming the most celebrated member of George Pierce Baker's famous ''47 Workshop.'' His first plays were published in 1914, and his first staged play, *Bound East for Cardiff*, was produced in 1916. It was followed by *Thirst*, produced by the Provincetown Players in the summer of 1917. It was that group that gave O'Neill his artistic arena and, with its move to New York, quickly established his reputation as the chief innovator in theater.

O'Neill then began a very prolific stretch of writing that lasted over a dozen years and vaulted him into the front rank of American playwrights. Through the 1920s, he penned a group of major

Eugene O'Neill

plays, including *Beyond the Horizon* (1920), *The Emperor Jones* (1920), *Anna Christie* (1921), *The Hairy Ape* (1922), *All God's Chillun Got Wings* (1924), *Desire Under the Elms* (1924), *The Great God Brown* (1926), *Strange Interlude* (1926), *Lazarus Laughed* (1928), *Dynamo* (1929), and *Mourning Becomes Electra* (1931).

O'Neill's personal grief helped shape his dramatic vision. Between 1920 and 1923, O'Neill's father, mother, and brother all died, leaving him deeply troubled. He attempted only one comedy, *Ah, Wilderness* (1933), concentrating instead on the grimmer side of life and relying heavily on the probing psychoanalytical theories of Sigmund Freud. He also mined his own life for his themes and characters, most obviously in his later plays, in which he clearly attempted to exorcise his subconscious familial guilt and sorrow.

O'Neill's reputation in the United States went into something of a decline after 1930, perhaps because his vigorous innovation and experimentation gave way to more morose autobiographical studies, some of which were not staged at the time. His international reputation remained high, however, and in 1936 he won the Nobel Prize in literature, only the second American at the time to have been so honored.

O'Neill and his third wife, Carlotta, went into relative seclusion in the late 1930s. Thereafter, in the 1940s, he was stricken with a degenerative neurological tremor which impaired his faculties and prevented him from undertaking new projects or completing work on his ambitious cycle of plays tentatively entitled "A Tale of Possessor Self-Dispossessed." However, he finished *Long Day's Journey into Night,* which many critics deem his crowning achievement. In the work's dedication to Carlotta, O'Neill indicated that he was finally able to pay homage to his family, the "four haunted Tyrones," and to write about his past "with deep pity and understanding and forgiveness."

In his last active years, O'Neill finished plays that now rank among his very best, including *The Iceman Cometh* (1946) and *A Moon for the Misbegotten* (1947). Other later plays include *A Touch of the Poet* (1957) and *Hughie* (1959), which, like *Long Day's Journey into Night,* were first produced posthumously. By the time he died in 1953, O'Neill had written over thirty significant dramatic works and solidified his reputation as America's premier dramatist.

PLOT SUMMARY

Long Day's Journey into Night is set in the living room of the Tyrones' shoreline summer home in New London, Connecticut, in August of 1912. The play begins in the morning and ends late at night on the same day.

The work is divided into four acts. It largely consists of painful disclosures and acrimonious exchanges among the four family members, as major crises mount and finally engulf the family in despair. Of central concern are Mary's relapse into morphine addiction, Jamie's continued descent into irreversible dissipation, and Edmund's grim discovery that he has tuberculosis and must enter a sanatorium.

Act One

The play, which opens just after breakfast, begins on a hopeful note, evident in the affectionate exchange between James and Mary Tyrone, but it is clear that Mary is being carefully watched by her family. Neither her morphine addiction nor Edmund's obvious ill health are honestly discussed. Instead, the characters fence around the truth with evasive banter, though, at times, resentment and

disappointment surface. Tyrone upbraids Jamie, his eldest son, for encouraging Edmund, the younger son, to follow in Jamie's dissolute footsteps. Jamie, ever critical of "the Old Man," in turn derides Tyrone as a miser, ultimately to blame for Mary's addiction and Edmund's ill health because of his penny-pinching reluctance to pay for competent doctors. To the father and sons, it becomes obvious that Mary is growing unstable, but she blames her edginess on a lack of sleep caused by Tyrone's snoring and the foghorn that sounded throughout the previous night. After the men leave to take up outside chores, Mary sinks into an armchair, clearly in a state of nervous agitation that threatens the last vestiges of her self-control.

Act Two, Scene One

The scene opens just before lunch. Edmund and Jamie sneak some of their father's whiskey and then resort to Jamie's usual trick of watering the remaining whiskey to disguise their actions. Their discussion shifts from Edmund's health to their fears about their mother, and Jamie grows distraught because Edmund has let Mary stay upstairs by herself. When she enters, it is evident to both of them that she has succumbed to the drug, smashing their hopes that she had finally shaken herself free of it. Jamie's sneering remarks about his father anger Mary, who excuses her husband's stinginess as the result of his hard life. She also fends off Jamie's insinuation that she has lapsed into her addiction again. Tyrone enters, and he soon realizes what has happened. After his sons exit for lunch, he remains behind with Mary, angry and defeated by her condition.

Act Two, Scene Two

The family returns to the living room after lunch. A telephone call from Dr. Hardy confirms the diagnosis of Edmund's sickness as tuberculosis. Edmund must keep an afternoon appointment with Hardy. Although the full truth remains hidden from Mary, her verbal attack on Hardy indicates that she knows that Edmund suffers from more than "a summer cold." She leaves to go upstairs, and it is clear to the rest that she is going to use more morphine. The father-son recriminations begin again, with Tyrone accusing both Jamie and Edmund of abandoning their Catholic faith to embrace damning alternatives: in Jamie's case, degeneracy, and in Edmund's, a gloomy and self-destructive philosophy. Edmund leaves and Jamie warns his father not to put Edmund in a second-rate sanatori-

A scene from the 1958 production at the Aldwych Theatre in London

um, prone as he is to look for the cheapest way out. Mary returns and, left alone with Tyrone, complains about her loneliness and Tyrone's tightfisted failure to provide a real home. She bitterly blames Tyrone's lifestyle for past disasters, including her difficult birthing of Edmund and postpartum pain, then begins to drift into the solace of her romanticized past, when she was in a convent school planning to become a nun or a concert pianist. Edmund returns and pleads with her to stop taking the morphine, but it is clearly to no avail. She can only try to make him stop blaming himself for her renewed addiction.

Act Three

It is early evening, and Mary has sunk further into her drug-induced detachment from reality, which, like the gathering fog outside, "hides you from the world." She is alone with Cathleen, the servant who had accompanied her on her automobile ride into town to obtain more morphine. She confides in the girl, treating her like a childhood friend while plying her with Tyrone's whiskey. She tells the servant about her early hopes and her romanticized first impressions of Tyrone. After Cathleen leaves to resume her duties, Tyrone and Edmund enter. Both have been drinking and continue to imbibe while Mary drifts through a reverie on Jamie's alcoholism, her early married life on the

itinerant hotel-hopping theater circuit, and her expensive satin wedding gown. When Tyrone leaves to fetch another bottle of whiskey, Edmund tries to tell his mother that he must enter a sanatorium, but she refuses to accept the truth, which, because her own father had died of consumption, she fears is a virtual death sentence. He voices wounding regret that he has "a dope fiend for a mother," but is immediately contrite and hurries away. The act ends in a confrontation between Mary and Tyrone over Edmund's condition. Mary refuses to eat dinner, claiming she is tired, and Tyrone then accuses her of slipping off to "take more of that God-damned poison."

Act Four

It is around midnight. Tyrone, morose and almost lost in an alcoholic stupor, awkwardly attempts to play solitaire. Edmund enters, also drunk, and is immediately accused of "burning up money" by leaving the lights on behind him. Edmund attempts to defy his father, and is quick to defend his brother against his father's ritual complaints about Jamie's debauchery. Edmund then launches into a self-pitying conceit about being "a ghost within a ghost," a soul lost in the comfort of the fog. His father only finds him morbid. Edmund continues, reciting depressing poetry and fueling his father's anger. They begin to play Casino, but they are constantly distracted from the cards by their concern for Jamie and their fear that Mary will get up and come downstairs. They also continue to drink, reflect on their lives, and trade a mixture of recriminations and affectionate concerns for each other. They discuss Mary and her romantic distortions of the truth about her earlier life in the convent and her father's wealth. Edmund then takes up Jamie's theme of Tyrone's stinginess, evident in Tyrone's effort to find an inexpensive sanatorium for Edmund. Tyrone offers his familiar excuse, arguing that his family poverty and experience as a child laborer instilled in him a desperate fear of the poor house, turning him into "a stinking old miser." He reveals his own deep regret that his fears led him to sacrifice his acting talent for a fixed but secure and very lucrative role in a popular melodrama. Edmund, in his turn, laments the loss of hope found in rare moments at sea, where life, however briefly, seemed to hold some meaning.

Jamie, drunk, lurches through the house and into the room as Tyrone, to avoid a confrontation, retires to the side porch. After recounting his adventure with Fat Violet in a local brothel, Jamie begins a painful confession in which he claims that his bitter resentment towards Edmund has caused him to try to drag Edmund into his own moral quicksand and turn him into a bum. He admits to having been jealous of Edmund and holding him responsible for Mary's addiction. His love for his kid brother, though stronger than the hate, will not stop him from wanting to see Edmund fail.

When Jamie seems to fall asleep, Tyrone returns and begins his litany of complaints about his oldest son, but he is interrupted when Jamie starts up and begins returning fire with caustic, sneering innuendos.

The men, worn down by drink and a lack of sleep, soon begin to doze, but they quickly grow alert when they hear the piano begin a badly rendered Chopin waltz in a nearby room. Mary, carrying her wedding gown on her arm, then makes the entrance the men have dreaded. She is obviously in a narcotic-induced trance, barely aware of her surroundings. She begins a detached and vacant reverie on her childhood dreams and hopes. The men remain immobilized, making only feeble attempts to break through to her, vainly reciting lines of verse that underscore the helplessness of their situation. Mary's reverie continues as the men sit quietly in their chairs and an indifferent curtain finally descends.

CHARACTERS

Cathleen

The "second girl," Cathleen is the Tyrone household maid, "a buxom Irish peasant" of about Edmund's age. She is dull, awkward, and slow but very amiable and totally unaffected. She shows no awareness that her familiarity is inappropriate for a servant, and her ingenuousness encourages Mary to treat her almost like an old school chum and confidant.

Gaspard
See James Tyrone

Jamie
See James Tyrone, Jr.

The Kid
See Edmund Tyrone

The Old Man
See James Tyrone

Edmund Tyrone

Edmund, the youngest son of James and Mary Tyrone, is twenty-three, ten years younger than his brother, Jamie. Thinner, and a bit taller than Jamie, Edmund more closely resembles his mother than his father. He also shares some of his mother's nervousness, evident in his hands. A fledgling journalist, he is also a poet. He is more of an intellectual than his brother and quickly becoming better read, but he has also seen something of the world, working on merchant ships as a common seaman and drifting through waterfront bars and flophouses. He has a deep and abiding love of the sea, but he also has a morbid view of life that his father finds deeply distressing. He has a special bond with Jamie, for whom he has a great affection. He is ill with tuberculosis, and the consumptive disease is evident in his gaunt frame, wracking cough, and sallow complexion.

James Tyrone

The sixty-five year old family patriarch, James Tyrone is a financially successful and handsome actor whose robust looks and bearing and make him

MEDIA ADAPTATIONS

- *Long Day's Journey into Night* was first adapted to film by Sidney Lumet, and starred Katharine Hepburn, Sir Ralph Richardson, Jason Robards, Jr., and Dean Stockwell. A black and white film, Embassy, 1962; available from Republic Pictures Home Video.

- *Long Day's Journey into Night* was produced again as a made for television film by Jonathan Miller, using Sinclair Lewis's adaptation of the play, and starring Peter Gallagher, Jack Lemmon, Bethel Leslie, and Kevin Spacey, in 1988; available from Lorimar Home Video/Vestron.

- A third version of the play, filmed at the Tom Patterson Theatre in Stratford, Ontario, Canada, was directed by David Wellington, and starred Peter Donaldson, Martha Henry, William Hutt, and Tom McCamus, Stratford Festival, 1996; not currently available.

---

appear more youthful. His popular success has not spoiled him, partly because he is a self-made man from a poor immigrant Irish family deserted by his father. His resulting fear of poverty has turned him into a man obsessed with money and owning property, always looking for bargains, even at the expense of his family's health. From that same heritage comes a lack of snobbery and pretension. He wears clothes to "the limit of usefulness," and thus appears somewhat shabby and careless in his dress. However, he does reveal the "studied technique" of an experienced actor and takes some pride in his powerful, resonant voice and his command of language. His wife's morphine addiction and his sons' profligate lives have made him both resentful and angry. Whiskey offers him some solace, but he is never able to escape the recrimination of his sons, who hold him partly responsible for their mother's drug addiction.

James Tyrone, Jr.

The oldest son of James and Mary Tyrone, Jamie, at thirty-three, shows the physical signs of his dissipation. He favors his father in appearance, but lacks the Old Man's robust vitality and graceful presence. He is an unabashed and unapologetic drunk, with a history of failing at most everything he has tried. He is also a womanizer, spending much of his time haunting saloons and brothels. Afflicted with a caustic cynicism and sneering manner, he mocks his father at every turn, blaming Tyrone's

miserly ways for most of the family problems. Though protective towards Edmund, he admits to a desire to corrupt him, to shape his brother in his own image, and he knows why. His beloved mother's use of morphine had begun after bearing Edmund, and a part of Jamie hates his brother as the source of her pain. For Tyrone, Jamie is nothing but a freeloading, ungrateful bum, quickly slipping beyond redemption. Jamie is at least honest enough to agree with that assessment of his character.

Mary Tyrone

Mary, wife to James Tyrone, at fifty-four, is several years younger than her husband. She is described as having a "graceful figure" with a distinctly Irish face, once pretty and "still striking." From the outset, it is clear that she is on edge, nervously fluttering her fingers, once beautiful but now gnarled by rheumatism. She has been addicted to morphine for several years, and has been in out of sanitariums, desperately trying to get free of her dependency. Under the influence of the drug, she escapes into an idealized version of her girlhood at a convent school, with dreams of becoming a nun or a concert pianist. She finds the real world lonely and depressing, offering little hope or joy. She cannot deal with unpleasant truths; for example, that her son Edmund might be suffering from something more serious than a cold. Still, she retains the "unaffected charm" and "innate unworldly innocence" of her youth, explaining her family's pro-

---

tective loyalty and love and crushing disappointment when she once more falls victim to her addiction.

THEMES

The plot of *Long Day's Journey into Night* focuses on a dysfunctional family trying to come to grips with its ambivalent emotions in the face of serious familial problems, including drug addiction, moral degradation, deep-rooted fear and guilt, and life-threatening illness.

Alienation and Loneliness

The Tyrone family is fragmented, and each of its members to some degree is alienated from the rest. The most obvious estrangement exists between Tyrone and Jamie, both of whom allow their bitterness to overwhelm whatever residual love and respect they have for each other. Jamie holds his father's tightfistedness to blame for Mary's addiction to morphine, while Tyrone cannot forgive what he sees as his son's gutter-bound dissolution. The two are barely civil to each other, and knowing the recriminations their encounters habitually bring, they simply try to avoid each other, especially when drink has dissolved their masks of civility.

More subtle is the ambivalent alienation that Jamie feels towards Edmund. He confesses that a part of him hates Edmund, from jealousy and an irrational association of Edmund's survival with their mother's desperate plight.

Most estranged and alienated of all is Mary. Her struggle with her addiction is desperately lonely, most of the time beyond the others' understanding or sympathy. She talks at length of her isolation, placing much blame on Tyrone for the itinerant life his acting career imposed on them. Under the influence of morphine, Mary drifts into her idealized past, cut off from the pain of her current life.

Deception

Deceptive masks are worn early in the play in an effort to evade unpleasant truths. The other members of the family try to keep Mary from knowing that Edmund is seriously ill, and Mary obviously attempts to deceive herself with the comforting belief that Edmund is only suffering from "a summer cold." Mary also attempts to hide her relapse into drug use with pathetic excuses that simply deepen the family's disappointment. The

deceptions even become trivial, in Jamie's efforts to deceive his father by watering down the whiskey, for example, or in Tyrone's efforts to hide his whiskey-fetching forays from the help.

More poignant are the self-deceptions, in which characters mask the truth from themselves. Clearly, the past into which Mary escapes is illusory, a romanticized but comforting distortion of truth. Even Jamie, cynical but honest, deludes himself in his search for personal redemption through alcoholism and whoring.

God and Religion

For Tyrone, a troubling problem is his sons' rejection of their Catholic faith, a foundation stone in their "shanty Irish" heritage. His complaints about their rejection of religion occasions Jamie's scoffing observation that Tyrone himself is a truant Catholic, which Tyrone must admit. He insists, though, that he still believes in God, which his sons do not. He is particularly upset with Edmund's godless and pessimistic view of life, claiming that it has been learned from reading depressing, atheistic poetry and philosophy.

Guilt and Innocence

Mary's illusory, drug-induced escape into her youth is partly a flight from guilt into a restored innocence and rediscovered faith. In their own ways, the other Tyrones try to unburden themselves of guilt and shame, either through expiation, as seen in Jamie's admission of his jealousy of Edmund, or in pleas for understanding, as seen in Tyrone's attempts to blame his selfish penny pinching on his early poverty. The play's tragic theme is that innocence can not be restored; each character must bear some guilt and pain, even to the grave's edge.

Loyalty

The loyalty of the three Tyrone men towards Mary has eroded because she has repeatedly dashed their hopes for her recovery, but their anger, hurt, and disappointment are an emotional index of their love for her. It is the common loyalty towards her that keeps the family together and explains why, for example, Jamie and Tyrone even tolerate each other.

Memory and Reminiscence

Mary is not the only one with regrets about the past. Tyrone is haunted by his impoverished childhood and his father's abandonment and eventual suicide. In one self-pitying confession, he expresses regrets for having given up the chance of becoming a great Shakespearean actor in order to take a lucrative but artistically unrewarding part in a popular melodrama.

Moral Corruption

Implicit in the responses to Mary's drug addiction is the belief that addiction was an indication of a weak moral will. Public disclosure of her behavior seems to be more threatening to the family than Jamie's disgraceful drinking, gambling, and whoring. In honest moments, Tyrone recognizes that the morphine is a poison and that Mary cannot control her need, but the moral stigma remains. Jamie's moral descent, buffered by his affection for his brother and mother, is treated as less of a social embarrassment, even by Tyrone.

Search for Self

The principal searcher in *Long Day's Journey into Night* is Edmund, O'Neill's alter ego. Both Mary and Tyrone escape to their pasts, Mary to her convent days and Tyrone to a time in his career when he might have resisted trading his talent for wealth. Edmund, having just begun a writing career as a poet and journalist, looks to a future when his drifting ends and he finds an elusive inner peace that he has glimpsed in rare moments at sea. The alternative is to follow Jamie, his dissolute doppelganger, down a self-destructive, unhappy path to a spiritual dead end.

Wealth and Poverty

Throughout *Long Day's Journey into Night*, Tyrone confirms the justice of Jamie's sneering attacks on him as a miser. Old Gaspard, as Jamie calls him, is obsessed with the cost of things, and is always looking for the cheapest alternative. He invariably equates the best with a bargain price, whether he is buying land, cigars, or automobiles, employing servants, or engaging the services of a physician.

On occasion, Tyrone's penny-pinching habits border on the comic. He cannot resist remarking on the most trivial of his marketplace triumphs, and he launches into diatribes about making the electric company rich while he wanders through the house turning off lights in rooms that others have abandoned. But there is real pathos, too, for some of the

TOPICS FOR FURTHER STUDY

- Investigate the history of the use of morphine and the problems of morphine addiction from the time of its chemical isolation from opium in 1806 to the present day.

- Research the development of sanatoria or hospitals devoted to consumptive diseases and their methods of treating tuberculosis prior to the development of modern vaccines and chemotherapy.

- Investigate the plight of Irish Catholic immigrants to America at the time of the potato blight famine that struck Europe in 1845.

- Select one or more of the poets, novelists, or playwrights mentioned or quoted in the play and investigate their literary legacy and influence on O'Neill.

- Research the state of the American theater at the end of the nineteenth century, particularly the negative effect that the profit motives of commercial theaters had on the quality of their productions.

family problems have their origin in Tyrone's misplaced values, which, in an honest moment, even he admits. Jamie never lets him forget that it was his reluctance to seek out a competent physician that led to Mary's addiction. Jamie fears, too, that Tyrone will attempt to find a bargain sanatorium for Edmund, and repeatedly warns his father against doing so.

Indirectly, Tyrone begs for understanding, even forgiveness, by recounting his hard beginnings in an Irish immigrant family, deserted by his father. His fears of landing in the poorhouse are honest enough, for they relate to that dreadful time, when he had to work twelve hours a day in a machine shop to help his family survive. Tyrone has little success in engaging his sons' sympathies, however. Although Edmund claims to understand his father better, both sons are weary of his stories and are largely indifferent to his past; their concern is with the end result of Tyrone's stinginess, not its cause.

STYLE

Long Day's Journey into Night is Eugene O'Neill's thinly veiled autobiographical study of a dysfunctional family disintegrating because of its inability to cope with drug addiction, life-threatening illness, shame, and guilt.

Dramatic Unities

Throughout the four acts of *Long Day's Journey into Night,* O'Neill preserves the unities of time and place. The setting remains the living room of the Tyrone's summer home in New London, Connecticut, and, in emulation of the classical practice, the action unfolds within a single day in August of 1912, starting in the early morning and ending around midnight. Each scene and act is a segment of that single day, and within each the progress of time is scrupulously faithful to the passage of real world time, relentless and impersonal.

Symbolism

O'Neill, within the realistic limits of his drama, uses symbolism very effectively. Of fundamental significance is the fog. It serves first as a mood enhancing but wholly natural phenomenon. At the beginning of the play, the fog of the night before has lifted, and the optimism of the Tyrone family is reflected in the day's early brightness. But by dinner time in Act Three, the fog has again rolled in, its presence announced by a foghorn "moaning like a mournful whale in labor." Its return suits the encroaching sense of futility and isolation of each of the main characters, particularly Mary. It is she who asks why the "fog makes everything sound so sad and lost."

At a more complex symbolic level, the fog has further significance. It is evoked as a metaphor in the rhapsodic self-scrutiny of Edmund, for example. Confiding in his father, Edmund claims that he desires to melt into the fog, to "be alone with myself in another world where truth is untrue and life can hide from itself," to become "a ghost belonging to the fog."

The fog is also a place of forgetfulness, a place where reality is dimmed, and the world is oddly distorted. It thus serves as a symbol of Mary's drug-

induced stupor and her escape into an idealized past that offers her a brief respite from pain.

Autobiographical Elements

The "haunted Tyrones" are dramatic portraits of O'Neill's real family, and the events of the play reflect a critical time in his life when he was about to enter a sanatorium with a mild case of tuberculosis. Like James Tyrone, O'Neill's father, James O'Neill, had been a highly successful actor, famous in the role of Edmund Dantes in a stage adaptation of Alexandre Dumas's *Count of Monte Cristo.* Like Mary, O'Neill's mother, Ella Quinlan, became addicted to morphine under circumstances that may have been like those described in the play. And, like Jamie, O'Neill's older brother was an alcoholic and struggling actor who literally drank himself to death after Ella O'Neill died of cancer. Many of the play's details are also rooted in fact, including the New London setting and the Tyrone family history.

Allusions

Although the drama is not rich in allusions to public events of the time, it does use references to several writers and often includes parts of poems and character references and lines from dramatic works woven into the dialogue. While the furniture in the living room is both sparse and shabby, its two bookcases are filled with volumes of writers past and present, carefully named by O'Neill in his stage directions and mentioned in the dialogue. Tyrone's preference is for Shakespeare, who is often quoted, while Edmund's is for more modern writers and philosophers, like Nietzsche, Dowson, Marx, Baudelaire, and Swinburne, writers that his father finds gloomy, morally repugnant, or anarchistic. Jamie, too, has read his share of literature. In the final act, it is he who quotes several lines from Swinburne's "A Leave Taking" in choric counterpoint to Mary's painful monologue.

Allusion is also made to the famous American actor, Edwin Booth. It is a point of great pride for Tyrone that he had once acted on stage with Booth, who thought highly of Tyrone's skill. But the memory is painful, for Tyrone is plagued by the belief that he traded his talent short for easy money.

Foreshadowing

Long Day's Journey into Night begins cheerfully enough. The day is bright, and the initial exchanges between Tyrone and Mary are affectionate and playful, but foreboding clues to the play's tragic turn are quickly introduced. Mary's behavior hints at her return to morphine use. We learn that she had spent a sleepless night and that her appetite is poor. She is obviously restless. She also seems slightly disoriented, even mildly hysterical. Her fluttering hands and obsessive concern with her hair, her inability to find her glasses—all these foreshadow her mounting loss of self-control.

Monologue

Lengthy monologues are used in *Long Day's Journey into Night* in at least two important ways: as reveries and confessions. Central are the reveries of Mary. As she plunges deeper into her drug-induced daze, she rambles on about the past into which she desperately wants to escape. At times she seems incoherent; she even babbles. In her final appearance, she begins a long, inchoate monologue, almost totally oblivious to the efforts of other characters to break through to her. Edmund's long poetic discourse on fog is both a sort of confession and a reverie, as is Tyrone's monologue on his earlier life in theater. Almost pure confession is Jamie's meandering fourth act monologue in which he starts explaining why he stayed with Fat Violet and ends with his admission that he has tried to corrupt Edmund.

Naturalism

Naturalism, which espouses a clinical approach in literature, is noted for its "slice of life" action lines. Such fiction often lacks closure, remaining open-plotted and inconclusive. Problems, like those in *Long Day's Journey into Night,* are left unresolved, hanging on and dragging the characters into an implied future beyond the scope of the work. Naturalistic works also tend to be grim. They strip away a character's sense of dignity to expose unpleasant truths that lie at uncomfortable depths, even below the character's conscious being. It is invariably a painful process, and it is one that is central to O'Neill's play.

Oedipus Complex

Often noted is the Freudian influence on O'Neill, particularly his espousal of the Oedipal attachment of sons to their mothers and sexual jealousy and enmity towards their fathers. Although a possible inner source of guilt in Edmund, the character whose behavior most clearly evidences a latent Oedipal guilt is Jamie. He seeks a surrogate mother among matronly prostitutes and reveals a bitter jealousy towards Edmund, his chief rival for Mary's affections in the Oedipal model outlined by Freud.

HISTORICAL CONTEXT

There are two historical periods relevant to *Long Day's Journey into Night.* The play was written between 1939 and 1941, but it is set in 1912, at a critical period in the author's own life, paralleling that of his fictional persona, Edmund Tyrone.

Public Events

Events of moment from the outside world do not intrude on the Tyrone family dialogue. For example, there is no mention of the April, 1912, sinking of the *Titanic,* which took over fifteen hundred passengers to their watery death, and was the greatest maritime disaster of the age. Nor is mention made of Captain Robert Scott's ill-fated expedition to the South Pole, which ended in March, 1912, when Scott and the last survivors died in a heroic attempt to reach awaiting shelter and provisions.

O'Neill's focus, relentlessly on the Tyrone family problems, simply made unnecessary the need for allusions to such important topical events. They are conspicuous only by their absence, a fact that contributes to the play's claustrophobic impact. An awareness of the outside world is reflected not in events but in the social consciousness of the Tyrones. They have a sense of living on the margins of respectability, not fully accepted by the "Yanks" because of Tyrone's impoverished, shanty-Irish, Roman Catholic heritage.

For the audience there is a foreshadowing of the impending American love affair with the automobile, which Henry Ford made possible when he introduced the Model T in 1908. By 1913, his company was able to sell the model for $500, putting it within the financial reach of most middle-class families. Tyrone, bound by his past, dislikes the second-hand auto he has bought for Mary, and he expresses his preference for the trolley and walking. Only Mary uses the car, and she must be driven by a paid chauffeur, to Tyrone's tight-fisted consternation. Clearly, the world is passing Tyrone by, as in real life it seemed to be passing O'Neill's father by.

A Battle of the Books

Two bookcases occupy the Tyrone living room. The first, small and plain, contains works by modern writers, many of them favorites of Edmund and Jamie: novels by Balzac, Zola, and Stendhal; plays by Ibsen, Shaw, and Strindberg; poetry by Rossetti,

COMPARE
&
CONTRAST

- **1910s:** World War I begins in the summer of 1914, with the United States joining the allies against Germany in 1917.

  1940s and 50s: O'Neill finishes *Long Day's Journey into Night* prior to America's entry into World War II on December 7, 1941. The Cold War with the Soviet bloc flares into open combat in Korea, a "police action" ending with an armistice agreement signed on July 27, 1953, four months before O'Neill dies. In 1956 the Soviet Union cracks down on dissidents in Poland and Hungary; that same year *Long Day's Journey into Night* wins O'Neill, posthumously, his final Pulitzer Prize.

  Today: The 1990s bring an end to the Cold War and to fears of a nuclear holocaust.

- **1910s:** The airplane, automobile, and motion pictures, all in their infancy, begin a radical transformation of daily American life.

  1940s and 50s: Films, with sound since 1928, are the most popular entertainment medium; commercial airlines continue to replace trains in distance passenger travel; and American houses start sporting double garages. By the 1950s, television becomes both popular and increasingly affordable; jet engines become common on commercial planes; and large finned automobiles with powerful engines streak through America on a growing network of parkways and highways.

  Today: Houses without at least two television sets grow rare; railroads continue a losing struggle to survive; and automobiles, while legally moving faster on interstate highways again, get smaller, more fuel-efficient, and ever more expensive.

- **1910s:** America begins reflecting an awareness of foreign movements in art and letters, of the French naturalists like Zola and Balzac, and the realistic drama of Ibsen, Strindberg, and Chekhov; O'Neill reveals that foreign influence in his very first plays.

  1940s and 50s: American readers remain drawn to the fiction of William Faulkner, Ernest Hemingway, John Steinbeck, and F. Scott Fitzgerald; the plays of Clifford Odets, Maxwell Anderson, Lillian Hellman, and Robert Sherwood also have a dedicated following, but O'Neill's reputation remains stagnant. By the 1950s, a host of postwar novelists and poets make their mark, challenging Faulkner and Hemingway, Frost and Eliot, for book stall space; the realistic problem play reaches its maturity in the works of Arthur Miller, Tennessee Williams, William Inge, and O'Neill, while avant garde rumblings are heard in the Off- and Off-Off Broadway wings.

  Today: Laurels in fiction are up for grabs; in theater, August Wilson, Sam Shepard, and David Mamet continue making an indelible mark.

- **1910s:** Through stricter federal laws governing drug use and the militant success of the Anti-Saloon League and the Women's Christian Temperance Union, America seeks to end drug addiction and alcohol abuse; achieves Prohibition with ratification of the Eighteenth Amendment in 1919.

  1940s and 50s: With prohibition repealed in 1933, America returns to imbibing alcohol, creating a new, post-World War II problem: the drunk driver; morphine still widely used as a pain killer. The Beat Generation brings "mind expanding" drugs like marijuana closer to the mainstream; middle-class America turns to tranquilizers to cope with depression; hard drugs begin to plague the inner cities; synthetics like methadone replace morphine in some medical applications.

  Today: Drug abuse remains a major problem, with crack cocaine and heroin an inner-city blight and marijuana use common everywhere in America, especially among the young; groups like Mothers Against Drunk Driving (MADD) help stiffen penalties for driving while under the influence, in some states upgrading repeat offenses to a felony.

Wilde, Dowson, and Kipling; and philosophical works by Nietzsche, Marx, Engels, and Schopenhauer. The second, larger, glass-fronted bookcase contains older works, including three sets of Shakespeare, sets of the romantic fiction of Dumas and Victor Hugo, fifty imposing volumes of the world's greatest literature, several major works of history and miscellaneous old plays, poetry collections, and Irish histories. This second, more venerable appearing bookcase contains the preferred readings of James Tyrone, Sr. There is but one common link: Shakespeare's picture adorns the wall above the plainer bookcase, implying that he holds a place of honor even in the hearts of the sons.

The rift that separates Tyrone and his sons, though firmly based in familial guilt and shame, has been widened by their disparate tastes in literature and philosophy. Throughout the play, literary allusions and quotations provide a dominant recurring theme in the emotionally charged rounds of repeated accusation and counter accusation. Clearly, Edmund's taste is for the realists and naturalists in fiction and drama, materialists and nihilists in philosophy, and fatalists and adherents to the detached, art-for-art's-sake school in poetry.

Tyrone finds Edmund's tastes deplorable, writers full of nothing but gloom and despair. He dismisses the lot of them as decadent, depressing, and godless. For him, Shakespeare reigns supreme. He even has a theory that the real Shakespeare was not English but an Irish Catholic.

O'Neill's real father, like Tyrone, was one of the last of the matinee idols, working in a theater that admitted little that was new or unconventional. Typical fare was warmed-over Shakespeare and heroic melodrama, works that provided lucrative vehicles for popular actors like James O'Neill but insulated the theater from the real world. Eugene O'Neill would change all that; influenced by the writers whose works rest on Edmund's bookcase, by the 1920s he would revolutionize the American theater.

Substance Abuse: Morphine and Alcohol

By 1912, responsible physicians had stopped the indiscriminate use of morphine as a pain killer and treatment for depression. New laws required pharmacists to dispense it only by authorized prescription, ending its unrestricted use. However, for many Americans like Mary Tyrone, the damage had already been done. Morphine and laudanum, another opium derivative, had left thousands addicted, and many faced the social stigma and disgrace that drug addiction finally involved.

The excessive use of alcohol was more widely tolerated, at least in men. The saloon was an established American institution by the end of the nineteenth century. It served as a working man's social club where males could imbibe, discuss the day's events, and wager on cards and billiards. Some of the saloons were also haunts for prostitutes, while others were outright bordellos; most, like their English pub counterparts, did not admit ladies.

Many saloon patrons, like Jamie Tyrone, were problem drinkers and gamblers, prone to violence, sexual promiscuity, or insolvency. Their excesses fueled the temperance reform movement, led and supported by a growing legion of women who wanted to protect families from "demon rum" and improve the nation's moral character and health. The movement would finally win a legal victory in 1919 with the passage and ratification of the Eighteenth Amendment. But the victory proved hollow. The ban on alcohol gave rise to illegal bootlegging, bathtub gin, and the infamous speakeasy, a Jazz Age substitute for the old saloon. Unlike the saloon, the speakeasies were patronized by men and the new generation of liberated "flappers," setting the model for the bars and nightclubs that went into legal operation when prohibition ended.

Tuberculosis

Tuberculosis, called "consumption" by the Tyrones, was a dread disease in 1912, claiming close to 100,000 American lives annually. Treatment, provided in special hospitals called sanatoria, was largely in an experimental stage of development. Although physicians knew that a germ caused the disease, they had no miracle cure. A few used x-ray treatments, but most tried to counter the disease's symptoms with prolonged rest, special diets, and an abundance of fresh air. Edmund, who discovers that he has consumption, faces a period of recovery in a sanatorium, just as O'Neill himself did in 1912.

The Great Depression

Prohibition ended in 1933, a half dozen years before O'Neill started writing *Long Day's Journey into Night*. Throughout the 1930s, America suffered a deep economic depression from which it had not completely recovered by the time O'Neill began the play. Although O'Neill's political sympathies were with the working class, he wrote what has been termed "private tragedy," not social-conscience polemics like Clifford Odets's *Waiting for Lefty* (1935) and other works of the leftist Group Theatre. In the 1930s, O'Neill's reputation went into a decline, despite the fact that he won the Nobel Prize for literature in 1936.

World War II

World War II commenced in 1939, when Nazi Germany invaded Poland. Two years later, on December 7, 1941, the United States entered the war when the Japanese bombed Pearl Harbor. Fortunately, by that time O'Neill had finished *Long Day's Journey into Night.* The War's impact and his declining health brought his writing to a near standstill. In 1943, in the middle of the war, O'Neill and Carlotta burned the fragmentary parts of his projected cycle of plays, which by then he knew he would never finish.

CRITICAL OVERVIEW

In 1956, the production of *Long Day's Journey into Night* by the Royal Dramatic Theatre in Sweden won much praise for O'Neill. Potential producers soon pressured Carlotta O'Neill to release the work for an American staging, and after several months she turned the play over to Jose Quintero and two associates. Quintero's earlier revival of *The Iceman Cometh,* which opened in May of 1956, had already prompted new enthusiasm for O'Neill. His New York production of *Long Day's Journey into Night,* coupled with the play's publication by the Yale University Press, fully elevated O'Neill's reputation and restored him to the front ranks of American dramatists.

Leading critics like Brooks Atkinson, Walter Kerr, Harold Clurman, and Joseph Wood Krutch proclaimed the play's power on stage. Kerr, for example, in his review in the *New York Herald Tribune,* called the play "a stunning theatrical experience," while *New York Times* critic Atkinson announced that with the production of *Long Day's Journey into Night* the American theater had reached "stature and size." But the critical vindication of O'Neill was not unanimous. Some reviewers subtly condemned the work with tepid praise. Others pondered the play's stage power in the face of what Stephen Whicher, reviewing the Stockholm production for *Commonweal,* claimed were "several

massive faults which should have destroyed it." Yet others paraded out old complaints about the playwright's heavy handed, awkward technique, tortured dialogue, painful self-flagellation, oppressive length, and morbid pessimism. One reviewer, Gilbert Seldes, commenting on the published play in *Saturday Review,* faulted the playwright's repetition, long speeches, "passion for reciting poetry," and his "desperate flatness of language." Another commentator, the *New Yorker*'s Wolcott Gibbs, complained that the play "is often as barbarously written as it is possible for the work of a major writer to be," and doubted the work's status "as a major contribution to the drama of our time."

The unabashed autobiographical content of *Long Day's Journey into Night* also troubled many critics, some of whom argued that the play simply failed to evoke the emotions appropriate to tragedy because, as C. J. Rolo maintained in the *Atlantic Monthly,* the characters were "not only devoid of heroic attributes" but "even lacking in ordinary dignity and strength." For Rolo, the play failed to produce what O'Neill himself referred to as the "transfiguring nobility of tragedy."

Artistically, O'Neill, a tireless innovator, always had to swim against some pretty strong critical currents. Noting what seem like obvious flaws in his work, some important critics have only grudgingly agreed to O'Neill's status as the dean American theater. There is, for example, Eric Bentley's famous quip: "He is the leading American playwright; damn him, damn all; and damning all is a big responsibility." Bentley's frustration with O'Neill partly stems from what has always bedeviled O'Neill's critics—the fact that his texts never seem to suggest the grandeur that their dramatizations often achieve on stage. Away from the magic of theater, under a reader's naked light, his plays can sometimes seem pedestrian and awkward, almost embarrassingly so.

That fact has made some writers circumspect in approaching O'Neill's published plays. Harold Clurman, reviewing the Yale text of *Long Day's Journey into Night* in the *Nation,* remarked that "O'Neill's plays are nearly always more impressive on the stage than on the printed page." O'Neill was "a faulty craftsman," perhaps, but, as Clurman noted, the Swedish production had held its audience transfixed for four and one-half hours, a performance length that modern audiences would normally find unendurable, barely tolerable in a great classic like Shakespeare's *Hamlet,* which litters the stage with corpses, but not in a play in which there is very little overt action and nothing is really resolved.

The length and perplexing content of *Long Day's Journey into Night* hardly made it common fare in community, regional, or even academic theaters, thus its great power on stage was largely unknown in America's heartland until 1962, when Sidney Lumet's film version appeared. The movie, running under three hours, edited out some of the original play, but what remained was hailed as a remarkable cinematic triumph that remained essentially faithful to the Broadway production of the play. The film version must be credited with once again making O'Neill popular and with revealing to its wide audience the great force that lies, not just in, but around O'Neill's words.

As Travis Bogard observed in his book *Contour in Time: The Plays of Eugene O'Neill,* in *Long Day's Journey into Night* O'Neill managed "a return to four boards and a passion," placing great faith in his actors, the interpreters of his text. For Bogard and many other critics, O'Neill's last works are his greatest, "the highest achievement of the American realistic theatre," and of these *Long Day's Journey into Night* is indisputably regarded as the best.

CRITICISM

John Fiero

In the following essay, Fiero discusses the differences between the printed and produced versions of O'Neill's play. Fiero is a professor of English at the University of Southwestern Louisiana and an actor.

By the time Eugene O'Neill's *Long Day's Journey into Night* hit the boards at Broadway's Helen Hayes Theatre, absurdist playwrights like Samuel Beckett and Eugene Ionesco had already begun an assault on language as an inadequate tool for authentic communication. In his play, written fifteen years earlier, O'Neill seems to have come to a similar conclusion, though in a much more familiar guise: his relentless and trenchant realism. Edmund, the playwright's persona in the baldly autobiographical play, seems to sum up O'Neill's belief as he concludes his long monologue in Act Four: "I just stammered. That's the best I'll ever do. I mean, if I live. Well, it will be faithful realism, at least.

Stammering is the native eloquence of us fog people.''

In Edmund's words lies the essence of the O'Neill paradox. No other playwright so highly acclaimed on stage is so often found flawed on paper. To the annoyance of many critics, *Long Day's Journey into Night,* often reputed to be O'Neill's crowning achievement, best illustrates that paradox. It is a text that, if merely read, seems to fall embarrassingly short of the glory it has achieved on stage. Unaided by the magic of the theater, at some disjointed and awkward places, the text does seem to stammer, lurch, and sputter along—but it does so at least partly by design.

Theater only admits to one cardinal sin—boring an audience. Literary trespasses, on the other hand, seem almost infinite. As the premiere production of *Long Day's Journey into Night* in Stockholm demonstrated, on the stage the play was absolved of its literary failings; its audiences sat through its four and one-half hour length, not just without complaint, but with unflagging attention and final approval. That fact perplexed some critics, including Henry Hewes, who in his *Saturday Review* assessment of the Swedish production and the published play ventured the opinion that O'Neill's work improved in translation. For him, the Swedish rendering gave "the play a movement and a music that it sometimes lacks in English." The raw English text, on the other hand, was permeated "with old arguments hashed, rehashed, and re-rehashed." For Hewes, there even seemed to be some emotional chord in the Swedish national character that O'Neill managed to strike, a chord, presumably, not found in the English-speaking world.

Hewes wrote on *Long Day's Journey into Night* again in the *Saturday Review,* after its Broadway opening, during which Quintero and company kept the American audience glued to their seats. The work proved every bit as stage worthy in English as it had in Swedish. For all its real or assumed literary sins, it struck, not just a Swedish, but some universal emotional chords. Hewes recanted. For him the play now became "enormously interesting," with "a breadth . . . that may make it the most universal piece of stage realism ever turned out by an American playwright."

The play's stage success may baffle but should not surprise those who read O'Neill's works with some sense of the transforming power of the stage. There is a time-tested truism of theater that says that

WHAT DO I READ NEXT?

- *A Moon for the Misbegotten*, produced in 1947, was written by O'Neill as a eulogy for his brother, Jamie, who is fictionalized as Jamie Tyrone in the play. As he is in *Long Day's Journey into Night*, Jamie is an alcoholic who seeks solace in the arms of a series of large women. The play deals with his hapless affair with Josie Hogan. It was a work that O'Neill finally came to loathe, possibly because his own son followed in his uncle's footsteps and committed suicide.

- *Trouble in the Flesh* (1959), is Max Wylie's graphic fictional account of Seton Farrier, whose life as the greatest dramatist of his day is clearly based on O'Neill's biography.

- *East of Eden* (1952), John Steinbeck's fictional saga of the Trask family investigates themes parallel to those treated in *Long Day's Journey into Night*. Based on the biblical story of Cain and Abel, the novel focuses on family depravity, sibling jealousy and rivalry, guilt, and forgiveness.

- *Death of a Salesman* (1949), Arthur Miller's great "tragedy of the common man," has some parallels with O'Neill's play, including the tragic consequences of material pursuits and the alienation of sons from their father. Miller's play is the principal rival claimant to *Long Day's Journey into Night* as America's greatest tragedy.

- *Buried Child* (1978), Sam Shepard's mythic study of a dysfunctional family riddled with guilt for the murder of a real or illusory child, with some parallels to O'Neill's *Long Day's Journey into Night* in its themes and retrospective method.

- *A Hatful of Rain* (1955), Michael V. Gazzo's play dealing with the impact of a veteran's drug addiction on the lives of his wife, father, and brother has thematic parallels to O'Neill's work. An excellent 1957 film version won Anthony Franciosa an Academy Award nomination for best actor.

---

many plays read poorly but play very well (and, of course, vice versa). In the case of *Long Day's Journey into Night,* the maxim may well have its greatest currency, for on paper, O'Neill's craftsmanship, in places, seems almost primitive and his expression flat and even hackneyed.

Yes, *Long Day's Journey into Night* suffers from a comparison with, for example, Arthur Miller's *Death of a Salesman.* Miller's "tragedy of the common man," from the same period, is generally considered the chief rival to O'Neill's play as the greatest tragedy of the American theater. *Death of a Salesman* reads very well, revealing a stylistic mastery presumed lacking in O'Neill's play. Miller's dialogue flows smoothly, even when Willy breaks into his hallucinatory conversations with Ben, as in Act One, when Willy plays cards with Charley while conversing with the specter of his dead brother. It is a marvelous piece of word stitching and

control. By comparison, O'Neill's dialogue often seems rough hewn, even crude, particularly in the sudden emotional lurches that move a character from angry recrimination to abject contrition, as in many of Jamie's lines. On paper, these sudden shifts may well seem jarring and forced, although even C. J. Rolo, otherwise hostile in his *Atlantic Monthly* review, characterized the emotional phrasing as "generally convincing."

Critics have carped about other problems with *Long Day's Journey into Night,* "the massive faults" that Stephen Whicher mentions. O'Neill has been damned for his crude technique, for the excessive incursion of borrowed poetry, for example, or his redundancy and attention-challenging prolixity. Some criticism, highly subjective, goes beyond technique to the play's content, its unrelieved gloom, its self-pitying characters, or its skeleton-rattling quest for personal absolution.

A play, of course, is not the text; it is the very thing on stage, a place where, in post-modernist terms, the text is repeatedly deconstructed to the bone. O'Neill, for all his real or imagined textual flaws, had an acute sense of the theater, the only proving ground of drama. In *Long Day's Journey into Night*, the playwright reveals his great faith in the interpretive artists of the living theater to find the play, not just in, but behind, between, and around his words. As Travis Bogard noted in his *Contour in Time: The Plays of Eugene O'Neill*, O'Neill's "ultimate 'experiment'" was to return to "a confident reliance on his actors." In both *Long Day's Journey into Night* and *A Moon for the Misbegotten*, Bogard claimed that "[e]verything, now, is in the role. An actor in these plays cannot hide behind personal mannerisms, clever business or habitual stage trickery. O'Neill has stripped all but the most minimal requirements from the stage, leaving the actors naked. They must play or perish."

Nakedness is the play's essential condition. Each character is ritually stripped of dignity and self-control as the outward mask of filial regard and concern falls away, exposing an array of conflicting emotions: love, jealousy, shame, guilt, hate—within whose endless jars truth resides. Characters almost immediately begin a ritual of repeated recriminations: the miserliness of James Tyrone, the apostasy and dereliction of Jamie and Edmund, the inability of Mary to escape from her addiction. The play thus becomes a crucible of pain, whose grinding pestle is the rude and abrasive language that resonates throughout. Characters stammer and babble because the polite and rational language of conversation cannot carry the overload of their discharging emotions. In their most poignant moments, Edmund grasps at the truth of his inner self in his own poetic metaphors, Mary escapes into narcosis, James Tyrone into self-pitying incoherency, and Jamie into the expropriated poetry of others. For each, normal discourse simply fails to bear adequate witness to the character's inner agony.

As John H. Raleigh noted in *The Plays of Eugene O'Neill*, throughout the play there is also "a continuous tension between the present and the past." In a ritual quest for absolution, each character is forced, at some point, to confront both. Although Mary seeks to restore her lost innocence in her romanticized girlhood, in Act Three she faces a moment of painful truth: "You expect the Blessed Virgin to be fooled by a lying dope fiend reciting words! You can't hide from her!" But, as Whicher observed in *Commonweal*, "the most poignant ef-

fect of the play is the counter-movement by which the mother retreats into illusion while the others move to a clear sight of truth." Ironically, that clear sight comes through alcohol, which thickens their tongues and numbs their minds. They face themselves honestly when least able to convey their honesty in lucid and coherent language.

The men try to cope with their current feelings by a protracted and self-critical examination of their past. Each has at least one confessional monologue, painfully linking the past to the present in an effort to expiate his human failings. James Tyrone, for example, explaining that his miserliness springs from his deep-rooted fear of poverty, evinces some self-disgust because he sold his acting talent short for material security. Although long and somewhat redundant, these speeches are necessary to explain the ambivalent feelings that *Eugene O'Neill and the Tragic Tension: An Interpretive Study of the Plays* author Doris V. Falk asserted "lead to tense, exhausting, and brilliant drama."

Much of what seems clumsy or primitive in the text becomes poignant on stage—the heavy-handed reliance on fog as symbol, for example, or Jamie's mood lurching between sneering accusations and instant regret. The physical gestures and objects, merely described in the play, become very important complements to the dialogue. In fact, the physical objects create a poignant effect in proportion to their very scarcity, particularly in the last act, when the Tyrone family tragedy seems somehow embedded in a single lighted bulb, a worn out deck of playing cards, a bottle of cheap whiskey, and an old, satin wedding gown. Oddly enough, some descriptions in stage directions, richly suggestive on the page, may be impossible to render in the theater. For example, as Mary sinks deep into her morphine-induced narcosis, her eyes grow increasingly brighter. In staging the play, the description can only serve to cue actors, to draw them to a physical focal point revealing Mary's relapse into her addiction and attendant isolation. On the other hand, the fog horn, beginning in the third act, takes on the force of a keening chorus of mourners, a powerful counterpoint to the characters' pain in its melancholic and desolate wail. Its power is only hinted at by the stage directions.

The O'Neill paradox is a troubling problem. Plays that pass into the realm of dramatic literature must ultimately survive as texts to be read, as fixed and permanent as fiction and poetry. The staged play, on the other hand, is ephemeral and forever

> SCENE BY SCENE THE
> TRAGEDY MOVES ALONG WITH A
> REMORSELESS BEAT THAT BECOMES
> HYPNOTIC AS THOUGH THIS WERE
> LIFE LIVED ON THE BRINK OF
> OBLIVION"

changing—right up to the final curtain of the play's last performance. O'Neill, a great innovator and experimenter, worked tirelessly to test the limits of the stage, not leave behind a canon of literary masterpieces. Unfortunately for his reputation, many of his plays, theatrical swans, are textual ugly ducklings, and, like his actors, must be played or run the grave risk of perishing.

Source: John Fiero, in an essay for *Drama for Students,* Gale, 1997.

Brooks Atkinson

In the following excerpt from a review of Long Day's Journey into Night *that originally appeared in the* New York Times *on November 8, 1956, Atkinson applauds both the play and the production, asserting:* ''Long Day's Journey into Night *has been worth waiting for. It restores the drama to literature and the theatre to art.''*

As drama critic for the New York Times *from 1925 to 1960, Atkinson was one of the most influential reviewers in America.*

With the production of *Long Day's Journey Into Night* at the Helen Hayes last evening, the American theatre acquires size and stature.

The size does not refer to the length of Eugene O'Neill's autobiographical drama, although a play three and three-quarter hours long is worth remarking. The size refers to his conception of theatre as a form of epic literature.

Long Day's Journey Into Night is like a Dostoevsky novel in which Strindberg had written the dialogue. For this saga of the damned is horrifying and devastating in a classical tradition, and the performance under Jose Quintero's direction is inspired.

Twelve years before he died in 1953, O'Neill epitomized the life of his family in a drama that records the events of one day at their summer home in New London, Conn., in 1912. Factually it is a sordid story about a pathologically parsimonious father, a mother addicted to dope, a dissipated brother and a younger brother (representing Eugene O'Neill) who has TB and is about to be shipped off to a sanitarium.

Roughly, those are the facts. But the author has told them on the plane of an O'Neill tragedy in which the point of view transcends the material. The characters are laid bare with pitiless candor. The scenes are big. The dialogue is blunt. Scene by scene the tragedy moves along with a remorseless beat that becomes hypnotic as though this were life lived on the brink of oblivion.

Long Day's Journey Into Night could be pruned of some of its excesses and repetitions and static looks back to the past. But the faults come, not from tragic posturing, but from the abundance of a great theatre writer who had a spacious point of view. This summing-up of his emotional and artistic life ranks with *Mourning Becomes Electra* and *Desire Under the Elms,* which this department regards as his masterpieces. . . .

Long Day's Journey Into Night has been worth waiting for. It restores the drama to literature and the theatre to art.

Source: Brooks Atkinson, in a review of *Long Day's Journey into Night* (1956) in *On Stage: Selected Theater Reviews from The New York Times, 1920–1970,* edited by Bernard Beckerman and Howard Siegman, Arno Press, 1973, pp. 378–79.

Stephen Whicher

In the following essay, Whicher provides a favorable assessment of the Swedish production of Long Day's Journey into Night, *and offers high praise for O'Neill's skill as a playwright, noting especially his talent for writing compelling drama that contains sensitive, moving insights into human nature.*

In accordance with the dying wish of Eugene O'Neill, his last play, *Long Day's Journey Into Night,* was given its world premiere in Stockholm by '' *Dramaten,*'' a group which has gained an international reputation for its distinguished productions of O'Neill plays over a period of thirty years. Their superb presentation of his ''last letter to the world'' makes clear that it is a *play,* and not a memoir cast in dialogue form as it has been characterized by certain American reviewers of the book.

It is true, as these reviewers point out, that the work has a great deal of autobiographical interest and emphasis. The Tyrone family which it depicts is O'Neill's own, and the story which he lays bare, a story of "the damned," is true to the facts as we know them. Furthermore, the mood of this last play is the same as that which dominates many of his earlier, largely autobiographical works—the mood of homelessness, the sense of helplessness, the death-longing, the constant background of the "ole davil, sea" which marked the plays of the S.S. Glencairn group, *Anna Christie, Beyond the Horizon* and, with varying disguises, *The Straw* and *All God's Chillun Got Wings.*

The significant fact, however, is not that the work contains autobiographical elements, but that O'Neill has transcended them so completely. The undeniable impact of its current Swedish production, for example, certainly cannot be explained by the self-revelation which the play contains. Audiences are not sitting on hard seats night after night, absorbed in this play for over four hours, just because it gives them information about O'Neill. Nor does its autobiographical element explain my own reaction. Starting with a prejudice against O'Neill, and watching its first performance with no knowledge of the play, I found my attention held from first to last, and was moved as one can only be, I would suppose, by real drama. Since then I have studied the English text of the play and have gone back to the stage production to find it just as gripping. If our definitions of tragedy do not fit this work, we should perhaps rethink our definitions.

For this reason, I can not agree with those critics of the play who speak of O'Neill's inability to cut, as if we had another *Look Homeward, Angel* on our hands. I predict that any future Maxwell Perkins who tries to cut this to the limits of an ordinary play will find that it can not be done.

The play as a whole is a solid, sinewy, exceptionally well-built piece of work. O'Neill has left us a big, powerful Something, like a yacht in the living room, which can't and won't be dismissed. Whether we think it ought to or not, this play does prove itself by the only proper test for a play: performance. It is gripping and moving theater.

That being the fact, we need to ask why, for it has several massive faults which should have destroyed it. It austerely ignores almost every means,

> IF OUR DEFINITIONS OF TRAGEDY DO NOT FIT THIS WORK, WE SHOULD PERHAPS RETHINK OUR DEFINITIONS"

including action, by which the usual play interests an audience. As Joyce, Proust, and Woolf have written novels that abandon story, so this is a tragedy that abandons "drama," and, further, it makes its journey on the usual square wheels of O'Neill's style, although some speeches are eloquent in context.

Furthermore, the fact remains that he asks actors to sustain and audience to respond to *one* emotion—helpless grief at hopeless loss—for nearly five hours. For all his skill and that of his interpreters, that is asking a great deal; by all rights it should have been much too much.

One reason why it is not is the play's masterly construction. Is there a *tour de force* like this in modern drama—a play that sustains mounting tension through so much talk and so little action, with no fantasy, spectacle, poetry, or play of ideas to help it on? In *Death of a Salesman* Arthur Miller uses flashbacks that contrast present and past with dramatic sharpness. A book that comes close to O'Neill's play in theme and mood, Faulkner's *The Sound and the Fury,* dazzles the reader with its juggling of the time sequence. O'Neill, hewing to the line of strict naturalism, foregoes all this, so that the past can enter his play only as narrated in the present. Yet the past is his subject, or a large part of it. The way he has solved a problem which no other dramatist would have attempted is a revelation of O'Neill's dramatic craft.

The chief reason for the play's success, however is the character portrayal. James and Mary Tyrone are two of the richest roles in dramatic literature. The whole interest of the play is in its character revelation. Its excitement consists in feeling ourselves penetrate steadily deeper into the lives of this family until we reach the full "pity, understanding and forgiveness for *all* the four haunted Tyrones" with which the author wrote. He not only makes us see, he makes us care; we value these people as they value each other. Nothing has impressed Swedish audiences more than the play's warmth. O'Neill has shown force and insight in other plays, but never this love and compassion for his characters.

Beyond the deep human interest, however, is the tone and mood of the whole, what we must call the religious dimension. O'Neill has constantly tried in his plays to treat the ''big subject,'' the Mystery beyond human life. One can argue that this is what has spoiled some of his work. Here he succeeds; he is not soft, as in *Moon for the Misbegotten,* nor abstract, as in *Lazarus Laughed* or *The Iceman Cometh.* An awareness of life as a mysterious shaping force, a vague dark enemy like the Boyg in *Peer Gynt,* rises quietly and naturally from the human situation and gives it tragic stature.

A word must be said of the chief device used to give this effect, the foghorn. Perhaps this ''sick whale in the back yard''—which the Swedes, not having our Moby Dick reflexes, translated ''sick elephant''—seems over-obvious in the reading. As handled by '' *Dramaten ,*'' however, that living yet inhuman voice in the background of the last two dark acts, punctuating and commenting on the action and calling us back, as it does the characters, to the thought of the fog and sea around us, has sometimes almost intolerable power. Of all the remarkable sound effects in O'Neill's plays, this is the finest.

But the catharsis of *Journey* is not to be achieved by a trick. In this work O'Neill passes his final judgment on the life he escaped—surely with relief—three years ago. As the night and fog close in, the characters struggle toward honesty, helped on by whiskey, which O'Neill uses here as elsewhere as a kind of truth serum. What they reach is hopeless resignation, helpless love, and a longing for death. Man can live by illusions, O'Neill says, and he can live by faith, which is probably the same thing, but ultimately neither is any good. The most poignant effect of the play is the counter-movement by which the mother retreats into illusion while the others move to a clear sight of truth. But she knows too: ''There is no other way I can stop the pain—*all* the pain.'' Nor can faith help. The father's Catholic belief is ''bog trotter'' superstition, scornfully rejected by his sons, who quote *Zarathustra:* ''God is dead.'' The mother's dream of recovering her innocent conventgirl's trust in the Virgin is pathetically futile. One call of the foghorn refutes her.

The climax of the play is Edmund's long speech in the fourth act about the ''high spots'' in his memories. ''For a moment I lost myself—actually lost my life. I was set free! . . . For a second there is meaning! Then the hand lets the veil fall and you are alone, lost in the fog again, and you stumble on toward nowhere, for no good reason!'' Remembering O'Neill's long effort to assert some ''meaning,'' ending with the ''electrical display'' of *Strange Interlude,* we can hear the sick older man summing up his life through the mouth of his younger self. ''I will always be a stranger who never feels at home, who does not really want and is not really wanted, who can never belong, who must always be a little in love with death!''

It may be that *Long Day's Journey Into Night* has succeeded in Sweden because this heartsick pessimism goes down easier here than it would in the United States. Anywhere it makes a strange tragedy. If we accept, for example, Francis Fergusson's formula for drama, that it begins in purpose and works through passion to perception, then we have to say that purpose survives here only as a long-abandoned illusion, that perception is essentially complete early in the play, and that nearly all we have is four acts of agony. This is, rather, a play of discovery, like *Oedipus,* but of discovery for the audience only; the characters have little left to discover.

Yet this may be *the* modern tragedy. In its passivity, its despair, its longing, its undramatic reduction of human life to meaningless suffering, and its agonized honesty, it strikes a keynote of our modern mood. If we are to write honestly, this is what we must face. If we are to work through to something more ''positive,'' this is what we must overcome. O'Neill's journey is also our own.

Source: Stephen Whicher, ''O'Neill's Long Journey'' in *Commonweal,* Vol. LXIII, no. 24, March 16, 1956, pp. 614–15.

FURTHER READING

Hayes, Richard. ''A Requiem for Mortality,'' *Commonweal,* Vol. 64, February 1, 1957, pp. 467-68.
     A belated review of the Broadway production of *Long Day's Journey into Night* praising both the play and the cast for achieving ''tragic nobility'' within a realistic framework.

McDonnell, Thomas P. ''O'Neill's Drama of the Psyche,'' *Catholic World,* Vol. 197, April, 1963, pp. 120-25.
     Argues that *Long Day's Journey into Night* is O'Neill's apotheosis in his quest for a tragedy of self, of his own tormented psyche.

Manheim, Michael. *Eugene O'Neill's New Language of Kinship,* Syracuse University Press, 1982.

This study's introduction, its chapter on *Long Day's Journey into Night,* and its appendix focused on the play's motifs offer solid help in interpreting the play.

Pfister, Joel. "The Cultural Web in O'Neill's *Journey,*" in *Staging Depth: Eugene O'Neill and the Politics of Psychological Discourse,* University of North Carolina Press, 1995, pp. 203-15.

Relates Mary from *Long Day's Journey into Night* to Ophelia in Shakespeare's *Hamlet* and Annie Keeney in O'Neill's earlier play, *Ile.*

Raleigh, John Henry. "O'Neill's *Long Day's Journey into Night* and New England Irish-Catholicism," *Partisan Review,* Vol. 26, no. 4, Fall, 1959, pp. 573-92.

A helpful background study that relates the "dualism of religion-blasphemy" that permeates the play to Catholicism and Irish myth.

SOURCES

Atkinson, Brooks. Review of *Long Day's Journey into Night, New York Times,* Vol. 47, November 8, 1956, p. 2.

Bogard, Travis. *Contour in Time: The Plays of Eugene O'Neill,* revised edition, Oxford University Press, 1988.

Clurman, Harold. "The O'Neills," *Nation,* Vol. 182, March 3, 1956, pp. 182-83.

Falk, Doris V. *Eugene O'Neill and the Tragic Tension: An Interpretive Study of the Plays,* Rutgers University Press, 1958.

Gibbs, Wolcott. "Doom," *New Yorker,* Vol. 32, November 24, 1956, pp. 120-21.

Hewes, Henry. "O'Neill: 100 Proof—Not a Blend," *Saturday Review,* Vol. 39, November 2, 1961, pp. 30-1.

Hewes, Henry. "O'Neill and Faulkner via the Abroad Way," *Saturday Review,* Vol. 39, October 20, 1956, p. 58.

Kerr, Walter. Review of *Long Day's Journey into Night,* in *New York Herald-Tribune,* November 8, 1956.

Raleigh, John Henry. *The Plays of Eugene O'Neill,* Southern Illinois University Press, 1965.

Rolo, Charles J. "The Trouble of One House," *Atlantic Monthly,* Vol. 97, March, 1956, pp. 84-5.

Seldes, Gilbert. "Long day's Journey into Night," *Saturday Review,* Vol. 39, February 25, 1956, pp. 15-16.

Whicher, Stephen. "O'Neill's Long Journey," *Commonweal,* Vol. 63, March 16, 1956, pp. 614-15.

A Man for All Seasons

ROBERT BOLT

1954

Robert Bolt's play *A Man for All Seasons* presents a "hero of the self" whose unwavering integrity collides with King Henry VIII's egoistic drive to wrench personal salvation and political permanence for the Tudor line from an unwilling, because politically cornered, Pope. The Pope refuses to condone an annulment for Henry's marriage to Catherine of Aragon (of Spain) having already dispensed with biblical law to permit him to marry her in the first place. Sir Thomas More ignores Henry's pleading demands, throws off the Duke of Norfolk's friendly advice, and places his family in jeopardy, because he cannot in good conscience submit his immortal soul to the commands of a mortal king. Neither does the political powder-keg that Henry's enemies may see More's obstinence as a signal for revolt convince him to submit. This crucible of moral standards takes place in the early sixteenth century, but Bolt contemporizes the drama by inserting an audience go-between, the Common Man, whose asides remind the viewer of More's relevance to twentieth-century heroism. The Common Man makes all too clear that the likes of a Sir Thomas More are as rare today as they were in Henry's VIII's kingdom.

AUTHOR BIOGRAPHY

Robert Bolt led a life very different from his sixteenth-century hero. After what he calls a "gloomy"

Robert Bolt with his wife, Sarah Miles, in 1990

childhood and a poor academic career, he spent a mind-opening year at the University before being recruited into the British army. A committed Marxist who considered the working class "morally and aesthetically beautiful" and Ascot (his emblem of the elite) "overprivileged, ugly, and pretentious," he joined the Communist Party in 1942, but quit after five years, disillusioned with the Party's inability to live up to his absolutist ideals (Hayman 10). Upon returning from service in World War II, he completed his university studies and earned a teaching diploma. Then followed eight years of school teaching. Bolt's first theatrical work, a children's nativity play, resulted in "an astonishing turning point" in his life. He made a conscious decision to make play writing his avocation and enjoyed his first success with *Flowering Cherry* in 1957. He wrote a radio play of *A Man for All Seasons* in 1954, then wrote the stage version in 1960, which was met with critical acclaim in London and New York. From then on he split his time between the stage and film, producing a successful film version of *A Man for All Seasons* in 1966 after having written two hit screenplays, *Lawrence of Arabia* in 1962 and *Dr. Zhivago* in 1965. His plays and films have earned awards—Academy Awards for Best Adapted Screenplay (*A Man for All Seasons*) and Best Picture, among others. A common theme that runs

through each of his works is the "drama of the threatened self" wherein a protagonist must choose between honoring his own integrity and bending to the demands of his society. The protagonist defends his choice in polished, witty dialogues that display admirable and rare moral fiber, scenes of remarkable dramatic clarity. After a disabling heart attack and stroke his productivity declined and he died in 1995.

PLOT SUMMARY

Preface

Robert Bolt, who took an honors Bachelor of Arts degree in history, provides a summary of the historical context of his play and defends his reasons for choosing Sir Thomas More as a "hero of selfhood" in an elegantly written Preface. He also explains his intention for the Common Man—to "draw the audience in, not thrust them away."

Act One

This drama set in the sixteenth century begins with a contemporary player, the Common Man. Dressed in black tights, he represents Adam, but he immediately steps into the role of Sir Thomas

More's steward, the first of many personas he will adopt. More enters with Richard Rich, a political opportunist; they debate whether a man can be bought, even by suffering. Then enter More's wife Alice, daughter Margaret, and good friend, the Duke of Norfolk. More gives Rich a goblet he received as a bribe, and Rich manages to obtain a position as Norfolk's librarian, although More warns him to stay out of politics and teach. At eleven o'clock More is called to Cardinal Wolsey on the King's business, ending the dinner party.

Wolsey asks More to review a letter to the Pope, but, as Wolsey suspected, More sees things with "that horrible moral squint" and disapproves of Wolsey's efforts to sway the Vatican. The issue is that King Henry, having already obtained papal approval to marry his brother's widow (for state reasons), now wants to annul this marriage (Catherine not having produced the necessary male heir) and marry again. As More puts it, Wolsey wants the Pope now to "dispense with his dispensation, also for state reasons." Wolsey seems sincere in his concern for the state—he fears an uprising as devastating as the Yorkish Wars if Henry cannot secure the Tudor line. Wolsey asks More if he will take his position as Lord Chancellor when he dies, and More agrees that he is at least a better candidate than Wolsey's secretary, Thomas Cromwell.

More meets Cromwell as he hails a boat home (the Common Man is boatman), and then meets Signor Chapuys, Ambassador to Spain, who reminds More that the Spanish King will be insulted if his aunt, Queen Catherine, suffers an insult at the hands of King Henry. When More arrives home, he finds William Roper, his daughter's suitor, there. Roper wants to marry Margaret, but More refuses him because of his heretical attitude (implying Lutheran ideology), toward the Church of England. He also refuses to reveal to his beloved family the nature of his nighttime errand.

The Common Man announces the death of Wolsey and the subsequent assignment of More as Lord Chancellor. Cromwell befriends Rich, hoping to find his familiarity with More politically useful.

Back at More's home, his family and Norfolk desperately seek More because the King is en route for a surprise visit. They find More at his vespers. The King arrives, shows his Latin inferior to Margaret's, brags about having steered a new ship here, and promises to stay for dinner. In the midst of his frivolity, Henry makes an offhand attempt to bring More around concerning the divorce. Henry admits that he needs More's support because More is "known to be honest." Finding More unmoveable, he announces coldly that he'll "brook no opposition." Abruptly upon the striking of eight o'clock, Henry departs; he has fled to Anne Bolyn's customary dance. Alice begs her husband Thomas to "be ruled" by his king, for his own safety. But More cannot acquiesce to ignore a sacrament of the church; to do so would put his own soul in peril. Roper, having now somewhat modified his views on the Church, enters into a debate with More between man's law and God's law. More expresses his belief that following God's law will save his soul, but that being a skilled forester in the "thickets" of man's law, he is not above resorting to legal hairsplitting to save his life. More chides Roper for anchoring to his principles, but pulling up anchor and moving elsewhere when the "weather turns nasty."

In a pub presided over by the Common Man, Cromwell extracts from Rich the potentially useful information that a woman tried to bribe More (unsuccessfully) and rewards Rich with a position as Collector of Revenues. When Rich warns Cromwell that he may have met his match in More, a man who "doesn't know how to be frightened," Cromwell retaliates by holding Rich's hand in the candle flame. The curtain comes down on Rich's pained observation, "You've enjoyed it!"

Act Two

Like Act One, Act Two begins with Common Man addressing the audience directly. This time he announces the passage of two years and reads from a history book a paragraph on the sixteenth-century British practice of "imprisonment without trial, and even examination under torture" as means to protect the Church of England.

More and Roper enter, now guardedly disputing whether the King has a right to declare himself the "Supreme Head" of the Church, as he has done. More hopes to take refuge in the phrase "so far as the law of God allows." Chapuys arrives to pressure More to resign as Lord Chancellor in protest of Henry's defiance of the Pope. Chapuys intimates that an armed resistance would follow such a signal from More. Norfolk comes in to announce that the Convocation (a church ruling body) has accepted Henry's terms, thus severing "the connection with Rome." Symbolically, More has Margaret remove his chain of office. Norfolk scorns More's preference for "theory" over patriotism. Alice wants at least to know why she must give up her status and household; but More will give neither her nor

Norfolk his reasons—to protect them. Now lacking the means to pay him, More lets the Common Man (as steward) go, saying he'll miss him. The steward asks the audience, "What's in me for him to miss?"

All exit and Norfolk and Cromwell enter the alcove. Norfolk tries to convince Cromwell to leave More alone in his silence, but Cromwell informs Norfolk that he too must help pressure More into supporting the state. The steward takes a position with Richard Rich.

The next scene takes place in More's home, now cold and less well appointed. Chapuys arrives on an official visit to deliver a letter of support from the Spanish King. More resolutely refuses to touch it, knowing that to do so would be seen as treason by Cromwell's agents. Rebuffed, Chapuys departs.

Roper, who has been outside gathering bracken for firewood, announces a caller demanding More's presence at Hampton Court to answer "certain charges." The scene changes to Cromwell's office, where Master Rich is present to record their conversation. In a roundabout manner Cromwell interrogates More, but fails to intimidate him. Shaken, More leaves and runs into Norfolk. More picks an argument with him, simply to spare his friend the pain of seeing him destroyed. Upon returning home More learns that Parliament has approved an oath of loyalty regarding the marriage. More's only hope is to find a loophole in the wording such that he can take the oath and also keep his conscience clear.

The next scene is a jail with More in it. The jailer, who is the Common Man, reads from a history book the upcoming executions of Thomas Cromwell, Howard Norfolk, and Thomas Cranmer (Archbishop of Canterbury) the death from syphilis of King Henry, and the prosperous life of Richard Rich and the Common Man himself. Norfolk, Cromwell, and Cranmer make one last ineffective attempt to sway More, as does his family. Despite More's legal maneuvering, he is outdone by an outright lie. On the witness stand, Richard Rich declares that More told him Parliament could not place the King at the Head of the Church. More responds sorrowfully, "In good faith, Rich, I am sorrier for your perjury than my peril." Norfolk as foreman reads the verdict: "guilty on the charge of High Treason." The Common Man as headsman performs the execution; blackout and the harsh sound of drums announce the beheading.

The Common Man makes a final aside to the audience suggesting one should not make trouble in

Orson Welles as Cardinal Wolsey and Paul Scofield as Thomas More in the film adaptation

life, adding "If we should bump into one another, recognize me."

CHARACTERS

Attendant to Signor Chapuys
The attendant is present to indicate the status of the Spanish Ambassador.

Signor Chapuys (sha-pwees)
Signor Chapuys, the Spanish Ambassador, at first glance appears to do little more in the play than walk on at key moments to testify to the piety and integrity of Sir Thomas More. He pays the boatman a few coins for revealing More's pious habits and he attempts to deliver a message from the King of Spain expressing the Catholic King's approval of More's resistance to Cromwell and the Reformation movement. More realizes that even reading the missive will be taken as evidence of treason, so he refuses to accept the envelope. Chapuys is flabbergasted because he has misread More's moral stance as a political one; this scene thus alerts the viewer

MEDIA ADAPTATIONS

- Robert Bolt's first version of *A Man for All Seasons* was a radio play produced for the BBC (British Broadcasting Corporation) in 1954. Three years later, BBC-TV televised the play.

- Robert Bolt adapted his play for the screen in 1966 and the Columbia film, starring Paul Scofield as More, Robert Shaw as King Henry VIII, and Orson Welles as Cardinal Wolsey, won 6 Academy awards, including Best Picture, Best Adapted Screenplay, Best Director (Fred Zinnemann), and Best Actor for Scofield, who had played the part on stage in London.

- In 1988 Charleton Heston directed and starred in a cable TV version of the play with Vanessa Redgrave and John Gielgud. This version has not enjoyed the popularity of the Zinnemann film.

to another of More's rigorous ethical standards. Chapuys's purpose in the play is to illuminate the political issues surrounding the taking of the King's oath. Chapuys informs More, much to More's dismay, that Yorkshire and Northumberland are ready to launch an insurrection (that Chapuys and his cohorts may have instigated) against Henry. His message indicates to More the gravity of his situation.

The Common Man

The Common Man is a pot-bellied, middle-aged man, a base and crafty figure who dons different costumes to enact the roles of More's steward, boatman, jailer, foreman of the jury, and executioner (called ''headsman''). He also serves as intermediary between the audience and the play, summarizing off-stage events and commenting on the meaning of the play, a device (often used by playwright Bertolt Brecht) meant to remind viewers of the play's artifice. Within the play, the Common Man represents the antithesis of Sir Thomas More in terms of his ethical motivation, yet he shares with More a talent for self-preservation. Leo McKern, the actor who played the Common Man in the London production, was quoted in *Gambill* as saying the role is ''one of the best ever written for a true character actor.''

Cranmer, Archbishop of Canterbury

Cranmer does not appear until More is jailed in the Tower. There he joins in with Cromwell and Norfolk in attempting to sway More. He fails as dismally as have the others. Cranmer swears the jailer in oath to report any treason spoken by More against the king, and quickly reminds the jailer not to perjure himself when Cromwell offers him fifty guineas if he brings forth any evidence. As Archbishop, Cranmer has the authority to absolve More of sins before his execution; but More, contemptuous of Cranmer's own morals, refuses his services at the gallows.

Thomas Cromwell

King Henry assigns Cromwell the unwelcome task of bringing More around to accepting the King's annulment to Catherine and his appointment as Head of the Church of England, called the Act of Supremacy. The historical Cromwell was an effective statesman who served his king well, though he was reportedly as shrewdly exploitive as Bolt portrays him. Cromwell enjoys the prestige and power of his official role as Cardinal Wolsey's solicitor and his unofficial role as ''ear to the King.'' However the assignment to convert More to Henry's way of thinking puts Cromwell into a precarious position. If he fails, he not only will have to execute an innocent man but he also runs the great risk of earning the King's disfavor. (In fact, the Common Man announces that only a few years after More's beheading, the historical Thomas Cromwell was executed, under the charge of High Treason.) Cromwell's only salvation lies in unhinging More from his allegiance to the salvation of his soul. He expresses his frustration over More's obstinacy in an invective against the soul: ''A miserable thing, whatever you call it, that lives like a bat in a Sunday School! A shrill, incessant pedagogue about its own salvation—but nothing to say of your place in the State! Under the King! In a great native country!''

Duke of Norfold

More's close friend the Duke of Norfolk is a worldly man who enjoys gaming and who recognizes his own ''moral and intellectual insignificance'' as compared to the likes of Sir Thomas, whom he admires greatly. Norfolk succumbs to pressure and ratifies the Act of Supremacy, thereby causing a rift between himself and More. Norfolk foolishly badgers More to relent and join the King's supporters, not realizing the depth of More's integrity, integrity being a smaller matter to the Duke. Norfolk coolly conducts the trial for High Treason against his former friend, never aware that More had eased his passage from trusted friend to state enemy by purposely offending him.

Howard

See Duke of Norfold

King Henry, VIII

Bolt portrays Henry in his exuberant youth, at the beginning of the period of corruption for which the historical Henry VIII is best known. The on-stage Henry is brash and impulsive; he makes an unannounced visit to More to try his own hand at bringing More around to his point of view on the Acts of Succession and Supremacy. Masking his real purpose, he playfully tries to match wits with the more serious scholar, Margaret, and then shores up his own confidence by boasting of his skills at dancing and boat steerage when she clearly out-ranks him. Failing in his match with the elder More as well, he impulsively turns his attention to the social pleasures of dinner. But this is a man whose affections turn on and off at the strike of a clock—he just as impulsively departs after hearing the 8 o'clock bells, in order not to miss Anne Bolyn's dance hour. To compound More's danger, the monarch is incapable of loyalty, and what he wants for himself become for him matters of state. His henchmen know that they might be next on his list of treasonous subjects, but cannot oppose his imperious will.

Alice More

Historically, Alice More was Sir Thomas's second wife, his first wife having died soon after giving birth to Margaret. In Bolt's play, Alice—illiterate, a great cook, and a delighted newcomer to nobility— never fully understands the full political and theological implications of her husband's moral stand, but she willingly accepts the severely reduced station in life imposed upon her by his downfall because of her unflinching admiration for and trust in her husband as a man.

Margaret More

The historical Sir Thomas More educated his daughter more thoroughly than was conventional. In the play, Margaret shows herself more erudite than King Henry, but she cleverly avoids upstaging him in a match of Latin wit. Margaret loves her father but is independent enough to love Will Roper, a young man whom her father initially dislikes because of his heretical ideas about the Church.

Sir Thomas More

Sir Thomas More is the central character of *A Man for All Seasons*. He is an intelligent man who enjoys life, loves his family, and respects his king. However, his fatal ''flaw,'' a deeply ingrained sense of integrity, causes him to choose death over compromising his soul. To Cardinal Wolsey, concerned for matters of the state, More's ethics are a ''horrible moral squint'' that prevent More from cooperating with the reigning powers of England. Sir Thomas More's decision to refuse Henry VIII did not come easily. Up until the Act of Supremacy and the oath Henry VIII required his countrymen to take, More had supported his king in both state and religious policy. Bolt also demonstrates the pain More's decision causes his family. Resigning the position of Lord Chancellor of England puts More's beloved family into poverty; continuing to defy his king puts them into disgrace. More is also a man who enjoys the humble pleasures of life—a good wine, the stuffed swan specially prepared for King Henry's unannounced visit, or the pudding Alice made him during the precious last minutes he spends with her. But none of this deters More in upholding his virtue and principles.

More is a man of deep religious convictions who counters Wolsey's concerns for the state by insisting that he'd rather govern the country by prayers. At the same time, he trusts the law to protect him on earth, and he considers it his God-given duty to become expert enough in legal intricacies to defend himself from the King. More says that God made Man capable of serving him ''wittily, in the tangle of his mind!'' Ultimately, More believed a man's duty was to sort out the conflicts between religion and state according to his own conscience, saying "In matters of conscience, the loyal subject is more bounden to be loyal to his conscience than to any other thing."

In his attempt to present the man with "an adamantine sense of self" Bolt carefully integrated many of More's own words, taking material from William Roper's biography of his father-in-law, from the writings of More's contemporaries, and from More's own writings.

Richard Rich

Richard Rich prostitutes his ethic for political advancement and perjures himself to secure his place of power. He begins humbly enough as librarian to More's friend the Duke of Norfolk. He quickly shows himself of use, however, to Cromwell, who gives him a position as Collector of Revenues in the hope of obtaining "tidbits of information" about Thomas More. Rich willingly tells him the little he knows, and when Rich seems rueful over his lost innocence, Cromwell assures him that playing the informer will grow easier as time goes on. Rich's cool-headed delivery of a complete lie at More's trial (saying that More, after refusing to reveal to anyone else his position on the King's naming himself Head of the Church, suddenly intimated it to Rich) proves Cromwell's prediction true.

William Roper

William Roper, suitor to Margaret More, is a young man who swings from a passionate Churchman to passionate Lutheran—and back again. More accepts his bid for Margaret's hand when Roper returns to the Church, but chides him for anchoring to his principles, but moving the anchor "when the weather turns nasty." Roper remains loyal to More throughout his trial, but betrays his own lack of moral conviction by urging More to go ahead and take the oath, a violation of principle More would never commit.

Will

See William Roper

Cardinal Wolsey

The aging Cardinal capitulates to Henry's pressure to seek an annulment of his marriage to Catherine. Fearing a bloody fight for the kingship if no heir appears to secure the King's lineage, Wolsey chooses to play the statesman in his position as Lord Chancellor of England. However, he fails to persuade the Pope to "dispense with his dispensation" that permitted Henry to marry his brother's widow Catherine, whose male offspring have not survived. Thus making it illegal and immoral for the King to marry Anne Bolyn and perhaps obtain the needed male heir. Wolsey's last act of naming More to replace him is puzzling because Wolsey well knew that More would not succumb as easily as he himself did; on the other hand he knew that More was possibly the one man in England capable of persuading the Pope.

Woman

Perhaps the same woman who tried to bribe Sir Thomas and failed, "the woman" stops him on his way up the gallows to chide him for a "false judgement" against her. More very quickly recognizes her and spiritedly rebukes her, saying that if he had the judgement to do again he would not change her sentence.

THEMES

Individualism

The historical More acted out of religious belief as well as integrity, and he became a saint for his forbearance. For Sir Thomas More, God—not a political sovereign self-appointed to head the Church—had jurisdiction over a human's soul, and More felt compelled to honor God's rule over an earthly king's command. Robert Bolt modernizes More's beliefs however. Robert Bolt's Thomas More tells his daughter that for a man to take an oath is to hold "his own self in his own hands," a sentiment more aligned with the individualism of the modern period, when Bolt wrote the play. Bolt's More equates the soul with the self, saying "a man's soul is his self," a statement that would have been as unfamiliar to the historical More as to any of his sixteenth-century contemporaries. It is essentially a modernist concept that the soul belongs not to God but to the individual and that the individual has a right (even an obligation) to express himself as an individual. Seeds of individualism certainly existed in More's time in the form of Humanism, a philosophy that emphasized the human element of life over the divine. Renaissance Humanists (led, in fact, by More and his Dutch friend Erasmus) looked to classical Greek and Roman thought and literature for models and urged humankind to embrace greater social responsibility. More and other Renaissance

TOPICS FOR FURTHER STUDY

- Some of the characters in the play alluded to a potential Yorkist uprising; which characters would have been affected by such an uprising and in what way? What bearing did the claims of the York family to the throne have on More's predicament?

- Rank in importance the following reasons for More's refusal to take King Henry's oath and explain how they contributed to his decision: religious conviction, personal integrity, concern for public morality. Add any other reasons you consider important.

- When Robert Bolt adapted his play for film, he eliminated the Common Man. What significance did the Common Man have in the play, and why do you suppose Bolt chose not to include him in the film version? If you have seen the film, explain what devices Bolt and the director used to replace the effect of the Common Man.

- What role did Henry VIII's Act of Supremacy play in the eventual Reformation of the Catholic Church and its official relationship to the State over the following centuries?

---

philosophers fused classical culture to Christian religious belief in order to improve human life on earth; however, it would take William Wordsworth's nineteenth-century egoism to galvanize the secular, individual self into the core of the human spirit as Bolt portrays it in Sir Thomas More.

Bolt's anachronistic torquing of More's philosophy goes hand in hand with his inclusion of the Common Man in the play, whose primary concern is not his moral self but his corporeal self. The Common Man changes outward identities as easily as he changes hats, but his essential, opportunist self remains the same. He serves as a foil to More's integrity and reinforces the heroism of More's martyrdom. For Bolt, a man who was by his own description "not a Catholic nor even in the meaningful sense of the word a Christian," More was a "hero of selfhood" because he "knew where he began and left off, what areas of himself he could yield to the encroachments of his enemies, and what to the encroachments of those he loved" (Bolt's Preface to the play, p. xi).

Ethics

A Man for All Seasons is a historical drama that explores the religious and personal ethics that led to Sir Thomas More's beheading in 1535. Sir Thomas

More believed in the supremacy of the Church in all things, both on earth and in the human spirit. He further believed the Pope to be the embodiment of God's law on earth. Because King Henry VIII had obtained papal approval of his marriage to Catherine (which defied biblical law in that she was his brother's widow), More had no objection to this marriage. But Henry came to believe that his marriage to Catherine was sinful and that his not having obtained an heir by her was obvious evidence of his state of sin. Thinking his soul was in peril and also desirous of an heir to continue the Tudor line, Henry VIII appealed to Pope Clement VII for a dispensation of his former dispensation in order to annul this marriage and make a new one with Anne Bolyn. The Pope, under pressure from Spain to uphold the union of Catherine with Henry, refused. Once again, More supported the Pope's decision, to the vast displeasure of Henry VIII. When Henry defied the papal decision and married Anne Bolyn in a civil ceremony, More did not attend. Without the needed annulment, Henry's new marriage placed him in deeper moral danger, that of bigamy. In desperation, King Henry pressured Parliament to declare the Act of Supremacy which placed him at the head of the Church of England and effectively demoted the Pope to merely the Bishop of Rome. The court of the Archbishop of Canterbury promptly annulled the marriage. More still could not in good conscience ratify Henry's Act, because he placed God's rule over that of the State—as far as More was concerned, the Act of Supremacy was not valid, nor was Henry's marriage to Anne Bolyn. More's obstinace infuriated Henry and also made him uneasy; he wanted the reassurance of More's approval and needed his public support. More sought refuge in the law, being expert at negotiating paths through forests of legal minutia. More is willing to compromise his ethics enough to take the oath if he can find a legal loophole to protect him. He tells his worried son-in-law Roper, ''An oath is made of words. It may be possible to take it. Or avoid it.'' He might have succeeded if not for the moral failing of Richard Rich, who perjured himself as witness in More's trial, making it possible for Henry to eliminate More's moral and ethical objections by eliminating More himself.

Law

In *A Man for All Seasons,* English law, lawmaking, and legal interpretation vie directly with God's law, law-making, and interpretation. Henry fights a political battle to secure the kingship of his heirs by pitting English law against papal law. He runs into opposition from Sir Thomas More, a brilliant lawyer with unimpeachable religious devotion. More's piety made his approval of Henry's marriage annulment the more critical to Henry's program. Even with legal matters well in hand, as self-declared Head of the Church of England (''as far as God's law allows''), Henry needed More's support in order to quell the objections of Yorkish and other nobles who stood ready to initiate a revolution to overturn the Tudor line of ascension that Henry represented and seemed unable to prolong. Under English law any legitimate child of Henry's was in direct line to ascend to the throne, but Henry, being only the second Tudor to rule, felt he needed a son to fortify his family's claim to the throne—this was not the time to introduce the notion of England being ruled by a queen. As Chapuys hints in the play, the families of the defeated noble lines in Yorkshire and Northumberland need little excuse to stage an armed resistance against a king they already wished to depose. Thus legality would assure peace among the nobles as well. Not content merely to have Parliament decree an Act of Supremacy making himself sovereign of both Church and State in England (effectively demoting the Pope to Bishop of Rome), Henry demanded that his followers pledge an oath supporting the Act.

At first More tries to find a legal loophole in the King's obligatory oath, telling William Roper, ''An oath is made of words. It may be possible to take it. Or avoid it.'' Failing to find a way to take the oath, More chooses to remain silent regarding the Act of Supremacy and the marriage. According to English law silence by default is always legally interpreted as assent. As long as he neither denies the oath nor gives his reasons for doing so, the King must legally assume his assent and therefore cannot legally commit him for treason.

The theme of law and its abuse are ironically foregrounded in the penultimate scene of *A Man for All Seasons* when Cromwell, in a characteristic display of patriotism but with unexpected enthusiasm, salutes the appearance of various coats of arms, proudly observing in rhymed couplets, ''What Englishman can behold without Awe, The Canvas and the Rigging of the Law!'' Richard Rich then defiles the lofty ideals of English law through perjury and sentences an innocent man to death.

STYLE

Symbolism

Robert Bolt consciously inserted symbolism about the sea and water as ''a figure for the superhuman context.'' In the play, references to currents and tides refer to shifts in the forces around More. Thus More's need to be steered by boat to see Wolsey or Cromwell or to return home indicates that he is at the mercy of others, whereas Henry VIII's boasting about steering a ship himself, albeit badly, indicates his arrogant usurpation of authority. In another manifestation of the sea image, More speaks to Roper of the ''currents and eddies of right and wrong'' as a sea he cannot navigate so simply as Roper does. More is ''set against the current of [his] times.''

The symbolism of clothing is another pervasive symbol in the play. From the very first scene, clothing represents identity that is simple to don or doff. For example, Roper demonstrates a religious about-face when at the beginning of Act 2 he appears dressed in black and wearing a large cross as a show of allegiance to the Church. In an earlier scene More refused him Margaret's hand in marriage because of his heretical views—now More says of him that he changes the anchor of his principles far too readily. The Common Man, too, nimbly changes clothing to change personas, although, unlike Roper, he remains anchored to the principle of selfish opportunism with his essential self intact. In one scene, sporting spectacles and carrying a book, he is the pedantic commentator; in another he dons a gray cap and condemns an innocent man to death; it's all a question of headwear. Only the last costume gives the Common Man pause—he balks at sitting in judgment of More. But once past this hurdle he shows no compunction about donning the mask of executioner. In preparation for the trial scene, the Common Man displays his many hats, setting them on poles (as More's head will soon be set on a pole for display) in front of a series of coats of arms of different proportions. While the hats suggest the common man's (meaning everyman's) mercurial nature, the coats of arms ironically allude to timeless, lofty ideals that none but More honor, and he does so with his life.

Chorus

During the sixteenth century the chorus, which had consisted of several actors in classical Greek times, was reduced to one actor who commented on and interpreted the action of the play before, after, and between scenes. For example, Shakespeare begins *Henry V* with an apologetic prologue in which a player asks the audience to embellish the stage props with imagination (''Piece out our imperfections with your thoughts. . . . Think, when we talk of horses, that you see them''). Modernist Bertold Brecht transformed the chorus to a new purpose; Brecht's ''chorus'' figures are alienating devices designed to remind the audience of the artifice of theater, thus distancing them from the play's action. Bolt adopts Bertold Brecht's use of the chorus, giving the concept yet another twist. Like a Brechtian chorus, the Common Man delivers a modern, self-reflexive, self-conscious judgment of the play: ''It is perverse! To start a play made up of Kings and Cardinals in speaking costumes and intellectuals with embroidered mouths, with me.'' But in opposition to Brecht's use of chorus figures, Bolt wanted the Common Man to draw in the audience, to provide someone with whom they might identify. Because he felt that his device failed, Bolt explained in his Preface why he included the Common Man and had him make frequent puns on the word ''common''—it was ''intended primarily to indicate 'that which is common to us all''' (xvii). Even though audiences chose to see the Common Man as vulgar and foreign and therefore not themselves, Bolt insists that he sometimes heard in their laughter a ''rueful note of recognition.''

HISTORICAL CONTEXT

The Ascension of the Tudor Monarchs

King Henry VIII was only the second Tudor king to rule in England, and he had good reason to worry about his ability to keep the throne in his family. Cardinal Wolsey alludes to the potential menace of two powerful families who alternated, captured, lost, and recaptured the kingdom for the thirty years prior to his father's reign when he says to Sir Thomas More, ''Do you favor a change of dynasty? D'you think two Tudors is sufficient?.'' The two houses were House of Lancaster, whose symbol was a red rose and the House of York, whose symbol was a white rose; their quarrels over the throne came to be called ''The War of the Roses.'' Henry Tudor, or Henry VII had fought with the Lancaster side, so he diplomatically arranged to marry a York, thus sealing a temporary truce between the families and beginning the Tudor dynasty. It was up to Henry VIII to continue the line.

Church Reform, Humanism, and Social Reform

The Church Reform issues (''forgiveness by the florin,'' temperance, duty to God) debated by Sir Thomas More and his son-in-law William Roper in *A Man for All Seasons* were not new concepts to the sixteenth century but were ideas that had been infiltrating the intellectual centers of Europe and steadily eroding the long-held Roman Catholic dominion since the fourteenth century. There were at least two fronts of attack on the Catholic hegemony. On one hand various Church Reform movements sought to eradicate widespread corruption among the priesthood, who numbered one in forty of England's total population and many of whom lacked education and moral superiority. On the other hand was Luther's Protestant movement, which was not so much a ''Reformation'' as a wholesale refutation of clerical authority. The Protestants denied Catholic clergy the power to absolve sin, insisting that God alone can offer salvation to humans. Protestants made God their ultimate authority. Because God did not make his authority directly known to man, the laity (not just the clergy) were left to interpret his intentions. This democratic line of thought, an attitude of empowerment for the layperson, resonated with the budding new philosophy of the Humanists (including More and his Dutch friend Erasmus), who sought to improve human life on earth by adhering to the lofty ideals of classical Greek and Roman cultures. With the chip-

COMPARE & CONTRAST

- **16th century:** Officially, all English citizens belonged to the Catholic Church and many attended its services. However, because the Roman Catholic service was entirely in Latin, few congregants fully understood it. Furthermore, the Church was losing authoritative ground due to inroads of Martin Luther's Protestantism and separate Church Reform movements to combat corruption of the clergy. Within a century, the Catholics would no longer hold a monopoly on European religion.

  1950-1965: The Catholic Church still served about one-third of English citizens and a majority of the populations of many European countries, even though the Church was losing popularity because of its hard stand on issues such as abortion, birth control, and clerical celibacy. In the ground-breaking Convocations of 1962 and 1965 the Church took measures to ''update'' its image and make the religion more appealing.

  Today: Although the Roman Catholic Church remains the largest organized religion in the world, only about one-fifth of England's citizens call themselves Catholic. The Roman Catholic Church has suffered fractionalizing due to its continued strict stance on abortion, birth control, clerical celibacy, euthanasia, and women in the priesthood. In undeveloped areas such as parts of Africa missionary efforts have resulted in phenomenal growth in Catholicism.

- **16th century:** Religious persecution was so widespread that America was colonized partially by English citizens seeking freedom to worship as they pleased. In England it was common for people to be charged as ''heretics'' (whether for religious or some other reason) and forced to wear a marker of their shame so that others could shun them; some were executed.

  1950-1960: In developed nations such as England and the United States, religious freedom was officially assured, although some groups suffered from prejudiced treatment. In communist countries, religion was actively suppressed by the state.

  Today: Religious freedom and diversity exist in most developed and third-world countries, even in formerly communist-held countries. Religious differences contribute, however, to the many ethnic conflicts worldwide, such as those in Bosnia, Liberia, and Rwanda.

- **16th century:** The charge of treason was routinely used to rid the ruler of unwanted persons in England as well as in other European countries. Henry VIII had John Fisher beheaded days before he executed Sir Thomas More, and Cardinal Wolsey died while under charge for High Treason.

  1950-1960: England sustained a clean record of providing its citizens with safety from unfounded charges of treason. However, things were otherwise in the United States. Although the United States promises due process of law and immunity from unfounded accusations, Senator Joe McCarthy made a sham of political tolerance and legislative integrity by leading a relentless persecution of intellectuals and filmmakers with any suspected ties to communism.

  Today: In England and the United States, along with most developed nations, it takes a strong case to condemn a citizen for treason or other crimes against the state.

---

ping away of Papal authority came a need for stronger state administration. A vested interest in state sovereignty underlay Henry VIII's urge toward independence from ecclesiastic rule, even if his immediate reason for breaking with the church was more political and more pressing. Henry was a good Catholic, had even defended the Church against the attacks of Martin Luther, but his need to cement the Tudor line with a male heir overrode his religious allegiance. He began to see flaws in Catholicism that he might otherwise have ignored. Over time, Church Reform affected everyday life, not just spiritual matters, as they paralleled and reinforced peasant revolts against the hardships of serfdom.

King Henry VIII

Because his older brother Arthur was in line for the throne, young Henry Tudor did not expect to be crowned king of England. However, when Henry was eighteen, Arthur died and Henry succeeded his vastly successful father. A marriage was arranged for Henry to Arthur's widow, Catherine of Aragon, to strengthen England's tie to her native Spain. Catherine had five children by him, but only one, a daughter, lived past infancy. Because having a male heir to whom Henry would turn over the English dynasty was seen by Henry and his most astute advisors as critical to the political stability of England, and because Henry came to believe that his wife's barrenness indicated that the Biblical punishment for marrying a brother's widow had befallen him, Henry sought to annul his marriage and form a new one with Anne Bolyn, daughter of a wealthy aristocrat. He defied Pope Clement VII and married Anne Bolyn in a civil ceremony that Sir Thomas More disdained to attend. When Henry failed to obtain More's approval of the marriage and the Act making him head of the Church of England, he had More executed. The historical More had prophetically written that despite his close friendship with the King, "If my head would win him a castle in France, it should not fail to fall." Three years and no sons later, Henry had Anne executed for infidelity. Henry would marry four more wives after Anne and execute one of them.

What began as a desire to arrange a divorce and marriage, ended with Henry overthrowing the authority of the Pope in England, dissolving hundreds of monasteries and nunneries (the latter to redirect funds to the Crown, the largest such redistribution since the Norman Conquest), and executing a large number of clergy who refused to accept his supremacy over the Pope's. Throughout his battle with the Church, Henry never ceased to be a devout Catholic and he actively suppressed heretics. In spite of his brutal egoism, Henry VIII succeeded in centralizing administration of England, effectively separating the realms of Church and State, and initiating the Reformation of the Church.

CRITICAL OVERVIEW

When *A Man for All Seasons* made its debut on the London stage at the Globe Theater on July 1, 1960, Robert Bolt had only one moderate theater success under his belt (*Flowering Cherry*). Therefore, to have earned the popular and critical acclaim he did for his Brechtian historical play was a significant achievement, and it catapulted the thirty-six-year-old into the theatrical limelight, where he was to remain for the next decade. The *Illustrated London News* called it a "brilliant play," one which let history have its moment on stage. The *New Statesman,* however, identified a complaint that would be leveled frequently at this play and at the 1966 screenplay—that it privileges history over psychological depth. Nevertheless, *A Man For All Seasons,* starring Paul Scofield as Thomas More, ran for 320 performances in London before moving on to a year-and-a-half run on Broadway, where it earned the Tony Award for best play and the New York Drama Critics Award for Best Foreign Play in 1962.

In New York critics found much to praise in the performances and in the script. Robert Brustein of the *New Republic* called it a drama of "remarkable intelligence, historicity, theatrical ingenuity, and good taste." Much of the theater in the early sixties fed the popular appetite for social significance, but Bolt's play stood on its own merit, or rather on the merit of its protagonist. Critics were somewhat split in their acceptance of a historical play that did not seem to care about today's social issues. While some critics applauded the portrayal of More as realistic and as struggling with an understandable dilemma, others took the opposite perspective, chiding Bolt for irrelevance. John McCarten of the *New Yorker* called the play "a sharp and brilliant portrait of a man who might just as easily be of our day as King Henry's." Howard Taubman called it " an ode to the best and noblest in man," and asserted that More "has a burning immediacy for our day." However, John Simon, writing for *Theater Arts,* felt that doctrinal differences in religious belief no longer carried much empathic weight, and charged the play guilty of missing an opportunity for deeper relevance. At the same time, Simon forgave the playwright for falling prey to the limitations of any historical play, being "forced to look at things a little more panoramically than profoundly."

Bolt eliminated the Common Man in the 1966 film version of *A Man for All Seasons,* perhaps because the device for providing scene cues in the was original 1954 radio play version was unnecessary in the medium of film. Whatever Bolt's artistic reasoning, his screenplay was a huge success. Directed by Fred Zinneman and once again starring Paul Scofield, the film won six academy awards (Best Picture, Best Actor for Scofield, Best Director, Best Adapted Screenplay, Best Cinematography, and Best Costume Design) and received nominations for two others. Charleton Heston's 1988 remake of the film had little effect on the eminence of Zinneman's production.

Over time, criticism has distilled to a view that Bolt's stage play is one of the best plays to address the issue of selfhood. Literary critics have focused, predictably enough, on Sir Thomas More and on the presence of the Brechtian device of the Common Man. There are some who see the Common Man as a polar opposite to and foil for More, a man who conspicuously lacks More's integrity. There are others, however, who observe that the Common Man also shares a significant characteristic with More—that of holding fast to one's principles. In More's case the principles are religious and personal integrity, while the in the case of the Common Man the principles are self-preservation and expediency. Anselm Atkins explained the concept linking the two men in *Modern Drama:* ''the Common Man is Everyman—and also—More. We each have a self and a theoretical ability to be true to it.'' To Arthur Thomas Tees, writing in the *University Review,* More and the Common Man must be weighed against each other in the context of tragedy, wherein ''the tragedy is not in the central figure but in the rejection of that figure by others around him.'' To Tees, ''More is a non-tragic hero; the Common Man is a tragic non-hero.'' Bolt has been categorized as both a ''traditionalist'' (Walker) and as a ''Brechtian'' (Fuegi) in terms of his theatrical style. There are elements of both schools in *A Man for All Seasons,* although Brecht's essential interest in moving the audience to commitment to social change is lacking. In Sir Thomas More's terms, the play is ultimately a ''humanist'' work, one that values human acts of beauty and integrity on earth.

CRITICISM

Carole L. Hamilton

Hamilton examines Bolt's play as a tribute to the ideal of selfhood. As Bolt himself described it,

Hamilton sees More's faith to his principles as a stand for individuality and preservation of the self.

In an elegant Preface to the script of *A Man for All Seasons,* Robert Bolt explains the historical background to Sir Thomas More's story of martyrdom at the hands of King Henry VIII. Bolt also explains his reasons for choosing a sixteenth-century theologian and statesman as a ''hero of selfhood'' in spite of having little interest himself in questions of Christian piety. For Bolt, ''virtue'' and ''selfhood'' have lost meaning in the modern era, where the self is ''an equivocal commodity.'' What fascinated Bolt about More was that he, unlike many of his contemporaries, considered the king's oath a serious contract, one that asked him to ''offer himself as a guarantee.'' More refused to take the oath because he disagreed with its premise (that the King could overrule God's Law) and because he took his own virtue and soul seriously. For More, to take an oath falsely would literally perjure his soul. Bolt translates this position into modern parlance to suggest that More refused also to perjure his ''self''—that he valued his faith in his own capacity for virtue. It is this capacity for virtue, where virtue is adherence to the self, that Bolt sees as a scarce commodity in the modern world. Bolt's story of More is about a man's fight for selfhood; it is also the story of how the modern loss of selfhood came to be.

Bolt, who belonged to the Communist Party for more than five years before becoming disillusioned with it, abhorred the growing consumerism in the 1950s in Great Britain and elsewhere. He agreed with Karl Marx that a society that placed too much emphasis on getting and spending, money would take on more importance than personal virtue. As Bolt asserts, ''We would prefer most men to guarantee their statements with, say, cash rather than with themselves.'' Critics have agreed with his assessment of the modern age and of Thomas More as a suitable hero. ''In a collective society the individual tends to become an equivocal commodity, and when we think of ourselves in this way we lose all sense of our own identity. More's refusal to take the oath is Bolt's way of asserting that even under the greatest of pressures man can exist unequivocally; that it is possible to live in the modern world without 'selling out','' wrote Robert Corrigan in *The New Theatre of Europe.* The modern period has been described as a period of moral bankruptcy; in such a world, the self is compromised at every turn. Thus Bolt turned to history for subject matter because ''modern man has become so trivial and

WHAT DO I READ NEXT?

- Thomas More's 1516 *Utopia* predates his fatal conflict with Henry VIII. The fictional account analyzes the ills of England before expounding upon ''Utopia'' (''nowhere''), a land run according to the ideals of Humanism.

- George Bernard Shaw's 1923 *Saint Joan,* concerns the martyrdom of Joan of Arc, whose sainthood made her a misfit in her society.

- Jean Anouilh's 1969 French drama, *Becket, Or the Honor of God,* like T. S. Eliot's 1935 *Murder in the Cathedral,* tells the story of another British Christian martyr, Thomas a Becket.

- In *Enemy of the People,* an early (1882) play by Henrik Ibsen, a town rejects and persecutes a doctor who warns the people that the town's lucrative baths are polluted.

- Plato's *Apology* (written between 371 and 267 BC) records Socrates's defense in his trial against the state for impiety and corrupting youth through his teachings.

- In Sophocles's *Antigone* (circa 400 BC), a young woman defies the king's prohibition against performing burial rites for her brother and suffers imprisonment for this act of loyalty. Jean Anouilh's 1942 adaptation of the same name is an allegory for France under Vichy rule.

- A scholarly account of the various stages of the Reformation of the English Church can be found in Christopher Haigh's 1993 *English Reformation: Religion, Politics, and Society under the Tudors.*

uninteresting that he has lost his power to involve us, while modern mass society has inhibited even the superior spirits from expressing themselves through significant action,'' according to Robert Brustein in the *New Republic.*

More believed in the ultimate supremacy of God. For More this was a fact and not simply a matter of allegiance. For More, God was supreme and nothing the King of England said or did could change this fact. More was also a loyal subject, and he supported the King's governance of the State and of the English Church. More helped Henry write a defense against Martin Luther and he turned down William Roper as suitor to his daughter until Roper mended his heretical views. But when it came to the King's ''Great Matter,'' as Henry's desire to annul his marriage to Catherine came to be known, More could not condone an act that the Pope expressly refused to sanction. In the Roman Catholic Church, the Pope is God's presence on earth and the Pope's decisions carry the weight of a decision by God. This was an especially significant factor in the early sixteenth century, when the Church and State were

intertwined in a way that is no longer conceivable. Popes routinely dispensed with inconvenient biblical laws to help monarchs make politically expedient marriages, and priests were routinely involved in matters of war. Cardinal Wolsey himself organized military campaigns as well as conducted peace talks with France. The relationship of the English king to the Pope enforced the king's authority in England and internationally. Unfortunately though for Henry VIII, Pope Clement VII could not please the English king because of another impingement of State upon Church: at the time hundreds of Spanish troops surrounded the Vatican and Clement VII dared not offend the Spanish king. The Pope refused Henry's request. Henry could not abide this, so he broke with Rome and declared the Act of Supremacy.

More considered the move an outright defiance of God's law. Finally breaking his vow of silence after an unfair trial, More declares, ''The King in Parliament cannot bestow the Supremacy of the Church because it is a Spiritual Supremacy!'' In other words, neither the Parliament nor the King had the authority to decree the Act of Supremacy in the first place. In fact, English law itself protected the Church from such violations of its jurisdiction, and More added, ''furthermore, the immunity of the Church is promised in Magna Carta and the King's own coronation oath.'' More was on firm ground both ecclesiastically and legally, but could not prevent either the King's violation of Church and State law, nor the irreversible chasm between Church and State that his Act would initiate. The creation of a separate, secular government would ultimately lead to the modern condition that Bolt found so lacking in virtue and selfhood that he resurrected a 400-year-old hero to salvage it.

Henry VIII's declaration of sovereignty over the Church in England was the first of many breaks between church and state that would take place over the next two centuries, thus shifting state governance from an abstract, transcendental mode of authority (derived from God) to a hierarchical, temporal authority (administered by humans). Thenceforth, the state would gradually break free of the connection to God, coincidentally eroding the reinforcing authority of God's endorsement of the monarch. It was a slippery slope that ultimately contributed to the paucity of moral virtue of the secular world: the absence of God in government translated to the possible absence of God at all. The lack of a transcendental authority, according to Bolt, also contributed to the modern loss of self, for, as Bolt hypothesizes in his Preface, ''It may be that a clear sense of the self can *only* crystallize round something transcendental.'' Certainly More's self is crystallized around a transcendental idea—the supremacy of God over man. The State was also crystallized around this transcendental idea, and Thomas More, foresaw that to remove this idea would prove as fatal for the world as it would for himself. In a final invective to Cromwell, More laments, ''It is a long road you have opened. First men will disclaim their hearts and presently they will have no hearts. God help the people whose Statesmen walk your road.''

Bolt clearly desired his audience to find connections in his historical play that would resonate with life in the modern world. He was quoted in the *English Journal* saying: ''The action of this play ends in 1535, but the play was written in 1960, and if in production one date must obscure the other, it is 1960 which I wish clearly to occupy the stage. The 'life' of a man like Thomas More proffers a number of caps which in this or any other century we must try on for size,'' In the play, More himself alludes to his heroism. Deploring those who rationalize taking the easy path, More tells his daughter, ''If we lived in a State where virtue was profitable, common sense would make us good, and greed would make us saintly. And we'd live like animals or angels in the happy land that *needs* no heroes.''

More was found guilty of High Treason after the perjurous testimony of Richard Rich, an immoral opportunist who sold his own soul for bureaucratic advancement—in other words, an archetypal ''modern'' man. The first appearance of Rich finds him prophetically asserting to More that ''every man has his price.'' In their argument (which may or may not have occurred between the historical More and Rich) Rich voices a modern preoccupation with self-interest over integrity and hard currency over ethical value. And yet, it is not Rich that Bolt means the audience to blame. Bolt repeatedly draws the viewer's attention to the Common Man, who, if not directly responsible for More's execution, represents the greater danger to the life expectancy of virtue. For it is the Common Man, performing the roles of foreman and headsman, who dutifully and thoughtlessly tenders the guilty verdict and dependably performs the execution. In effect, the Common Man silently condemns the life of morality, as symbolized by Thomas More, or as Corrigan expressed it, the Common Man ''judges and executes the heroes of selfhood.''

In one of the few encounters More has with him, the Common Man expresses his wish simply to ''keep out of trouble.'' More turns away, disgusted by the man's refusal to take a moral stance, saying ''Oh, Sweet Jesus! These plain, simple men!'' The interchange carries the added emphasis of ending abruptly with sudden music and a swift change of scene. The epilogue provides a final podium for the Common Man, who reiterates his philosophy and attempts to impose it on the audience; ''don't make trouble,'' he warns. The effect is meant ironically, to chide the audience *not* to follow his advice.

But the medium of theater places implicit emphasis on the first, literal meaning of the Common Man's words: theater does not ''make trouble.'' Nor does passively watching this morality play compel the audience to take a stance like that taken by More. Far from it. The price he paid for virtue was his life. The audience, on the other hand, has just bought virtue for the price of a theater ticket. Theater-goers may walk away, feeling a special affinity for a man like Thomas More, passively and tragically failing to recognize themselves in the Common Man, who passively and tragically facilitated More's demise. For the modern period, too absorbed with the loss of self to commit to virtue, commends itself simply for *recognizing* virtue when it sees it, and that seems to be enough. With no simple means to practice virtue first-hand, modern human-kind prefers to practice it via the arts; it is part of the general dilution of moral values. In a consumer culture, morality, virtue, and ethical goodness are not transcendental ideas around which to crystallize a self, but thoughts that sponsor feelings of ''vague humanitarianism,'' moments of mental virtue that are never translated into action.

The theater, and plays such as Robert Bolt's *A Man for All Seasons* feed the modern appetite for snacks of virtue, small acts of recognizing virtue that can be consumed in the theater, the movie theater, and conveniently at home, on television. Bolt meant his play to stir the consciences of his audience, but in actuality, his play does no more than solace them.

Source: Carole L. Hamilton, in an essay for *Drama for Students,* Gale, 1997.

Kenneth Tynan

The following excerpt contains Tynan's review of A Man for All Seasons, *which originally appeared in the* Observer *in 1960. Following the text of Tynan's review is Bolt's response to certain points made by Tynan in his review; this appeared in the next edition of the* Observer. *Following Bolt's article is Tynan's response to it. The discussion in this excerpt centers around Tynan's contention that Bolt is more concerned with Thomas More's personal character and opinions than he is with the historical significance of More's ideas or the time in which the events chronicled in the play took place.*

A dramatist, screenwriter, and critic, Tynan was a prominent figure in English theater during the 1950s and 1960s.

In *A Man for All Seasons,* Robert Bolt has chopped the later career of Sir Thomas More into a series of short and pithy episodes, each of which is prefaced by a few words of comment and explanation, addressed directly to the audience. Changes of scene are indicated emblematically, by signs lowered from the flies; and the style throughout inclines rather to argument than to emotional appeal. There is no mistaking whose influence has been at work on Mr Bolt; the play is clearly his attempt to do for More what Brecht did for Galileo.

In both cases, the theme is persecution, and the author's purpose is to demonstrate how authority

" MR BOLT LOOKS AT HISTORY EXCLUSIVELY THROUGH THE EYES OF HIS SAINTLY HERO"

enforces its claims on the individual conscience. More was a victim of the Reformation; Galileo, a century later, fell foul of the Counter-Reformation; and both men, being contented denizens of our planet, were extremely reluctant to embrace martyrdom. Each found himself the servant of two masters. Galileo had to choose between science and the Pope, More between the Pope and the King; and each of them, after years of hair-splitting and procrastination, ended up by choosing the Pope— Galileo because he feared for his body, More because he feared for his soul. According to Brecht, Galileo was disloyal to the new science, and is therefore to be rebuked; according to Mr Bolt, More was loyal to the old religion, and is therefore to be applauded.

It is hereabouts that the two playwrights part company. I have no idea whether Mr Bolt himself is a religious man, but I am perfectly sure that if someone presented him with irrefutable evidence that every tenet of Catholicism was a palpable falsehood, his admiration for More would not be diminished in the smallest degree, nor would he feel tempted to alter a word of the text. The play's strongest scenes, all of which occur in the second half, are those in which More, employing every resource of his canny legal brain, patiently reminds his inquisitors that silence is not to be equated with treason, and that no court can compel him to reveal or defend his private convictions. His position, in short, is that he takes no position; and I have no doubt that we are meant to draw an analogy between More and those witnesses who appear before the Un-American Activities Committee and take the Fifth Amendment.

As a democrat, I detest such coercive investigations into a man's innermost ideas; as a playgoer, however, I feel entitled to know what his ideas are, and how he arrived at them. Here, where Brecht is voluble, Mr Bolt is mum. If, upon completing *Galileo,* Brecht had suddenly learned that his protagonist's hypotheses were totally untrue, he would either have torn up the manuscript or revised it from start to finish. From Mr Bolt's point of view, on the other hand, it matters little whether More's beliefs were right or wrong; all that matters is that he held them, and refused to disclose them under questioning. For Mr Bolt, in short, truth is subjective; for Brecht it is objective; and therein lies the basic difference between the two plays.

Compare them, and it soon becomes obvious that Mr Bolt's method is the more constricting. Since there can be no battle of ideologies, he must reduce everything to personal terms; the gigantic upheavals of the Reformation dwindle into a temperamental squabble between a nice lawyer who dislikes divorce and a lusty monarch who wants an heir. Our attention is focused on the legal stratagems whereby More postponed his martyrdom, and distracted from the validity of the ideas that got him into trouble to begin with. The play contains some muscular period writing, especially in the scene where More deliberately insults his old crony, the conformist Duke of Norfolk, in order to absolve him from the responsibility of breaking off their friendship; and it is history's fault, not Mr Bolt's, that his hero came to grief so much less dramatically than Brecht's. (More's fate was sealed by a perjured witness; whereas it was Galileo himself who laid low Galileo.) At bottom, however, *A Man for All Seasons* is not so much a play as an essay in hagiography. Mr Bolt looks at history exclusively through the eyes of his saintly hero. Brecht's vision is broader: he looks at Galileo through the eyes of history.

The direction, by Noel Willman, skips swiftly around a permanent setting (by Motley) of impenitently Swedish-modern design. Leo McKern plays the Chorus, a bellicose, time-serving oaf whom the programme labels, somewhat rudely, 'The Common Man'. Beery and button-holing, Mr McKern gives a reekingly good account of a highly tendentious role.

Where More himself is concerned, Mr Bolt has indulged in a lot of simplification. He has banished More the scurrilous pamphleteer, More the earthy pleasure-lover, and More the vernacular comic, whom C. S. Lewis has called 'our first great Cockney humorist'. What remains is More the gentle reasoner, and this Paul Scofield plays to the hilt, at once wily and holy, as unastonished by betrayal as he is by fidelity. He does the job beautifully; but where, in this obsequious piece of acting, is the original Scofield who burst upon us, some twelve years ago, like exquisite thunder? Perhaps time has

tamed him, or security, or something unassertive in his cast of mind. It is true that he has never given a bad performance; but it was not in negatives like this that we formerly hoped to praise him. We were looking for greatness. The power is still there, though it has long been sleeping; may it soon revive and transfix us (1960).

The above review provoked a comment from Robert Bolt which was published in the next edition of *The Observer*. It ran:

'Mr Tynan's certainly fair and probably generous notice of my play raises incidentally a philosophic question of practical importance. I am grateful for the comparison he drew between *A Man For All Seasons* and *Galileo*—indeed I impudently challenged it by misquoting Brecht's most celebrated line at the climax of my own play. It is where the plays diverge that Mr Tynan makes the proposition which I want to query: "For Mr Bolt, in short, truth is subjective; for Brecht it is objective; and therein lies the basic difference between the two plays."

'I only roughly understand what is meant by "objective truth". It is presumably a truth which remains true regardless of who does or doesn't hold it to be true. It seems a very religious concept. But in the present context Mr Tynan's point is clear enough: "If, upon completing *Galileo*, Brecht had suddenly learned that his protagonist's hypotheses were totally untrue, he would either have torn up the manuscript or revised from start to finish." Is this Mr Tynan's guess, or did Brecht himself say he would? For what it means is that the worth of this play about Galileo is conditional upon the correctness of Galileo's hypotheses. I don't believe this, and I don't believe Mr Tynan does, really. Thus:

The difference between the hypotheses of modern cosmology and the hypotheses of Galilean cosmology is already quite as sharp as the difference between the Galilean and the Aristotelian. If the Galilean hypotheses were "true" and showed the Aristotelian to be "untrue" then by the same token the Galilean are now shown to be untrue. If the Galilean hypotheses are untrue then, according to Mr Tynan, *Galileo* should be torn up or rewritten. In fact, Mr Tynan and I both think it a great play.

'Or, if this comparative view of the truthfulness of successive hypotheses is insufficiently "objective" for Mr Tynan, let us anticipate the dawning of that day when every feature of the Galilean cosmology has been discarded in favour of others. (I take it Mr Tynan does not deny the possibility of such a thing. If he does, he has a kindred spirit, not in Galileo but the Cardinal Inquisitor.) If that day is tomorrow, will Brecht's absorbing, profound and illuminating play at once become boring, superficial and dull? It will continue to be as absorbing, profound and illuminating as it in fact is. But where can these virtues now reside? What is it that is left when the ''objective'' truth of Galileo's beliefs is removed from the play *Galileo?* Just Galileo. And that is what Brecht's play is about, as mine is about More.

'There are many differences between the two plays (apart I mean from the obvious one in sheer stature), but the *basic* difference is this. Both men were passionately and to their core convinced. Both were required by Authority to deny themselves. One complied; the other refused.

'Brecht's play shows the frightful price which may have to be paid for that compliance—the reduction of the man in his own estimation to a status where he has only the right to scratch himself and eat. My play shows the frightful price which may have to be paid for that refusal to comply—the end of life on any terms at all.

'Both plays are about uncommon individuals but both are also about organised society. As the essence of organised society, I have taken, quite overtly I think, the structure of the Law. An act of perjury in a trial for High Treason seems to me not altogether undramatic but in this case it has a wider significance, too. More, as Mr Tynan emphasises, put his trust in the Law, that is, in organised society; this act of perjury, engineered by the Court, showed how the appointed guardians of society were ready to crack it open and let in anarchy to maintain their own advantages. As for the passive bulk of society, those with no immediate responsibility for what is done, I don't think my portrait of the Common Man is ''rude'' or ''tendentious''; he is not actively malignant; under similar circumstances could either Mr Tynan or myself be sure of doing better?

'Here is the practical bearing of all this: Any society needs a conservative and a radical element. Without the first it flies apart, without the second it putrefies. The conservative can be taken for granted, for it only needs acceptance and a good working substitute for acceptance is sloth. But the radical rejects the *status quo,* and unless this is done in the name of a definite vision of what an individual human person is, and is not being allowed to be, rejection degenerates to a posture, no less complacent than the Establishment itself. I think this is our

present position. Much ink, perhaps some blood, will flow before we arrive at a genuinely modern, genuinely credible vision of what a human person is. But I think that any artist not in some way engaged upon this task might just as well pack up and go home. The personal is not ''merely'' personal.'

I replied as follows:

Mr Bolt's dissenting gloss on my review of *A Man for All Seasons* is a healthy phenomenon; it is always cheering when a playwright shows that he cares more about the ideas he is expressing than about the number of paying customers he can induce to listen to them. But while I respect Mr Bolt's motives, I cannot swallow his conclusions; they seem to me to be founded on premises that expose, quite poignantly, the limitations of our Western approach to historical drama.

Mr Bolt surveys his chosen slice of the Tudor era with the right end of the telescope firmly clapped to his eye: what he sees is Sir Thomas More, in dominant close-up, with everything else out of focus. A hint, now and then, is lightly dropped that More's obduracy was not only a crafty individual challenge to Tudor law but a social and political threat to the whole process of the English Reformation. Once dropped, however, these hints are rapidly swept under the carpet and forgotten. Mr Bolt is primarily absorbed in the state of More's conscience, not in the state of More's England or More's Europe.

Brecht, on the other hand, though he gives us an intimate study of Galileo's conscience, takes pains to relate it at every turn to Galileo's world and to the universe at large. In short, he uses the wrong end of the telescope as well. He naturally worries about 'what an individual human person is'; but he also worries about the society into which that person was born, and the contributions he made (or failed to make) towards improving it. Brecht's play deals with Galileo *and* the postponed dawn of the age of reason. Mr Bolt's play deals with More, *tout court.*

As to the matter of 'objective truth': what concerns Brecht is Galileo's contention that the earth revolved around the sun, and I am not aware that anybody has yet disproved it. If they had, I have no doubt that Brecht would have written a different play, possibly based on the arrogance of scientists who fail to verify their hypotheses, or on the ways in which hubris can stunt the growth of enlightenment. 'The truth', as he never tired of insisting, 'is concrete'; Galileo is in possession of a useful, concrete, revolutionary truth, which authority compels him to deny.

Does Mr Bolt seriously think that Brecht would have devoted the same attention to a man who held that the earth was a saucer-shaped object created in the seventh century A.D.? That, too, would have constituted a heresy, and the Church would unquestionably have silenced anyone who sought to spread it. Under pressure, the heretic might well have recanted, and thereby reduced himself, as Mr Bolt says of Galileo, 'in his own estimation'. But what about the estimation of history? Heartless though it may sound—and the theatre, where suffering is feigned, is the last stronghold of permissible heartlessness—I must confess that I am more interested in a persecuted scientist whose beliefs are demonstrably true than in one whose beliefs are demonstrably false.

Mr Bolt makes no such distinctions. For him, the mere fact of belief is enough, and Sir Thomas's martyrdom would have been just as tragic if the point at issue had been his refusal to admit that two plus two equalled four. We are expected to sympathise with him simply and solely because he declines to reveal his convictions. It is here that Mr Bolt and I part company. There may be evidence of temperamental bias in my preference for oppressed heroes with whose opinions I agree; but I don't think I am acting unfairly when I demand that heroes should define their opinions, regardless of whether I agree with them. Brecht tells us precisely what Galileo asserted, and why he asserted it; and the play grows out of the explanation. Mr Bolt tells us nothing about More's convictions or how he came to embrace them. In the second act Norfolk asks him whether he is willing to abandon all he possesses because of 'a theory'—namely, the idea that the Pope is St Peter's descendant.

'Why, it's a theory, yes; you can't see it, can't touch it; it's a theory,' More replies. 'But what matters to me is not whether it's true or not but whether I believe it to be true, or rather not that I *believe* it but that *I* believe it. . . . I trust I make myself obscure?'

That is as close as we get to knowing what More believes, and why. It is not, in an age as pragmatical as ours, nearly close enough. By way of a footnote; I concede that people like Mr Bolt and myself might easily behave, in comparable circumstances, as corruptly and boorishly as the character played by Leo McKern. What is 'rude' and 'tendentious' is that a character who is the essence of boorish corruption should be labelled 'The Common Man'.

Source: Kenneth Tynan, ''Theatre'' in his *Right and Left: Plays, Films, People, Places, and Events,* Atheneum, 1967.

Howard Taubman

In the following review, which originally appeared in the New York Times *on November 23, 1961, Taubman offers a positive assessment of* A Man for All Seasons, *noting Bolt's skills as a writer and his ability to present his plot and characters in a manner that allows the audience to form its own opinions regarding the people and events depicted.*

In *A Man for All Seasons* Robert Bolt has written a play that is luminous with intelligence and steely with conviction.

The central figure of this work, which arrived last night at the ANTA Theatre, is Sir Thomas More, the lawyer and scholar, who would not yield to the expediency required by his sovereign, Henry VIII. The theme of the play is the pressure that a community of friends and foes brings to bear on a man who can do no other but listen to the still, small voice of his conscience.

A Man for All Seasons is written with distinction. It combines in equal measure the dancing, ironic wit of detachment and the steady blue flame of commitment. With its commingling of literary grace, intellectual subtlety and human simplicity, it challenges the mind and, in the end, touches the heart. For it is not only about a man for all seasons but also about an aspiration for all time.

Mr. Bolt, a young English playwright, has written a chronicle play, using the fluid structure of the Elizabethan narratives and adding to it a chorus in the tradition of the Greek dramas. This chorus is The Common Man. It is his proposition that ''the sixteenth century is the century of the common man, as are all centuries.''

This Common Man, who serves at one time or another as servant, boatman, jailer, foreman of a jury and executioner, is an engaging rogue. Played with wonderful sharpness, humor and familiarity by George Rose, he is the shrewd, nimble comic fellow who knows how to adapt to his environment and look after himself. Not a bad fellow at heart, not even heedless, he is merely cautious. Who except the Sir Thomas Mores can cast the first atone at him?

Mr. Bolt sports with The Common Man, using him not only for sharp-witted, disenchanted comment but also for a helping hand with changes of scene. With Sir Thomas the author does not trifle. His steadfastness is rooted in wisdom, and his words are the warm, mellow, penetrating expression of a sad, knowing observer of the world and its ways.

By the standards of neatly plotted drama, there is a basic weakness in the conception of Sir Thomas. For when we meet him, years before his end, his character seems to be fixed in its perception and courage. As he moves down the inevitable road to destruction, the early traits are re-enforced. There is no fatal flaw in him.

But one feels that Mr. Bolt's intention is to use Sir Thomas More's fate as the gauge of man's desperate ever-renewing predicament. Mr. Bolt is not writing a tragedy in the conventional sense but recalling history with pungency, letting us draw whatever contemporary lessons we may. And he is careful to observe that there are many, that the cap may be worn where it fits. . . .

"We are dealing with an age less fastidious than ours," says one of Mr. Bolt's characters. Well, are we? This fine, meaty play will stir you and cause you to ask further questions of your own.

Source: Howard Taubman, "Drama Based on Life of Thomas More Opens" (1961) in *On Stage: Selected Theater Reviews from The New York Times, 1920–1970,* edited by Bernard Beckerman and Howard Siegman, Arno Press, 1973, pp. 439–41.

FURTHER READING

Alvarez, A. "The Price of Period" in British *New Statesman,* Vol. 60, July 9, 1960, p. 46.
    An early review of the original London stage play that calls the play a "historical romance," too "cozy" for real dramatic tragedy.

Atkins, Anselm. "Robert Bolt: Self, Shadow, and the Theater of Recognition" in *Modern Drama,* Vol. 10, September 1967, pp. 182-88.
    Atkins equates More with the Common Man, "a striking example of the coincidence of opposites," in that both of them live by the principle to preserve the self.

Brustein, Robert. "Chronicle of a Reluctant Hero" in the *New Republic,* Vol. 145, no. 24, December 11, 1961, pp. 280-30.

> MR. BOLT IS NOT WRITING A TRAGEDY IN THE CONVENTIONAL SENSE BUT RECALLING HISTORY WITH PUNGENCY"

A positive review of the New York play that sees Bolt's play as an effective model for the rebirth of the chronicle history.

Carper, Gerald Carper "Dramas of the Threatened Self" in *Video Classics of American Film,* September, 1989.
    A summary of Bolt's major works that demonstrates their common themes about "of the threatened self."

Duprey, Richard A. "Interview with Robert Bolt" in the *Dalhousie Review,* Vol. 48, Spring, 1968, pp. 13-23.
    Bolt explains his choice of More as a man in conflict over selfhood and sees two choices for modern man: accepting a world without moral standards or returning to Christian morals.

Fuegi, John. "Robert Bolt" in *Contemporary British Dramatists,* edited by James Vinson, St. James Press (London), 1973.
    An essay that identifies the two major influences on Bolt's work as Brecht and the cinema.

Gambill, Thomas C. *The Drama of Robert Bolt: A Critical Study,* Kent State University, 1982.
    A study of Bolt's plays as a representative of the drama of the "angry young men" and the influence of Bertolt Brecht.

Hayman, Ronald. *Robert Bolt,* Heinemann, 1969.
    A slim volume that includes an interview with Robert Bolt about his life, chapters critiquing six of his plays, and a follow-up interview in which Bolt responds to the play critiques.

McCarten, John. "The Reluctant Martyr" in the *New Yorker,* Vol. 37, no. 42, December 2, 1961, pp. 117-18.
    A positive review of the New York production praising Bolt realistic portrayal of More.

McElrath, Joseph R. "The Metaphoric Structure of *A Man for All Seasons* " in *Modern Drama,* Vol. 14, 1972, pp. 84-92.
    A detailed analysis of the metaphor of the sea and land that Bolt mentions in his Preface and that pervades the play.

Peachment, Chris. *London Times,* October 23, 1986.
    A retrospective view of Bolt's work that finds much of merit in it.

Simon, John. "Play Reviews: *A Man for All Seasons*" in *Theater Arts,* Vol. 46, no. 2, February, 1962, pp. 10-11.
    A favorable review suggesting that although the play is limited by attempting too much historical scope; it is "intelligent, pungent, and absorbing."

Tees, Arthur Thomas. "The Place of the Common Man: Robert Bolt: *A Man for All Seasons*" in the *University Review,* Vol. 36, October, 1969, pp. 67-71.

Tees describes the Common Man's function as foil to More. They are polar opposites in that while More is a "non-tragic hero" (having no fatal flaw), the Common Man is a "tragic non-hero."

Trewin, J. C. "Two Morality Playwrights: Robert Bolt and John Whiting" in *Experimental Drama,* edited by William A. Armstrong, Bell and Sons, 1963, pp. 103-27.

An analysis of Bolt's plays as successful studies of social conscience in the individual. Trewin likes the plays but calls Bolt's explanatory preface a distraction.

Tucker, M. J. "The More-Norfolk Connection" in *Moreana,* Vol. 33, 1972, pp. 5-13.

Tucker reveals that Bolt has distorted the role that the historical Duke of Norfolk played in More's demise and describes the relationship history shows they had.

Walker, John. "Top Playwrights" in the *Sunday Times Magazine,* November 26, 1978.

In this special edition devoted to British theater, Walker's essay groups fifty British playwrights under six categories, "wits and dandies," "traditionalists," "individualists," and so on.

SOURCES

Corrigan, Robert, editor. "Five Dramas of Selfhood" in *The New Theatre of Europe,* Dell, 1962, pp. 9-31

Taubman, Howard. Review of *A Man for All Seasons* in the *New York Times,* Vol. 23, November, 1961.

The Miracle Worker

WILLIAM GIBSON
1957

Initially written for television, *The Miracle Worker* by William Gibson first aired in 1957. After it was warmly received by television audiences, it was rewritten for the stage and opened on Broadway in 1959 at the Playhouse Theatre. Although some of the reviews were mixed, the audience response was very favorable and during its run the first production of *The Miracle Worker* rarely failed to fill the 1,000 seat theatre.

Drawing heavily from letters written by Anne Sullivan in 1887, as well as from Helen Keller's autobiography, William Gibson constructed a drama around the events that took place when Helen Keller and her teacher, Anne Sullivan, first met in the 1880s. The exchanges that take place in *The Miracle Worker* are all derived from factual events that Gibson has woven together to construct a fluid, emotionally real, depiction of the "miracle" Anne Sullivan was able to work: teaching Helen Keller language.

Audiences and critics alike were most drawn to *The Miracle Worker*'s honest and emotionally vivid portrayal of the relationship between Annie (as she is called in the play) and Helen. The actors' intense energy and commitment to truth in the scenes of physical struggle between Annie and Helen were held as the most memorable moments of the play when it first opened on Broadway. Audiences found the story of Annie's struggle to teach Helen language and her eventual success life affirming and

uplifting. Surrounding the major themes of change and transformation and language and meaning is basic integrity and emotional honesty. These two elements are the strongest reasons that *The Miracle Worker* is so popular among audiences and has been called an American Theatre classic.

AUTHOR BIOGRAPHY

William Gibson was born in the Bronx, New York, on November 13, 1914, the son of George Irving, a bank clerk, and Florence (Dore) Gibson. Gibson spent his childhood in New York City and eventually attended the City College of New York, where he studied from 1930 until 1932. After graduation, Gibson moved to Kansas, supporting himself as a piano teacher while pursuing his interest in theatre. It was in Topeka, Kansas, that Gibson had his earliest plays produced. Most of these early works were light comedies; two of them were later revised and restaged: *A Cry Of The Players* and *Dinny and the Witches,* both in 1948. Shortly after his time in Kansas, Gibson met a psychoanalyst named Margaret Brenman; the two were married on September 6, 1940, and eventually had two sons, Thomas and David.

Gibson's first major critical and popular success in New York was *Two for The Seesaw,* which opened on Broadway in 1958. He was praised for the play's brisk dialogue and the compassion with which he endowed the characters. However, it is Gibson's second Broadway production, *The Miracle Worker,* for which he is best known.

Gibson first became fascinated with Anne Sullivan and her triumph as Helen Keller's teacher while reading the letters that Anne Sullivan wrote in 1887 describing her experiences in the Keller household. It was these letters and also Nella Brady's biography, *Anne Sullivan Macy,* that inspired Gibson to write about Anne Sullivan's accomplishments. Gibson first attempted to write *The Miracle Worker* as a solo dance piece but wrote it as a television play for the series *Playhouse 90,* which was produced by CBS. After *The Miracle Worker* was warmly received when it aired on CBS on February 7, 1957, Gibson received offers to adapt it for stage and film. He decided to write it for the stage because he wished to have more artistic control over the production. Although it opened to mixed reviews, positive press and word-of-mouth led to *The Miracle Worker*'s success on Broadway.

The Miracle Worker was adapted as a feature-length film starring Anne Bancroft as Annie and Patty Duke as Helen in 1962, and was again produced for television in 1979 with Patty Duke playing the role of Annie and Melissa Gilbert as Helen.

After *The Miracle Worker,* Gibson continued to write for the theatre and became a member of the Dramatists Guild. However, after *Golden Boy* (1964), which was a musical adaptation of Clifford Odets's play of the same name, Gibson largely withdrew from the New York theatre scene. It was during this time in the 1960s and 1970s that he founded and became president of the Berkshire Theatre Festival in Stockbridge, Massachusetts. Gibson did return to the New York stage, however, during the 1980s; *The Monday after the Miracle,* his sequel to *The Miracle Worker* opened on Broadway on December 14, 1982, at the Eugene O'Neill Theatre. *The Monday after The Miracle* was a much darker piece than its predecessor and garnered poor reviews and attendance; it closed after a short run. *The Miracle Worker* continues to be Gibson's best known work and is the drama on which his reputation rests.

PLOT SUMMARY

Act One

The Miracle Worker is set in the 1880s and begins at the Keller home in Tuscumbia, Alabama. It is night, and three adults stand around the lamplit crib of the infant Helen Keller: her parents, Kate and Captain Arthur Keller, and a doctor. They are discussing a serious ailment which Helen has just barely survived. While the Captain sees the doctor out, Kate makes the horrifying discovery that because of the illness, the child can no longer see nor hear. The next scene introduces Helen's Aunt Ev and unsympathetic half-brother James, and reveals that in the five-and-a-half years since the first scene Helen has become a willful, feral child, indulged in everything because denial brings tantrums and no one knows how to teach her decent behavior. The Captain and Kate argue about Helen, he saying that after so many doctors have failed it is a waste of money to hire more, while she is unwilling to give up. The Captain relents, and a desperate inquiry leads eventually to "a suitable governess" from Boston, a young woman named Annie Sullivan.

The next scene shows Annie in Boston, preparing to leave the Perkins Institute for the Blind, where as a patient she moved from blindness to partial vision. She is 20, stubborn, humorous, and haunted by the loss of her younger brother, Jimmie, who died after they were separated at an orphanage. Arriving in Alabama, Annie is met at the station by Kate and the sarcastic James. Kate is apprehensive because of Annie's youth, but Annie assures her that youthful energy will help in the task ahead, and says she has another asset as well: "I've been blind." The women begin to warm to each other. Back at the Keller home, Annie irks the Captain by refusing to let him take her suitcase. She meets Helen, and immediately makes Helen understand that the suitcase is to go "up." Together, Annie and Helen get it upstairs to Annie's room while Kate, appreciating what she has just seen, placates the Captain. Upstairs, Annie teaches Helen to hand-spell "doll" and "cake" to get each, then is outsmarted when Helen hits her in the face with the doll and runs out the door, locking Annie in. Unable to find the key, Annie must be humiliatingly "rescued" with a ladder brought to her window. After dinner, Annie finds Helen at her favorite place, the water pump in the yard. Thinking she is alone, Helen brings forth the "vanished" bedroom key from her mouth and gleefully drops it down the well. Annie smiles, with "great respect, humor, and acceptance of challenge," and enters the house, leaving Helen alone as the lights dim to end Act One.

Act Two

As Act Two begins, Helen is spilling and breaking things in Annie's room. Annie, using sign language, stubbornly spells the name of each broken item into Helen's hand. Entering, Kate asks Annie if this has any meaning for Helen. Annie says it will have none until Helen understands what a word—a name—is. Asked why she then persists in the silent struggle, Annie shows her resilience and humor by replying, "I like to hear myself talk!" Alone that night, Annie experiences one of her frequent memory-trips back to the orphanage, the crones who made life there hateful, and her forced and final parting with her brother.

At breakfast, Helen's improper behavior (she runs about the table, placing her hands on the others' food) sparks a confrontation between the Captain—whose practice is to ignore Helen so that the family (mainly him) can converse—and Annie, who insists that all such indulgence of Helen must stop. Annie asks to be left alone with Helen. There follows the longest and most famous onstage fight

William Gibson

in American theatre, unresolved even after several scripted pages of battle because the lights change from the dining-room to the yard, where the family awaits the outcome. Eventually, Helen staggers from the house, bumps into her mother's knees, and clutches them. Then comes Annie, battered but smiling, to report her victory. Helen has eaten from her own plate. With a spoon. And folded her napkin.

The Captain, angry at Annie and her treatment of his daughter, wants to fire the young teacher but is persuaded by Kate and Aunt Ev to grant Annie's request to isolate herself and Helen in the garden house for an entire week. Annie's plan is to make Helen dependent upon her for everything, thus forcing Helen to communicate with her, thus opening the only way for her to truly become Helen's teacher. While the Kellers take Helen on a long drive so she won't know on returning that she is at home, the "Garden House" theatrically appears in the back yard before the eyes of the audience, through the use of lighting, props, and furniture. Helen throws a fit at being left alone with Annie, then subsides exhausted. She won't let Annie touch her, but Annie gets her curiosity by hand-spelling to a servant child, and communication is re-established. That done, Helen is put to bed, and a striking stage setting ends Act Two: each of the Kellers is picked out by a shaft of moonlight, listening as Annie sings a lullaby to the unhearing Helen.

Act Three

Act Three begins as the deadline for the end of the "Garden House" experiment approaches. Helen is clean and disciplined and has learned to hand-spell many words to get treats, but Annie frustratedly feels that she has accomplished little more than "fingergames—no meaning." Helen has gestures and concepts—she touches her cheek to signify her mother—but has yet to connect these with the movements of Annie's fingers in her palm. Annie begs for another week, but the Kellers, seeing the improvements but not the gap left to close, refuse. Annie insists on keeping Helen until six, the official deadline, but as the time dwindles we see the harrowing effect of the ordeal on Annie. Helen will not give or receive affection and shows no signs, even as Annie desperately spells more words into her hands, of moving past fingergames to the universe of language and communication. At the stroke of six, the Garden House disappears before our eyes, Kate claims Helen and carries her out of sight, and Annie, alone at the end of her struggle, remembers again the loss of Jimmie and repeats a line often heard in that connection, "God owes me a resurrection."

Returned to her family, Helen acts up at dinner, and the family indulges her despite their assurances to Annie that they would not. Helen throws a pitcher of water on Annie, and Annie grabs up Helen and the pitcher and stalks out, vowing to make Helen refill the pitcher. The Captain angrily rises to go out and fire Annie, but James, the sarcastic idler, shows he has understood Annie by going to the door and resolutely standing up to his father, who despite his anger is finally impressed with his son.

In the yard, Annie is forcing Helen to pump water, meanwhile spelling w-a-t-e-r into Helen's hand, and "Now," as Gibson says, "the miracle happens." Helen has the breakthrough Annie has prayed for, and runs around the yard touching, and learning from Annie the names of the pump, the stoop, the trellis, and more. Annie calls out, and the scene is joined by the Kellers, the servants, and their children. Helen learns to spell "Mother" and "Papa," and the family kneels to her in tears. Then Helen gropes her way across the yard to Annie, to learn what her "name" is. Annie spells it to Helen, who spells it back: "Teacher." Helen shows the depth of the miracle of her understanding by getting from her mother the keys Annie had used to lock her out or in, and bringing and giving them to Annie. The onlookers withdraw, leaving Annie and Helen alone onstage. Annie, who had sworn never to love again after the loss of Jimmie, spells into Helen's hand, "I love Helen," adding verbally her last words to Jimmie: "Forever and ever." Then she and Helen, hand in hand, cross the yard to go in to dinner.

CHARACTERS

Anagnos (ah-nah-nyose)

Anagnos, described by Gibson as "a stocky bearded man," is Annie's counselor at the Perkins Institution for the Blind. It is Anagnos who places Annie in the Kellers's home as a governess for Helen. He is loving and kindly with Annie, but he can also be stern when necessary.

Annie

See Anne Sullivan

Aunt Ev

Aunt Ev is described by Gibson as "a benign visitor" who serves as a catalyst for the Kellers's first contact with the Perkins Institute. Aunt Ev is a talkative woman who often tries to be helpful, but who can be a bit intrusive. She sometimes oversteps her place as a visitor in the Keller household and at one point even threatens to take matters into her own hands.

Blind Girls

The "Blind Girls," who range in age from 8 to 17 years old, are the girls at the Perkins Institution with whom Annie has the closest relationship. Together they are like sisters: excited, lively, and loving. The youngest of the girls has difficulty accepting Annie's departure to the Kellers. When Annie is leaving, it is the Blind Girls who give her the smoked glasses that became Annie's trademark. They also give Annie a doll to give to Helen.

Doctor

The doctor opens the play with Helen's parents, Kate and Arthur. He is an elderly man who provides comforting words to Helen's parents after their child has just come out of a high fever caused by what the Doctor calls "acute congestion of the stomach and brain."

Keller

See Captain Arthur Keller

Captain Arthur Keller

Captain Keller is referred to by Gibson as "a hearty gentleman in his forties" and throughout the play displays the greatest measure of doubt in Annie's ability to teach his daughter. Keller is a newspaper publisher who possesses much power, both in the business world and in his own home. Nothing is done and no decisions are made in the Keller household without his consent. When Annie first arrives on the scene, Keller is extremely skeptical of her abilities, especially because of her young age. He is also not used to Annie's forthrightness and considers her to be rude and unladylike. Throughout *The Miracle Worker* Annie fights the constant battle to win Captain Keller's acceptance in order to keep her job, but she does not win his respect until after she has worked her "miracle" with Helen.

Helen Keller

Helen, the recipient of the miracle that is worked in the play, is the six-and-a-half year old daughter of Kate and Arthur who is left deaf and blind after a serious illness as an infant. Her struggle to communicate and relate to the world around her necessitates the arrival of Annie to the Keller household. Despite her handicaps, Helen is a girl of exceptional intellect and cleverness, but it is her lack of restraint that leaves her thrashing around the world in which she lives without any focus or discipline. During the action of the play, the emphasis is mostly on Helen's battle of wills with Annie. Annie tries to get Helen to connect the hand symbols that she teaches her with the world around her. At the climax of the play, this connection is finally made with a substance that Helen remembers from a time in her infancy prior to her illness, namely water.

James Keller

James, Captain Keller's son from a previous marriage, is described by Gibson as "an indolent young man." James is often flippant and sarcastic, largely due to his inner turmoil. With all of the

Patty Duke as Helen Keller in the pivotal scene at the well

attention being paid to Helen and the baby, James is easily hurt and wears this hurt openly. When Annie arrives he is at first skeptical but eventually becomes one of her strongest supporters. This support reveals itself as important in Annie's struggle to prove to Captain Keller that she is a capable teacher.

Kate Keller

Defined at the play's beginning as "a young gentlewoman with a sweet girlish face," Kate Keller develops into a woman consumed with guilt over her daughter Helen's condition. She is patient and gentle with Helen, but when Annie arrives Kate must learn that it is sometimes necessary to use force while trying to teach her daughter. At first Kate has a difficult time letting Annie take control of Helen's discipline, but after witnessing Annie's success with Helen in two short weeks at the Keller household, Kate realizes that she must let go, relying upon her strength to help her do the best thing for her child.

Martha

Martha, a young African-American child, is playful and curious, and can also be a bit bossy,

MEDIA ADAPTATIONS

- *The Miracle Worker* was originally written for television and produced on CBS's *Playhouse 90* in February of 1957. Teresa Wright starred as Annie and Patty McCormack portrayed Helen.

- The film version of *The Miracle Worker* was produced in 1962 by Metro-Goldwyn-Mayer. It was adapted by Gibson himself, directed by Arthur Penn, and stars Anne Bancroft as Annie and Patty Duke as Helen—both leads in the original Broadway production of the play. The film is available on videocassette.

- The 1979 television remake of *The Miracle Worker,* which stars Patty Duke as the teacher Annie and Melissa Gilbert as Helen, is available on videocassette from Warner Home Video. The production bears noting, as the same script used for the original *Playhouse 90* production was used for this remake.

especially with Percy. In the scenes that she shares with Helen, Martha is both amazed and terrified by Helen's behavior.

Offstage Voices

The ''Offstage Voices'' in *The Miracle Worker* serve different functions at different times in the play, but they are always directly related to Annie and her struggle. One of the recurring voices is ''Boy's Voice,'' which is the voice of Annie's dead younger brother, Jimmie. This voice, along with the others, represents Annie's internal struggle with feelings of guilt, her motivation to succeed with Helen, and her will to continue living her own life.

Percy

Percy is a young African-American child who seems to be a bit younger than Martha. Although Percy is frightened of Helen, he becomes directly involved in Helen's education while he is staying in the garden house with Annie and Helen.

Servant

An African-American man who is a servant who helps with some of the heaviest labor around the Keller household. This servant has no lines in the play, and serves mainly to help change the set and move the large and weighty items that Viney, Percy, and Martha cannot move themselves.

Annie Sullivan

Annie Sullivan is the ''miracle worker'' to which the title of the play refers. She first appears while she is still at the Perkins Institution for the Blind, where she has lived as a pupil since she was a child. Everything that she has learned, including the sign language that she later uses with Helen, she has learned at Perkins. When Anagnos asks her to become Helen's governess, as requested by the Keller family, it is her first job. At the age of twenty, Annie takes her first step out of the Perkins Institution and into her adult life. From the first moment that she enters the Keller household, Annie is met with skepticism and doubt, mostly because of her young age and lack of experience. This, however, does not deter her from what she feels must be done. When Annie and Helen first meet, Helen is a spoiled child who, because of her family's pity, is allowed to do whatever she pleases. Annie's first challenge is simply to get her to respond to discipline. After that, her time is devoted to teaching Helen hand symbols in the hope that she will eventually connect them with the objects and people around her, and thus learn ''language.''

The other characters in the play also offer their own challenges to Annie. Captain Keller almost fires Annie because of what he calls her ''Yankee'' attitude, and they are constantly at odds with each other over the way that she treats Helen. It is only through clever manipulation that Annie is able to bide time until she can successfully prove herself to him. James Keller, in his usual sarcastic way, finds Annie's methods laughable at first, but he is eventually won over. Kate Keller also meets Annie with skepticism, but she is in such pain over Helen's condition that she is willing to let Annie have whatever she needs in order for Helen to have a better life.

The character who has the most direct effect on Annie throughout the play, however, is her own conscience, represented by the Offstage Voices. These voices represent Annie's past experiences and give her the motivation that she needs to succeed with Helen. Alone, these voices present the only direct threat to Annie's confidence and strong will. The most powerful of them all is the voice of her younger brother, Jimmie, whose death Annie blames on herself. Annie is not able to silence his voice until the end of the play, when the ''miracle'' finally happens and she clutches Helen to her promising to love her ''forever and ever,'' just as she once promised Jimmie.

Viney

Viney, an African-American woman, is a servant in charge of the daily housework and meals in the Keller household. She is cheerful, practical, and very adept at her job. Viney is also very loving and protective with the Keller children, and although Mildred, the Kellers's baby, is obviously her favorite, she appears to love Helen very much. It is difficult for Viney to know what to do with Helen and how to communicate with her.

THEMES

In simplest terms, *The Miracle Worker* is the story of how one person can enter the lives of others and change them forever. During the course of the play, Annie Sullivan enters the Keller household and through her work to teach Helen—who is deaf, mute, and blind—language, ends up changing all of the characters's perceptions of the world, as well as changing her own world-view. By the end of the play the ''miracle'' that she works, teaching Helen language, has a direct effect on everyone's life and the way in which they live it.

Change and Transformation

The first overriding theme of *The Miracle Worker* is that of change and transformation. The characters of the play very much want to change their lives but are unsure of the extent to which they are willing to transform themselves. When Annie first comes to the Keller household to help with Helen, the Kellers are desperate for any change in their relationship with Helen. Once Annie begins to take charge of the situation, however, she meets with resistance. Mr. Keller is unaccustomed to her brash manner and is reluctant to give her control of Helen, while Kate finds it difficult to watch someone else take charge

TOPICS FOR FURTHER STUDY

- Discuss the use of food and drink as significant parts of the action of *The Miracle Worker*.

- The end of *The Miracle Worker* has been described by some critics as ''too sentimental.'' Do you agree? What, then, does ''sentimental'' mean?

- Read *Two for the Seesaw*. What are the qualities of Anne Bancroft as an actress that would prompt directors to cast her as the heroine of two such different plays as *The Miracle Worker* and *Two for the Seesaw?*

- How many kinds of sign language are used in the U. S.? Research the methods of hand-spelling used with people who are both deaf and blind

of her daughter's discipline. Annie is a very stubborn woman who does not give up easily and is able to manipulate both parents into letting her have the chance to prove herself; however, she must fight tooth and nail for this privilege again and again throughout the course of the play.

Throughout the play small changes are made within the lives of the characters, but the true transformation does not occur until the climax of the play when the ''miracle'' takes place. It is when Helen finally connects the simple hand symbols that Annie has been teaching her with actual objects and people that everything else falls into place. Helen's is utterly changed as she rushes around asking Annie the names of different objects and people. Mr. Keller and Kate finally realize the significance of Annie's methods and are able to believe in what can be done. It is also during this last scene that Kate is finally, after a difficult struggle, able to give Helen to Annie. Gibson describes this in the play's stage directions as ''a moment in which [Kate] simultaneously finds and loses a child.'' Annie's transformation is complete when she can no longer hear the voices of her past haunting her; Annie then realizes that she can devote herself to loving and teaching Helen without and fear or doubt.

Language and Meaning

It is during the climactic scene at the end of Act Three that the second major theme, language and meaning, is resolved. The importance of language is first emphasized in an early scene between Kate and Annie, shortly after Annie's arrival. Kate begins by asking Annie what she plans to teach Helen and Annie answers, "First, last, and—in between, language. . . . Language is to the mind more than light is to the eye." Annie is actually quoting someone else's words at this point, but it is obvious that she realized the significance of it because she was once blind herself and has benefitted from the language that she has learned. The question for Annie is how and whether it is possible to teach Helen language and its meaning.

In the beginning, the work that Annie does with Helen is simply a matter of discipline and repetition. Annie must first struggle to control Helen's extremely strong will, which had never been challenged prior to Annie's arrival. Once Annie begins to have progress in this area she is able to begin teaching Helen hand symbols for different objects. The hand symbols, at first, are just a repetition game to Helen, who does not make any connection between symbol and object; Annie hopes that through this repetition Helen will eventually start to connect the symbols with actual objects in her world. Annie's doubts about whether this method will work, however, are strong and eventually Annie realizes that it is necessary for Helen to depend on her for everything; only then will Helen be motivated to use the symbols that Annie teaches her. Annie convinces the Kellers to give her complete control over Helen and she then uses every method from repetition to force to resentment to keep Helen interested in learning. Annie's methods hold Helen's interest, but Annie expresses her realization of their inadequacy when she tells Helen: "Now all I have to teach you is—one word. Everything."

The final connection between language and meaning does come, but not until it seems that all the work that Annie has been in vain. After living secluded in the garden house for two weeks with Helen and Percy, Annie has no choice but to let Helen go back to the Kellers. In a short scene at the dinner table, Helen begins to recede back into her old ways. Annie will have none of it, and in a final battle of wills with Helen over spilled water, she inadvertently helps Helen make that huge leap of connecting language to the world around her. In the triumphant scene at the water pump, Annie can finally exclaim about Helen that "She knows!" It is during this one scene that the themes of change and transformation and language and meaning come together in a demonstration of the power of love and determination and the strength of the human will.

STYLE

Flashback

The most striking aspect of the construction of *The Miracle Worker* is the style in which the play is written. Although realistic in tone, *The Miracle Worker* often makes use of cinematic shifts in time and space to illuminate the effect of the past on the present in a manner analogous to Arthur Miller's *Death Of A Salesman*. It is clear that Gibson was influenced by *Death Of A Salesman*, which was written in 1949, especially in terms of his use of flashback and stage space. The realistic tone of *The Miracle Worker* comes through in the dialogue, which is similar to the way that people talk to each other in real life. It is Gibson's use of flashback that brings about many of the cinematic shifts within the linear action of the play. The first of these flashback scenes occurs at the play's opening, when the audience learns how Helen Keller first became deaf and blind. The scene depicts the incident which sets the wheels in motion for the rest of the events in the play. Right after this scene, the audience is taken into "real" time and the action proceeds chronologically.

After this initial scene, the use of flashback in *The Miracle Worker* changes. Unlike *Death Of A Salesman*, in which the characters actually step into the past and play out scenes, Gibson uses offstage voices whenever he wants to set past events against the action of the present. Gibson uses this device solely with the main character, the miracle worker herself, Annie Sullivan. These voices from the past help the audience to understand why Annie does the things that she does while working with Helen in the Keller home. By using these voices, the audience is able to hear and see into Annie's mind. These moments are also the only time that the point of view of the play changes. Most of the time, as in most plays, the action unfolds before the audience's eyes as it happens and not through any particular character. However, in the flashback scenes in which Gibson uses offstage voices, the point of view changes because the audience is getting a glimpse of the past through the mind of Annie Sullivan.

Setting and Use of Space

The cinematic style that Gibson uses also can be seen with the setting of the play and the use of stage space. Gibson's use of stage space is also very similar to Arthur Miller's in *Death Of A Salesman*. Both playwrights establish a particular setting as a base for reality in their plays, in which only the basics are used. In *The Miracle Worker,* Gibson uses only the items that are actually used during the action of the play to establish the Kellers's home, such as the water pump and doors with locks. Anything that is not actually used by the characters in the play should only be suggested. Both playwrights use this particular technique so that the characters can enter into other areas of the play without having to do complicated set changes that would ruin the fluid motion of the play. As Gibson states in the script: "The convention of the staging is one of cutting through time and place, and its essential qualities are fluidity and spatial counterpoint." By using this convention, the audience is quickly taken from the Keller home to the Perkins Institution for the Blind, the train station, or the garden house, without disturbing the action of the play.

With the use of this staging convention, characters occupying different areas of the stage can affect one another. This can be seen early in the play when Annie is at the Perkins Institution where she is preparing to leave to go to the Keller home. In the scene, Annie is hearing the offstage voices of her past when Anagnos calls out her name, quickly bringing her back to the present. At this point, Annie answers him by calling out "Coming!" At the same moment, Kate, who is in the Keller home, catches the word "coming" and "stands half turned and attentive to it, almost as though hearing it." This is a prime example of how Gibson uses the space of the stage to bring worlds in the play together in order to show the effects that they have on each other. In production, the careful use of lighting helps to make these shifts in setting clear to the audience, as if a world is unfolding before their eyes instead of the action being interrupted for a change of set. This keeps the audience involved and helps to make them a part of the world of the play, which is similar to the way film directors use crossfades and other editing devices to manipulate their audience's attention.

Honesty

Although the cinematic style that Gibson uses in *The Miracle Worker* works very well, it is important to note that Gibson placed great importance on the play truthfulness. No matter what devices Gibson used in *The Miracle Worker,* honesty is apparent in his technique. Without honesty, whether dealing with the characters' relationships or the dramatic conflicts that arise in the action of the play, the audience will not connect with the play. It is due to the play's honesty that Gibson is able to use flashback, cinematic shifts, and other devices in order to inspire the audience and pull them into the world of Annie Sullivan and Helen Keller. The audience is able to believe in and care about what is happening in the world of the play because of the honesty with which Gibson endows every character and situation in *The Miracle Worker.*

HISTORICAL CONTEXT

Prejudice and Fear in America during the 1880s and 1950s

The Miracle Worker was written in the United States during the late 1950s, which was the beginning of a period of change in American society. The country had just witnessed the paranoia of the McCarthy hearings, during which many theatre artists were charged with participating in "un-American" activities, or simply accused of being Communists. The mid- to late 1950s also witnessed the beginning of the Civil Rights movement in the southern U.S., including in Alabama, where *The Miracle Worker* is set. In American theatre, audiences had seen the crumbling facade of the American dream in the plays of Tennessee Williams and Arthur Miller. All of these aspects are a part of *The Miracle Worker* in its form, origin, and focus.

Although the subject of *The Miracle Worker* is not the paranoia of possible Communist invasion or the civil rights of African Americans in the 1950s, both of these factor into an underlying theme of the play: prejudice and fear. In the play, the prejudice and fear that arise from misunderstanding are brought to light. The most obvious example of this is the way in which the Kellers treat Helen. They use Helen's handicap as a reason to treat her with pity and for their reluctance to discipline her. The Kellers's fear and ignorance of Helen's condition cause them

COMPARE
&
CONTRAST

- **1880s:** Alabama and the rest of the South just finished living through the period of Reconstruction (1865-77) which followed the Civil War. Southerners were suspicious of the North's methods and ideas, including rights for African Americans.

  1950s: Alabama attracts international attention as the birthplace of the Civil Rights Movement. The Southern Christian Leadership Conference (SCLC), led by Martin Luther King, Jr., helped the black community to mobilize and plan a strategy to realize their goals, which included desegregation and voting rights.

  Today: The United States government and much of American society has adapted to accommodate and promote the ideas of Martin Luther King, Jr. and the Civil Rights Movement. There are still some citizens, however, who choose to keep their racist and separatists beliefs even though the law does not support them. Subversive groups such as the Ku Klux Klan continue to exist and promote their message of hatred and division.

- **1880s:** African Americans in the South struggle to find their place in society. Most work as servants in the households of the wealthy white families.

  1950s: The practice of segregation led to little opportunity for African Americans to receive higher education and advance to well-paying careers.

  Today: African Americans hold positions at all levels of business in the U.S. Nevertheless, racism continues to be a problem in American society. Great steps have been taken since the dawning of the Civil Rights Movement, but much is left to be done to lessen the racial problems in the United States.

- **1880s:** Sign language, like the hand symbols that Annie uses in *The Miracle Worker*, is introduced to American society. It is met with strong resistance and nongesticulating schools continue to hold prominence.

  1950s: The invention of the tellatouch enables a sighted caller to communicate with a deaf-blind person who can read braille.

  Today: More technological advances continue to be developed to help the visually and hearing impaired communicate effectively within a hearing and sighted society.

- **1880s:** Almshouses or asylums are used to house America's outcasts and disabled where they are used for forced labor to help defray maintenance costs. The Perkins Institution for the Blind (founded by Dr. Samuel Gridley Howe in 1832) continues to offer an alternative to asylums, as well as teaching the visually and hearing impaired.

  1950s: Blind and deaf students attend public schools with non-disabled students. Special day and residential schools are also common and continue to receive funding to help meet the needs of deaf and blind students as well as their teachers.

  Today: The Americans with Disabilities Act was passed in 1990 to address the needs of the disabled, from education and employment to telecommunications and public services.

---

to underestimate Helen's intelligence, and allow them to treat her like an animal.

Prejudice is also clearly present in the relationships that Captain Keller has with Annie and Viney. *The Miracle Worker* is set in the southern U.S. in the 1880s, shortly after the Reconstruction following the Civil War. During this period, the South resented the North's methods and ideas, especially those concerning the treatment and rights of former slaves. This view is dramatized in the play with the relationship Captain Keller has with Viney; he is very short with Viney, and does not appreciate when she offers her opinion of the changing circumstances in the Keller household after Annie's arrival. Viney displays a fear of Captain Keller and is unsure of her place in their relationship. The suspicion and resentment of the North by the South is seen in *The Miracle Worker* with the arrival of Annie, who is from the North and her relationship with Captain Keller. From the beginning, Captain Keller establishes himself as a man of the South while he is discussing the Battle of Vicksburg with his son James during Annie's first breakfast with the Kellers. The Battle of Vicksburg lasted for 47 days and ended with the victory of the North, led by Ulysses S. Grant, on July 4, 1863. Grant became famous for his ruthless determination during this Civil War battle and Captain Keller later compares Annie's stubbornness with Grant's. Captain Keller's prejudice and resentment can be seen in his remarks about Grant's drunkenness; therefore, his comparison of Annie and Grant can be construed as negative. Captain Keller is also fearful of Annie's methods because of her young age and the fact that she herself is virtually blind. In these examples, Gibson is displaying deeply rooted prejudices common among many Americans.

American Theatre in the 1950s

During the 1950s, the American theatre saw many plays dealing with the problems of American society and the disenchantment that people sometimes experienced while trying to pursue the "American Dream." Arthur Miller's *Death Of A Salesman* (1949) is often considered a modern tragedy because of the depth of one simple man's struggle in American society. This play in particular had an effect upon the theatre structure and form of *The Miracle Worker*. In his play, Gibson uses flashback and past events to punctuate the action that is unfolding on stage in "real" time, as the audience is watching. Other artistic trends such as the use of psychological truth as a basis for the characters' conflicts and motivation were seen in plays like Tennessee Williams's *A Streetcar Named Desire* (1947). Gibson follows this trend as well in his use of offstage voices in *The Miracle Worker,* which represent Annie's subconscious and give her the motivation to do the difficult things that she does. By the end of the 1950s, however, these trends began to fade away as plays began to take nonrealistic and existential paths; an example of which is *Waiting For Godot* by Samuel Beckett.

The late 1950s were a difficult time in the U.S. for many people. Fear and prejudice were relevant themes in many aspects of American life, especially in the South. Some people were reluctant to change and desperately tried to hold on to their idea of American society, while others around them cried out for their own place in the world while expressing their views of what American society should be. Eventually, many Americans allowed change to enter their lives and like the Kellers in *The Miracle Worker* learned and grew together in the process.

CRITICAL OVERVIEW

When *The Miracle Worker* first opened on Broadway on October 19, 1959, it was an instant popular success. Despite mixed reviews from the press, it had no trouble attracting 1,000 theatergoers a night during the length of its run. *The Miracle Worker* was William Gibson's second play to be produced on Broadway, and because of its success with the public, it is also the play for which he is best known and the one on which his reputation as a playwright rests.

The positive critiques of *The Miracle Worker* focus mostly on Gibson's honest and unsentimental treatment of the relationship between Helen and Annie. Gibson is praised for the wit and humor that he brings to the situation, and for the emotional purity with which he endows the struggle to bring Helen into the world around her by teaching her language. Much has been written about the acting out of the play's youthfulness and vigor by Anne Bancroft, who played Annie Sullivan, and Patty Duke, who played Helen Keller. Both of these actors were praised for the concentration, stamina, and passion that they brought to the play, especially during the now famous struggle between the two of them in the dining room. Next to the climactic scene by the water pump at the end of the play, this scene in the dining room is the one that critics and theatergoers remember most vividly. The pure, raw emotional energy of this moment in the play can, as critic Richard A. Duprey maintained, "work marvelous things in the soul." It is this emotional connection with the audience that kept the play well attended during its Broadway run and is largely why it continues to be produced today.

Most of the negative criticism that *The Miracle Worker* received was concerning the structure of the play itself. Critics expressed that what was characterized as an uneven and clumsy structure was a result of the play's adaptation from a television script. Some critics went as far as to say that Gibson sometimes confuses playwriting with psychological counseling and although emotionally rewarding, *The Miracle Worker* is a less than perfect drama. Gibson's use of offstage voices came under fire from some critics as well. These criticisms of the structure of the play, however, never seem to come without praise of other areas of Gibson's talent. In Richard Hayes's review of *The Miracle Worker* in *Commonweal,* he praised the play's ''affirmations of the human spirit,'' but declared: ''One recognizes the content of the moment, of the experience, but is released into nothing else: essentially, it is a *fact* to which one has responded. That the fact may be a gratifying demonstration of human worth is, in itself, aesthetically irrelevant.'' Other critics echoed Hayes's sentiments, arguing that although it offers an emotionally satisfying night of theatre, *The Miracle Worker* does little to further the artistic development of drama as a genre.

Overall, the popular success and positive criticism of *The Miracle Worker* have continued to eclipse the negative criticism that it has received, and have helped establish its reputation as a classic American play and one of the most life-affirming dramatic works to come out of the 1950s. Robert Brustein summed up Gibson's positive reputation when he observed in the *New Republic* that ''Gibson possesses substantial literary and dramatic gifts and an integrity of the highest order. In addition, he brings to his works authentic compassion, wit, bite and humor, and a lively, literate prose style equaled by few American dramatists.''

CRITICISM

Stephen Coy

Coy is a retired educator who has continued his instruction of drama with numerous contributions to textbooks and journals. In this essay he proposes that a reader/viewer can obtain an excellent overview of Gibson's theatrical skills by reading/seeing The Miracle Worker.

William Gibson has published fiction, poetry, plays, and autobiography, but he is best known for two stage works: *Two for the Seesaw,* a successful comedy-drama produced on Broadway in 1958; and *The Miracle Worker,* a classic American play—and later a popular television play and film.

Though not ranked alongside Eugene O'Neill, Arthur Miller, and Tennessee Williams, Gibson has carved an impressive niche for himself and will not be overlooked by history. The distinguishing features of his work are an uninhibited combination of humor and seriousness, often with a touching emotional effect; an elegance of style which resides not in fancy language but in a fine-tuned sense of the absolutely appropriate word or gesture; a flexibility of approach which permits him to move from solid realism to an almost Shakespearean use of the stage's capabilities; and a notable skill in orchestrating dialogue, actor movement, sound, and especially lights to produce effective theatrical moments.

Some of these aspects of Gibson's ability will become apparent in this analysis. But all of his skills, and some of his weaknesses, can be seen better by reading the entire text of *The Miracle Worker*—and best by seeing a decent stage production.

The Miracle Worker is certainly Gibson's best known and most widely-produced drama. What is not commonly known is that the play was originally created as a drama for television: it first appeared on *Playhouse 90* on February 7, 1957, with Teresa Wright as Annie Sullivan and Patty McCormack (known for her role in the Broadway play *The Bad Seed*) as Helen Keller. The stage version, with Patty Duke as Helen and Anne Bancroft as Annie, began its Broadway run in 1959. The story next became a motion picture, adapted by Gibson and directed by Arthur Penn. The film won Academy Awards for Bancroft as best actress and Duke for best supporting actress, as well as nominations for Gibson, Penn, and Costumer Ruth Morley. Completing a circle more odd than vicious, *The Miracle Worker* resurfaced as a television feature production in 1979. The chief reason for this revival was apparently to give Patty Duke, now a grown woman, a turn on the other end of the seesaw: she played Annie to the Helen of Melissa Gilbert, who is best known for her role on the television series *Little House on the Prairie.*

The Miracle Worker is a well-titled play. It tells part of the story of Helen Keller, who, though blind and deaf from childhood, became a noted writer, public figure, and source of inspiration for many people. However, the title refers not to Helen and her miracles—they are still in the future when the play ends—but to her teacher, Annie Sullivan. The story concerns the first year in the professional life of Annie (formerly blind herself but partially cured through many operations before she was out of her teens) and her extraordinary efforts in one short year to make a teachable child out of the utterly spoiled, crafty animal that Helen had become.

The play is based on real lives, and Gibson feels strongly that the necessary "shaping" of the material for the stage must not interfere with its basic truth or reality. He cites biographies of Helen Keller and Anne Sullivan Macy in his foreword to the play, and says, "The main incidents of the play are factual: I have invented almost nothing of Helen's, or of what passes between her and Annie, though often I have brought together incidents separated in time."

Space too is telescoped in the play. Gibson describes the stage as being divided into two areas by a diagonal line. The area upstage of this line is on raised platforms and always represents the Keller house; inside we see, down right, a family room, and up center, elevated, a bedroom. The downstage area is neutral ground; when not simply the yard of the Keller home, it "becomes" various places at various times—The Perkins Institute for the Blind in Boston, the Garden House, and so forth. In this downstage area, near center stage, is a water pump. Readers interested in stage design will recognize the similarity of this arrangement to that of Miller's *Death of a Salesman,* with the Loman household on levels upstage and the downstage area serving as back yard, offices, a restaurant, and other venues of the play. A paradoxical concept of staging—one area stays reliably the same, the other is fluid—was becoming acceptable to American audiences. It should particularly be noted that Gibson has placed the water pump near the center of the entire stage area, reflecting the fact that the pump, Helen's favorite spot and the place where the most crucial dramatic moment of the play occurs, is central to the play itself.

Movement in time and space onstage is accomplished by the use of properties and set pieces (the Garden House where Annie isolates herself with Helen is assembled onstage before the eyes of the audience), by the movements of the actors, and by changes in the lighting. How Gibson unites these theatrical tools shows the confidence and control of his craftsmanship: in one remarkable sequence, the audience is taken, in a few seconds of stage time, from a crowded farewell party for Annie in Boston

WHAT DO I READ NEXT?

- *The Story of My Life,* by Helen Keller. Learn what this miracle worker accomplished.

- *Anne Sullivan Macy,* by Nella Brady. A fascinating account of Sullivan's life, and an examination of what happens to a life that climaxes at the age of twenty-one.

- *The Seesaw Log,* by William Gibson. This the author's own account of the entire process of getting *Two for the Seesaw* produced on Broadway. There is not to be found a funnier or more truthful book about the farce, the frustrations, and the sheer lunacy of big-time commercial play production.

- *The Joy of Signing,* by Lottie L. Riekehof. An illustrated guide to sign language that provides a working understanding of the language of the deaf.

to a solitary moment in which Annie hears, from the past, the voice of the younger brother from whom she was tearfully separated at an orphanage, to a voice summoning her for departure, to the sounds of train travel, to the Keller home where Annie is awaited. Technically, these rapid changes may seem like mere film editing, but the special quality of the stage for these transitions—its specifically spatial counterpoint—is seen when Annie starts into her painful memory as the party laughter recedes; and when Annie answers, "Coming!" to the voice summoning her for the train—and Helen's mother Kate, "far away" in Alabama, "stands half turned and attentive to (Annie's voice), almost as if hearing it."

The essential conflict in *The Miracle Worker* is between Annie and Helen, with Annie trying her every resource—humor, patience, cruelty, kindness, and above all perseverance—to make Helen communicative enough so that the teaching process can, in earnest, begin. But while that conflict is the core of the play, there are important secondary conflicts. Helen's father has given up on the child, while her mother, Kate, refuses to do so. Of doctors trying to treat Helen, the Captain says:

> KELLER: Katie, how many times can you let them break your heart?
>
> KATE: Any number of times.

Kate's attitude makes her an ally of Annie's, and she often intervenes to prevent Keller from firing the upstart Irish girl. But the Captain is completely authoritarian, and Annie's high-handed ways with the entire household regarding their treatment of Helen—no more being "bountiful at her expense"—leaves him angry and unaccepting for most of the play. If trying to reach Helen is the ultimate test of Annie's native wit, guile, and stamina, then her confrontations with the Captain are the test of her integrity and her faith in her methods; for it is because of her thorny refusal to budge from her standards that she is threatened with the loss of her job and her pupil.

A more subtle problem surfaces between Kate and Annie. In making Helen totally dependent upon her as the conduit of all communication, particularly during the period in which the two are completely isolated in the Garden House, Annie inevitably puts herself in the position of mother to the child. This change makes the women not antagonists but simply uncertain about how to behave. This is seen poignantly near the end of the play, when Helen makes her first real breakthrough. Just as the struggle appears lost, Helen starts to work the pump in the Keller yard and the "miracle"—her mind learning to name things—happens as she feels the water and the wet ground. Annie and the others realize what is happening as Helen, possessed, runs about touching things and learning their names, finally, to her parents' great joy, the words "Mother" and "Papa." The frenzy slows as Helen realizes there is something she needs to know, gets Annie to spell it for her, and spells it back. It is the one word which more than any other describes the subject of *The Miracle Worker:* "Teacher."

But Annie's discomfort is not yet banished. As Helen's parents fall to their knees to embrace her, Annie "steps unsteadily back to watch the three-some" in their family-shared joy and wonder. The pain of Annie's loss of her brother Jimmie, present in recurrent memories throughout the play, had led her to say that she could never love another human being and that God owes her a resurrection. In reaching Helen, she finds that she is capable of love. But it is not clear whether the resurrection is of Annie, restored to full humanity, or of Jimmie, since

Annie now sees Helen as a sister rather than a daughter, conveniently removing Annie as a kind of mother-competitor to Kate. The play ends with Annie saying to Helen, as she used to say to Jimmie, that she loves her "forever and ever." She says this as the two are the last to leave the stage, and it is a moment of intense emotional power.

Powerful as it is, this ending reflects one of the weaknesses of Gibson as a playwright: he has often been accused, and not without justice, of excessive sentimentality. There are critics who feel that the basic material and conflicts of *The Miracle Worker* are themselves so powerful that the addition of poor, pathetic Jimmie, whose offstage whimperings we hear (through Annie's memory) many times during the play, is a sort of emotional overkill. Helen's breakthroughs at the end of the play are intensely moving, and together with Annie's discovery that she can, at last and indeed, love Helen, they are enough to render unnecessary the emotional baggage of Jimmie's "presence" in the play. It must be said in fairness, however, that many critics, honoring the indisputable power of the play, do not find it over sentimental.

There is one other aspect of the play which may keep it, not in reading but in terms of actual production, from realizing its full potential. It suffers from what might be called the "Lear Syndrome." The actor John Gielgud is supposed to have said that if you are young enough to play the demanding title role in William Shakespeare's *King Lear,* you are not old enough to understand it, and vice versa. The part of Helen simply cannot be played by most child actresses: any girl young enough to play Helen at six is unlikely to understand the character except shallowly; and any child actress who can understand Helen, and go convincingly from savagery to lovability, is likely to be not only intelligent but very willful and nearly impossible to direct. This may sound trivial, and is certainly not a criticism of the play as literature. But we remind ourselves that plays are created to be performed first (and read secondarily) and that anything which hurts their possibilities for production must be recognized.

Whatever Gibson's (debatable) weaknesses as a playwright, they are overshadowed by his virtues: skillful characterization, psychological sensitivity, humor, strong dramatic conflicts, and a craftsman's control of the working tools of theatrical production.

Source: Stephen Coy, in an essay for *Drama for Students,* Gale, 1997.

Walter Kerr

In this excerpt, Kerr praises Gibson's skill in telling an emotionally gripping story while avoiding the pitfalls of melodrama.

Kerr is an American dramatist, director, and critic who won a Pulitzer Prize for drama criticism in 1978.

If it is sometimes difficult to make ugliness palatable, it is even more difficult to make goodness persuasive.

All audiences love to have their emotions stirred in the theater, and all audiences hate to have their emotions stirred too easily. The greatest danger author William Gibson faced in telling the story of Helen Keller in *The Miracle Worker* was that of arousing the quick, instinctive resentment of people who might come to feel that they had opened their hearts to a setup.

The materials for too many tears, too easily drawn, were there. The child Helen Keller, deaf, dumb, and blind, was at once an object of pity. We were apt to be on guard, determined not to surrender our compassion too swiftly, when we met her. Annie Sullivan, her twenty-year-old nurse and teacher, invited very nearly the same obvious sympathy: she was orphaned, unlettered, the victim of haft a dozen operations on her own eyes. The spectacle of these two misfits, cut off from the kindness of the rest of the world and from each other as well, moving in sorry circles toward a moment of communication that might never come, was in one sense irresistible; in another sense it was the very sort of patent bid for pathos that generally causes us to set our jaws, stiffen our backs, and defy The Little Match Girl herself to make us cry.

Mr. Gibson won our consent to the harrowing adventure, and then our open surrender to the full-throated chords it dared to sound, by one right stroke of craftsmanship. He did not deal tenderly with images that were already rich in wistful appeal. He dealt roughly with them.

The most direct question posed during the earlier stages of the evening, as a harassed family tried to cope with the small inarticulate monster that moved among them, was spoken by one of Helen Keller's parents to the other.

''Do you like her?'' was the question. It was not answered, though the silence, of course, constituted an answer in itself. Love, perhaps, was possible, in some dim maternal way, for the pale, spastic crea-

A scene from the 1979 television movie

ture whose fingers went flying like thousand-leggers over the faces around her, searching out frantic identifications. But honesty forbade the pretense of liking. Patty Duke played the near-animal who crawled like a frightened crab across an Alabama front yard to hurl a stolen key into a well and then pound herself fiercely on the head as a sign of secretive delight. And she played with a taut mouth drawn back from defiant teeth, with hands that were quicker to strike than they were to receive caresses, with a directionless energy that was doubled by a despair she could not understand.

Nor was any sentiment wasted on the problems Anne Bancroft faced when, as the inexperienced Annie Sullivan, she settled down to the task of breaking a fierce, unintelligent will. ''A siege is a siege'' said this indestructible battering-ram, rolling up her sleeves and lunging at the locked fortress with a ferocity that might have distressed Attila. There was a long pantomime passage in the middle of the second act during which Miss Bancroft was determined that Miss Duke would eat her dinner, eat it with a spoon, and thereafter fold her napkin. Miss Duke was ready to kick, scratch, bite, tear chairs to splinters and the tablecloth to rags before any such eventualities took place. No known holds were barred, no shreds of flesh spared; the sounds were

> THE GREATEST DANGER AUTHOR WILLIAM GIBSON FACED IN TELLING THE STORY OF HELEN KELLER IN *THE MIRACLE WORKER* WAS THAT OF AROUSING THE QUICK, INSTINCTIVE RESENTMENT OF PEOPLE WHO MIGHT COME TO FEEL THAT THEY HAD OPENED THEIR HEARTS TO A SETUP"

the sounds of bodies grunting under impact and of furniture cracking under assault; two naked wills wound up on their knees, like dogs panting twice before moving in to the kill; the holocaust was total, not merely physical but spiritual.

When it was over, Miss Bancroft quietly reported to the waiting parents, ''The room's a wreck but her napkin is folded.'' And there was almost more strength in the quiet statement than there had been in the desperate donnybrook. Miss Bancroft's command of her own powers was absolute; and when she touched us she did it not by begging but by the assertion of a rigid, almost brutal, rectitude.

Certain questions of art may be raised about play and production. Should Mr. Gibson have carried along with him, from the television original, a subjective sound track native to another medium? Hadn't he compromised his own honesty by casting six children who were actually blind in one very short sequence in order to introduce, through their attractiveness, an appeal that had nothing to do with the quality of his writing? Had he drawn too steadily not on what was pathetic in his materials but on what was artificially dramatic around them, stretching some of his family tensions beyond the point of profitable return? I think he may have done all of these things, though without essential damage to what was, and is, essentially important: the excitement of watching a mind wrenched, by main force, into being.

Source: Walter Kerr, *The Miracle Worker,* in his *The Theater in Spite of Itself,* Simon & Schuster (New York), 1963, pp. 255–57.

Robert Brustein

In this essay, Brustein analyzes The Miracle Worker *and Gibson's motivations for writing the play.*

Brustein is an American drama critic and the artistic director of the American Repertory Theater Company.

Near the conclusion of *Two for the Seesaw,* the rambunctious street urchin, Gittel Mosca, is gently informed that ''after the verb to love, to help is the sweetest in the tongue.'' William Gibson, setting aside more serious concerns to anatomize the sweeter, softer virtues, has thus far dedicated his dramatic career to the definition and conjugation of these two verbs.

For, like the play which preceded it, *The Miracle Worker*—written with the same wit and mounted with equal competence—is essentially a two-character work about the relationship of kindness to love. The time has been set back to the 1880's, the seesaw has been freighted from New York to Alabama, and precariously balanced upon it now are an afflicted child and a 20-year-old Irish girl from Boston; yet, the two plays are clearly lifted from the same trunk. In outline, both works are about the redemption and education of a helpless little ragamuffin by a more experienced, vaguely guilty mentor which results in a mutual strengthening of character. Here the ragamuffin is not a Jewish dancer from the Bronx, but the child Helen Keller, while the helping hand belongs not to the disconsolate divorce, Jerry Ryan, but to Helen's gifted teacher, Annie Sullivan. On the other hand, everybody's motivation remains constant. Annie's conscience-pangs over her desertion of her dying brother, for example, recall Jerry's uneasiness over his desertion of his wife, and both expiate their guilt through ''help,'' unswerving dedication to the welfare of another. To press the parallel further, both plays rely excessively on extra-dramatic devices: *Two for the Seesaw* on a persistently clanging telephone, *The Miracle Worker* on a garrulous loudspeaker. And, despite the excellence of the writing, both plays impress me less as dramas of conflict than as socio-psychological essays on the subject of interpersonal relations.

The Miracle Worker documents a historical occurrence: Helen Keller's transformation from a hopelessly untidy, aggressive, isolated, willful animal, possessed only with a sense of touch, into a disciplined, well-groomed human being about to enter the world of languages. The factual story contains only two disclosures of a dramatic nature. Since one of them (that Helen has become deaf and blind from an infant disease) is expended in the opening moments, the bulk of the play consists of Gibson's filler. Some of this filler is purely theatrical: Helen and Annie engage in what are surely the most epic brawls ever staged-in the course of these highly entertaining improvisations, ink is eaten, food is spit, faces are slapped, plates are broken, water is thrown, and general havoc prevails. Some filler is designed for edification: Annie lectures Helen's parents on the dangers of permissive child-rearing (Helen has been badly spoiled), and, in an ill-defined subplot, a cowardly son learns at last to command the love and respect of his stern father by asserting himself. It is Gibson's penchant for instructing his characters in "mature" behavior which disturbs me most. In common with most playwrights of the modern school, love operates in his plays with all the intensity of an ideology, and the only development his people are permitted is a more accurate apprehension of the proper way to show affection.

In consequence, no event occurs in *The Miracle Worker* which is not somehow identified with love. Take the last scene, the other factual disclosure of the story and the "miracle" towards which everything moves. From history, we know that Helen Keller suddenly made the connection between words and things essential for learning language while pumping water from a well. On the stage, this discovery issues in a perfect orgy of embraces. The child pumps the water, grunts out the word, scurries back and forth along the length of the stage, rings a bell wildly, embraces her mother, kisses her once cold, now loving father, and finally offers her love to Annie whom she has hated throughout the action. As for Annie, finally permitted to express the affection she has purposely withheld, she spells out on the child's hand, "I love Helen . . . forever and ever," and the curtain descends.

What is one to say about this? Mr. Gibson's motives are undoubtedly impeccable, his heart is rooted in the proper place, and, though he dances on the edge of Sentiment's soggy slough, he rarely falls in. In its homiletic genre, the play is solid species, and it has been given an admirable production. Arthur Penn has conducted the action with spontaneity, truth, and flow; George Jenkins has provided a functional, multi-story set; and the acting-in a season plagued by miscasting-is all fine, particularly by Anne Bancroft, now a top notch comic-pathetic actress with a mime's expert control of her

> "MR. GIBSON'S MOTIVES ARE UNDOUBTEDLY IMPECCABLE, HIS HEART IS ROOTED IN THE PROPER PLACE, AND, THOUGH HE DANCES ON THE EDGE OF SENTIMENT'S SOGGY SLOUGH, HE RARELY FALLS IN"

neck, hands, and facial muscles, and by Patty Duke, a sniffing, sniveling, staggering, moaning Helen who can transform a well-ordered room into Hiroshima in a matter of seconds. But I am afraid I am churlish enough not to respond very strongly to Human Documents, or Testaments to the Human Spirit, or even to Profound Convictions that Man will Endure and Prevail, unless they are accompanied by a good deal more grit, a good deal more mystery, and a great deal more information about the dark places of human motivation than we are given here.

I say this with regret because, although his craft is still a little shaky, Gibson possesses substantial literary and dramatic gifts, and an integrity of the highest order. In addition, he brings to his works authentic compassion, wit, bite, and humor, and a lively, literate prose style equalled by few American dramatists. (Annie's moving tribute to words, while appropriate for a character concerned with communication, is clearly a reflection of Gibson's own love affair with the English language.) Since Gibson is one of a handful of theater writers who does not have to apologize for his dialogue, he can afford a faithful production which does not have to apologize for the play.

But his weakness for inspirational themes, if not suppressed, will inevitably doom him to the second rank. That Gibson has intelligence, tough-mindedness, and a capacity for indignation, nobody who reads *The Seesaw Log* will deny, but his dramas persistently follow the safer, more familiar road of routine wisdom and spiritual uplift. Like most dramatists of his generation, Gibson confuses playwriting with psychological counseling; unlike most of them, he is capable of much more. His potential is large but it will never be fulfilled until he can find more compelling sources for his view of man than the cheery chapbooks of Horney and Fromm, until he can examine the more dangerous truths which lie beneath the comforting surface of the skin.

Source: Robert Brustein, "Two for the Miracle," in the *New Republic,* November 9, 1959, pp. 28–29.

FURTHER READING

Atkinson, Brooks. "*Miracle Worker:* Two Strong Minds and Two Strong Players" in the *New York Times,* November 1, 1959, p. 1.
>A favorable review of the play's Broadway premiere. Atkinson finds favor with both Gibson's material and the performances of the lead actresses.

Contemporary Literary Criticism, Volume 23, Gale, 1983.
>Provides an overview of Gibson's work, providing criticism on a number of his plays, including *The Miracle Worker.*

Dictionary of Literary Biography, Volume 7: *Twentieth Century American Dramatists,* Gale, 1981.
>An overview of Gibson's career, with insights into a number of his works.

Tynan, Kenneth. "Ireland Unvanquished" in the *New Yorker,* Vol. XXXV, no. 37, October 31, 1959, pp. 131-36.
>A mixed review of *The Miracle Worker* that ultimately finds the play somewhat exploitive.

SOURCES

Brustein, Robert. "Two for the Miracle," in *The New Republic,* Vol. 144, no. 19, November 9, 1959, pp. 28-29.

Duprey, Richard A. "An Enema for the People" in his *Just Off the Aisle: The Ramblings of a Catholic Critic,* Newman Press, 1962, pp. 135-46.

Hayes, Richard. "Images" in *Commonweal,* Vol. LXXI, no. 10, December 4, 1959, p. 289.

The Mousetrap

AGATHA CHRISTIE
1952

The Mousetrap was initially performed as a radio play in 1952 and was broadcast by the BBC with the title *Three Blind Mice.* The radio play had been commissioned in 1947 by Queen Mary, who was a Christie fan. The forty-five minute play was based on a short story on which Christie had been working; however, audience reaction was so positive that Christie went back to work on the script, elaborating on it, and with its first performance on October 6, 1952, *The Mousetrap* became a stage play. After a seven-week tour, the play opened in London at The Ambassadors Theatre on November 25, 1952. The play later transferred to St. Martin's Theatre in London on March 23, 1974 and has been running there ever since. *The Mousetrap* has broken several records for its continuous theatrical run since its opening, and it is estimated that more than four million people had seen the play by the time its twenty-five year anniversary was celebrated in 1977. After another twenty years of performances it is safe to speculate that an additional three to four million people have probably sat in the dark and tried to puzzle out the identity of the murderer. Performances of *The Mousetrap* continue to benefit from tourists who seek out the play both for its artistic merits and for the joy of being part of a theatrical tradition. Christie signed over the royalties from the play to her grandson at its opening in 1952. It is thought that he has become a multi-millionaire from the royalties of this one property alone.

AUTHOR BIOGRAPHY

Agatha Mary Clarissa Christie also wrote as Agatha Christie Mallowan and under the pseudonym Mary Westmacott. Christie was born September 15, 1890, in the seaside resort town of Torquay, Devon. She was educated at home by her mother until age sixteen and later studied piano and voice in Paris. Christie was an avid reader who knew by the time she was a teenager that she wanted to be a writer, but it took a dare from her sister to force Christie into writing her first novel. *The Mysterious Affair at Styles* was published in 1920 and sold only a few thousand copies, but the novel's publication and the seventy dollars that Christie earned was enough to encourage her writing. For the next half dozen years Christie wrote steadily, turning out novels and building a readership among enthusiastic mystery buffs. But it was the publication of *The Murder of Roger Ackroyd* in 1926 that caught the attention of the reading public. Although Christie's plots had always been unfailingly clever and well-constructed, this newest novel created a murderer who was so far above suspicion and required such analytical skill to solve that Christie's popularity as a mystery writer and novelist was immediately assured.

Christie's novels have introduced such timeless and popular detectives as the Belgian Hercule Poirot; the genteel, elderly Miss Jane Marple, and the adventurous and lucky couple Tommy and Tuppence Beresford. Among the best known Hercule Poirot novels are *Murder on the Orient Express*(1934), *The A.B.C. Murders* (1936), and *Death on the Nile* (1937). The most popular Jane Marple mysteries include *What Mrs. McGillicuddy Saw!* (1957), *A Murder is Announced* (1959), and *The Mirror Crack'd* (1962). The Beresfords, who solve crimes more through luck than deductive thought, are featured in such works as *The Secret Adversary* (1922), *Partners in Crime* (1929), and *By the Pricking of My Thumbs* (1968). Christie's novels are distinctive in that they present complex puzzles designed to misdirect the reader's attention from the most important clues. The solution is often the least expected or anticipated one, but, upon reflection, always makes perfect sense.

Christie was a prolific writer who turned out more than a hundred novels and short stories. She was also a playwright who published more than a dozen plays. Among the best known are *Ten Little Niggers* (produced in the United States as *Ten Little Indians*) and *Witness for the Prosecution*. Under the pseudonym Mary Westmacott, Christie published several romance novels, and in a departure from fiction, she published a book of poetry (*Poems*, 1973) and two autobiographical works, *Come, Tell Me How You Live* (1946) and *An Autobiography* (1977).

Christie was married twice. Her first marriage to Archibald Christie in 1914 ended in divorce in 1928. Her mother's death and problems in her marriage led to the most mysterious element in Christie's life when, in December 1926, Christie disappeared. After a nation-wide and very public search, Christie was located ten days later in a hotel at Harrogate. She was registered under the name of her husband's alleged mistress. Both Christie and her husband refused comment, but they were divorced soon after. Christie married Max Edgar Lucien Mallowan in 1930. She had one child, a girl, from her first marriage. Christie was a recipient of several awards, including the New York Drama Critics Award in 1955 for *Witness for the Prosecution*. She was named a Commander of the British Empire in 1956 and Dame Commander, Order of the British Empire in 1971. Christie died in England on December 24, 1977.

PLOT SUMMARY

Act One, scene i

The play opens with a radio account of a woman murdered in London. Mollie and Giles have just opened a small guest house and inn with property that Mollie has inherited from her aunt. The action begins on their first day of business and with their first guests. Christopher Wren is the first guest to arrive. He is enthusiastic about the house and praises both the style and decor. Mrs. Boyle is the second guest to arrive, and she arrives complaining that a taxi did not meet her at the train (although she never provided an arrival time). The third guest to arrive, Major Metcalf, is carrying her luggage when he enters the hall a few moments later. Mrs. Boyle's complaints about everything, including the lack of servants and experienced hosts, result in Giles offering to cancel her stay, but she declines and insists she will stay.

Miss Casewell arrives next with news that the snow is worse, and they are all likely to be snowed in for some days. She brings a newspaper account of the murder earlier that afternoon and joins with Wren and Giles in speculating about the murderer. There is a knock at the door and Mr. Paravicini arrives claiming to be stranded in the storm and seeking a room. Mr. Paravicini announces that the roads are so snowed in that that there will be no further arrivals or departures. His strange pronouncement that the inn is just "perfect" makes Mollie and Giles uneasy.

Act One, scene ii

This scene takes place the next afternoon. Mrs. Boyle is still complaining, but Major Metcalf is happy with the excellent breakfast and lunch and tells her so. Mrs. Boyle is writing a letter and Major Metcalf is reading when Wren enters and quickly exits again to seek quiet in the library. Soon after, Miss Casewell enters and turns the radio up loudly enough to force Mrs. Boyle out of the room. Wren again enters claiming to have fled Mrs. Boyle in the library. Wren and Miss Casewell talk, and she lets slip that she had a poor, deprived childhood too awful to think about.

The phone rings, and the local police superintendent claims he is sending a policeman over and that Giles should follow his orders. At the mention of the policeman, Miss Casewell flees the room clearly upset. Once again, Mrs. Boyle enters to complain about the heat, leading Giles to rush off and put more coal in the furnace. Mrs. Boyle tells Mollie that Wren's story and name sound "fishy" and she thinks Mollie should check his references. Paravicini enters and warns Mollie that she should get references before she lets guests stay. He tells her that she can never tell who is a murderer, robber, madman, etc. At the same time he continues to leer suggestively at Mollie. Later, Mollie lets it slip about the police calling. At the news, Mrs. Boyle is disturbed; Metcalf is incredulous. Paravacini, who has been attending the fire, is startled enough to drop the poker.

Just then, Sgt. Trotter arrives on skis. Major Metcalf goes to use the phone and discovers that the line is dead. After his entrance, Trotter assembles everyone to tell them that he has been sent to provide police protection and alleges that someone present may be connected to the murder of a woman

Agatha Christie

in London. The murdered woman was a local woman, who with her husband, was imprisoned for a number of years in connection to a child-neglect case. The woman and her husband were found guilty of actions that resulted in the death of one of the three children who had been mistreated while in their foster care. Clues left at the scene of the murder indicated that there may be two more possible victims. Trotter claims that the murderer may be one of the other two children who survived, a young man and woman—both in their twenties. Clues left at the scene have led Trotter to the guest house. Trotter asks everyone present if any of them have any connection to the child's death so many years ago, but all present deny it. At that, Trotter goes off to search the house, and the guests begin to speculate about the murder and the possible identity of the murderer. Metcalf says that he knows that Mrs. Boyle was the magistrate who sent the children to live with those foster parents.

Sgt. Trotter returns from inspecting the house and states that he is going to phone his supervisor with a full report. When told that the phone lines are dead, Trotter remarks that they may have been cut. He sends Giles upstairs to check the other extension but not until he has mentioned that the killer may be among the guests. With everyone out of the room,

A playbill from the St. Martin's Theatre where Christie's play continues its record-breaking run

Trotter follows the telephone wire and crawls out the window searching for a cut end. Mrs. Boyle returns to the room and rushes over to close the open window. Just then, someone else enters the room. The lights are turned off and a scuffle and gurgles are heard. Mollie enters, turns on the light, and Mrs. Boyle's body is seen on the floor.

Act Two

Trotter is interrogating all present. Everyone claims to have been alone; no one saw anyone else as they responded to Mollie's cries for help. All their alibis sound slightly suspicious. Both Mollie and Giles are suspicious of one another because both hid the fact that they were in London the previous day. Trotter talks to Mollie alone and asks her about how well she knows her husband and about her knowledge of the abused children. Trotter tries to make Mollie think that Giles could be the surviving brother bent on revenge. But Mollie points out the murderer could even be the children's natural father since no one has any idea of where he is and that Trotter could be looking for a middle-aged man and not a young man. After Trotter leaves the room, Wren enters quite distraught and convinced

that Trotter will try to pin it all on him. He discloses that Wren is not his real name and that he is not an architect. Mollie tells Wren that she has an unhappy, even horrible, memory in her past, too, but does not disclose what it is. Giles enters and finds Wren comforting Mollie. He misunderstands and accuses Mollie of having had a longstanding affair with Wren. Mr. Paravicini enters as the Ralston's are quarreling and announces that Trotter cannot find his skis. Everyone enters the room and all deny knowing anything about Trotter's skis. Trotter resumes interrogating everyone about their knowledge of the murder or the child's death years earlier.

Trotter speaks to everyone individually, and then tells them that he wants each one to reconstruct their actions during Mrs. Boyle's murder, with one exception. Trotter wants each person to do what another claimed to be doing. Mollie is to play "Three Blind Mice" on the piano as Mr. Paravicini did during the murder. After a few moments Trotter calls Mollie back into the room. At first, Trotter accuses Mollie of withholding personal knowledge of the child's murder. Trotter pulls a gun out of his pocket and reveals that he is Georgie, the dead child's older brother. It was he who murdered the woman in London and Mrs. Boyle. Trotter drops the revolver and reaches out to strangle Mollie. He is interrupted by Miss Casewell, who tells him that she recognizes him as her brother Georgie. She leads him away telling him that she's going to take him somewhere where he will get the kind of help he needs. Metcalf enters the room with the other guests and tells them that Georgie has been sedated. He explains that he knew that Georgie was not a policeman because he, Metcalf, was the policeman. Metcalf also divulges that Paravicini is a crook. And Mollie and Giles reveal that each was in London to buy an anniversary gift for the other. The play concludes with Mollie crying out that her pie is burnt.

CHARACTERS

Mrs. Boyle

Mrs. Boyle is a large imposing woman in a bad temper; she complains about everything. She is disapproving of every effort that Mollie and Giles produce to make her comfortable. She surveys everything with displeasure and looks at her surroundings disapprovingly. Mrs. Boyle was a magis-

MEDIA ADAPTATIONS

- Although a number of Christie's plays and novels have been adapted for film and television and even by other playwrights, *The Mousetrap* has never been adapted in any other format. Although the play is based on a radio script (*Three Blind Mice*, broadcast by the BBC) there is no tape of that broadcast known to exist. Students wishing to explore Christie's work on film might consider Public Broadcasting's series *Mystery*, which has adapted several of the Hercule Poirot and Jane Marple mysteries for television. A large number of these PBS films are now syndicated on the Arts & Entertainment (A & E) channel.

- *Ten Little Indians*, based on Christie's novel *Ten Little Niggers*, has been filmed at least three times. It was first produced in 1965 by Associated British & Pathe Films. The play was filmed again in 1975 and in 1989. The latter two productions are available on video.

- Christie's *Death on the Nile* was filmed by Paramount in 1978. The film offered an all-star cast of Hollywood actors and won several awards for costume design. Hercule Poirot was played by Peter Ustinov.

- *Witness for the Prosecution* has been filmed twice. The theatrical release was filmed by United Artists in 1957 and is considered the best of the Christie film adaptations. The film, staring Charles Laughton, Tyrone Power, and Elsa Lanchester, won several Academy Awards, including Best Picture, Best Director (Billy Wilder), and Best Actor (Laughton).

---

trate at some point. The audience learns just before she is murdered that Mrs. Boyle was the magistrate who sent three children to live with foster parents. The children were all abused and the youngest killed, but she disavows any responsibility for the tragedy.

Miss Casewell

Miss Casewell is described as a young woman who is masculine in appearance and with a masculine voice. She claims not to have lived in England for some years, since she was twelve to thirteen years of age, but she is mysterious about where she does live. Mollie thinks Miss Casewell peculiar, and Giles doubts she is a woman. Wren and Miss Casewell talk, and she lets slip that she had a poor, deprived childhood too awful to think about. The audience learns in the final scene that Miss Casewell was one of the children who was abused so many years earlier. It was her younger brother who was killed. She also discloses at the play's conclusion that she returned to England to find her older brother, Georgie.

Georgie

See Detective Sergeant Trotter

Major Metcalf

Major Metcalf is middle-aged, square-shouldered, military in manner and bearing. He is friendly and very polite, and serves as a good counter to Mrs. Boyle during the play's first act. The audience learns in the final scene that Metcalf is a policeman who is at the guest house undercover to help find a murderer and to provide protection to the possible victims.

Mr. Paravicini

Mr. Paravicini is foreign, dark, and elderly with a small flamboyant mustache. For those in the audience who are familiar with Agatha Christie's other works, Paravicini seems to be a slightly taller edition of Hercule Poirot, which may serve to confuse some members of the audience. Paravicini claims to be lost after his car overturned in a snow drift. He is much taken with himself—first leering at Mollie and then providing a dramatic reading of his untimely arrival in a storm with no luggage. The audience learns at the play's conclusion that he is a con man or crook.

Giles Ralston

Giles is described as arrogant, attractive, and in his twenties. He has been married for one year to Mollie. Their courtship lasted only three weeks. Giles is jealous of the attention that Wren showers on Mollie. The audience knows little about Giles and it is revealed that Mollie also knows little about Giles.

Mollie Ralston

Mollie is a tall, pretty young woman in her 20s. She has been married for one year to Giles. Mollie knew him for only three weeks before they married. Mollie inherited the house from her aunt and then decided to turn the property into a guest house. Both husband and wife are inexperienced at running an inn and have no idea what they are doing. The audience learns in the last scene that Mollie was a teacher years earlier and that she was the teacher of a young boy who was murdered by his foster parents. The child had written to Mollie for help, but she was ill and never received the letter. She is haunted by this child's death.

Detective Sergeant Trotter

Detective Sergeant Trotter is a cheerful, common-place young man who arrives at the guest house on skis. He has a slight cockney accent. Trotter spends most of his time on stage explaining to the other characters (and to the audience) the motive for the murder of the woman in London. He is supposedly there to protect the guests in the household and to find the murderer. However, in the final act, Trotter pulls a gun out of his pocket, threatens to shoot Mollie, and reveals that he is Georgie, the older brother of a child who was murdered by his foster parents. Georgie and his sister were neglected and abused by the same people. It was Georgie/Trotter who murdered the woman in London and Mrs. Boyle. He is not really a policeman, but only assumed that disguise to gain entry to the guest house. Miss Casewell recognizes him because of his habit of twisting a lock of his hair

when nervous. At the end of the play, she sedates him and takes him away to be confined where he can be treated for his emotional illness.

Christopher Wren

Christopher Wren is the first guest to arrive. He is described as a wild-looking neurotic young man; his hair is untidy and long. Wren is also quick to confide and child-like. He also has a knowledge of and appreciation for fine furniture. Wren is friendly and likes to cook. But he is also nosy and prone to gossip, reflecting his interest in people. Wren claims to be an architect and to have been named after the seventeenth-century architect, Christopher Wren by his parents in an effort to promote an interest in architecture. He sings nursery rhymes at odd moments during the play. Wren arrives with a suitcase so light that Giles thinks it is empty. After Mrs. Boyle is murdered, Wren is quite distraught and convinced that Trotter will try to pin both murders on him. Later, he discloses that Wren is not his real name and that he is not an architect. But he doesn't volunteer any information about who he really is. His character is mysterious and the audience learns little of substance about him

THEMES

The Mousetrap begins with the murder of a mysterious woman in London. The action takes place in a guest house thirty miles from London where a house full of suspects have gathered and where a second murder is about to be committed.

Appearances and Reality

At the heart of any mystery lies the question of what is real and what is not. This is particularly true of *The Mousetrap*, which relies on disguise to confuse the audience. The detective in the mystery genre is suppose to be the outsider, the member of the cast with whom the audience can most closely identify. But in this play, the appearance of the detective does not fulfill the audience's expectations, since the reality is that the detective is the murderer. Christie is playing with a genre which the audience thinks is predictable in its basic form,

TOPICS FOR FURTHER STUDY

- Agatha Christie's plays and novels are often set in the English countryside and take place in an indeterminate time. This gives them a sort of timeless quality that keeps the plots and characters from appearing dated and, perhaps, accounts for her continued popularity. Discuss the importance of setting, place, and time in respect to Christie's work. Do you think that this timelessness adds to the complexity of the puzzle that readers and audiences must solve?

- Critics appear to be divided on Christie's appeal as a feminist. Some think her female characters intelligent and resourceful, while others think that Christie relies on stereotypes that present women as dependent on men, consumed with their appearance, and unable to think beyond how to attract a man. Examine how the women in *The Mousetrap* respond to both criticisms.

- After the war, much of England and almost all of London lay in ruins, and a huge effort at rebuilding the country was undertaken. Research this period and comment on whether you agree with some critics who think that the popularity of *The Mousetrap* derives from the need of a populace to escape into entertainment. If you think this is the case, how then, do you account for the play's popularity nearly fifty years later?

- The mystery genre is said to date from Edgar Allan Poe, but some critics credit Christie with having had the greatest influence on the genre's development. Research Christie's influence on other mystery writers and decide for yourself if this credit is deserved.

---

forcing them to employ analytical skills beyond the accustomed.

Death

Death provides both the opening of this play and the transition between acts. And yet, in one sense, death is almost the least important aspect of the play; solving the murder is the crucial element. Christie's first victim is unknown to the audience and the second is a complaining obnoxious woman whom the audience gladly sacrifices in the struggle to unearth a murderer. Thus, death becomes almost abstract, a necessary action to advance the plot but not an action which causes the audience any grief. The result is that death, rather than assuming a central position of importance in the play, becomes only a necessary contrivance which the author employs to entertain. However, in a second way, death has a separate importance. The motivation for the deaths that occurs during the play is the death of a small boy years earlier. It is this death that leads to the others, and since both victims are in some way responsible for the death of the child, once again the audience is able to absolve itself of any caring for the two female victims. And so, Christie provides a complexity to the theme of death that requires her audience to look beyond the obvious.

Justice and Injustice

This play can also be described as a search for justice. The two murder victims are responsible for the death of a young child and the abuse of his siblings. The murderer has decided that justice has not been provided through social and legal means and so decides to dispense justice himself. The difficult question for Christie is how to make the murderer sympathetic without sacrificing law. She does this by making the initial murder an innocent child who suffered greatly. The first victim is the foster mother who was responsible for the child's death. The second victim is the magistrate who placed the boy in foster care. Christie adds to the second victim's appeal as a sacrifice for justice by giving her an unattractive personality. And to stack the deck further against the two female victims, she makes the murderer friendly and attractive, but emotionally and mentally disturbed. Accordingly, the audience is sympathetic to him and uncaring about the victims. In the end, justice has the appearance of having been served: the deranged young man is taken away to be treated and a sympathetic potential victim has been saved.

Order and Disorder

To establish a venue for murder, Christie creates a scenario that dismisses order from the stage and instead establishes disorder. She does this first with the snow storm that strands all the guests. The second step is to remove any chance of communication with the outside authorities. To do this the phone lines are cut, and the house is isolated. Next the detective's skis have disappeared and the audience realizes that the detective is stranded and unable to seek help. And finally, the guests and their hosts begin to fall apart and their veneer of civility is cracked enough for the audience to begin suspecting any or all of them to be a murderer.

Punishment

Modern audiences are conditioned to expect punishment as a response to crime. But for Christie, punishment depends more on circumstance than the crime committed. Although Georgie/Trotter has dispensed his own idea of punishment to his two murder victims, the audience is given ample reason to dislike the victims and like their murderer. The plot makes clear that Georgie is also a victim, and so his removal to a treatment center at the play's conclusion is a resolution the audience endorses. Generally, most audience members will feel that Georgie has suffered a great deal and that he is deserving of sympathy rather than condemnation. A second glance at the play reveals that he has almost claimed a third and more innocent victim, but since Mollie has not been injured (she leaves the stage unhurt and more concerned with her burned pie than her near death), the audience is permitted and encouraged to direct all its sympathy to the young man who was more victim than victimizer.

Revenge

Like punishment, revenge is the motivating force behind Georgie's deception. He is seeking revenge for his brother's death and revenge for the injuries he suffered. The two murder victims are unsympathetic characters, while the murderer is portrayed as both likable and emotionally unstable.

All of these elements lead the audience to recognize and sympathize with the young man when he is unmasked at the play's conclusion. Forgotten is the fear and conflict that permeated the last act. But, since the last act takes place only ten minutes after the second victim's murder, presumably, their collective fear was not great. In fact, Christie leaves the audience with an understanding that all the guests are once again engaged in common-place activities.

Sanity and Insanity

Insanity is offered as both a mitigating reason for Georgie's actions and a justification for the murder of two people. Throughout the play the murderer is referred to several times as a homicidal maniac, but the connotation of maniac is someone who is unbalanced. In fact, the definition of maniac is a madman, a lunatic, someone who is violently insane. After Trotter is unmasked as Georgie, the audience, who has come to like the young man, is quick to accept that he is insane. Indeed the conclusion reveals that he is not going off to prison, but instead, he has been sedated and will be confined somewhere for treatment. His insanity is justified by the circumstances of his childhood. And it is a solution with which the audience is comfortable.

STYLE

The Mousetrap is a two-act play written in the mystery genre. The play employs a remote, isolated location in which a group of suspicious people have gathered. It becomes readily apparent that some are not who they seem to be and that most have something they are hiding.

Act

A major division in a drama. In Greek plays the sections of the drama were signified by the appearance of the chorus and were usually divided into five acts. This is the formula for most serious drama from the Greeks to Elizabethan playwrights like William Shakespeare. The five acts denote the structure of dramatic action. They are exposition, complication, climax, falling action, and catastrophe. The five-act structure was followed until the nineteenth century, when Ibsen combined some of the acts. *The Mousetrap* is a two-act play. The exposition, complication, and climax are combined in the first act with the story of the child's murder and the murder in London and in the final minutes of act one when Mrs. Boyle is murdered. The falling action and catastrophe are combined in the second act with the realization that a murderer is in the house and that Trotter is Georgie.

Catharsis

Catharsis is the release of emotions, usually fear and pity. The term was first used by Aristotle in his *Poetics* to refer to the desired effect of tragedy on the audience. Many critics cite *The Mousetrap* as cathartic because Christie subverts the mystery genre by making the detective the murderer. The unexpected ending provides an exciting release for the audience, who think they have the murders solved only to discover how wrong they have been,

Character

A character is a person in a dramatic work. The actions of each character are what constitute the story. Character can also include the idea of a particular individual's morality. Characters can range from simple stereotypical figures to more complex multi-faceted ones. Characters may also be defined by personality traits, such as the rogue or the damsel in distress. ''Characterization'' is the process of creating a lifelike person from an author's imagination. To accomplish this the author provides the character with personality traits that help define who she will be and how she will behave in a given situation. For instance, Trotter is likable and represents authority. But in the play's conclusion the audience learns that Trotter does not represent authority—he represents insanity.

Genre

Genre is a term for the categorization of literature. Genre is a French word that means ''kind'' or ''type.'' Genre can refer to both the content of literary work—such as tragedy, comedy, or pastoral—and to the forms of literature, such as drama, novel, or short story. This term can also refer to types of literature such as mystery, science fiction, or romance. *The Mousetrap* is a drama, but it is also a mystery.

Plot

The pattern of events in a narrative. Generally plots should have a beginning, a middle, and a conclusion, but they may also sometimes be a series of episodes connected together. Basically, the plot provides the author with the means to explore primary themes. Students are often confused between the two terms; but themes explore ideas, and plots simply relate what happens in a very obvious manner. Thus the plot of *The Mousetrap* is a snow storm that isolates a group of people, one of whom is a murderer. But the themes are those of insanity and revenge.

Scene

Scenes are subdivisions of an act. A scene may change when all of the main characters either enter or exit the stage. But a change of scene may also indicate a change of time. In *The Mousetrap,* the second scene of Act I occurs the next afternoon and thus indicates the passage of time in the play.

Setting

The time, place, and culture in which the action of the play takes place is called the setting. The elements of setting may include geographic location, physical or mental environments, prevailing cultural attitudes, or the historical time in which the action takes place. The location for *The Mousetrap* is Monkswell Manor, a small guest house thirty miles from London. The action begins in the late afternoon and concludes the following afternoon; both acts take place in the Great Hall of the Manor.

Suspense

Quite simply, suspense is the anticipation of an action occurring. It is a major device in mystery since suspense is what keeps the audience interested in the resolution of the action. In a play such as *The Mousetrap,* suspense is more than curiosity, since members of the audience may already be familiar with the play's resolution. Suspense heightens the audience's reaction to characters, either sympathetic or not. It also provides the audience with an opportunity to prove their analytical skills superior to the author's. Dissecting the clues is an important ritual for theatre-goers for whom solving the mystery is the whole purpose of seeing the play.

HISTORICAL CONTEXT

Agatha Christie's *The Mousetrap* opens in theatres during a period marked by post-World War II rebuilding, a new monarchy, food shortages, and the threat of communism. The giddiness that greeted the end of the war has been replaced by the realities of rebuilding the country. Whole sections of the nation have been destroyed in the bombings of the war, and London, in particular, is undergoing

COMPARE & CONTRAST

- **1952:** Elizabeth II succeeds her father George VI to the throne. During her reign the British Empire will decline from forty nations to no more than twelve with Elizabeth having a voice only in England.

  Today: Elizabeth II is celebrating twenty-five years as England's queen. For the monarch, the scandals of her royal children have caused many of her subjects to question the expense of maintaining a royal household.

- **1952:** Britain tests an atomic bomb on October 2, thus joining the United States and the Soviet Union as a nuclear power.

  Today: Testing of nuclear weapons has been banned by most developed countries, and a greater awareness of the ecological damage and health risks inherent in testing leads to increasing pressure on the remaining nations who still test nuclear bombs to cease their testing.

- **1952:** Jonas Edward Salk tests a vaccine designed to combat the epidemic of polio. Salk's live virus vaccine will eventually be replaced by Albert Bruce Sabin's oral vaccine.

  Today: Polio has been almost completely eradi-

  cated in first-world countries such as Britain and the United States. Now the controversy focuses on whether to continue with a vaccine that has the potential of causing the disease in a small number of recipients of the vaccine.

- **1952:** *Singing in the Rain* is the big Hollywood musical released this year. It spoofs Hollywood in the twenties and provides a musical score that will be nominated for an Academy Award.

  Today: Hollywood releases few large musicals. Disney Studio's animated film musicals have largely replaced big-budget productions. Andrew Lloyd Webber's *Evita* is a notable exception but has only moderate box office success.

- **1952:** Playwright Lillian Hellman defies the congressional committee investigating communism and refuses to supply information that might lead to further "witch hunts."

  Today: A movie version of Arthur Miller's *The Crucible*, written as a condemnation of the communist witch hunts, is a box office failure. Reviewers argue that the topic appears dated.

---

a rebirth. In England, the king who has guided Great Britain through the war years dies on February 6, 1952. His daughter, Elizabeth, ascends the throne replacing George VI to become only the second Elizabeth to wear the crown. Food is in such short supply in England that 53,000 horses were consumed for food in the previous year to feed a population that now exceeds fifty million people. And in London, a four-day smog kills more than four thousand people. Meanwhile, the threat of communism hangs over everyone. The war that humbled Germany has loosed the threat of communism on the world, and this is particularly noticeable in the United States where congressional inquiries into the "Red Threat" continue for a third year.

In contrast to the difficult realities outside the theatre's door, inside the Ambassadors Theatre the atmosphere is decidedly different. On stage, the only concern about food is that caused by the snow storm, and Giles is confident that if the store of tins in the cupboards should prove inadequate, the hens in the outbuilding will meet any need. No one will go hungry, and indeed, the conversation frequently focuses on food, the preparation of meals, and the guests satisfaction with what is offered at the table. Monkswell Manor is entirely satisfactory according to at least one guest. The house is untouched by the bombing that destroyed London only thirty miles away. The furniture is comfortable and stylish and although the house is difficult and expensive to heat (a universal complaint about British homes), Giles keeps piling on the coal.

Of course a short distance away in London all that burning coal added to the growing problem with automobile emissions is causing smog that endangers the health of its urban population. Nevertheless, at Monkswell Manor smog is not a problem. A snow storm that has reached blizzard proportions may prove to be more of a danger to those inside the house than the smog that exists in London.

In fact, the stage setting of *The Mousetrap* effectively removes the audience from the real world outside. Christie creates an escape from the problems that plague England. At a time when other writers are lamenting the lost innocence of a world and creating a literary tradition that reflects the ruins of London, Christie is still offering an escapist literary journey for her fans. In a discussion that examines a new post-war literary tradition, Andrew Sanders maintains that Christie's play "tells us something about the resilience of certain theatrical conventions and styles." These conventions, Sanders argues, "have been selected so as not to offend the sensibilities of audiences happy with a pattern of light-hearted banter." Theatre patrons who want to escape the troubles that plague the country will keep Christie's play on the London stage long after John Osborne's *Look Back in Anger* has completed its run.

CRITICAL OVERVIEW

When Agatha Christie's *The Mousetrap* opened in London's West End on November 25, 1952, few theatre-goers anticipated that the play would become a fixture for the next half-century. The *Times of London* review of the play's opening at the Ambassadors Theatre noted that "the piece admirably fulfills the special requirements of the theatre." That is, there is a good assortment of suspects and potential victims assembled on stage and each is easily identifiable. The reviewer for the *Times* noted that these people "provide the colour, the mystification, the suspects, and the screams" and that "all fit the play as snugly as pieces in a jigsaw puzzle." The audience would find that *The Mousetrap* fits nicely into the Christie tradition: "No sooner have

we, following the precepts of our old friend Poirot, peered back into the past—for this is what is known, rather grandly, as a revenge tragedy—and found in the present a suitable couple for the child victims of long ago, than the ingenious pattern shifts, and we are back where we started."

This inability to out-think Christie and solve the crime is part of what keeps audiences flocking to see this play. The run at Ambassadors Theatre lasted twenty-two years; in 1974, *The Mousetrap* moved to St. Martin's Theatre to continue its successful theatrical course.

The Mousetrap finally opened off-Broadway on November 5, 1960, at the Maidman Theatre. At its New York opening, *New York Times*'s reviewer Lewis Funke observed that "a good in-the-flesh whodunit has been overdue." While observing that the play was not a "blood-curdling experience," Funke noted that "it is the Christie skill and polish in throwing you off the scent that keeps the entertainment going." "*The Mousetrap*," Funke stated, "will not exactly shakes you up, but neither will it let you down." While neither the *Times of London* review or the *New York Times* provided the kind of "don't miss it" or "Four Stars" review that many theatre patrons come to expect of a play that is as wildly successful as *The Mousetrap* has proved to be, both papers did pronounce the suspense and clever plotting worth a visit. Apparently the public agrees. The play is simply a well-constructed mystery that holds the audience's attention from the first moment and offers enough theatrical "red herrings" to keep the audience guessing until the play's conclusion.

Throughout the play's run in London, note of its longevity has appeared almost yearly in the *Times of London*. As the play neared its fortieth year of continuous performance, Robin Young, writing in *Times,* considered the play's continued success, observing that "the solution [to the murder] . . . is unorthodox enough to be unguessable, and unguessable enough to be unforgettable. The play has seeped into our collective consciousness as a national challenge." That the public has responded to this "national challenge" is evident in the six-month wait to get tickets. As Young stated, one reason that the play has remained interesting and fresh so many years after its opening is attributed to the yearly change in cast and director. A performance of *The Mousetrap,* Young remarked, has become an "essential part of the London itinerary, right up with the Houses of Parliament and the Tower of London." In the United States, however, the play has never achieved similar status. Nevertheless, the play still remains complex and intriguing forty-five years after its initial performance. In fact, when an attempt was made a few years ago to publish a novel loosely based on the play, called *Three Blind Mice,* public clamor halted the book's publication. A book, it was argued, would reveal the identity of the murderer. And so the mystery remains to delight and entertain London audiences.

CRITICISM

Sheri Metzger

Metzger is a Ph.D. with an extensive background teaching drama. In this essay she assesses critical response to Christie's play and praises the writer's dramatic skills.

J. C. Trewin remarked in *Agatha Christie: First Lady of Crime* that it often astonishes critics and theatre reviewers that after so many years on the London stage *The Mousetrap* "can still be acted before audiences with no idea of its development or climax." Not only critics but audiences have kept the secret of the whodonit and they have done so, Trewin argued, in tribute to Christie's work. Part of the appeal is in the reliability of the puzzle. Christie fans know they can rely on a solution that is plausible and yet one that completely escapes them until the play's conclusion. The least likely suspect is too often the murderer, or is he? It is the solving of that equation that keeps audiences guessing and coming back for more. And it is that complexity and familiarity that account for the play's longevity.

Trewin maintained that characterization was less important to Christie than action, that many of her characters were stereotypes who might have as readily been identified by numbers as by name. These stock characters might have easily been "transferred as needed, from plot to plot, hall to manor, court to vicarage . . . they rarely had a life of their own." Perhaps to some degree that is true. Devoted readers of Christie will recognize Mrs. Boyles, Miss Casewell, Mollie, Giles, and Major Metcalf as fa-

miliar characters. But after more than a hundred novels, short stories, and plays, that familiarity is what readers and audiences are seeking. It is the accustomed that creates comfort and why Christie's work endures. But, I would agree that it is the plot, the action, the murder, and its solution that keeps the fan returning for more. It is the pleasure derived from solving the puzzle that keeps the audience in their seats.

Christie relied on narration and plot and eschewed the technology that is identified with so many other mystery writers. *The Mousetrap* employs no sliding panels or hidden staircases to enliven the action. There are no devices to create illusion; there are only the words and actions of ordinary people to offer clues. If, indeed, a murderer can be defined as ordinary. The lack of gadgets to distract the audience and Christie's reliance on a world of upper class gentry are two components that account for her longevity, according to Russell Fitzgibbon. In a chapter of his *The Agatha Christie Companion* that examines Christie's appeal, Fitzgibbon synthesized several critical responses to Christie. In one section, he examined criticism of Ian Fleming's use of technology. Christie's supporters argue that Fleming's use of technology is so quickly outmoded that his work is easily and quickly dated, and conclude that Christie, who ignored any technology more advanced than the radio, is timeless in her appeal. But Fleming's supporters counter with the assertion that Christie's work appears dated because she relies upon an antiquated setting and life-style that no longer exists in England, and consequently, the popularity of her work will inevitably decline.

In response to both these views, Fitzgibbon asserted that Fleming's technology is mechanical and impersonal, while Christie uses "the personalities, the emotions, and the general intangibles she found in the social world she knew so well." The lengthy theatrical run and enduring popularity of *The Mousetrap* would seem to support Fitzgibbon's argument. The comforts of the Victorian upper class may no longer exist in England, and this is especially true in the wake of World War II, but the public's need to escape to that earlier realm is apparently even greater today than it was in the 1920s when Christie first began to re-create that world.

It is the characters who deceive the audience and who provide the clues that enable the fans to

WHAT DO I READ NEXT?

- Tom Stoppard's *The Real Inspector Hound* (1968) is one of several parodies of *The Mousetrap*. Stoppard employs many of the familiar Christie elements of the mystery play: the setting, the plot, the country house. And like Christie, Stoppard relies up an unexpected plot twist to keep the audience guessing.

- The evolution of the mystery play is evident in Anthony Shaffer's *Sleuth* (1970). Shaffer relies on illusion to replace the central themes of victim, murderer, and detective. Rather than simply trying to analyze the clues and solve the puzzle, audiences must first try to determine exactly what has happened. Little is as it appears initially.

- Ira Levin's *Deathtrap* (1978) is another play that relies on illusion to fool an audience that cannot rely upon character, setting, or language to provide the necessary clues to solve the mystery.

- *Ten Little Niggers* (1943) is another Christie play that enjoyed success with its audiences. Christie

had so many people dying on stage that she initially had difficulties getting the play produced. When it finally appeared on stage, the play proved to be very popular especially in New York where it had a longer run than in London. The play's distasteful title was later changed to *Ten Little Indians*.

- Christie's *The Hollow* (1951) deviates from some of her other plays, since the murder occurs later in the play, by which time the audience is absolutely eager to se the victim dispatched. The dialogue is enjoyable and the puzzle lives up to Christie standards of enjoyment.

- *Witness for the Prosecution* (1953) is often cited as Christie's craftiest and most elaborate play. This play is often noted for its courtroom scene, something not often seen in a Christie work. The ending is startling and very much appreciated by the audience.

---

solve the puzzle. As Trewin noted, the characters are often stock and interchangeable; but David Grossvogal maintained in *Art in Crime Writing: Essays on Detective Fiction* that it is their very reliability, their ordinariness that attracts Christie fans. Her public ''knew these people without having encountered them and they were therefore exactly suited to [our] expectations.'' The actual murder, stated Grossvogal, ''was trivial enough'' and ''antiseptic.'' A Christie murder lacks the corruption and messiness of a Mike Hammer or Sam Spade crime scene, but Grossvogal acknowledged that ''there were always half a dozen compelling reasons to kill the victim—and as many evident suspects.'' This is certainly true of *The Mousetrap*.

Mrs. Boyle establishes at her entrance that she is going to make her stay at Monkswell notable. Her constant complaining in the face of Mollie's earnest desire to help quickly makes her a victim the

audience wants to murder. Christie makes sure that everyone on stage has the appearance of a suspect; all are hiding something and everyone acts suspicious, except detective Trotter. But an aware Christie audience will expect these characters, anticipate their entrance, and concentrate on the action to provide the clues.

Much of the criticism that has focused on Agatha Christie in recent years has delved into the issue of whether Christie can be defined as a feminist or if the depiction of women characters in her work reveals that she was an anti-feminist. Marty Knepper attempted to respond to this controversy by examining the body of Christie's work in the *Armchair Detective*. Knepper did admit that there is sexism in some of Christie's work but asserted that ''Only a writer with a healthy respect for women's abilities and a knowledge of real women could create the diversity of female characters Christie does. Her women characters display competence in many fields, are not all defined solely in relation to men, and often are direct contradictions to certain sexist 'truisms' about the female sex.'' Knepper continued by presenting examples from Christie's work that span several decades and character types. While acknowledging that Christie has created women who are flawed and who are even murderers, Knepper maintained that the greater majority of women are strong, intelligent, clever, successful characters. Knepper concluded that ''Christie, while not an avowed feminist, let her admiration for strong women, her sympathy for victimized women, and her recognition of society's discrimination against women emerge in the novels written during the decades of the twentieth century more receptive to feminist ideas (such as the 1920s and World War II years), while Christie, always concerned with selling her novels to mass audiences, relied more on traditional (sexist) stereotypes and ideas about women in the more conservative and anti-feminist decades (such as the 1930s).'' In applying Knepper's theory to *The Mousetrap* it becomes clear that in this play Christie's feminism is not easily defined. Mrs. Boyle is a magistrate. That she apparently was not always good at it could be argued as anti-feminist, but then, men were not always good magistrates either. But her constant complaining is a greater problem, since complaining has historically been attributed to women as a negative trait. And, since it makes her an unsympathetic character, her murder is almost welcomed by the audience. Mollie co-owns the guest house with her husband and on the surface seems a competent business woman. But she is easily led by Trotter to question her husband's honesty, becomes a near victim, and is in need of rescuing at the play's conclusion. Miss Casewell is described as mannish in appearance, and Giles even questions if she is a woman at one point. Is this a positive depiction of a single woman? It depends on the critics vantage point. Critics can choose to point out that Miss Casewell's appearance implies that she is strong and in command. While other critics might ask why Christie could not create a single woman who is both strong and feminine. But as M. Vipond noted of Christie's feminism in *International Fiction Review*, ''to generalize about sexual roles is to lose that touch of reality,'' the depiction of ''familiar patterns and types'' that draws the audience to Christie's work. There is much to be said for simply enjoying the characters as they are presented than in dissecting them to reveal Christie's feminist agenda.

When a play is as successful as *The Mousetrap* it is perhaps inevitable that its success will spawn parodies. Marvin Carlson looked at the influence of Christie's play in an article that appeared in *Modern Drama*. Carlson began by noting that with the advent of newer forms of mystery, Christie's play is ''taking on an increasingly anachronistic tone.'' He maintained that the mystery play has not lost its popularity, but rather, that the mystery play has evolved into something very different, a comic thriller. One of the first of the comic parodies of detective fiction was Tom Stoppard's *The Real Inspector Hound* (1968), which, Carlson maintained, used Christie's play as a model because it was both familiar and popular. Stoppard makes use of Christie's ''trick'' of making the detective the murderer. The public expects a certain resolution to a mystery, but in *The Mousetrap,* the expected is subverted when the detective, whom the audience thinks they can count on to be eliminated as a suspect, is revealed as the murderer. Stoppard parodies Christie by elaborating upon this ''trick.'' Although Christie has disguised the murderer as a detective, she has also disguised the detective as a suspect. In the end the murder is solved by the real detective and the mystery play remains rooted in its traditional garb. But in Stoppard's play, the disguised detective is not really a detective but is another murderer disguised as a detective. The complexity and ridiculousness of it all creates the comedy for the audience. Carlson observed that Stoppard's play eventually led to other comedy thrillers such as *Sleuth* (1970) and *Deathtrap* (1978), both of which went on to be successful films. However, it is worth noting that while Carlson found *The Mousetrap* ''anachronistic,'' its theatre run continues long after the comic thriller has left the stage.

Finally, the question remains why *The Mousetrap* has endured so long as a fixture in London's West End theatre district. Trewin attempted to answer a question for which there is no clear response, and he acknowledged that he has ''no dramatic reply. . . . People keep on going.'' He compares it to a sort of Stonehenge complete with legends, but Trewin also recognized that the play is a ''really efficient thriller'' that represents an ''untouched fragment of 1952.'' If Trewin's premise is to be accepted, then fans of Christie have elevated *The Mousetrap* from an entertaining puzzle to a tourist attraction that represents a world that disappeared more than 45 years ago.

Source: Sheri Metzger, in an essay for *Drama for Students,* Gale, 1997.

John Wren-Lewis

In this excerpt, Wren-Lewis discusses Christie's record-breaking play and offers some theories on the secret of its success.

Wren-Lewis is a critic for various publications and a lecturer in the Department of Religious Studies at the University of Sydney, Australia.

The longest-running play in human history is now well into its forty-first year on the London stage. Agatha Christie's detective-thriller *The Mousetrap,* which celebrated the fortieth anniversary of its opening on November 25th last year, has now become almost a British National Monument. When I went to its opening night, to see the young Richard Attenborough playing the detective, we were still only just emerging from the shadows of World War Two. The possibility that forty years on I'd be in Australia wasn't in my mind then, but even more remote was any thought that the play could still be going near the end of the century. And I don't think the idea crossed anyone else's mind either; Agatha Christie herself, interviewed on the then-phenomenal occasion of the play's tenth anniversary, said she had expected a run of no more than three months and was greatly buoyed by the assurance of impressario Peter (now Sir Peter) Saunders that it was good for at least a year! ...

The extraordinary success of *The Mousetrap* would imply that it contains some particularly acute, nerve-touching insight about the origin of evil in the human psyche, and I believe this to be indeed the case. For the play gives a very special twist to the ''least likely suspect'' theme, a twist anticipated occasionally in earlier stories (for example, in more than one by G. K. Chesterton), but never (to my knowledge) before put into drama-form, the mode which appeals most directly to the mythopoetic imagination. After all these years of exposure on the London stage, I don't think I shall be giving away any secret by mentioning what that twist is (and anyway, the characteristic of a really significant mythic theme, as I believe this to be, is that it retains its appeal even when the ''plot'' is common knowledge.) At the end of *The Mousetrap,* the detective himself, the young policeman who appears as the protector of the innocent and as the guardian of law and order, turns out to be the murderer. And here I find a clear echo of a theme expressed in different ways in many of the world's ancient stories about

''THE EXTRAORDINARY SUCCESS OF *THE MOUSETRAP* WOULD IMPLY THAT IT CONTAINS SOME PARTICULARLY ACUTE, NERVE-TOUCHING INSIGHT ABOUT THE ORIGIN OF EVIL IN THE HUMAN PSYCHE''

the Fall, but most clearly in the one which, more than any other, has exercised emotional appeal across many different cultures, the biblical story in which the Loss of Eden comes about because of a ''snaky'' temptation to assume a divine role of moral guardianship, ''knowing good and evil.''

I would translate this idea as a diagnosis that the responsibility for humanity's unnatural destructiveness lies with the very element in the psyche that purports to aim at harmony, the moral impulse—not that it is too weak, as conventional social wisdom assumes, but that it usurps power and tries to control all other impulses by judging and repressing. It was an insight central to William Blake's attempts to uncover the true essence of Christianity in his mythic epics: ''The punisher alone is the criminal of Providence.'' And this too is surely something we are in a better position to understand today than any earlier generation, thanks to the detailed investigations of psychologists and sociologists. There is now ample evidence that behind all really violent and destructive human behaviour, whether it be the ridiculously excessive ambitions of the military conqueror or the empire-building of the capitalist, or the sadism of tyrants great or small, or the insatiable violence of the rapist, or the blind destructiveness of the hoodlum or child-batterer, there lies a screaming protest on the part of some much'more limited desire that has been repressed by an overweening morality, in society, in the family, or in the individual psyche itself. And on the other, outer side of the coin, egoistic and aggressive urges become really dangerous and outrageous precisely when they are moralised and amplified by righteous indignation. The Inquisition really did think that they were saving souls, and while mere greed or ambition would never lead any sane person to plunge the world into nuclear winter, a holy war might easily do so, on the judgement that it is better to be dead than red or, in more topical terms, better to have a nuclear holocaust than to submit to the Great Satan of American Capitalism.

"Better to rule in Hell than serve in Heaven" were words which Milton put into the mouth of Satan himself. His poem followed much Christian tradition in linking the Biblical story of Paradise Lost with another ancient tale, giving it, in the process, a definite "whodunnit" flavour of its own, by suggesting that the serpent was just a disguise for the cosmic Mr. Big—Lucifer, the Archangel of Light, who subverts humanity in the course of trying to usurp the role of God. The moral impulse, or "conscience," could indeed be described as the angel (the messenger) of light in the human psyche, and this story unmasks its constant tendency to get above itself and rule the roost instead of simply serving life. Thus a vicious circle is created, because repression and moralisation exaggerate the very impulses they claim to control, and thereby give "conscience" the excuse for attempting still more repressive measures and expressing still more moral outrage against others. This was why Blake went beyond Milton's interpretation of the story and represented Satan as having to all intents and purposes already taken over the place of God in most religions by making them agents of repressive moralising, rather than of salvation. That, he argued, was why Jesus of Nazareth "died as a reprobate . . . punished as a transgressor"—because he had seen what was going on in the world and tried to reverse the process by urging "mutual forgiveness of each vice," only to have his name and image taken over in turn in the service of repression and indignation.

The Mousetrap doesn't attempt to pursue the story into those depths: its villain simply gets killed at the end, much as in most other "whodunnits." But Chesterton did try to take that extra step: Father Brown never sought punishment or death for his villains, but unmasked them only as a first step in trying to redeem them. And for Blake that was the ultimate goal both in society and in the psyche itself, to "have pity on the Punisher" and restore the moral sense to its proper role as servant of life, by subordinating its judgements to forgiveness. He had the mystic vision that while no individual can hope to make more than a small impact on the destructive patterns of society by pursuing this goal, determined exposure of satanic judgementalism within the psyche will open up direct experience of eternity even in the midst of the world's still-unresolved conflicts. He identified this as "the Everlasting Gospel of Jesus"; yet he also insisted that "All Religions are One" prior to satanic perversion—and in our own day his insight, expressed in different terms, has been the core "gospel" of Krishnamurti, who stood apart from all formal religion: he urged the regular practice of "nonjudgemental choiceless awareness" as the way of opening to the eternal. Maybe he wasn't a detective-story buff for nothing.

The ending of any detective-story after the unmasking of the villain is inevitably something of an anticlimax (a post-climax, perhaps?), and in my view one of Blake's most profound insights was that the unmasking of the Great Originator of Sin in human life brings something of the same feeling. Like the Wizard of Oz, pretension is the essence of Lucifer's power in the world and in the psyche: unmasked, he becomes something of a joke:

> Truly, My Satan, thou art but a Dunce,/ And dost not know the Garment from the Man.

Perhaps that was what Chesterton was getting at, in a different idiom, when he said that if humanity were to be suddenly struck with a sense of humour, we would find ourselves automatically fulfilling the Sermon on the Mount. And perhaps, too, this is why the motivation of the crime in *The Name of the Rose* is the suppression of humour. So do join me as a detection buff, for the sheer fun of it, and go and see *The Mousetrap* if you're in London—it's fun even if you do know the ending.

Source: John Wren-Lewis, "Adam, Eve, and Agatha Christie: Detective Stories As Post-Darwinian Myths of Original Sin" in the *Chesterton Review,* Vol. 19, no. 2, May, 1993, pp. 197–99.

Eric Shorter

Finding The Mousetrap *to be conventional and often uninspired, Shorter assesses the play's lengthy theatrical run.*

Once upon a time (and a very good time it was) the Abbey's Lady Gregory said: 'We went on giving what we thought good until it became popular'. No better motto could be found for theatrical managers, but how many heed it? The motto now is to give what the manager thinks will be popular until it is generally thought good. Hence *The Mousetrap*. It must be good because it has run for so long.

Agatha Christie's thriller has now been on for 21 years. It has broken every conceivable theatrical record. It has made its manager's West End reputation. It has been visited by successive generations of playgoers. It has caused annual celebrations to be held. It has seen the coming and going of over 150 actors and actresses. It has become a mecca for American visitors ('Gee, look,' said one on the night I went, 'there's George from Philadelphia—well, what d'you know?').

What indeed does anybody know to explain the tenacity of this routine, country house whodunnit? *The Mousetrap* has been running at the cosy Ambassadors for so long that not many playgoers can remember to have seen anything else at that address; and yet not many seem to have seen it. This is the oddness, the challenge, the strangeness, the mystery of the longest running mystery in the history of the theatre. Why has nobody (so to speak) seen it? Of course you find critics here and there who saw it, even on its first night. Others recall the roughly annual changes of cast in the spirit of men recalling Hamlets and Macbeths. 'Did you ever see Dickie Attenborough?' they ask in much the manner of my elders who would tell me as a boy that if I hadn't seen Tree or Irving or Forbes-Robertson there wasn't much point in bothering with the Gielguds or Oliviers. What standards, after all, could I possess?

Well I have to admit that until the other night I had no standards at all for *The Mousetrap*. It was just something that had been running at one of my favourite small theatres since the Flood. I had never much liked whodunnits anyway since I could never bring myself to care who had done it; and since my memories of this theatre had always been witty— Gingold and Crisham and Kendall in revue (*Sweet and Low, Lower* and *Lowest*) or the two Hermiones in Coward's *Fallen Angels*— why sully them with a coach-party teaser? So I resisted it for 21 years. It did not need much effort.

No one ever asked me in all that time if I had seen it. Nor did I ask them. Somehow *The Mousetrap* was never a subject of dinner table conversation, at any rate not in my part of the world; and

"AND THE IDEA OF THE THRILLER? TIMELESSLY CONVENTIONAL"

although Agatha Christie is not a name to sneeze at the play itself never struck its author either as having contained the seeds of immortality.

Whether those seeds are to be found in the text or the performance, the theatre or its position, its management or its publicity, is a question which nobody can answer for sure. We know the manager is a keen and inventive publicist. Hence those huge cakes, club ties, and other efforts to capitalize on the show's success. Mr. Peter Saunders is the first to acknowledge that he has never missed a promoter's trick in keeping *The Mousetrap* baited.

Then, there is the theatre itself, one of the smallest in the West End circuit. It has a good position, just off Cambridge Circus. and of course, it doesn't take much filling anyhow. And this, for some observers, is the rub—that one of the West Ends most conveniently placed small playhouses should have been commandeered for such an orthodox thriller over such a long period. The argument goes that if so many people want it, let them see it in a bigger house; thus proving the need of it.

It is an argument based on the necessity for cosy theatres (of which London has so few compared to Paris) to be kept for new plays of some artistic ambition or revivals of limited appeal. The idea is that once a play has recovered its basic costs it shall not obstruct the flow of others which cannot otherwise get a central hearing. Therefore to have kept *The Mousetrap* going for 21 unbroken years at one of the handful of theatres seating under 500 is considered to have been an act of managerial self-indulgence without parallel in the history of the drama. And the transfer of it in the spring to the St. Martin's signified not an attack of conscience but merely the expiry of Mr. Saunders's lease on the Ambassadors. In any case the St. Martin's happens to be next door, and though it seats 550 instead of 450 it is still one of the few small West End playhouses.

During the 21 years the new drama in Britain acquired a reputation for social, political and moral urgency which could only find expression in smaller playhouses—at least until its authors had made their names—while one of the likeliest theatres for testing such talents was given over in seeming perpetuity to a trivial, if well-turned, thriller containing not so much as a line to tickle the moral, political or social fancy of anyone over 10. Mr. Saunders is merely bored by such objections. 'Where are all these new plays?' he will ask you as he once asked me over lunch at the Ivy (just opposite the Ambassadors); and at the time, not being myself a manager, I could not point them out. He maintains that if a manager wants to put a play on (and often at the last minute they funk London) there is usually a suitable theatre.

Meanwhile *The Mousetrap* looks like running for ever to the advantage of everyone associated with it from Mr. Saunders to Peter Cotes who directed it in 1952 and whose fees have since exceeded £30,000 but who has not been back to see it since. The author herself has taken nothing in royalties since she made them over from the start to a nephew then aged 10. And it all began because the BBC wanted something by Agatha Christie, at Queen Mary's request, to celebrate Queen Mary's 80th birthday. So Mrs. Christie ran up a short story called *Three Blind Mice* which she subsequently stretched into a play. Since that title had been used for a pre-war piece, heads were scratched to find another; and finally the author's son-in-law came up with *The Mousetrap* (and its Shakespearean echoes from the play-within-a play in *Hamlet*). Today, of course, at each revival of *Hamlet* an extra snigger can be counted on during the play scene—as if Shakespeare had culled the idea from Mrs. Christie.

And the idea of the thriller? Timelessly conventional. Into the lounge hall of a snowed-up panelled, home counties hotel just opened by a diffident young couple drift a careful assortment of independent types (grave, comical, foreign, peculiar, chatty, silent and so forth), one of whom is in due course bumped off. Thereafter suspicion falls, with the help of red herrings, on the survivors variously in turn; and before the final unmasking a mild degree of curiosity, even excitement, certainly tension is aroused. The suspense, if not intense, is agreeable; and the plotting is unquestionably neat.

What is questionable is the quality of the acting which struck me as not rising to the proverbial level of rep. Most reps I know of could do better but of course they are not allowed to try—any more than a film can be made—until what Mrs. Christie originally guessed might be 'quite a nice run' comes to an end. In our time? Our children's? Ever? Why in fact must the show go on? Only an Act of Parliament will ever stop it. . . .

Source: Eric Shorter, "Quite a Nice Run" in *Quarterly Theatre Review,* No. 112, Spring, 1974, pp. 51–53.

FURTHER READING

Blain, Virginia, Isobel Grundy, and Patricia Clements, editors. *The Feminist Companion to Literature in English,* Yale University Press, 1990, pp. 207-8.
   This reference work provides an encapsulated biographies of major women writers, noting their contribution to women's literature.

Carlson, Marvin. "Is There a Real Inspector Hound? Mousetraps, Deathtraps, and the Disappearing Detective" in *Modern Drama,* Vol. 36, no. 3, September, 1993, pp. 431-42.
   This article notes the influence of Christie's play on later theatrical parodies. Carlson compares *The Mousetrap* to Tom Stoppard's *The Real Inspector Hound* (1968), Ira Levin's *Deathtrap* (1978), and Anthony Shaffer's *Sleuth* (1970).

Fitzgibbon, Russell H. *The Agatha Christie Companion,* Bowling Green University Press, 1980.
   Fitzgibben's work is considered by many to be one of the most complete resources assembled on Christie. The text includes a detailed biography, a discussion of Christie's work, and critical reviews.

Funke, Lewis. "*Mousetrap* Arrives," in the *New York Times,* November 7, 1960, p. 46.
   Funk's review provides an enthusiastic recommendation for the first New York City performance of Christie's play.

Gilbert, Michael. "A Very English Lady" in *Agatha Christie: First Lady of Crime,* edited by H. R. F. Keating, Weidenfeld & Nicolson, 1977, pp. 51-78.
   Gilbert offers readers an easy-to-read biography of Christie that is gossipy in tone and focuses on many of the writer's private moments. The article is accompanied by photographs and newspaper duplications that add authenticity to the text.

Grossvogel, David I. "Death Deferred: The Long Life, Splendid Afterlife, and Mysterious Workings of Agatha

Christie'' in *Art in Crime Writing: Essays on Detective Fiction,* edited by Bernard Benstock, St. Martin's Press, 1983, pp. 1-17.

Grossvogel argues that Christie is the one author who has done the most to shape detective fiction as the public knows it, focusing on Hercule Poirot as a model for the ideal detective.

Knepper, Marty S. ''Agatha Christie: Feminist'' in *The Armchair Detective,* Vol. 16, no. 4, Winter, 1983, pp. 398-406.

Knepper argues that Christie should be included in a list of feminist writers by attempting to answer the questions: ''What are the characteristics of a feminist writer?'' and ''What are the characteristics of an anti-feminist writer?''

Sanders, Andrew. *The Short Oxford History of English Literature,* Clarendon Press, 1994.

Sanders offers a look at the social and political climate of postwar England. He observes that theatre patrons weary of the rebuilding of their nation after the end of World War II sought out Christie's play as escapist entertainment.

Times of London, November 26, 1952, p. 12.

Uncredited, enthusiastic review of the opening of *The Mousetrap* at Ambassadors Theatre on November 25, 1952.

Times of London, July 31, 1991, p. 13.

This unnamed writer ponders the longevity of Christie's play and concludes that the play has become a ''national challenge.''

Trewin, J. C. ''A Midas Gift to the Theatre'' in *Agatha Christie: First Lady of Crime,* edited by H. R. F. Keating, Weidenfeld & Nicolson, 1977, pp. 131-54.

Trewin examines several of Christie's plays and provides a knowledgeable insight into their construction.

Vipond, M. ''Agatha Christie's Women'' in *International Fiction Review,* Vol. 8, no. 2, Summer, 1981, pp. 116-23.

Vipond argues that Christie's women possess strong qualities that identify them as bright and competent.

Young, Robin. ''Fresh Blood as *Mousetrap* Enters its 40th Year'' in the *Times of London,* November 25, 1991, p 7.

This article, which appears on the thirty-ninth anniversary of the play's debut, celebrates Christie's work as an institution that has now become a tourist attraction.

'night, Mother

MARSHA NORMAN

1983

'night, Mother, written in 1981, was Marsha Norman's fifth play. The work received generally favorable reviews when it was first produced on stage in 1983. Among the numerous honors bestowed upon the play, it was awarded the 1983 Pulitzer Prize for drama. Critics have lauded the play for its emotional honesty and realistic dialogue, with much of the praise focused on the play's unflinching depiction of a family—specifically a mother and daughter—in crisis. This lack of sentimentality and the play's focus on the loneliness and emptiness of the two women's lives are often cited by those praising 'night, Mother. In contrast, those who did not like the play most often complain that it is drab and lacks any significant development in its two characters. While this was not intended as a condemnation of the play, dissenting critics also said that those reviewers who praised the play so lavishly were over-reacting to a dramatic work that was adequate but not great—let alone deserving of a Pulitzer. On balance, however, 'night, Mother was well-received, by audiences and critics alike, for its realism and honesty.

When 'night, Mother premiered in Canada in 1984 the notices were favorable. Although reviewers in the United States had not generally reviewed the play as feminist, Canadian critics did note that the work presented men only as peripheral characters in the women's lives and that women were central to the play's themes. Although the topic of 'night, Mother is unhappiness that results in suicide,

Norman manages to interject some macabre humor through sharp dialogue. Despite its impartial (even negative) stance toward suicide, 'night, Mother nevertheless became a source of controversy due to its inclusion of that subject. The issue was intensified by the Pulitzer Prize going to the play. Yet Norman's work is viewed by most as a depiction of a failed mother/daughter relationship, a chronical of the daughter's deep unhappiness, and, ultimately, her inability to deal with her lot in life. In this sense the play is valued as both a gritty work of fiction and a cautionary tale that has bearing on real life.

AUTHOR BIOGRAPHY

The isolation and loneliness of life, topics of her play 'night, Mother, are issues that are familiar to Marsha Norman, since they spring from her own childhood. Norman was born September 21, 1947, in Louisville, Kentucky. Her family chose to isolate Norman rather than expose her to ideas that challenged their own as religious fundamentalists. She received a B.A. from Agnes Scott College in Georgia in 1969, and a M.A. from the University of Louisville in 1971. Norman worked with gifted and emotionally disturbed children for two years at Kentucky State Hospital. She has been married three times and has two children.

By 1976 Norman was working full time as a writer contributing articles to a local newspaper. Her first play, Getting Out (1977) is based on a woman she knew while working at Kentucky State Hospital. In 1978 she was awarded a National Endowment for the Arts grant that enabled her to work with the Actors' Theatre in Louisville (ATL), an influential organization that produces the work of up and coming playwrights. Norman quickly followed with three more plays written during her association with ATL: Third and Oak: The Laundromat [and] The Pool Hall (1978), Circus Valentine (1979), and The Holdup (1980). From 1980 to 1981, she also served as a resident director with the company. She wrote 'night Mother after moving to New York City with her second husband, theatrical producer Dann Byck.

Other plays that Norman has written include Traveler in the Dark (1984), Sarah and Abraham (1988), and D. Boone (1992). She has also written the book and lyrics for two musicals, the children's production The Secret Garden (1991), and The Red Shoes (1993). In 1987 Norman published her first novel, The Fortune Teller. She also authored two teleplays, In Trouble at Fifteen (1980) and Face of a Stranger (1991). In 1986, she adapted her own work for the film version of 'night, Mother, which was produced by Universal Pictures and starred Sissy Spacek.

Norman received the American Theatre Critics Association award for the best play produced in regional theatre in 1977-78 for Getting Out. That work also brought Norman the John Gassner New Playwrights Medallion, the Outer Critics Circle, and the George Oppenheimer-Newsday Award in 1979. Norman received a Pulitzer Prize for drama for 'night, Mother in 1983; the play was also honored with the Susan Smith Blackburn Prize, a Tony Award nomination for best play, and the Elizabeth Hull-Kate Warriner Award from the Dramatist Guild. She also received a Tony award for Best Book of a Musical in 1991 for The Secret Garden. In addition to her work on the film adaptation of 'night, Mother, Norman has written several unproduced screenplays.

PLOT SUMMARY

'night, Mother takes place in the living room and kitchen in the rural home of mother Thelma Cates and her daughter, Jessie. The play follows real time as displayed on a clock on stage. The hour and a half length of the play matches exactly the hour and a half of dialogue and action between Thelma's opening lines and her final call to Jessie's brother to inform him of his sister's death.

'night, Mother opens with Jessie Cates asking her mother for a piece of plastic sheeting and for the location of her father's gun. After Jessie finds the gun hidden away in an old shoe box in the attic, she begins cleaning the weapon. As she does, she calmly tells her mother that it is her intention to commit suicide later that evening. She accompanies this announcement with a stream of idle chatter that describes the ease with which she has purchased the ammunition and even had it delivered to their rural home. Thelma, is at first disbelieving. When she realizes that Jessie is serious, she attempts to dissuade her. Taking little note of her mother's arguments, Jessie continues with her preparations for death. She cleans the refrigerator and instructs her mother on how to order groceries, how to use the washer and dryer, and when to put out the garbage. She tells Thelma that she has stopped delivery of the

Marsha Norman with her husband, Dann Byck, in 1983

daily paper, ordered her favorite candy for her, and arranged to continue the delivery of milk—although her mother prefers soda or orangeade. Jessie has even prepared a Christmas list of gift suggestions for her brother for the next several years.

To keep her mother busy and to create a semblance of order, Jessie asks her to make some hot chocolate for them—yet neither women drinks it because neither likes milk. The purpose in making the chocolate, clearly, was to distract her mother from the announcement Jessie has just made. While these activities are going on, Jessie keeps up a flow of gossip about her mother's friends and her family. This gossip reveals to the audience that Jessie is in her thirties, divorced, unemployed, and that she hates her life. It also reveals that her mother's closest friend will no longer visit her because Jessie's presence makes her uncomfortable. The dialogue paints a picture of a mother who has assumed an air of helplessness so that she can provide a purpose in life for her daughter. She can do the little things that Jessie does for her, obtaining her prescibtions and shopping, yet she allows her daughter to assume these chores.

Jessie sees herself as having no future. She is an epileptic who only leaves their rural house to go to the hospital after a seizure. She is divorced from a

man she still loves, but the audience learns that when given the ultimatum of either continuing her smoking habit or quitting and staying with her husband, Jessie chose smoking. We learn from Thelma, however, that the husband, Cecil, was unfaithful, having had an affair with a neighbor's daughter. Jessie's son, Ricky, is a thief and a drug addict, and while Jessie's mother thinks the boy will outgrow these tendencies, Jessie sees little hope. That lack of hope is the crux of this one act play. Jessie tells her mother that she is committing suicide because she sees no point in continuing with a life as empty as hers has become. She can visualize only another fifty years of the same emptiness and can see no point in continuing. Jessie uses the metaphor of a bus trip to describe the reason for killing herself. She states that it does not matter if you are fifty blocks from your stop when you get off because for her the stop will be the same right now as it will be in those fifty blocks/fifty years. Jessie's is a life that, from her perspective, holds no promise and no future.

Jessie's mother, Thelma, divulges family secrets in her attempt to stop Jessie's planned suicide. She tells Jessie that her seizures are not the result of a fall from a horse but that she has had them from early childhood. Thelma also tells her daughter that the epilepsy is inherited and that her father also suffered from the disease. As Thelma reveals how empty her marriage was, the audience learns of Thelma's jealousy of her daughter's close relationship with her father. As her husband lay dying, Thelma left him to watch the western series *Gunsmoke* on television, since he refused to talk to her. Yet she asks Jessie what she and her father said to one another in those last moments just before he died. Thelma refused to share her husband's last minutes and cannot understand why her daughter did not make the same choice.

Their interaction makes clear that Thelma and Jessie love one another, but, to Jessie, her mother's love is not reason enough to continue living. Thelma pleads with Jessie; she cajoles her with stories, and offers to change their lives. The desperation of the mother is clear, as is her love for her daughter. In the last moments of the play, a desperate Thelma clings to her impassive daughter and is pushed aside as Jessie leaves the room with the muted farewell "'night, Mother." She goes and locks herself in her room. The play ends with the sound of a gunshot followed by Thelma's grief-stricken call to her son.

CHARACTERS

Jessie Cates

Jessie is somewhere in her mid-thirties or early forties. She suffers from epilepsy, and this, combined with her perceived failure in relationships, provokes her decision to commit suicide. She views this act as the ultimate means of asserting control over her life. She has an ex-husband whom she still loves. Her marriage was precipitated by her mother—if not outright arranged—when Thelma hired Cecil to build a porch she did not need. Jessie has a son, Ricky, who is a petty thief and has problems with drugs. For most of her life Jessie's epilepsy has made it impossible for her to work. As the play's action begins, drugs seem to have brought the disease under control, yet Jessie is too frightened of the outside world to venture into it. She sees her life as empty, without purpose, and without a future; an existence that is utterly beyond her control to alter. Jessie has suffered several losses: the death of her father (perhaps the closest relationship in her life), the break-up of her marriage, an absent son whom she regards as a failure, and the death of her dog. Her combined depression and fear of interaction with people other than her mother has led her to

believe that the future holds no hope of change or any increase in autonomy; Jessie feels that she is a puppet acting out a life over which she has no authorship.

Thelma Cates

Thelma is Jessie's mother. She is a widow and has one other child, a son named Dawson who lives with his wife. In the course of the play, she reveals that she never loved Jessie's father and that they had little communication. She spends much of her time on needlework, and her creations clutter the family home. At first appearance she seems to be an elderly woman dependent on her daughter for many everyday necessities. It becomes clear through the course of the play, however, that she has allowed Jessie to take over these chores, not because she is incapable, but because she felt that Jessie needed a purpose.

At Jessie's announcement that she intends to commit suicide, Thelma displays a series of emotions: disbelief, anger, fear, desperation, and, finally, a degree of acceptance. She loves her daughter and makes every attempt to talk her out of killing herself. Yet there are intimations throughout the play that many of Jessie's problems may have been caused by Thelma's behavior toward and treatment of her daughter.

Mama
See Thelma Cates

Mother
See Thelma Cates

THEMES

Alienation and Loneliness

Alienation and loneliness are important themes in *'night, Mother.* Jessie has become totally isolated as a result of her epilepsy and her failed attempt at raising a family. Her mother hid the disease to protect Jessie, but in doing so, she also isolated the child from the world. She is so alone that the only way she can meet a man and marry is for her mother to hire him to so some construction work on the house. Jessie cannot work because of her disease and by the time her epilepsy is under control, she is too frightened and set in her ways to attempt life in the outside world. Jessie's decision to kill herself results from the isolation and loneliness of her life.

MEDIA ADAPTATIONS

- *'night, Mother* was adapted for film in 1986, with a screenplay by Norman and directed by Tom Moore. The film starred Sissy Spacek as Jessie and Anne Bancroft as Thelma. Although produced by Aaron Spelling, who is best known for melodramatic television series such as *Beverly Hills 90210* and *Melrose Place,* the film is true to the content of Norman's original text. Criticism has centered on Spacek and Bancroft as too glamorous to portray the simple, average women depicted in the play. The film received mixed reviews. It is available from MCA/Universal Home Video.

Free Will

Jessie's choice to kill herself is her attempt to take control of her life. In a small way she took control when she chose smoking instead of her husband, but that provided a bitter and hollow victory, since she still loved Cecil. Her epilepsy and her mother's efforts to shelter her from any knowledge of her disease in some way deprived Jessie of the free will to make decisions about her disease and, more broadly, her life. Free will means assuming responsibility for an individual's actions and an acceptance of the consequences; Jessie's choice of suicide is her effort to assert control and act upon the free will that she feels has been absent from her life.

Death

The theme of death—by definition the utter lack of life—lies at the center of *'night, Mother.* Preparation for her death is the reason for Jessie's actions and the purpose behind the dialogue that carries the play's action. It is her effort to provide closure that motivates Jessie to tell her mother of her pending suicide. The play is an hour and a half of preparation for the act of dying. The audience also sees and hears the emotions that are usually reserved for after the death of a loved one: the pain, the grief, the fear, the anger, and the reluctant acceptance.

Human Condition

The human condition is often identified as a component of the basic human need for survival. In *'night, Mother,* Thelma's hour and a half effort to save her daughter's life reveals much about the nature of the human condition. The audience is given a glimpse of the nature of the Cates's lives, their pain and anguish and the barren quality of their existence as Thelma tries to find a reason to deter her daughter's suicide. That Jessie can so easily dismiss her mother's pleas and offers of help discloses that there is no single reason as to *why* she wants to die; in Jessie's mind the overwhelming sensation is that there is no single reason for her to continue living.

Identity

An important issue for Jessie is her attempt to create an identity. She tells her mother that her brother calls her "Jess like he knows who he's talking to." She also says that her son Ricky is "as much like me as it's possible for any human to be"; Jessie identifies them both as failures. She so identifies herself with her husband that when he decides to leave her she writes herself a note telling her what she knows he feels. Jessie's identity is so tied up in the identities of those she loves—and she is too weary to attempt to assert a new identity in life—that she feels the only way to separate herself is through death.

Limitations and Opportunities

Jessie's choice to die is a direct result of the lack of opportunity in her life. She can see no future and no change and thus no purpose in her continued existence. Her epilepsy and her life's choices have resulted in an existence bound by limits and lost

TOPICS FOR FURTHER STUDY

- Research the issues surrounding the right to die. Jessie makes the choice to commit suicide but indicates that she makes this choice because she has no compelling reason to live. How does this reasoning fit the argument that proponents of an individual's right to die present?

- In *'night, Mother* Jessie identifies herself in relationship to her father, husband, son, and especially her mother; she appears to have no identity of her own. Comment of Jessie's struggle to create an identity separate from these family members. Is suicide the only means available to her?

- The emptiness of her life is an oppressive force for Jessie. Discuss the issue of alienation and isolation that defines Jessie's life.

- Many critics have been divided in their reviews of *'night, Mother*. One reviewer actually noted that men seemed particularly unaffected and unsympathetic to Jessie's plight. Are women more sympathetic? And do they identify with these two women because they, too, are familiar with the mother-daughter dynamics? Or is this a play that transcends gender stereotyping?

---

opportunities. Although her disease is now under control, a lifetime of limitations have conditioned Jessie to not look beyond the moment. Suicides are often characterized as individuals who cannot see that they have another choice. Jessie certainly fits this model.

Natural Law

Natural law is often described as the survival of the fittest (as Charles Darwin notes in his study of evolution *The Origin of Species*). It can be applied as simply an evolutionary term that accounts for the survival of one species over another. It is sometimes used to account for why one individual survives and another does not. Certainly there are applications to *'night, Mother,* since not all epileptics commit suicide (most lead normal lives that involve active socialization and work), nor do all women who are divorced or have failed personal relationships kill themselves. Jessie's death can be described as keeping with the natural law of survival—it should be noted, however, that it is Jessie who feels the world holds no place for her, not vice versa. Were she willing to make the effort, it is clear that Jessie could function in and be a part of the world. The manner in which natural law plays a part in the play is wholly created in Jessie's mind; part of her reasoning is that

she is not strong enough—she has been condition to believe—that she is too weak to live.

Success and Failure

Success and failure are important themes in *'night, Mother* because they account for the reasons behind Jessie's actions. Jessie chooses suicide to escape a life that is empty and which she sees as likely to remain empty. While she does not describe her life as a failure, it is clear from her failed marriage and her son's behavior that she sees little reason to celebrate her life achievements as successes. She regards her life as a failure and even describes her inability to work as a failing. That she cares for her mother cannot be regarded as a success, since Jessie also recognizes that her mother allows Jessie to care for her as a means to keep her busy, not out of any actual need.

STYLE

'night, Mother occurs in real time. Jessie states her intention to commit suicide in the play's opening moments. The remainder of the play focuses on Jessie's preparations for death, her mother's efforts

to dissuade her, and an examination of the emptiness and isolation of Jessie's life.

Act

A major division in a drama. In classic Greek plays the sections of the drama were signified by the appearance of the chorus and were usually divided into five acts. This is the formula for most serious drama from the Greeks to the Romans, as well as to Elizabethan playwrights such as William Shakespeare. The five acts denote the structure of dramatic action. They are exposition, complication, climax, falling action, and catastrophe. The five act structure was followed until the nineteenth century when Henrik Ibsen combined some of the acts. 'night, Mother is a one act play. The exposition, complication, climax, falling action, and catastrophe are combined in one act when Jessie reveals her intention to kill herself. The drama—and the elements of the traditional five acts—plays out during the next ninety minutes.

Analogy

Analogy is a comparison of two things. Often something unfamiliar is explained by comparing it to something familiar. In 'night, Mother Jessie uses the analogy of a bus trip for her future years as a means to explain why she is going to kill herself.

Character

A character—by strict definition—is person in a dramatic work. The actions of each character are what constitute the story. Character can also include the idea of a particular individual's morality and other traits that shape and define their personality. Characters can range from simple stereotypical figures (a New York City cab driver or a brisk, smart-aleck waitress) to more complex ones. "Characterization" is the process of creating a life—forging a person from an author's imagination. To accomplish this the author provides the character with personality traits that help define who she will be and how she will behave in a given situation. For instance, Thelma is initially made to seem silly and helpless. As the action progresses, however, Thelma reveals that she is actually quite capable and rather than a doddering old woman, is a shrewd and calculating person.

Dialogue

Dialogue is a conversation between two or more people. In 'night, Mother dialogue assumes the role of debate. Jessie and her mother engage in a debate over whether she is justified in planning a suicide. One important feature of this play is that the dialogue is realistic. Mothers and daughters (and others in close, long-term relationships) do talk in a sort of conversational short-hand that evolves over a number of years. Jessie and Thelma engage in just this sort of dialogue, which enhances the reality of the action rather than interfering with it.

Drama

A drama is often defined as any work designed to be presented on the stage. It consists of a story, of actors portraying characters, and of action. But historically, drama can also consist of tragedy, comedy, religious pageant, and spectacle. In modern usage, a "drama" (like the "Drama" section of a video store) is something that explores serious topics and themes but does not achieve the same level as tragedy. 'night, Mother incorporates aspects of drama according to this definition, while also working in elements of tragedy.

Naturalism

Naturalism was a literary movement of the late nineteenth and early twentieth centuries. This is the application of scientific principles to literature. For instance, in nature behavior is determined by environmental pressures or internal factors, none of which can be controlled or even clearly understood. There is a clear cause and effect association: either the indifference of nature or biological determinism influence behavior. In either case, there is no human responsibility for the actions of the individual. European Naturalism emphasized biological determinism, while American Naturalism emphasized environmental influences. Jessie's realization that she has inherited her father's epilepsy is a component of naturalism.

Plot

This term refers to a pattern of events that make up a story. Generally plots should have a beginning, a middle, and a conclusion, but they can sometimes be made of a series of episodes connected together (as director Quentin Tarantino did with his film Pulp Fiction, which strings a series of episodes into one larger plot). Basically, the plot provides the author with the means to explore primary themes. Students are often confused between the two terms; but themes explore ideas, and plots simply relate what happens in a very obvious manner. The plot of 'night, Mother revolves around Jessie's preparations to commit suicide. But the themes are those of identity, death, choice, and loneliness.

Realism

Realism is a nineteenth century literary term that identifies an author's attempt to portray characters, events, and settings in a realistic way. Simply put, realism is attention to detail, with description intended to be honest and frank at all levels; at its best, realism will provoke recognition in an audience. There is an emphasis on character, especially behavior. In 'night, Mother, the dialogue between Thelma and Jessie is recognizable as real to the audience. These are events, people, and a home that, as Norman hopes, will be familiar to the audience. The living room and kitchen are similar to one found in most homes in America. Thelma is familiar to most women, and her fears of losing her daughter are universal.

Setting

The time, place, and culture in which the action of the play takes place is called the setting. The elements of setting may include geographic location, physical or mental environments, prevailing cultural attitudes, or the historical time in which the action takes place. The location for 'night, Mother is an unnamed midwestern city. The action begins in the evening and concludes ninety minutes later; the one act takes place in the living room and kitchen of the Cates's residence. Norman's situation is created to be universal, so the time is relatively unimportant, and the location could be any town, the evening any evening. Norman states in her stage directions that she does not want either character identified by setting, dress, or regional accent. They are simply two women who could be anyone.

Unities

The three unities of dramatic structure include unity of time, place, and action. The unities are generally credited to the Greek playwright Aristotle, who defined them in his *Poetics*. The "unity of time" refers to all the action taking place within one twenty-four hour period. Since 'night, Mother takes place during a ninety minute period without intermission, this play adheres to the unity of time. The "unity of place" limits the action to one location, in this case, the Cates's living room and kitchen. The most important is the "unity of action." The action should have a beginning, a middle, and an end. In 'night, Mother the action begins with Jessie's announcement that she will commit suicide. The mid-

dle details her mother's attempts to dissuade her and her preparations for death; the end is the shot that concludes the play. Thus 'night, Mother adheres to all three unities.

HISTORICAL CONTEXT

Alienation, Isolation, and Anorexia

Although the United States had more than 228 million people in the early 1980s, Americans still largely defined themselves as human beings who were self-reliant and in control of their own destiny. The search for autonomy in a country where government has become so huge and intrusive is a concern for many people. But the question of autonomy is of particular interest to women who by the last half of the twentieth century were attempting in large numbers to assert themselves as individuals. One important issue for women occurred in the early 1980s, when the Equal Rights Amendment failed to be ratified. This sent a message to women that equality still remained an elusive factor in their lives. This is particularly evident in the increasing numbers of women who show symptoms of eating disorders. Women and young girls who suffer from anorexia or bulimia often cite the issue of control as a motivating factor in their eating patterns. In adopting anorexia as a means of control, women are often starving themselves to death. This is a passive means of suicide. A woman need not use a gun or another weapon such as pills; rather she can die through neglect. The intent is the same, but the means offers a long-term effort at assuming control. The correlation between anorexia and suicide is evident with Jessie. Much of 'night, Mother focuses on food but only with regard to Jessie's mother. Jessie does not consume the candy and junk food that permeates the Cates's home. In fact, Jessie's mother complains that Jessie never did like to eat. This line offers a clue that connects Jessie to other women trapped by anorexia: Jessie represents the image of a woman attempting to regain control.

Women Smokers

Since women have historically been defined as property, first of their fathers and, later in life, of their husbands, it is perhaps understandable that modern women should seek a means to define themselves as free individuals. By the early 1980s, women smokers were out-numbering their male counterparts. This trend did not evolve out of any particular love for cigarettes. Instead women began smoking for a complex set of reasons. The image of success that is evoked by cigarette advertisers certainly played a role: women could share in the same successful world populated by men. But another reason may have been that smoking represents choice. A primary argument to emerge from the women's struggle of the 1960s and 1970s was a woman's right to choose. Whether that choice involved birth control, employment, or smoking mattered little. In fact for women, smoking became a right that was not legislated and was not dependent on men. When Jessie is asked to choose between her husband and smoking, she chooses smoking. Quite simply, smoking became a freedom of choice that Jessie found lacking in her life; it represented autonomy in her life. Given the choice between smoking, which she decided to do on her own, and staying with Cecil, whom she married as a result of her mother's arrangments, Jessie opts for one of the few things she came to on her own.

Right to Die

If anything, the right to die has become an even larger issue in the fifteen years since Norman wrote *'night, Mother.* Technology and its ability to keep a body alive long after the brain ceases to function is an important impetus for those who claim the right to die. In 1981, the case of Karen Ann Quinlan was still recent news. Quinlan was a young woman who suffered major brain trauma. Although her brain was unable to monitor basic bodily fuctions such as breathing, life support machines kept her alive. Her family fought to have her life support withdrawn, arguing that Karen's quality of life was negligible. This issue has persisted in the 1990s with the prominence of Dr. Jack Kevorkian, a retired pathologist from Michigan who has assisted people in committing suicide if they are terminally ill or in chronic, unrelievable pain. Those who support right to death issues consistently state that it is a person's choice to end their own life if they deem it devoid of value. While Jessie is not terminally ill or brain dead, the manner in which she percieves her situation—through a cloud of depression—is analogous to those seeking euthanasia (which means merciful death): she feels that her quality of life is negligible. Jessie chooses to die, not because she is ill or mentally deficient in some manner, but because she has the right to choose. Norman makes clear in her text that there is no primary reason for Jessie's choice. But what she does offer is a woman who chooses to act rather than be acted upon: there is no reason for Jessie to die except that she chooses to do so. In her neutral description of Jessie, Norman is

creating a woman who could be anyone. She is also forcing her audience to question the choice of who has a right to die. The play inevitably evokes that discussion, since Norman has set her play in an indeterminate time and place. Again, Jessie's choice to commit suicide can be discussed within the larger issue of individual autonomy. Jessie could easily be lost as an individual. In deciding to die, she sets herself apart and creates an identity of her own.

CRITICAL OVERVIEW

'night, Mother was first produced in January of 1983, at the American Repertory Theatre in Cambridge, Massachusetts. This first production received favorable reviews with many of the reviewers focusing on the honesty of the relationship between mother and daughter. William Henry, who commented on Norman's realistic dialogue in his *Time* review, referred to the characters' speech as ''spare, suspenseful, and entirely honest.'' Henry continued, praising Norman's script as ''miraculously free of melodrama.'' However, the critic credited the performance of Kathy Bates as Jessie, whose ''deceptive calm gives the play its force,'' with elevating the production above the ordinary. Other critics also praised the cast which included Bates and Anna Pitoniak as Thelma. As further proof of the play's success, Norman was awarded the first Susan Smith Blackburn prize, which is given annually to a woman playwright, in January, 1983.

Two months later, *'night, Mother* opened on Broadway with the same cast. Again the reviews were mostly favorable, but a few critics did wonder what merited all the fuss. Although many reviwers continued to praise the play's realistic depiction, detractors of the play based their disfavor on the argument that the play was so realistic as to be ordinary. In his review for the *Nation,* Richard Gilman stated that *'night, Mother* has nothing wrong with it, but that there is ''not much to get excited about either.'' Gilman refers to Thelma as ''silly, self-indulgent and totally reliant on her daughter in practical matters''; he describes Jessie as ''heavy-set, slow-moving and morose.'' (Gilman imposed Bates's reality on to the character of Jessie who is meant only as a representative type; Norman neither describes nor alludes to Jessie's weight in the play; rather she states in her stage direction that Jessie is ''pale and vaguely unsteady physically.'') Gilman did state that he found the play "interesting as a moral inquiry" into the right to die issue but that the dialogue off-sets this point with conversation that is commonplace and predictable. For other critics the play is a manipulation of the audience. For example, Stanley Kauffman, writing for the *Saturday Review,* claimed that Jessie's statement regarding her intention to kill herself is purely an act of vengeance and that the ninety minutes spent in preparation are intended as torture. Instead of a heroine, Jessie becomes a "vengeful neurotic." That the audience sympathizes, cares about these characters, or despairs for them is, in Kauffman's view, a manipulation of the audience by Norman. However, the dissenters were in the minority. Most critics and the public favored the play enough that it had a ten month run on Broadway. As a further endorsement, *'night, Mother* was awarded the 1983 Pulitzer prize for drama.

In April 1984, the play opened off-Broadway still with the original cast. The play has since been produced by touring companies and in regional theatres across the United States. Although American critics had not labeled *'night, Mother* as feminist, Patricia Keeney Smith, in her review of the Canadian production (which opened in October, 1984) did note that the play was "a story of women, full of valour, irony and liberating laughter."

When *'night, Mother* was eventually adapted for film, Norman wrote the screenplay. The film received mixed reviews from several of the same critics repeating their earlier reviews of the theatrical production. And although Norman had emphasized in her stage directions that the women were indistinguishable from any other women, much of the criticism of the film focused on the two actresses playing Jessie and Thelma, Sissy Spacek and Anne Bancroft, respectively. Critics either embraced the two as ideal for the parts or rejected them as the worst possible choices. The film was a commercial success, but that may have been in large part due the marketability of its stars.

CRITICISM

Sheri Metzger

Metzger holds a Ph.D. and has a strong background in literature and drama education. In this essay she discusses issues of identity and autonomy.

A critical issue in *'night, Mother* is the relationship between Jessie and her mother, Thelma. It is evident in Jessie's preparations for her suicide that she regards herself as her mother's primary caretaker. Jessie is responsible for her mother's diet, for the maintenance of the home, and for her mother's health, or so her Thelma lets her believe. In assuming so much control over her mother, Jessie has reversed the mother-daughter relationship and has become a mother to her own mother. It is little wonder, then, that she cannot imagine an identity separate from her mother's. In deciding that she will kill herself, Jessie is finally establishing an identity of her own and setting a boundary between them that her mother cannot cross. When Jessie announces her decision to kill herself at the end of the evening that she sets in motion a series of events that must end with her death; there is never any doubt that Jessie will die at the play's conclusion because it is necessary for her to die to free herself. The choice she makes is one that only she can make; her mother has no say in the matter. Their dialogue establishes that this may have been the first significant decision Jessie has ever made independent of her mother.

Jessie has always been bound to her mother. She left her mother's home to marry the man her mother selected for her, and, when that marriage failed, she returned home to her mother. And with the example of her parent's unhappy and uncommunicative marriage before her, Jessie accepted that a retreat to her mother's house was her only option. According to developmental psychology, adult maturation is partially achieved through a separation from parental figures, as a person acquires independence and the ability to make independent decisions. This maturation process has been lacking in Jessie's life. She has been sheltered and protected, kept isolated in her mother's home, and closeted with only her family to provide socialization. Consequently, a complete break from her family is the only option if Jessie is to become an individual; the tragedy of this play is that for Jessie suicide is the only avenue to this independence.

The isolation of an existence without friends and a lack of the socialization that accompanies the emotional and physical growth of most young women is an important feature of Jessie's loneliness. The emptiness of her life is the primary reason she offers for her decision to kill herself. And it is the one argument her mother cannot combat. In the series of objections that Thelma raises regarding Jessie's suicide, the closest she can come to dealing with her

Anne Bancroft as Mother and Sissy Spacek as Jessie in the film adaptation

daughter's loneliness is her suggestion of a dog to provide companionship.

Thelma recognizes and understands Jessie's isolation. She has lived a long time with solitude. Any thought that her daughter would provide companionship evaporated when Jessie demonstrated that she preferred the company of her silent father; but since Jessie, too, has a propensity for silence, it is unlikely that Jessie could ever have provided Thelma with a substantial form of companionship. Instead of conversation, Thelma has satisfied her social needs and combated her loneliness with needlepoint, junk food, and candy. But for Jessie, the craving for something more in her life cannot be satisfied with food or cross-stitching. Indeed, Thelma states that Jessie has never been interested in eating. She needs to fill an emptiness that food cannot satisfy. And like many people who commit suicide, Jessie Cates sees this as the only option left to her; it is the only way to cancel a life filled with hopelessness, helplessness, and emptiness.

In an essay in *Modern Drama* that examines Jessie's need to establish her identity and autonomy, Jenny S. Spencer began by noting the different responses that men and women had to a performance of *'night, Mother* which she attended. She observed that men found the play predictable and

without tension. They were not surprised by the suicide. But Spencer noted that the women with whom she spoke found the play realistic and disturbing. On some level, women can empathize and identify with both Jessie and Thelma. Spencer argued that when Jessie articulates her inability to change her life—"[I] cannot make it better, make it work. But I can stop it"—she is trying to establish some control over her life. This speech establishes the purpose motivating Jessie's decision. It provides her with authority, with autonomy, with identity. Spencer maintains that Jessie's suicide, "self-negating as it is, will specifically address that need to protect, to fix, to determine her identity."

That Jessie lacks an identity is evident from the information given regarding her past. She identifies so strongly with the husband she has lost but still loves that, when he left her, she wrote a note to herself justifying his choice and signing his name. She explains this by saying that she knew how he felt. She excuses her son's behavior by asserting that he is like her and thus doomed to failure. Jessie's self is so a part of her husband and child that she cannot exist separately from them. Thelma further robs Jessie of an identity when she tells Jessie that she is just like her father. She is silent as he was silent, but more importantly, the source of

WHAT DO I READ NEXT?

- Kate Chopin's *The Awakening* (1899) is a novel that illuminates the heroines struggle to establish an identity separate from that of her father, husband, and son. Choice, free will, and suicide are important issues in this text.

- Tillie Olson's short story, "I Stand Here Ironing" (1961) is concerned with the relationship between a mother and daughter. Olson relates events common to all women and explores how those events can serve to trap mothers and daughters in a relationship not of their making.

- Beth Henley's *Crimes of the Heart* (1982) depicts a mother and three daughters who struggle to create an identity that is not defined by their mother's suicide. Henley's play examines the other side of suicide—that of the child who must contend with guilt and unresolved questions when a parent chooses to kill herself.

- "To Room Nineteen," Doris Lessing's 1963 short story presents a woman who subordinates her identity to the needs and identities of her husband and children. Her choice to abandon her family by committing suicide can promote a compelling discussion about free choice that often focuses on gender.

- Carolyn Heilbrun's text, *Writing A Woman's Life* (1988) examines how women's lives are written, how the events, decisions, and relationships that define women's lives are told and presented to the public. This book provides the reader with an understanding of the struggle the writer must undertake to create a text. Individual chapters provide interesting insights into some of the most famous women writers of the last century and can help more advanced students develop an appreciation for the art of writing and perhaps instill a desire to write.

---

her disability, her epilepsy, is inherited from him; she has his disease. Even the epilepsy that she thought resulted from a fall from a horse is not her own. As she sees the situation, there is no part that is wholly hers. And, of course, she is also her mother. Jessie has become her mother, not only because she is now Thelma's caretaker, but because daughters are always bound in some inexplicable way to their mothers.

As Jessie's identity cannot be detached from her mother's, Thelma's cannot be isolated from Jessie's. Thelma's fear is the one that nags at all mothers: if my child dies, will I cease to be a mother? As Spencer observed: "Mama is engaged in the immediate struggle to save her child's life, a struggle in which her own identity is equally at stake." *'night, Mother* is not a play about suicide. It is a play, as Spencer wrote, "about mothers and daughters, about feminine identity and feminine autonomy." The realism of Norman's dialogue speaks to mothers and daughters who can immediately identify with the conflict and tensions that define the Cates's lives. Consequently, women recognize themselves in the dialogue, whereas men see and hear little with which to identify.

As *'night, Mother* is played out on stage, the audience is made aware of the passing of time. The play is constructed in one act without intermission. The clocks on stage display real time. Although time is advancing, in many ways the clocks also serve as a kind of countdown. When time runs out, the shot will sound and Jessie will die somewhere off stage. The tension in the audience quickens during this period. As Mama's arguments are met with resistance, the audience becomes aware that Jessie's suicide is inevitable. Serving as counterbalance to this tension is Thelma's almost growing, though unnerving, acceptance of Jessie's decision. She does try a succession of arguments designed to change Jessie's mind, but when they fail, the two begin a conversation about how Thelma should report the death, who she should call, and how she should behave at the funeral. The conversation assumes an even more macabre tone when Mama says, ''I'll talk about what I have on, that's always good. And I'll have some crochet work with me.'' The matter-of-fact nature of this conversation indicates that Thelma also realizes the inevitability of Jessie's loss and her attention turns to how to cope.

In an essay that examines Thelma's reliance on oral gratification as a substitute for emotional involvement, Laura Morrow asserted in *Studies in American Drama* that ''mama prefers surface to substance.'' That is, Thelma uses immediate gratification—in her case candy and junk food—as a means to deny reality. Chatter serves much the same purpose. Mama cannot understand the silence of her husband and her daughter. She cannot understand that both use silence as a means of reflection. Mama, on the other hand, uses conversation in place of thought. It is simply easier for her to talk than to think. That Jessie recognizes these traits in her mother is evident in the preparations she makes before her death. Her immediate concern is with food. Jessie instructs her mother on how to order food and when to have it delivered. She orders a supply of her mother's favorite junk food and candy. Jessie even anticipates that her mother won't eat the foods that she needs and insists that the milkman continue to deliver milk—even if her mother objects. But Jessie is also aware of her mother's other hunger, and so she suggests other people with whom Thelma can have conversations. Jessie's brother Dawson and his wife can also provide company, but Mama rejects this because they only have Sanka (instant coffee). Once again, food takes priority in her life. And yet, it is clear to the audience that Thelma loves Jessie and that Jessie returns that love. The audience can only assume that their love for one another is not enough for Jessie to transcend a lifetime of disappointment and pain.

'night, Mother is a profoundly disturbing play that forces its audience to confront the darker issues that arise in some families. And although Norman conditions the audience to expect it, the offstage sound of the gunshot at the play's end has a power and a shock all its own.

Source: Sheri Metzger, in an essay for *Drama for Students*, Gale, 1997.

Sally Browder

In this excerpt, Browder examines the relationship between the mother and daughter characters in 'night, Mother, *comparing them to traditional parent/child roles.*

A frequent author on themes of personality and development, Browder is a clinical psychologist and program director specializing in women's psychiatric treatment.

In a nondescript house in anonymous America a conversation unfolds between two women. In the course of this routine and quiet evening at home the revelation shared by one offers up a jolting portrayal of a personal relationship and power. Jessie, a woman in her late thirties or early forties, announces to her mother that she is going to kill herself at the end of the evening. In the ensuing dialogue Thelma, her mother, moves from scoffing disbelief to the stunned realization that her daughter is serious.

No crisis has precipitated this decision. Indeed, nothing has happened at all. But Jessie explains her growing recognition that the prospects for her future are as bleak as her life has been disappointing and filled with failure to that point. She has lived with her mother for a long time. Divorced, alienated from her criminal son, struggling with—and only recently having gained some control over—her epileptic seizures, she lives in a world isolated from outside support and friendship. The father she loved as a child has died. She is not close to, indeed resents, her older, domineering brother and his wife. Jessie explains that she has been thinking about suicide for years and has chosen this moment simply because she now feels good enough to do it. As she relates in poignant understatement, ''I'm just not having a very good time and I don't have any reason to think it'll get anything but worse. I'm tired. I'm hurt. I'm sad. I feel used.''

The power of the play *'night, Mother* lies in its relentless movement toward the final gunshot. No matter how much we do not want to believe it will come, we are forced to share with the mother a growing realization that the evening will end with Jessie's death. Death lends to all of human existence an urgency and poignancy, a sense of meaning that arises from the awareness that life will not last. In Jessie's case the knowledge and control over the timing of that end and its immediacy are themselves the source of meaning never before existent in her life. Her suicide arms her with a power, a sense of control over her life. It is the lens through which she offers a view of her existence, an existence so fraught with detachment and boredom that she chooses to continue meticulously in the tedious business of its day-to-day routine until that moment when she shuts it off. But when her life is compressed within the boundaries of that evening, what emerges are a few hours of honesty and intensity that burst like a meteoric glimpse of what this mother-daughter relationship is and what it might have been.

When Jessie chooses suicide, she not only defines the boundaries of her existence, she draws the boundaries between mother and daughter as well. She makes a choice that is not her mother's choice. Thelma does not disagree with Jessie's view of life. She, too, has had her share of disappointments. Her marriage was unhappy and she carries an unreasonable guilt that she was somehow responsible for Jessie's epilepsy. She acknowledges the unattractiveness of her life: "We don't have anything anybody'd want, Jessie. I mean, I don't even want what we got, Jessie". Her life is characterized by limitations, by a sense of detachment and resignation that would have her observe that "there's just not that much to things that I could ever see". But while she does not understand it, she is resigned to getting through life, helped, so to speak, by her attempts to sweeten her existence with dishes of candy scattered throughout the house.

Jessie's decision is a repudiation of her mother's choices. It is her one clear statement that she will not be like her mother. This is in striking defiance of the mother's assumption of oneness in their relationship, an assumption that allows her to say presumptuously, "Everything you do has to do with me, Jessie: You can't do anything, wash your face or cut your finger, without doing it to me". In the end she cannot even keep her daughter alive.

As we are left to wonder how this daughter came to see all of the elements of her life as indicative of failure and alienation, and how this mother's experience contributes to this conclusion, we have only the evidence of this brief, private conversation. As Jessie says, "You're it, Mama. No more." The horrible bleakness of life, the emptiness Jessie experiences is not a peculiarity of female existence. But the significance of the mother-daughter relationship in the daughter's sense of powerlessness is unique to women. This play is not merely about the perils of parenthood or, more specifically, even the precariousness of motherhood in regard to

> THE POWER OF THE PLAY
> 'NIGHT, MOTHER LIES IN ITS
> RELENTLESS MOVEMENT TOWARD
> THE FINAL GUNSHOT"

daughters. It is about the problem and the elusiveness of autonomy, one of the stages on which the drama of human development unfolds. . . .

At some point, most mothers and daughters recognize that they are pitted in an ageless struggle by their mutual efforts to maintain their relationship in its earliest form or to alter it. Like a complicated primitive dance, they perpetually pull together and move apart. The daughter resists her mother's attempts to control her life, yet at the same time resents the mother for what the mother has not been able to provide for her. The mother, on the other hand, simultaneously pushes her daughter away, in an effort to teach her not to expect nurturance but to give it and yet strives to protect and cling to her daughter, to claim her as an extension or possession. From this struggle emerges the opportunity for daughters to make their own choices, develop a sense of themselves, and participate in relationships as more equal partners.

For daughters, and thus for all women, the struggle is played out continuously in relationships. It is the choice between security and risk, loyalty and self-assertion, submission and power. They must choose to replay intricate patterns of dependency and need or courageously engage in equitable partnerships. Given the unique dynamics of this first important relationship, women are in greatest peril of failing to develop an adequate sense of meaning and autonomy when they confront the temptation to accept a sense of meaning assigned to them by others, assigned to them initially by their mothers.

This is the tragic realization to which Jessie comes too late. Jessie's isolation and exclusive reliance upon her mother as sole companion are insufficient to provide her with a sense of self, to provide her with a sense of power, a sense of meaning in life: "What if you are all I have and you're not enough?" "It's somebody I lost, all right, it's my own self. Who I never was, or who I tried to be and never got there. Somebody I waited for who never came. And never will.''

The healthy course, to participate in relationships as an equal partner rather than as a dependent or recipient, requires giving up the security of an unequal relationship. It requires being strong and hopeful about one's own future while tolerating the pain of knowing the limitations and diminishment of the one with whom one may be most identified. It also implies staying around to confront the consequences of honesty, something of which Jessie's choice of suicide relieved her.

Honesty is a casualty of unequal relationships. The lack of honesty in mother-daughter relationships is not always intentional or malicious and usually arises out of a desire to protect. Mothers alter the truth in an effort to shield their daughters from what well may be a harsh reality. In doing so, however, they fail to equip their daughters to deal with reality, whatever it may be. I am reminded of a friend's story of how, as a young girl, she could not tolerate spending even one night away from home. When she called home her mother always insisted that everything was fine in the same tone of voice she always used, even in the presence of disaster. The mother's reassurances became red flags that pitched the young girl into a frenzy of anxiety and fear.

If Thelma is at fault, it is only in believing she could provide everything for this daughter, that she alone could be enough. So pervasive is this expectation, that even Jessie shares it, only realizing the bitter consequences of it on the evening of her death. She says of the decision to return to live with her mother, ''If it was a mistake, we made it together.''

In the end, whatever this particular mother did would have been wrong, just as whatever any mother does is wrong. As long as she is made to feel ultimately responsible for her daughter's well-being, a mother is thrust into unyielding, conflicting expectations. She encourages her daughter's dependency and identification with her while struggling with her own ambivalence about rearing a child who may serve to remind her of her own limitations. She must enable the daughter to develop a sense of self-sufficiency while being charged by society to engender qualities that may not contribute to a sense of power or well-being. The qualities that we think of as characterizing a good mother are not necessarily qualities that enable young daughters to attain autonomy. Mothers either love their children too much or not enough. And their daughters either love or hate them whatever they do.

As the interaction moves on to its jarring conclusion, we sense the inevitability of its outcome. It is not that there was anything missing from this relationship, though this might be a more reassuring assessment. Jessie and Thelma were not more or less honest than most other mothers and daughters. This mother did not deprive her daughter, at least not any differently from the ways many mothers deprive their daughters when they pass on to them their insecurities and needs and sense of resignation. Nevertheless, Thelma is left to wonder what she could have done wrong, just as she has wondered all her life how she could have altered the reality of her daughter's epilepsy or failed marriage or any other experience in life she could not have controlled. Thelma's helpless questioning mirrors our own disturbing questions. How could it have been possible for Jessie to feel a sense of anticipation in her life of good things to come rather than the certainty of failure and deprivation? Confronted with such a small universe and a limited set of options, how could she have developed a strong enough sense of self to survive?

In the end, the only reality we can know is that self which we cannot help being, the self known first in that most primary of relationships, the private affair between mother and daughter, those two selves that merge and painfully pull apart and that ultimately cannot bear the burden of existence for each other. But the frightening prospect of randomness in this relationship is that it can lead in either of two ways. As that relationship is reenacted again, for every daughter, in all subsequent relationships, one either learns the courage to experience meaning in life and the power of a separate self, experienced in relation to others, or one shares the painful expression of this woman's reality—that the only power one has is the power to say no.

Source: Sally Browder, '''I Thought You Were Mine': Marsha Norman's 'night, Mother,'' in *Mother Puzzles: Daughters and Mothers in Contemporary American Literature*, edited by Mickey Pearlman, Greenwood Press, 1989, pp. 109–13.

Richard Gilman

In this review, Gilman admires the artistic merits of 'night, Mother *yet, in light of the play's subject matter, questions the accolades bestowed upon Norman's work.*

Gilman is an American educator and critic whose works include The Making of Modern Drama *(1974) and* Decadence: The Strange Life of an Epithet *(1979).*

The hyperbole machine is operating on Broadway again. Upon a modest two-character play with nothing flagrantly wrong with it—but not much to get excited about either—the reviewers have lavished nearly their whole stock of ecstatic adjectives, to which encomiums a Pulitzer Prize has just been added. Even before Marsha Norman's *'night, Mother* reached New York City, Robert Brustein likened it to *Long Day's Journey Into Night.* (That Brustein's American Repertory Theater had given the play its premiere, in Boston, might have had something to do with that wild comparison.) Well, O'Neill's best play and Norman's do have something in common: they both bring us unpleasant news about the family.

The play takes place one evening in a house "way out on a country road" in the South. A middle-aged woman and her thirtyish daughter live here. The mother is silly, self-indulgent and totally reliant on her daughter in practical matters; the daughter is heavyset, slow-moving and morose. Early in the evening she informs her mother that she is going to kill herself that night. "I'm tired," she says. "I'm hurt. I'm sad. I feel used." From then on the play details the mother's frantic efforts to dissuade her daughter and the young woman's stolid insistence on carrying out her plan.

The mother makes absurd suggestions: the daughter could take up crocheting; they could get a dog, rearrange the furniture. The younger woman grimly makes her preparations, showing her mother where things are in the kitchen, telling her how to pay the bills and so on. As the mother begins to grasp her daughter's seriousness, her arguments become the "reasonable" ones any civilized person would make, but the daughter beats them back, saying she wants to turn life off "like the radio when there's nothing on I want to listen to."

Up to this point the play is moderately interesting as a moral inquiry (do we have the right to kill ourselves?) and moderately effective as a tale of suspense. But then the women begin to talk about the past, the daughter's childhood in particular, and what emerges is commonplace and predictable. I don't mean their lives are commonplace and predictable—that's a given—but dramatically the play falls into domestic cliche. The mother confesses that she and her husband, the girl's father, had no

love for each other and, in response to the daughter's lament, says, "How could I know you were so alone?"

Next we learn that the daughter suffers from epilepsy. She says it's in remission and isn't the reason she's killing herself, but the fact of the illness, and especially the fact that the mother for a long time hid the truth about it from her, enters our consciousness as a diminution of mystery. So too does the daughter's admission that her own husband left her partly because she refused to stop smoking.

The effect of these revelations is that the suicide becomes explicable on the one hand—epileptics, neglected children and abandoned wives have a hard time "coping"—and ludicrous on the other—if nicotine is more important than marriage, what can you expect? The play might have had a richness, a fertile strangeness of moral and philosophical substance, had the suicide been undertaken as a more or less free act; had Norman not offered as the executor of this fascinating, dreadful decision a character with so many troubles. When the shot sounded (from behind a bedroom door) I wasn't startled, dismayed or much moved; it was all *sort of* sad, *sort of* lugubrious.

Norman writes cleanly, with wry humor and no bathos. Kathy Bates as the daughter and Anne Pitoniak as the mother give finely shaded performances. But the only way I can account for the acclaim. *'night, Mother's* been getting, besides the hunger for "important," "affecting" dramas that gnaws at our educated theatergoers, is that this domestic tragedy doesn't succumb to the occupational disease of its genre: an "uplifting" or at least a consoling denouement. But what a negative virtue that is, and what a comment on our impoverished theater! Yes, the play's *honest,* yes it's sincere; but have we reached the point where we find such minimal virtues something to rave about?

Source: Richard Gilman, review of *'night, Mother* in the *Nation,* Vol. 236, no. 18, May 7, 1983, p. 586.

FURTHER READING

Brown, Linda Ginter, Editor. *Marsha Norman: A Casebook,* Garland (New York), 1996.

This is a collection of essays that explore different aspects of Norman's work. The collection includes essays on the Norman plays *'night, Mother, Getting*

NORMAN WRITES CLEANLY, WITH WRY HUMOR AND NO BATHOS"

Out, Third and Oak, The Holdup, Traveler in the Dark, Sarah and Abraham, and *The Secret Garden.*

Burkman, Katherine H. "The Demeter Myth and Doubling in Marsha Norman's *'night, Mother*" in *Modern American Drama: The Female Canon,* edited by June Schlueter, Faileigh Dickinson University Press, 1990. p 254-63.

Burkman examines the nature of the mother-daughter relationship in *'night, Mother* by comparing Jessie and Thelma to the mythic Demeter and Persephone.

DeMastes, William W. "Jessie and Thelma Revisited: Marsha Norman's Conceptual Challenge in *'night, Mother*" in *Modern Drama,* Vol. 36, no. 1, 1993, pp. 109-19.

DeMastes examines feminist criticism of Norman's play and concludes that feminist who have condemned the play as subordinate to male constructs of realism should take another look at the play, which demonstrates that feminist writers can use realism to tell a woman's story.

Hart, Lynda. "Doing Time: Hunger for Power in Marsha Norman's Plays" in *Southern Quarterly,* Vol. 25, no. 3, Spring, 1987, pp. 67-79.

Hart examines how food and the hunger to escape a repressive and oppressive life are central to several of Norman's plays. Among the plays she examines are *'night, Mother* and *Getting Out.*

Henry, William A. "Reinventing the Classic" in *Time,* February 7, 1983, pp. 85.

Henry offers a positive review of Norman's play that commends the dialogue and the casting of Kathy Bates as Jessie.

Morrow, Laura. "Orality and Identity in *'night, Mother* and *Crimes of the Heart*" in *Studies in American Drama* Vol. 3, 1988, pp. 23-39.

Morrow examines the relationship between mothers and daughters and the search by daughters to create an identity separate from their mother's. The author compares these two plays and concludes that food and orality are important devices for both Norman's play and Beth Henley's *Crimes of the Heart.*

Smith, Raynette Halvorsen. "*'night, Mother* and *True West:* Mirror Images of Violence and Gender" in *Violence in Drama,* edited by James Redmond, Cambridge University Press, 1991. pp. 277-89.

Smith claims that violence and gender stereotyping in both Norman's play and Sam Shepard's *True West* function to deconstruct gender myths of feminine masochism of which both Norman and Shepard have been accused.

Spencer, Jenny S. "Norman's *'night, Mother:* Psycho-drama of Female Identity" in *Modern Drama,* Vol. 30, no. 3, September, 1987, pp. 364-75.

Spencer explores Jessie's struggle to establish her own identity, one separate from her father, husband, son, and mother. Spencer concludes that Norman's play is more about mothers and daughters and female autonomy than it is about suicide.

Wolfe, Irmgard H. "Marsha Norman" in *American Playwrights since 1945: A Guide to Scholarship, Criticism, and Performance,* edited by Philip C. Kolin, Greenwood, 1989. p 339-48.

Wofle provides a production history, including excerpts from reviews of Norman's plays. A bibliography is also included.

SOURCES

Gilman, Richard. "Review of *'night, Mother*" in the *Nation* May 7, 1983, pp. 585-86.

Kauffman, Stanley. "More Trick than Tragedy" in the *Saturday Review,* Vol. 9, no. 10, September-October, 1983, pp. 47-48.

Smith, Patricia Keeney. "Theatre of Extremity" in *Canadian Forum,* April, 1985, pp. 37-40.

The Odd Couple

NEIL SIMON
1965

When *The Odd Couple* appeared on Broadway in March of 1965, Neil Simon was already a fairly well-known playwright. His successful comedy, *Come Blow Your Horn,* had initiated his Broadway career in 1961 and *Barefoot in the Park* in 1963 had been an even bigger hit. But *The Odd Couple,* with its unforgettable pair of mismatched roommates, made Simon a cultural phenomenon, and he subsequently became in his own lifetime the most commercially successful playwright in the history of theatre. After its long run on Broadway, *The Odd Couple* was turned into a successful film in 1968 and then became a popular television series (on the American Broadcasting Company network) running from 1970 to 1975. Thus, Oscar Madison and Felix Ungar, the ''odd couple'' of the title, were steadily prominent in the popular entertainment industry for ten years and, as a result, became a part of American culture. Though some may forget which one was ''sloppy'' and which one ''neat,'' almost everyone understands the phrase ''odd couple'' as a way of describing a mismatched pair. The television show is still syndicated in reruns, the movie version appears frequently on television, and regional and local theatre groups mount productions of the play with great regularity. In 1985 Simon responded to the continued popularity of his odd pair by writing a female version for Broadway, in which all the characters' genders were reversed. Though not as popular as the original play, this new version helped perpetuate the ''odd couple'' as one

of the most memorable pair of characters in the history of commercial theatre.

AUTHOR BIOGRAPHY

Neil Simon was born on July 4, 1927, in the Bronx, New York, the younger son of a father who sold cloth fabric to the dress manufacturers in Manhattan's garment district. At the age of fifteen Simon teamed with his older brother Danny to write comedy sketches for the annual employee party of a Brooklyn department store; their success in this endeavor convinced Simon that he wanted to be a comedy writer. He and Danny eventually wrote sketches for popular radio and television shows, but the partnership split in 1954 and Neil went on to write for television comedians like Sid Caesar, Garry Moore, Phil Silvers, Red Buttons, and Jerry Lewis.

Though successful enough to earn two Emmy Awards for television writing in 1957 and 1959, Simon found writing for television unfulfilling and in the fall of 1957 began working, in his spare time, on his first play. *Come Blow Your Horn,* based on his relationship with Danny and their parents, took him three years to write, and he went through twenty-two completely different versions. When the finished *Come Blow Your Horn* finally appeared on Broadway in 1961, however, its success launched Simon's playwriting career. His second comedy, *Barefoot in the Park* (1963), was based on the life he and his first wife, Joan Baim, had lived in a small apartment in New York City's Greenwich Village. With a young Robert Redford in one of the lead roles this comedy was even more successful than his first. In his third and most famous comedy, *The Odd Couple,* Danny served as the model for the meticulous Felix Ungar. By all standards, the play was an enormous success. By the mid–1960s Neil Simon was rich, successful, and very famous. He was so prolific with his comedy hits in the late 1960s and early 1970s that he sometimes had as many as four shows running simultaneously on Broadway.

In 1973, Joan, Simon's wife of twenty years, died of cancer. Simon subsequently married actress Marsha Mason, who would star in several productions of his work. His *Chapter Two* (1977) was based on Simon's complex emotional response to Joan's death and his second marriage. While still a comedy, this play represents a turning point in Simon's career, introducing more serious shadings to his palette. Many of his subsequent plays adopted this new pattern and from 1983 to 1986 a trilogy of such autobiographical plays—*Brighton Beach Memoirs, Biloxi Blues,* and *Broadway Bound*—won Simon greater praise from critics. In the 1990s, his fourth decade of playwriting, Simon's success continued, and in 1996 he published the first half of his memoirs, *Rewrites,* which covers the period from his birth to the reception of *Chapter Two.*

PLOT SUMMARY

Act I: *The Initial Poker Game*

The Odd Couple opens on a hot summer night in the large, twelfth-floor apartment of New York City sportswriter Oscar Madison. A few months earlier, before Oscar's wife left him, the apartment had reflected the modest luxury of its Riverside Drive neighborhood on the Upper East Side of Manhattan. But the apartment is now a mess because Oscar is very sloppy and his weekly poker game is in progress. Dirty dishes, empty bottles, half-filled glasses, ashtrays, and other messes created by the poker game have been added to the discarded clothes, old newspapers, magazines, mail, and disarrayed furniture that are part of Oscar's everyday sloppiness.

As the curtain rises on this smoke-filled room we see Murray, Roy, Speed, and Vinnie around the poker table. They are concerned about the unusual lateness of one of their regular poker players, Felix Ungar. Oscar enters from the kitchen with food for his buddies, the phone rings. It's Oscar's wife complaining about his overdue alimony payments. Two more phone calls, one from Murray's wife and another to Felix's wife, Frances, inform everyone that Felix is missing because earlier in the day his wife declared an end to their twelve-year marriage. The poker players worry that the sensitive Felix might be contemplating suicide, and when he finally arrives at Oscar's apartment they try to pretend that everything is normal while simultaneously interpreting everything Felix does as a preamble to suicide. Felix admits that earlier in the day he swallowed a whole bottle of pills but then vomited them up. After heartfelt expressions of concern, Murray, Roy, Speed, and Vinnie go home, and

Oscar tries to console Felix, massaging his neck and back, pouring him a drink. When Felix hums and hops from leg to leg, bellowing like a moose to clear his ears, we get an indication of the eccentricity that might have led his wife to expel him. Felix confesses that he was unbearably obsessive about such things as petty finances, cleaning house, and cooking. Oscar sympathizes by describing the traits that led his wife to leave him. He invites Felix to move in with him, admitting that he doesn't like living alone. Felix agrees, imagining all the ways he can help Oscar—from fixing things to cooking and cleaning. During this discussion, Felix's wife calls but only to find out when Felix is coming back for his clothes (she wants to have the bedroom repainted). Felix declares his acceptance of the failed marriage and starts to clean up Oscar's apartment, responding to Oscar's goodnight by calling Oscar by his wife's name, Frances.

Act II, Scene 1: The Second Poker Game

Two weeks later, about eleven at night, another poker game is in session, but this time the apartment is immaculately clean. Felix appears from the kitchen with carefully prepared food and reminds all the players to use their coasters to preserve the carefully applied finish on the table. Some of the players, like Vinnie, are quite pleased with the new atmosphere. Others, like Oscar and Speed, are aggravated by the excessive concern for tidiness. The game breaks up prematurely and Murray is the last to leave, commenting on how happy he thinks Oscar and Felix must be living the bachelor life. But in the argument that ensues following Murray's departure, Oscar makes it clear that he is very unhappy living with the excessively tidy Felix. He asserts that Felix is obsessive about controlling things, including his own emotions, and ought to loosen up, relax, and have more fun. But when Felix tries to express his anger by throwing a cup against the door, he hurts his shoulder. Oscar's plan for loosening up and having more fun is to invite to dinner two attractive sisters from the upstairs apartment. Gwendolyn and Cecily Pigeon are British (they say "solicitor" instead of "lawyer"). Oscar met them on the elevator a week earlier, and he is eager to get to know them better. Felix, however, feels a loyalty to his estranged wife that makes "dating" seem wrong to him. Following an argument, Felix finally relents and agrees to help entertain the Pigeon sisters—

Neil Simon in 1988

provided he can cook the dinner. He calls his wife to ask for her recipe for London broil.

Act II, Scene 2: An Evening with the Pigeon Sisters

A few days later, about eight at night, the dining room table is set elegantly for four. Felix is in the kitchen when Oscar enters cheerily. But Felix is angry because Oscar had told him he would be home at seven and that the sisters would arrive by seven-thirty. The dinner, planned for eight o'clock, is nearly ruined. Gwendolyn and Cecily arrive and they all sit, but Felix does not join the conversation until he comments, quite inappropriately, on the weather. When Oscar goes into the kitchen to fix drinks, Felix becomes the center of attention for the Pigeon sisters and tells them how much he misses his wife and children. This is not what Oscar had in mind for trying to romance the women, but Gwendoyn and Cecily find Felix "sensitive." When Oscar comes from the kitchen with their drinks all three are crying. Felix rushes into the kitchen to inspect his burned London broil and when he dejectedly returns, Gwendolyn and Cecily suggest that they all go upstairs to their apartment for dinner. The sisters leave to prepare but Felix tells Oscar he won't go because it would mean being unfaithful to his wife and children. Oscar goes upstairs alone,

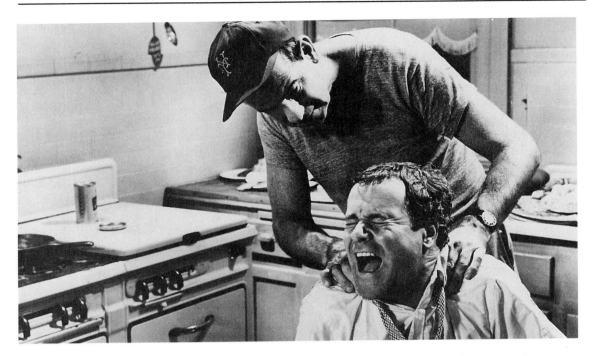

Walter Matthau as Oscar attempts to relieve some of Felix's tension by giving him a massage

angrily accusing Felix of being unwilling to change, suggesting sarcastically that if he wants to commit suicide the apartment is indeed twelve floors from the pavement.

Act III: The Last Poker Game

The next evening, about seven-thirty, the apartment is set up for yet another poker game. Felix is vacuuming when Oscar comes in, still angry about the previous evening's failure with the Pigeon sisters. They argue and Oscar begins to sabotage Felix's efforts at cleaning, finally throwing a plate of linguini against the kitchen wall. Oscar gets Felix's suitcase and demands that Felix move out. Felix leaves just as the other poker players arrive. His friends are worried about him but have started to play poker nonetheless. The doorbell rings and Gwendolyn, Cecily, and Felix appear. They have come for Felix's things because he is going to move in with the Pigeon sisters for a few days until he gets settled. Oscar and Felix shake hands just as Oscar's wife calls on the phone. Oscar sent her money to pay all his alimony, and he expresses a desire to talk with her again. As he is going out the door, Felix promises to come back for the next week's poker game. The poker game begins and Oscar admonishes the players to be careful of their cigarette butts.

CHARACTERS

Oscar Madison

Oscar Madison is the "messy" half of this famous "odd couple." Oscar takes pity on his best friend, the newly separated and nearly suicidal Felix Ungar, and invites Felix to live with him in his New York City apartment. Within two weeks, however, Oscar regrets the invitation. The 43-year-old Oscar is carefree, pleasant, and very appealing as a character. When asked by one of the poker players what kind of sandwiches he's serving, Oscar looks under the bread and says, "I got brown sandwiches and green sandwiches." The green, he says, is "either very new cheese or very old meat." At the end of the play there is a suggestion that Oscar's experience with Felix has provoked a change in his personality because Oscar's last words in the play are an admonishment to the poker players to be less messy. In both the original Broadway stage production in 1965 and in the movie version of 1968, Oscar

MEDIA ADAPTATIONS

- *The Odd Couple* was adapted by Simon himself as a 1968 film starring Walter Matthau as Oscar and Jack Lemmon as Felix. Gene Saks, who directed the stage version, also directed the film—which is very faithful to the play script, though occasionally expanded to include street scenes in New York City. In technicolor, running 106 minutes, available from Paramount Home Video and at many video rental stores. A videodisc (Laservision) version is also available from Paramount.

- An animated cartoon called *The Oddball Couple* premiered in September of 1976 on ABC and was based on the odd couple concept as it featured a slob-like dog named Fleabag and a fussy cat named Spiffy, both freelance magazine writers.

- *The Odd Couple* was adapted as a 30 minute television show that ran on ABC from September of 1970 to July of 1975 and included 114 episodes. Jack Klugman played Oscar and Tony Randall played Felix, but in the series many other characters—like Oscar's secretary, Myrna, and Felix's daughter, Edna—had to be invented to satisfy the need for greater variety. Available in reruns on some cable television channels like Nickelodeon.

- *The Odd Couple* was adapted again by ABC in October of 1982 as another 30 minute television series called *The New Odd Couple* and ran until June of 1983 with black actors Demond Wilson and Ron Glass playing Oscar and Felix. Most episodes were simply recast versions of previous *The Odd Couple* scripts.

was played by Walter Matthau. In the five-year television series beginning in 1970, Oscar was played by Jack Klugman.

Murray

Murray, one of the poker players, is a policeman and a methodical, even slow, thinker. He is also very gentle and caring, and demonstrates the most concern for Felix. Murray is fairly unflappable, but he is also a bit simple and naive.

Cecily Pigeon

Cecily Pigeon is a little more uninhibited than her sister, Gwendolyn; she is the one who makes such suggestive remarks as,''Oh, we've done spectacular things but I don't think we'd want it spread all over the telly.''

Gwendolyn Pigeon

Though the Pigeon sisters seem almost indistinguishable, Simon describes Gwendolyn as the "mother hen." Like her sister Cicely, Gwendolyn is in her 30s, British, attractive, and works as a secretary for the Slenderama Health Club. She is a little slower mentally than her sister—she has trouble remembering Felix's name.

Roy

Roy is Oscar's accountant and a man with an acute sense of smell. He is the poker player who complains most about air quality and bad odors in Oscar's apartment. In the second act he storms from the game because the fastidious Felix has put disinfectant on the playing cards.

Speed

As his name implies, Speed is always in a hurry. He is the impatient poker player —sarcastic, complaining, and even a little mean. As the curtain rises on Murray shuffling the cards with agonizing slowness, the caustic Speed has the play's sharp first line: ''Tell me, Mr. Maverick, is this your first time on the riverboat?''

Felix Ungar

Felix Ungar is the "neat" member of the "odd couple," originally played on Broadway by Art Carney (he also played the character Norton on the popular Jackie Gleason television comedy *The Honeymooners*). In the movie, the role was rendered by Jack Lemmon, and in the television series Tony Randall portrayed Felix. A 44-year-old news writer for CBS, Felix responds to his wife's decision to end their marriage by considering suicide, but in Simon's comic world, attempted suicide is funny rather than serious; the compulsively tidy Felix sends his suicide note to his wife in a telegram. Oscar claims that Felix's problem is an obsession with control and urges Felix to "let loose" once in a while, to do something he "feels" like doing rather than always doing what he thinks he's "supposed" to do. At the end of the play, when Felix accepts the invitation from the Pigeon sisters to stay in their apartment, he is perhaps demonstrating a less conventional aspect of his personality.

Vinnie

Vinnie, the last of the poker players, is nervous and eccentric. At the initial poker game he is constantly checking his watch because he wants to leave early—he's departing for a vacation in Florida (in July) the next morning.

THEMES

Order and Disorder

When two good friends newly separated from their wives decide to live together, the arrangement fails miserably because the two friends have personal habits and domestic lifestyles that are diametrically opposed. Felix likes to live in an extremely ordered and tidy living space while Oscar not only tolerates living in disorder and messiness but even seems to prefer it.

Simon is more interested in creating compelling character types and raucous laughter than he is in investigating ideas, but to the extent that *The Odd Couple* deals with theme it focuses on the friction between radically different personalities. There is never a sense that either Oscar or Felix is "right" and the other is "wrong." They are simply different and attempting to live together was a bad idea. Oscar initiated the idea because he was lonely and concerned for Felix, but in his carefree approach to life he did not anticipate the conflict that should

have been apparent from his knowledge of Felix's habits. Oscar describes Felix as "a panicky person" obsessed with controlling everything in his life. Specifically, Felix panics when he is confronted with disorder in any form, and he attempts to "fix" things by restoring his concept of order thus giving himself the illusion of control. When Felix accepts the invitation to live with Oscar, he characteristically adopts the very behavior patterns that drove his wife to dismiss him. At the end of Act I, Oscar repeatedly asks Felix to go to sleep, but Felix insists on staying up to clean, saying he needs pencil and paper "to start rearranging my life." He says, "I've got to get organized," and the malleable Oscar finally gives in. When Felix unconsciously calls Oscar "Frances," Felix's wife's name, it is clear that Felix is looking to Oscar as some sort of substitute for the relationship he had with his wife.

Public vs. Private Life

Oscar and Felix are best friends, but before moving in together they share only a public life with one another. When they finally share a living space, they discover that the pressures of private life are much more demanding. The transition from "good friends" to pseudo "husband and wife" tests compatibility in a way that only experience can prove. The same living space and the experience of round-the-clock sharing magnifies differences and makes the discord inescapable and intolerable. Oscar and Felix were certainly aware of their personality differences before they lived together, but they encountered these differences only briefly in their public relationship, largely at the Friday night poker game. In Act III, when Oscar throws Felix's suitcase on the table and insists that Felix leave, he says, "all I want is my freedom." Even with his unusual tolerance for disorder, Oscar cannot live in inescapable proximity with behavior that is so different from his own. He admits that it's not a question of right or wrong: "It's not your fault, Felix. It's a rotten combination."

Very clearly, Simon is suggesting that heterosexual marriages can also suffer from the same hopeless conflicts when they exchange a "public" relationship for an intimate and "private" one. Simon communicates this theme by drawing attention to the way the relationship between Oscar and Felix is very much like a marriage. In Act I, when Oscar is trying to convince Felix to take advantage of his offer, he says, "I'm proposing to you. What do you want, a ring?" In the second scene of Act II, Oscar and Felix sound like the cliched married

TOPICS FOR FURTHER STUDY

- Compare the movie version of *The Odd Couple* with the television series. Which is more effective and why? How does each differ from the stage play?

- Research to discover how rising costs have affected Broadway and how economic pressures have contributed to the dichotomy between commercial entertainment and art in American theatre.

- Read several theoretical discussions that attempt to define comedy philosophically, as distinct from laughter, and then apply your definition of comedy to *The Odd Couple,* your favorite television sitcom, and to a Shakespearean comedy.

- Identify the techniques that Simon uses in *The Odd Couple* to establish the conflict between Oscar and Felix by the end of Act I, to intensify that conflict in Acts II and III, and to resolve the conflict by the end of the play.

couple when they argue—"If you knew you were going to be late, why didn't you call me?" Similarly, the opening of Act III, when Oscar and Felix are not "talking," perfectly mimics the archetypal marriage spat. When Oscar tells Felix he must leave, he says, "it's all over, Felix. The whole marriage. We're getting an annulment." And Felix responds, "Boy, you're in a bigger hurry than Frances was."

Simon strengthens this aspect of the theme by calling attention to the marital and near-marital relationships that surround Oscar and Felix. It's clear that Speed's marriage has its rocky moments because he compares the aggravation he feels in the poker game to the aggravation he gets at home. Murray responds to Oscar's pretending on the phone that he is having an affair with Murray's wife by saying, "I wish you *were* having an affair with her. Then she wouldn't bother *me* all the time." Murray perhaps speaks for the general skepticism about marriage by saying, "twelve years doesn't mean you're a *happy* couple. It just means you're a *long* couple." In contrast with these rocky relationships, Vinnie appears to have a happier marriage, dedicated as he is to his frequent travels with his wife. In direct contrast to Oscar and Felix, the Pigeon sisters seem to live together without serious conflict—perhaps because, unlike Oscar and Felix, they are so much alike.

Finally, Simon puts this theme into perspective by using the public relationships between the poker players as a backdrop for Oscar and Felix. The poker players meet once a week and as a result know one another well, but their apparent camaraderie is never tested by the more demanding situation of living together over a long period of time. And Simon is careful to show that their relationships are filled with potential conflict and tension due to personality differences. The irascible Speed, for example, seems always on the verge of quitting the group. But at the end, even Felix vows to come back to the next poker night. He's not going to "break up" the game because "marriages may come and go, but the game must go on."

Change and Transformation

The only way that marriages survive is through the compromise that must occur when inevitable conflicts arise. Oscar and Felix's experience shows that some conflicts are too great for compromise, but they point the way toward the necessity for compromise by demonstrating slight changes in their personalities by the end of the play. Oscar's change becomes clear when he receives a phone call from his ex-wife and reveals that he paid up his alimony in full. He says, "you don't have to thank me. I'm just doing what's right." Oscar's relationship with his wife and son appear to be improving because he has become a more responsible husband and father. And, of course, he ends the play with his admonition to the poker players to "watch your cigarettes, will you? This is my house, not a pig sty."

The change in Felix is much more mysterious. Moving in even temporarily with the Pigeon sisters, nearly total strangers, is something Felix would not have been able to do when the play began. But is he merely "loosening up" as Oscar suggested he ought to? Or is he making a huge change and considering a romantic relationship with either or both of the sisters? As he gathers his things in Oscar's apartment, Felix passes the poker players and smiles in a way that is open to interpretation. When he moves in with Gwendolyn and Cecily will he try to tidy up their lives the way he attacked Oscar's? There is no way to know, but it is clear that he has gone through some kind of change for he asks Murray to tell his wife that "if I sound different to her, it's because I'm not the same man she kicked out three weeks ago."

While the play's ending leaves Oscar and Felix's future relationship open to some speculation, it seems reasonable to assume that the two men will not live together again. It is interesting to note then, that the popular television series presumed a different scenario. In the television situation comedy version of *The Odd Couple,* Oscar and Felix remain roommates, each having reached a kind of mutual tolerance for the other's idiosyncracies. The series did, however, preserve much of the friction between the two characters, in order to maintain comical conflicts similar to the play. This is something of a reversal of Simon's suggested outcome, but one that can be seen as necessary to perpetuate a weekly comedic series.

STYLE

Conflict

In November of 1963, Simon sold the screen-rights for *The Odd Couple* to Paramount Pictures before he had even written a single word of the play upon which the movie was eventually based. In his memoir, *Rewrites,* Simon quotes the single sentence he and his agent used to close the deal: "'Well, it's about two men who are divorced, move in together to save money to pay their alimony, and have the same fights with each other as they did with their wives.'"

This anecdote illustrates the effectiveness of the play's main dramatic conflict. One sentence was all Paramount needed to know that Neil Simon could deliver another hit. The inherently funny conflict between the fussy Felix Ungar and the messy Oscar Madison is subtly established by the end of Act I, is effectively intensified in Act II and the beginning of Act III, and then finally is resolved by their separation and small changes in personality at the end of the play. The conflict is comically ironic because the solution the two men come up with for their separate divorces ends up creating yet another kind of divorce.

In Simon's memoir he recounts that the most difficult part of writing the play was writing the resolution of the conflict in Act III. From the beginning of the rehearsal period, it was clear that the first two acts were effective but that the third act was a disastrous failure. This last act did not get a satisfactory rewrite until well after the first out-of-town performances had begun and Simon had realized that the key to resolving the conflict was bringing the Pigeon sisters back into Act III.

Character

What was not obvious in Simon's one-sentence synopsis for Paramount is that the conflict was based on the clash of extremely different personality types. Ultimately, it is the creation of Oscar and Felix as an "oil and water" mix that makes it possible for *The Odd Couple* to be tremendously funny.

Simon creates these contrasting character types with the effective use of theatrical detail, most notably with carefully crafted dialogue. Sometimes it is the words of the character himself that establishes the "type" as when when Oscar enters hurriedly in Act I carrying a tray with beer, sandwiches, a can of peanuts, and already opened bags of pretzels and chips. In the visual context of the slovenly apartment, Oscar's balancing act with the snacks already characterizes him as the probable source of the living room mess but his opening words very subtly reinforce this impression. The impatient poker players ask Oscar if he's "in" or "out," that is, whether or not he plans to play this hand. "I'm in! I'm in!" Oscar says, "Go ahead. Deal!" Vinnie asks, "Aren't you going to look at your cards?" and Oscar answers, "What for? I'm gonna bluff anyway." The messy condition of Oscar's apartment has prepared the audience to understand his carefree type immediately, and his opening words characterize him perfectly with elegant economy.

Sometimes Felix and Oscar are effectively characterized by what others say about them. The third line of the play, for example, is Roy's "Geez, it stinks in here," a line that is quickly followed by Vinnie's, "What time is it?" Roy's line implies that the yet-to-appear host is the main cause of the mess they find themselves in, an impression he solidifies with a later line, "You know, it's the same garbage from last week's game. I'm beginning to recognize things." Felix doesn't enter until nearly half-way through the first act, but when he does the following comment from Murray has already characterized Felix as one who organizes his life in a way very unlike Oscar—"Hey, maybe he's in his office locked in the john again. Did you know Felix was once locked in the john overnight. He wrote out his entire will on a half a roll of toilet paper! Heee, what a nut!"

As fictional creations, Oscar and Felix, like the other characters in the play, are "types" rather than multifaceted characters. They mostly embody single, predominating traits—as in Oscar the carefree, irresponsible, and sloppy type and Felix the precise, uptight, and extremely orderly type. Multifaceted characters are generally considered more artistically sophisticated, but character "types" can be used to great artistic purpose, as in the novels of Charles Dickens for example. Simon draws his character types precisely, using carefully crafted dialogue to reveal their characteristics.

Comedy

When one thinks of comedy one thinks first of laughter, and the *The Odd Couple* generates belly laughs, mainly because of the verbal cleverness captured in its "one-liners." The "one-liner" is a short response in which the character's retort surprises because of exaggeration or incongruity. For example, when Murray agrees to eat the "brown" sandwich that Oscar brings out of the kitchen, Roy says, "are you crazy? His refrigerator's been broken for two weeks. I saw milk standing in there that wasn't even in the bottle." The laugh comes from the surprising and exaggerated image of milk so sour it has become a solid substance. Simon perfected his skill at one-liners writing for television shows in the 1950s and no dramatist has ever been more adept at this skill. It has, however, been something of a hindrance to his reputation as a serious artist. Though audiences have been enthusiastic in their response to Simon's comedies, critics have generally been less admiring, often citing the reliance on "one-liners" as a cheap trick more appropriate to the world of sitcom entertainment than the world of art.

HISTORICAL CONTEXT

Vietnam

1965 was a period of considerable turmoil in the United States because President Lyndon Johnson, despite his claims to the contrary, was escalating U.S. involvement in Vietnam and many citizens (mostly young people) were protesting, especially on college campuses around the nation. In February, a month before *The Odd Couple* opened on Broadway in March, U.S. bombers were retaliating against North Vietnamese forces for attacks on American military advisors in South Vietnam. By March the first deployment of U.S. combat troops was landing in Da Nang and student protests had begun to mushroom. In May, a nation-wide student protest including more than 100 U.S. colleges proclaimed its opposition to the war. Despite this public outcry, Congress authorized the use of U.S. ground troops in direct combat operations and by the end of June full-scale combat involving American troops had commenced. Continued anti-war rallies ultimately divided the American public between "hawks" and "doves," those who supported the escalation of the war and those who opposed it. Often these lines divided on grounds of age and education, with college faculty and students usually leading the ranks of the "doves." As draft calls were doubled to enlist troops for Vietnam, university enrollments rose sharply with young men taking advantage of the draft deferral for college students as a way of avoiding military service.

Racial tensions

Adding to the turmoil created by Vietnam were continuing tensions over race relations. In Selma, Alabama, throughout February and March, Martin Luther King Jr. was leading civil rights protests against state regulations that limited black voter registration. Demonstrations were marred by violence as 200 Alabama state police used whips, night sticks, and tear gas to control the largely black crowds. The Governor of Alabama at the time, George Wallace, finally refused police protection for the demonstrators and President Johnson responded by sending 3,000 U.S. National Guard troops to Selma. Elsewhere, in New York City's Harlem, on February 21, civil rights activist Malcolm X was assassinated by black extremists as he prepared to deliver a speech asserting the need for peaceful coexistence between blacks and whites. In the Watts section of Los Angeles in August, race riots erupted in this predominantly black section of

COMPARE
&
CONTRAST

- **1965:** The divorce rate stood at 2.5% per 1,000 people, down from its high after World War II but up from a lower rate in 1960. The divorce rate had risen from 0.9% in 1910 and had jumped dramatically during the second World War to 3.5% in 1945, peaking in 1946 after the war had ended but then dipping steadily to 2.2% in 1960.

  Today: The divorce rate stands at around 4.6% per 1,000 people, down from its all-time high of 5.3% in 1981. The rates had risen steadily from 1965 and into the 1970s before peaking and starting another decline in the mid 1980s.

- **1965:** The issue of racial prejudice dominated the news and the social consciences of the American people, but there was no evidence of black characters in the lives of Oscar, Felix, or their poker-playing buddies. The issues of gender consciousness and homophobia were much less prominent, and, in this social climate, few, if any, considered it homoerotically suggestive that two bachelors chose to live together.

  Today: Though the issue of racial prejudice is still very much "in the air," it has now been joined or even eclipsed in importance by the issues of feminism and homophobia. Increased awareness of gay issues has made many people more observant of homosexual subtext, and the relationship between Oscar and Felix can, on some levels, be perceived as homoerotic. The feminist movement can also be seen as a factor in Simon's decision to create a "female" version of the play in 1985. In 1982, ABC produced a second sitcom version of the play that featured black actors in the roles of Oscar and Felix.

- **1965:** America was becoming deeply mired in the Vietnam conflict and open hostilities at home over the war would dominate the rest of the decade, culminating in the National Guard opening fire on Kent State University student protestors, killing four and wounding eight on May 4, 1970.

  Today: The memories of Vietnam still weigh heavily on America's psyche, though the 1991 Persian Gulf War was seen by many as a ritualistic military victory that in part exorcised the ignominy of that earlier military failure. Novels, plays, and popular films about Vietnam began appearing in the mid 1970s and became so numerous in the 1980s and 1990s that an entire genre of Vietnam War literature has arisen.

- **1965:** The "cold war" begun in the early 1950s was still raging and Communist Russia was seen as a great and dangerous political and military power.

  Today: The fall of the Berlin Wall in November of 1989 signaled the economic and political decline of Russia, which is now splintered into many independent states and is suffering from internal dissension and severe economic problems as it attempts to assimilate the Western concepts of democracy and free market capitalism.

- **1965:** Stock prices and trading volume reached an all-time high, with the Dow-Jones industrial average gaining about 11% in 1965 to finish the year at a historic high of 969.

  Today: After a major "crash" in 1987, the stock market continues to climb to dizzying heights, fueled by "baby-boomer" investors who worry that they will not have sufficient funds for retirement. In the greatest "bull" run in the history of the market, the Dow-Jones industrial average flirted with the 7,000 mark and some analysts predicted a 10,000 point Dow by the year 2000 while others predicted another crash of monumental proportions.

- **1965:** Simon's opening allusion to "Mr. Maverick" was funny for his audience because the hit television series starring James Garner and Jack Kelly as Bret and Bart Maverick had just ended its 124 episode run on ABC in 1962.

  Today: A new generation has become familiar with the Maverick character through the popular 1994 movie starring Mel Gibson as Bret Maverick and Jodi Foster as his spunky romantic interest. James Garner, the original Bret Maverick, took a supporting role in the film as Marshal Zane Cooper and lent considerable nostalgia to the film for an older generation of viewers.

the city and nearly 10,000 rioters destroyed 500 square blocks of the city and caused an estimated $40 million of damage. In 1965, race relations in America were obviously volatile and even dangerous to peace and public safety.

"Flower Power"

An idealistic youth culture in America responded to this turmoil by asserting its belief in the power of a non-denominational spiritual awareness. Poet Allen Ginsberg coined the term "flower power" when anti-war demonstrators responded to Oakland city police with a strategy of non-violence. Images of young people inserting daisies in the barrels of police anti-riot weapons helped popularize the epithet. Identifying more with Eastern religions than with traditional Christianity, these "flower children" embraced "love" and "peace" as attainable foundations for social and political order. This movement was led by "gurus" like Ginsberg, the Hare Krishnas, and Harvard psychology professor Timothy Leary, who espoused the use of consciousness-altering drugs such as LSD and marijuana.

The Insulated World of Simon's Play

As with most of his comedies, Simon's *The Odd Couple* is not seriously concerned with the social, political, and cultural climate of the times in which he wrote. Simon admits that he is not a "political" writer but said in *Rewrites:* "[I] hope that my plays become a documentation of the times we lived in, at least from the perspective I had to view it all." *The Odd Couple* might document an upper-middle-class New Yorker's world in 1965 but it would certainly be a very insulated world, quite unconnected to the significant turmoil most of the country was experiencing outside of Oscar's apartment.

It is most likely that this insulated quality derives from Simon's dedication to light, comedic entertainment, a desire to provide the audience with an engaging but untroubling evening of laughter and sentiment. In fact, *The Odd Couple* might even have been designed to provide its audience with an escape from the sometimes gruesome realities that were taking place on the street and being reported on the evening news. As with most of Simon's comedies, *The Odd Couple* is a pleasant night in the theatre rather than a disturbing or even thought-provoking one. Its most "serious" issue is divorce, and, in the spirit of light comedy, divorce is treated as a human experience without significantly troubling consequences or ramifications.

CRITICAL OVERVIEW

The Odd Couple has been Neil Simon's greatest popular success, running for 964 performances in its Broadway debut and then spawning a popular movie version, an even more popular television series, and eventually a kind of sequel or "female version" that tells the same story with the genders reversed. Added to these successes is the fact that all of these manifestations of his play have entertained the public for more than thirty years as regional and amateur theatre groups continue to perform both versions of his play and television stations rerun the movie and sitcom series. But Simon has always been more popular with audiences than he has been with critics—who tend to classify him as a merely entertaining comedy writer rather than as a serious artist with a comic vision.

In 1965, *The Odd Couple* was Simon's third straight comedy hit (the 1962 musical *Little Me* had been less successful with audiences despite Simon's collaboration as librettist). The critics had responded in 1961 to his first Broadway hit, *Come Blow Your Horn*, with reserved praise, finding it (in *New York Times* critic Howard Taubman's words) a pleasant "confection," a play with "hilarious moments" that "aims low" and only seeks "to entertain." This would become the general critical opinion of Simon's work throughout his career, as his next two hits, *Barefoot in the Park* and *The Odd Couple*, gathered basically similar responses. Through succeeding decades the critical response might vary slightly from play to play but the overall assessment stayed roughly the same. Consistently recognized as a sound theatrical craftsman and a genuinely funny writer, the critics nonetheless found Simon lacking in intellectual and emotional depth and often reduced him to the simple epithet, "gag-man."

Reviewing the original Broadway production of *The Odd Couple*, Taubman found the opening scene "one of the funniest card sessions ever held on a stage" and the play's humor "unflagging" but labelled the play finally as a "farce," and not of the "higher art" of "true comedy." Taubman's appreciation of the play's hilarity was thorough and genuine but he finally had to separate himself from the audience's more unreserved applause.

Some critics, like Walter Kerr, have been kinder to Simon during his career; Kerr, for example, once called Simon "a man of sense, using just the jigger and a half of substance that will make a decent drink.'' Other critics, like subsequent *Times* writers Frank Rich and John Simon (no relation), have been generally harsher. John Simon once proclaimed that Neil Simon's work was ''devoid of ideas'' and ''an outrage . . . against human intelligence and art.'' He admitted that ''audiences, of course, may find trash to their taste; but the critic's first task is to identify it as such. Then, if people still want to eat it, let them; only let no one pretend it's food.'' Academicians have generally been harshest of all when they deign to comment on such a popular writer. College and university professors well-studied in classic comic dramatists like Shakespeare and Moliere (pronounced ''Mole-yair'') and even more contemporary writers like Alan Ayckbourn (pronounced ''ache-born'') and Joe Orton have often been brutal with Simon. For example, in the third edition of *Contemporary Dramatists,* Martin Gottfried admits that ''Neil Simon must be reckoned with if only because he is the most popular playwright in the history of the American theatre'' but adds that ''Simon is generally dismissed as a hack.'' Similarly, Gerald Berkowitz, writing in *Players* magazine begins by declaiming that ''Neil Simon is a critical embarrassment . . . it is universally agreed that [his plays] offer no specific insights into the human condition.'' But even critics as harsh as these must admit to certain strengths in Simon's comedies, most notably the indisputable fact ''that a Neil Simon comedy makes the audiences laugh, and [that] this laughter is louder, longer and more constant than that produced by any other modern dramatist,'' according to Berkowitz.

On the other hand, Simon has had his champions. In fact, two book-length critical assessments of his work are both quite effusive in their praise. Edythe McGovern, in her *Neil Simon: A Critical Study,* puts Simon in a class with writers like Moliere and George Bernard Shaw, who ''successfully raised fundamental and sometimes tragic issues of universal and therefore enduring interest without eschewing the comic mode.'' Of *The Odd Couple* McGovern asserts that Simon has ''captured the essence of incompatibility among humans who repeat again and again their self-defeating patterns of personality.'' In *Neil Simon,* Robert Johnson asserts that ''Neil Simon has not received as much critical attention as he deserves,'' and that ''Simon's work also explores a larger number of serious themes and points of view than he is credited with presenting.'' Johnson concludes that ''Oscar and Felix's attempt to share living quarters . . . is the

most captivating dramatization of incongruity Simon has yet created.''

The individual interested in Neil Simon's comedies can come to his or her own opinion about the merit of Simon's comedy or about *The Odd Couple* in particular by seeking out learned definitions of comedy and comparing them to a multitude of works in literature and in the popular media.

CRITICISM

Terry Nienhuis

Nienhuis is an associate professor of English at Western Carolina University. Here he discusses the mechanics of humor, Simon's facility with comedy, and the playwright's struggle to be recognized as more than a gag writer.

Neil Simon has been so successful financially and has become so popular with audiences that there is only one ambition left for him—to be taken seriously as an ''artist.'' The reluctance of critics to give him this respect continues to goad Simon and *The Odd Couple* is a worthy ground for examining this issue because it is his most famous play and still quite typical of his best work.

In the long history of English and American cultures there has always been a dichotomy between entertainment and art, but this cultural division and conflict has been intensified in America in the twentieth century as popular media have become more powerful and pervasive in American life. The radio, movies, television, cable television, and the wide availability of video recordings have made popular entertainment and popular culture an increasingly powerful force as we approach the beginning of a new century. Alongside or even against this rising tide of popular culture and entertainment stands a declining interest in books, in reading, and in classic literature. In some circles this situation is taken very seriously, as in the well-known book by social critic Neil Postman, *Amusing Ourselves to Death: Public Discourse in the Age of Show Business.* Postman claims that the public's demand for entertainment has trivialized and even in some cases destroyed the culture's capacities for rational discourse and careful analytical judgment. He compares the situation in twentieth-century America to the one in Aldous Huxley's futuristic novel, *Brave New World,* where ''people will come to love their oppression, to adore the technologies that undo their capacities to think.''

Putting such diatribes aside, it is still clear that in the comedies of Neil Simon in general and in *The Odd Couple* in particular there is much to enjoy and admire. Initially, there is Simon's verbal wit and his capacity for creating raucous laughter: *The Odd Couple* might be Simon's most perfectly funny play. Those who study laughter analytically tell us that laughter usually comes from surprise—from our perception of incongruity, our delight in superiority, and our relief when forbidden subjects are brought out into the open so we can experience a release of psychic tension. In *The Odd Couple* our laughter comes predominantly from the surprise and perception of incongruity that occurs when we encounter Simon's famous ''one-liners.''

For example, in the play's initial poker scene Murray chides Oscar for not paying his alimony, asking Oscar if it doesn't bother him that his kids might not have enough to eat, and Oscar retorts: ''Murray, *Poland* could live for a year on what my kids leave over from lunch!'' This exaggeration takes us by surprise on many levels and can cause wild laughter in a typical audience. Psychologically, we probably are also laughing because we recognize that alongside the surprising incongruity there is a certain truth to Oscar's remark—that Oscar's wife still has plenty of money and that American children are very frequently spoiled. This is one way the comic one-liner can be described—sharp surprise from perceiving wild incongruity followed by a cognitive recognition that there is a paradoxical truth in the incongruity. The surprise catches our attention and the recognition gives us the pleasure of understanding. However, with Simon the weak link in the equation is usually with the recognition element. His one-liners are often fairly shallow on the cognitive side.

Compare, for example, a ''one-liner'' from Shakespeare. In *Romeo and Juliet* Mercutio has been fatally stabbed by Tybalt and Romeo says, ''Courage, man, the hurt cannot be much'' and Mercutio replies, ''No, 'tis not so deep as a well, nor so wide as a church door, but 'tis enough, 'twill serve. Ask for me to-morrow, and you shall find me a grave man.'' This will be funny even in the context of Mercutio's death because the incongruities are so striking, but the difference is that the ''recognition'' part of the one-liner is so much more important than the surprising incongruity. Mercutio's quip is a sad reminder of our own

WHAT DO I READ NEXT?

- Any of the plays of Britain's Alan Ayckbourn, who is often referred to as the ''British Neil Simon'' because of his commercial popularity, his ability to create laughter, and his prolific number of hits. More respected by critics, Ayckbourn is signficantly more daring technically and much more profound in his use of comedy than Simon.

- *Taking Laughter Seriously,* by John Morreall, SUNY Press, 1983. A concise discussion of the psychological elements that underlie laughter, with a concluding chapter discussing humor as a way of looking at life.

- *The Gingerbread Lady* (1970), *God's Favorite* (1974), *Chapter Two* (1977), or *Lost in Yonkers* (1991) as examples of Neil Simon plays that work with darker materials and make more of an attempt to balance humor with seriousness.

- *The Sunshine Boys* (1972) for another fascinating Neil Simon ''pair,'' this time two, old, vaudevillian comics who have a love-hate relationship with one another.

mortality, a recognition that even a vital (though perhaps rash) human being like Mercutio can get caught very easily by mortal circumstances. Death will finally make the merry Mercutio ''grave.'' As Mercutio pays a price for his exaggerated vitality, perhaps too great a price to our way of thinking, Shakespeare insists that even in our laughter we must consider life in all its complexity. Even when he is being very funny, Shakespeare is more interested in the cognitive side of humor than he is in the belly laughs.

But Simon can also be appreciated for his exquisite theatrical craftsmanship; he is very adept at creating the effects he wants to achieve. The opening poker scene in *The Odd Couple* is a perfect example. Simon knew that if he established Oscar and Felix's poker-playing buddies as an interesting

Jack Lemmon as the tidy Felix and Walter Matthau as the sloppy Oscar in a scene from the film

and varied group before he introduced Oscar and Felix themselves he would be able to prepare his audience much more effectively for the entrance of his main characters. And with characteristic theatrical skill Simon does this from the first moment of the play. The play opens with the striking visual impression of Oscar's messy and smoke-filled apartment and of Murray, Roy, Speed, and Vinnie sitting around the poker table with two chairs empty. Vinnie has the largest stack of poker chips and one of the early jokes will be Speed's impatience at Vinnie's desire to leave early with his winnings. Vinnie is nervously tapping his foot and checking his watch but Speed is even more impatient, an emotion that will be highlighted throughout the play by Oscar's eventual reaction to living with Felix. Roy is watching Speed and Speed is glaring "with incredulity and utter fascination" at Murray, who is shuffling the cards with aggravating slowness. Thus, Simon creates tremendous theatrical interest and laughter even before anyone has spoken a word. With this tableaux established so exquisitely, Speed's line, which opens the play, creates a laugh that few comic playwrights can so easily create: Speed "cups his chin in his hand," "looks at Murray," and says, "Tell me, Mr. Maverick, is this your first time on the riverboat?" Already the audience is hooked.

They want to know about these men and how they relate to one another. They wonder who will fill the two vacant chairs. And when Oscar finally arrives on stage, it has been clearly established that one of the missing chairs belongs to an eccentrically fussy person named Felix and that the messy condition of this apartment is a result of the carefree attitude of the host. Even Simon's critics usually agree that in terms of play construction and theatre craft, Neil Simon takes a back seat to very few comic dramatists.

However, the critics have also been quick to point out that craftsmanship is only part of dramatic artistry. The most important aspect of art is what the writer has to say about human experience. The critics often refer to Simon as a mere "gag-man," and if laughter were the deciding factor in evaluating comedy, Simon's quality would be much easier to discern. Someone could simply use a machine to measure the audience's laughter, and the longest and loudest guffaws might easily declare Simon the greatest of comic writers. But more academic critics have implied that volume and duration of laughter are not sufficient and perhaps not even necessary conditions for great comedy. In fact, many great comic moments provoke smiles rather than laughter and sometimes comedy even evokes pathos. What is essential to a great comedy appears to be not laughter but a provocative comic vision.

What is a "comic vision"? It is an approach to comedy that includes not only laughter but also a thoughtful, even philosophical way of looking at the human experience. The eighteenth-century English politician and man of letters Horace Walpole once said that "this world is a comedy to those that think, a tragedy to those that feel." The tragic vision has been defined in many ways but perhaps tragedy shows us that our defeats can be partial victories. The comic vision, on the other hand, might show us that our victories always imply partial defeat, if for no other reason than that we can never completely extinguish our follies or life's hardship and pain. In the most powerful comedies, the happy ending always has an alloy of harsh reality, as in the ending of Shakespeare's *Much Ado about Nothing,* for example, where many lovers are paired up and happy but the noble Don Pedro is left conspicuously alone.

Some of Simon's comedies have flirted with darker materials, plays like *The Gingerbread Lady* (1970), *God's Favorite* (1974), and *Lost in Yonkers* (1991), but they have been unconvincing for audiences and critics alike. Simon seems to lack the intellectual and emotional depth to tread in such waters, and *The Odd Couple* is yet another example. Johnson reports that Simon "originally envisioned *The Odd Couple* as 'a black comedy,'" but there is nothing left of that original conception. Oscar and Felix are lovable eccentrics and their conflict has no convincingly serious or thought-provoking elements. This is perhaps clearest at the end when Oscar talks on the phone with his wife. Here Oscar becomes a merely sentimental hero as he turns over a new leaf and reveals that underneath he was always a better person than he appeared to be. Felix, on the other hand, departs shrouded in a little more mystery, but Simon does not exploit the thematic possibilities in this mystery and simply terminates the conflict between Oscar and Felix with an echo of the joke that closed Act I. Oscar and Felix address one another by their wives' names, saying, "So long, Frances. So long, Blanche." The audience will laugh once more at this verbal surprise because yet another incongruity has struck them. However, after the laughter passes there is no significant recognition phase where the incongruity reveals something thought-provoking and profound about Oscar, Felix, or human life in general.

Source: Terry Nienhuis, in an essay for *Drama for Students,* Gale, 1997.

Howard Taubman

In this review, Taubman recounts the Broadway debut of The Odd Couple *and praises Simon's comedic skills.*

The opening scene in *The Odd Couple,* of the boys in their regular Friday night poker game, is one of the funniest card sessions ever held on a stage.

If you are worried that there is nothing Neil Simon, the author, or Mike Nichols, his director, can think of to top that scene, relax. The main business of the new comedy, which opened last night at the Plymouth Theatre, has scarcely begun, and Mr. Simon, Mr. Nichols and their excellent cast, headed by Art Carney and Walter Matthau, have scores of unexpected ways prepared to keep you smiling, chuckling and guffawing.

Mr. Simon has hit upon an idea that could occur to any playwright. His odd couple are two men, one divorced and living in dejected and disheveled splendor in an eight-room apartment and the other to be divorced and taken in as a roommate.

One could predict the course of this odd union from its formation in misery and compassion through its disagreements to its ultimate rupture. Mr. Simon's way of writing comedy is not to reach for gimmicks of plot; he probably doesn't mind your knowing the bare outline of his idea. His skill—and it is not only great but constantly growing —lies in his gift for the deliciously surprising line and attitude. His instinct for incongruity is faultless. It nearly always operates on a basis of character.

Begin with that poker game. Mr. Matthau, the slovenly host, is off stage in the kitchen fixing a snack while Nathaniel Frey, John Fiedler, Sidney Armus and Paul Dooley are sitting around the table on a hot summer night, sweating and grousing at the luck of the cards. The burly Mr. Frey is shuffling awkwardly, "for accuracy, not speed," and the querulous Mr. Fiedler, the big winner, talks of quitting early.

The cards are dealt. Mr. Matthau walks in with a tray of beer and white and brown sandwiches. They're brown in his scheme of housekeeping because they're either new cheese or very old meat. As he opens the beer cans, sending sprays of lager over his guests (surely a Nichols touch), the dealer inquires whether he intends to look at his cards. "What for," Mr. Matthau, the big loser, grumbles, "I'm gonna bluff anyhow."

> NEIL SIMON'S INSTINCT FOR INCONGRUITY IS FAULTLESS. IT NEARLY ALWAYS OPERATES ON A BASIS OF CHARACTER"

The sixth member of the Friday night regulars, Mr. Carney, is missing. Evidently he has been away from his known haunts for 24 hours, and a phone call from his wife informs his friends that she hopes he never turns up. Since they know that he is a man who takes such blows seriously, they fear that he will do something violent to himself.

With Mr. Carney's arrival as Felix, the discarded husband, the principal action begins. Mr. Carney is truly bereaved, a man of sorrows, His eyes are stricken. his lips quiver, his shoulders sag. Even poker gives way before his desolation. The players are too concerned about possible moves by Felix toward self-destruction. When at last they go home, they depart softly and gravely like chaps leaving a sick room.

Mr. Matthau as Oscar, the host, consoles Felix, massaging away the spasms in his neck and enduring the moose calls with which the unfortunate fellow clears ears beset by allergies. Nothing much happens during the rest of the act except that these two inevitably blunder into a domestic alliance, but there is scarcely a moment that is not hilarious.

The unflagging comedy in the remainder of the play depends on the fundamental switch—of the odd couple. Felix is a compulsive house keeper, bent on cleaning, purifying the air and cooking. When the gang assembles for its poker game, Felix has special treats ready for snacks.

Mr. Carney handles the housewifely duties with a nice, delicate, yet manly verve. But he is strict. When he serves a drink to Mr. Frey, he wants to know where the coaster is. The answer—and this is Mr. Simon, the marks–man at firing droll lines—is, "I think I bet it."

Mr. Matthau for his part is Wonderfully comic as a man who finds his companion's fussy habits increasingly irksome. He walks about with a bearish crouch that grows more belligerent as his domestic situation becomes both familiar and oppressive.

There is a marvelous scene in which he and Mr. Carney circle each other in mutual distaste—Mr. Matthau looking like an aroused animal about to spring and Mr. Carney resembling a paper tiger suddenly turned neurotic and dangerous.

To vary the humors of the domestic differences, Mr. Simon brings on two English sisters named Pigeon—yes Pigeon, Gwendolyn and Cecily—for a date with Oscar and Felix. The girls induce more laughter than their names promise. Carole Shelley and Monica Evans are a delight as the veddy British and dumb Pigeons.

Mr. Nichols's comic invention, like Mr. Simon's, shines through this production and the comfortable Riverside Drive apartment invoked by Oliver Smith's set. Just a sample: Mr. Carney left alone with the Pigeons is as nervous as a lad on his first date. When one of the girls takes out a cigarette, he hastens to her with his lighter and comes away with the cigarette clamped in its mechanism.

The Odd Couple has it made. Women are bound to adore the sight of a man carrying on like a little homemaker. Men are sure to snicker at a male in domestic bondage to a man. Kids will love it because it's funny.

Source: Howard Taubman, review of *The Odd Couple,* in the *New York Times,* March 11, 1965 .

Walter Kerr

In this review of the play's original Broadway run, Kerr lauds The Odd Couple *as a greatly entertaining evening of theatre.*

Kerr was a longtime reviewer for the New York Times, *as well as the author of several book-length studies of modern drama, he was one of the most influential figures in the American theater.*

I'm sorry the Moscow Art players have returned to Russia. I'd like them to have seen the first-act poker game in *The Odd Couple.*

I don't necessarily say they'd have learned anything from it. I just feel pretty sure they'd have liked it. It has so much interior truth. Director Mike Nichols has staged an absolute summer festival of warm beer, sprayed toward the ceiling like those terraced fountains municipal designers are so fond of, and I suppose we can credit author Neil Simon with providing the sandwiches. The sandwiches have been made of whatever was left over in host Walter Matthau's long-defrosted refrigerator. ("it's either very new cheese or very old meat'' Mr. Matthau volunteers as he offers his cronies a choice between brown sandwiches and green) and the members of the party are happy enough to munch them as they gripe, growl, snarl, and roar over their hands, their wives, their lives, and the high cost of losing.

This is where the art comes in. Instead of isolating each one of Mr. Simon's dozens of laugh-lines and milking it for all it's worth, director Nichols flings all the gags into the pot together, letting them clink and spin like so many chips, until everything overlaps and you can't tell life from lunacy. Nat Frey shuffles the pack as though he were crushing glass in his strong bare hands, John Fielder sings his piping little song about having to leave by twelve until it takes on the piercing sound of counterpoint from another planet, Sidney Armus and Paul Dooley fling their arms up and their cards down like men freshly accused of treason, and Mr. Matthau grunts and bellows in his homespun way to put a moose-like bass under the whole hot summer-night orchestration. The interplay is true, blue, and beautiful.

After the poker game comes the play, which is jim-dandy, ginger-peachy, and good. Mr. Matthau is a divorced man, which is why he is able to have all his friends in on Friday nights and also why the eight-room apartment looks like one of those village bazaars at which underprivileged citizens can exchange their old refuse. (Oliver Smith has caught in his setting just the right muddy and mottled note for ramshackle bachelor quarters, with the trousers back from the cleaners hanging where they ought to be, from the bookshelves, and with a nice fat hole burned in the what used to be the best lampshade).

Into the dissolute comfort and the brawling bliss of Mr. Matthau's menage comes a thin note of warning. One friend, who turns out shortly to be Art Carney, hasn't shown up. News is received that he, too, has left his wife. Furthermore, he is threatening suicide, sort of. Now it is time for Mike Nichols to set his mother-hen actors pacing, pacing, pacing the floor, as they brood and cluck and worry inordinately about their deeply disturbed buddy. When Mr. Carney does finally appear, the rush to save him from himself—all windows are locked tightly against jumping, and he is scarcely allowed to go to the bathroom alone—is sympathetic, solicitous, and rough as a maddened hockey game. We may not have had as funny a first act since "The Acharnians."

Naturally, Mr. Matthau and Mr. Carney now settle down as roommates, making as nice a couple as you'd care to meet if they could only get along. Mr. Carney is death on dust and a fast man with an Aerosol bomb (one reason his wife threw him out is that he always insisted on recooking the dinner) and he drives Mr. Matthau stark, staring mad. In short, both of them might just as well have wives, and that constitutes the meat, the moral, and the malicious merriment of this brief encounter.

The contest thins out a bit, I am honor bound to say, during the second act, while Mr. Carney worries desperately over his London broil and reduces a couple of visiting pigeons (they're girls, they're sisters, and their name is Pigeon) to tears. But the repeated joke is at least a good joke, the Pigeon sisters ultimately prove to be funny and useful, Mr. Simon's comic invention keeps re-igniting, and the poker players are coming back, so I wouldn't even notice if I were you.

Now a word about Mr. Matthau, and I do hope the Moscow Art is listening. Mr. Matthau could play all of the parts in "Dead Souls" with one hand tied to one foot and without changing makeup. He is a gamut-runner, from grim to game to simple hysteria, and when he finally does have his long overdue nervous-breakdown, with his voice sinking into his throat like the sun in the western sea, he is magnificent. Of course, he is good, too, impersonating an orangutan as he leaps furniture in his wild desire to make certain alterations in Mr. Carney's throat, and again when he shows his old pal the door (only to be haunted by the memory of that despairing face and by a parting remark that he comes to think of as The Curse of the Cat People). But perhaps our man is best of all when he is merely intimating contempt in his sneering dark eyes, with a baseball cap peaked backwards on his untidy head and his face curled in scorn until it looks like the catcher's mitt.

We mustn't overlook Mr. Carney, who is immensely funny quivering his lip like an agitated duck, clearing his ears by emitting foghorn hoots, and clawing his hands through what is left of his hair to indicate pride, despair and all of the other seven deadly virtues. His problem is tension ("It's tension. I get it from tension. I must be tense," he says) and ours is to keep from laughing through the next good line.

It's a good problem to have, and I urge you to drop in on *The Odd Couple* any night at all, Fridays included.

Source: Walter Kerr, in a review of *The Odd Couple* in the *New York Herald Tribune,* March 11, 1965.

An insightful analysis of Simon's comedies in general (through *Biloxi Blues*) including perceptive commentary on *The Odd Couple.*

FURTHER READING

Bryer, Jackson R., editor. *The Playwright's Art: Conversations with Contemporary Dramatists,* Rutgers University Press, 1995, pp. 221-240.
> Interview with Simon responding to questions as varied as "how did you get started writing plays?" to "how do you feel about theatre critics?"

Johnson, Robert K. *Neil Simon,* Twayne, 1983.
> The second and currently last book devoted to Simon's work; includes chapter on *The Odd Couple.*

McGovern, Edythe. *Neil Simon: A Critical Study,* Frederick Ungar, 1978.
> First book-length discussion of Simon; includes chapter on *The Odd Couple.*

Simon, Neil. *Rewrites,* Simon & Schuster, 1996.
> Simon's autobiography through his writing of *Chapter Two.* Offers some interesting insights into his inspirations and writing processes.

Weise, Judith. "Neil Simon," in *Critical Survey of Drama: English Language Series,* edited by Frank N. Magill, Salem Press, 1985.

SOURCES

Berkowitz, Gerald M. "Neil Simon and His Amazing Laugh Machine," *Players Magazine,* Vol. 47, no. 3, February-March, 1972, pp. 110-113.

Gottfried, Martin. "Simon, (Marvin) Neil," in *Contemporary Dramatists,* 3rd edition, St. Martin's Press, 1982.

Kerr, Walter. "A Jigger and a Half" in his *Thirty Plays Hath November,* Simon & Schuster, 1969, pp. 297-301.

Konas, Gary, editor. *Neil Simon: A Casebook,* Garland, 1997.

Simon, John. "Bad Things" in *New York,* January 13, 1975, pp. 54-55.

Taubman, Howard. Review of *Come Blow Your Horn* in the *New York Times,* February 23, 1961, p. 31.

Taubman, Howard. Reviews of *The Odd Couple* in the *New York Times,* March 9, 1965, p. 50; March 21, 1965, p. 1.

A Raisin in the Sun

LORRAINE HANSBERRY
1959

A Raisin in the Sun was first produced in 1959 and anticipates many of the issues which were to divide American culture during the decade of the 1960s. Lorraine Hansberry, the playwright, was an unknown dramatist who achieved unprecedented success when her play became a Broadway sensation. Not only were successful women playwrights rare at the time, but successful young black women playwrights were virtually unheard of. Within its context, the success of *A Raisin in the Sun* is particularly stunning.

In part because there were few black playwrights—as well as few black men and women who could attend Broadway productions—the play was hindered by a lack of financial support during its initial production. Producers hesitated to risk financial involvement in such an unprecedented event, for had the play been less well-written or well-acted, it could have suffered an incredible failure. Eventually, however, the play did find financial backing, and after staging initial performances in New Haven, Connecticut, it reached Broadway.

Compounding the racial challenges the play posed was its length of nearly three hours as it was originally written. Because audiences are not accustomed to plays of such length, especially by a newcomer, a couple of significant scenes were cut from the original production. (These scenes are sometimes included in later renditions.) These scenes include Walter's bedtime conversation with Travis

and the family's interaction with Mrs. Johnson. In addition, the scene in which Beneatha appears with a "natural" haircut was eliminated in the original version primarily because Diana Sands, the actress, was not attractive enough with this haircut to reinforce the point of the scene. This scene would become more crucial as cultural ideas shifted.

AUTHOR BIOGRAPHY

Born in Chicago in 1930, Lorraine Hansberry was the youngest of four children. Her father, Carl Hansberry, was a successful real estate agent—and his family hence middle-class—who bought a house in a previously all-white neighborhood when Lorraine was eight years old. His attempt to move his family into this home created much tension, since Chicago was then legally segregated. Subsequently, however, as a result of Carl Hansberry's lawsuit, the Illinois Supreme Court declared these housing segregation laws unconstitutional.

After high school Hansberry attended the University of Wisconsin, where she studied drama, and the Art Institute of Chicago, where she studied painting. She moved to New York in 1950, supporting herself through a variety of jobs including work as a reporter and editor, while she continued to write short stories and plays. Before completing *A Raisin in the Sun,* she attempted three plays and a novel. During this period, she also met and married her husband, Robert Nemiroff, a white man who shared Hansberry's political perspective. They were divorced in 1964.

When Hansberry began *A Raisin in the Sun,* she titled it *The Crystal Stair,* which is also a line in a poem by Langston Hughes. The eventual title under which the play was and is performed is taken from Hughes's famous "A Dream Deferred." The play achieved its Broadway debut in 1959—it was the first play by a black woman to be produced in a Broadway theater. Several other "firsts" occurred because of this production; for example, Hansberry was the youngest playwright and first black playwright to win the New York Drama Critics Circle Award. This was a particularly rewarding honor, since Eugene O'Neill and Tennessee Williams, two of America's most prominent playwrights, also had plays on Broadway at this time. This version of *Raisin in the Sun* ran for 530 performances. A film version for which Hansberry had written the screen-

play was also released in 1961. She was nominated for the Screen Writers Guild award for her work.

Hansberry began another play, *The Sign in Sidney Brustein's Window.* Although it was less successful, it ran on Broadway for 101 performances. It closed on the day of Hansberry's death, January 12, 1965. At the age of 35, after a remarkably brief illness, Hansberry died of cancer.

PLOT SUMMARY

Act I, Scene One

The opening scene of *A Raisin in the Sun* occurs on a Friday morning when the members of the Younger family are preparing to go to school or work. During this scene, as in the opening scene of most plays, several key pieces of information are revealed. The family's inadequate living situation is conveyed through the fact that they share a bathroom with other tenants in their apartment house and through the fact that Travis must sleep on the sofa in the living room. As crucial, Walter's conversation elicits the fact that Mama is expecting a significant check in the mail the following day—life insurance paid to them because Mama's husband and Walter and Beneatha's father has died. The tension over money is also evident when Ruth refuses to give Travis fifty cents he needs for school. Walter gives him the money, along with an additional fifty cents to demonstrate that the family is not as poor as Ruth claims. Ironically, however, when Walter leaves for work, he will have to ask Ruth for carfare since he has given all his money to Travis.

During breakfast, Walter discusses the liquor store he wants to buy with the money Mama will receive. The other family members are hesitant to invest money with Walter's friends. Walter becomes increasingly frustrated, but when he expresses his longing for a more independent life and a career beyond that of chauffeur for a white man, Ruth and Beneatha discount his desires. Beneatha reminds him that the money belongs to Mama rather than directly to them, but her response is disingenuous because she already knows Mama plans to save some of the money for Beneatha's school tuition.

After the others leave, Ruth speaks to Mama about Walter's hopes. Mama is hesitant for at least two reasons—she does not approve of liquor, and she would like to buy a house for the family. This possibility excites Ruth, and within this conversation, Mama reveals why this dream is so significant to her. During this conversation, Beneatha states that she has another date with George Murchison, a young man she doesn't particularly like. This puzzles Mama since George comes from a wealthy family. The conversation grows more tense, however, when Beneatha defies her mother regarding religion, making statements Mama considers to be blasphemous. The scene concludes when Ruth suddenly faints, an act that will be explained later.

Act I, Scene Two

This scene occurs the following morning, with most of the family cleaning house and waiting for the mailman. Ruth, however, has gone out, and Mama implies that it might be because she's pregnant. Beneatha states that she's about to receive a visitor, Joseph Asagai, from Nigeria. There follows a discussion of European colonialism in Africa—although Mama appears somewhat ignorant, Beneatha's knowledge seems particularly new and her attitude self-righteous. At this point, Ruth returns and confirms that she is pregnant. Although Mama is pleased, Ruth and Beneatha think of the child as simply another financial burden.

They are diverted from their conversation when Beneatha spies Travis outside chasing a rat with his friends. During this confused moment, Asagai arrives. He critiques Beneatha because she has straightened her hair according to the style of the time. He suggests that she is a racial assimilationist—that is, that she aspires to white values. Simultaneously, he asserts that a woman's primary sense of fulfillment should come from her role as a wife.

After Asagai leaves, the mailman arrives with the check. Walter returns home, more frustrated than ever, especially when Mama urges him to go talk to Ruth. Mama is concerned because Walter is going "outside his home to look for peace" and because the "doctor" Ruth has gone to see is an abortionist. Although she expects Walter to be outraged at this possibility, he seems by his silence to agree that abortion would not be such a bad idea.

Act II, Scene One

Later that day, Beneatha appears in an African gown Asagai has given her. Walter is drunk and wants to act like an African warrior. George Murchison arrives to pick up Beneatha, but he is displeased at her appearance and refuses to take her

Lorraine Hansberry in 1959, the year of A Raisin in the Sun*'s Broadway debut*

seriously. She is, he says, "eccentric." Walter responds to George antagonistically, describing him as wearing "faggoty-looking white shoes." Ruth understands that something has gone drastically wrong, and that whatever she and Walter once shared, that love is gone.

Mama returns home, stating that she has been doing business downtown. She has in fact bought a house—located in Clybourne Park, an entirely white neighborhood. She bought that house not because she wanted to make a political statement but because it was big enough for her family and within her price range.

Act II, Scene Two

In this scene, Mrs. Johnson, a neighbor, arrives, ostensibly to congratulate the Youngers on their impending move. Within the conversation, however, she brings up recent bombings of houses belonging to black families moving into previously all-white neighborhoods. Within this conversation, Mama reveals herself to have more militant feelings than she had previously expressed. When Walter confesses that he has not been to work for three days, Mama begins to rethink her decision and eventually offers some of the money to Walter so that he can buy the liquor store and ''be the head of this family from now on like you supposed to be.''

Act II, Scene Three

At this point, the family mood has improved considerably. Ruth and Walter have gone to the movies for the first time in years, and Ruth has bought curtains for the new house. In the midst of their excitement, a white man knocks at their door, introducing himself as Karl Lindner, from the ''New Neighbors Orientation Committee.'' Although he attempts to present himself not as racist but merely reasonable, his goal is to buy the house back from the Youngers, who refuse his offer. After he leaves, Beneatha asks, ''What they think we going to do— eat 'em?'' Ruth responds, ''No, honey, marry 'em.''

To celebrate their good fortune, the family has bought Mama a set of gardening tools, but in the midst of their celebration, Bobo, a friend of Walter's arrives. He reveals that Willy, their mutual friend and potential business partner, has disappeared with all of their money. Mama is especially outraged because the money represented everything for which her husband had suffered. The scene ends with the family as dejected as they had been joyous at the beginning.

Act III

Walter has gone to Karl Lindner's apparently to accept his offer, but when Lindner arrives, the family has regained its determination to move. The movers arrive. The play concludes on an ambiguous note—for although the family is moving, their life in Clybourne Park will likely be difficult.

CHARACTERS

Joseph Asagai

Joseph Asagai is a friend of Beneatha's who has been out of town all summer. He is from Nigeria and introduces Beneatha to Nigerian culture. He brings her a native African dress, for example, and also encourages her to let her hair grow naturally rather than have it straightened—although this encouragement is phrased in terms of an insult. He, in other words, introduces issues that would become prominent in the United States during the decade following the production of this play (issues related to African American pride and heritage). On the other hand, he discourages Beneatha from acting independently as a woman, arguing that the only

true feeling a woman should have is passion for her husband.

Bobo

Bobo is an extremely minor character. He appears near the end of the scene to convey the bad news that his and Walter's friend has absconded with their money. He feels as dejected as Walter since the amount of money he had contributed consisted of his entire savings.

Mrs. Johnson

Mrs. Johnson is a neighbor of the Youngers, and she is portrayed as nosy and manipulative. In her primary scene, she appears to be jealous of the Youngers's good fortune and seems to want to ruin it for them by raising their fears. In some versions of this play, her role is eliminated.

Karl Lindner

Karl is a white man and the represent of the Neighborhood Welcoming Committee for Clybourne Park, where the Youngers plan to move. Although Karl attempts to present himself as a reasonable man, he has racist motives in attempting to persuade the Youngers not to move to his neighborhood. Although he himself might not commit violence, his goals are consistent with those who would commit violence in order to keep neighborhoods segregated.

Mama

See Lena Younger

George Murchison

George is Beneatha's date, though she doesn't take him seriously as a future mate. In the elder Youngers's eyes, his primary attractive quality is his access to wealth. Yet his presence also raises the issue of class tensions within the black community. He claims to have no interest in African culture and is exactly the opposite of the idealist Joseph Asagai.

Beneatha Younger

Beneatha is the younger sister of Walter, the daughter of Mama, sister-in-law of Ruth, and aunt of Travis. Throughout the play, she struggles for an

A scene from A Raisin in the Sun

adult identity, determined to express her ideas but often failing to do so tactfully. She dates a wealthy college friend, George Murchison, whom she describes as boring, in part because he is so conventional. She is also interested in Joseph Asagai, another college acquaintance whose home is Nigeria. She eventually follows his desire that she should adopt a more native African style. Also significant to the play is her desire to be a doctor, a goal for which she will need some of the money Mama has inherited.

Lena Younger

Mama's role in the play is quite significant. She is a woman with dreams but also with the wisdom to know when to act on them. She receives a $10,000 insurance payment as a result of her husband's death and longs to buy a more comfortable house for her family. Yet when she realizes how much a business would mean to Walter, she gives him a substantial portion of the money, hoping this will encourage him to live more fully. She is also, however, a woman of strong conviction, as is apparent in the scene when Beneatha suggests that God is imaginary but more significantly in the scene when Walter seems to agree with Ruth regarding the

abortion. At this point, she recognizes that her family's enemy has been transferred from their culture to their own hearts. Mama is clearly the source of the family's strength as well as its soul.

Ruth Younger

Ruth is married to Walter and hence the daughter-in-law of Mama and sister-in-law of Beneatha. She is the mother of Travis. She clearly loves her husband and family but also clearly feels the stress of poverty. Although she is enthusiastic about the family owning its own home, she urges Mama to help Walter invest in the liquor store because it means so much to him. During the course of the play, Ruth realizes she is pregnant and considers seeking an abortion, which would have been illegal at the time. By the end of the play, the implication is that Ruth will have this baby and that the family will direct its energy away from self-destruction.

Travis Younger

Travis is the son of Walter and Ruth. His role in the play is minor; he serves primarily as a foil permitting the other characters to raise the issues of the play. He is at the cusp of adolescence, simulta-

MEDIA ADAPTATIONS

- *A Raisin in the Sun* was released as a film by Columbia Pictures in 1961. Its cast included Sidney Poitier, Ruby Dee, Claudia McNeil, Diana Sands, and Louis Gossett Jr. This version was produced by David Susskind and Philip Rose. This film is distributed by Columbia Tristar Home Video.

- An American Playhouse version of the play was released for television in 1989. It is distributed through Fries Home Video and stars Danny Glover, Esther Rolle, and Starletta DuPois, and is directed by Bill Duke.

- Another video which was originally a filmstrip provides a supplment to the play. It is also called *A Raisin in the Sun* and is available from Afro-American Distributing Company.

- A cassette sound recording of the play is available from Harper Audio. It stars Ossie Davis, Ruby Dee, Claudia McNeil, Diana Sands, and Lloyd Richards. This cassette was produced in 1972.

---

neously attempting stereotypic adult masculine reticence and longing for childlike affection. He is received affectionately by the other characters.

Walter Lee Younger

Walter is the son of Mama, the husband of Ruth, the brother of Beneatha, and the father of Travis. He works as a chauffeur, a job he finds unsatisfying on a number of levels but most particularly because he does not desire to be anyone's servant. Although he is in his mid-thirties, his living situation encourages him to believe he is perceived nearly as a child. He longs to invest his father's insurance money in a liquor store because he wants to achieve financial success through his own efforts. When his friend runs off with the money, Walter feels particularly hopeless. Ironical-

ly, however, he achieves a sense of himself as an adult and leader of his family in part through this event. By standing up to Karl Lindner when it would have been easier to accept Lindner's financial offer, Walter asserts himself forcefully into his culture—and although his choices may make his life difficult in some ways, he will not be spiritually defeated.

THEMES

Race and Racism

The clear primary theme of *A Raisin in the Sun* has to do with race and racism. The Youngers live in a segregated neighborhood in a city that remains one of the most segregated in the United States. Virtually every act they perform is affected by their race. Ruth is employed as a domestic servant and Walter as a chauffeur in part because they are black—they are the servants, that is, of white people. They are limited to their poorly maintained apartment in part because they have low-paying jobs but also because absentee landlords often do not maintain their property. Travis chases a rat, while Beneatha and Mama attempt to eradicate cockroaches, both activities which would not occur in wealthier neighborhoods.

The most significant scene which openly portrays racism, however, is the visit with Karl Lindner. Although he does not identify himself as racist, and although his tactics are less violent than some, he wants to live in an all-white neighborhood—and he is willing to pay the Youngers off to stay out of white neighborhoods. This type of racism is often dangerous because it is more easily hidden.

Prejudice and Tolerance

Closely related to the theme of race and racism is the theme of prejudice and tolerance. Karl Lindner and his neighbors are clearly prejudiced against black people. Yet other forms of prejudice and intolerance also surface in the play. Walter responds to George Murchison aggressively because George is wealthy and educated; educated men seem to Walter somehow less masculine. Similarly, although Joseph Asagai encourages Beneatha to feel proud of her racial identity, he discourages her from feeling proud of her intellectual abilities because he believes professional achievements are irrelevant to a proper woman.

Civil Rights

Also related to the theme of race and racism as well as to the theme of prejudice and tolerance is the theme of Civil Rights. Although this play would debut before the major Civil Rights movement occurred in the United States during the 1960s, it raises many of the issues that would eventually be raised by the larger culture. ''Civil Rights'' generally refer to the rights a person has by law—such as the right to vote or the right to attend an adequate schools—and are often also referred to as human rights. The central civil rights issue in this play is, of course, the idea of segregated housing. Mama Younger has the money to pay for a house she wants, but people attempt to prevent her from doing so because of her race. At this moment, she is not trying to make a political point but rather to purchase the best house available for the money. Houses available in her own ghetto neighborhood are both more costly and less well-kept.

American Dream

The ''American Dream'' includes many ideas, but it is primarily the belief that anyone who comes to or is born in America can achieve success through hard work. Walter Younger aspires to achieve part of this American Dream, but he is frustrated at every turn. Although he is willing to work hard, opportunities for him are few because he is black. His culture has relegated him to the servant class. When some money does become available to him, his business opportunities are also few—for few businesses historically thrived in minority neighborhoods. Yet by the end of the play, whether or not he achieves the American Dream, he does achieve a sense of himself as an individual with power and the ability to make choices.

Sex Roles

While questions of race are certainly prominent in the play, an equally significant, if less prominent, issue involves gender. Mama understands that in order to experience himself as an adult, Walter must experience himself as a man—that is, he must be the leader of a family. Of course, in order for Walter to be the leader, the women must step back. And even within their stations as servants, Walter and Ruth's roles are further divided according to their sex—Walter is the chauffeur, Ruth the domestic servant. More blatantly, however, Joseph Asagai asserts that women have only one role in life—that of wife and presumably mother. And although Beneatha longs to be a doctor, she is also caught up

TOPICS FOR FURTHER STUDY

- Research segregation laws that applied to various U.S. cities in the 1950s. Examine the arguments people made in efforts to change these laws.

- Investigate the history of a particular neighborhood with which you are familiar. Analyze how its ethnic composition has shifted over decades or centuries and discuss the causes and effects of those shifts.

- Write an argument for or against owning or investing in a liquor store. Try to use specific examples or statistics in your essay. Consider the ethical as well as economic issues involved.

- Research the recent history of Nigeria. Compare its national events with the predictions Joseph Asagai makes in the play.

- Compare how extended families functioned in the 1950's (or another time period of your choice) with the way they function today.

in the romance of potentially being Asagai's wife. This tension points out the fact that individuals can be exceptionally progressive in one area of their lives while being much less progressive in other areas.

STYLE

Setting

Among the most important elements of *A Raisin in the Sun* is its setting. Because the Youngers are attempting to buy a new home in a different neighborhood, their current apartment and neighborhood achieve particular significance. The play takes place in a segregated Chicago neighborhood, ''sometime between World War II and the present,'' which for Hansberry would be the late 1950s. In other words, the play occurs during the late 1940s or the 1950s, a time when many Americans were prosperous and when some racial questions were beginning to be raised, but before the Civil Rights movement of the 1960s.

More specifically, the play occurs in the Youngers' apartment, which Hansberry describes in detail: "Its furnishings are typical and undistinguished and their primary feature now is that they have clearly had to accomodate the living of too many people for too many years." The furnishings, that is, come to represent the hard lives of the characters, for though everything is regularly cleaned, the furniture is simply too old and worn to bring joy or beauty into the Youngers' lives, except in their memories. Other details of the setting also contribute to this closed-in feeling: the couch which serves as Travis's bed, the bathroom which must be shared with the neighbors.

Allusion

Two significant allusions are prominent in this play—one literary and one historical. The title of the play, *A Raisin in the Sun,* is taken from a poem by Langston Hughes, "Harlem." Langston Hughes was a prominent African American poet during the Harlem Renaissance, a period during the 1920s when many African American writers achieved considerable stature. The poem asks whether a dream deferred, or put off, dries up "like a raisin in the sun" or whether it explodes. During the play, Mama realizes that some members of her family are drying up, while others such as Walter are about to explode, and she realizes that their dreams can be deferred no longer.

The other major allusion is to Booker T. Washington, who is quoted by Mrs. Johnson as saying "Education has spoiled many a good plow hand." Booker T. Washington was a prominent African American during the late nineteenth century; perhaps his most well-known speech is his "Atlanta Exposition Address." Washington argued that Negroes should not aspire to academic education but should learn trades such as mechanics and farming instead. He also suggested that Negroes should not agitate for political rights and that while the races might intermingle for business purposes, they should live separate social lives. His primary opponent during this time was W. E. B. DuBois, who argued for equality and desegregation. Within the context of the play, Washington is understood as a negative example.

Climax

The climax of a work of literature occurs at the point when the tension can get no greater and the conflicts must resolve. In longer works, there may be several points of heightened tension before the final resolution. The climax of *A Raisin in the Sun* occurs when Karl Lindner visits the house for the second time, when Walter is about to accept his offer but changes his mind. The audience understands that while the Youngers may now achieve their dreams, their lives in this racist culture will remain difficult.

Foreshadowing

Foreshadowing occurs when a later event is hinted at earlier in the work. This occurs in *A Raisin in the Sun* when Ruth faints at the end of Scene One. This is a standard, almost stereotypic, way to convey pregnancy, which Ruth will confirm later in the play—and which will become significant through the family's response to it.

Symbolism

A symbol is an object that has value in itself but also represents an idea—something concrete, in other words, that represents something abstract. One of the symbols in *A Raisin in the Sun* is Mama's straggly plant. She wants to take this to the new house, although she plans to have a much more successful garden there, because this plant "expresses ME." Though the plant has struggled to live and seems to lack the beauty for which it would ordinarily be valued, it is significant to Mama because it has survived despite the struggle, as her family has survived.

HISTORICAL CONTEXT

The Civil Rights Movement of the 1950s

A Raisin in the Sun directly addresses the issue of segregated housing in the United States. While many neighborhoods remain effectively segregated today, such segregation was legally enforced during the 1950s. Despite several Constitutional Amendments subsequent to the Civil War, African Americans were denied many civil rights a full century later. In 1954, the case of Brown vs. Board of Education was tried in Kansas; it reached the United States Supreme Court in 1955. The Court found that segregated education was inherently unequal edu-

COMPARE & CONTRAST

- **1950s:** Schools and neighborhoods were racially (and sometimes ethnically) segregated, often by law. These laws received several major court challenges during this decade; many of the laws were declared unconstitutional.

  Today: Many neighborhoods and schools remain segregated despite legal and cultural attempts to reverse this situation. On the other hand, many schools, including prestigious universities, are completely integrated. Yet Affirmative Action, the practice through which this integration was in part achieved, is currently being challenged in several states.

- **1950s:** The computer microchip was invented by an employee of Texas Instruments and began to be widely produced. This invention would come to revolutionize the technological industry. Computers and computerized products were generally limited to military and industrial purposes and were not common household products. Computers that did exist were much larger than an average-sized living room.

  Today: Nearly every American home contains one—or more likely several-products that rely on computer microprocessors. These include not only personal computers complete with modems but also digital watches and clocks, compact disc players, and remote control devices for televisions and videocassette recorders.

- **1950s:** Senator Joseph McCarthy held his famous Senate hearings which attempted to demonstrate Communist infiltration of many U.S. institutions, including the Army. Although he is eventually censured by the Senate, these hear-

ings destroy the lives of many apparently innocent Americans.

  Today: With the fall of the Berlin Wall, the demise of the Soviet Union, and the internal conflicts in many Eastern European countries, Communism is no longer perceived as a threat by most Americans. The United States has emerged as the single world superpower.

- **1950s:** Dr. Jonas Salk developed the polio vaccine; this and other medical advances significantly decreased the rate of childhood illness by the end of the decade.

  Today: Many childhood illnesses have been controlled in the United States, although the infant mortality rate remains comparatively high for a developed country. Other illnesses, however, such as cancer and AIDs (Acquired Immune Deficiency syndrome), have become more prominent and receive considerable attention within the medical community as well as within the general culture.

- **1950s:** The Universal Copyright Convention occurred when most Western nations agreed to protect the copyright of work produced in each other's countries. For example, a novel originally printed in England could not be reprinted in the United States without the author's permission.

  Today: Most nations respect the idea of copyright. However, the rise of the internet has complicated this issue, since it is now so easy to distribute copyrighted material in this new form. New laws are likely to be written regarding the electronic ownership of material.

cation, effectively outlawing the practice of "separate but equal" school systems. Also in 1955, the Montgomery bus boycott occurred, with blacks and some whites refusing to ride city buses that forced blacks to sit in the back. In 1958, the public schools in Little Rock, Arkansas were closed by the Gover-

nor in an attempt to defy the Supreme Court's ruling. In 1959, the bus system of Atlanta, Georgia, was integrated, although the Governor asked riders to continue "voluntary" segregation. Ironically, in that same year, the United Nations voted to condemn racial discrimination anywhere in the world.

By the 1960s, Civil Rights demonstrations became common and resulted in much new legislation, although cultural implementation of those ideas would take much longer.

Literature and Arts in the 1950s

Artistically and culturally, the 1950s are commonly thought of as a repressed decade, often with good reason. It wasn't until 1959, for example, that *Lady Chatterly's Lover* by D.H. Lawrence was permitted to be distributed in the United States. Definitions of obscenity shifted during this decade, as did many other cultural assumptions.

A Raisin in the Sun was only one of several significant plays which opened on Broadway during this period. Others include *Sweet Bird of Youth* by Tennessee Williams, *The Zoo Story* by Edward Albee, and *The Miracle Worker* by William Gibson. Musicals that year included *Once upon a Mattress* starring Carol Burnett and *Gypsy* starring Ethel Merman and Jack Klugman. *The Sound of Music* also premiered starring Mary Martin.

Significant works also appeared in other forms of literature. E. B. White published his famous version of William Strunk's *The Elements of Style,* a grammar book that has become a standard in composition. Philip Roth published his collection of short stories, *Goodbye, Columbus,* while Saul Bellow published *Henderson the Rain King.* In Germany, Gunter Grass published his masterpiece, *The Tin Drum.*

Daily Life in the 1950s

Although the 1950s are known as a decade of prosperity, a significant number of Americans still lived in poverty. A study published by the University of Michigan demonstrated that 30% of families lived on or below the poverty line in 1959. In 1958, U.S. unemployment reached nearly 5.2 million. Simultaneously, some extremely wealthy Americans were able to avoid paying income taxes completely.

Because of technological discoveries, many aspects of daily life changed during the fifties. American automakers began to manufacture compact cars and computers began to be developed. Television became a popular source of home entertainment. People began to do the majority of their shopping at supermarkets rather than at small markets. Frozen orange juice concentrate became a popular item as did "heat and eat" frozen dinners (often called TV dinners).

Popular movies released in 1959 included *Ben Hur* starring Charlton Heston, Alfred Hitchcock's *North by Northwest* starring Cary Grant and Eva Marie Saint, and *The Diary of Anne Frank* with Millie Perkins and Shelley Winters. Rock and roll fans were saddened by the deaths of Buddy Holly and Ritchie Valens. Other musical performers included Paul Anka and Neil Sedaka. Perhaps the most famous toy ever—the Barbie doll—was also introduced this year; it would not be until 1968, however, that a black version of the doll would be produced.

CRITICAL OVERVIEW

A Raisin in the Sun is easily Lorraine Hansberry's best-known work, although her early death is certainly a factor in her limited oeuvre. From its beginning, this play was critically and commercially successful. After a brief run in New Haven, Connecticut, it opened on Broadway in 1959, where it ran for 530 performances. Although this was the first play written by a black woman to appear on Broadway, it received the New York Drama Critics Circle Award. A later adaptation won a Tony Award for best musical in 1974.

Newspapers reviewers were lavish in their praise of this performance. According to Francis Dedmond in an article published in *American Playwrights since 1945,* various critics complimented the work's "moving story" and "dramatic impact" as well as the play's "honesty" and "real-life characters." Magazine writers were equally enthusiastic. According to an article in *Plays for the Theatre,* this play is "one of the best examples" of work produced by minority playwrights during the late 1950's and 1960's.

Because of this early success, the play was translated into more than thirty languages and performed on stage as well as over the radio in several countries. To celebrate its twenty-fifth anniversary in 1983 and 1984, several revivals occurred. Reviewers remained enthusiastic.

Critics agree that this is a realistic play that avoids stereotypic characters. This realism permitted the black characters to be understood and sympathized with by a primarily white audience. By avoiding extremist characters—by creating Karl Lindner as a nonviolent if prejudiced man rather than as a member of the Ku Klux Klan for example—Hansberry was able to persuade her audience of the constant if subtle presence and negative effects of racism. According to Glendyr Sacks in the *International Dictionary of Theatre-1: Plays,* "Interest in the play . . . was undoubtedly fuelled by the unusual experience, for a Broadway audience, of watching a play in which all but one character was black. Furthermore, the tone of the play was not didactic. Its values were familiar, . . . and to some extent audiences and critics, both predominantly white, must have felt some relief that the protest implicit in the play was not belligerent." While some contemporary critics would suggest that realism is outdated, others argue that the play's influence on subsequent black works has been highly pervasive. Literature can be politically and culturally challenging, in other words, even if its form is conventional. Because the play is not overt in its protest, some later critics viewed it as assimilationist, an ironic situation since the play itself protests against assimilationism.

Some critics, however, did critique *A Raisin in the Sun* for its realism. Gerald Weales, in an article published in *Commentary* in 1959, claimed that "The play, first of all, is old fashioned. Practically no serious playwright, in or out of America, works in such a determinedly naturalistic form." He continued, "in choosing to write such a play, she [Hansberry] entered Broadway's great sack race with only a paper bag as equipment." He also suggests that the plot is "mechanical" and "artificial." His criticism, however, seems to be primarily against the genre in general rather than against Hansberry's manipulation of it. The tone of this article indicates that no realistic play would win Weales's favor. By the end of his article, he does concede that *A Raisin in the Sun* is a good play with "genuinely funny and touching scenes throughout."

Hansberry herself responded to the reception of her play in an article she published in the *Village Voice* in 1959. She occasionally appeared amused at both the type and amount of response her play received. Some critics, she suggested, seem to think that any negative reaction at all would be inherently racist, while others seem to disdain emotional appeals in literature in general. On the other hand, she stated that the play has been "magnificently understood." She suggested that her characters choose life and hope despite the fact that the culture in general seems enamored with despair because the Youngers and people like them have had "'somewhere' they have been trying to get for so long that more sophisticated confusions do not yet bind them."

Despair, in other words, is a luxury they cannot afford.

In part, though, this play remains popular specifically because of its realism. It presents characters whose values and goals are emotionally accessible to virtually any American audience, yet who through their eventual dignified responses to their situation achieve heroic status. Perhaps Hansberry's greatest contribution to subsequent drama was her ability to present black characters as admirable figures.

CRITICISM

L. M. Domina

Domina is a poet and author who also teaches at Hofstra University. In this essay Domina examines both the racial and gender roles played out in Hansberry's drama.

In many ways, *A Raisin in the Sun* seems to forecast events that would transpire during the decade following its initial production and beyond. The play raises issues of racial interaction and justice, as well as gender roles, class, and the nature of the American dream. It situates these questions, however, within the context of individual choice and individual heroism. Each of the characters in this play attempts to achieve a meaningful life within a struggle against cultural impediments, and an analysis of the characters' responses to racism will reveal the nature of their heroic qualities.

When the play opens, the Younger family has no clear leader. Its power structure is complicated, especially in terms of American norms. Because the American nuclear family was unabashedly patriarchal in the 1950's, Walter would seem to be the head of the household. Yet although he might (or might not) make the most money, he is not the family's breadwinner in the traditional sense, since Ruth and occasionally Mama also work. At this point in history, most married women—especially most white married women—did not work outside the home. Although these norms varied by race, white norms were so culturally dominant that they were aspired to even by members of other races. Despite his positions as husband and father, Walter continues to live because of economic necessity in his mother's house. And even Travis knows that he can make extra money by delivering groceries, an activity his mother forbids because of his age.

WHAT DO I READ NEXT?

- *Native Son* by Richard Wright, which was published in 1940, opens with a scene in which a family attempts to kill a rat. The protagonist, Bigger Thomas, becomes a chauffeur and eventually kills the daughter of his boss.

- The *Selected Poems of Langston Hughes,* published in 1987, contain much of the work Hughes published, including the poem ''Harlem.'' Hughes's poems both protest injustice and celebrate beauty.

- *To Be Young, Gifted, and Black* is a collection of autobiographical writings by Lorraine Hansberry published after her death in 1969. It remains one of the most well-known autobiographies of the 1960s.

- *Coming of Age in Mississippi,* published by Anne Moody in 1968, is the story of one young woman's work during the Civil Rights movement. It focuses particularly on voter registration in the American South.

- *Up from Slavery* is a collection of autobiographical essays by Booker T. Washington, published in 1901. Although he is often considered a hero, he seems to argue for ''separate but equal'' social arrangements between the races.

- *The Souls of Black Folk* by W. E. B. DuBois was published in 1903. DuBois presents a more radical argument than Washington, and he predicts that ''the problem of the Twentieth Century is the problem of the color line.''

Regardless of the details, though, Walter obviously cannot support this family alone.

It is Mama who has the money, though only because of an imminent insurance payment due her because of her husband's death. Although the other characters agree that this check is rightfully Mama's, they also each speculate about how it should be used. They also, though, claim an implicit right to it, since as Walter says, ''He was my father, too.'' Yet this check will ironically be the catalyst for a shift in the family's leadership responsibilities, from Mama to Walter. As Mama says, Walter will ''come into his manhood'' when he begins to make decisions for the family at the end of the play. This phrase is telling, however; Walter cannot achieve adulthood without achieving ''manhood'' with its gendered implications. Walter cannot be a man, in other words, unless he is making decisions for women. His success at the end of the play, therefore, depends on a sexism that is simply more explicit when it is presented by Joseph Asagai.

Asagai is a Nigerian man studying in the United States. Although he discusses ideas with Beneatha, whom he begins to date, he also argues that ''between a man and a woman there need be only one kind of feeling. . . . For a woman that should be enough.'' Implicitly, for a man that feeling exists but need not be enough. Even if Beneatha can escape the subjugation of American racism through a return to Africa, in other words, that return itself implies a subjugation to male authority.

Yet Beneatha is herself ambivalent regarding her own dreams. Speaking with Asagai, she describes a childhood incident in which a friend, Rufus, was seriously hurt: ''I remember standing there looking at his bloody open face thinking that was the end of Rufus. But the ambulance came and they took him to the hospital and they fixed the broken bones and they sewed it all up.'' Beneatha is so amazed at this ability—and at the hope it offers—that she aspires to perform medical wonders herself. ''I always thought it was the one concrete thing in the world that a human being could do,'' she says. ''Fix up the sick, you know—and make them whole again. That was truly being God.'' Asagai critiques this last statement: ''You wanted to be God?'' But Beneatha clarifies her point: ''No—I wanted to cure.'' Asagai on the other hand claims to live the dreams of the future. Relying on the most romantic of cliches, Asagai urges Beneatha to return to Africa with him: ''three hundred years later the African Prince rose up out of the seas and swept the maiden back across the middle passage over which her ancestors had come.'' Beneatha's last lines in the play occur when she is telling Mama of this proposal, though she seems to misunderstand Asagai's implications. ''To go to Africa, Mama—be a doctor in Africa,'' she says. She apparently doesn't realize that Asagai's understanding of her as an African princess is inconsistent with her vision of herself as an African doctor; he wishes her to be a subservient wife to him according to male-dominated social mores.

A major distinction, however, between Asagai's interpretation of gender roles and Mama's turning the leadership of the family over to Walter is the place of dignity in each decision. Asagai's statement that ''for a woman it should be enough'' to have a husband will have the effect of limiting Beneatha's dignity, of precluding her from completely realizing her dreams. Mama's manipulation of circumstances so that Walter can ''come into his manhood'' has the effect of increasing his dignity and providing a venue for him to realize his dreams.

For to the extent that the play reveals the effects of racism, it considers racism specifically within the context of a particular family's dreams. Mama makes her decisions, in other words, based on her love for her family rather than primarily on an ideological opposition to segregation. ''I just tried to find the nicest place for the least amount of money for my family,'' she says to Walter when he objects to her choice. ''Them houses they put up for colored in them areas way out all seem to cost twice as much as other houses.'' And it is eventually the family members' ability to live by their own decisions rather than to simply react to the decisions of others which affords them their greatest dignity. When Walter appears entirely to give up, Beneatha says of him, ''That is not a man. That is nothing but a toothless rat,'' recalling the rat Travis had chased in the alley with his friends. ''There is nothing left to love'' in him, she tells her mother. But Mama disagrees: ''There is *always* something left to love.''

The audience will recall that Mama cares for all living things, even those that do not seem to thrive. *Characters in 20th-Century Literature* described Mama as a ''commanding presence who seems to radiate moral strength and dignity.'' According to Hugh Short in an article published in the *Critical Survey of Drama,* ''the theme of heroism found in an unlikely place is perhaps best conveyed through the symbol of Lena's plant. Throughout the play, Lena has tended a small, sickly plant that clings tenaciously to life despite the lack of sunlight in the apartment. Its environment is harsh, unfavorable, yet it clings to life anyway—somewhat like Walter, whose life should long ago have extinguished any trace of heroism in him.''

Walter finally realizes that ''There is *always* something left to love,'' even in himself, when he remembers his own father's pride. He declines Lindner's offer because ''my father—my father— he earned it for us brick by brick. . . . We don't want to make no trouble for nobody or fight no causes, and we will try to be good neighbors.'' Walter realizes that just as his dreams cannot be realized for him by others, neither can they be destroyed for him by others. He rises into renewed dignity not simply because he has access to some money but because he has a renewed sense of himself. According to Qun Wang in *Reference Guide to American Literature,* ''even though Lena represents the family's link to the past and tradition, she is very supportive of her children's choices for the future.'' Throughout the play, Mama has been trying to lead Walter into the realization of his own dignity, and it is finally through her forgiveness and trust that he achieves it.

Earlier, Mama had assumed certain things about her children's pride because of the example she and her husband had set. Although she had recognized that ''Something eating you [Walter] up like a crazy man,'' it is only when Walter passively agrees with Ruth's decision regarding the abortion, however, that Mama, in her shock, begins to realize how desperate he feels. He is not like his father after all: ''I'm waiting to hear how you be your father's son. Be the man he was . . . I'm waiting to hear you talk like him and say we a people who give children life, not who destroys them.'' When Walter fails to respond, Mama is indignant: ''you are a disgrace to your father's memory.'' She considers him a disgrace not only because he won't argue against Ruth's proposed abortion, but because his motive seems to be financial; he has become obsessed with money rather than remembering the values she and his father sought to teach him. Here, Mama begins to realize that she must actively intervene if Walter is to find the inner resources to honor his father's memory. In relinquishing her role as matriarch, she therefore actively participates in the renewal of Walter's hope.

It is in this sense that the characters are heroic. In choosing life, they defy their struggle. In defying their struggle, they refuse the possibility of defeat.

Source: L. M. Domina, in an essay for *Drama for Students*, Gale, 1997.

Gerald Weales

In this appraisal of Lorraine Hansberry's A Raisin in the Sun, Weales examines the play's dramatic qualities and offers his ideas as to why it won the New York Drama Critics' Award in 1959.

Weales is an American drama critic; he is a winner of the George Jean Nathan Award for drama criticism and the author of numerous books on drama.

On the day that the New York Drama Critics' Award was announced, a student stopped me as I walked across the campus—where I pass as an expert on the theater—and asked a sensible question. Had *A Raisin in the Sun* won because it was the best play of the year, or because its author, Lorraine Hansberry, is a Negro? Even if the play is a good one (and, with reservations, I think it is), even if it were indisputably the best of the year, the climate of award-giving would make impossible its consideration on merit alone. Whenever an award goes to a playwright who is not a veteran of Broadway or to a play which is in some way unusual, the special case is almost certainly as important a factor in the voting as the play itself. The only contender this year that might have been chosen on its own merits (of which I think it has very few) was Tennessee Williams's *Sweet Bird of Youth.* Had *J. B.* got the award—and the smart money assumed it would and assumed, correctly, that it would also get the Pulitzer— special consideration would have derived from the image of Archibald MacLeish as the poet invading Broadway, and from the critical piety that longs for verse on the commercial stage. Had *A Touch of the Poet* got the award, respect for O'Neill as America's greatest playwright and the suspicion (unfounded) that this is very likely the last full-length play to be unearthed from the O'Neill papers and put on stage would have received ballots along with the play itself. It is, then, only sensible to assume that Lorraine Hansberry's being a Negro, and the first Negro woman to have a play on Broadway, had its influence on the voting critics.

Even if the balloting had been purely aesthetic, the award to Lorraine Hansberry would have been greeted as the achievement of a Negro—hailed in some places as an honor to American Negroes, dismissed in others as a well-meaning gesture from the Critics' Circle. Such reactions are inevitable at this time. Any prominent Negro—Marion Anderson or Jackie Robinson or Ralph Bunche—becomes a special hero to the Negro community an example of what a Negro can be and do in the United States; such figures are heroes, also, to white Americans who feel a sense of guilt about what the average American Negro cannot be and do. Lists are still compiled, I suppose, of prominent American Jews or famous Americans of Italian or German or Irish origin, but they are no longer urgently needed, by in-group or out, as are the lists of the successful American Negroes. So long as the Negro remains an incompletely integrated part of American society (equal but separate, in the non-legal meaning of the phrase), the achievements of singer, baseball player, or diplomat may be admired as such, but his race will not be ignored—by Negro or white.

The Negro artist and intellectual is particularly marked by this situation. Ralph Ellison and James Baldwin, for example, admirable writers both, are Negro writers in a way that Saul Bellow and Herbert Gold are not Jewish writers. A critic may note, as Richard Chase did recently in COMMENTARY, that in *Henderson the Rain King* for the first time Saul Bellow does not use Jewish characters, but this is not the kind of operation that followed Baldwin's *Giovanni's Room,* by which it was possible to view the book as a Negro novel without Negro characters.

The playwright who is a Negro is faced with a special problem. Broadway has a tradition of Negro shows, inevitably folksy or exotic, almost always musical, of which the only virtue is that Negro performers get a chance to appear as something more than filler. The obvious reaction to such shows is the protest play, the Negro agit-prop, which can be as false to American Negro life as the musicals. A playwright with serious intentions, like Miss Hansberry, has to avoid both pitfalls, has to try to write not a Negro play, but a play in which the characters are Negroes. In an interview (*New York Times,* March 8, 1959), Miss Hansberry is reported as having said to her husband before she began *Raisin,* "I'm going to write a social drama about Negroes that will be good art." However good the art, unfortunately, the play will remain, in one sense, a Negro play. The *Times* interview made quite clear that Miss Hansberry was aware that she was writing as much for the American Negro as for the American theatre. Similarly, an article on Sidney Poitier, the play's star, in the *New York Times Magazine* (January 25, 1959), made the point that Poitier avoided roles that might "diminish the Negro's stature as a human being." Whatever his ambitions as an artist, the Negro playwright, like the Negro actor, is still forced into a propaganda role. The publicity for *A Raisin in the Sun,* the news stories about it, the excitement it stirred up among Negroes (never until *Raisin* had I seen a Philadelphia theatre in which at least half the audience was Negro) all emphasize that it is a play written by a Negro woman about Negroes, a fact which could hardly have been forgotten when the Critics' Award was passed out.

Having suggested that objectivity is impossible with respect to *A Raisin in the Sun,* I should like to make a few objective remarks about it. The play, first of all, is old-fashioned. Practically no serious playwright, in or out of America, works in such a determinedly naturalistic form as Miss Hansberry in her first play. The semi-documentary movies that cropped up at the end of World War II, and then television, particularly in the Chayefsky school of drama, took over naturalism so completely that it is doubtful whether the form will ever again be comfortable in the theater. It is now possible to accept on stage the wildest fantasy or the simplest suggestion; but the set that pretends to be a real room with real doors and real furniture has become more difficult to accept than a stylized tree. Ralph Alswang's set for *Raisin,* as murky and crowded and gadgety as the slum apartment it represents, is ingenious in its detail; but the realistic set, like the real eggs the young wife cracks for an imaginary breakfast, reaches for a verisimilitude that has become impossible. *Raisin* is the kind of play which demands the naturalism that Miss Hansberry has used, but in choosing to write such a play, she entered Broadway's great sack race with only a paper bag as equipment. Her distinction is that she has won the race this year, which proves, I suppose, that narrow naturalism is still a possible—if anachronistic—form.

If the set suggests 1910 and Eugene Walter, the play itself—in its concentration on the family in society—recalls the 30's and Clifford Odets. It tells the story of the Younger family and their escape from a too-small apartment on Chicago's South Side to a house in which they have space and air and, unfortunately but not insurmountably, the enmity of their white neighbors. The conflict within

" *A RAISIN IN THE SUN* IS A FIRST PLAY AND A GOOD ONE; MORE IMPORTANT, IT HAS HOLD OF ONE OF THE CENTRAL DRAMATIC PROBLEMS OF OUR TIME"

the play is between the dreams of the son, Walter Lee, who wants to make a killing in the big world, and the hopes of his mother and his wife, who want to save their small world by transplanting it to an environment in which it might conceivably flourish. The mechanical means by which this conflict is illuminated—the insurance money, its loss, the representative of the white neighborhood association—are completely artificial, plot devices at their most devised. Take the loss of the money, for example. From the first moment that Walter Lee mentions his plans for a profitable liquor store, his connections, the need for spreading money around in Springfield, the audience knows that the money will be stolen; supposedly, in good naturalistic tradition, the audience should sit, collective fingers crossed, hoping that he might be spared, that the dream might not be deferred and shrivel, like a raisin in the sun, as the Langston Hughes poem has it. I found myself, fingers crossed, hoping that the inevitable would not come, not for the sake of Walter Lee Younger, but for the sake of the play, of which the solid center was already too hedged with contrivances. No one's crossed fingers did any good.

Of the four chief characters in the play, Walter Lee is the most complicated and the most impressive. He is often unlikable, occasionally cruel. His sense of being trapped by his situation—class, race, job, prospects, education—transfers to his family, who become to him not fellow prisoners but complacent jailers. Their ways of coping with their condition are his defeats, for to him the open-sesame that will release him (change his status? change his color?) is money. The play is concerned primarily with his recognition that, as a man, he must begin from, not discard, himself, that dignity is a quality of men, not bank accounts. Walter Lee's penchant for taking center stage has forced his wife to become an observer in his life, but at the same time she is an accusation. For most of the play she wears a mask of wryness or the real cover of fatigue, but Miss Hansberry gives her two scenes in which the near-hysteria that lies beneath the surface is allowed to break through. The mother is a more conventional figure—the force, compounded of old virtues and the strength of suffering, that holds the family together. She is a sentimentalized mother figure, reminiscent of Bessie Burgess in *Awake and Sing,* but without Bessie's destructive power. The daughter, who wants to be a doctor, is out of place in this working-class family. Not that her ambition does not belong with the Youngers, but her surface characteristics—the flitting from one expensive fad to another—could not have been possible, on economic grounds alone, in such a household. Although Miss Hansberry, the daughter of a wealthy real estate man, may have enjoyed poking fun at a youthful version of herself, as reported in the *Times* interview, the result of putting the child of a rich man into a working-class home is incongruous.

Despite an incredible number of imperfections, *Raisin* is a good play. Its basic strength lies in the character and the problem of Walter Lee, which transcends his being a Negro. If the play were only the Negro-white conflict that crops up when the family's proposed move is about to take place, it would be an editorial, momentarily effective, and nothing more. Walter Lee's difficulty, however, is that he has accepted the American myth of success at its face value, that he is trapped, as Willy Loman was trapped, by a false dream. In planting so indigenous an American image at the center of her play, Miss Hansberry has come as close as possible to what she intended—a play about Negroes which is not simply a Negro play.

The play has other virtues. There are genuinely funny and touching scenes throughout. Many of these catch believably the chatter of a family—the resentments and the shared jokes—and the words have the ring of truth that one found in Odets or Chayefsky before they began to sound like parodies of themselves. In print, I suspect, the defects of *Raisin* will show up more sharply, but on stage—where, after all, a play is supposed to be—the impressive performances of the three leads (Poitier, Ruby Dee, and Claudia McNeil) draw attention to the play's virtues.

A Raisin in the Sun deserved the Critics' Award as much as any other play of this season, and more than most. That statement, however, is as much an accusation of the season as it is praise of the play. Every fall, when the advertisements begin to bloom

in the pages of the New York *Times,* I am filled again with certainty that something is about to happen on Broadway. Every spring, when the results are in, I am aware of a dream deferred, a raisin shriveled. This season, however, has been duller than most. I cannot recall any moment of real excitement. There were small pleasures, small merits, but no revelations. The one real experiment in form, Shimon Wincelberg's *Kataki,* a full-length monologue play (and it came from television), was put quietly to sleep by tepid reviews. It is perverse to expect something really fine, I suppose. The Ibsens, the Shaws, the Chekhovs have always been the exceptions in the theater and they have had to make their way against the theater itself. The Broadway business is at present congenial to adaptations of novels and television plays, to mechanical comedies, to the Pinero-like seriousness of William Inge and Robert Anderson, to anything that is safe, even though a high percentage of the safeties turn out to be bombs.

American fiction, it seems to me, is alive now and aware of its life. American drama, except perhaps for musical comedy (*Candide,* after all, is the best American play in many years), is, if not dead, often deadly—and does not particularly care that it is. Arthur Miller is the only one of the postwar American playwrights whose concern with the theater is likely to engender excitement and he, perhaps wisely, works slowly and appears infrequently. Even Tennessee Williams, whose mixture of old expressionism and new neuroticism once had vitality, seems now mechanical in his flamboyance; *Sweet Bird of Youth,* for all its acclaim, looked to me like the same old rabbit out of the same old hat. There is something sad about the fact that the Critics' Award went to a play that not only uses an outdated form, but often uses it clumsily. I do not want to disparage Miss Hansberry's achievement with *A Raisin in the Sun.* It is a first play and a good one; more important, it has hold of one of the central dramatic problems of our time. If one were to compare her with Chekhov, however, as Brooks Atkinson did in his review, the comparison could hardly be as flattering as the *Times* critic made it. I hope that Lorraine Hansberry will go on to write more plays and that all of them will be as good as or better than *A Raisin in the Sun,* but I do not expect to find in them any real hope for a vital American theater. *A Raisin in the Sun* is the best play of the year, but the American theater today is an old man in a dry season. Where does that leave us? Waiting for fall, of course.

Source: Gerald Weales, "Thoughts on *A Raisin in the Sun,*" in *Commentary,* Vol. 27, no. 6, June, 1959, pp. 527–30.

Kenneth Tynan

In this review, originally published in the March 21, 1959, issue of the magazine, Tynan offers his assessment of A Raisin in the Sun*'s debut performance, praising the play's dramatic virtues.*

A dramatist and screenwriter, Tynan served as drama critic for the New Yorker *from 1958 to 1960.*

The supreme virtue of *A Raisin in the Sun,* Lorraine Hansberry's new play at the Ethel Barrymore, is its proud, joyous proximity to its source, which is life as the dramatist has lived it. I will not pretend to be impervious to the facts; this is the first Broadway production of a work by a colored authoress, and it is also the first Broadway production to have been staged by a colored director. (His name is Lloyd Richards, and he has done a sensible, sensitive, and impeccable job.) I do not see why these facts should be ignored, for a play is not an entity in itself, it is a part of history, and I have no doubt that my knowledge of the historical context predisposed me to like *A Raisin in the Sun* long before the house lights dimmed. Within ten minutes, however, liking had matured into absorption. The relaxed, freewheeling interplay of a magnificent team of Negro actors drew me unresisting into a world of their making, their suffering, their thinking, and their rejoicing. Walter Lee Younger's family lives in a roach-ridden Chicago tenement. The father, at thirty five, is still a chauffeur, deluded by dreams of financial success that nag at the nerves and tighten the lips of his anxious wife, who ekes out their income by working in white kitchens. If she wants a day off, her mother-in-law advises her to plead flu, because it's respectable. ("Otherwise they'll think you've been cut up or something.") Five people—the others being Walter Lee's progressive young sister, and his only child, an amiable small boy—share three rooms. They want to escape, and their chance comes when Walter Lee's mother receives the insurance money to which her recent widowhood has entitled her. She rejects her son's plan, which is to invest the cash in a liquor store; instead, she buys a house for the family in a district where no Negro has ever lived. Almost at once, white opinion asserts itself, in the shape of a deferential little man from the local Improvement Association, who puts the segregationist case so gently that it almost sounds like a plea for modified togetherness. At the end of a beautifully written scene, he offers to buy back the

> THE SUPREME VIRTUE OF *A RAISIN IN THE SUN* IS ITS PROUD, JOYOUS PROXIMITY TO ITS SOURCE, WHICH IS LIFE AS THE DRAMATIST HAS LIVED IT"

house, in order—as he explains—to spare the Youngers any possible embarrassment.

His proposal is turned down. But before long Walter Lee has lost what remains of the money to a deceitful chum. He announces forthwith that he will go down on his knees to any white man who will buy the house for more than its face value. From this degradation he is finally saved; shame brings him to his feet. the Youngers move out, and move on; a rung has been scaled, a point has been made, a step into the future has been soberly taken.

Miss Hansberry's piece is not without sentimentality, particularly in its reverent treatment of Walter Lee's mother, brilliantly though Claudia McNeil plays the part, monumentally trudging, upbraiding, disapproving, and consoling, I wish the dramatist had refrained from idealizing such a stolid old conservative. (She forces her daughter, an agnostic, to repeat after her, "In my mother's house there is still God.") But elsewhere I have no quibbles. Sidney Poitier blends skittishness, apathy, and riotous despair into his portrait of the mercurial Walter Lee, and Ruby Dee, as his wife, is not afraid to let friction and frankness get the better of conventional affection. Diana Sands is a buoyantly assured kid sister, and Ivan Dixon is a Nigerian intellectual who replies, when she asks him whether Negroes in power would not be just as vicious and corrupt as whites, "I *live* the answer." The cast is flawless, and the teamwork on the first night was as effortless and exuberant as if the play had been running for a hundred performances. I was not present at the opening, twenty-four years ago, of Mr. Odets' *Awake and Sing!,* but it must have been a similar occasion, generating the same kind of sympathy and communicating the same kind of warmth. After several curtain calls, the audience began to shout for the author, whereupon Mr. Poitier leaped down into the auditorium and dragged Miss Hansberry onto the stage. It was a glorious gesture, but it did no more than the play had already done for all of us. In spirit, we were up there ahead of her.

Source: Kenneth Tynan, in a review of *A Raisin in the Sun* (1959) in the *New Yorker,* Vol. 69, no. 15, May 31, 1993, pp. 118, 122.

FURTHER READING

Dedmond, Francis. "Lorraine Hansberry" in *American Playwrights since 1945: A Guide to Scholarship, Criticism, and Performance,* edited by Philip C. Kolin, Greenwood, 1989, pp. 155-68.

This is a thorough article which provides an assessment of Hansberry's reputation through her career. In addition, it includes a useful resource list.

Hansberry, Lorraine. "Willie Loman, Walter Younger, and He Who Must Live" in the *Village Voice,* Vol. IV, no. 42, August 12, 1959, pp. 7-8.

Hansberry discusses positive and negative responses to her play and compares it to *Death of a Salesman* by Arthur Miller.

Howes, Kelly King, editor. "Lorraine Hansberry" in *Characters in 20th Century Literature, Book II,* Gale, 1995, pp. 204-09.

This article approaches the play through an analysis of its characters. It provides an extensive discussion of each of the characters and compares them to other significant characters in American literature.

Sacks, Glendyr. "Raisin in the Sun" in *International Dictionary of Theatre-1: Plays,* edited by Mark Hawkins-Dady, St. James Press, 1992, pp. 649-50.

This article is a basic plot analysis which provides some cultural context.

Short, Hugh. "Lorraine Hansberry" in *Critical Survey of Drama,* edited by Frank Magill, Salem Press, 1994, pp. 1086-94.

This article discusses *A Raisin in the Sun* in the context of Hansberry's other plays. Describing this play as the most successful, Short analyzes it according to its theme of heroism.

Wang, Qun. "A Raisin in the Sun" in *Reference Guide to American Literature,* edited by James Kamp, St. James Press, 1994, pp. 1031-32.

This article briefly describes the major characters as well as situates Hansberry as a playwright within the canon of American literature.

Weales, Gerald. "Thoughts on *A Raisin in the Sun*" in *Commentary,* Vol. 27, no. 6, June, 1959, pp. 527-30.

This review is among the more negative Hansberry received. Weales critiques the traditional form of the play, suggesting that the form guarantees stereotypes despite the qualities of the play that Weales himself praises.

The Rez Sisters

TOMSON HIGHWAY
1986

When *The Rez Sisters* was first performed in 1986, Canadian and American audiences took note of this new and offbeat play by Native North American playwright Tomson Highway. A Cree Native of Manitoba, Canada, Highway wanted to make life on the reservation (or 'the rez') seem ''cool'' and ''show and celebrate what funky folk Canada's Indian people really are.'' His goals were met with this play, which received high praise (winning the Dora Mavor Award for best new play in Toronto's 1986-87 theater season and being named a runner-up for the Floyd F. Chalmers Award for the outstanding Canadian play of 1986). *The Rez Sisters* also proved to be a commercial success, playing to sold-out audiences during a cross-Canada tour from October to February of 1988. Audiences found Highway's portrait of seven ''rez sisters'' to be, as William Peel called them in *Canadian Theatre Review,* ''a striking cast of characters who reveal both blemishes and beauty'' and who ''possess, on the whole, great human dignity.''

The play spans a summer in 1986, when seven women (all related by birth or marriage) decide to travel to Toronto to participate in ''THE BIGGEST BINGO IN THE WORLD.'' Each woman offers the audience a different attitude toward life on the reservation—as well as their individual dreams of escaping it. From Pelajia Patchnose, who hopes to win enough money to bring paved roads to ''Wasy'' (their reservation), to Emily Dictionary, an ex-biker whose rough-and-ready outlook creates some

friction in the group, these characters display the natural desire to rise above their surroundings and create a better world for their children and each other.

The Rez Sisters was lauded for its realistic portrayal of these distinct personalities. On a larger scale, Highway was hailed for creating a work that made Native North American life accessible as well as entertaining to a wide audience.

AUTHOR BIOGRAPHY

A "rez" man himself, Tomson Highway has transformed the spiritual and cultural lessons of his youth into drama. He was born in Manitoba, Canada, on his father's trap-line ("in a tent, like all his brothers and sisters") on December 6, 1951 (some sources cite 1952). He spoke only Cree until the age of six, when he was sent to study at a Roman Catholic boarding school. He stayed there until he was 15, visiting his family only two months each summer. After finishing grade nine, Highway was sent to high school in Winnipeg, where he lived with various white foster parents. He graduated in 1970.

Since he was a "musical prodigy" in high school, Highway next spent two years at the University of Manitoba studying piano—a pursuit that he continued the following year, studying to be a concert pianist in London. After this year abroad, Highway returned to Canada, where he continued his studies at the University of Manitoba and the University of Western Ontario (from where he graduated with a Bachelors of Music Honors in 1975). However, he stayed an extra year to complete the English courses required for a Bachelors of Arts degree; during this time, he met and worked with James Reaney, one of Canada's more respected playwrights and poets.

With his studies completed, Highway followed his humanitarian impulses and began seven years' work with The Native Peoples' Resource Center in London, Ontario, and The Ontario Federation of Indian Friendship Centers in Toronto. It was during this time that he traveled extensively through the reservations of Canada, meeting and observing scores of Native people in streets, bars, prisons, and friendship centers. Upon turning thirty, Highway began his career as a playwright, presenting his work to Native audiences on reservations and in urban community centers. With the 1986 premiere of *The Rez Sisters,* Highway's artistic career began to blossom.

Speaking of his inspiration in creating *The Rez Sisters*'s female protagonists, Highway remarked to the Toronto *Globe and Mail*'s Ray Conlogue, "I am sensitive to women because of the matrilineal principle of our [Cree] culture, which has gone on for thousands of years. Women have such an ability to express themselves emotionally. And as a writer, you've got to express emotion." This "expression of emotion" found in *The Rez Sisters* proved impressive: the play received numerous honors and played to sold-out audiences across Canada. After its success, Highway wrote a collection of monologues, *Aria* and his "flip-side" to *The Rez Sisters, Dry Lips Oughta Move to Kapuskasing* (1989), which features seven Indian men. Like its counterpart, *Dry Lips* won numerous awards, including four Dora Mavor Moore Awards. Highway served as the artistic director of Native Earth Performing Arts, Inc., Toronto's only professional Native theater company, until 1992. He also cowrote *The Sage, the Dancer, and the Fool,* with Rene Highway and Bill Merasty in 1989.

PLOT SUMMARY

Act One

The Rez Sisters opens on a late August day on the Wasaychigan Hill Indian Reserve (or as its residents refer to it, "Wasy") on Manitoulin Island, Ontario. Pelajia Patchnose is found nailing shingles to her roof, with the assistance of her sister, Philomena Moosetail. Pelajia's first line, "Philomena. I want to go to Toronto," reveals her desire to escape what she sees as her dull life in "plain, dusty, boring old Wasy." "Everyone here's crazy," she complains. "No jobs. Nothing to do but drink and screw each other's wives and husbands and forget about our Nanabush" —who is also known as "The Trickster," a mythological spirit that observes (and sometimes enters into) the action of the play. After complaining more about the fact that there are no paved roads in Wasy, Philomena lifts her sister's spirits with her wit (and by falling off the roof). Annie Cook, their half-sister, arrives and the three talk of their beloved hobby: bingo. Eager to run to the post office, where a parcel awaits her, Annie leaves and the two remaining sisters talk of how the bingo games in Wasy "are getting smaller and smaller all the time."

The scene changes to Marie-Adele Starblanket's house (down the hill from Pelajia's), where she is throwing stones at Nanabush, disguised as a seagull. When Nanabush tells her "As-tum [Come]," she replies, "I can't fly away. I have no wings. Yet." Her conversation is interrupted when her sister-in-law, Veronique St. Pierre, enters with her mentally disabled adopted daughter, Zhaboonigan Peterson. Veronique and Marie-Adele discuss a used car purchased by an acquaintance before moving onto a more serious topic: Marie-Adele's cancer. Veronique questions Marie-Adele about who will take care of her fourteen children after she "goes to the hospital"; Marie-Adele replies that her husband, Eugene, will carry this load. The topic shifts to the real motive of Veronique's visit: to tell Marie-Adele that she heard a rumor that "THE BIGGEST BINGO IN THE WORLD" is coming to Toronto and to ask Marie-Adele if she wants to play. Annie arrives, learns of the upcoming bingo game, and all four of them walk together to the post office. On the way, Marie-Adele, Annie, and Veronique pause to tell the audience about their hopes for the upcoming game: Marie-Adele wants to buy an island where she can live with her family, Annie hopes to buy a complete country-music record library, and Veronique imagines herself cooking for everyone over a brand-new stove.

Arriving at the post office (which doubles as a general store), the women meet Emily Dictionary (Annie's sister and half-sister of all the others). Described as "one tough lady," Emily is an ex-biker who lived in California for years but has returned to Wasy. Instigated by only a few remarks, the women all begin a massive, free-for-all war of insults in which their suspicions and jealousies of each other are revealed to the audience. While the women bicker, Zhaboonigan wanders outside and talks to Nanabush, telling him of a time when she was sexually abused by two white boys. After the women stop fighting, Annie opens her parcel and finds a Patsy Cline record (a gift from her daughter) and the confirmation of the rumor regarding "THE BIGGEST BINGO IN THE WORLD," which will take place in Toronto on September 8. Marie-Adele reads a letter from a hospital in Toronto, confirming her appointment for tests on September 10. The women decide to travel to Toronto, play bingo, take Marie-Adele to undergo her tests, and then return. But when they ask their local Band Council for a loan (which would enable them to rent a car), their request is refused.

Act Two

In order to think of ways to raise enough money for their trip, the seven women hold a meeting in Pelajia's basement. They decide to use Eugene's van, but they also realize that they will need a total of $1,400 in order to pay for food and expenses. To raise this money, the women undertake a variety of odd jobs, presented to the audience in a long and humorous pantomime sequence. Finally, the money is raised and the women enter the van that, they hope, will take them to the $500,000 bingo jackpot.

En route to Toronto, the women have various conversations while others sleep; from these conversations, the audience learns about their respective pasts, hopes, and fears. Philomena, for example, explains that September 8 holds a special significance for her, since it is the birthday of her child that she had to give up as soon as it was born. Annie tells of her boyfriend Fritz, a Jewish country singer whom she hopes will marry her. Suddenly, a tire blows out and must be replaced. As the women change the tire, Marie-Adele wanders off and is attacked by Nanabush in the form of a nighthawk. Understanding that this is an omen of her death, Marie-Adele begs him for mercy: "Oh no! Me? Not yet. Give me time. Please."

Once the tire is changed, they resume their trip and conversations. Marie-Adele tells of Eugene's distress over her condition, which Pelajia explains with, "There's only so much Eugene can understand . . . He's only human." Emily then reveals why she returned to Wasy: her lover, a member of her all-female biker gang, was killed on a San Francisco highway. The tension in the van is almost unbearable, until Emily acknowledges her gratefulness to the others. Relieved, she gives a "high-five" to Zhaboonigan and the stage transforms onto the site of the long-awaited bingo game.

The Bingo Master—who is also Nanabush, this time in a new disguise—greets the women and the audience, who actually play a warm-up game of bingo with the cast. However, once the actual big-money game begins, the women express their distress at their lack of fortune. Finally, they rush the grandstand and destroy the bingo machine while "out of this chaos emerges the calm, silent image of Marie-Adele waltzing romantically in the arms of the Bingo Master." The Bingo Master suddenly changes into the nighthawk and carries Marie-Adele to the spirit world, signifying her death.

The action then returns to Wasy, where the six women sing the Ojibway funeral song over Marie-

Adele's grave and then talk at the store. As a kind of renewal in the face of Marie-Adele's death, Emily announces that she is pregnant with "Big Joey's" (a local man's) child. Veronique assumes the role of mother to Mare-Adele's children and is seen cooking for them on the departed sister's stove. The play's final scene occurs at the same place it began: Pelajia's roof, where she is still nailing shingles and joking with Philomena (who did win enough money to buy a new toilet). As Pelajia considers all of the changes for which she will work on the reserve, Nanabush dances to the beat of her hammer, unseen by her but appearing "merrily and triumphantly" to the audience.

CHARACTERS

Annie Cook

The 36 year-old sister of Marie-Adele and half-sister of Pelajia and Philomena, Annie hopes to be a country singer and someday marry her boyfriend, Fritz, who is a Jewish country musician. She delights in gossiping about the activities of "Big Joey," a local man who sleeps with a variety of women. Her daughter, Ellen, lives in a neighboring town with her boyfriend and writes her to tell her about the upcoming bingo game in Toronto.

Emily Dictionary

Recently returned to the Wasy reservation, Emily is the 32 year-old sister of Annie (and half-sister of Pelajia and Philomena). Described as "one tough lady," Emily's coarse language and rough exterior are the results of an abusive ten-year marriage and the death, years later, of a female lover in San Francisco. Her rough exterior gradually gives way as her relationship with her traveling companions deepens. At the play's end she reveals that she is pregnant and that Big Joey is the father.

Philomena Moosetail

Philomena is Pelajia's 49 year-old sister and the voice of practicality among the seven women. She is lighthearted and often cracks jokes. She hopes to win enough money to buy a toilet that is "big and white and very wide." Late in the play, she reveals that she once had to give up her child.

Nanabush

The traditional "Trickster" that features prominently in Cree and other Native American and North American culture, Nanabush is, according to Highway, "as pivotal and important a figure in the Native world as Christ is in the realm of Christian mythology." Described as "essentially a comic, clownish sort of character," Nanabush "teaches us about the nature and the meaning of existence on the planet Earth." In the play, Nanabush appears disguised as a seagull, a nighthawk, and the Bingo Master. It is he who takes Marie-Adele to the spirit world when she dies at the bingo game. ("Nanabush" is the Ojibway name for the Trickster.)

Pelajia Patchnose

The natural leader of "the rez sisters," the 53-year-old Pelajia Patchnose dreams of a life away from the reservation the women refer to as Wasy. After her return from the bingo game, she decides (as Dennis W. Johnston describes in *Canadian Literature*), to use her leadership talents "to genuinely improve conditions on the reserve rather than just to complain about them."

Zhaboonigan (zah-boon-i-gan) Peterson

Zhaboonigan is the 24 year-old mentally disabled adopted daughter of Veronique. Her parents died in a "horrible car crash" twenty-two years ago and Veronique has raised the girl since then. Only she and Marie-Adele can see Nanabush when he appears; in one instance, she tells the Trickster of a time that she was sexually abused by two white boys.

Veronique St. Pierre

The 45 year-old sister-in-law to the other women, Veronique complains about her alcoholic husband when not caring for Zhaboonigan Peterson, her adopted daughter, who has mental deficiencies. After Marie-Adele's death, Veronique moves into the Starblanket home to care for the fourteen children and cook for them on Marie-Adele's stove, an example (like her adopting Zhaboonigan) of her sweet nature and concern for others' well-being.

Marie-Adele Starblanket

Suffering silently from cancer, the 39 year-old Marie-Adele is the "mother figure" of the play. She lives with her husband, Eugene, and her fourteen children, for whom she hopes to win enough money to buy an island paradise where they can live "real nice and comfy." She dies during the bingo game in Toronto, where her spirit is symbolically transported to the spirit world.

THEMES

Appearances and Reality

In *The Rez Sisters,* seven women travel from their Indian reserve to Toronto in order to participate in "THE BIGGEST BINGO IN THE WORLD." Each woman has her own dreams of what winning the bingo jackpot will bring them. Annie hopes for enough money to "buy every single one of Patsy Cline's records" and "go to all the taverns and night clubs in Toronto and listen to the live music." Philomena hopes for a new toilet that is "big and wide and very white." Marie-Adele wishes for "the most beautiful incredible goddamn island in the whole goddamn world." Veronique desires "the biggest stove on the reserve." Finally, Pelajia wants to build "a nice paved road" in front of her house, since their "old chief" has done nothing to help her realize this dream. Each woman's dreams of wealth are linked to their desires to make life at Wasy more bearable—or, in the case of Marie-Adele, escape "the rez" entirely.

However, when the women arrive in Toronto, luck does not favor them. Despite the fact that Philomena plays with twenty-seven cards, she only wins $600 and the others return empty-handed after charging the bingo machine in their fury. (Marie-Adele does not return at all, dying during the bingo game.) Rather than complain about their hard luck, however, the "rez sisters" realize that these dreams cannot be realized by chance alone and that they need to focus on the changes that they can accomplish themselves. Speaking at the funeral of Marie-Adele, Pelajia states:

> Well, sister, guess you finally hit the big jackpot. Best bingo game we've ever been to in our lives, huh? You know, life's like that, I figure. When all is said and done. Kinda' silly, innit, this business of living? But what choice do we have? When some fool of a being goes and puts us Indians plunk down in the middle of this old earth, dishes out this lot we got right now. But, I figure we gotta make the most of it while we're here. You certainly did. And I sure as hell am giving it one good try. For you. For me. For all of us. Promise. Really.

The remaining women learn to work in order to improve their lives on "the rez": Veronique takes

TOPICS FOR FURTHER STUDY

- Research the appearance of the Trickster in Native American and Native Canadian cultures and compare his depiction in various myths to his appearance in *The Rez Sisters.*

- Research how many Native Americans and Canadians were forced to live on reserves (reservations). Find accounts of life on these reserves. Compare and contrast these accounts with the depiction of Wasy in *The Rez Sisters.*

- Research the effects of Christianity and missionaries on Native American and Native Canadian life. Describe the degree to which you think these effects have caused many Native people to lose touch with their spirituality.

- Research they ways death is depicted in various cultures. Compare and contrast these depictions with the Cree perception of death that is presented in *The Rez Sisters.*

care of Marie-Adele's children, Annie vows to practice her singing in order to become a star, and Pelajia accepts her position on her roof, hammering away for a better tomorrow. As Philomena tells Pelajia early in the play, "This place is too much in your blood. You can't get rid of it. And it can't get rid of you." The literal and metaphorical journey depicted in *The Rez Sisters* reflects the women coming to understand the importance of these words. Perhaps the clearest sign that the sisters are moving in the right direction is the final appearance of Nanabush as Pelajia works on her roof; he "dances to the beat of the hammer, merrily and triumphantly."

Friendship

In her essay on *The Rez Sisters,* in *Books in Canada,* Carol Bolt remarks that, when seeing the play, audiences feel as if they "have been a part of an extraordinary, exuberant, life-affirming family." This reaction is due to Highway's creation of characters that reflect the value of friendship and a close community. The fact that all of the women are either sisters, half-sisters, or sisters-in-law suggests that they have known each other for a long time; throughout the play they behave in a comfortable, familiar manner, joking and gossiping with each other. Even those women who profess dislike for each other (such as Annie and Veronique) still *talk* to each other, realizing the fact that severing any ties between them would be worse than being annoyed by each other's idiosyncracies.

When a war of words erupts between the women, they throw the worst insults they can imagine at each other: Philomena calls Annie a "slime"; Emily calls Annie a "slippery little slut"; Veronique tells Annie she is a "sick pervert"; Pelajia calls Marie-Adele "a spoiled brat"; Marie-Adele tells Veronique that she is like "some kind of insect, sticking insect claws into everybody's business"; and Annie mocks Pelajia for thinking that she is "Queen of the Indians." However, despite these bitter retorts, a day later they are all working together, trying to raise enough money for their trip to Toronto. And during their drive, the women confess their secret fears and try to provide each other emotional comfort. Despite their gossip and tendency to quarrel, Highway's characters share an unspoken realization that they need each other for stability and support.

Supernatural

Observing the action of the play is Nanabush, the "trickster" that plays a large role in many Native mythologies and cultures. "We have a mythology that is thousands and thousands of years old," Highway explained to Hartmut Lutz in *Contemporary Challenges: Conversations with Canadian Native Authors.* Highway described the trickster to the *Globe and Mail*'s Conlogue as "central to our system of spiritual belief. It's a connection to this great energy, or God, which most people only perceive in moments of extreme crisis. Or when they are close to death, and can see into the spirit world." In *The Rez Sisters,* only Marie-Adele and Zhaboonigan can recognize Nanabush in his various disguises, suggesting that the former is "close to death" and that the latter, despite her mental handicap, is more perceptive and open to the spirit world than the other women. On her way to Toronto, Marie-Adele is confronted by Nanabush, who warns her of her upcoming death; however, her ascension into the spirit world (in the arms of the Bingo Master) proves to be a breathtaking journey. By placing Nanabush onstage for most of the play,

Highway suggests that the Trickster may be fading from modern Native's memories but is in fact still very much a part of their everyday lives.

STYLE

Setting

When Pelajia Patchnose, at the opening of the play, tells her sister that she wants to leave Wasy and "go to Toronto," Philomena replies, "But you were born here," as if this is reason enough for her to stay. As the play progresses, however, the audience learns that this *is* reason enough; one of the play's chief issues is that home is where the heart is; how a group of people learn to respect their homeland and stand up to the challenges that make their lives' difficult—rather than run off to a different place. "This place is too much inside your blood," Philomena tells Pelajia. "You can't get rid of it. And it can't get rid of you." The sisters frequently lapse into Cree, such as when Pelajia says, "Aw-ni-gi-naw-ee-dick [Oh, go on]" to Philomena or when Marie-Adele and Nanabush conduct an entire conversation in the same language.

Creating the play to occur in a specific place with its own language and identity reflects one of Highway's chief artistic concerns: "I believe that a sense of place applies to everybody," he said in an interview with Robert Enright in *Border Crossings.* "Where you come from, where your roots are—all that is extremely strong. I don't think that anybody is able to get rid of it." Unlike other plays with indeterminate settings, *The Rez Sisters* emphasizes Wasy to show that the setting is as important and as central to the play as the characters.

Characterization

One of the chief appeals of *The Rez Sisters* is its array of colorful characters—the manner in which Highway presents his "sisters" is worth noting. Each of the women presents a different point of view about life on the rez. Pelajia, for example, thinks of a world elsewhere, where her "old man" would not have to "go the hundred miles to Espanola just to get a job." Philomena is more down-to-earth and practical, as suggested by her desire for a nice new toilet (and her casual opening of the bathroom door to yell at the other women while she is sitting on an old one). Annie is the town gossip, prying into the affairs of others. Emily is a contrast to her friends because she is tougher and more cynical, at first appearance less concerned with the others' welfare. Marie-Adele is tender and faces her impending death with great dignity. Veronique frets over her own childlessness but still cares for her adopted daughter, Zhaboonigan: a mentally disabled young woman whose honesty and joy springs forth to relieve the play's most tense situations. Denis W. Johnston has written in *Canadian Literature* that the play's complexity "lies not in its plot, but in a sophisticated pattern of character revelation and development." By offering his audience such a wide variety of characters and attitudes, Highway is able to more fully explore life "on the rez" and the dreams of those who live there.

Symbolism

The foremost symbol used in the play (the one that opens and closes the story) is Palajia's hammer, which is first seen when she is attaching shingles to her roof. Unhappy with her life at Wasy, the hammer symbolizes the toil and labor that Pelajia associates with the rez. She also uses the tool to threaten the other women, in which case it becomes a symbol of her aggression and her role as a leader to the women. At their meeting in Pelajia's basement, Emily uses the hammer as a gavel, bringing order to their chaotic plans. Finally, as Johnston has remarked, Pelajia is using it at the end of the play, again on her roof, but with an important difference: now "her hammer has become a badge of purpose rather than just a physical tool." Tracing the way that Pelajia uses her hammer is like tracing the ways in which her character changes; it serves as a symbol of her growth and accepting responsibility to transform and improve her corner of Wasy. With it, she will rebuild her life and the lives of her "rez sisters."

HISTORICAL CONTEXT

Describing the initial reaction to *The Rez Sisters,* Highway remarked to *Canadian Literature*'s Johnston, "I'm sure some people went to [the play] expecting crying and moaning and plenty of misery, reflecting everything they've heard about or witnessed on reserves. They must have been surprised. All that humor and optimism, plus the positive values taught by Indian mythology." These values are found in the attitudes of the women towards both Wasy and each other, and the best way to explore the cultural context of *The Rez Sisters* is to consider

what its author has said about the role of spirituality and mythology in Cree and other Native cultures. 1986 saw the disaster at the Soviet Union's Chernobyl nuclear power plant (which is estimated to cause anywhere from 6,500 to 45,000 future deaths by cancer caused by radiation); as if commenting on this tragedy, during his tenure as artistic director for the Native Earth Performing Arts, Inc., Highway once stated, "At a time in our history, as a community of human beings, when the world is about to get literally destroyed, and all life forms have a very good chance of being completely obliterated—at a crucial time like this, Native people have a major statement to make about the profound change that has to come about in order for the disaster to be averted." The statement to which Highway refers here is, of course, the play itself, which offers viewers a look at the spirituality of seven women and how this spirituality plays a role in their daily lives.

In several interviews, Highway has talked at length about the Trickster (who appears in *The Rez Sisters* as Nanabush), his role in Native culture and the effect of Christianity on Native beliefs. The Trickster "occupies a central role for us," Highway told Conlogue in the *Globe and Mail,* "just as Christ does for [Christians]. But there are three important differences. Trickster has a sense of humor. He was never crucified. And he is neither male nor female." (The Trickster's sense of humor is found in *The Rez Sisters,* for example, when he transforms into the showy and bombastic Bingo Master.) "The way of Nanabush is the way of joy and laughter," Highway said in *Maclean's.* "Contrast that with Christianity—the way of pain and tears." Highway sees one of his artistic goals as reacquainting Native people with their own mythologies, which, as he stated in *Contemporary Challenges,* were "almost destroyed or . . . obliterated by the onslaught of missionaries." Describing the reaction to his second play, *Dry Lips Oughta Move to Kapuskasing,* Highway told Enright in *Border Crossings* that he was "shocked to discover that main-stream audiences knew more about the size of Elizabeth Taylor's breasts . . . than they did about their own systems of gods and goddesses."

This is not to say that only Native audiences can learn from Highway's depiction of Native spirituality; on the contrary, Highway has studied many mythologies from around the world and seeks to educate non-Native audiences about the way and teachings of Nanabush: "We're not a highly intellectualized or highly technologized society," he told Enright, "but we haven't sacrificed our spiritual centre."

While only two of his "rez sisters" can recognize Nanabush, this does not imply that the others have lost touch with their spiritual heritage: other characters speak of legendary figures, such as Windigo, a giant and Bingo Betty, a local ghost who haunts "the rez," "hovering in the air above the bingo tables, playing bingo like its never been played before." However, Highway is not implying that one culture is superior to another or more inherently "right"; rather, as he told Bemrose in *Maclean's,* he feels that, "If we could combine the best of both cultures [Native and Western] we could create something really beautiful: a society that isn't structured to pollute or hoard bombs." An interesting historical footnote to this comment is that, in 1986, a stalemate occurred in the nuclear disarmament talks between President Ronald Reagan and Soviet Party Secretary Mikhail Gorbachev, illustrating just how important "hoarding bombs" is to much of the world.

CRITICAL OVERVIEW

The Rez Sisters was first performed at the National Canadian Centre of Toronto on November 26, 1986. Critical response to the play was overwhelmingly positive. In a 1987 edition of *Canadian Fiction Magazine,* Daniel David Moses stated, "The majority of Native people, forced to inhabit ignored, economically disadvantaged areas called reserves, are not encouraged to regard their own lives as important. The accomplishment of *The Rez Sisters* is that it focuses on a variety of such undervalued lives and brings them up to size." Thomas King, who published an excerpt from the play in his anthology *All My Relations: An Anthology of Contemporary Canadian Native Fiction,* applauded Highway for his portrayal of the "rez" community and his ability to present a community as "the intricate webs of kinship that radiate from a native sense of family."

Highway has also received acclaim for his positive and optimistic look at his characters, as well as the way that he presents the inner lives of these women to the audience. Carol Bolt, writing in *Books in Canada* called the play a "freewheeling, unforgettable journey in terrific company, the Rez sisters, all of them full of energy and honesty and dreams and life." Writing in a 1990 edition of the

Canadian Theatre Review, William Peel echoed Bolt by saying that Highway "has carved out a number of memorable portraits" and that his "achievement lies not only in the characters he has created, but in his masterful orchestration of the action through which these characters are revealed." Indeed, his skill at characterization has won Highway his greatest acclaim: in *Canadian Literature,* Denis W. Johnston states, "A reading of some of the women's individual stories—a character's 'through-line' in theatrical terminology—will help to demonstrate how the strength of the play depends on cyclical character journeys rather than on the plot line."

Praise has also been sung for Highway's ability to emphasize the culture of his Native characters in a manner that is accessible to non-Native audiences. John Bemrose, writing in *Maclean's* called Highway a playwright "who has learned to straddle two worlds with more grace than most people manage in one." The Toronto *Globe and Mail*'s Conlogue praised Highway's art on similar grounds, stating that "Highway embodies the customary contradictions of living in two worlds at once, native and white, but he embodies them with a special intensity because, simply put, he is outrageously talented." Johnston remarked that although the play is one that is concerned with Native women, it is also a play with a universal message "about people and their dreams and their fears. That these people happen to be Native women, reflecting some problems of their particular place in contemporary society, asserts one feature only of the play's appeal."

When *The Rez Sisters* was brought to the New York Theater Workshop in New York City, it received a negative review in the influential *New York Times.* As critic David Richards wrote: "All of the play's shortcomings, and none of [Highway's] assets, are readily apparent . . . [Highway] plots scenes clumsily and states points baldly. When the dialogue is supposed to be ribald, it rarely rises above the level of adolescent bathroom humor." However, Richards's review mainly finds fault with the production rather than the play: "the drama, which has won numerous awards in Canada, has to be more surprising than this ramshackle staging would suggest." He further stated that "Mr. Highways' strongest gift, an ability to capture flamboyant personalities with their defenses down, remains largely unexploited" because "few of the [actresses] show any signs of theatrical sophistication. Raw gusto, more than anything else, distinguishes their collective endeavors."

Despite such negativity, Highway's ability to offer a glimpse of Native life without alienating non-Native audiences is one of the reasons why the play was nominated for—and awarded—the Dora Mavor Moore Award for best new play of the 1986-87 Canadian theater season. (The play was also chosen as a runner-up for the Floyd S. Chalmers Award for outstanding Canadian play of 1986). In addition to these prizes, *The Rez Sisters* was selected (in 1988) as one of only two productions to represent Canada at the Edinburgh Festival.

CRITICISM

Daniel Moran

Moran is an educator with significant experience in the instruction of drama and literature. His essay on Highway's play explores the themes of character, womanhood, and community that lead the sisters to appreciate one another and their reserve.

Terence, the popular playwright of ancient Rome, once wrote that "Fortune favors the bold." While this may be true in some cases, none of the bold women in Highway's *The Rez Sisters* seem particularly "favored" by Fortune or anything else for that matter. Pelajia, for example, opens the play by voicing her desire to leave: "I want to go to Toronto." Veronique complains of her drunken husband. Emily was beaten by her husband for ten years, then left only to experience death in a new relationship. Annie lost her sweetheart to her own sister, Marie-Adele, who is now stricken with cancer. And Philomena, who seems the most jovial of the group, secretly wonders about the child she was forced to give up twenty-eight years before. All of the women hope that, by winning the bingo jackpot, they will be able to realize their dreams and improve their lives. What Highway suggests, however, is that real change cannot be found by the luck of a bingo machine (or more succinctly, money); rather, it must come from within the women themselves. As the women journey from Wasy to Toronto, they embark on a spiritual and emotional journey as well, returning with a fresh attitude, ready to affect real change.

The play begins with a depiction of the women's lives at "plain, dusty, boring . . . old Wasy," the "rez" where most of the action takes place. Pelajia is hammering shingles on her roof and complaining that Wasy needs paved roads "so that

people will stop fighting and screwing around and Nanabush [the Trickster] will come back to us because he'll have paved roads to dance on.'' She continues to describe Wasy as a place where everyone is "crazy" because there are "no jobs" and "nothing to do but drink and screw each other's wives and husbands and forget about our Nanabush.'' Gossip is a favorite pastime on the rez, as seen when Annie enters and begins asking if anyone heard that "Gazelle Nataways plans to spend her bingo money to go to Toronto with Big Joey.'' Their love of gossip seems to benefit them, however, when they learn that, in Toronto, "THE BIGGEST BINGO IN THE WORLD'' will be played for a $500,000 jackpot. Their reactions to this news displays their feelings of claustrophobia living in Wasy: Marie-Adele, for example, hopes to use her future winnings to buy an island "with pine trees and maple trees and big stones and little stonelets'' where she can live "real nice and comfy'' with her husband and her fourteen children. Similarly, Annie plans on discovering life off of the rez, in Toronto, where she can feel sophisticated and "drink beer quietly—not noisy and crazy like here.'' As pointed out by David Richards of the *New York Times,* the women's desperation to escape is evidenced by the repetitive phrase they each use, "When I win,'' rather than, "If I win.'' The Delaware playwright Daniel David Moses has written that these women (and many real women like them) were never "encouraged to regard their own lives as important,'' and the opening scene of the play reveals this fact.

Highway's emphasis on the characters of Native women suggests that he is exploring the ways in which their drive for success differs from that of their male counterparts. In the *Globe and Mail,* Highway said that he is "sensitive to women because of the matrilineal principle in [Cree] culture, which has gone on for thousands of years.'' When examined from a distance, one can see that these women fit the roles of various "types'': Annie is the local busybody; Emily is the masculine biker; Philomena is the rez's comic relief; Marie-Adele is the mother figure; Veronique is the bitter gossip; and Zhaboonigan, Veronique's mentally disabled adopted daughter, is an outsider that is loved but cared for out of a sense of pity and duty. In offering these various character types, Highway creates a model of a community, where all sorts of women need to accept each other if their lives are ever to improve. There are no men in *The Rez Sisters,* although several are discussed by the women. The picture that the women's dialogue paints of the rez

WHAT DO I READ NEXT?

- *Dry Lips Oughta Move to Kapuskasing,* Highway's 1989 "sequel" to *The Rez Sisters.* The opposite view of *Rez, Dry Lips* focuses on seven men who play hockey (instead of bingo), a female Nanabush, and the dark tragedy that overshadows their lives.

- *The Sage, the Dancer, and the Fool* is a 1989 Highway play, written in collaboration with Rene Highway and Bill Merasty. In it, the playwrights feature Native oral traditions through the use of minimal sets.

- Barry Lopez's text *Giving Birth to Thunder, Sleeping with His Daughter: Coyote Builds North America,* (published by Andrews & McMeel, 1978) is a collection of stories about the Trick-

ster figure in native cultures. The title refers to "Coyote," an animal form that Nanabush assumes in many legends.

- *They Came Here First: The Epic of the American Indian,* by D'arcy McNickle. Considered to be the first anthropolgist to chronicle Native literature, Cree novelist, biographer, and ethnohistorian McNickle's book is a comprehensive look at the cultural development of Native races.

- Many of American poet Emily Dickinson's *Collected Poems* feature people who encounter death in some form; a comparison of the way that death is portrayed here and in *The Rez Sisters* could prove interesting.

---

men suggests that they will be of little help in healing the rez: Veronique's husband, Pierre St. Pierre, never provides his family with any money because he "drinks it up"; Big Joey is a womanizer who spends his days with other men's wives; Wasy's Band Leader has been making empty promises about community improvements (such as the new road Pelajia wants) for years, yet he never fulfills these promises; Henry Dadzinanare, Emily's ex-husband, beat her "every second night for ten long ass-fuckin' years." Highway's use of an all-female cast (except for Nanabush, who, due to his nature, can be played by either a male or female actor) serves to remind the audience that, although the play looks at universal human issues (such as death and love), he is offering a woman's perspective on these issues—a perspective that the audience sees change as the play proceeds.

One of the ways that Highway illustrates the changes in the sisters' attitudes is his depiction of the van ride to Toronto. At one point in this literal and figurative journey, Marie-Adele wanders off while the others fix a flat tire. She is greeted by Nanabush, this time in the guise of a nighthawk, who approaches and then attacks her as an omen of

her impending death. Her frantic cries reveal her complete and total fear:

> "What do you want? My children? Eugene? No! Oh no! Me? Not yet. Not yet. Give me time. Please. Don't. Please don't. Awus [go away]! Get away from me! Eugene! Awus! You fucking bird! Awus! Awus! Awus! Awus! Awus!"

Following this, she has "a total hysterical breakdown"; later in the van, she tells Pelajia, "een-pay-seek-see-yan [I'm scared to death]." To comfort her, Emily and Pelajia must face death almost as squarely as Marie-Adele herself, causing them to grow stronger as individuals and sisters. As Bolt remarked on this scene in *Books in Canada,* "We have seen the sisters raging at each other in a remarkable sequence, a riot of every conceivable insult," but now they are "gentlest with each other" because "their journey has taken them simply and directly to the heart of the matter." Their conversation with Marie-Adele causes Emily to consider the presence of death in her own life and understand how it has affected her: when her lover committed suicide in San Francisco, Emily "drove on. Straight into daylight. Never looked back." Now, however, in the safe haven of the van, Emily can be honest with herself and others and find the comfort she would never solicit but desperately needs.

The appearance of Nanabush in the previously described scene is a reminder to the audience that the women's spirituality is another of Highway's artistic concerns. "Nanabush" is the Ojibway name for the Trickster, a central figure in Native mythology. Throughout *The Rez Sisters,* Nanabush observes the action, seen only by Marie-Adele and Zhaboonigan (because their suffering has brought them closer to the spirit world). At first, Marie-Adele toys with Nanabush (in the guise of a seagull), who asks her to "fly away" with him. Her response, "I can't fly away. I have no wings. Yet," reveals her desire to escape but also her failure to fully understand the reason for Nanabush's visit: he has come to guide her to her death, a fact that Marie-Adele is not yet ready to accept. When he appears to Zhaboonigan, she describes to him a time when she was sexually molested: "They ask me if I want ride in car. . . . Took me far away. Ever nice ride. Dizzy. They took all my clothes off me. Put something up inside me here." Zhaboonigan, in a sense, can be seen as a symbolic character, representing the "rape" of Native pride and culture by white civilization and society; as if reflecting this idea, Nanabush "goes through agonizing contortions" while listening to her story. "The missionaries think they've killed off the Trickster," Highway told Conlogue in the *Globe and Mail,* "but we don't think so. To my mind, the Trickster has been passed under the table for two hundred years." Part of Highway's purpose in writing *The Rez Sisters* is to reawaken his audience's awareness of Nanabush and bring him out from "under the table."

The climax of the play, the actual bingo game, features a theatrical device that links the viewers even more closely with the characters, breaking down the wall between the audience and the actors: viewers play a "warm-up" bingo game (using cards supplied in their programs). The "theatrical daring" of this device has been praised by Moses in *Canadian Fiction,* who explained, "We literally play along, experiencing for ourselves the Rez Sisters' passion." The purpose of this device, however, is also to lure the audience into *thinking* like the sisters, to intensify their hope that Annie's B-14 (the number she needs to complete her bingo card) will be called. Of course, it never is, and the sisters, exploding in frustration, storm the bingo machine as if to protest what they see as the unfair hand of fortune.

While this occurs, Marie-Adele is escorted away from the melee by the Bingo Master, who "waltzes romantically" with her, says, "Bingo" in her ear, and then transforms into the nighthawk: Nanabush in dark feathers. In his essay in *Canadian Literature,* Johnston remarked that Marie-Adele "comes to accept her own death in the same way that she accepted life, gently and with love." Her death here is the central event of the play: before the numbers are called, Highway has the actresses arranged at a long bingo table, featuring Veronique's "good luck" crucifix and lit "so that it looks like 'The Last Supper.'" This is a Christian image, to be sure, but one that many non-Native viewers are able to understand. Like Christ, Marie-Adele accepts her death with grace: "beautiful soft . . . darkwings . . . come and get me . . . wings here . . . take me." The connection here is clear: as Christ died to create great changes in his followers' minds and hearts, the death of Marie-Adele will do the same for her "disciples" at Wasy.

The final scenes of the play illustrate these effects in a number of ways. Veronique has moved into Marie-Adele's house to care for her children; now she has a home with everything that Pierre St. Pierre's drunkenness has withheld from her. Her previous "small-mindedness," commented Johnston, "was a symptom not of having too little love to bestow, but rather of having too few people on whom to bestow it." Annie has decided to practice and pursue her dream of a country-music career. Emily reveals to everyone that she is pregnant with Big Joey's baby, as if fate has compensated for the loss of Marie-Adele; while Emily is unimaginable as a mother when she first enters the play, she is now a little softer and the implication here is that motherhood will allow her to express more openly the love and compassion that was reawakened during the sisters' journey. The most notable transformation is Pelajia's, who stands at Marie-Adele's grave and realizes that complaining will not help anyone: "Kinda' silly, innit, this business of living? But. What choice do we have?" To put her new perspective into action, Pelajia climbs atop her roof again and begins hammering at her shingles, but this time in a different state of mind: when asked by Philomena if she still wants to leave Wasy and go to Toronto, she replies, "Well . . . oh . . . sometimes. I'm not so sure I would get along with him if I were to live down there. I mean my son Tom." Her acceptance of herself and the rez is growing stronger, and, as if to bless her conversion, Nanabush makes a final appearance on her roof, dancing ''merrily and triumphantly'' to the beat of her hammer. The ''good fortune'' that the Rez Sisters so desperately hoped for was, in fact, to *lose* ''THE BIGGEST BINGO IN THE WORlD.'' Losing at bingo (and, more importantly, losing Marie-Adele) has forced them to reevaluate their lives and take the responsibility of change upon themselves.

Source: Daniel Moran, in an essay for *Drama for Students,* Gale, 1997.

Carol Bolt

In this positive review, Bolt recounts the action of The Rez Sisters.

Tomson Highway's *The Rez Sisters* takes us from the Wasaychigan Hill Indian Reserve on Manitoulin Island to the World's Biggest Bingo in Toronto. It's a free-wheeling, unforgettable journey in terrific company, the Rez sisters, all of them full of energy and honesty and dreams and life.

There is Pelajia Patchnose, who wants paved roads ''so people will stop fighting and screwing around and Nanabush will come back to us because he'll have paved roads to dance on.'' There's Annie Cook, who wants to go to Toronto to go to all the record stores, listen to all the live bands ''and drink beer quietly, not noisy and crazy like here.'' There's Philomena Moosebait, who wants only a toilet ''big and wide and very white.'' And there's Marie-Adele Starblanket who has cancer and who counts her 14 children on the posts of her white picket fence: ''Simon, Andrew, Matthew, Janie, Nicky, Ricky, Ben, Mark, Ron, Don, John, Tom, Pete, and Rosemarie.'' Marie-Adele longs for an island, ''the most beautiful, incredible island in the whole goddamn world'' for her 12 Starblanket boys and two Starblanket girls. In all, there are seven vital, remarkable women; and we also meet Nanabush, the trickster, disguised as a seagull, a disturbing spirit whom only Marie-Adele and the mentally disabled girl, Zhaboonigan Peterson, can see.

> ZHABOONIGAN: Don't fly away. Don't go. I saw you before. There, there. It was a. Screwdriver. They put a screwdriver inside me. Here. Remember. Ever lots of blood. The two white boys. Left me in the bush. Alone. It was cold. . . . Ever nice white bird you . . .

Wasaychigan Hill is ''plain, dusty, boring . . . old Wasy'' where the ''old man has to go the hundred miles to Espanola just to get a job'' and the ''boys . . . Gone to Toronto. Only place educated Indian boys can find decent jobs these days.'' It is also a world full of poetry and spirits, ''where on

certain nights at the bingo . . . you can see Bingo Betty's ghost, like a mist, hovering in the air over the bingo tables, playing bingo like it's never been played before,'' and where Nanabush courts Marie-Adele, dancing with her, begging her to fly away with him.

Marie-Adele tells him she has no wings ''. . . Yet.'' Besides, she is going to Toronto. For tests. And to play the biggest Bingo in the world with her five sisters.

It is when the women start out for Toronto, driving through the night, that the story becomes most haunting. While the others stop to change a tire blown out on the pitch-dark midnight highway, Marie-Adele meets the Night Hawk, the dark side of Nanabush. He reminds her that she's dying and she's terrified. She talks about her husband, Eugene:

> I could be really mad, just raging man just wanna tear his eyes out with my nails when he walks in the door and my whole body goes ''k-k-k-k'' . . .

She talks about ''the curve of his back, his breath on my neck, Adele, *ki-sa-gee-ee-tin oo-ma,* making love, always in Indian, only. When we still could. I can't even have him inside me anymore. It's still growing there. The cancer.''

''Pelajia,'' she explains in Cree, '' *Een-pay-seek-see-yan.* Pelajia, I'm scared to death.''

The six women continue together toward Toronto as Pelajia tries to comfort Marie-Adele.

> You know, one time, I knew this couple where one of them was dying and the other one was angry at her for dying. And she was mad because he was gonna be there when she wasn't and she had so much left to do . . .

We have seen the sisters raging at each other in a remarkable sequence, a riot of every conceivable insult. Now, when they're gentlest with each other, when their journey has taken them simply and directly to the heart of the matter, the stage erupts again. Nanabush, in disguise as the Bingo Master, lets everyone in the audience play one warm-up game on the bingo cards included with each program.

Whoever wins this warm-up game, it isn't the Rez sisters. Then the biggest bingo in the world is called, for the big pot they all want, (''A HALF MILLION smackeroos! If you play the game right''). They do everything they can to win. Philomena plays 27 cards. But when they realize it isn't going to work, they storm the stage, complaining that the game is unfair. It's a wonderful moment of theatre, as the Bingo Master changes to the Night Hawk and waltzes away with Marie-Adele.

The Rez sisters return to the reserve without Marie-Adele. Although the play's final sequence seems empty without her, perhaps we are feeling the same loss the characters feel. After all, for two hours we have been part of an extraordinary, exuberant, life-affirming family.

Source: Carol Bolt, ''No Wings Yet'' in *Books in Canada,* Vol. 18, no. 2, March, 1989, p. 26.

Drew Taylor

In this article, Taylor gives an overview of the Native North American theatre from which Tomson Highway's The Rez Sisters *emerged.*

Each summer, members of the Native Theatre School—the only one of its kind in Canada—develop a new production at their farm in Heathcote, Ont., and then take it on the road. Audiences on Indian reserves enjoy the plays, whether they deal with urban teenagers or movie stereotypes of Indians, says school director Cathy Cayuga: ''They laugh aloud—they understand the absurdities.'' But when her troupe performs for white audiences, they are often greeted with confusion. Added Cayuga: ''People are terribly self-conscious—afraid to laugh.'' Few Canadian plays successfully cross the boundary between native and white experience. Those that have, such as *The Ecstasy of Rita Joe,* have been written or coauthored by whites. Until Manitoba-born Cree playwright Tomson Highway's *The Rez Sisters,* which opened last week at the Great Canadian Theatre Company in Ottawa, the imaginative landscape claimed by Canada's dedicated band of native theatre professionals has been unmapped territory for the rest of the country.

The Rez Sisters premiered at the Native Canadian Centre in Toronto a year ago, was runner-up for a Floyd S. Chalmers Award for outstanding Canadian Play in 1986 and won a Dora Mavor Moore Award for Best New Play 1986/87. The play follows seven women who leave their reserve—or ''rez'' in native slang—on Manitoulin Island, Ont., to visit the world's biggest bingo game in Toronto. Their banter, sometimes tough, sometimes wryly humorous, reflects the staccato rhythms of the playwright's native Cree tongue. Highway attributes his drama's success to its director, Larry Lewis, and to its actors. But the play, which will soon tour throughout Western Canada, also marks a turning point in native arts generally. Said Highway: ''We're enter-

''*THE REZ SISTERS*'S PRIMARY GOAL IS NOT TO ENTERTAIN A MASS AUDIENCE BUT TO MAKE CONNECTIONS WITH INDIGENOUS CULTURES TORN APART BY SOCIAL CHANGE''

ing a second wave. Exactly 25 years ago Norval Morriseau's first solo exhibition of paintings started a revolution by sharing the sacred stories beyond our communities. Now we are extending that, taking the oral traditions into theatre and three dimensions.''

Highway is artistic director of Native Earth Performing Arts, Inc., one of the country's 12 full- and part-time native performing groups. Some are based in cities, such as Vancouver's six-year-old Spirit Song Native Indian Theatre Company, which runs ambitious training programs in theatre arts and mounts at least one new production a year. Others are reserve-based companies, such as the De-Ba-Jeh-Mu-Jig Theatre on Manitoulin Island. The group's name—''storytellers'' in Ojibwa—reflects its focus on translating legends for the enjoyment of both reserve audiences and summer tourists.

Blake Debassige, president of De-Ba-Jeh-Mu-Jig, distinguishes between the contemporary dramas produced by urban-companies and what his group does, which he calls ''the romantic tradition—an extension of telling stories round the campfire.'' Because those traditions were suppressed for centuries by white missionaries, some native activists say that the act of resurrecting legends is just as revolutionary as creating gritty new works. Once, native theatre took highly sophisticated forms: when Capt. James Cook arrived on Canada's west coast in 1778, he found Nootka Indians using masks, props, trapdoors, lighting and smoke effects in their religious dramas. But between 1884 and 1951 performing many theatrical celebrations was punishable under the Criminal Code.

Changes to the code marked the beginning of a renaissance. So did reports of growth in indigenous peoples' theatre in the Caribbean, Scandinavia and the South Pacific. In 1980 and again in 1982 delegates from those cultures converged in Ontario for the Indigenous Peoples' Theatre Celebrations, creating an international support network that still persists. Native Theatre School director Cayuga has studied community theatre in Jamaica, and the school tour last year included two Carib Indians and a Lapp, or Sami, from Sweden.

Despite the success of *The Rez Sisters,* it is at the community level that native theatre will continue to flourish. That is because its primary goal is not to entertain a mass audience but to make connections with indigenous cultures torn apart by social change. Even *The Rez Sisters* performs a healing role. The play's only male character is Nanabush— in Ojibwa legend, the trickster who is also something of a Christ figure, an intermediary between humanity and the world of the spirit. Said Highway: "When the white man came to this continent, Nanabush passed out under the table of The Silver Dollar [a bar in Toronto]. Our responsibility as native artists is to sober him up."

Source: Drew Taylor, "Legends on the Stage" in *Maclean's,* Vol. 100, no. 42, October 19, 1987, p. 69.

FURTHER READING

Bemrose, John. "Highway of Hope," in *Maclean's,* Vol. 102, no. 19, May 8, 1989, p. 62.
    Although he mainly focuses on Highway's *Dry Lips Oughta Move to Kapuskasing,* Bemrose does offer some valuable quotations from Highway on the differences between the Cree language and English.

Conlogue, Ray. "Mixing Spirits, Bingo, and Genius," in the Toronto *Globe and Mail,* November 21, 1987, p. C5.
    Conlogue explains how *The Rez Sisters* reflects Highway's concerns as a Native and as an artist, touching upon such topics as the Trickster, racism and the "matrilineal principle" in Native literature.

Enright, Robert. "Let Us Now Combine Mythologies: The Theatrical Art of Tomson Highway," in *Border Crossings,* Vol. 1, No. 4, December, 1992, pp. 22-27.
    This is a long and thorough interview in which Enright and Highway discuss the playwright's childhood, study of folklore, and the effects of Christianity on Native spiritual life.

Johnston, Denis W. "Lines and Circles: The 'Rez' Plays of Tomson Highway," in *Canadian Literature,* Nos. 124-25, Spring-Summer, 1990, pp. 254-64.
    This is a very perceptive and valuable essay in which Johnston discusses the stylistic and thematic similarities and differences between *The Rez Sisters* and *Dry Lips Oughta Move to Kapuskasing.* Each play is analyzed in great detail.

King, Thomas, editor. *All My Relations: An Anthology of Contemporary Canadian Native Fiction,* McClelland and Stewart, 1990.
    An excellent anthology of Native fiction. King was the first to publish Highway's work in a major anthology, and his introduction offers some perspectives on the playwright's work.

Lutz, Hartmut. "An Interview with Tomson Highway," in *Contemporary Challenges: Conversations with Canadian Native Authors,* Fifth House Publishers, 1991.
    In this interview, Highway discusses the role of mythology in Native life.

Peel, William. Review of *The Rez Sisters* in *Canadian Theatre Review,* No. 65, Winter, 1990, pp. 62-64.
    Peel explores the narrative structure of *The Rez Sisters* and explains how Highway creates his "memorable portraits" throughout the play.

SOURCES

Edgar, Kathleen, editor. "Tomson Highway" in *Contemporary Authors,* Vol. 151, Gale (Detroit), 1996, pp. 244-45.

Moses, Daniel David. *Canadian Fiction,* 1987.

Richards, David. "Bingo As the Way of Escape, at Dismal Odds" in the *New York Times,* January 5, 1994, pp. C15, C21.

Rosencrantz and Guildenstern Are Dead

Rosencrantz and Guildenstern Are Dead, Tom Stoppard's best-known and first major play, appeared initially as an amateur production in Edinburgh, Scotland, in August of 1966. Subsequent professional productions in London and New York in 1967 made Stoppard an international sensation and three decades and a number of major plays later Stoppard is now considered one of the most important playwrights in the latter half of the twentieth century.

Recognized still today as a consistently clever and daring comic playwright, Stoppard startled and captivated audiences for *Rosencrantz and Guildenstern Are Dead* when he retold the story of Shakespeare's *Hamlet* as an absurdist-like farce, focusing on the point of view of two of the famous play's most insignificant characters. In Shakespeare's play, Rosencrantz and Guildenstern are little more than plot devices, school chums summoned by King Claudius to probe Hamlet's bizarre behavior at court and then ordered to escort Hamlet to England (and his execution) after Hamlet mistakenly kills Polonius. Hamlet escapes Claudius's plot and engineers instead the executions of Rosencrantz and Guildenstern, whose deaths are reported incidentally after Hamlet returns to Denmark. In Stoppard's play, Rosencrantz and Guildenstern become the major characters while the *Hamlet* figures become plot devices, and Stoppard's wildly comic play becomes the story of two ordinary men caught up in events they could neither understand nor control.

TOM STOPPARD

1966

Stoppard's play immediately invited comparisons with Samuel Beckett's *Waiting for Godot* and also brought to mind George Bernard Shaw, Oscar Wilde, and Luigi Pirandello. ''Stoppardian'' is now a recognizable epithet that suggests extraordinary verbal wit and the comic treatment of philosophical issues in often bizarre theatrical contexts.

AUTHOR BIOGRAPHY

Tom Stoppard (pronounced Stop-pard, with equal accents on both syllables) was born Tomas Straussler in Czechoslovakia on July 3, 1937. His name was changed when his mother married British army major Kenneth Stoppard after the death of the boy's father. Educated from the age of five (in English) in India and from the age of nine in England, Stoppard left school at seventeen to become a journalist before deciding in 1960, at the age of twenty-three, to become a full-time writer.

Before becoming an ''overnight'' sensation with *Rosencrantz and Guildenstern Are Dead,* Stoppard worked as a free-lance writer and drama critic in London, writing stage plays, television plays, radio plays, short stories, and his only novel, *Lord Malquist and Mr. Moon.* The turning point in his writing career came in 1963 when his agent, Kenneth Ewing, wondered in casual conversation who the King of England might have been during the time of Shakespeare's *Hamlet.* The question prompted Stoppard to write a one-act verse burlesque entitled *Rosencrantz and Guildenstern Meet King Lear,* and when Stoppard participated in a writing colloquium for young playwrights in Berlin in 1964 he submitted a version of this text.

Stoppard eventually discarded from this play most of the verse and the references to King Lear, gradually focusing on events in Hamlet's Elsinore. In August of 1966, Stoppard helped direct the first production of the play in Edinburgh. Though the play was ''done in a church hall on a flat floor'' with ''no scenery'' and ''student actors,'' influential London theatre critic Ronald Bryden perceived the play's potential and wrote that Stoppard's play was ''the best thing at Edinburgh so far'' and that ''it's the most brilliant debut by a young playwright since John Arden.'' Bryden's review convinced the National Theatre in London to produce the play and Stoppard soon vaulted into international prominence.

Since his phenomenal success with *Rosencrantz and Guildenstern Are Dead* Stoppard has produced a large body of work that critics continue to find intelligent, erudite, witty, and filled with verbal pyrotechnics. A number of early critics questioned whether this dazzling surface was supported by genuine profundity and many early critics found Stoppard's plays coldly analytical rather than emotionally powerful. But *The Real Thing* in 1982 and *Arcadia* in 1993 seemed to deliver the kind of pathos his highly intellectual ''philosophical farces'' might have been lacking. Though not unanimously acclaimed by critics today, Stoppard is undeniably a major figure in contemporary drama. He has also written a number of adaptations of plays in foreign languages and several screen plays, including a feature film version of *Rosencrantz and Guildenstern Are Dead* in 1990.

PLOT SUMMARY

Act I

Two minor characters from Shakespeare's *Hamlet* are travelling to the court of King Claudius and have paused on the road to play a coin-tossing game of ''heads or tails.'' The one named Rosencrantz has just won for the 70th consecutive time, each time betting on ''heads.'' Rosencrantz is embarrassed to be winning so much money from his friend, Guildenstern, but Guildenstern is more concerned with the apparent violation of probability in this phenomenal run. After the string gets to 76, Guildenstern begins throwing the coins more absent-mindedly as he speculates on the possible philosophical and even religious explanations for this amazing streak.

Guildenstern suggests four possibilities for this run of ''heads,'' including simple luck since every toss has the same 50/50 odds no matter what has happened earlier. He helps Rosencrantz recall that this day began with a messenger from King Claudius insisting that they come to Elsinore, where their friend Hamlet had gone some time earlier. They hear music in the air and are soon joined by a troupe of actors, ''tragedians,'' whose leader (the Player) tries to solicit money from them in exchange for a performance.

When the Player suggests an entertainment that implies sexual participation, Guildenstern is angered but Rosencrantz is eventually intrigued and tosses a coin on the ground, asking ''what will you do for that?'' The Player and Guildenstern bet on whether the coin has fallen heads or tails, exchanging tosses until the Player finally chooses tails and loses. After the Player refuses to bet any longer on the coin toss, Guildenstern tricks him into betting that the year of his birth doubled is an odd number (any number doubled is even). When the Player loses, the troupe has no money to pay the wager and must perform for free. As they are readying themselves, Rosencrantz notices that the last tossed coin turned up tails.

A sudden change of light on stage indicates a shift from the present exterior scene to an interior scene in Elsinore Castle where Hamlet and Ophelia enter and perform actions from Shakespeare's famous play. Rosencrantz and Guildenstern try to leave, but Claudius, Gertrude, and the rest of the court enter speaking Shakespearian verse, trapping the two men into playing the roles they are assigned in *Hamlet.* Rosencrantz and Guildenstern learn that King Claudius wants them to find out why Hamlet is acting so strangely. When the characters from Shakespeare's play leave, Rosencrantz and Guildenstern (now in the castle at Elsinore) are as baffled as before. To prepare for their interrogation of Hamlet, Rosencrantz initiates a question and answer game and then Guildenstern pretends to be Hamlet while Rosencrantz questions him. The first Act ends as Hamlet appears and welcomes Rosencrantz and Guildenstern to Elsinore.

Act II

As characters from *Hamlet* continue to come and go, Rosencrantz and Guildenstern ruminate about their continued confusion. Eventually, the Player arrives and complains about how the two courtiers disappeared (in Act I at the lighting change) when his troupe was performing. He complains that as actors he and his troupe need an audience to complete their sense of identity. Hamlet has asked the tragedians to perform *The Murder of Gonzago* and since the Player seems to be ''a man who knows his way around,'' Guildenstern asks for advice. The Player tells them to accept uncertainty as a natural part of human life. As Rosencrantz and Guildenstern speculate about their future, the question of control, and the nature of death, Claudius and Gertrude re-enter and once again sweep Rosencrantz and Guildenstern into their Shakespearean roles. As the characters from *Hamlet* come and go, the acting troupe eventually returns to rehearse *The Murder of Gonzago,* but this rehearsal is interrupted by scenes involving other characters from *Hamlet* and gradu-

Tom Stoppard

ally evolves beyond the rehearsal of *The Murder of Gonzago* as it appears in *Hamlet* to a summary of events that occur later in the play, including the death of Polonius and the deaths of Rosencrantz and Guildenstern themselves. Rosencrantz and Guildenstern don't quite understand that it is their own deaths being enacted, but Guildenstern is rattled by the suggestion and accuses the actors of not understanding death. A blackout brings the action back to *Hamlet* and the frantic conclusion of *The Murder of Gonzago.*

Suddenly it is sunrise, the next day, and Claudius enters and commands Rosencrantz and Guildenstern to accompany Hamlet to England. As Rosencrantz and Guildenstern wonder about how to find Hamlet, he appears, dragging the body of Polonius. They join their two belts to capture him, but Hamlet evades them as Rosencrantz's trousers fall down. Eventually, Hamlet is brought to Claudius by others and the stage lighting changes once more to reveal that Rosencrantz and Guildenstern are again outdoors. They are taking Hamlet to England.

Act III

Act III opens in pitch darkness with soft sea sounds and sailor voices indicating that Rosencrantz and Guildenstern are on a boat. Gradually, light

Rosencrantz and Guildenstern are joined by the Player (center) as they contemplate the meaning of their existence

pirates attack the ship and in the confused battle that follows Hamlet, the Player, and Rosencrantz and Guildenstern leap into the three barrels. After the fight is over, only the Player and Rosencrantz and Guildenstern reappear. Hamlet is now gone, but as Rosencrantz and Guildenstern look at the letter again they discovered that the letter Hamlet substituted now instructs the King of England to put them to death. All the players reemerge from one of the barrels and form a menacing circle around Rosencrantz and Guildenstern. The Player offers philosophizing words, but the enraged Guildenstern snatches a dagger from his belt and stabs the Player in the throat, appearing to kill him. However, the dagger is retractable, the Player rises, and the tragedians act out several kinds of deaths as the light dims, leaving only Rosencrantz and Guildenstern on stage. Rosencrantz proclaims that he has "had enough" and disappears. Guildenstern calls for his friend, realizes he's gone, and disappears himself.

Immediately, the stage is flooded with light and the characters appear from the tableau of corpses that ends Shakespeare's tragedy. An Ambassador from England announces that Rosencrantz and Guildenstern are dead, and Hamlet's friend, Horatio, ends the play by pointing out that "purposes mistook [have] fallen on the inventor's heads."

reveals three large barrels and a huge, gaudily striped umbrella on the deck of the ship. After they discover that Hamlet is sleeping behind the umbrella, Rosencrantz and Guildenstern open the letter from Claudius that they are to present to the King of England when they deliver Hamlet. They are surprised to discover that the letter orders the King of England to put Hamlet to death, but Guildenstern philosophizes that "death comes to us all." Hamlet arises from behind the umbrella, blows out a lantern, and the stage goes to pitch black again and then moonlight, which reveals Rosencrantz and Guildenstern sleeping. While they sleep, Hamlet takes the letter from them, substitutes another, and retires again behind the umbrella, blowing out the lantern and bringing darkness again to the stage.

When light returns, it is morning and Hamlet is relaxing under the umbrella. Rosencrantz has also decided not to worry about what the letter does to Hamlet. They hear music and the tragedians reappear, all climbing (quite impossibly) out of the three large casks on deck. The Player explains that they had to "run for it" because their production of *The Murder of Gonzago* offended the King. Suddenly,

CHARACTERS

Alfred

Alfred is a Stoppard invention who does not appear in Shakespeare's play. Alfred is a small boy, one of the six tragedians, who is highlighted in Stoppard's play because he is forced to play the feminine roles in drag and finds his cross-dressing very humiliating.

Ambassador

The Ambassador from England appears in both plays but only at the end to announce that the orders to execute Rosencrantz and Guildenstern have been carried out.

Claudius

In Shakespeare's play, Claudius, Hamlet's uncle, secretly murders Hamlet's father, marries Hamlet's mother, and sends for Rosencrantz and Guildenstern to gather information on Hamlet's behavior as Hamlet mopes around the court. After Hamlet

MEDIA ADAPTATIONS

- *Rosencrantz and Guildenstern Are Dead* was made into a feature film in England in 1990 starring Gary Oldman as Rosencrantz, Tim Roth as Guildenstern, and Richard Dreyfuss as the Player. Stoppard adapted the script to the screen and directed the film himself. The film is in technicolor and runs 118 minutes and is available to rent from select video stores and for purchase from Buena Vista Home Video or Facets Multimedia. It was named the best picture at the Venice Film Festival in 1991 but met with a lukewarm reception in the United States.

- In 1972, Kenneth Friehling provided a 38 minute audio cassette commentary on the play for the Everett/Edwards Modern Drama Cassette Curriculum Series out of Deland, Florida.

---

kills Polonius, Claudius orders Hamlet escorted to England by Rosencrantz and Guildenstern, where orders in a sealed letter are supposed to have Hamlet killed.

Gertrude

In both Shakespeare's and Stoppard's plays, Gertrude is Hamlet's mother and the new wife of King Claudius.

Guildenstern

In Stoppard's play, Guildenstern is the more philosophical and intellectual of the two courtiers who double as minor characters in Shakespeare's play and major characters in Stoppard's. The opening sequence of coin tossing vexes Guildenstern because he craves order and predictability in the universe. The apparent violation of probability in coin tossing drives him to seek an explanation but he attempts to remain calm when no satisfactory answers arise. He has a wry sense of humor, can be quite sarcastic, and is resilient, though he is also quick to anger and subject to panic or despondency when he finally feels overwhelmed. Guildenstern likes to hear himself talk and often rambles at length, sometimes without making a lot of sense. He frequently uses parables and analogies to attempt to understand the mysteries that confront him and he likes verbal games as a way of working things out. Wary and nervous, he likes to stay in control and questions more than his friend, Rosencrantz, whom he often badgers but ultimately is trying to protect and support with optimism whenever possible.

Hamlet

The hero of Shakespeare's tragedy, Hamlet is a relatively minor character in Stoppard's play, where he drifts in and out performing actions and speaking lines from his classic role as the melancholy Dane. In Stoppard's play, Hamlet is eventually portrayed more playfully as he lounges in a deck chair in Act III.

Horatio

Horatio is Hamlet's best friend in Shakespeare's play. In Stoppard's comedy he exists only to deliver the last speech of the play.

Ophelia

Ophelia is the daughter of Polonius, who is one of the King's counselors in *Hamlet*. Ophelia is Hamlet's ''girlfriend'' in both Shakespeare's and Stoppard's plays. Almost all of her Shakespearean lines are omitted in *Rosencrantz and Guildenstern Are Dead* as she mimes most of her scenes.

The Player

If the Player has a counterpart in Shakespeare's play he is the actor who performs the Pyrrhus speech for Hamlet in Act II, scene ii. In Stoppard's play this character is the leader of the wandering troupe of actors who perform *The Murder of Gonzago* and a major character because he speaks so clearly and forcefully about reality and theatrical illusion. Proud of his acting craft but frustrated by his lack of financial success and his dependence on audience, the Player is self-assured, intense, but also sad. Like Guildenstern, the Player is philosophical but he is also practical, pragmatic, and resilient. A man experienced in the ways of the world, the Player accepts uncertainty more easily than anyone else in the play.

Polonius

In both Shakespeare's and Stoppard's plays, Polonius is the father of Ophelia and is killed by Hamlet when Hamlet mistakes him for the King. Polonius is portrayed in both plays as old, garrulous, and occasionally foolish.

Rosencrantz

Rosencrantz is a minor character in Shakespeare's *Hamlet* and one of the two major characters in Stoppard's unusual version of Shakespeare's story. In Shakespeare's play, Rosencrantz is one of Hamlet's university friends from Wittenberg. With Guildenstern, he is summoned by King Claudius to come to Denmark because Hamlet, after returning to Denmark for his father's funeral and his mother's wedding, began acting quite strangely. Rosencrantz helps Guildenstern spy on Hamlet for Claudius and then is assigned with his friend to take Hamlet to England after Hamlet kills Polonius. When Hamlet returns to England, he reports to his friend Horatio that on the ship to England he discovered Claudius's letter ordering his death. He substituted a letter ordering the deaths of Rosencrantz and Guildenstern and escaped the ship when pirates attacked it. In *Hamlet,* Rosencrantz and Guildenstern are such nondescript characters that Claudius and his queen Gertrude can't distinguish between them.

In Stoppard's play, Rosencrantz is the more timid of the two courtiers and considerably less reflective and philosophical than his friend, Guildenstern. At the beginning of the play Rosencrantz is winning on every toss of the ''heads or tails'' game and is embarrassed to be taking so much money from his friend but is either oblivious or unconcerned about how unusual this streak of ''heads'' might be. He is relatively unreflective, naive, innocent, even simple-minded and slow intellectually. He often ''tunes out'' when Guildenstern rambles in his philosophical talk but he is very sensitive and concerned about his friend's unhappiness. Usually, he doesn't question as much as Guildenstern, but when he understands their situation he generally

feels more overwhelmed. However, when he senses approaching death, Rosencrantz is quietly resigned.

Soldier

In both plays a soldier talks with Hamlet and identifies the Norwegian military commander, Fortinbras, as he marches his troops across Denmark toward Poland. Hamlet admires Fortinbras for his bravery and Fortinbras succeeds to the throne in Denmark after both Claudius and Hamlet die.

Tragedians

The tragedians who perform *The Murder of Gonzago* in *Hamlet* are more childlike and playful in Stoppard's comedy, where they play musical instruments as well as miming their roles in *The Murder of Gonzago.*

THEMES

Human Condition

Stoppard's *Rosencrantz and Guildenstern Are Dead* blends two stories—Shakespeare's *Hamlet* and Stoppard's own version of how the two courtiers might have felt and behaved after they were summoned by King Claudius to spy on their schoolmate, Hamlet.

When Stoppard decided to write about Rosencrantz and Guildenstern he was free to give them personalities of his own because Shakespeare had hardly given them any personalities at all. He was also free to let them speak in a more colloquial language and to elaborate on aspects of their lives that Shakespeare did not specify, such as what they might have done with Hamlet on the ship to England. But once Stoppard chose to blend his story with Shakespeare's, Rosencrantz and Guildenstern were fated to die at the end of Stoppard's story because they die at the end of Shakespeare's. Stoppard uses this literary fatalism as a metaphor for the fate that awaits all human beings—the inevitability of death.

The play begins with Stoppard's story, as two very un-Shakespearean courtiers flip coins as they pause on the road to Elsinore. The extraordinary suspension of the laws of probability that permits over 100 coins to land ''heads'' before one lands ''tails'' indicates that there is something special about this day. And when a coin finally lands ''tails'' Rosencrantz and Guildenstern are immedi-

TOPICS FOR FURTHER STUDY

- Compare Shakespeare's *Hamlet* with *Rosencrantz & Guildenstern Are Dead* to see how Stoppard used the play as a source. What did he include, what did he leave out, and why? Research the conclusions of scholars on the relationship between the two texts to confirm and enlarge your findings.

- Read psychologists and psychiatrists on the human attitudes toward death, perhaps beginning with Elisabeth Kubler-Ross's *On Death and*

Dying. Compare what you learn in your research to what is implied in *Rosencrantz & Guildenstern Are Dead*.

- Read Samuel Beckett's *Waiting for Godot* as an example of Theatre of the Absurd. Compare it to Stoppard's *Rosencrantz & Guildenstern Are Dead* and decide how they are similar or different in tone and theme. Research the conclusions of scholars on the applicability of Absurdism to Stoppard's play to support your conclusions.

---

ately swept out of Stoppard's story and back into Shakespeare's, from which they originally came. Once they are placed in Shakespeare's story, their fate is sealed. They will die at the end, even though they shift back and forth from the Shakespearean to the Stoppardian story. What was special about this day is that it set in motion the events that would lead to their deaths.

Fate is something that has already been decided, something humans have no control over, something that will happen whatever human beings do, and the literary fatality that comes from entering a world where events are already decided gives Stoppard the metaphor he needs for human fate. Though they resist accepting the fact, human beings are doomed to die as soon as they enter the world.

When the tragedians first arrive in Stoppard's story, Guildenstern says "it was chance, then . . . [that] you found us," and the Player says, "or fate." Subsequent references to "getting caught up in the action" of the Shakespeare play are frequent, as are references to not having any "control." And when the Player says in their dress rehearsal for *The Murder of Gonzago* that "everyone who is marked for death dies," Guildenstern asks, "Who decides?" and the Player responds, "*Decides*? It is *written*."

Art and Experience

Stoppard elaborates on the theme of fate by exploring the relationship between art and experi-

ence. Throughout the play, he uses the tragedians and their spokesperson, the Player, to emphasize that art can create an illusion that is often more real and convincing than the experience of ordinary life.

The tragedians specialize in portraying death on stage, but Guildenstern argues that their version of death is not "real." The Player responds by saying that the fictional representation of death is the only version that human beings will believe. He recalls the time he arranged for one of his actors condemned to be hanged to meet his execution on stage. However, to his surprise, the audience jeered and threw peanuts at this "real death" and the actor couldn't accept his fate calmly, crying the whole time, "right out of character."

Sigmund Freud asserted that human beings are psychologically incapable of seeing themselves as dead. When we come close to dying in our dreams we wake up or alter the dream so we become spectators ourselves, and as soon as we exist as spectators we have not in fact died. In art, however, we can experience death vicariously and safely, testing our reactions to it in a way that paradoxically rehearses us for our own death while further distancing us from the reality of it. Playing the role of spectators is perhaps as close as humans can ever get to accepting the reality of their human mortality.

This assertion is demonstrated most effectively in Act III, when the frustrated Guildenstern attacks the Player and seems to stab him fatally in the neck with a dagger. Like Rosencrantz and Guildenstern, audience members initially unaware of the retractable blade in the stage dagger will experience a moment of shock when it appears that a real death has taken place on stage. But almost immediately we remember that we are at a play and that this death cannot possibly be real. When the Player comes to his feet to the applause of his fellow tragedians, the audience laughs in relief, as does Rosencrantz, who applauds and calls for an encore.

Death

The theme of humans denying their own mortality also helps to explain a number of problematic points in the play. When, for example, Rosencrantz and Guildenstern discover that the letter from Claudius orders Hamlet's death, the generally sympathetic and pleasant pair distance themselves from the fact and justify their non-involvement. As disagreeable and unheroic as this behavior might be, it is in keeping with Stoppard's theme. Guildenstern justifies his non-involvement by feigning acceptance of "the designs of fate," and Rosencrantz's denial of responsibility is capped with a phrase that adumbrates the end of the play—"If we stopped breathing we'd vanish." Even more problematical, perhaps, is their behavior after discovering the revised letter that orders their own deaths. Shakespeare's pair were probably ignorant of the letter's contents and surprised by their executions. Rosencrantz and Guildenstern realize they are delivering their own death warrants and do nothing to avoid it. But quite in character, Rosencrantz simply avoids thinking about it—"All right, then. I don't care. I've had enough. To tell you the truth, I'm relieved," while Guildenstern continues to look for explanations and escape routes—"there must have been a moment. . .where we could have said— no." His final words are either a continued denial of the reality of his death or an acceptance of his status as a literary character—"well, we'll know better next time."

Stoppard's theme is probably best summed up by the speech that Rosencrantz makes in Act II about lying in a coffin. Quite out of the blue he says to Guildenstern, "do you ever think of yourself as actually *dead,* lying in a box with a lid on it? Quite honestly and significantly, Guildenstern says "no" and Rosencrantz echoes his response. But then the usually dim-witted Rosencrantz touches on the essential problem—"one thinks of it like being *alive* in a box, one keeps forgetting to take into account the fact that one is *dead* . . .which should make all the difference. . .shouldn't it? I mean, you'd never *know* you were in a box, would you? It would be just like being *asleep* in a box." When human beings attempt to think about their deaths, they assume some kind of continued consciousness. Ironically, Rosencrantz demonstrates in this speech the very kind of thinking he has just categorized as "silly." After characterizing death as a kind of sleep, he associates death with a mortal dream state, complete with the possibility of waking to full consciousness and a sense of helplessness—"not that I'd like to sleep in a box, mind you, not without air." Unable to conceptualize his own death he refuses to fully accept that "for all the compasses in the world, there's only one direction, and time is its only measure."

STYLE

Comedy

One of the most distinguishing features of Stoppard's *Rosencrantz and Guildenstern Are Dead* is the way it moves in and out of the plot of Shakespeare's *Hamlet* and changes tone as it does so. While Shakespeare's play has many moments of rich humor, it is basically serious and tragic, while Stoppard's treatment of the Shakespearean story is distinctly comic, even farcical.

Much of Stoppard's comedy comes, then, from the implicit contrast with Shakespearean solemnity. As the most famous tragedy of the most respected playwright in the history of the world, *Hamlet* conjures up an image of high seriousness, but when we meet Stoppard's courtiers at the beginning of his play they are casually flipping coins and speaking in colloquial, informal prose rather than Shakespearean verse. The rag-tag tragedians add even more contrast with Shakespearean seriousness, especially when they descend in their financial desperation to the suggestion of a pornographic exploitation of little Alfred. However, when the two courtiers are sucked into the Shakespearean action and must mingle with characters speaking Shakespearean blank verse, they begin speaking the same way and the sharp contrast with their informal speech creates a comical effect both going and coming. Their inability to escape the *Hamlet* plot is comic, as is what appears to be a posturing attempt to fit into it when they can't escape. Finally, they are comic when they deflate again to their non-heroic stature after the

Hamlet characters disappear. In their first entry into the Shakespearean world, Stoppard indicates that the two courtiers are "adjusting their clothing" before they speak, and as they use the lines given them in Shakespeare's play, their inflated style is comic because it seems postured and implies desperate ineptitude. Then, back in their Stoppardian world, they are once again comically unheroic, as Rosencrantz whines, "I want to go home," and Guildenstern puts on his comical bravado, unconvincingly attempting to appear in control.

But if Rosencrantz and Guildenstern are comically foolish because they seem overwhelmed by the power of the Shakespearean world, they are also comically noble because their ordinary presence seems eventually to deflate that Shakespearean high seriousness. It is as if their ordinary, prosaic quality begins to acquire a nobility of its own, and in contrast the Shakespearean characters eventually begin to sound exaggerated, even a little silly. This impression finds its culmination in Act III, when Hamlet is discovered lounging under a gaudily striped umbrella, reduced to something not quite classically Shakespearean. There is thus in Stoppard's play a kind of comic victory for the underdog, perhaps most clearly expressed at the beginning of Act II when Rosencrantz responds to Hamlet's esoteric Shakespearean language by saying, "half of what he said meant something else, and the other half didn't mean anything at all." Generations of readers and theatre goers who have silently struggled at times to understand the demanding dialogue of "the world's greatest playwright and the world's greatest play" chuckle as the ordinary man speaks up.

Parody

Thus, we are led also to parody as a source of Stoppard's humor in *Rosencrantz and Guildenstern Are Dead.* Stoppard's references to other literary texts are numerous and subtle, but parody as a literary style frequently imitates a serious work in order to demean it. Stoppard's parody is distinctive because it is generally quite respectful and affectionate toward its source rather than critical.

Apart from his parodic use of Shakespeare's *Hamlet,* Stoppard is most clearly parodying Samuel Beckett's *Waiting for Godot,* whose two main characters, Vladimir and Estragon, play word games and "pass the time" as they wait for someone who never arrives. Beckett's play begins on a country road that is distinctly nondescript, so when Stoppard specifies in his opening stage directions that "two Elizabethans [are] passing the time in a place with-

out any visible character" it is sufficient to recall *Waiting for Godot* for those who are very familiar with the Beckett classic. However, if this reference is missed, Stoppard includes another reference later in the play that is even less mistakable. Near the end of Act II, when Hamlet is dragging Polonius's body across the stage, Rosencrantz and Guildenstern unfasten their belts and hold them taut to form a trap for Hamlet. This comes to naught as Hamlet avoids them, but the parodic comedy sparkles when Rosencrantz's trousers fall down, recalling a similar scene at the end of *Waiting for Godot.* The parody is not intended to satirize Beckett's play or either pair of characters. If anything it ennobles both, paying respects to Beckett's genius, as in an "homage," and dignifying the silliness of Rosencrantz and Guildenstern. With his buddy's trousers comically gathered at his ankles and facing another complete failure, Guildenstern says quite simply, "there's a limit to what two people can do."

Apart from the simple pleasure of recognition that such parody provides a knowing audience, this parody enlarges the suggestiveness of Stoppard's text. His two ordinary men are not to be taken as victims of an absurdist world, as Beckett's are. Rosencrantz and Guildenstern live in a simpler world where the inevitability of death is not tragic but a natural part of life. If human beings can calm their minds, they will realize that it is "silly to be depressed" by death, that "it would be just like being *asleep* in a box." When, at the beginning of the play, Rosencrantz exults that eighty-five consecutive winning calls of heads has "beaten the record," Guildenstern says "don't be absurd," and the clever allusion to Beckett speaks volumes to those who catch the joke.

HISTORICAL CONTEXT

The Turbulent Sixties and Stoppard as a Political Playwright

The year 1966, like rest of the mid-1960s, was extremely turbulent both socially and politically. U.S. involvement in the Vietnam War, for example, aroused world-wide protest as the Chairman of the U.S. Senate Foreign Relations Committee, J. W. Fulbright, challenged the legality of America's military involvement in Southeast Asia and even Pope Paul VI pled for an end to hostilities. In America, the National Organization for Women (NOW) was founded by Betty Friedan to gain equal rights for

COMPARE & CONTRAST

- **1966:** Vietnam is becoming a full-scale military conflict. By year's end, 389,000 U.S. troops are in South Vietnam and the bombing of North Vietnam is already extensive, despite growing protest to the war in the U.S. and abroad.

  Today: The U.S. "defeat" in Vietnam continues to plague the national sense of self-esteem. Though full diplomatic and cultural relations with Vietnam have resumed, the American memory of failure and ignominy has yet to be exorcised.

- **1966:** The Women's Liberation Movement is gaining momentum as Betty Friedan, author of the influential *The Feminine Mystique* in 1963, organizes the National Organization for Women (NOW) and becomes its first president.

  Today: Women have gained a new place in society. Through the rise in two-income families and the extensive development of day-care facilities, women have taken a dramatically increased role in the work force, moving from domestic positions into direct competition with men, though female salaries are statistically lower.

- **1966:** The American Civil Rights Movement is backed by the wide-sweeping 1964 Civil Rights Act, aspects of which are contested in a number of southern states that resist school integration. Alabama Governor George Wallace signs a state bill on September 2 that forbids Alabama's public schools from complying with desegregation guidelines.

  Today: African Americans enjoy far greater economic, social, and political mobility, and school integration is commonplace in America. Former Governor Wallace, an unsuccessful candidate for the presidency of the United States in 1968 and 1972, is now partially paralyzed and confined to a wheelchair as a result of an assassination attempt in May of 1972.

- **1966:** French President Charles de Gaulle proposes that Europe strive for more economic and political independence from the powerful domination of the United States and Russia, announcing on March 11 that France will withdraw her troops from NATO (The North Atlantic Treaty Organization) and requests that NATO remove all its bases and headquarters from French soil.

  Today: Russia has become much less powerful politically, economically, and militarily as various regions within the former Soviet empire assert their independence and Russia suffers major economic setbacks. The United States perhaps dominates Europe most powerfully in its exportation of popular culture, with European countries enthusiastically embracing Western clothing, entertainment, and life styles.

- **1966:** After 8 years in power, South Africa's prime minister Henrik F. Verwoerd is assassinated on September 6 and succeeded a week later by Balthazar Johannes Vorster, who vows to continue the policies of apartheid (pronounced "ah-par-tate," it is a system of racial segregation and white dominance) in South Africa.

  Today: After decades of resistance from the white minority, apartheid is overthrown in South Africa in 1996 when the former political prisoner Nelson Mandela is elected president in a free election and a new national constitution brings a non-racial democracy to the country.

- **1966:** California's Bank of America creates the BankAmericard and Master Charge is created in response by New York's Marine Midland Bank, ushering in the era of the credit card. By the end of 1966, there are 2 million BankAmericard holders.

  Today: BankAmericard has become Visa, Master Charge has become MasterCard, and the credit card has become a way of life world-wide. In the United States alone, banks solicited 2.7 billion credit card applications by mail in 1995, roughly 17 for every American between the ages of 18 and 64. The average credit card debt per household has risen from $649 in 1970 to nearly $4,000 in 1996.

women, and the civil rights movement for American blacks was spurring race riots in Cleveland, Chicago, and Atlanta. The 1964 Civil Rights Act was being openly defied by Southern states refusing to desegregate schools and the University of Mississippi's first black graduate, James Meredith, was shot while participating in a Mississippi voting rights march. Meanwhile, Massachusetts voters elected Edward Brooke the first black U.S. senator since Reconstruction. Closer to home for Stoppard, England was responding to demands for independence from Rhodesia and conflicts heated up between Protestants and Catholics in Northern Ireland.

But in the midst of this social and political turmoil, *Rosencrantz and Guildenstern Are Dead* displays no interest in the social and political issues of its time. And for many years after his initial success, Stoppard seemed to write from a steadfastly apolitical point of view, claiming, perhaps puckishly, that "I must stop compromising my plays with this whiff of social application. They must be entirely untouched by any suspicion of usefulness. I should have the courage of my lack of convictions."

As a result, the work following *Rosencrantz and Guildenstern Are Dead*—including such plays as *The Real Inspector Hound* (1968), *Jumpers* (1972), and *Travesties* (1974)—seemed to a number of critics to lack political and social awareness. Stoppard's drama was seen by many as dazzling in its display of ingenuity and word play and interesting in its often arcane subject matters but ultimately superficial. Influential British theatre critic Kenneth Tynan summed up this assessment succinctly, calling Stoppard "a cool, apolitical stylist," referring to *Travesties* as "a triple-decker bus that isn't going anywhere."

But in a flurry of plays in the late 1970s, starting with *Every Good Boy Deserves Favor* (1977), Stoppard silenced these critics by writing several plays dealing explicitly with political issues and themes. *Every Good Boy Deserves Favor* is set in a Russian prison hospital where one of the inmates is imprisoned for his political beliefs. *Professional Foul* (1977) is set in Czechoslovakia and deals with political dissidents in a totalitarian society. *Night and Day* (1978) takes place in a fictionalized African country and examines the role of the press in a dictatorial third-world country while *Cahoot's Macbeth* (1979) concerns the repression of theatre in Czechoslovakia. Though not considered major plays in the Stoppard canon, these works clearly demonstrated Stoppard's capacity for engaging contemporary social and political issues.

The Tradition of the Theatre of the Absurd

When *Rosencrantz and Guildenstern Are Dead* appeared in 1966, its possible connections to the Theatre of the Absurd were seen immediately, in part because of Stoppard's conscious echoing of Beckett's classic *Waiting for Godot*. But subsequent assessments have suggested that Stoppard's connection with this literary context is more problematical than initial identifications would have suggested.

The Theatre of the Absurd arose after World War II and flourished in the 1950s and early 1960s, initially and especially in France in the works of Eugene Ionesco (E-on-S'-co), Jean Genet (Shuhnay'), and Samuel Beckett. These and other playwrights rejected the concept of a rational and ordered universe and tended to see human life as absurd and lacking purpose. To express this vision effectively, these dramatists tended to eliminate reassuring dramatic elements like logical plot development, realistic characterization, and rational dialogue, replacing them with bizarre qualities that forced audiences to experience absurdity first hand.

And in 1968, Stoppard acknowledged the impact that Beckett and others had had on writers of his generation, saying "it seemed clear to us, that is to say the people who began writing about the same time that I did, about 1960, that you could do a lot more in the theatre than had been previously demonstrated. "Waiting for Godot"—there's just no telling what sort of effect it had on our society, who wrote because of it, or wrote in a different way because of it."

By the mid-1960s, the Theatre of the Absurd had lost much of its shock value and was already becoming outmoded, taking its last flourish in America from the early work of Edward Albee. But in 1966 and 1967, many critics saw Stoppard as a late example of this absurdist movement, with Charles Marowitz asserting in May of 1967 that Stoppard's play eventually became "a blinding metaphor about the absurdity of life."

However, later assessments have suggested that Stoppard uses the Theatre of the Absurd more for comic effects than philosophical meaning. Critics like William Gruber eventually observed that Rosencrantz and Guildenstern are given the opportunity for meaningful action (when they discover the letter condemning Hamlet) and lack the courage or character to act responsibly. And in *Beyond Absurdity: The Plays of Tom Stoppard* (1979), Victor Cahn makes the case that "*Rosencrantz and Guildenstern Are Dead* is a significant step in moving theatre out of the abyss of absurdity." Though certainly working in the context of the absurdist theatre movement of the 1950s and early 1960s, Stoppard's first major drama must not be too easily subsumed under its heading.

CRITICAL OVERVIEW

When *Rosencrantz and Guildenstern Are Dead* premiered in Edinburgh and London in August of 1966 and in April of 1967, Tom Stoppard was immediately recognized as a major contemporary playwright. The cleverness in the concept of the play, its verbal dexterity, and its phenomenal theatricality brought its first reviewer, Ronald Bryden, to call it "the most brilliant debut by a young playwright since John Arden." Later, in London, Irving Wardle, writing for the *Guardian*, said that "as a first stage play it is an amazing piece of work," and in New York, Harold Clurman, reviewing the play in *Nation*, echoed the general sentiment by calling Stoppard's play a "scintillating debut." And Clive Barnes, the highly influential critic for the *New York Times*, asserted in October of 1967 that "in one bound Mr. Stoppard is asking to be considered as among the finest English-speaking writers of our stage, for this is a work of fascinating distinction."

However, as enthusiastic as critics were for this dazzling first effort, they also had some very clear reservations. Generally, they thought Stoppard's play somewhat derivative, too closely linked to Beckett's *Waiting for Godot,* for example. Bryden found the play "an existentialist fable unabashedly indebted to *Waiting for Godot*" and the appreciative Clurman called it "*Waiting for Godot* rewritten by a university wit." Also in New York, an appreciative Charles Marowitz writing for the *Village Voice* added, "my only objection is that without the exhilarating stylistic device of the play-beneath-the-play, the play proper would be very much second-hand Beckett." Michael Smith, also writing for the *Village Voice,* applauded the play, saying "the writing is brilliantly clever, the basic trick inspires a tour de force, and the play is great fun," but added, "the drawback is Stoppard's attempt to

push it to deep significance. The early part of the play repeatedly echoes "Waiting for Godot" in sound and situation but entirely lacks its resonance."

Another reservation the critics voiced was the suggestion that the play's verbal dexterity and ingenious theatricality might have been all it had to offer, that underneath the dazzling surface there was very little of substance and that the play was ultimately shallow. This was suggested by Philip Hope-Wallace reviewing the first London production for the *Guardian* when he said, "I had a sensation that a fairly pithy and witty theatrical trick was being elongated merely to make an evening of it." And despite his generous praise for Stoppard's play, Charles Marowitz added that "much of its cross-talk is facile wordmanship that benefits accidentally from ambiguity."

Writing somewhat after the initial critical response to the play, critics Robert Brustein and John Simon summed up this ambivalent response. Brustein wrote, "I advance my own reservations feeling like a spoilsport and a churl: the play strikes me as a noble conception which has not been endowed with any real weight or texture," and in a now often quoted remark, Brustein calls Stoppard's play "a theatrical parasite, feeding off *Hamlet, Waiting for Godot* and *Six Characters in Search of an Author*—Shakespeare provided the characters, Pirandello the technique, and Beckett the tone with which the Stoppard play proceeds." Similarly, critic John Simon writing for *The Hudson Review* admitted that "the idea of the play is a conception of genius" but also saw it as "squeezing large chunks of Beckett, Pinter, and Pirandello, like sliding bulges on a python as he digests rabbits swallowed whole," finally reducing Stoppard's play to "only cleverness and charm."

More than 30 years later, this ambivalent assessment continues to hang over Stoppard's work in general and over *Rosencrantz and Guildenstern Are Dead* in particular. In varying degrees, critics have leveled similar charges upon successive major plays—*Jumpers (1972), Travesties (1974), The Real Thing (1982),Hapgood (1988),* and *Arcadia (1993),* frequently assessing them as excessively concerned with cleverness and the arcane, too cerebral, lacking in genuine emotion, and ultimately shallow when measured against a very high standard of art and genius. However, the duration and accomplishments of Stoppard's career has finally affirmed his status as a major playwright. By the time Stoppard had written *Jumpers* and *Travesties*, Jack Richardson, writing in *Commentary* in 1974, had to admit Stoppard's pre-eminence: "since *Rosencrantz and Guildenstern,* a play I admired but found a little too coy and dramatically forced in its darker moments, Stoppard has come closer and closer to a successful wedding of theatrical artistry and intelligence. He is already the best playwright around today, the only writer I feel who is capable of making the theatre a truly formidable and civilized experience again."

In the context of a brilliant career, *Rosencrantz and Guildenstern Are Dead* continues to be a formidable achievement. Even by 1973, Normand Berlin, writing in *Modern Drama,* could assert that Stoppard's first major play had "acquired a surprisingly high reputation as a modern classic." And within a decade of its first appearance, *Rosencrantz and Guildenstern Are Dead* had enjoyed over 250 productions in twenty different languages. Though a number of critics now feel that *Rosencrantz and Guildenstern Are Dead* is perhaps not Stoppard's best play—that some of his later work have been more complex, polished, and mature—Stoppard's first major play remains his most popular and his most widely performed.

CRITICISM

Terry Nienhuis

Nienhuis is an associate professor of English at Western Carolina University. In this essay he postulates that Stoppard's themes of uncertainty and confusion make his play appealing to twentieth century audiences who easily identify with his characters' doubts and fears.

The Twentieth Century could easily be summed up as an Age of Uncertainty. When it began, nearly one hundred years ago, religious certitude was already eroding, and the process has continued steadily as we approach the twenty-first Century, leaving many more human beings unsure about the existence of an all-powerful, all-knowing, and all-loving divine being who guarantees the order and rationality of the universe. Two unprecedented world wars and the unleashing of atomic weapons have even made us uncertain about the continued existence of the planet. And the highly influential Freud

has subtly contributed to our uncertainty with his essential message that much of what motivates us remains below the surface of our normal awareness. Perhaps most paradoxically, science, the paragon of certainty, has dominated the Twentieth century, but as its discoveries advance our knowledge on both telescopic and microscopic scales science also reveals how much more we don't know and thus adds to our collective sense of uncertainty. From large issues to small, from public policy to personal lives, from those who are highly educated to those who are not, a feeling of uncertainty has come to typify our age.

This sensitivity to uncertainty may very well account in part for the enormous and continued appeal of *Rosencrantz and Guildenstern Are Dead* because Stoppard's play focuses quite comically and movingly on this very issue. It is ultimately a play about ordinary people overwhelmed by confusion and uncertainty. In fact, in an interview with Giles Gordon in 1968, Stoppard explains that the genesis of the play came from his interest in the way Rosencrantz and Guildenstern "end up dead without really, as far as any textual evidence goes, knowing why. Hamlet's assumption that they were privy to Claudius's plot is entirely gratuitous. As far as their involvement in Shakespeare's text is concerned they are told very little about what is going on and much of what they are told isn't true. So I see them much more clearly as a couple of bewildered innocents rather than a couple of henchmen, which is the usual way they are depicted in productions of *Hamlet.*

This tale of "bewildered innocents" begins on the day they have been summoned by a king's messenger to appear at the Danish court. The messenger gave them no explanations or directions, simply orders, and their first encounter with King Claudius leaves them not much more enlightened. Speakers of colloquial prose in Stoppard's story, Rosencrantz and Guildenstern are bombarded with Claudius's Elizabethan rhetoric and Stoppard's humor in this opening confrontation with the *Hamlet* world includes the ordinary person's admission that much of this Shakespearean language can seem incomprehensible. That it seems so to Rosencrantz and Guildenstern is obvious. As soon as the *Hamlet* characters have left, Rosencrantz wails, "I want to go home" and Guildenstern attempts to calm him by saying, "Don't let them confuse you," even though he is as confused and uncertain as his friend. After stuttering his reassurances to Rosencrantz,

WHAT DO I READ NEXT?

- Stoppard's *The Real Thing (1982)* is a more conventional play about love and marriage. It was very popular and convinced critics that Stoppard could write with more emotional impact and with less reliance on clever, verbal pyrotechnics.

- Shakespeare's *Hamlet (1601)*, the obvious source for Stoppard's play, is a nearly inexhaustible resource for comparisons with *Rosencrantz and Guildenstern Are Dead*.

- Stoppard clearly acknowledged Samuel Beckett's *Waiting for Godot (1952)* as a major influence on *Rosencrantz and Guildenstern Are Dead*. Beckett's classic play is about two men ''passing the time'' as they wait for someone who never arrives. There are many similarities as well as differences between the two plays.

- Luigi Pirandello's play, *Six Characters in Search of an Author (1921)*, is another example of ''a play within a play'' and the most famous literary investigation into how fictional life and real life relate to one another. As actors rehearse a play, six fictional characters from an unfinished play mount the stage and demand to have their story represented and resolved.

- *The Importance of Being Earnest (1895)*, by Oscar Wilde, is the classic example of the epigrammatic verbal wit that Stoppard is renowned for and which he first displayed so brilliantly in *Rosencrantz and Guildenstern Are Dead*.

- *On Death and Dying (1969)* by Elisabeth Kubler-Ross is a classic investigation into the human attitudes toward death. She describes five stages of dying that move from denial, anger, bargaining, and depression to acceptance.

- Sigmund Freud was a provocative commentator on human attitudes toward death, and though nearly every educated person is familiar with Freud's basic ideas, few have actually read him. A very short and readable essay of astounding sensitivity called ''On Transcience'' (1916) is perhaps a good place to start in reading Freud.

Guildenstern asks, ''Has it ever happened to you that all of a sudden and for no reason at all you haven't the faintest idea how to spell the word—'wife'—or 'house'—because when you write it down you just can't remember ever having seen those letters in that order before. . .?'' All of us have probably had this quirky experience of uncertainty and Stoppard's evocation of it helps the audience identify with his beleaguered heroes. Rosencrantz says, nostalgically, ''I remember when there were no questions'' and Guildenstern responds with, ''There were always questions. To exchange one set for another is no great matter.'' And Rosencrantz perhaps responds for a twentieth Century audience when he concludes, ''Answers, yes. There were answers to everything.'' The concept of God was once the answer to everything, but with that concept in question in the modern world, nothing, not even science or technology, has come to take its place.

Guildenstern responds to his friend's nostalgic memories of certitude by pointing out that all of the answers now are ''plausible, without being instinctive.'' In other words, in the modern world (the world of Stoppard's Rosencrantz and Guildenstern) probability replaces certitude as the ontological coin of the realm—what human beings can count on as being true. Guildenstern goes on to say that ''all your life you live so close to truth, it becomes a permanent blur in the corner of your eye,'' which recalls his ''unicorn'' speech and the notion that what we regard as ''real'' is simply what's familiar—''reality, the name we give to the common experience.'' After their first meeting with Claudius and the Danish court, the certainty that Rosencrantz and Guildenstern feel is very minimal—''that much is certain—we came.'' Ironically, however, Guildenstern's continued attempt to reassure his friend in this pivotal scene leads him to stumble across the only certainty that is available to all human beings—the certainty of one's own mortality. Guildenstern says, reassuringly, "The only beginning is birth and the only end is death—if you can't count on that, what can you count on?" Thus Stoppard brings his investigation of uncertainty home to his audience. On the practical level in the lives of Rosencrantz and Guildenstern the questions without answers are questions like "why were we sent for, what are we supposed to do, where's Hamlet, what should we say to him, what's his problem, and where are we going now?" As these fictional characters struggle comically with an uncertainty that seems to govern in small matters, they are gradually being drawn to their deaths and it is in their deaths that the audience can fully share their concern for uncertainty. Few of us will engage in and experience the uncertainties of power politics, but all of us will face, like Rosencrantz and Guildenstern, the uncertainties we feel about our own mortality.

All of this concern for certainty and uncertainty is clear from the beginning of *Rosencrantz and Guildenstern Are Dead* when, in one of the play's most striking and important images the coin tossing game defies the laws of probability. When over 100 coin tosses turn up a consecutive run of "heads" rather than the customary mixture of "heads" and "tails," Guildenstern is disturbed because the run is not "normal" or what humans are accustomed to. He has been thrust into a world he does not feel certain about. Ironically, the run of "heads" has produced a kind of certainty ("heads" turns up every time) but Guildenstern can't trust this certainty because it defies what he is familiar with. As he recalls their previous coin-tossing, he recalls that the familiar uncertainty in their game, the "luck" or randomness of the "heads" and "tails," came out to a roughly 50/50 percentage that created a new kind of certainty. Just as "the sun came up about as often as it went down, in the long run, . . . a coin showed heads about as often as it showed tails."

After the coin-tossing game introduces the issue of uncertainty, the addition of the tragedians and especially the Player reinforces the theme and makes it much more explicit. To some extent out of necessity, the tragedians live more easily with uncertainty . They are out of fashion theatrically and must be ready to perform whatever an audience will pay to see. They also make their livelihood improvising and blurring the distinction between illusion and reality, so they have more toleration for uncertainty about reality. When Guildenstern complains

about their uncertainty in Act II, the Player says, "Uncertainty is the normal state. You're nobody special." His advice is to "Relax. Respond . . . Act natural . . . Everything has to be taken on trust; truth is only that which is taken to be true. It's the currency of living. There may be nothing behind it, but it doesn't make any difference so long as it is honored."

The tragedians also serve to connect the issue of uncertainty to the question of mortality. Their expertise is in portraying death and they are relatively more comfortable with the certainty of mortality. They even felt casual enough with it to attempt using the actual execution of one of their actors on stage when the action in one of their plays called for a hanging. As the Player understates it quite simply near the end of the play, "In our experience, most things end in death." They also understand from their experience portraying death on stage that human beings believe more in the familiar illusion of mortality than they do the frightening actuality of it. When Guildenstern says, "You die so many times; how can you expect them to believe in your death," the Player responds, "on the contrary, it's the only kind they do believe. They're conditioned to it." He understands that given the human denial of their own mortality, fictive experiences are the only way to create "a thin beam of light that, seen at the right angle, can crack the shell of mortality."

As it winds down to its conclusion, Stoppard's play focuses on this relationship between fictive death, real mortality, and the question of uncertainty. Early in the play the audience shares a feeling of uncertainty with Rosencrantz and Guildenstern when they are as much baffled by the results of the coin-tossing game, the eccentricities of the tragedians, and perhaps even by the rapid-fire Elizabethan verse of the *Hamlet* characters. During these periods of the play, the audience develops an empathy for the two heroes, identifying with their confusion and lack of certainty. But late in Act II, the tragedians present their version of *The Murder of Gonzago* and predict quite explicitly how Rosencrantz and Guildenstern will die: "a twist of fate and cunning has put into their hands a letter that seals their deaths." At this point, even if they don't know the *Hamlet* story, the audience must accept the deaths of Rosencrantz and Guildenstern. But Rosencrantz "does not quite understand" what he has witnessed and finally says, "yes, I'm afraid you're quite wrong. You must have mistaken me for someone else." More aware but equally denying, Guildenstern simply gets angry and challenges the Player: "you!— What do *you* know about *death*?" However, the audience is implicated in this denial as well, for it is a metaphor for their own refusal to accept the most certain thing in their lives. As the Player tells about his experience with the actor in his troupe actually hanged on stage during a performance, he paints a picture of an audience that could not accept real death in a place where they had become accustomed to fictive death—"audiences know what to expect, and that is all that they are prepared to believe in." From this point until the end of the play, Stoppard's audience is forced to watch fictive characters acting out the denial of their mortality. At the same time, the audience is invited to compare its own attitude toward the certainty of death with the one demonstrated by Rosencrantz and Guildenstern. When the play is over, they have witnessed yet another pair of fictive deaths and maybe have advanced ever so slightly toward being prepared for their own.

Source: Terry Nienhuis, in an essay for *Drama for Students*, Gale, 1997.

Joseph Hynes

In this excerpt, Hynes avers the greatness of Stoppard's Rosencrantz and Guildenstern are Dead, *while also discussing the debt of gratitude the play owes to not only William Shakespeare's* Hamlet, *but to such absurdist works as Samuel Beckett's* Waiting for Godot.

At the top of his form, Tom Stoppard writes tragicomedies or comic ironies. Stoppard's top form has given us *Rosencrantz and Guildenstern Are Dead* (1967) and *Arcadia* (1993), contenders for the finest postwar English-language drama, and in neither case generic comedy, since comedy includes importantly a limited, socially satisfying resolution over and above the laughs. Because the recent brilliance of *Arcadia* happily implies that Stoppard may give us much more, I do not think of these two plays as bookends enclosing his life's work. At the same time, however, a close look . . . will provide a useful awareness of Stoppard's dramatic structures and methods as well as of his preoccupations as a man of his century, his extraordinary sense of humor, and his commitment to the history of ideas as humanity's river.

Rosencrantz and Guildenstern Are Dead (hereafter *R&GAD*) gets a big and essential head start from the fact that *Hamlet* tends to be more or less a part of the cultural equipment of anyone reading or seeing *R&GAD*. Indeed, I can only suppose that Stoppard's play must be confusing or even incomprehensible to one who has not heard of the Shakespeare tragedy.

As a writer of the 1960's, Stoppard in this play was also indebted to Beckett's *Waiting for Godot.* Like Beckett's Gogo and Didi, Rosencrantz and Guildenstern are two minor characters among history's *dramatis personae.* Their puzzled, funny, painful, perhaps not hopeless search is for meanings, answers, causes, reasons. They spend their time, like many moderns, not deriving answers but playing the game of "Questions." Also like Didi and Gogo, one of them is weaker than the other, and they encounter Shakespeare's troupe of players where Beckett's pair meet Pozzo and Lucky. Both couples wait to find out what it's all about. Beckett's couple hope that Godot will turn up as promised (they seem to recall) and will explain things. Stoppard's team remember being "sent for" in the dark of night by a faceless messenger from court, told to report to the king, and made to cool their heels while agonizing over what they're meant to be and do, and where they will end up. The condition of all four resembles that of Sartre's existential loner, or indeed that of the early medieval bird flying from an unknown place of origin through a lighted mead-hall to an unknown destination. Each couple wants to know the significance of the relatively lighted interval.

Another debt is to the make-believe realm of Jean Genet's *The Balcony* and, farther back, the plays of Pirandello. For Stoppard is out to dissolve any fourth wall, any notion that art and life are distinct. *R&GAD* insists, frighteningly and delightfully, that art *is* life, illusion *is* reality, the mirror gives us whatever truth may be, acting *is* the way it is. For the imagination generating this play, as implicitly for the metafictions of the 1960's—I think especially of Doris Lessing's *The Golden Notebook,* Vladimir Nabokov's *Pale Fire,* and John Fowles's *The French Lieutenant's Woman* —Hamlet's famous soliloquy is reworded by implication to read "to seem or not to seem." We are to forget about "to be," about objective facts or truth on any significant level.

All of this abstraction barely suggests, of course, the brilliant dramaturgy with which Stoppard delights our eyes and ears in the theater. To start, we might remember that Rosencrantz and Guildenstern are such walk-on characters in Shakespeare's play as to be omitted altogether by some directors trying to save time. These two appear only seven times in *Hamlet.* Stoppard upends Shakespeare by putting these walk-ons at center stage, from which they are virtually never absent. The effect created is that *Hamlet* appears to be going on in the wings of Stoppard's play and intrudes only seven times on *R&GAD*. A couple of not-too-bright Oxbridge (or Heidelberg) undergraduates on a bare Beckettian stage speak 1960's colloquial prose except where Hamlet, Claudins, Polonius, Gertrude and Company drop in from time to time to speak Shakespeare's blank verse at and with them.

R&GAD operates from the premise that "all the world's a stage." To drive home this point Stoppard makes strategic use of the Player and his troupe, who play a small, if necessary, part in *Hamlet*. Early on the Player recognizes Rosencrantz and Guildenstern as "fellow artists." Neither they nor the audience know at the time precisely what the Player means, but we all gradually learn, as Hamlet does, that "thinking makes it so."

On several occasions the Player explains and demonstrates that what we see constitutes the real for us. When Guildenstern grows impatient with what he regards as the frivolous pretense of these actors, and cries out in desperation that they only pretend to die but can know nothing of real death, of ceasing to be, he seizes the Player's dagger and stabs him with it. At that moment, Rosencrantz, Guildenstern, the troupers, and the entire audience are hushed and staring at the fallen Player. When the Player then rises to the applause of his fellows he has clearly proven his point about the truth of seeming-to-be. Rosencrantz and Guildenstern *and the audience* have been smitten with Stoppard's thesis and we all share the realization that we are "fellow artists" inevitably in that we spend our lives constructing our own meanings. The fourth wall is gone and we and the *other* actors are one in the human condition.

But what is this renowned human condition? In this play we must work at Stoppard's definition by juggling Calvin, Saint Augustine, and Sartre. In other words, the familiar issue of determinism vs. free will underlies this play and keeps it percolating in our heads long after the performance.

The principal manifestation of this age-old debate occurs after the Player informs Rosencrantz and Guildenstern that the troupe members are not free to "decide" what they perform, for "It is *written*." "The bad end unhappily, the good unluckily. That is what tragedy means." Then in about one page he paraphrases what seems to be *The Murder of Gonzago*, the play within the play of

> " WE'RE ALL AFRAID TO DIE,
> ESPECIALLY WITHOUT BEING SURE
> OF WHY WE'VE LIVED"

Hamlet, which is the play within Stoppard's play. As both Rosencrantz and Guildenstern fear, however, and as we viewers realize, the Player is actually paraphrasing Shakespeare's play, from the murdering of Hamlet's father right through to the final switching of letters that culminates in the king of England's killing Rosencrantz and Guildenstern.

This occasion frightens Rosencrantz and Guildenstern, combined as it is with their operating almost totally in the dark and with their play-opening experience of watching 94 consecutive coins violate the law of probability by coming up heads. But it engenders more than fear in the audience. We know, of course, that Stoppard's title marks his limitations: he cannot change the outcome that has been "written" by Shakespeare. That much is determined.

Beyond Stoppard's being confined by his predecessor, however, lie a number of similar questions about artistcreators and their creatures. How did Shakespeare alter his source? Who authored Shakespeare? In what sense is Stoppard "written"? Can we clearly separate Shakespeare's source from him as maker of *Hamlet,* or are artist and artifact inevitably blended and blurred, as in the case of Stoppard's choosing to have his Player *create* the play that turns out to be Shakespeare's *Hamlet,* featuring the Player and Stoppard's title-figures? Where do the mirrors and the onionskin layers of seeming begin and end? Perhaps finally (if such an adverb applies here), we in the audience want to know whether we are as doomed, as "written," as Calvin and the Player assert and as Rosencrantz and Guildenstern feel.

This sense of doom descends at the end of Stoppard's play, which, as always, coincides in some sense with Shakespeare's. Just as Stoppard anticipates Shakespeare by having the Player invent *Hamlet,* so he alters *Hamlet* by having Rosencrantz and Guildenstern read Claudius's letter condemning Hamlet to death, choose not to inform Hamlet of this command, and then read and decline to act upon

Hamlet's substituted letter ordering their own deaths. In these ways some elbow-room is given for variations or choices within fixed limits, but outcomes are nonetheless determined as "written."

In view of such tight metaphysical or theological confinement, how are we to read Rosencrantz and Guildenstern's final attitude, and what is to be our own attitude? An answer may be attempted in two parts.

First, ambiguity coats the term "final attitude," for, inasmuch as Rosencrantz and Guildenstern are artifacts, they do not end. They are potentially susceptible to as much literary analysis and criticism as is *Hamlet*. Indeed, Stoppard is having a good time with the whole critical industry, present company included. For the play suggests an additional layer of applied significance for every reader or viewer who takes in *R&GAD* and tries to make it mean. Thus the play, like *Hamlet* or anything else created, will go on acquiring significance indefinitely. So much for finality, then, at least aesthetically.

Second, Rosencrantz and Guildenstern and we would seem to be restricted to a certain few conclusions. We can accept the plain deterministic reading of *all* creation and creatures. Rosencrantz seems to take this view and to be glad to know at last where the royal ship, beyond his control, is taking him. He likes certitude and is tired. Guildenstern's "Now you see me, now you—" [blackout] appears to comment on anyone's quick mead-hall flight between darknesses. It is hard to know whether he is suggesting a view of his own demise or is remarking on the wondrous technical expression of snuffing it.

Or perhaps we can join the Player in an acceptance of whatever creative leeway is available to us, and enjoy such limited freedom within our cages. Augustine's view would be that, although we cannot work it out rationally without religious faith, the Creator's knowing our outcome and our choosing it are not contradictory. We simply cannot know the mind of God, and we err gravely if we assume that mind to function as ours does.

The only other option would seem to be Sartre's. That is, if we cannot *know* anything of what lies outside the mead-hall, then in effect nothing lies outside it and we had better attend to the business of making choices for the only life we can be sure of. Therein, says Sartre famously, we will find and exercise the only meaningful freedom, to which we are condemned.

Obviously Stoppard does not twist our arms to force us into buying one of these views in isolation from the others. He does, however, force us to consider or reconsider all of them. More strikingly, as he dissolves the form-content dichotomy, he creates an illusion of oneness, of ultimate inseparability, among life on stage, life in the wings, and life out front. Whatever this life is, we are clearly all in it together, mirrors and all, jokes or no jokes. We laugh a great deal at Stoppard's humorous ingenuity, but we eventually experience our modern middle-class human unity with Elizabethan–Danish royalty and two movingly klunky courtiers. We're all afraid to die, especially without being sure of why we've lived. In the end do we submit fatalistically to our death, or do we freely choose to embrace it? And how are we to contemplate and—in Stoppard's case—express the difference?

Source: Joseph Hynes, "Tom Stoppard's Lighted March" in the *Virginia Quarterly Review,* Vol. 71, no. 4, Autumn, 1995, pp. 643–47.

Clive Barnes

In this positive review of Rosencrantz and Guildenstern are Dead, *which was originally published on October 17, 1967, Barnes praises playwright Stoppard's scholarship and intricate wordplay.*

Barnes is a well-known theatrical critic best known for his reviews in the New York Times.

It is not only Hamlet who dies in *Hamlet*. They also serve who only stand and wait. Tom Stoppard's play *Rosencrantz and Guildenstern are Dead,* which opened last night at the Alvin Theater, is a very funny play about death. Very funny, very brilliant, very chilling; it has the dust of thought about it and the particles glitter excitingly in the theatrical air.

Mr. Stoppard uses as the basis for his play a very simple yet telling proposition; namely that although to Hamlet those twin-stemmed courtiers Rosencrantz and Guildenstern are of slight importance, and that to an audience of Shakespeare's play they are little but functionaries lent some color by a fairly dilatory playwright, Rosencrantz and Guildenstern are very important indeed to Rosencrantz and Guildenstern.

This then is the play of *Hamlet* not seen through the eyes of Hamlet, or Claudius, or Ophelia or Gertrude, but a worm's-eye view of tragedy seen from the bewildered standpoint of Rosencrantz and Guildenstern.

We first see them on a deserted highway. They have been summoned to the King's palace; they do not understand why. They are tossing coins to pass the time of day. The ordinary laws of chance appear to have been suspended. Perhaps they have been. Destiny that has already marked out Hamlet for such a splendid, purple satin death, is keeping a skimpy little piece of mauve bunting for poor Guildenstern and gentle Rosencrantz. They are about to get caught up in the action of a play.

Their conversation, full of Elizabethan school logic and flashes of metaphysical wit, is amusing but deliberately fatuous. Rosencrantz and Guildenstern are fools. When you come to think of it, they would have to be. Otherwise they might have been Hamlet.

As they talk, the suspicion crosses the mind (it is a play where you are encouraged to stand outside the action and let suspicions, thoughts, glimmers and insights criss-cross your understanding) that Mr. Stoppard is not only paraphrasing *Hamlet,* but also throwing in a paraphrase of Samuel Beckett's *Waiting for Godot* for good measure. For this is antic lunacy with a sad, wry purpose.

Like Beckett's tramps, these two silly, rather likable Elizabethan courtiers are trying to get through life with a little human dignity and perhaps here and there a splinter of comprehension. They play games with each other and constantly question not their past (probably only heroes can afford that luxury) but their present and their future. Especially their future.

On the road they meet the strolling players, also, of course, for the plot is a mousetrap seen from the other side of the cheese, on the road to Elsinore. The leading Player, a charming, honest and sinister man, invites the two to participate in a strolling play. They, with scruples, refuse, but in fact they cannot refuse—because in life this precisely is what they have done.

Mr. Stoppard seems to see the action of his play unfolding like a juicy onion with strange layers of existence protectively wrapped around one another. There are plays here within plays—and Mr. Stoppard never lets us forget that his courtiers are not only characters in a life, but also characters in a play. They are modest—they admit that they are only supporting players. But they do want to see something of the script everyone else is working from.

It is one of Mr. Stoppard's cleverest conceits of stage, craft that the actors re-enacting the perform-

"MR. STOPPARD IS NOT ONLY PARAPHRASING *HAMLET,* BUT ALSO THROWING IN A PARAPHRASE OF SAMUEL BECKETT'S *WAITING FOR GODOT* FOR GOOD MEASURE"

ance of *Hamlet* that is, in effect, dovetailed into the main section of the play, use only Shakespeare's words. Thus while they are waiting in the tattered, drafty antechamber of the palace for something to happen, we in the audience know what is happening on the other side of the stage. As one of them says, "Every exit is an entry somewhere else."

Finally reduced to the terminal shrifts of unbelief, it seems that Rosencrantz and Guildenstern realize that the only way they can find their identity is in their "little deaths." Although on the final, fateful boat they discover the letter committing them to summary execution in England, they go forward to death, glad, even relieved.

It is impossible to re-create the fascinating verbal tension of the play—Mr. Stoppard takes an Elizabethan pleasure in the sound of his own actors—or the ideas, suggestive, tantalizing that erupt through its texture. Nor, even most unfortunately, can I suggest the happy, zany humor or even the lovely figures of speech, such as calling something "like two blind men looting a bazaar for their own portraits." All this is something you must see and hear for yourself.

When the play had its first professional production in London in April of this year it was staged by the British National Theater, and to an extent this version has been reproduced here by its original and brilliant director, Derek Goldby. Helped by the tatterdemalion glories of Desmond Heeley's setting, the richness of his costumes, and Richard Pilbrow's tactfully imaginative lighting, the play looks very similar. But whereas the supporting players in London—the Hamlet, Claudius and the rest—could well have played their roles in Shakespeare as well as in Stoppard, here there is understandably less strength.

However, the mime roles or the players (expertly devised by Claude Chagrin) are superbly done,

Paul Hecht is remarkably good as the chief Player (although I would have welcomed a touch more menace) and Brian Murray and John Wood provide virtuoso portrayals as Rosencrantz and Guildenstern.

Mr. Murray, blandly exuding a supreme lack of confidence, and Mr. Wood, disturbed, perhaps more intellectually than viscerally, play against each other like tennis singles champions. And luckily this is a game where neither needs to win and both can share the trophy.

This is a most remarkable and thrilling play. In one bound Mr. Stoppard is asking to be considered as among the finest English-speaking writers of our stage, for this is a work of fascinating distinction. Rosencrantz and Guildenstern LIVE!

Source: Clive Barnes, in a review of *Rosencrantz and Guildenstern are Dead* (1967) in *On Stage: Selected Theater Reviews from the New York Times, 1920–1970* , edited by Bernard Beckerman and Howard Siegman, Arno Press, 1973, pp. 500–02.

FURTHER READING

Bareham, T., editor. *Tom Stoppard:* Rosencrantz and Guildenstern are Dead, Jumpers, Travesties: *a Casebook,* Macmillan, 1990.
> Contains interviews with Stoppard, general assessments of his work, reviews of early productions, and excerpts from critical studies.

Cahn, Victor, L. *Beyond Absurdity: The Plays of Tom Stoppard,* Associated University Presses, 1979.
> In a long section on *Rosencrantz and Guildenstern are Dead,* Cahn contrasts Stoppard's play with the traditional Theatre of the Absurd.

Gordon, Robert. *Rosencrantz and Guildenstern Are Dead, Jumpers, and The Real Thing: Text and Performance,* Macmillan, 1991.
> Part of a useful series that focuses on the performance aspects of plays. The sections on *Rosencrantz and Guildenstern Are Dead* include one that describes and comments on its first professional production at the Old Vic in 1967.

Harty, III, John, editor. *Tom Stoppard: A Casebook,* Garland, 1988.
> Three essays on the play, including invaluable essays by William E. Gruber and J. Dennis Huston that discuss how Stoppard uses the Shakespearean text.

Hayman, Ronald. *Contemporary Playwrights: Tom Stoppard,* Heinemann, 1977.
> A very readable critical study that includes a short chapter on Stoppard's first major play and a valuable interview with the author.

Jenkins, Anthony, editor. *Critical Essays on Tom Stoppard,* G. K. Hall, 1990.
> Includes four important essays on the play and an especially valuable interview with Stoppard.

Londre, Felicia Hardison. *Tom Stoppard,* Frederick Ungar, 1981.
> A scholarly assessment of Stoppard's work through the late 1970s, including a chapter on *Rosencrantz and Guildenstern Are Dead.* Accessible for most students.

Matuz, Roger, editor. *Contemporary Literary Criticism,* Vol. 63, Gale, 1991.
> A very thorough compendium of excerpts from the most important criticism on *Rosencrantz and Guildenstern Are Dead.* An excellent place to start for an overview of interpretations of the play.

Perlette, John M. "Theatre at the Limit: *Rosencrantz and Guildenstern Are Dead* in *Modern Drama,* Vol. 28, no. 4, December, 1985, 659-69.
> An essential essay for understanding the complexities of Stoppard's thematic treatment of death.

Rusinko, Susan. *Tom Stoppard,* Twayne, 1986.
> A very accessible introduction to Stoppard that includes a short chapter on *Rosencrantz and Guildenstern Are Dead.*

Sales, Roger. *Rosencrantz and Guildenstern are Dead,* Penguin, 1988.
> A thorough, book-length analysis of the play that effectively summarizes and comments on the action of both Stoppard's and Shakespeare's play before setting *Rosencrantz and Guildenstern Are Dead* into the context of Stoppard's other work and Beckett's *Waiting for Godot.*

Twilight: Los Angeles, 1992

ANNA DEAVERE SMITH

1993

Twilight: Los Angeles, 1992 is the fourteenth part of Anna Deavere Smith's work in progress, *On the Road: A Search for American Character,* begun in 1983. The play's unifying focus is the civil unrest in Los Angeles following the April, 1992, verdict in the first Rodney King trial, presented from the perspective of the wide range of persons that Smith interviewed. The actress-playwright interprets a limited number of these actual people in her solo performances, editing and rearranging her raw material as she deems appropriate.

Although she conducted about 175 interviews for the project, in her one-woman performances Smith limits her *dramatis personae* to between twenty-five and forty-five personalities, depending on her production venue. Her choices have varied as Smith has worked on her command of the diverse people that she represents.

Twilight: Los Angeles, 1992 began its premier run on May 23, 1993, in Los Angeles, at the Center Theatre Group/Mark Taper Forum, which had commissioned the work. It received almost unanimous critical acclaim, and it has since gained favorable notice in subsequent productions in Princeton, New Jersey, and in New York, Washington, D. C., and London, England. It has also garnered several honors, including Obie, Drama Desk, and Outer Critics Circle awards and two Antoinette Perry nominations.

Although *Twilight: Los Angeles, 1992* was also nominated for a Pulitzer Prize, the Pulitzer jury disqualified it on the grounds that it was not fictional and could only be performed by the interviewer-playwright herself. More than anything else, that decision reflects a critical inability to pigeonhole the work into some familiar category. The play's kinship with the documentary is unquestioned, but it simply escapes any easy classification. Its intention is clear, however; the piece documents a critical time of racial division and civil unrest, not to place blame for what happened, but to help the process of healing through a kaleidoscopic and sympathetic rendering of different viewpoints.

AUTHOR BIOGRAPHY

In *On the Road: A Search for American Character,* the series of plays to which *Twilight: Los Angeles, 1992* belongs, Anna Deavere (Duh-veer) Smith set out, as she says, "to capture the personality of a place by attempting to embody its varied population and varied points of view in one person— myself." Her series is a work-in-progress, its aim being the isolation of *the* American character through the dramatization of its many voices, the "different people" who "are shaping it." But her quest is partly a voyage of self-discovery, too, a shaping of her own role as a black woman writer, actress, and teacher.

Anna Deavere Smith was born in Baltimore, Maryland, on September 18, 1950, the oldest child of Deavere Smith and Anna Young Smith. Her father owned a coffee and tea business, and her mother was an elementary school principal. During her early years, Anna's upbringing was largely restricted to a segregated community, giving her few opportunities to meet the various kinds of people that she would later depict in her plays. However, she did sharpen one skill for which she seemed to have a natural gift—mimicry. That talent earned her a reputation as a bit of a mischief maker, though she never got in any serious trouble.

It was not until she attended Western High School that she began making friends with people of different ethnic backgrounds, especially the Jewish schoolmates whom she befriended. She has credited that school experience with giving her the sympathy necessary to depict persons with diverse ethnic and cultural heritages in her work. That sympathy re-

mained latent but strong after she graduated from Western in 1967.

Smith continued her education at Beaver College in Glenside, Pennsylvania, just outside Philadelphia. She first studied linguistics, but grew increasingly restless with the academic regimen in the face of the domestic strife of the late 1960s. She did graduate from Beaver, but did not really begin to find her professional niche until she inadvertently began taking acting classes at the American Conservatory Theatre in San Francisco. While apprenticing as an actor and director in that city's theaters, Smith earned an M.F.A. from the Conservatory, then moved to New York, where she supported herself by working for KLM Airlines and taking bit parts in soap operas.

In 1978, Smith took a position as a drama teacher at Carnegie-Mellon University, in Pittsburgh. It was there that she began developing her fundamental technique of characterization. She sought a way to free herself from the "method school of acting" that stressed the internalization of a role through the process of identifying with the character. She turned, instead, to the more objective method of depicting real people, an idea that came to her when watching Johnny Carson interview a series of diverse guests on the Tonight Show. She began taping interviews to challenge her acting students with the task of impersonating the speech and verbal mannerisms of the interviewed subjects.

Smith's interview method and her interest in American diversity led, in 1983, to the start of her main work, *On the Road: A Search for American Character.* Smith has also pursued an acting and teaching career that has taken her to several cities and several schools, including New York University, Yale University, the University of Southern California, and Stanford University, in Palo Alto, California, where she has served on the theater faculty since 1990. She has appeared in secondary roles in major films and taken her one-woman shows across America. She has also won several prizes and awards, including Tony and Obie awards and, in 1996, a much-coveted MacArthur Foundation fellowship.

PLOT SUMMARY

In the conventional sense, *Twilight: Los Angeles, 1992* has no plot or story line at all. The work consists of a series of monologues, the words of real persons interpreted by Smith in her dual role as playwright-performer. The monologues are edited redactions made up from interviews that Smith conducted in the aftermath of the events that seriously divided the Los Angeles community in the wake of the Rodney G. King beating on the night of March 3, 1991.

The playwright, to remind both her audiences and her readers of the issues, provides a ''Time Line'' in production playbills and the published work. The Time Line is a chronological outline of the important events referenced by the various voices in the play. It is that which provides the ''story.'' The major occurrences from that Time Line are summarized below.

1991: March 3-15

On March 3, after stopping King for speeding, members of the LAPD (Los Angeles Police Department) severely beat and arrest him. George Holiday, a nearby resident, captures the episode on video tape and distributes it to television networks, which repeatedly show it in broadcast news. Three days later, LAPD Chief Daryl F. Gates calls the King beating an ''aberration'' as the community clamors for his resignation. King is released from custody, and on March 15, four LA policemen—Sergeant Stacey Koon and officers Laurence Powell, Timothy Wind, and Theodore Briseno—are charged with a felony and arraigned for their part in the beating.

1991: March 15-26

On the night of March 15, fifteen-year-old Latasha Harlins, an African-American girl, is shot to death by Korean-American Soon Ja Du in a South LA liquor outlet. On March 26, on the same day that the four officers charged in the King beating enter an innocent plea, Soon Ja Du is arraigned for murder.

1991: April 1-July 22

On April 1, Los Angeles mayor Tom Bradley empowers a special commission under Warren Christopher to investigate the LAPD. Three days later, the LA Police Commission places Gates on leave, but he is immediately reinstated by the City Council. On April 7, Gates takes disciplinary action against the four indicted officers, firing Wind and suspending the other three. The Christopher Commission releases its report on July 9, recommending

Anna Deveare Smith

that Gates and the whole Police Commission resign. On July 16, the Police Commission orders Gates to reinstate his assistant chief, David D. Dotson, whom Gates had forced to step down after Dotson complained of the chief's failures to discipline police officers. About a week later, Gates announces his intention of retiring in 1992.

1991: July 23-November 15

On July 23, the Second District Court of Appeal orders a change of trial venue for the four LAPD officers charged in the King case. Some two months later, the prosecution in the trial of Soon Ja Du begins presenting its case. On October 11, the court finds Soon guilty of involuntary manslaughter. A month later, on November 15, she is sentenced to five years' probation, four-hundred hours of community service and a $500 fine.

1991: November 26-29

Judge Stanley Weisberg names Simi Valley in Ventura County as the Rodney King trial venue. Three days later, on November 29, LAPD officers kill a black man, leading to a confrontation with about a hundred housing-project residents in the Watts area of LA.

A playbill from the Cort Theatre for Smith's play

1992: February 3-April 29

Pretrial motions precede the actual trial of the four LAPD officers in the Rodney King case, which begins with opening arguments on March 4, before a jury lacking a single African-American. Two weeks later the prosecution rests its arguments. On April 13, Briseno admits that King was never a threat to the arresting officers. Meanwhile, on April 16, Willie L. Williams is named as Gates's successor as police commissioner. On April 23, the King-trial jury begins its deliberations, returning a verdict on April 29. The officers are found innocent, except for one charge against Officer Powell for the excessive use of force. The verdict, which results in a mistrial, is widely publicized on television.

The feared reaction comes the same day. A peaceful protest rally of over two-thousand people at a South-Central LA church breaks into violence, spreading in a widening circle of shootings, beatings, and looting. Vandalism eventually leads to arson, engulfing a large section of central LA in fire. Reginald Denny, a white truck driver, is pulled from his cab and severely beaten in an episode caught on video tape and broadcast on television. LA Mayor Bradley declares a local emergency, and Governor Pete Wilson orders out the National Guard.

1992: April 30-May 11

On the next day, April 30, Bradley imposes a curfew for the whole of LA, but the looting and burning of stores continues in various sections of the city as the violent protest continues. Meanwhile, the Justice Department announces its intent to investigate further the possible violation of Rodney King's civil rights.

Beginning on May 1, the LA community tries to restore order. A peace rally draws over a thousand persons, mostly Korean-Americans. On May 2, city crews start the clean-up, while volunteers carry food and clothing into the devastated areas. Thirty thousand residents march in Koreatown, calling for an end to racial discord.

On May 3, the *Los Angeles Times* announces the toll paid by the community: 58 dead, almost 2,400 injured, over 12,000 arrested, 3,100 businesses damaged. By May 4, with National Guard troops patrolling the streets, LA citizens start back to work and school, but some cannot return because looted and vandalized businesses remain closed. LAPD officers begin rounding up illegal immigrants suspected of looting or other riot-related crimes. LA officials turn suspects over to the Immigration and Naturalization Service for deportation.

On May 8, the troops begin withdrawing from LA, while the Crips and Bloods, two major LA gangs, agree to truce terms. Three days later, the LA Board of Police Commissioners names William H. Webster to chair a commission created to study the LAPD's response during the riots.

1992: May 12-December 14

On May 12, three of the "L A Four"—Damian Williams, Antoine Miller, and Henry Watson—are arrested for the April 29 beating of Reginald Denny. Gary Williams surrenders to the LAPD later on the same day. The L A Four are arraigned on May 21, charged with thirty-three violations for their attacks on thirteen motorists, including Denny. Meanwhile, various demonstrations continue. On May 25, Korean grocers meet with leaders of the Bloods and Crips to fashion an alliance. On May 30, Gates resigns at Chief of the LAPD and Willie Williams takes his place.

Over the summer and into December, protests continue, but violence is minimal. In October, the Webster Commission concludes that the LAPD's internal problems inhibited a quick response to the civil unrest. In the same month, the Black-Korean alliance breaks off, and on December 14, trouble erupts again when the Free the L A Four Defense Committee demonstrates at the site of the Denny beating.

1993: January 22-August 4

On January 23, ten charges against the L A Four are dismissed, but not the charge of attempted murder. Shortly thereafter, on February 3, the King civil rights trial of the four LAPD officers begins; it concludes two months later, on April 17. Briseno and Wind are acquitted. However, Powell and Koon are found guilty, and on August 4 are sentenced to a thirty-month term in federal prison.

1993: August 19-December 7

On August 19, the trial of the L A Four begins. It lasts about three months, although the final arguments begin early on, in late September. Jury problems force a verdict delay, as Judge Ouderkirk has to dismiss two jurors in early October. Convictions follow on October 18. Although acquitted of the more serious charges, on December 7, Damian Williams is sentenced to a maximum prison term of ten years for his attack on Denny.

CHARACTERS

Character Introduction

Although Smith interviewed about 175 people in her research for *Twilight: Los Angeles, 1992,* in the published work containing their monologues she includes just under a third of them. In any given performance of her play, she further limits the number of persons depicted but had included some who are not in the published work. An example is Maria, Juror #7 in the second Rodney King trial, who was interviewed and added to the Mark Taper Forum production of the play two weeks after it opened. Another example is the opera diva Jessye Norman.

There is actually no set cast of characters in *Twilight: Los Angeles, 1992.* As she deems appropriate, Smith selects the cast from her gallery of choices both to fit her specific audience and her artistic aims of the moment.

Theresa Allison

The founder of Mothers Reclaiming our Children (Mothers ROC), Theresa Allison is also the mother of gang-truce negotiator Dewayne Holmes. She explains that her organization started after the

MEDIA ADAPTATIONS

- As of the spring of 1997, among Smith's plays making up her *On the Road* series, only *Fires in the Mirror: Crown Heights, Brooklyn and Other Identities* had been produced for media presentation. However, since her success with *Twilight* and *Fires,* Smith has appeared on television and radio as speaker, debate moderator, and interviewed guest. She has also taken supporting roles in major films, including Mrs. Travis in *Dave* (1993), produced by Warner Bros., and Anthea Burton in *Philadelphia* (1993), produced by Tri-Star.

- *Fires in the Mirror* was directed by George C. Wolfe for PBS's *American Playhouse* and aired on television in April, 1993, featuring Smith in solo performance; video is available from the Public Broadcasting System (PBS).

killing of her nephew, Tiny, who was shot in the face. She speaks of the unjust system, and her belief that Tiny was actually shot by officers dressed as gang members, two of whom she calls ''Cagney and Lacey.'' She recalls the day of the shooting as looking ''like the crucifixion of Jesus.'' It was a day, too, that changed some happy people to ''hurting people.'' She goes on to tell how her son, Dewayne, was arrested and how she and her friends surrounded the police cruiser, fearful that the cops wanted to kill him. He was set free but was marked thereafter and was eventually picked up and sentenced for a crime that Theresa insists he did not commit.

Anonymous man

An unnamed white juror in the first Rodney King trial, this soft-spoken man breaks into tears as he recalls his ambivalent feelings about the verdict and its aftermath. He speaks of the personal confusion and the threats on his life. Most agonizing was a letter received from the KKK offering the jurors its support and extending an offer of membership.

That invitation shamed the man and left him remorseful.

Twilight Bey

A slight, graceful young black, Twilight Bey is a member of the Crips gang and one of the organizers of the truce between the Crips and the Bloods, a rival gang. He speaks very confidently of his youth, as a community "watchdog," and of the significance of his name as indicating that he has "twice the knowledge of those my age." He relates his name to the idea of limbo, as somehow being caught in a place ahead of his time, and he talks about what he sees at night, the drug-addicted "walking dead" and the young kids beating up elderly people at bus stops. He is also the titular character of the play, partly because what he says about limbo—a place between darkness and understanding—is an appropriate thematic metaphor for the entire work.

Big Al

See Allen Cooper

Elaine Brown

A woman in her early fifties, Elaine Brown is the former head of the Black Panther Party and author of *A Taste of Power*. She grieves over the fact that the protesters took to the street with no plan, just rage. She says that commitment must be based "not on hate but on love," and that change cannot be brought about by a "piss-poor, ragtag, unorganized, poorly armed" and "poorly led army."

Allen Cooper

A large, ex-gang member and former convict, Big Al is an activist in the nation-wide truce movement. He offers a defensive litany on life in the LA ghetto, where even a bubble gum machine packs a gun and nothing spells trouble 'til the black man gets his hands on it." He repeatedly says, "You gotta look at history, baby." He sees the African American as victim, and questions whether Reginald Denny might have driven his truck into the black neighborhood as an "intimidation move."

Reginald O. Denny

Reginald Denny, the white truck driver beaten and shot at during the LA riot, describes what little he remembers of the experience. He is "upbeat" and "speaks loudly." He admits to being unaware of the King verdict and its aftermath until visitors came to speak with him at the Daniel Freeman Hospital. He talks about Jesse Jackson, Arsenio Hall, and the four people who rescued him—Titus, Bobby, Terry, and Lee—with whom he feels "a weird common thread in our lives." He describes what he has seen on video tapes and what his rescuers have told him. He talks about a room in a future house that will be a memorial, "a happy room," one where "there won't be a color problem." Denny seems hopeful and remarkably free of bitterness.

Sergeant Charles Duke

Sergeant Charles Duke is a member of the LAPD Special Weapons and Tactics Unit and a defense witness in both trials of the officers who beat Rodney King. Duke explains that Officer Laurence Powell mishandled his baton while beating Rodney King, making his blows weak and ineffective. He laments that "upper- body control holds" were outlawed in 1982 as inhumane, even though they provided a better method of subduing suspects on drugs. He relates, too, that he had tried to find alternatives to the use of batons but was rebuked for his efforts. He believes that Chief Daryl Gates wanted to provoke a law suit to prove that the City Council and Police Commission had made a mistake in banning older choke holds techniques.

Elvira Evers

Elvira Evers is a Panamanian woman, who, during the rioting, while pregnant, is shot and taken by ambulance to St. Francis Hospital. Doctors operate to trace the bullet's course and deliver her baby girl via Caesarean section. The baby has the bullet lodged in her elbow, but it is successfully removed. Describing the events, Elvira remains remarkably unemotional.

Daryl F. Gates

Daryl F. Gates, Chief of the LAPD during the rioting, attempts to explains his absence from his post after the verdict in the first Rodney King trial. He was meeting with a group opposed to Proposition F, but claims to have been in constant contact with his office. He admits that he should have left immediately, but doubts that his presence in LA would have mattered. "I should have been smarter," he confesses, but primarily because he gave his critics ammunition to use against him. He resents having become "the symbol of police oppression in the United States," and finds it very unjust.

Mrs. Young-Soon Han

A Korean immigrant and former owner of a liquor store, Mrs. Han angrily remarks on the treatment and status of Korean Americans. She bitterly argues that black Americans fare better, and then talks of justice and violence. Although she wishes that Asians and blacks could live together, she sees "too much differences" preventing community peace and harmony—a fire that "canuh burst out anytime."

Angela King

Angela King, the aunt of Rodney King, in a relatively long monologue, relates her unsettled family life to the film *Carmen,* starring Dorothy Dandridge and Harry Belafonte. She discusses her closeness with her brother, Rodney's father, recalling childhood anecdotes. She explains that they were raised without racial hatred and that now she seeks justice for the beating of her nephew. She is particulary upset by the defendants' lack of remorse and the efforts of the authorities "to make you look bad to the people." She is convinced her phone is tapped but that there is nothing she can do about it.

Maria

Juror #7 in the second Rodney King trial, Maria, a lively black woman, gives a no-holds-barred account of her fellow jurors, whom she unmercifully parodies as "brain-dead." She gives a hilarious description of the group's interactive workings as they strive to cooperate in their joint obligation as jurors.

Julio Menjivar

A native of El Salvador, Julio Menjivar is a man in his late twenties. A bystander, he describes the arrival and behavior of the National Guard during the unrest, claiming that guardsmen almost shot his mother, sister, and wife, then rounded the residents up and hauled them by bus to jail. He describes his fright, his prayers, and his unhappiness with having a criminal record.

Katie Miller

A big black woman with a powerful voice, Katie Miller claims that the looters and vandals in Koreatown were not blacks but Mexicans. Although she did not engage in looting, she went "touring" with friends after the rioting. She is sarcastic and very angry with local newscaster Paul Moyer because he called the looters of an I. Magnin store "thugs." She is outraged because the media seem to suggest that looting in the poor sections of LA

was vindicated, but not in "a store that rich people go to."

Paul Parker

Paul Parker, the Chairperson of the Free the L.A. Four Plus Defense Committee, argues that the defendants charged with attacking Reginald Denny were victimized because it was a black-on-white affair, and that the authorities would go "any extremes necessary" to gain a conviction. He takes intense pride in his African-American heritage, and warns that as long as there is no justice for blacks, there will be no peace for whites.

Rudy Salas, Sr.

Rudy Salas, Sr., a sculptor and painter, is a large man of Mexican descent. Partly deaf, he wears a hearing aid in both ears. His deafness resulted from a police beating back in the 1940s. Rudy retains hatred for "gringo" policemen and other whites, whom he refers to as "my enemy." He calls the feeling "insanity," and knows it is a waste, but he can not help it. He is convinced that whites fear "people of color," and he relishes their discomfort. He indicates that his hatred has been fortified by the experiences of his sons.

Second anonymous man

This well-dressed, handsome man, an unidentified Hollywood agent, starts out by remarking that the anticipated unrest from the King trial verdict did not at first dampen his "business as usual" activities. He noted the gossip and tension among his white, upper-middle class associates, but panic did not set in until the rioting began, when the flight of working whites from downtown LA lacked only "Godzilla behind them." He admits that the verdict was unfair, and that he started to "absorb a little guilt." He was saddened by the television coverage showing people destroying their own neighborhoods.

Stanley K. Sheinbaum

Stanley K. Sheinbaum, former president of the LA Police Commission, is seventy-three, with "the smile and laugh of a highly spirited, joyous, old woman." He speaks in two monologues In the first, he talks of "these curious people," the gang members at a truce meeting he had witnessed with Congresswoman Maxine Walters. He is troubled by the assumption that the gangs are always the enemy, and that he must be on a side that prevents understanding. In the second monologue, he recalls driving downtown after the King verdict and seeing a black woman driving on the freeway holding a hammer in her hand, which spelled "trouble." He recalls encountering Chief Daryl Gates leaving the police garage as he arrived, then being inside LAPD headquarters when the first rock came through a plate-glass window.

Judith Tur

A ground reporter, Judith Tur gives a running commentary on the beating of Reginald Denny as video taped from a helicopter by John and Marika Tur. She describes the event as "like being in a war zone," and becomes very angry at the "real brave men" who beat and tried to shoot Denny. She tells of her own hard life to explain why she has little sympathy for the rioters, who, she charges, are "really taking advantage."

Maxine Waters

Maxine Waters is a U. S. Representative from the 35th District in California, representing South-Central LA. She is an "elegant" woman and powerful orator. She vents her anger with Washington's insensitivity to inner-city problems and describes how she crashed an exclusive White House meeting on the issue to speak her mind to President Bush.

Henry Keith Watson

One of the L.A. Four accused in the attack on Reginald Denny, Keith Watson, twenty-nine, escaped punishment when acquitted in the subsequent trial in October of 1993. Defending his anger and the burning and looting of the rioters, he says that "justice didn't work."

Cornel West

A scholar, Cornel West relates the civil turmoil to analogous issues, including the frontier and the gunfighter and the "deep machismo ethic" of a "gangsterous orientation" seen in the character of Sylvester Stallone's Rambo and rap music. He argues that blacks are "playing exactly the same game," attempting to "outbrutalize the police brutality." He notes that black women remain subjugated because of the machismo and laments the end of the Black Panther movement and the loss of the "internationalism and multiracialism" that it represented. He maintains that "conservative forces" have held the civil rights movement in disarray.

Elaine Young

An experienced realtor, Elaine Young has sold many homes to Hollywood stars. She has also received publicity because of her problems with silicone implants. During the rioting, fearful of being alone, she goes to the Beverly Hills Hotel, staying until early morning on three consecutive days. After being interviewed at the Polo Lounge, she receives an accusative letter from a man who calls her "a dumb shit bimbo" for her flippant lack of concern over the unrest. That clearly upsets her.

THEMES

Actual events provide the focus and stated or implied reference point for all of the monologues that make up *Twilight: Los Angeles, 1992*. The main incidents are the beating of Rodney King; the verdict in the first trial of the LAPD officers involved; the ensuing civil unrest, including the shooting, burning, and looting; the beating of Reginald Denny; the second King trial and verdict; and the hearing and verdict in the L.A. Four trial.

Anger and Hatred

Closely related to themes of race and racial prejudice, anger and hatred have a powerful, resonating presence in *Twilight: Los Angeles, 1992*. Some of the persons, like Rudy Salas, Sr., the Mexican artist, seem almost consumed with hatred. His is directed against "gringos," especially white police officers. His anger is shared by others, mostly by inner-city blacks and Latinos who resent the treatment afforded them by the LAPD, what Theresa Allison calls "the hands of our enemy, the unjust system."

Atonement and Forgiveness

Some of the more reflective voices in *Twilight: Los Angeles, 1992* express a prayer or hope that what LA citizens experienced throughout the unrest will give way to a future reconciliation and community harmony and peace among different ethnic groups. It is the "room" that Reginald Denny plans for his future house, a room that is "just gonna be people," where a person's race will not matter. It is the hope, too, of Otis Chandler, former publisher of the LA *Times*. He believes that someday LA can become "a safe, pleasant city, for everybody, re-

TOPICS FOR FURTHER STUDY

- Investigate the controversy that arose in 1991, when a white actor, Johnathan Pryce, was chosen for the lead role in the Broadway production of Alan Boublil and Claude-Michel Shonberg's musical *Miss Saigon* (1989). Relate the controversy to Smith's practice in her one-woman interpretations of racially diverse characters.

- Research the influence of the Los Angeles civil unrest and subsequent events such as the O. J. Simpson murder trial in debates over the need to reform the American jury-trial system.

- Investigate the causes and effects of the riots in the Watts district of Los Angeles in the summer of 1965 and the subsequent report of the Kerner Commission. Relate your findings to the civil unrest resulting from the Rodney King trial in 1992.

- Research the role of Anna Deavere Smith in the

controversy arising from August Wilson's keynote speech before the Theatre Communications Group in June 1996, in which the celebrated playwright argued the need of a separate and autonomous black American theater.

- Investigate the influence of the Los Angeles disturbances of 1992 on popular and underground culture, including "gangsta rap" and politically-incorrect humor.

- Investigate the depiction of ethnically-mixed, inner-city neighborhoods in recent film and media treatments, including Spike Lee's *Do the Right Thing* (1989).

- Investigate the excessive use of force over the last decade by law enforcement agencies in Los Angeles or any other large American city and what steps have been taken, if any, to rectify the problem.

---

gardless of where they live or what they do or what the color of their skin is." The new harmony would be the community's atonement for the past, and it would have to involve forgiveness.

Others are far more pessimistic, however. There is, for example, Mrs. Young-Soon Han, who believes that racial hatred still burns deeply and can ignite at any time, although, as a Korean, she would like to find a way to live together with blacks. And there are those like Gladis Sibrian, Director of the Farabundo Mart National Liberation Front, who believe that "there is no sense of future, sense of hope that things can be changed."

Civil Rights

The failure of the first Rodney King trial to produce an acceptable verdict led to a second, federal trial on the grounds that the LAPD officers had violated King's civil rights. The issues of civil rights and justice thus lie at the core of the play's matter, and the idea that minority groups have been

denied those rights is echoed by various persons. According to Mike Davis, writer and urban critic, the thrust of the civil rights movement was to insure equality for everyone, but, ironically, even privileged whites are losing rights to police-enforced laws that limit such freedoms as movement and the right of assembly. Another figure, Bill Bradley, a U.S. Senator from New Jersey, recounts the experience of a black friend who was stopped by LAPD officers while riding in a car with a white woman. The friend was forced to lie face-down on the ground and was questioned while an officer held a gun to his head. Bradley laments that the "moral power" of the law firm where his friend was interning was not invoked by the firm's partners. Without that moral coercion, the laws that give us all citizens equal rights remain only theoretical.

Class Conflict

Although the central conflict associated with the LA turmoil was based in racial divisions, there is clearly a relationship between race relations and economic class, particularly in the distinction between the impoverished inner-city residents "of color" and wealthy suburban whites. Some of the bitterness of the blacks and Latinos is based on what is perceived as class privilege, not just race. For example, much of Katie Miller's anger is directed against the implicit assumption by the media that the poor people who looted the I. Magnin store on Wilshire Boulevard were "thugs," inferior to the rich people who shopped there. She deplores the "give me your money and get out of my face" attitude of inner-city store owners who lack any respect for their customers.

Fear

One response to the LA turmoil was fear, a feeling prevalent among whites but also expressed by many others. The rage that gripped the rioters and looters induced panic in white people like the Hollywood agent (Anonymous Man #2); Elaine Young, the realtor; and the co-ed at the University of Southern California (Anonymous Young Woman). Paula Weinstein, a movie producer, remembers "watching rich white people guard their houses and send their children out of L.A. as if the devil was coming after them." As Owen Smet reports, after the riots, latent fears almost doubled the business of the Beverly Hills Gun Club, because "there's no place safe in LA County, daylight *or* dark."

Some of the minority people found a positive thing in the fear felt by whites. Rudy Salas, Sr., for example, takes great personal pleasure in the fear that whites have of minorities. Others, like Paul Parker, see the white fear as a catalyst for achieving racial justice.

Guilt and Innocence

To some extent, culpability goes hand in hand with fear in *Twilight: Los Angeles, 1992*. As the Hollywood agent remarks, the "victims of the system," the ones burning and looting, "got the short shrift." He admits that he "started to absorb a little guilt" for what was happening. Shame also seems to overwhelm the juror in the first Rodney King trial when talking about the KKK letter of support for the jurors.

Too often, though, guilt is deflected through a displacing of personal responsibility. For example, LAPD Chief Daryl Gates, criticized for slipping off to a Republican fund raiser during the crisis, rationalizes his behavior and complains of being vic-timized as a "symbol of police oppression," despite his excellent record and work he "had done with kids."

Justice and Injustice

Many of the figures in *Twilight: Los Angeles, 1992* talk of justice, especially in the context of victimization. For the blacks, the first Rodney King trial resulted in a travesty of justice, and many others agreed with that assessment, believing the verdict wrong. The civil unrest started from a protest against that injustice. For Theresa Allison and others, the struggle of the inner-city blacks is against injustices largely perpetuated by police brutality. With sad anger, she asks: "Why do they have so much power? Why does the system work for them? Where can we go to get the justice that they have?" These are questions which *Twilight: Los Angeles, 1992* can simply raise, not answer.

Law and Order

The riot erupting in the wake of the verdict in the first Rodney King trial represented a basic breakdown of law and order, as described by Compton Fire Department Captain Lane Haywood and others. While some officials remark on ways the breakdown could have been anticipated and prevented, Congresswoman Maxine Waters, speaking at the First African Methodist Episcopal Church, proclaimed that "whether we like it or not, riot is the voice of the unheard."

For some, like Julio Menjivar, the efforts to restore law and order involved the misuse of power by both the LAPD and the National Guard, which, he claims, victimized his family and unjustly arrested him. Such complaints against the abuse of power by the police thread through the remarks of many of the inner-city minority speakers. Measured against these, Sergeant Charles Duke's conclusion that the lawlessness arose from improper or inadequate use of force to maintain peace seems tragically discordant.

Prejudice and Tolerance

Racial intolerance also threads through the speeches of various persons and is intrinsically bound to other themes. L.A.'s ethnic diversity still lies at the root of some of its problems. Images of white cops and black or Latino victims are common in the accounts, but so too are statements of mutual intolerance voiced by the blacks and Korean Americans. For Paul Parker, the chairperson of the Free the LA Four Plus Committee, "the Koreans was like the Jews," store owners from an earlier era, and targets of much of the black rage.

Race and Racism

Obviously related to questions of anger and intolerance, racial identity is a very important theme in *Twilight: Los Angeles, 1992*. Implicit in the work is the paradoxical idea that cultural diversity is both a source of a community's discord and its potential strength, a potential that far too few seem to realize. Many of the speakers are racial apologists, defenders of their ethnic heritage, in which they take pride. The dark side of that pride is racial insularity, a powerful impediment to the creation of a community in which race consciousness no longer exists. Spokespersons too easily place blame elsewhere, outside their own race. The shame is that, like Theresa Allison and Michael Zinzun, they are often justified by what happened.

Victim and Victimization

A feeling of victimization is ubiquitous in Smith's drama. It lies at the root of all complaints about injustice and is the source of much of the frustration and anger. It is expressed by members of all involved minorities—black, Latino, and Korean. It is, for example, the focus of Mrs. Young-Soon Han's poignant litany. The former owner of a liquor store destroyed in the riots, she complains that "Korean immigrants were left out from society and we were nothing." It is a charge paralleled in the monologues of blacks and Latinos, too. It is sometimes tied to the idea of revenge, justifying the carnage of the rioting. That is the message of Paul Parker, for example, and it is the warning of Congresswoman Maxine Waters, who insists that people who have "been dropped off everybody's agenda" will grow angry and take to the streets to vent their anger and frustration.

STYLE

Twilight: Los Angeles, 1992 has no narrative thread defining its structure. Its kinship is with eye-witness accounts reported in the media or responses to questions asked by a talk-show interviewer. The "story" behind the play consists of the actual events that occurred in Los Angeles over a two-year period. These include the beating of Rodney King, the trial and verdict in the ensuing trial, the violent community reaction, the beating of Reginald Denny, the federal Rodney King trial, and the trial and outcome of "L.A. Four" accused of the attempted murder of Denny.

Colloquialism

The language of *Twilight: Los Angeles, 1992* is not the invention of the playwright. It consists of the actual words used by the real people that she interviewed, and it reflects various dialects and levels of command of English. For many of the figures, English is an adopted language, thus many speeches are rich with unidiomatic expressions and non-standard grammar. Smith's characters talk like real people because they are real people, and Smith as playwright-performer captures the colloquial cadences and texture of their speech in her literal transcriptions. In the case of Chung Lee, President of the Korean-American Victims Association, she even uses a figure who speaks Korean that must be translated by his son. As with her other "characters," Smith studied Lee's speech and renders his voice verbatim in her performances.

Documentary

Twilight: Los Angeles, 1992 has been called a work of "documentary theater." The events discussed by the "characters" are real, as are the characters themselves. Smith's method is journalistic, but it is made dramatic by her on-stage renderings or performance of the real persons she depicts. On paper, her work is a collection of monologues compiled from her interviews. Her own voice is removed and her questions merely implied. On stage, Smith strives for objectivity and completely obscures her role as interviewer as she adapts the character and voice of those she had interviewed. Speaking of the published text of *Twilight: Los Angeles, 1992*, Smith says her book "is first and foremost a document of what an *actress heard* in Los Angeles," and that her "performance is a reiteration of that."

Monologue

Almost all the characters in *Twilight: Los Angeles, 1992* present themselves in monologues in isolation from the rest of the *dramatis personae*. There is, in fact, a total absence of dialogue, the usual engine and necessary method of advancing story in dramatic form. The nature of the monologues varies greatly, as do the voices presenting them. Some are very articulate, rational, and coherent, while others are charged with emotion and often inchoate. The content of the monologues also varies greatly, running a gamut from self-vindication to heated diatribes against perceived injustices.

Narrative

Drama, as a presentational form, unfolds in the here and now, and it ordinarily uses narrative primarily for exposition and the reporting of offstage actions. A common character in much traditional drama is the "messenger," who, for example, reports the outcome of a battle that cannot be depicted on stage. To some degree, the characters in *Twilight: Los Angeles, 1992* are all messengers, and the events they allude to or describe are things that have happened in the offstage world of South-Central Los Angeles. They are somewhat like media commentators and interpreters, not actors in a unfolding scene. It precisely for this reason that Smith's drama defies traditional classification.

Stream of Consciousness

Smith faithfully renders what her subjects have actually said in their interviews with her. She removes only her own voice. Although the monologues are not interior stream-of-consciousness monologues, some of them are similar to that narrative technique in their free association of ideas. They are full of non-sequiturs, hesitation, and verbal hemming and hawing. That impromptu, unrehearsed quality is fundamental to the documentary authenticity of the work.

Symbolism

There is really no symbolism in *Twilight: Los Angeles, 1992,* at least not in the ordinary sense. Symbolism suggests a conscious artistry on the part of the writer, but Smith as writer is primarily a reporter and arranger. Her artistry is largely the interpretive artistry of theater, revealed in her performance of the voices that she has objectively recorded. Still, there is a sort of emblem in the concept of "twilight," a word used not only because it is the name of her titular figure, Twilight Bey, but also because it is used by others to suggest a kind of condition, the limbo of which Bey speaks. Twilight sees himself as "stuck in limbo," a place between dark and light. For him, light is the "knowledge and wisdom of the world," while darkness, although not negative, means a narrower perspec-

tive, of, as he says, "just identifying with people like me and understanding me and mine." That limbo, that twilight, seems equally descriptive of the condition of the City of Los Angeles and its people.

Urban Realism

Twilight: Los Angeles, 1992, with its focus on the problems of a great metropolis, is a work of urban realism. Like traditional narratives dealing with life in ghettos and slums, the work shows the plight of many inner-city residents, people who have to live with despair, anger, and frustration, subjected as they are to drive-by shootings, unemployment, drug trafficking, police brutality, economic exploitation, and a host of other problems. It does not, of course, suggest ways to solve the problems. Instead, it offers an almost clinical study of their effect on the lives of the people whose voices Smith gives public hearing on stage.

HISTORICAL CONTEXT

When Anna Deavere Smith first began her *On the Road* series of plays in 1983, the Soviet Bloc had begun disintegrating, and the Cold War was quickly winding down. It officially ended during the administration of President George Bush. Anticipated peace benefits did not really materialize, however, even though an economic recovery from a recession had begun by 1993, the year in which President William Clinton entered the Oval Office and Smith completed *Twilight: Los Angeles, 1992.* Domestic violence, drug trafficking, and other criminal activity continued to plague the United States, as did global disasters affecting foreign policy. Not all the problems were man made, however.

Natural Disasters Take Toll in U.S. and Abroad

In August of 1992, Hurricane Andrew hit the Homestead area of South Florida, killing 15, leaving 250,000 homeless and causing $20 billion in property damage. In the same year, flooding in Chicago and a violent Nor'easter striking East Coast states caused considerable damage and loss of life.

In the next year, another violent storm struck the Eastern Seaboard in March, claiming 240 lives and causing extensive property damage. In the summer, flooding of the Mississippi and Missouri Rivers took 50 lives and destroyed an estimated $12 billion in property and crops.

Abroad, by 1992, famine in Somalia had killed over 300,000 people, and the ensuing anarchy prompted President Bush to send U. S. troops into Somalia under a United Nations mandate. Civil wars in Sudan, Angola, and Mozambique also created mass starvation. The next year, violent rains and earthquakes took over 20,000 lives in areas of India and Bangladesh.

Terrorism Hits America's Homeland

At home, the United States got its first serious taste of the kind of terrorist activities that have plagued many foreign countries. On February 26, 1993, a bomb set by Islamic fundamentalists at New York's World Trade Center killed six and forced 100,000 persons to evacuate the twin towers. Unlike the violence of the Los Angeles rioting, arising from domestic problems, the attack on the World Trade Center was prompted by the foreign policy of the United States. It was also premeditated, not a spontaneous reaction to a specific perceived injustice.

Many Americans Remain in Poverty

The plight of the "unheard" inner-city minorities for whom Smith provides a voice in *Twilight: Los Angeles, 1992* is reflected in the fact that in 1993 over ten percent of all Americans had to depend on food stamps to get enough to eat. The total number, 26.6 million, was the highest in the program's history. Clearly, the improving economic picture was not helping the nation's poor, many of whom lived in urban slums like South-Central Los Angeles.

Efforts to Control Gun Sales Continues

In an on-going effort to reverse the growth of violent crime, including urban drive-by shootings, the federal government passed the "Brady Bill," signed into law on November 30, 1993. The law requires a five-day waiting period in the purchase of handguns. Earlier in the same month, the Senate passed a bill banning the manufacture and sale of assault-style automatic weapons, despite a major campaign launched by the National Rifle Association to prevent its passage. Demands for controls increased in the wake of the Long Island Railroad train attack by Colin Ferguson, who, on December

7, 1993, gunned down several commuters, leaving five dead and eighteen wounded.

Abortion Issue Continues to Divide America

Domestic violence in the United States was hardly limited to the economic and racial problems contributing to the upheaval in Los Angeles. America was divided over the issue of legalized abortion, for example. On March 10, 1993, during a demonstration outside a women's clinic in Pensacola, Florida, an anti-abortion advocate shot and killed Dr. David Gunn. Activists burned down or sprayed other abortion clinics with noxious chemicals in protest of an "abortion on demand" policy.

Siege of Branch Davidian Cult at Waco Ends in Disaster

Anti-government groups, including private militias, continued to spring up in the United States, as did some religious cults with similar political agendas. The Branch Davidians, led by David Koresh, stood off a 51-day siege by government agents in Waco, Texas. On April 19, 1993, when stormed by federal law enforcement agents using tear gas, the cult members set fire to their compound, killing over 80 cult members, including two dozen children. The event contributed fuel to the anti-government activity that continues to afflict the nation.

CRITICAL OVERVIEW

Anna Deavere Smith's *Twilight: Los Angeles, 1992* has garnered considerable critical acclaim through its production history, stretching from venues in Los Angeles and New York to Washington, D. C. and London, England. Its success in theaters far removed from the play's focus and epicenter, the Spring, 1992, civil upheaval in South-Central Los Angeles, attests to its power to transcend the topicality of its content—the real-world social problems that have led P. J. Corso and others to call her play a "docudrama."

For some critics, in her *On the Road* series, of which *Twilight: Los Angeles, 1992* and *Fires in the Mirror* are the most compelling and successful parts, Smith has created what a reviewer in *Time* claims is "a new art form." But what that new form is remains very controversial. So, too, does Smith's classification as a writer.

In analyzing *Twilight: Los Angeles, 1992* and other pieces from *On the Road,* some critics have pondered over this very issue. For Chris Vognar, the question is "what to call her? Actress/playwright? Anthropologist/ethnographer?" Smith's text, after all, is primarily an archive of the actual words of real people who lived through and in or near the turmoil that began with the beating of Rodney King and exploded into the South-Central Los Angeles rioting and looting. Smith compiled and arranged the monologues from interviews that she conducted with these people, leading some to discuss her role as writer as largely that of a journalist or "oral historian" in the mold of her acknowledged mentor, Studs Terkel. The argument was rehashed by the 1994 Pulitzer Prize jury in drama, which removed *Twilight: Los Angeles, 1992* from consideration, as Sean Mitchell reported, because "its language was not invented but gleaned from interviews." It was also the opinion of the jury that the work could be performed only by Smith, because she alone conducted the interviews.

That critical caveat is not so troubling to those who see Smith as a "performance-playwright" and concentrate on her stage artistry rather than her compiled, inanimate text. Part of Smith's skill is revealed in the dramatic tapestry of disparate voices that she weaves in performance. As Jan Stuart notes, "Smith lines up her characters in a boldly ironic juxtaposition," threading her way through what Robert Brustein calls the "victims, victimizers, and viewers" that she depicts.

More an arranger than a composer perhaps, but Smith, for most reviewers, has nevertheless worked theatrical magic in the various productions of *Twilight.* Almost no critic denies Smith's mimetic skills, her great artistic gift in depicting a broad spectrum of characters through what Monica Cortes calls "acting otherness." Martin Hernandez describes her as a "human chameleon, embodying each character with astounding flexibility." Through sudden shifts in her posture, gesture and voice, accompanied by minor, quick-change adjustments in dress, Smith transforms herself from one person into another, crossing chasms of race, gender, age, and class in the blink of an eye. Describing her technique, Richard Schechner claims that Smith "works by means of deep mimesis, a process opposite to that of 'pretend.'" He maintains that she "incorpo-

rates" her characters and that her method "is less like that of a conventional Euro-American actor and more like that of African, Native American, and Asian ritualists."

More of a sticking point for interpreters of her play is Smith's assumed purpose in *Twilight* and other plays in her *On the Road* series. Most credit Smith with admirable objectivity and basic fairness. Michael Feingold argues that the playwright-actress arranges her materials "so that we see all sides" equitably. Smith "never tilts this balance," he maintains, but moves "inside the anger and hate" of her diverse characters to find "sources of potential community" and the possibility of repairing "our shredded social contract." From this critical vantage point, Smith is a shaman-healer, helping a community and the nation bind up the wounds of class and racial discord.

There are, however, dissenting voices. For Stefan Kanfer, Smith's play is flawed because it advances "an illiberal agenda concealed by a mask of objectivity." He claims that "every member of a minority group is given a shred of dignity, a credible plea of despair," while the depicted whites are shown only as "brutes," "fools," or "insensitive naifs." From this point of view, Smith is biased, and her true agenda is not to heal but to place blame and, presumably, invoke white guilt.

Others, like Robert Brustein, while crediting Smith with "an objective ear," draw pessimistic conclusions from her play and performance. Noting that "hate" and "enemy" are "the operative words" of the play, Brustein claims that *Twilight* "leaves us with a shocking sense of how America's hopes for racial harmony were left burning in the ashes of South-Central L.A." That, of course, is not so much an indictment of the play as it is of society.

The most troubling critical question is whether there is in fact a play without the playwright. As Mitchell says, "it is hard to imagine an Anna Deavere Smith show without Anna Deavere Smith." When read, the matter she enlivens in performance is, according to Mitchell, "only a little more fruitful than trying to read *A Chorus Line* or *Phantom of the Opera.*" Furthermore, as Kanfer points out, the final fate of two of the white police officers who beat Rodney King and the $3.8 million civil-suit award granted him "tend to vitiate the impact" of Smith's play. Can her play text survive Smith herself and its ever-increasing distance from the events that inspired it? Only time will tell.

CRITICISM

John Fiero

Fiero is an experienced actor and a professor at the University of Southwestern Louisiana. In this essay he discusses Smith's skill as a performer of her own material and its role in the effectiveness of her play.

On January 27, 1997, at the New York Town Hall, Anna Deavere Smith moderated a debate between playwright August Wilson and theater pundit Robert Brustein over Wilson's position that black American playwrights should work within a theater exclusively devoted to black culture. Wilson had taken particular umbrage with the practice of "color-blind-casting," especially as it pertains to casting black actors in "white" plays. According to Henry Louis Gates, Jr., in Wilson's view, "for a black actor to walk the stage of Western drama was to collaborate with the culture of racism," to demean, and to rob the actor of his or her true and distinct identity.

Whether or not Wilson is in some ways "an unlikely spokesman for a new Black Arts movement," as Gates maintains, he has championed a view that seems diametrically opposed to what Smith practices in her multi-cultural, mimetic art. Described by Sharon Fitzgerald as "Anna of a thousand faces," Smith dons the character of her interviewed subjects without a nanosecond's regard for the politically-correct idea that actors should portray only what their birthright entitles them to portray. In her one-woman performances of *Twilight: Los Angeles, 1992,* she has impersonated an imposing array of real people of different color, sex, national origin, socioeconomic class, political complexion, and age—shedding and donning character guises like a human chameleon.

Her purpose, too, seems antithetical to what Wilson preaches. As Lauren Feldman argues, "Smith inspires us to scrutinize common constructions of race, our own complicity in the events that continue to shape American race relations, and the role of the arts in reproducing or deconstructing social stereotypes." Thus, in searching for *the* American character, Smith has elected to deal with actual people at critical junctures in their lives, when their identities and even their lives are at risk. Moreover, she maintains that if American theater is to "mirror society" honestly, it "must embrace diversity." To that end, she crowds her dramatic canvass with portraits of diverse people caught in moments of reflection on an emotionally charged and violent set of real events. Hers is an assimilative aim, to synthesize such diverse voices into a "more complex language" which "our race dialogue desperately needs." In contrast, Wilson's separatist aim seems completely inimical to such a race dialogue.

The niggling question is whether that more complex language is inherent in the text of *Twilight: Los Angeles, 1992* or in the artistry of Smith as actress—or whether, indeed, the two can ever be separated. She has been credited with silencing "all the questions about racial identity in race-specific plays." For William Sun and Faye Fei, Smith has evolved "a unique genre" that allows her to pirouette convincingly through her characterizations without benefit of masks or makeup. Her range is simply extraordinary, covering a "full spectrum that runs between opposite racial, political, and ideological poles." In one moment, she is a white, middle-aged male, such as former LAPD Chief Daryl Gates; in the next, through a "morphing" of her face, gestures, posture, and, most of all, her voice, she becomes a female, like Elvira Edwards, the young Panamanian mother, or Elaine Brown, the over-fifty, former head of the Black Panther Party. Then, in a wink of the eye, she is a man again, but this time a proud and angry man, like Mexican-American artist, Rudy Salas, or the old Korean immigrant, Chung Lee, who can only speak in his native tongue. While a backdrop video screen provides footage of the Los Angeles rioting and beatings of Rodney King and Reginald Denny, the remarkable metamorphoses themselves are usually aided with only the barest theatrical amenities: slide projections identifying each character by a caption, name and, brief identifier; some minimal adjustments in stage and hand properties; and some slight costume changes, usually involving only one or two items of dress, like a hat and a shirt, or a pair of shoes and a jacket.

Her rendering of these "characters" has earned Smith warm praise from critics and audiences alike. She has repeatedly awed theater patrons with her rare mimetic gifts, leading more than one commentator to remark on her virtuosity. She has also been praised for her boldness, for her crossing of race, gender and language barriers, for finding and mining the humor that somehow survives the cataclysmic events behind the work, and for her innovative blending of theater arts, journalism and social sci-

WHAT DO I READ NEXT?

- *Fires in the Mirror: Crown Heights Brooklyn and Other Identities* (1992), like *Twilight: Los Angeles, 1992* is from Smith's *On the Road* series and employs the same technique. Its focus event is the rioting in the Crown Heights area of Brooklyn after the accidental killing of a black child by a Jewish rabbi. Text available as an Anchor Book from Doubleday.

- *The Hunger Wall*, is a collection of poems by James Ragan, inspired by the Los Angeles civil unrest of 1992 and the peaceful breakup of the former Czechoslovakia a month later (Grove Press, 1995).

- *Spell #7* (1979), a play by Ntozke Shange, offers a tremendous contrast to Smith's work in technique, although both writers are African American women interested in efforts to find an identity in a white-dominated culture.

- *Let Us Now Praise Famous Men* (1941), James Agee's photo-essay study of Georgia sharecroppers gives voice to the anonymous, unheard common man as Smith does in her *On the Road* series of plays.

- *Working* (1974) and *Coming of Age* (1995), two anthologies of oral histories compiled by Studs Terkel, the common man's historian, which rec-ord the voices of ordinary folk interviewed by the author. Smith acknowledges Terkel as one of her mentors; *Coming of Age* is available from The New Press; *Working* is available from Ballantine Books.

- "The Street Scene" (1938), Bertolt Brecht's brief essay on primitive "epic theater," which excludes the "engendering of illusion" that characterizes traditional theater. Critics have discussed Smith work in terms of Brecht's theories and practice.

- *I Am a Man* (1995), by OyamO (Charles Gordon), a play about the 1968 Memphis sanitation workers' strike, deals with the civil rights struggle from the perspective of the "unheard," common man to whom Smith also gives a voice. The focus is on T. O. Jones, a sort of Everyman who sets out to right social injustices.

- *The Coming Race War in America: A Wake-Up Call*, by syndicated columnist Carl T. Rowan, investigates the nation's "violent decline" and the lack of change for the vast majority of minority Americans since the civil rights upheaval of the 1960s (available from Little, Brown, 1996).

---

ences into that unique genre identified by scholars Sun and Fei.

Wisely, Smith does not depict herself as a character. She simply discards her real persona, the writer who spent countless hours interviewing her subjects. Furthermore, as Michael Feingold remarks, at some point early on in her performance, the actress, Anna Deavere Smith, paradoxically "disappears," leaving just "men, women, and children, talking in a torrent of diverse languages, living out their anger, their pain, their injuries and resentments and joys and fears." Each character speaks in a monologue, seldom, if ever, making reference to Smith or revealing the inquiry-response format of the interview process. She delivers their words "verbatim to an audience that often includes her 'characters' themselves," as Sun and Fei have noted. Her great skill in "acting otherness" has convinced even the most dubious members of her audience that she "can be as true as, or even truer than" those real persons she presents to the critical ear and eye.

In the final analysis, Smith does not really disappear during performance. She cannot and does not try to replicate her subjects through elaborate theatrical cloning. The audience is never invited to penetrate any sort of disguise, because, in truth, she never really dons one. Maskless through each of her portrayals, she maintains, however tenuously, her own identity, not as writer but as actress. Furthermore, it is her persistent presence as a *black* actress that provides a powerful counterpoint to her dramatic portrayals. This "simultaneous presence of performer and performed" is what Richard Schechner calls "doubling," a quality "that marks great performances." That is part of Smith's "shamanic invocation," a way of inviting the audience to "allow the other in, to feel what the other is feeling," a way of achieving an extraordinary degree of empathy.

Smith's play text does not, of course, consist of her own words. As she has indicated, in *Twilight* she has assembled a "document of what an *actress* heard in Los Angeles." In doing so, says Monica Cortes, she "shares the authority of authorship with the community that is the subject of her piece." Using the actual language of people who normally remain unheard, Smith gives them significant weight, shouldered by the "authority" of their shared authorship.

Yet, because she only recorded what others said, some have questioned her legitimacy as a playwright. Such reservations arise from a strict adherence to a single-author concept, what Iris Smith labels the "modernist notion of authorship." An alternate model, coming into its own of late, is what she calls "the theater collective," a method by which "play *writing* is intertwined with play *staging,* and often done by the same actors, directors and artists." Although Anna Smith acts in solo performance, she has worked extensively with dramaturges as collaborators, and has continued to deal with *Twilight* as a theatrical work in progress, not something forever restricted to the order or inclusiveness of a text which is at once both more and less the play. For critic Smith, Anna Smith qualifies as one of those "willing to risk losing control over the work, if the text can go out and do good work in the world."

Good work is surely the playwright's aim. She admits to a polemical purpose, to demonstrate that we "must reach across ethnic boundaries" to achieve some sympathetic understanding in the race dialogue she so fervently seeks. She also admits to being political, the inevitable legacy of her gender and race. "I am political without opening my mouth," she says; "my presence is political."

Therein may lie the rub. Smith has expressed an interest in having other actors perform her play, perhaps an ensemble of players. But one must wonder if other interpreters of the text could or would do justice to her purpose—the promotion of a new community dialogue. Sandra Loh, who maintains that Smith's cross-ethnic depictions involve an "ironic twist," argues that the actress-playwright could never get away with "impersonating" her array of sexually and racially mixed characters "if she were a white heterosexual male." Probably not, but more to the point, if the play were interpreted by a white actor, male or female, its meaning would certainly drift off Smith's intended course, thanks to unavoidable nuances that would result from the "doubling" effect of which Schechner writes.

One must also question whether anyone who has not dealt one-on-one with the real people of Smith's docudrama could, as Lauren Feldman remarks, "capture the characters with the same convincing compassion." One suspects that, at the least, Smith herself would have to coach the audacious actor who attempts to follow in her solo-performance footsteps. That possibility, like the community's memory of the events behind the play, is transitory. It also gives rise to Feldman's question: "will *Twilight* lose force with each additional degree of separation?" The answer is probably "yes," but it will not really matter if the race dialogue that Smith seeks is in authentic progress.

Source: John Fiero, in an essay for *Drama for Students,* Gale, 1997.

Robert Brustein

In the following review, noted drama critic Brustein examines Smith's work in Twilight: Los Angeles, 1992, *taking particular note of the multicultural issues that surrounded the Los Angeles riots.*

The most cogent commentators on our stormy times have unquestionably been not the columnists but the cartoonists, which is another way of noting that representational satire has more capacity than political commentary to relieve the pressures of a fractious age. On stage two inspired performers have recently been offering their own perspectives on the issues that divide us, and while the African American Anna Deavere Smith and the Jewish Jackie Mason seem worlds apart in tone, attitude, focus and ethnicity, they each provide more perspective on the nature of our discords than an army of op-ed pundits.

It is true that Smith might be more accurately described as a sociologist than as a satirist. Both in her previous *Fires in the Mirror,* which covered the Crown Heights affair, and in her current piece at the Joseph Papp Public Theater, *Twilight: Los Angeles, 1992,* which deals with the riots in South-Central L.A., she has drawn her material from interviews with the actual participants in those events. Still, Smith is not only an objective ear but a characterizing voice, and just as she shapes her text through editing and selection, so she achieves her emphasis through gesture and intonation. During the course of the evening the actress impersonates forty-six different people, capturing the essence of each character less through mimetic transformation, like an actor, than through the caricaturist's body English and vocal embellishments. Just look at her photographs: you'd never guess from any of those contorted head shots that she's an extremely handsome young woman.

Smith's subjects divide essentially into victims, victimizers and viewers, though it is sometimes difficult to determine which is which. If the former L.A. Police Chief Daryl Gates (defending himself against charges that he permitted the riots to rage while attending a fundraiser) and Sergeant Charles Duke (complaining that Officer Lawrence Powell was "weak and inefficient with the baton" because he wasn't allowed to use the "choke-hold") are clearly the patsies of the piece, the rioters, looters, gang members and assailants often appear more sinned against than sinning. A white juror in the first Rodney King trial—asked by a reporter, "Why are you hiding your heads in shame?"—is appalled to receive approving calls from the KKK. Keith Watson, one of those acquitted of beating Reginald Denny, justifies his rage and the burned-out vacant lots by saying "justice didn't work," while Paul Parker, chairperson of the Free the L.A. Four Defense Committee, charges "You kidnapped us, you raped our women...you expect us to feel something for the white boy?" One gringo-hating Latino, ranting against the "peckerwoods" and "rednecks" who have persecuted his family, expresses pleasure in the way Mexicans are able to terrify whites. Another Latino is encouraged by a policeman to "go for it, it's your neighborhood." A black woman "touring" in the white neighborhood loots I. Magnin because she finds it "very offensive" that rich stars should feel protected from rioting.

Then there are the other victims: the Asian shopkeepers who, in those tumultuous days, lost 90 percent of their stores and a number of their family members. At the same time that a spokesperson for a young black girl shot by a Korean shopkeeper (who was acquitted) is raging against Asians, Mrs. Young Soon Han, a former liquor store owner, speaks of her disenchantment with blacks. There were none in the Hollywood movies she saw in Korea; she thought this country was the best. Now "they" have destroyed the shops of innocent merchants simply because "we have a car and a house.... Where do I find justice? What about victims' rights?" Another store owner, inveighing against shoplifting and looting, remarks, "After that, I really hate this country, I really hate—we are not like customer and owner but more like *enemy.*"

"Enemy" and "hate" are the operative words of *Twilight.* With each ethnic group bristling at the other, one might think "cultural diversity" had become a euphemism for race war. A Mexican woman reporter, told her life is in danger, replies: "How could they think I was white?" The African American Parker boasts how "we burnt down the Koreans—they are like the Jews in this neighborhood." And this is countered not by appeals for tolerance but by counsels of caution, like those of Elaine Brown, former Black Panther, reminding the gun-brandishing, swash-buckling looters about America's willingness to use its power: "Ask Saddam Hussein."

To judge by the interviews in *Twilight,* however, the Los Angeles riots caused a lot of soul-searching, and considerable guilt, among some white Americans. The experience certainly stimulated considerable generosity from Denny, who, pleading for recognition as a person rather than a color, expresses profound gratitude to the black people who risked their lives to save him. By contrast, others, such as a reporter named Judith Tur, wonder why South-Central blacks can't be more like Magic Johnson or Arthur Ashe, adding that "white people are getting so angry, they're going back fifty years." A suburban real estate agent named Elaine Young, who has had thirty-six silicone surgeries on her face, whines that "we don't have the freeway, we can't eat anywhere, everything's closed," meanwhile defending her decision to hole up in the Beverly Hills Hotel.

These are easy targets; and it is true that *Twilight* sometimes lacks the dialectical thickness, as well as the surprise and unpredictability, of *Fires in the Mirror.* Lasting over two hours, it seems too long *and* too short for its subject. The L.A. riots were a response to violence and injustice by means of violence and injustice, and the paradox still to be explored is how looting and burning Korean stores and destroying your own neighborhood, not to mention racial assaults on innocent people, could become acceptable means of protest against inequity and racism. With most of them still in shock, few of Smith's respondents are in a position to examine the irrationality of such acts unless, like Shelby Coffey, they cite "a vast, even Shakespearean range of motives."

Smith makes some effort to penetrate these motives by ending her piece with a poetic reflection by a gang member on the "limbo" twilight of crack addicts, but the metaphor somehow seems inadequate. Still, if she has not always gone beyond the events of this tragedy, she has powerfully dramatized a world of almost universal tension and hatred. George C. Wolfe's elaborate production, with its videos of King's beating and films of Los Angeles burning, is probably more appropriate for the coming Broadway move than for the stage of the Public. But it leaves us with a shocking sense of how America's hopes for racial harmony were left burning in the ashes of South-Central L.A.

Source: Robert Brustein, "P.C.—or Not P.C." in the *New Republic,,* Vol. 210, no. 18, May 2, 1994, pp. 29–31.

Jan Stuart

Stuart praises Smith's writing and acting work in the following review, noting her skill with multiple and complex characters.

Toward the end of her heroic docu-theater event about the police beating of Rodney King and its violent aftermath, Anna Deavere Smith does something very, very clever.

Having impersonated dozens of participants in the 1992 Los Angeles maelstrom for some two hours, Smith steps into the shoes of Maria, a juror in the second Rodney King trial. We like Maria. She's theatrical, a spiky, pull-no-punches sort with a few choice words reserved for her fellow jurors. "Brain-dead," for starters.

One by one, Maria takes aim and caricatures each of her colleagues with their psychic pants down, constructing before our eyes a devastating archetype of group dynamics and the tortuous process by which strangers plow beyond their dissimilarities to get something done. Maria's impromptu

> *TWILIGHT* LEAVES US WITH A SHOCKING SENSE OF HOW AMERICA'S HOPES FOR RACIAL HARMONY WERE LEFT BURNING IN THE ASHES OF SOUTH-CENTRAL L.A."

performance is a panic—cathartically, bust-agut funny; as our laughter subsides, it may occur to us that the jury's breakthrough mirrors our own progress as we make our way through *Twilight: Los Angeles, 1992.*

The Maria monologue, indeed, is a microcosm, a summing-up of the experience of watching this challenging "one-person" show. Following the model of *Fires in the Mirror,* Smith's journalistic kaleidoscope of the Crown Heights riots, *Twilight: Los Angeles, 1992* distills dozens of interviews she conducted with players in recent events. African- and Asian-American, white, rich, poor, women, men, brain-dead and alive, the contrasting perspectives pile up before us, each of them so steadfastly believing in the correctness of their positions. Well before it's over, we begin to wonder how anything as implicitly harmonious as a verdict is possible in a multicultural soup such as the United States.

The soup thickens as Smith moves away from Crown Heights and into the L.A. of *Twilight,* whose ethnic and class tensions reflect the broader spectrum of American culture directly affected by the King beating. The racial cauldron of *Twilight* spills over into the shooting of a 15-year-old African-American girl by a Korean-American shopkeeper, as well as the riot attack on white truck driver Reginald Denny that followed the trial of the four officers charged with beating King.

Sliding deftly between interviewees with the suggestive turn of a sweater, Smith lines up her characters in a boldly ironic juxtaposition that recalls the inspired oral histories of Studs Terkel and the political documentaries of Marcel Ophuls. The back-to-back proximity of her subjects provokes two responses: At first we notice the seemingly unbridgeable divide from one monologue to the next; then we are struck by the unexpected bonds.

SMITH LINES UP HER CHARACTERS IN A BOLDLY IRONIC JUXTAPOSITION THAT RECALLS THE INSPIRED ORAL HISTORIES OF STUDS TERKEL AND THE POLITICAL DOCUMENTARIES OF MARCEL OPHULS"

Reginald Denny, sweet-tempered, forgiving, a bit out of it, seems a world away from Paul Parker, the shrewd, rage-driven head of the defense committee for Denny's attackers. As we listen more, we begin to see the synchronicity in their notions of justice; the urgency with which each of them argues their cases is thrilling.

The heightened complexity of Smith's L.A. terrain is matched by a newfound subtlety in her performance (in contrast to George C. Wolfe's booming, projection-happy staging) and a more ambitious use of transcripts. Where *Fires* hugged to a formulaic procession of individual arias, *Twilight* often splices as many as three witnesses into a seamless rush of testimony, working up a fierce, cinematic intensity.

If Smith occasionally tosses us a few sacrificial lambs for those with the guilty need to feel superior (a braying, facelifted real-estate agent who hides out at the Beverly Hills Hotel for the duration of the riots), she discourages the easy laugh and the foregone conclusion. Mostly, Smith gets us to listen. She validates, vigorously and humorously, the other side of the coin. She wants us to entertain the possibility of ambiguity.

By the time Maria launches into her tour-de-force vaudeville of a jury's A.A.-style confessional, we understand that we have already witnessed the same process. *Twilight: Los Angeles, 1992* is group therapy on a national scale based on the belief that we each have to dump our ugly personal baggage out on the table for all to see, before we can then get down to the difficult business of healing. Smith shows us how to do that with a breathtaking collage of real-life people who make us want to stand up and cheer, then sit back down and reflect.

Source: Jan Stuart, " *Twilight:* Group Therapy for a Nation" in *Newsday,* March 24, 1994.

FURTHER READING

Brustein, Robert. "P.C.—or Not P.C.," *The New Republic,* Vol. 210, no. 18, May 2, 1994, pp. 29-31.
　　A review of the Joseph Papp Public Theater production of *Twilight: Los Angeles, 1992* arguing that Smith might be better classified "as a sociologist than artist." Brustein divides her figures into "victims, victimizers and viewers."

Corso, P. J. "Anna Deavere Smith," AFROAM-L Archives, October 24, 1994. http://www.afrinet.net/~hallh/afrotalk/afrooct94/0546.html, February 16, 1997.
　　Corso relates Smith's method and matter to the work of Bertolt Brecht but argues that the commercial success of her work inhibits its value as a catalyst for social change.

Cortes, Monica Munoz. "The Works of Anna Deavere Smith: An Exploration of Otherness," *95 McNair Journal.* http://www.aad.berkeley.edu/95journal/MonicaCortes.html, January 15, 1997.
　　Relates performance theory based on theories of Sigmund Freud and Jacques Lacan to Smith's "theater of otherness."

Feingold, Michael. "Twilight's First Gleaming" in the *Village Voice,* Vol. 39, no. 14, April 5, 1994, pp. 97, 100.
　　A very favorable review of the *Twilight: Los Angeles, 1992* staged in New York in which Feingold praises Smith's "triple ability" as interviewer, writer, and actress.

Feldman, Lauren. "A Constellation of Character," *Perspective,* http://hcs.harvard.edu/~perspy/may96/twilight.html.
　　A review of *Twilight: Los Angeles, 1992* discussing the Smith's staging of the work and its evolution as the playwright's sense of race-relations have changed.

Fitzgerald, Sharon. "Anna of a Thousand Faces" in *American Visions,* Vol. 9, no. 5, October-November, 1994, pp. 14-18.
　　Discussing both *Twilight: Los Angeles, 1992* and *Fires in the Mirror,* article covers both Smith's onstage techniques and motives in her writing.

Gates, Henry Louis, Jr. "The Chitlin Circuit" in the *New Yorker,* Vol. 72, no. 45, February 3, 1997, pp. 44-55.
　　Gates discusses August Wilson's position on the need for a separatist black theater while chastising him for never having been a "Chitlin Circuit" playwright.

Kanfer, Stefan. "Twilight Tragedies" in the *New Leader,,* Vol. 77, no. 5, May 9, 1994, pp. 22-23.
　　A review that finds Smith's play flawed by its "illiberal agenda concealed by a mask of objectivity" and its "unwieldy" material.

Kroll, Jack. "Fire in the City of Angels" in *Newsweek,* Vol. 121, June 28, 1993, pp. 62-63.

A very favorable review of the Mark Taper Forum production of *Twilight: Los Angeles, 1992,* applauding Smith as "the most exciting individual in American theater right now."

Lewis, Barbara. "The Circle of Confusion: A Conversation with Anna Deavere Smith" in *Kenyon Review,* Vol. 54, no. 4, Winter, 1993, pp. 54-64.
Although this interview relates primarily to *Fires in the Mirror,* it gives insights to Smith's artistic aims and the influence of Ntozake Shange and George Wolfe on her work.

"Lives Altered Forever" in *Time,* Vol. 141, June 28, 1993, p. 73.
A review of the Mark Taper Forum production of Smith's play, finding the play "sprawling" in its coverage but flawed in its impression that blacks acted almost alone in the rioting and looting.

Martin, Carol. "Anna Deavere Smith: The Word Becomes You" in the *Drama Review,* Vol. 37, no. 4, Winter, 1993, pp. 45-62.
An interview conducted with Smith, focusing on *Fires in the Mirror,* but covering Smith's technique and purpose in her whole *On the Road* series.

Mason, Susan Vaneta, editor. "Theatre Review" in *Theatre Journal,* Vol. 46, 1994, pp. 111-18.
A collection of reviews of the Mark Taper Forum production of Smith's play, the article presents an array of opinions from performance artists, writers, and critics.

Mitchell, Sean. "The Tangle over *Twilight*" in *Los Angeles Times,* June 12, 1994, pp. 7, 48.
Mitchell addresses the controversy that arose over the classification of Smith's work as journalism or art.

Schechner, Richard. "Anna Deavere Smith: Acting as Incorporation" in the *Drama Review,* Vol. 37, no. 4, Winter, 1993, pp. 63-64.
Schechner describes Smith's method of creating and performing her work as a sort of "shamanism."

Smith, Anna Deavere. "Metaphor's Funeral" on the National Endowment for the Arts website, http://arts.endow.gov/Community/Features/Smith.html, January 15, 1997.
Given as a speech before a meeting of the National Council on the Arts, Smith claims to desire a "theatre that reclaims performance" and laments the fact that "conversation has collapsed."

Smith, Anna Deavere. "Not So Special Vehicles" in *Peforming Arts Journal,* Vol. 50/51, May-September, 1995, pp. 77-92.
Printed text of a keynote address delivered in 1993 at a meeting of the Association for Theatre in Higher Education, this speech discusses ethnocentric theater and the danger of "specialness" in the arts.

Smith, Iris. "Authors in America: Tony Kushner, Arthur Miller, and Anna Deavere Smith" in *Centennial Review,* Vol. 40, no. 1, Winter, 1996, pp. 125-42.
Smith discusses two "models" of theater authorship: the lone author, represented by Miller, and the "theater collective," as represented by Kushner and Smith.

Stuart, Jan. "*Twilight:* Group Therapy for a Nation" in *Newsday,* March 24, 1994.
Stuart reviews the Joseph Papp Public Theater staging of Smith's play, applauding Smith's skill in providing the audience "with a breathtaking collage of real-life people who make us want to stand up and cheer, then sit back down and reflect."

Sun, William H., and Faye C. Fei. "Masks or Face Re-Visited: A Study of Four Theatrical Works Concerning Cultural Identity" in *Drama Review,* Vol. 38, no. 4, Winter, 1994, pp. 120-32.
This article relates the mask to the problem of ethnic identities in plays and role interpretations. Although its focus is on the PBS, *American Playhouse* televised production of *Fires in the Mirror* (April 28, 1993), it argues that Smith's work has "silenced" the problems of "racial identity in race-specific plays."

Vognar, Chris. "Quite an Impression" in the *Daily Californian* website, http://www.dailycal.org/Issues/09.29.95/smith.txt, February 16, 1997.
A brief tribute to Smith's work, praising her achievement as performance-playwright and her ability to go beyond "mere language and into the realm of the personality and the soul."

Wald, Gayle. "Anna Deavere Smith's Voices at Twilight" in *Postmodern Culture,* Vol. 4, no. 2, January, 1994. Website at hhttp://jefferson.village.virginia.edu/pmc/issue.194/review-1.194.html, January 22, 1997.
A review of *Twilight: Los Angeles, 1992* as staged at the McCarter Theatre in Princeton, New Jersey, this piece offers an extensive description of Smith's performance technique.

Visit to a Small Planet

GORE VIDAL

1957

If a visitor from another galaxy happened to land on earth to observe the United States firsthand, what kind of impression would the country make on a complete stranger to the human race? This is the question posed in Gore Vidal's *Visit to a Small Planet,* a comedy subtitled as *A Comedy Akin to a Vaudeville.* Originally presented as a television play in 1957 (it had a New York City stage premiere in the same year), the satirical play follows the exploits of Kreton, an alien who lands on Earth, hoping to catch a glimpse of the American Civil War only to find that "something went wrong with the machine"; he has landed in the Manassas, Virginia, of the mid-twentieth century, outside of the Spelding family's home. Upon learning that it is not 1861, Kreton nevertheless decides to stay and observe human behavior: "You are my hobby," he tells the Speldings, "and I am going native."

Unlike film aliens such as E.T. or the creatures in *Close Encounters of the Third Kind,* Kreton is no lovable Martian. Arrogant, selfish, and patronizing, he is determined to make his stay memorable by starting a full-scale war between the United States and the Soviet Union (the setting being the days of the Cold War, when trust between the U.S. and U.S.S.R. was distinctly lacking). "I admit I'm leaping into this on the spur of the moment," he admits at the end of Act I, "but we're going to have such good times!"

Vidal's play pokes fun at the post-World War II fear of Communism and the ''Red-baiting'' (Senator Joseph McCarthy's house hearings on Un-American Activities) common in the late 1950s, as well as military paranoia and the rising importance of television in American life. Using Kreton as the satiric personification of America's ugly underbelly, Vidal's play employs a common science-fiction scenario to explore not alien but American life.

AUTHOR BIOGRAPHY

Describing himself as America's ''current biographer,'' Vidal's work has been widely applauded for its depth of satire and biting wit. Named Eugene Luther Vidal upon his birth—October 3, 1925— at the United States Military Academy in West Point, New York, Vidal grew up in an elite family, the son of an aeronautics instructor and the grandson of Oklahoma Senator Thomas P. Gore. As a child, he attended the Phillips Exeter Academy in New Hampshire and enlisted in the Army upon his graduation in 1943. World War II proved to be the inspiration for his first novel, *Williwaw* (1946), a critically well-received look at a military transport ship during the war. His next novel, *In a Yellow Wood* (1947), was similarly received; it was the publication of *The City and the Pillar* (1948), however, that gained him his first taste of notoriety (due to the novel's frank depiction of homosexuality). Although he was now a somewhat controversial figure, his next five novels were neither critical or financial bonanzas.

1964's *Julian,* however, helped Vidal gain new critical and popular success. The first of his many historical novels, *Julian* is the ''autobiography'' of the fourth-century Roman emperor who tried to abolish Christianity. Vidal's method of mingling historical fact and his own brand of wry fiction became one of his trademarks: other historical novels such as *Washington, D.C.* (1967); *Burr* (1973); *1876* (1976); *Lincoln* (1984); *Empire* (1987); and *Hollywood* (1990) feature this fact plus fiction approach to exploring and satirizing contemporary issues. His 1992 novel, *Live from Golgotha: The Gospel According to Gore Vidal,* imagines the effects of television coverage of Christ's crucifixion in order to satirize today's media and press. In addition, Gore has written numerous plays, screenplays (including an adaptation of Tennessee Williams' *Suddenly Last Summer*), twelve books of

Gore Vidal

essays (such as 1992's *Screening History*), and a series of mysteries under the pseudonym Edgar Box. He has also written a memoir, *Palimpsest,* which was published in 1995.

Vidal has always been interested in the connections between public and private life as well as the ways in which history is shaped by those whose motives seem (at best) questionable upon close examination. His outspoken manner and penetrating wit soon earned Vidal a status that goes beyond author. He is thought of as a social commentator, a celebrity as much as a writer. Although *Visit to a Small Planet* is not his most famous or critically favored work, it is representative of Vidal's wit and desire to satirize American political, sexual, and social life.

PLOT SUMMARY

Act I

Visit to a Small Planet opens with a view of television news commentator Roger Spelding's comfortably middle-class home near Manassas, Virginia. General Tom Powers, a friend of Roger's, is explaining to him that an Unidentified Flying Object (UFO) has, for the last twelve hours, been spotted hovering over the Spelding's home. When Roger dismisses the idea, Powers convinces him to look outside—which he does, seeing the craft. Roger, who was planning to announce to a television audience that UFOs do not exist, panics and asks Powers for permission to break the story. The general refuses, stating that this information is "classified."

Ellen, Roger's nineteen year-old daughter, then appears on the terrace with her boyfriend Conrad Mayberry, whom Roger dismisses as "the boy farmer." She and Conrad discuss their plans for the future; these plans are interrupted, however, when the UFO lands outside the house. The hatch opens and Kreton, the visitor from outer space, enters the room. He looks very human, sporting side-whiskers and the garb of an 1860s gentleman. Kreton asks the Speldings to take him to General Robert E. Lee. After some confusion, Kreton explains that he has been studying the inhabitants of Earth as a "hobby"; he hoped to see the Civil War Battle of Bull Run. He soon realizes, however, that he must have set the wrong coordinates for his time-traveling spacecraft. Invited by Roger (who hopes to interview him on his television show) to come inside, Kreton accepts, thrilled with the prospect of seeing "a real house."

General Powers returns with an aide and in Roger's study begins questioning Kreton. We learn that Kreton is not only from another planet but from another dimension, one where its inhabitants do not die and have the power to read minds—a power that Kreton demonstrates on the general. After being ordered by Powers to search Kreton's ship, the aide returns, explaining that the door has been shut and that there has been "some kind of invisible wall" constructed around it. When asked by Powers how he managed to create this force field, Kreton dryly responds, "I don't think I could ever explain it to you." Powers then announces that no one present is allowed to leave the house. The general presses his investigation of Kreton, speculating that he "has been sent here by another civilization for the express purpose of reconnoitering prior to invasion." Kreton denies that he has been "sent here" by anybody—but then explains that *he* intends to "take charge" of the entire world. When Powers attempts to arrest him, Kreton surrounds himself with another invisible force-field. The curtain closes as the audience hears all of the characters' thoughts and Kreton saying, "Tomorrow will be a wonderful day for all of us. Sleep tight!"

Act II, Scene 1

The next morning Kreton is found in the living room examining a globe and talking to Rosemary, the Speldings' cat, whose thoughts he can also read and understand. Roger has left for Washington with General Powers, Reba (Roger's wife) has received permission to go shopping and Conrad is still asleep upstairs. Ellen brings Kreton his breakfast, which he refuses because he never eats. He also tells Ellen that the inhabitants of his world have given up reproducing, since they never die. Finally, he explains that after they "wiped out" diseases such as scarlet fever, mumps, and the common cold, the inhabitants of his planet rid themselves of "the ultimate disease:" passion. As a result, Kreton explains "We feel nothing. We do nothing. We are perfect." Ellen learns that this lack of passion or any strong emotion is what initially led Kreton to travel to earth and escape his dull commander, Delton 4.

Ellen and Kreton grow friendlier, and Ellen convinces the alien to give her a lesson in the mind-tricks that he has been using throughout the play. Eventually, she is able to levitate a vase over the fireplace mantle for a few seconds, much to the surprise of Conrad, who watches in awe. Kreton next begins thinking about how he will take over the planet, deciding against "drying up one of the smaller oceans" or "monkeying around with the moon" in favor of a more subtle trick. At that moment, the audience sees the aide (who is stationed on the porch) watch in disbelief as his rifle leaps from his hands into the air. Kreton explains that he has just made *all* of the rifles in the world levitate for fifteen seconds.

General Powers returns and tells Kreton that he has been recently "classified as a weapon" and that the United States government expects him to furnish "a comprehensive list" of his "various mental powers." Roger enters with the alarming news that "at eleven twenty-six this morning every rifle in the Free World was raised fifteen feet in the air and the lowered again." Never considering the possibility that this was one of Kreton's tricks, Roger concludes, "It's the Russians, obviously." Kreton then explains the real purpose of his latest trick to the cat: "Well, I do believe I have started a war. . . . After all, that's what I came down here to see!"

Act II, Scene 2

Roger delivers a newscast from his study, interviewing General Powers, who tells the viewing

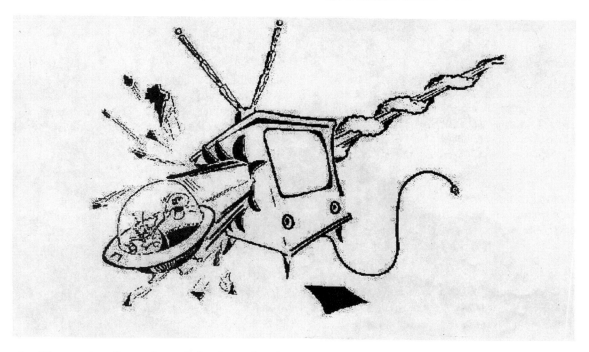

An illustration from the original production

audience that "it doesn't look good." Upstairs, Kreton enjoys his first bath while Roger informs Conrad—an avowed pacifist who hates all forms of war—that he should enlist in the Army. Conrad refuses and asks Ellen to marry him, but she refuses on the grounds that Conrad lacks "drive." Kreton comes downstairs, wearing full Confederate Army garb, and begins testing Conrad's pacifism by singing a series of patriotic songs. Conrad remains unmoved. As a last resort to incite Conrad's "primitive" urge to fight, Kreton broadcasts the mind of Powers's aide as he looks at Ellen; when Conrad hears these thoughts that refer to Ellen as "the babe with the crazy build," he attacks the aide and Kreton watches the fistfight, delighted. Ellen is also impressed and agrees to marry Conrad because of this display of love. As the young lovers exit, Powers enters and is told by Kreton that he has (again using the powers of his mind) "arranged a sneak attack" of United States bombers on Russia. In exactly forty-seven minutes, the world will reach "zero hour."

Act III

It is a half-hour later, and Kreton has transformed the Speldings' living room into a command center, using toy planes and soldiers to simulate the upcoming destruction. Powers reports that the Russian military is "completely mobilized" and enjoys a last drink with Kreton. Conrad and Ellen beg Kreton to stop the upcoming war, but Kreton explains that "war is not only fun," but "creative," since so many of humanity's great inventions were made during wartime. Ellen then tricks Kreton into telling her how he would contact his leader, Delton 4, if he so needed; Kreton's answer, "concentration," inspires her to attempt a "mind-trick" similar to the one she performed in Act II. As the cast rushes about the stage, Ellen sits on the sofa repeating, "Delton 4 . . . Delton 4 . . . Delton 4," until Kreton's leader arrives in answer to this call. Dressed in a suave morning suit, Delton 4 thanks Ellen for the warning and explains that Kreton "is a rarity" among those of his planet, for "he is morally retarded and, like a child, regards this world as his plaything." He also tells the cast that Kreton had "escaped from his nursery" and that he will take him back home. Kreton says goodbye, remarking that he actually envies earthlings for "being so violent . . . so loving . . . so beautifully imperfect" and "so much happier" than they realize. Once the aliens leave, time shifts back to the exact moment before Kreton arrived, leaving the characters with no memory whatsoever of the events that have just taken place.

CHARACTERS

Delton 4

A leader of Kreton's unidentified home planet, Delton 4 is an alien who enters the play at the end, after he is summoned by Ellen Spelding. He explains that Kreton is "morally retarded" and "was able to escape from his nursery." He apologizes for Kreton's actions and takes him home.

Kreton (kree-tahn)

Arriving on Earth from a distant planet in another dimension, Kreton is the "visitor" alluded to in the play's title. Like others who inhabit his home planet, Kreton never needs to eat, is immortal, and never has sex—immortality has negated the need for reproduction, and their culture has eliminated passion (sex for pleasure) as a societal evil. Through the powers of his mind, he is able to read the thoughts of others, create invisible force-fields, and cause objects to levitate. Kreton arrives hoping to witness a Civil War battle, but because of a navigational error, he lands in 1957. He invades the home of Roger Spelding and shows a great interest in the day-to-day lives of earthlings, calling them his "hobby." In order to create some excitement for himself, Kreton plays a prank that, he is sure, will cause a worldwide nuclear war. He sees the earth as a playground and hopes that a war will allow him to see the ways that "primitive" humans behave. As a character, he is a curious mix of super intellectual and wide-eyed child.

Conrad Maybery

Ellen's boyfriend, Conrad, is a mild-mannered young farmer. A pacifist (who resents all forms of war), Conrad contrasts the political views of both Roger Spelding and General Powers. One of the play's comic scenes features Kreton attempting to provoke feelings of agression within Conrad—which he eventually does, with a soldier whose thoughts about Ellen are broadcast by Kreton. Vidal uses Conrad to lampoon those who conveniently use pacifism as an excuse for their lack of direction and laziness.

General Tom Powers

General Powers is the Army commander assigned to investigate the spacecraft seen hovering over the Speldings' home. Complaining that he doesn't want this assignment and would rather return to his "Laundry Project" (where he oversees the washing and drying of the military's uniforms), Powers suspects that Kreton may be a "hostile alien" who has been sent by a "foreign power" to begin an invasion of the United States. His character is frequently used by Vidal to poke fun at paranoid military attitudes, officious bureaucrats, and the prevalent fear of Communism found in 1950s America.

Ellen Spelding

Ellen is Roger's daughter, a bored college student who wishes for the opportunity to do "something important" like "save the world." She convinces Kreton to teach her how to perform some of the "tricks" with her mind that he can do, and she eventually uses these skills to contact Kreton's superior, Delton 4, and halt the war that Kreton has planned. She also focuses her romantic attentions on Conrad, a local farmer of whom her father disapproves. Ellen is the embodiment of youthful optimism and idealism. She is the only character that Vidal abstains from making look foolish.

Reba Spelding

Reba is Roger's wife and Ellen's mother. Her biggest concern in the play is that fact that Kreton's spacecraft has landed in her rose garden. In Reba, Vidal is making fun of the 1950s ideal of the perfect housewife, a domestic-minded woman obsessed with presenting the perfect image embodied by everything from her delicious apple pie to her beautiful, well-behaved children.

Roger Spelding

A news commentator who believes that UFOs do not exist, Roger's opinions are immediately reversed when his home is visited by an alien from another dimension. He is constantly thinking about the possible ratings his television show will receive when he "breaks" the story of Kreton's visit. When not thinking about his own potential fame, Roger is found scolding Ellen, his daughter, for her choice of a boyfriend. Roger represents the growing role that television has in American society. Already by the 1950s, television had become an important source of information, bestowing considerable status and power on those who controlled it. This explains Roger's eagerness to interview Kreton; his first instinct is not to protect his family from possible harm but to secure the television rights to the alien visitation.

THEMES

Politics

The plot of *Visit to a Small Planet* concerns Kreton, an alien visitor, who invades a middle-class home in 1957 America. After he announces his plans to engage the world in a full-scale war for his own entertainment, the characters respond to this threat in ways that reveal their political ideas and ideals. Kreton has used his powers of mind to levitate all of the rifles in the world for fifteen seconds and both General Powers and Roger Spelding assume the Russian Army is behind the stunt. Roger explains to his television audience that the Russians have "launched a new anti-gravity force which suspended all the rifles in the free world some fifty feet off the ground." He continues by stating, "late this afternoon . . . Moscow, in an obvious move to avert suspicion, accused the United States of lifting all the rifles in the Communist world one hundred seven feet off the ground." Later, Powers asks Kreton if the United States can officially announce his arrival, for they would like him (and themselves) to "get the best possible break, publicity-wise." These are only some of the ways in which Vidal mocks the United States/Soviet rivalry as well as the then-prevalent American fear of Communism.

Earlier examples of political paranoia occur when Kreton is interviewed by Powers. He tells the alien, "you'll die if it turns out you're a spy or a hostile alien or something like that" and that he suspects Kreton to be "sent here by an alien race to study us, preparatory to invasion." Kreton, however, is above such trivial concerns as land acquisition, and his cool indifference to Powers exacerbates the General's rage. Later, Powers informs Kreton that he has been "classified as a weapon" and that the Pentagon expects a detailed list of his "powers." *Visit to a Small Planet* satirizes politics, revealing the insincerety of its highest ranking officials. Vidal presents politics as little more than a forum for ego-satisfaction and personal gain. Ultimately, Vidal's play invites viewers to notice the fear and suspicion that play such a large role in modern politics while also highlighting what he seems to see as a contradiction in the phrase, "military intelligence."

Patriotism

Closely connected to Vidal's political issues is his examination of patriotism. While author Samuel Johnson once defined patriotism as "the last refuge of a scoundrel," *Visit to a Small Planet* shows how different people define "love of one's country."

MEDIA ADAPTATIONS

- *Visit to a Small Planet* was adapted as a film by Edmund Beloin and Henry Garson, with Jerry Lewis as Kreton. Released by Paramount in 1960. Available on video.

When he first suspects Kreton of being the representative of a foreign country, General Powers attempts to display his patriotism by telling him, "if your people are thinking of an invasion they should know that we're ready for them. We'll fight them with everything we've got. We'll fight them with the hydrogen bomb, with poison gas, with broken beer bottles if necessary. We'll fight them on the beaches; we'll fight them in the alleys." Powers equates "patriotism" with military might and assumes that his definition of the term—and his fervid devotion to American—will intimidate Kreton.

After Kreton's threat of war becomes more of a possibility, Roger tells Conrad that he should enlist in the Army; Conrad, however, refuses because he "doesn't want to fight anybody." His pacifism directly opposes General Powers's display of "rough and ready" American spirit. This shocks Kreton, who asks, "Do you love your country?" When Conrad says that he does, Kreton's response shows his own understanding of American patriotism: "Then don't you want to slaughter its enemies?" After Conrad shakes his head, Kreton states, "that's the wrong answer. That is not a proper mid-twentieth century sentiment." Vidal is using Kreton as a way to illustrate Conrad's pacifism and suggest that not *all* patriots and "good Americans" equate "loving one's country" with a desire to "slaughter its enemies." Kreton begins singing old military songs in order to stir patriotic emotions within Conrad; when these fail, he begins evoking names from popular legend and entertainment: "Davy Crockett stood by his guns! Remember the Alamo! Remember the Maine! Remember Errol Flynn on the Burma Road!" However, none of these have any effect. Conrad's attitude towards war is meant

TOPICS FOR FURTHER STUDY

- Vidal's subtitle for the play is *A Comedy Akin to a Vaudeville*. Locate sources that describe what vaudeville theater was like and explain how the play resembles this faded American theatrical form.

- Research the McCarthy trials and the impact they had on American life. Compare and contrast your findings with the way that Vidal presents the fear of Communism in his play.

- The nuclear war that Kreton almost causes can be compared to the Cuban Missile Crisis of 1962, a nuclear standoff between the U.S. and the Soviet Union. Research this topic and compare the role that then President John F. Kennedy played in averting this disaster.

- Research the history of American television and explain what major changes in broadcasting took place in the 1950s.

---

to be seen as a more reasonable form of patriotism than that offered by General Powers. Kreton's inability to understand Conrad's ideas shows the alien's simplistic view of what patriotism entails.

Sex

A subplot of the play involves Conrad and Ellen's love affair. When the play begins, they are planning to check into a hotel under the names "Mr. and Mrs. Ollinger"; they have even filled a suitcase with old telephone books and plan on telling Roger that they are "going to the movies." Their furtive sexual scheming is mocked by Kreton, who tells them that, on his planet, sex does not exist, since they have rid themselves of all forms of passion. Throughout the play, Vidal explores American attitudes toward sex by having Kreton attempt to discover why Americans make such a fuss over it. When he asks Ellen if he can watch (for scientific purposes) her "tangle" with another man and is informed by her that his request is "disgusting," the mind-reading alien responds, "but . . . but it's

on your minds so much I simply assumed it was all quite public." Ellen explains that, in America, "we do *think* an awful lot about sex, but we're not supposed to talk about it and we only do it when nobody's looking." This attitude toward even the mention of sex is questioned by both Vidal and Kreton, who remarks, "these primitive taboos. You revel in public slaughter, you pay to watch two men hit each other repeatedly, yet you make love secretly, guiltily and with remorse." This conversation is one in which the audience is invited to question what Vidal sees as a contemporary contradiction: talking about violence is perfectly acceptable and decent, while sex is a forbidden topic and is reduced to a "primitive taboo."

STYLE

Satire

"Satire" is any work of art that uses ridicule, humor, and wit in order to criticize and provoke change in human nature or social institutions; satire can be found anywhere from Shakespeare (*Measure for Measure*) to an editorial newspaper cartoon. Vidal is widely known as a satirical writer, and *Visit to a Small Planet* is a work that strengthens such a reputation: when Kreton, an alien visitor, invades a middle-class Virginia home, the characters react to him in ways that showcase their fears and frustrations with their own lives. The play examines (and pokes fun at) contemporary ideas about war, the fear of "foreign" invasion, and attitudes toward sex. Vidal ridicules military bureaucracy and paranoia through General Powers, the influence of television on American life with Roger Spelding, and, in general, the irrational, "primitive" impulses that often govern our lives. Through the eyes of Kreton, an alien with little understanding of American life, Vidal is able to offer his viewers an "objective look" at our society and attitudes—as well as a commentary on how odd (or even silly) these ideas and attitudes may be.

Setting

Rather than offer his audience a play about aliens that occurs on another planet, Vidal offers his viewers a look at how *we* would seem "alien" to an extraterrestrial visitor. To accomplish this, Vidal sets his play in a modest, middle-class home, allowing Kreton, the alien, to see a "typical" American family whose concerns are television, college, sex, marriage, and patriotism. Doing so emphasizes how odd many Americans would seem to a "visitor" unaccustomed to our quirks, values, and everyday way of life.

Stereotype

One of Vidal's most prominent satirical targets here is the United States military (and in a larger sense, that American government) and the way that it approaches any form of alien (or foreign) life. In drama, a "stereotype" character is an exaggeration of a certain type of person, such as the lovelorn poet, the disaffected teenager, or the dorky nerd with tape holding his glasses together. General Powers is a stereotype of the American military commander, and Vidal forms this stereotype with a variety of traits. For example, the play begins with him complaining to Roger Spelding that he has been assigned to investigate the appearance of Kreton's spaceship: "Strat-Air tosses it to Major General Spotty McClelland (he's Com Air Int now) who lobs it straight at me so by the time I get back from luncheon I find I've been TD'd C.O.S. Priority 1-A the hell and bloody UFO deal dumped right in my lap." The General's use of so many acronyms and jargon-laden speech parodies the language employed by the military. Adding to this stereotype is the General's complete fear and suspicion of anyone foreign. At first suspecting Kreton of being "a spy sent here by an alien race," the General eventually accepts the fact that Kreton is from another planet, but not before he tells him that the Pentagon has "classified him as a weapon" because he can create force fields that will "put radar out of business." The General's inability to see Kreton as anything except a possible weapon to be used against enemies of the United States marks him as a stereotype of one-track military minds.

To a certain extent the other characters, with the exception of Ellen, represent stereotypes as well. Roger is a typical broadcaster, more interested in the next "big story" that will elevate his status than he is with the welfare of his family. Likewise, his wife, Reba, is more concerned with the family's outward appearance and how others in the neighborhood will perceive them (her worries that Kreton may have trampled her garden when he landed) than any real threat to their lives. Reba is a stereotype of the unrealistic 1950s housewife ideal—like June Cleaver on the *Leave It to Beaver* television series—a woman who cooks, cleans, and gardens, yet still looks fresh as a daisy twenty-four hours a day. While Vidal sympathizes more with his views than the other characters, Conrad is still the butt of many jokes about unmotivated young men who half-heartedly fly the flag of pacifism.

Black Humor

"Black humor" refers to comedy created by means not usually regarded as proper subjects for laughter. For example, although *Visit to a Small Planet* is a comedy, the plot concerns an impending nuclear war and the destruction of the entire world for one person's amusement. Although this seems like an odd subject for a series of jokes, Vidal uses the characters' reactions to this event to satirize modern attitudes towards warfare and violence. Vidal's play seems to suggest that any objective visitor to our nation would find many of our ideas and actions ludicrous and, therefore, funny. By using a "typical American family," Vidal also turns the mirror to the audience, letting them see how ridiculous they might act in a similar situation.

HISTORICAL CONTEXT

McCarthyism and American Life

The mid-1950s marked the height of Americas' "Red Scare"—a widespread fear of Communism that reached its peak in the investigations of the House Un-American Activities hearings, led by Senator Joseph McCarthy (a Republican from Wisconsin). In 1950, McCarthy advised President Harry Truman that the State Department was staffed with many Communists and Communist sympathizers. In addition, he suspected that a great number of Communists were working in fields that might influence public opinion, including the film and television industries. In the following years, McCarthy performed what was often called a "witch hunt" to prove the degree to which he felt Communists had infiltrated levels of American society. His hearings grew into popular, televised events where he and others would "Red-Bait" the accused; many entertainers and writers found themselves "blacklisted" (refused employment) either for their often inconsequential Communist affiliations or for refusing to cooperate with what they saw as McCarthy's unconstitutional methods. Events such as the Soviet Union's 1956 invasion of Hungary served to fan McCarthy's fire. McCarthy died in 1957 but not before receiving the formal censure of the United States Senate for his hearings on alleged subversion in the U.S. Army.

COMPARE
&
CONTRAST

- **1950s:** American fear of Communism increases, spurred by the U.S.S.R.'s signing of a 30-year pact with Communist China (in 1950), North Korea's invasion of South Korea (1950), the passing of the McCarran Act which calls for severe restrictions against allowing Communists into the United States or of immigrants who have belonged to totalitarian organizations (1950), and the mid-decade McCarthy hearings that attempt to uncover Communist infiltration in all levels of American society.

  Today: Communism has ceased to be viable world power. The former Soviet Communist empire is now broken into smaller nations, each with its own form of government. The Communist-controlled state of East Germany faded with the reunification of East and West Germany and the fall of the Berlin Wall. China remains the only large country to still employ Communist principles.

- **1950s:** Nuclear power rises as both a global and national concern; the United States tests the Hydrogen bomb in 1952 and electric power is first created by atomic means in 1955.

  Today: Although the threat of nuclear devastation has been somewhat allayed by the breakdown of the Soviet Union, many politicians and leaders still call for increased disarmament. Nuclear power has become more a part of American life, despite a horrible 1979 scare at Three Mile Island, Pennsylvania and, in 1986, the world's worst nuclear accident at the Chernobyl Power Station (in the Soviet Union), where 133,000 are evacuated and clouds of fallout affect all Europe.

- **1950s:** Science-fiction becomes a popular (although somewhat critically dismissed) art form: initially sparked by Orson Welles's 1938 radio production of H. G. Wells *The War of the Worlds,* which caused considerable panic, American interest in extraterrestrial life is found in Ray Bradbury's successful collection of stories, *The Martian Chronicles.*

  Today: Science-fiction is an established genre for many writers and filmmakers: novelists such as the late Robert A. Heinlein and Arthur C. Clarke are popular favorites; films such as *E.T., the Extra-Terrestrial* (1982) and the re-release of the *Star Wars* trilogy break box-office records; *The X-Files,* a television show about FBI agents investigating alien and other unexplained activity on earth, becomes a highly-rated and critically-successful series (ironically, the show plays upon paranoia and suspicion of government conspiracy—elements prevalent in the red-baiting 1950s).

- **1950s:** Television becomes a major force in American political and social life: in 1955, there are 33.5 million television sets in American homes. In 1957, NBC presents the first video-taped national broadcast: the Eisenhower/Nixon inauguration.

  Today: By 1995, there are 95.9 million television sets in American homes; cable TV and satellite dishes are offering greater services, choice of programming and access to worldwide news. The American public has become more and more demanding about the immediacy of their information. Live events such as the O. J. Simpson murder trial are watched by millions worldwide.

Like Arthur Miller's *The Crucible* (1953), *Visit to a Small Planet* attacks (although in a more comic vein) this prominent fear of Communism. On his newscast announcing the impending war with the Soviet Union, Roger Spelding warns, "[Soviet Premier] Nikita Krushchev and his gang" that "Mother-and-Father-America are ready." General Powers suspects Kreton of being an "alien spy" sent to the United States to "reconnoiter preparatory to invasion"; his fear of Kreton's origins is a metaphorical look at the red-baiting occurring in the McCarthy hearings. The characters' overall paranoia provoked by Kreton's visit reflects the prominent fear of Communist invasion found in 1950s America, described by Kreton as "the wonderfully primitive assumption that all strangers are hostile."

Nuclear Weapons and Warfare

While nuclear power is now a part of contemporary American life, such was not always the case. Electric power was first produced from atomic energy in Idaho in 1951 and the first United States hydrogen bomb was exploded, at Edniwetok Atoll in the Pacific, in 1952. At this point, nuclear power was something strange and frightening to many Americans; however, atomically generated power was first used in the United States (in Schenectady, New York) in 1955. A growing concern over what nations possessed the knowledge and resources necessary for creating "the bomb" became a routine topic for newscasters, writers, and citizens. Underground "bomb shelters" were also being sold to American homeowners who wanted to avoid the dangers of a possible atomic attack.

Visit to a Small Planet reflects the growing American concern over the possibly of nuclear war. When Kreton's initial attempt at triggering a global war succeeds, General Powers warns him that the Russians "got the bomb, too," to which Kreton replies, "Oh, I hope so!" His attitude toward atomic warfare as "exciting" and a cause for delight contrasts the terror of such an event taking place in the 1950s. Even more indicative of this fear is the way that Kreton begins the war: by causing every rifle in the world to levitate for a few seconds, Kreton plays a prank that causes the two major world powers to prepare for war. The idea of a war being started over such a "minor" event reflects the popular idea of "the button," which would, in the imagination of many Americans, be pressed by a mad foreign leader for an insignificant reason. The fear being that the fate of millions lies in the hands of one or two men's hands.

CRITICAL OVERVIEW

Visit to a Small Planet was originally written as a television script; its success in this medium convinced Vidal that it could be reworked for the stage. The play premiered on Broadway in 1957 to critical and commercial success. Brooks Atkinson, writing for the *New York Times,* wrote that, "as a writer of comedy, Gore Vidal is foolish and funny." Atkinson called the play "uproarious." He also noted the fact that, although Vidal had to make his television script longer for the stage, "the padding does not show," for Vidal "makes us look ridiculous in a low comedy carnival that has its own insane logic and never runs out of ideas." Atkinson concluded his review by remarking that *Visit to a Small Planet* is "a topsy-turvy lark that has a lot of humorous vitality. The tone is low; the entertainment highly enjoyable."

After its New York success, the play was made into a film starring Jerry Lewis as Kreton, the alien visitor. However, acclaim for the film was not sung as loudly as before. Writing for the *New York Times,* Howard Thompson stated that while he viewed the play as "fairly contrived stuff, cleverly turned on one obvious, running gag," the film version falls below the play for several reasons. The first is Lewis himself, who offers only "business as usual, the Lewis way." Complaining that Lewis lacked the talent to fill Kreton's role, Thompson writes that, "Mr. Vidal's brightest idea of all—that the visitor is a highly civilized bird, curious about us bumbling earthlings—is cut right down to Lewis size." A second reason for the film's failure is that General Powers, "the target of the playwright's devastating cracks about Pentagon static," has been removed entirely from the film.

The film's lack of success, however, did not hurt Vidal's reputation (the fact that he did not write the screenplay also helped him escape critical censure). In fact, praise of his wit has been something to which the versatile writer has grown accustomed throughout his career. Called "a scathing critic of every aspect of American life," (according to *Magill's Survey of American Literature*) and a writer whose work is described in *The Cambridge Handbook of American Literature* as both "tart" and "penetrating," Vidal has enjoyed a great amount of success and time in the literary spotlight. He is routinely praised for his "outspokenness in satirizing social mores and institutions," whether this satire arises in his plays, novels or essays. While not categorized as a major American playwright, Vidal is certainly regarded as a major American literary figure who, for forty years, has produced a body of work that is noted for its sheer volume, breadth of topics and genres it covers, and the lively critical discussions that it has engendered. While *Visit to a Small Planet* never received the acclaim or amount of criticism that his historical novels or essays on

American history have, it nonetheless stands as a representative example of Vidal's satirical mind and desire to uncover the attitudes and assumptions of Americans.

CRITICISM

Daniel Moran

Moran is an author and educator. His essay discusses Vidal's facility with satire.

Gore Vidal once labeled himself America's "current biographer," and *Visit to a Small Planet* can certainly be read and enjoyed as a satirical chapter in the political and cultural biography of the United States. Satire creates its effects by mocking human behaviors and assumptions in an effort to raise a reader or viewer's awareness of what the satirist sees as their foolishness. The satire of this play hits many "targets," such as American attitudes toward sex, military incompetence, bureaucracy, and paranoia. It also pokes fun at the fear of "Communist infiltration" and slogan-spouting patriotism. By using an alien visitor, Vidal is able to provide a "fresh look" at what he sees as modern American issues that deserve our examination. The play's humor derives largely from its suggestion that any such objective look at Americans would reveal them to be very silly people, "absolutely" as Kreton, the alien, observes, "wallowing in the twentieth century."

The play's opening scene immediately establishes its satirical tone. General Powers is complaining about his position to Roger Spelding, and his fear that other military staff members "mean to destroy" his career: he speaks of Lieutenant General Claypoole's assigning him the investigation of a possible UFO because it is "too hot" for him to handle. He sees himself as "the innocent victim of conspiracy and intrigue" because "Claypoole has been trying to get [his] corner office with the three windows and the big waiting room." Powers would rather spend his time on what he sees as the Army's more "important" work—the new "Powers Mobile Laundry Unit-K" project. *This* is Powers's chief concern, and the earnestness with which he describes it reveals the Army's love of bureaucracy and emphasis on seemingly unimportant matters: "Lot of big decisions to make in that area: kind of soap to use, things like that. Decided finally on

snow-chip flakes. Fine lather. Good detergent. Doesn't harm the fabric *and* has bluing already built in." The silliness of Powers's concerns are heightened when, fearing that the United States will go to war with the U.S.S.R., he states, "if there's one thing that destroys an army's morale and discipline, it is a major war" because the soldiers "lose more damned sheets and pillowcases." To General Powers, no fate is worse than discovering that "your laundry's a wreck"; to the audience, his "militarization" of the laundry is seen as a satirical jab at the concerns of military leaders.

A second theme raised in the opening conversation is the value that we inhabitants of this "small planet" place on television and the publicity it can create. When he hears of Powers's investigation, Roger (a newscaster) begs him for permission to "break the story," which Powers refuses due to the "Revised Espionage Act." However, Roger is not the only character concerned with his public image. Later in the play, Powers tells Kreton that the United States would like to "announce [his] arrival ourselves" in order to "get the best possible break, publicity-wise." Roger, too, tells Kreton that he "would certainly like to interview" him on television while he's "down here"; his news ratings are more important to him than the fact that his own home has become the site for an extra-terrestrial visitation—or that this visitor wants to watch humankind destroy itself. The most obvious mockery of the way that television operates is when Roger begins his broadcast—in which he plans to announce the impending war between the world's two superpowers—with "Mother-and-Father America, have you had your milk today? Pour yourself a glass of Cloverdale, the milkier milk" and then segues into the topic at hand with, "and what sort of a day has it been? Well, it's been quite a day. Not since those dark hours before Munich has the free world been so close to the precipice of total war." The banality with which Roger speaks of possible atomic destruction is an exaggeration of the way in which modern newscasters speak of two completely different topics (such as milk and nuclear war) in the same breath and with the same gravity ("A fire killed several hundred people today . . . and here are tonight's winning lottery numbers!"). After interviewing Powers (who chuckles and admits that "it doesn't look good"), Roger concludes his broadcast as he began it: after describing the upcoming war as a test of "the morale of a free people," he smoothly asks, "Mother-and-Father-America, have you had your milk today?" Clearly,

WHAT DO I READ NEXT?

- Arthur Miller's 1953 play *The Crucible* presents the chaos of a Salem witch trial as a way to explore the effects of McCarthyism on the lives of Americans.

- Eugene Burdick and Harvey Wheeler's suspense novel, *Fail-Safe*, was an incredible success when published, largely because of its theoretical look at what would happen if an accident caused six American atomic bombers to attack the U.S.S.R. without the chance of being recalled.

- *Julian* is Vidal's 1965 novel that made him a celebrity. This is the first of his historical fiction works; in it, readers follow the exploits of the fourth-century Roman Emperor who tried to abolish Christianity.

- Vidal's *Washington D.C.* (1967) is a historical novel that spans the eras of the New Deal and McCarthyism.

- *The Best Man: A Play of Politics* is Vidal's 1960 play (revised in 1977) that looks at a campaign race for political office and those affected by it.

- *Live from Golgotha,* Vidal's 1992 satire of the television industry in which he imagines modern "coverage" of Christ's crucifixion.

- Rita Kleinfelder's *When We Were Young: A Baby Boomer Yearbook* (1993) contains interesting information about the political, social, and cultural lives of mid-twentieth-century Americans.

- Jeff Kisseloff's *The Box: An Oral History of Television* (1995) presents the history of the medium in a conversational, easy-to-follow format.

- *Breakfast of Champions,* Kurt Vonnegut's 1973 novel, offers (like *Visit to a Small Planet*) a top-down satirical look at American politics, government, and sexual mores.

no disaster can supersede or displace the truly powerful force of American advertising.

Despite these jokes and jabs, it is Kreton, the visitor, who supplies most of the play's satirical attacks. Dressed in the outfit of an 1860s gentleman, he enters the play hoping to witness the Civil War's Battle of Bull Run but instead sees something more amazing: an everyday American family. Explaining that, in terms of his own planet's evolution, civilization on earth is "just beginning," Kreton decides to "go native" and study the "primitive" earthlings. His first observation is one that highlights the pettiness that makes up so much human interaction: "I expected to hear everybody talking about great events: battles, poets, that kind of thing, but of course you don't. You just squabble among yourselves." More "squabbling" ensues when Kreton attempts to learn about sex: when he is told by Ellen that his scientific interest in seeing her make love to Conrad is "disgusting," the mind-reading alien responds, "oh? But . . . but it's on your minds so much I simply assumed it was all quite public." Ellen explains that earthlings are very private about their sexuality and Kreton's response, "you pay to watch two men hit one another repeatedly, yet you make love secretly, guiltily and with remorse," illustrates the apparent contradiction in American morality: violence is a perfectly acceptable topic (and even a form of entertainment) but sexuality (and the act of human creation) is a "primitive taboo." Like General Powers's emphasis on the Laundry project, Vidal is again highlighting what he sees as an odd distribution of values.

The values of Conrad, Ellen's boyfriend and a confirmed pacifist, are also placed under scrutiny. One of Vidal's "set-pieces" in the play is Kreton's attempt to evoke Conrad's "primitive" side through the mention of patriotic slogans and the singing of patriotic songs; he believes that "all primitives can be lashed to fever-pitch by selected major chords" and that even a "peace-loving man who grows English walnuts" can be made to embrace the idea of total war. Kreton begins by singing a few verses of "There's No Place Like Home"; when this fails, he switches to "Yankee Doodle," "When Johnny Comes Marching Home" and the World War II anthem, "Comin' in on a Wing and a Prayer." Vidal's satire here is aimed against the "patriotism" found in such songs, which, when sung by the alien, seem hollow and silly: as the unmoved Conrad says after Kreton tells him, "it's for Mother," "Then let Mother go fight." However, Kreton does discover a way to incite Conrad: by broadcasting the thoughts of a soldier guarding the house—who desires Ellen—Conrad starts a fistfight which Kreton finds thrilling. Conrad is then characterized by Kreton as "a pacifist with a hard right, a stealthy left jab and a sly knee to the groin." Even the most staunch pacifist can display "blood lust," and the human tendency to resort to violence (described by Kreton as "complete reversion to type") is offered to the audience as a topic worthy of mockery and humor.

Despite his apparent perfection, however, Kreton possesses a major fault that serves as Vidal's final word on the play's issues. When talking to Ellen, Kreton says that, on his planet, the inhabitants can control time with their minds, communicate telepathically, and have rid themselves of every disease (including the common cold). But they have also wiped out "the great killer itself: passion," in an effort to eradicate "love-nest slayings, bad temper" and "world wars." The effects of this destruction of passion are described in Kreton's remark, "and now . . . we feel nothing. We do nothing. We are perfect." Perfect as they may seem, the inhabitants of Kreton's planet also find life "terribly dull"—which inspires Kreton to travel to earth and begin a world war in the first place. In one of his conversations with Rosemary, the Speldings's cat, Kreton explains that he "dotes on people" because of their "primitive addiction to violence" and "because they seethe with emotions" which he finds "bracing and intoxicating." His desire to "wallow shamelessly in their steaming emotions" reveals Vidal's attitude toward his characters and their values: despite the fact that they may behave in ridiculous ways and engage in irrational fighting, at least human beings have emotional lives that, at the very least, make life *interesting*. At the end of the play when Kreton is retrieved by his superior, Delton 4, he tells the Speldings, "oh, how I envy you. . . . For being so violent . . . so loving . . . so

beautifully imperfect. And so much happier than you know." Even a "Laundry Project" coordinator or a bumbling broadcaster has a more fulfilling existence than the most "perfect" of aliens. Despite all of the jokes at humanity's expense, it is Vidal's fondness for humanity as a whole that prevents the satire from ever becoming too bitter or the faults he points out from being seen as irredeemable.

Source: Daniel Moran, in an essay for *Drama for Students*, Gale, 1997.

Wolcott Gibbs

In the following review, New Yorker *drama critic Gibbs offers a mild endorsement for the expanded stage production of Vidal's television play.*

There is enough material in *A Visit to a Small Planet,* by Gore Vidal, for roughly an hour and a half of fine, fantastic comedy. It is somewhat unfortunate that the play at the Booth is obliged to go on for about fifty minutes longer than that, forcing the author to fill in this considerable gap either by stretching out genuinely comic situations almost to the breaking point or by writing in scenes that seem to contain rather less humor than desperation. The extra stuffing, presumably to be explained by the fact that the script is an expansion of one that was originally employed on television, is frequently irritating, but it isn't really calamitous, and I'm sure that you'll have a very pleasant time with Mr. Vidal's cheerful little report on the day the Spacemen came. In neither style nor invention can *A Visit to a Small Planet* be compared with Noel Coward's *Blithe Spirit,* which also dealt with supernatural callers but did so with a precise, sustained, and chilling wit certainly beyond Mr. Vidal's powers and probably even a trifle foreign to his natural disposition. Within its limitations, however, his play is a remarkably lively and agreeable piece of work, and it has the further merit of providing two highly—if not, indeed, outrageously—gifted comedians, Cyril Ritchard and Eddie Mayehoff, with parts just about perfectly suited to their talents.

The story you are asked to contemplate is concerned with the dreadfully disturbing things that are going to happen sometime next summer in a charming old house belonging to a celebrated newscaster near Manassas, in Virginia. The trouble begins with the landing of a flying saucer on the lawn and the emergence from it of a fascinating stranger, whose name is Kreton. This man is not from Mars, a planet that, in fact, he regards as almost impossible socially, but from some immensity beyond our present poor conception of time and space, and he belongs to a race that, having abolished food and sex, along, of course, with death, inevitably has a good deal of time for travel. His own hobby, as it happens, is the Earth, whose inhabitants amuse him in many ways but especially in their unique capacity for violence. Having hoped to arrive in time for the Battle of Bull Run, he has come equipped with the appropriate costumes, including an extremely handsome Confederate uniform, but his navigation proved faulty, and though he hits the right place, the date, to his embarrassment, is nearly a hundred years off. Deprived of the quaint old war he came to look in on, he can think of nothing to do but start a nice new one of his own, and he has just about finished his arrangements when, happily, his superiors whisk him back to the infinite.

It is quite a plot, combining, as you can see, satire with fantasy, and on the whole Mr. Vidal has done very nicely with it. His achievements are fairly difficult to describe. One particularly enchanting scene, for instance, shows Kreton trying to arouse the proper martial ardor in a young man by singing him a medley of the most terrible war songs ever written; another, involving some interesting sound effects, demonstrates his ability to read a whole stageful of minds simultaneously; another finds him in an intimate conversation with a cat, agreeing with her, as I got it, that it is no more disgusting to eat mice than to eat bacon; and still another pictures a Pentagon general doing his desperate best to fill in—naturally, in quadruplicate—a set of official forms classifying his guest and explaining the purpose of his visit in suitable military language. I might go on with these notes indefinitely, but it is obvious that the quality of the original is almost completely lacking in them, and it seems both superfluous and unkind to tax you further. It is probably enough to say that while I could do without a few things, such as a burlesque newscast that struck me as at once tedious and familiar, and a couple of not too exhilarating sequences devoted to young love, I found most of the play considerably funnier than anything else that has turned up this year.

The performances given by Mr. Ritchard, as Kreton, and Mr. Mayehoff, as the general, are in hilarious contrast. Although the action of the play takes place in 1957 and his own garb is that of 1861, Mr. Ritchard's conduct is basically that of a Restoration fop, and this wonderfully mannered elegance is the best of all attitudes for a man engaged in what can only be described as a slumming expedition.

> "WITHIN ITS LIMITATIONS, VIDAL'S PLAY IS A REMARKABLY LIVELY AND AGREEABLE PIECE OF WORK"

Mr. Mayehoff's technique is broader, being modelled more or less on that of the grampus, and no one is better equipped to impersonate a soldier whose tongue can never hope to keep up with one of the slowest minds in the world. At one point, for reasons that escape me now, he has occasion to imitate a mobile laundry unit, and not since Reginald Gardiner gave his famous impression of the sounds made by wallpaper has the art of mimicry reached a more peculiar height. The others in the cast, which Mr. Ritchard took the professional risk of directing himself, include Philip Coolidge, as the newscaster; Sibyl Bowan, as his empty-headed wife; and Sarah Marshall and Conrad Janis, as a pair of young lovers, whose sexual abandon Kreton finds very stimulating—a point of view I couldn't always share. They are all quite satisfactory in these subordinate assignments.

Source: Wolcott Gibbs, "Out of Nowhere" in the *New Yorker,* Vol. 32, no. 52, February 16, 1957.

Jack Gould

In the following review of the original television broadcast of Visit to a Small Planet, *Gould offers a favorable appraisal of Vidal's play.*

Visit to a Small Planet, seen on Sunday evening via the National Broadcasting Company, was welcome good fun, something off the beaten path in television drama. Not only was it satirical fantasy, a most rare video commodity but also it was satirical fantasy in which all the pieces fitted together.

Gore Vidal, the author, wrote about a gentleman from another dimension who is fascinated by the helpless earth people. Cyril Ritchard portrayed the visitor with great style and relish. And Jack Smight, the director, made sure everyone in the control room kept tongue in cheek. The fruit of their labors was a production that on the whole was an amusing adult lark, a decided credit to the Television Playhouse.

" NOT ONLY WAS *VISIT TO A SMALL PLANET* SATIRICAL FANTASY, A MOST RARE VIDEO COMMODITY BUT ALSO IT WAS SATIRICAL FANTASY IN WHICH ALL THE PIECES FITTED TOGETHER"

In Mr. Vidal's play the gentleman from some place else is Mr. Kreton, who doesn't disclose his home planet but merely notes he certainly doesn't come from dreary Mars. He arrives in a flying saucer that contains only a straight chair, not elaborate instrument panels. Electronics, it seems, are for primitives.

Upon landing in the back yard of a news commentator's home, Mr. Kreton, who is attired in the dress of the Civil War period, takes over first the household, then the United States Army and finally "the world organization." He has the power to know what other people are thinking, which proves especially sticky for an Army general accustomed to having a situation in hand. Kreton has less luck in penetrating the mind of the world body's secretary general; constant attendance at international conferences has muddled the secretary's thoughts.

Mr. Kreton explains to the earth people that they will not be civilized for a thousand years and will thrive only on violence and savagery. To keep them contented and happy he will start a war and the children may stay up a little late to see the bombing. He is deaf to the entreaties of the earth people, including the general, that they are trying to outgrow war.

In the nick of time another emissary arrives in a saucer. Kreton has broken the rules of some place else; it is forbidden to tamper with the past because the residents of the neighboring planet are descendants of earth people. Poor Mr. Kreton made a mistake and thought he was coming to earth in 1860, not 1960.

Kreton takes his leave somewhat sorrowfully. After all, with a little luck, he might go back into history and restage the Civil War so that this time the South won. But the earth people of today can only face a thoroughly dull existence, just peace and more peace.

Mr. Vidal got across his points of social commentary but never lost his sense of humor and light touch. Much of his dialogue was extremely bright and his characterizations rang true.

As Kreton, Mr. Ritchard was a perfect choice. He lent credibility to the visitor from outer space yet at the same time made his audience feel party to a theatrical romp. Alan Reed caught both the humor and poignancy of the general and Theodore Bickel was persuasively sincere in the small yet vital role of the world organization secretary. Edward Andrews was straightforward as the news commentator.

Mr. Smight's direction was inventive and deft and responsible for many a chuckle in its own right. This was especially apparent in the closing shot of one flying saucer hopping and skipping through the sky with carefree abandon.

Source: Jack Gould, in a review of *Visit to a Small Planet* in the *New York Times,* Vol. 104, no. 35536, May 11, 1955, p. 42.

FURTHER READING

Contemporary Literary Criticism, Gale (Detroit), 1985, pp. 402-12
    A critical overview of many of Vidal's works, this reference entry addresses the author's background and his work in a variety of genres.

Pemberton, William E. "Gore Vidal," in *Magill's Survey of American Literature,* Vol. 6, Marshall Cavendish, pp. 1998-2008.
    Another overview of Vidal's career with critcal analysis of the author's major works.

SOURCES

Atkinson, Brooks. Review of *Visit to a Small Planet* in the *New York Times,* February 8, 1957, p. 18.

Salzman, Jack, editor. "Gore Vidal," in *The Cambridge Handbook of American Literature,* Cambridge University Press, p. 248.

Thompson, Howard. Review of *Visit to a Small Planet* in the *New York Times,* April 14, 1960, p. 34.

Waiting for Godot

SAMUEL BECKETT

1952

Though difficult and sometimes baffling to read or (even) view, *Waiting for Godot* is nonetheless one of the most important works of our time. It revolutionized theatre in the twentieth century and had a profound influence on generations of succeeding dramatists, including such renowned contemporary playwrights as Harold Pinter and Tom Stoppard. After the appearance of *Waiting for Godot,* theatre was opened to possibilities that playwrights and audiences had never before imagined.

Initially written in French in 1948 as *En Attendant Godot,* Beckett's play was published in French in October of 1952 before its first stage production in Paris in January of 1953. Later translated into English by Beckett himself as *Waiting for Godot,* the play was produced in London in 1955 and in the United States in 1956 and has been produced worldwide. Beckett's play came to be considered an essential example of what Martin Esslin later called "Theatre of the Absurd," a term that Beckett disavowed but which remains a handy description for one of the most important theatre movements of the twentieth century.

"Absurdist Theatre" discards traditional plot, characters, and action to assault its audience with a disorienting experience. Characters often engage in seemingly meaningless dialogue or activities, and, as a result, the audience senses what it is like to live in a universe that doesn't "make sense." Beckett and others who adopted this style felt that this

disoriented feeling was a more honest response to the post World War II world than the traditional belief in a rationally ordered universe. *Waiting for Godot* remains the most famous example of this form of drama.

AUTHOR BIOGRAPHY

Samuel Beckett was born near Dublin, Ireland, on April 13, 1906. During his school years he was more interested in athletics than in academics, but he became excited about the study of French and Italian near the middle of his university career at Trinity College, Dublin, and ultimately graduated with honors in December, 1927. After graduation Beckett attempted to teach school but found teaching very unpleasant. He then sought to make his living as a writer but gained only modest success with his poetry, criticism, and prose during the 1930s and 1940s. However, at the end of 1948, as a diversion from his work on a novel, Beckett wrote *Waiting for Godot* in less than four months and the tremendous impact of this and subsequent plays in the 1950s turned him into an international celebrity. His monumental career as a playwright was born and it continued to overshadow his highly respected work as an experimental novelist.

In 1928, when Beckett had taken up residence in Paris as a school teacher, he met the great Irish short story writer and novelist James Joyce, author of *Dubliners, A Portrait of the Artist as a Young Man,* and *Ulysses.* For a number of years in the 1930s Beckett worked closely with the already famous Joyce as Joyce labored on his revolutionary masterpiece, *Finnegans Wake.* Joyce's erudition, esoteric word play, and elusiveness of meaning were qualities that Beckett was striving for in his own work, and when Beckett turned to drama as his major form of expression these aspects of his style intensified. *Waiting for Godot* stunned audiences with its bare set, unusual dialogue, slight plot, and bizarre characters, but subsequent plays became even more unusual. Throughout his writing career, Beckett was most interested in "minimalism," the attempt to create the greatest artistic effects with the least means possible. Beckett's plays got shorter and shorter until he eventually wrote a piece called *Breath* that lasted forty seconds and consisted of the sound of a single inhalation and exhalation of breath accompanying the rising and falling of the lights on a littered stage.

During World War II, Beckett lived in southern France and was active in the French Resistance, an underground movement fighting against the German occupation of France. Some have seen *Waiting for Godot* as a reflection on this period of Beckett's life. Beckett died of respiratory failure in Paris on December 22, 1989, and is considered by many to be one of the most innovative, daring, and revolutionary dramatists of the twentieth century. In 1969 he was awarded the Nobel Prize for Literature for "a body of work that, in new forms of fiction and the theatre, has transmuted the destitution of modern man into his exaltation."

PLOT SUMMARY

Act I

On a country road, at evening, near a tree with no leaves, a middle-aged man named Estragon (nicknamed Gogo) sits on a low mound struggling to remove his boots. He is soon joined by his friend, Vladimir (nicknamed Didi), who is glad to see him again and who recalls the story of the two thieves crucified with Christ and wonders whether it was true that one of them was chosen to be saved.

Estragon suggests that they leave this place but Vladimir reminds him they must stay because they are waiting for Mr. Godot. They debate whether this is the right place or time for their meeting, but their discussion tires Estragon and he falls asleep. After Vladimir wakes Estragon they decide that they might pass the time while they wait by hanging themselves, but the lone tree in sight seems too frail to hold them and they argue over who should hang himself first.

Two more characters enter—a man named Lucky, who carries a heavy load and has a rope around his neck, and a domineering man named Pozzo, who whips Lucky forward. The frightened Estragon and Vladimir huddle together and Estragon asks if Pozzo is Mr. Godot, but Pozzo, who claims to own the land they are on, intimidates Estragon and Vladimir into disavowing their connection with Godot. Pozzo proposes to stay with these two men and orders Lucky to provide what he needs to sit and relax. As Pozzo eats chicken, Estragon and Vladimir inspect Lucky; Estragon sees the chicken bones that Pozzo has thrown on the ground and is given permission to gnaw on them. Pozzo explains that he is taking Lucky to the fair to sell him, and when Lucky hears this he begins to weep, but when

Estragon brings Lucky a handkerchief for his tears Lucky kicks Estragon violently in the shin.

Vladimir exits to urinate, and, after he returns, Pozzo asks if Estragon and Vladimir would like Lucky to entertain them by "thinking," but Lucky's thinking turns out to be a long, almost nonsensical monologue. Pozzo and Lucky announce their departure, do not move, but then finally manage to leave, and Vladimir and Estragon comment on how the visit from Pozzo and Lucky helped pass the time while they waited for Godot. Finally, a boy enters, addresses Vladimir as Mr. Albert, and delivers the message that Mr. Godot will not be coming this evening but will surely come tomorrow. After the boy leaves, Vladimir and Estragon also decide to leave but, after declaring their resolve, do not move.

Act II

The next day, at the same time and place (the tree now has four or five leaves), Vladimir enters in an agitated state and sings a circular kind of song about a dog. Estragon enters, feeling gloomy about the beating he reports he has suffered, and he and Vladimir agree to say that they are happy, though they do not appear to be. They rededicate themselves to waiting for Godot, and Estragon suggests they could pass the time by contradicting one another or by asking one another questions. After a number of diverting exchanges, Vladimir sees Lucky's hat, left from yesterday, and he and Estragon do a vaudeville "bit" exchanging hats until Vladimir throws his own on the ground. Vladimir suggests they pretend to be Pozzo and Lucky, which they do with limited success, but when the game sends Estragon offstage, he quickly returns, frantically announcing that "they" are coming. Vladimir thinks this means that Godot is coming but Estragon's fear finally overtakes Vladimir as well and they look for a place to hide. The tree offers little in the way of cover. Estragon calms down and suggests that they simply watch carefully. They then discover another game, calling one another names, and they insult one another until Estragon comes up with the ultimate insult, calling Vladimir a "critic." After this game ends, they explore other diversions until they are interrupted by another visit from Pozzo and Lucky.

On this visit, Pozzo is blind and bumps into Lucky after they enter, knocking them both down. Estragon asks if it is Godot who has arrived, but Vladimir is simply happy that they now have com-

Samuel Beckett

pany as they wait for Godot. Pozzo is quite helpless, unable to get up from the ground, and Vladimir engages in a long philosophical discourse on whether he and Estragon should help Pozzo get up. In attempting to lift Pozzo, Vladimir falls himself and when Estragon attempts to help Vladimir up both end on the ground. With all three seated and unable to rise, Vladimir announces that "we've arrived . . . we are men." Vladimir and Estragon's next effort to rise is effortless and they help Pozzo to his feet, supporting him on each side. Pozzo begs them not to leave him. In response to Pozzo's question, "is it evening," Vladimir and Estragon scrutinize the sunset and conclude that they have indeed passed another day. Pozzo asks about Lucky, his "menial," who seems to be sleeping, and Estragon advances toward Lucky somewhat fearfully, remembering the kick in the shins he received the day before. For revenge, Estragon kicks the sleeping Lucky but hurts his foot in the process as Lucky awakes. Estragon sits and goes to sleep. Vladimir engages Pozzo in conversation and Pozzo claims no memory of a visit the day before. As Pozzo prepares to leave, Vladimir asks him what he does, blind, if he falls where no one is there to help him. Pozzo says, "we wait till we can get up. Then we go on." Vladimir asks if Pozzo will have Lucky sing or "think" again before they leave, but Pozzo reveals

A scene from the 1955 production in London

that Lucky is now "dumb," or mute, incapable of making sounds—"he can't even groan." Vladimir is confused because it seems to him that just yesterday Lucky could speak, but Pozzo is aggravated by the concept of time. For him, time is a meaningless concept; he says that the moments of our lives are like a light that "gleams an instant, then it's night once more." With those words, Pozzo and Lucky leave. Soon after they leave the stage, they fall down again.

Vladimir wakens Estragon, who is annoyed because he was dreaming that he was happy. Vladimir wonders how much of what he takes to be true is maybe some kind of dreaming. A boy enters, addressing Vladimir again as Mr. Albert, and announces that Godot will not be coming this evening but will be coming (without fail) tomorrow. The boy says he wasn't the one who came yesterday, though he seems to be to Vladimir. When Vladimir makes a sudden leap at the boy, the boy is frightened and runs off. Immediately, the sun sets, the moon rises, and Estragon awakes. Estragon talks of leaving but Vladimir reminds him they must wait for Godot to come tomorrow. They notice that everything is dead except the tree. They speculate again on the idea of hanging themselves but see that they lack a proper rope for it. When they try to use

Estragon's belt for a rope, his pants fall down to his ankles. When they test the belt, it breaks. They decide that they can bring a stronger rope tomorrow. Vladimir says, "Well? Shall we go?" and Estragon ends the play by saying, "Yes, let's go." The final stage direction says, "They do not move."

CHARACTERS

Mr. Albert
See Vladimir

Boy

The messenger who arrives near the end of each act to inform Vladimir and Estragon that Mr. Godot will not arrive is simply called "boy." Timid and fearful, he addresses Vladimir as Mr. Albert and admits in the first act that Pozzo and his whip had frightened him and kept him from entering sooner. He claims that he tends goats for Mr. Godot and that Godot is good to him, though he admits that Godot beats the boy's brother. On each visit the boy claims to have not seen Vladimir and Estragon before. In the second act the boy reports that he thinks Godot has a white beard.

MEDIA ADAPTATIONS

- A 1990 videotape production of *Waiting for Godot* is available from The Smithsonian Institution Press Video Division as part of a trilogy that includes productions of *Endgame* and *Krapp's Last Tape.* Performed by the San Quentin Drama Workshop, the production of *Waiting for Godot* includes Rick Cluchey as Pozzo. Act I on the first tape lasts 77 minutes and Act II on the second tape lasts 60 minutes. The whole trilogy is presented under the title Beckett Directs Beckett but only because it is based on Beckett's original staging for theatre.

- The 1987 film *Weeds,* starring Nick Nolte, is based loosely on the experience of Rick Cluchey in San Quentin prison. Sentenced to life imprisonment without parole for kidnapping, robbery, and aggravated assault, Cluchey witnessed the famous San Quentin production of Beckett's play, became an actor, organized a prison drama group, and was eventually released after twelve years to become an accomplished interpreter of Beckett's characters on stage and in film.

- A 45-minute black and white version of Act II is available from Films for the Humanities (Princeton, NJ, 1988; orig. 1976) and features Zero Mostel, Burgess Meredith, and Milo O'Shea in a production directed by Alan Schneider, director of the ill-fated American premiere in Miami.

- A 50-minute lecture by Bert States entitled *"Waiting for Godot* : Speculations on Myth and Method,'' was recorded on audiocassette in 1976 by the Cornell Literature Forum.

- A 36-minute lecture on audiocassette by Kathryn Ludwigson entitled "Beckett's View of Man in *Waiting for Godot* and *Endgame*,'' was made in 1972 by King's College. Part of a series entitled Christianity and Literature Cassettes, this lecture compares Beckett's description of modern man as lost and disoriented with the biblical view of man and points out passages in the dramas analogous to biblical texts.

- A 35-minute audiocassette program on the play by Lois Gordon as part of the Modern Drama Cassette Curriculum series was created in 1971 by Everett/Edwards of Deland, Florida.

- On June 26, 1961, a British television production of the play was broadcast with Peter Woodthorpe as Estragon and Jack MacGowran as Vladimir and directed by Donald McWhinnie. Beckett was not pleased with the production, feeling that the containment of the action in the small television frame misrepresented the drama of "small men locked in a big space.''

- A 24-page musical score for a 10-minute performance entitled "Voices,'' based on the play, was published in 1960 by Universal Edition (London) and attributed to Marc Wilkinson. The score features a contralto voice singing in English and German and an instrumental ensemble of flute, clarinet, bass clarinet, and violoncello.

Didi

See Vladimir

Estragon (Es-tra-gon)

Estragon is one of the two men (often referred to as "tramps'') who are waiting for Mr. Godot. He is the first to appear in the play and is more docile and timid than his friend Vladimir; Estragon usually follows Vladimir's lead. At times assertive, Estragon is more emotional and volatile than Vladimir but less engaged—he gives up more easily, does a lot of sleeping, likes to dream, and forgets more easily. He even forgets Godot's name at one point. He is confused more frequently than Vladimir and is more frequently afraid—perhaps because he is the one more often beaten and physically abused by others. He has bad feet, which hurt him in his too-small boots and which smell when he has his boots off. He is more skeptical and questions more than Vladimir, doubts Godot more, and is more often anxious to leave or to travel separately from his friend. Estragon, along with Pozzo, does the eating in the play. If Estragon and Vladimir are Laurel and Hardy, Estragon is Stan Laurel, the skinny one who is frequently confused, frightened, and whiny.

Gogo
See Estragon

Lucky

Lucky is the miserable slave or "menial" whom Pozzo drives on stage in Act I and blindly follows in Act II, but while Pozzo's fortune and character changes Lucky's remains fairly similar. In the first act he is an abused beast of burden, an automaton carrying a huge load and suffering from neck abrasions where Pozzo violently jerks his halter. Lucky is understandably sad and quiet, but he is also loyal to Pozzo, eager to please, and violent himself when Estragon gets near enough to be kicked. His "thinking" seems full of a desperate energy that may come from an attempt to communicate his sadness. In the second act Lucky is mute and mostly sleeps. Lucky has long white hair that falls down around his face.

Pozzo (Po-dzo)

Pozzo is the bald, brutal, insensitive, and overbearing figure who intimidates Estragon and Vladimir in the first act of the play after he drives his "slave," Lucky, onto the scene. Pozzo is a sadistic bully with a large body and a huge voice who violently abuses Lucky, both physically and psychologically, forcing Lucky with whip and halter to serve his every whim and need. In the first act Pozzo seems wealthy, self-assured, and powerful. However, in the second act, Pozzo is blind and a much different person. He still has Lucky on a rope and calls him his "menial," but Pozzo now is timid, frightened, vulnerable, and helpless as he falls to the ground and cannot rise without assistance.

Vladimir (Vlad-eh-meer)

Vladimir is the more forceful, optimistic, and resilient of the two "tramps" waiting for Mr. Godot, but he is also sensitive, easily hurt, and quickly frustrated. He is extremely caring and protective of his friend, Estragon, and he more courageously expresses his outrage at Pozzo's mistreatment of Lucky. He usually leads Estragon in their games to "pass the time" and he initially represents the pair when strangers like Pozzo and the boy appear. Vladimir is the one most confident that Godot will appear and the most insistent that they meet their obligations by waiting. He is more of a thinker and philosopher than Estragon and he remembers the past much more clearly, though his memory frustrates him when other people don't remember things the way he does. He sometimes becomes angry in these situations but occasionally doubts his own certainty. This more intellectual quality leads Vladimir to be more deeply brooding and gloomy but also more persistent than his friend. Vladimir has stinking breath and kidney problems. If Estragon and Vladimir are Laurel and Hardy, Vladimir is Oliver Hardy, the fat one who does the "thinking" but is frequently dead wrong.

THEMES

Human Condition

In this richly evocative "story" about two men who wait for another who never comes there are so many possible themes it is difficult to enumerate them. Those that are readily apparent include the issues of absurdity, alienation and loneliness, appearance and reality, death, doubt and ambiguity, time, the meaning of life, language and meaning, and the search for self. But one theme that encompasses many of these at once is the question of the human condition—who are we as humans and what is our short life on this planet really like?

We appear to be born without much awareness of our selves or our environment and as we mature to gradually acquire from the world around us a sense of identity and a concept of the universe. However, the concept of human life that we generally acquire may be fraught with illusions. Early in his life Beckett dismissed the Christian concept of God and based his concept of the human condition on the assumption that human existence ends in the grave, that our most monumental achievements are insignificant measured by the cosmic scales of time and space, and that human life without illusions is generally difficult and sad. Vladimir and Estragon live in a world without comforting illusions about human dignity, the importance of work and achievement, the inevitability of justice, or the promise of

TOPICS FOR FURTHER STUDY

- Research the following three topics: the French Resistance during the German occupation of France in World War II, Beckett's personal role in that Resistance movement, and interpretations of *Waiting for Godot* that suggest Beckett is using the play to reflect on his war experience.

- Research the production of *Waiting for Godot* at San Quentin penitentiary in November of 1957 and discuss the conditions under which unsophisticated audiences can understand and respond enthusiastically to Beckett's play.

- Find places in the text of *Waiting for Godot* where the play is clearly funny. Then find places where the humor is less obvious but still quite rich. Finally, research the concept of "black humor" and describe the sense of humor that you find in *Waiting for Godot.*

- Research as many different productions of *Waiting for Godot* as you can and classify what these productions reveal about differences in presentation and interpretation. Then describe the features of a production that you would undertake.

- Compare the Existentialist and Christian interpretations of the play and decide which one seems to you more faithful to the text that Beckett wrote.

---

an afterlife of eternal bliss. They live in a world where almost nothing is certain, where simply getting your boots off or sleeping through the night without having to urinate is a pretty significant achievement. They live in a world where violence and brutality can appear at any time, often victimizing them directly. They live without amenities, find joy in the smallest of victories, and are ultimately quite serious about their vague responsibility to wait for this mysterious figure who may or may not come and who may or may not reward them for their loyalty. It is a life lived on the razor's edge of hope and sadness.

Strangely enough, Pozzo often voices most clearly what Beckett might have called the reality of this world. In Act I, for example, Estragon feels pity for the abused and weeping Lucky, who is sobbing because Pozzo has said aloud that he wants to "get rid of him." As Lucky sobs, Pozzo brutally says, "old dogs have more dignity." But when Estragon goes with a handkerchief to wipe his tears, Lucky kicks him violently in the shins and it is now Estragon in pain. Pozzo then offers this observation: "he's stopped crying. [To Estragon.] You have replaced him as it were. [Lyrically.] The tears of the world are a constant quantity. For each one who begins to weep, somewhere else another stops. The same is true of the laugh. [He laughs.] Let us not then speak ill of our generation, it is not any unhappier than its predecessors. [Pause.] Let us not speak well of it either. [Pause.] Let us not speak of it at all.''

As Beckett dismissed what most of us take for granted, he eventually dismissed language itself as a reliable source of security. Ironically, this man of words ultimately mistrusted them. He knew that the word could never be counted on to convey meaning precisely and that linguistic meaning was always an approximation. Thus he shows Vladimir and Estragon spending most of their time dancing around words, attempting vainly to pin them down, to use them as guiding stars as best they can. At the end of the play, for example, Vladimir is struck by Estragon's suggestion that much of what Vladimir "knows" might be as unreliable as Estragon's dreams, and Vladimir launches into a poetic monologue that begins, "Was I sleeping, while the others suffered? Am I sleeping now?" But when he ends this lyrical moment of introspection he simply says, "what have I said?" This is a world where even words fail to wrestle our lives into consistently coherent patterns of meaning, a world where the human condition is radically insecure but where the struggle to find meaning is perhaps the only nobility left for us.

Friendship

It is tempting to see Beckett as a "nihilist," as someone who believed that there was nothing of value or meaning in human life, but the friendship of Estragon and Vladimir clearly offers us something positive and even uplifting in the difficult world of Beckett's play. In the unconventional banter of these two men it is sometimes easy to miss the intensity of their symbiotic relationship, but close attention to the theatrical qualities in their exchanges will show that they care deeply for one another and in many ways need one another to survive in their inhospitable world. Beckett, of course, is not sentimental about friendship—he is stubbornly realistic about everything he sees—but on the whole the relationship between Estragon and Vladimir is an important focus for understanding Beckett's most famous play.

In many places in the action Vladimir and Estragon bicker, misunderstand, and even ignore one another, but in other places their relationship is clearly tender, such as in the moment of Act II when Vladimir covers the sleeping Estragon with his coat. But if one were to focus on one moment in detail the most logical place to start might be the entrances of the two men at the beginning of the play. As the play begins, Estragon is sitting on a mound trying to take off his boot. Estragon and Vladimir have been separated overnight, but Beckett doesn't expect us to worry about why they have separated, any more than he expects us to give a moment's thought as to how they first met or how long they have known one another. It is enough to know that they are friends and that as the play begins Estragon is alone on this country road struggling to get his boots off. He finally gives up, saying "Nothing to be done," and at that moment Vladimir enters and responds to his friend's words as if he had been there from the start of Estragon's struggle—"I'm beginning to come round to that opinion," says Vladimir. The ease with which they are together again, as if they never were parted, is indicated deftly in the seamlessness of that second line of the play. Vladimir then says, more directly, "I'm glad to see you back. I thought you were gone forever" and though the line is spoken casually the clear implication is that losing Estragon forever would have created a very considerable hole in Vladimir's life. Vladimir expresses concern over Estragon's beating, then quickly shifts into one of his annoyingly condescending roles as Estragon's protector. Vladimir talks, almost as if he simply enjoys hearing the sound of his own voice, while Estragon resumes the struggle with the boot.

Eventually, Estragon succeeds in removing his boot and it could easily be suggested that he does so in part because of the mere presence of his friend. It is certainly no accident that just as Vladimir echoes Estragon's opening phrase, "Nothing to be done," Estragon "with a supreme effort succeeds in pulling off his boot." The removal of the boot, of course, is mundane. As Vladimir says, "Boots must be taken off every day." But in Beckett's careful art, the removal of the boot with the indirect emotional support of a friend is a metaphor for anything we attempt to do in our lives. In this life we face difficulties in the simple execution of daily affairs and ultimately we must face them alone or in the company of others who struggle as we do.

STYLE

Theatre of the Absurd

The seemingly endless waiting that Estragon and Vladimir undertake for the mysterious Godot has made Beckett's play one of the classic examples of what is called Theatre of the Absurd. The term refers both to its content—a bleak vision of the human condition—and to the style that expresses that vision. The idea that human life lacks meaning and purpose, that humans live in an indifferent or hostile universe, is frequently associated with Existentialist writers like the French philosophers Albert Camus (Kam-oo) and Jean-Paul Sartre (Sart). But when these two writers expounded their ideas in novels and plays, they generally used traditional literary techniques—that is, life-like characters; clear, linear plots; and conventional dialogue. But with writers like Beckett or the French dramatist Eugene Ionesco (E-on-es-co), the style is not an arbitrary choice but rather a necessary complement to the vision itself.

Beckett and those who adopted his style insisted that to effectively express the vision of absurdity one had to make the expression itself seem absurd. In other words, the audience had to experience what it felt like to live in an absurd world. Thus, the familiar and comforting qualities of a clear plot, realistic characters, plausible situations, and comprehensible dialogue had to be abandoned. In their place Beckett created a play where bizarre characters speak in what sometimes appears to be illogical, banal, chit chat and where events sometimes appear to change with no apparent logic. In *Waiting for Godot,* for example, this quality is embodied in its most extreme form in Lucky's first act monologue where he demonstrates his "thinking." For two full pages of text, Lucky goes on like this: "I resume alas alas on on in short in fine on on abode of stones who can doubt it I resume but not so fast I resume the skull to shrink."

Many of the play's original audience members and critics probably came to *Waiting for Godot* expecting something more traditional than Lucky's speech and were not able to adjust to what they were confronted with. Even today's reader may need a gentle reminder about expectations. As Hugh Kenner suggested at the outset of his book *A Reader's Guide to Samuel Beckett*, "the reader of Samuel Beckett may want a Guide chiefly to fortify him against irrelevant habits of attention, in particular the habit of reading 'for the story.'" For, as Martin Esslin explained in *The Theatre of the Absurd*, "*Waiting for Godot* does not tell a story; it explores a static situation. 'Nothing happens, nobody comes, nobody goes, it's awful.'" Or, as Kenner put it, "the substance of the play is waiting, amid uncertainty. . . . To wait; and to make the audience share the waiting; and to explicate the quality of the waiting: this is not to be done with 'plot.'"

Black Humor

Perhaps the easiest and also the most difficult thing to experience clearly in *Waiting for Godot* is its sense of humor. It's the easiest thing to experience because once one accepts the play on its own terms *Waiting for Godot* is wildly funny. But the play's humor is also the hardest thing to experience because the reputation of Beckett's play has created another set of expectations—that its dark vision must be taken with utmost seriousness.

However, a quick look at the subtitle of the play reveals that Beckett called it "a tragi-comedy in two acts," and this delicate balance between tragedy and comedy is probably the most essential ingredient in the play. Numerous critics have pointed out that *Waiting for Godot* is full of pratfalls, classic vaudeville "bits" like the wild swapping of hats in Act II, and the patter of comedians such as this from Act I:

> Estragon: [Anxious.] And we? Vladimir: I beg your pardon? Estragon: I said, And we? Vladimir: I don't understand. Estragon: Where do we come in? Vladimir: Come in? Estragon: Take your time. Vladimir: Come in? On our hands and knees. Estragon: As bad as that?

Hugh Kenner has even discovered what appears to be a "source" for the farcical dropping of trousers that ends the play. He pointed out that in

Laurel and Hardy's film *Way Out West* (1937) this dialogue occurs:

> Hardy: Get on the mule. Laurel: What? Hardy: Get *on* the mule.

At the end of *Waiting for Godot* we have:

> Vladimir: Pull on your trousers. Estragon: What? Vladimir: Pull on your trousers. Estragon: You want me to pull off my trousers? Vladimir: Pull ON your trousers. Estragon: [Realizing his trousers are down.] True. [He pulls up his trousers.]

Black Comedy is laughter that is generated by something truly painful. When we are led to laugh at tragedy or real suffering like death or the genuinely horrific, we are in the world of Black Comedy. In *Endgame* Nell says, "nothing is funnier than unhappiness." Beckett leads us to laugh because it may be the only viable response to extreme anxiety. In *Waiting for Godot,* of course, what follows the "trouser" passage above is the quite serious and even solemn concluding lines of the play—"they do not move."

HISTORICAL CONTEXT

The French Resistance Movement during World War II

Beckett wrote *Waiting for Godot* in the late months of 1948, three years after Allied forces had liberated France from German occupation, and some scholars suggest that his war experience might have served as an inspiration for the play. After German military forces had successfully invaded and occupied Northern France in the spring of 1940, a nominally free French government had been established in the South at Vichy and an underground French Resistance movement arose that attempted to frustrate and undermine German control of France. Beckett joined the Resistance movement in Paris in September of 1941 and helped pass secret information to England about German military movements. When an infiltrator began uncovering the names of Resistance members in Beckett's group, Beckett and his companion (later his wife) Suzanne had to flee Paris and travel into the South, where they eventually found refuge in the small village of Roussillon, near Avignon. In the French version of the play, this village is named as the place where Vladimir and Estragon picked grapes, an activity that Beckett and Suzanne actually engaged in. This has led some scholars to suggest that Vladimir and

COMPARE
&
CONTRAST

- **1954:** Less than a decade after the U.S. military unleashed the frightening power of the atomic bomb in 1945, Russia and the United States began harnessing nuclear energy for peaceful uses. The first nuclear power station began producing electricity for Soviet industry and agriculture on June 27 at a station 55 miles from Moscow at Obninsk. In August, the U.S. Congress gave the approval for U.S. private industry to participate in the production of nuclear power.

  Today: The production of electricity through nuclear power plants has grown tremendously but has failed to become the dominant power source it was envisioned to be, in part because of the perceived dangers of nuclear power plants. Nuclear accidents at Three-Mile Island near Harrisburg, Pennsylvania, in 1979 and at Chernobyl near Kiev, Russia, in 1986 increased opposition to reliance on nuclear energy production.

- **1954:** Large corporations begin to use computers to facilitate business activities.

  Today: The world has been transformed by computers as they power and guide everything from wrist watches to space shuttles. The World Wide Web has virtually interconnected everyone on the globe by creating an ''information super highway.''

- **1954:** The first color television sets are introduced into the United States by RCA. Color reception is of unreliable quality but RCA will dominate the new market until 1959, when Zenith and others use the courts to challenge RCA's virtual monopoly.

  Today: The black and white television is almost a collector's item and the transition is being made in the United States to the new digital television technology that will eventually make analog television sets obsolete. Digital television will provide a revolutionary clear image that delivers a ''movie'' quality picture.

- **1954:** Ray Kroc, a milkshake salesman in California, discovers a very successful but small California hamburger chain. He buys franchising rights from the owners, the McDonald brothers, and begins building his golden arches fast-food empire.

  Today: McDonald's is the largest fast-food chain in the world with nearly 20,000 restaurants in approximately 100 countries.

- **1954:** France asks the United States to help French troops surrounded at Dien Bien Phu in Indochina (Vietnam). President Eisenhower acknowledges the importance of containing Communist aggression in Southeast Asia but refuses to provide U.S. airpower to help relieve the siege.

  Today: The United States was gradually drawn into the Vietnam conflict (while the French withdrew) until the United States under President Lyndon Johnson severely escalated U.S. involvement in the mid-1960s. Public anti-war sentiment ultimately forced American politicians to withdraw from the war without winning it militarily and the United States perhaps still suffers psychologically for its perceived defeat in the Vietnam.

Estragon can, at least in part, represent Beckett and Suzanne in flight from Paris to Roussillon or the two of them waiting in an extremely dangerous form of exile for the war to end. In Roussillon, Beckett earned food and shelter by doing strenuous manual labor for local farmers, eventually working for a small local Resistance group, and trying to keep his identity hidden from the Germans occupying outlying areas. After the war, Beckett was awarded two French medals, the Croix de Guerre and the Medaille de la Reconnaissance, for his contributions to the war effort.

Indeterminate Time and Place in Beckett's Play

More importantly for Beckett's art, however, is that *Waiting for Godot,* on the whole, clearly detaches itself from particular aspects of the historical and cultural context in which Beckett wrote in order to universalize the experience of Vladimir and Estragon. And it achieves this universal quality initially by placing the two figures in an indeterminate setting and time. As the play opens, the setting and time is simply described as "A country road. A tree. Evening." In the second act, the description is simply, "Next day. Same Time. Same Place." This backdrop is left unspecified in order to emphasize that the action of the play is a universal "situation" rather than a particular series of events that happened to a particular set of characters.

At one time in our century this waiting could have stood for South Africans waiting for apartheid to end in their native land. More than a half century after the unleashing of atomic energy, this waiting could still represent our fears of nuclear catastrophe. On a more personal level, many know what it is like to wait for news of a test for cancer. But all of these specific situations reveal how specificity can reduce the poetic evocativeness of Beckett's waiting to a mundane flatness. The unspecified nature of what Vladimir and Estragon wait for is what gives Beckett's play its extraordinary power.

The peculiar quality of Vladimir and Estragon's waiting, of course, is that they wait with only the vaguest sense of what they are waiting for and that they wait without much hope while still clinging to hope as their only ballast in an existential storm. But even this narrower description of the play's "waiting" leaves many possibilities for corresponding situations. For example, one of the most famous productions of *Waiting for Godot* perhaps reveals most clearly how the indeterminate time and place of the play permits it to speak to a wide variety of audience experiences. In *The Theatre of the Absurd* Martin Esslin examined the famous 1957 production of *Waiting for Godot* at San Quentin penitentiary. Prison officials had chosen Beckett's play largely because it had no women in it to distract the prisoners, but the San Francisco Actors' Workshop group that was performing the play was obviously concerned that such an arcane theatrical experience might baffle an audience of fourteen hundred convicts. Much to their surprise, however, the convicts understood the play immediately. One prisoner said, "Godot is society." Another said, "he's the outside." As Esslin reported, "a teacher at the prison

was quoted as saying, 'they know what is meant by waiting . . . and they knew if Godot finally came, he would only be a disappointment.'" An article in the prison newspaper summarized the prisoners' response by saying, "We're still waiting for Godot, and shall continue to wait. When the scenery gets too drab and the action too slow, we'll call each other names and swear to part forever—but then, there's no place to go!" Esslin concluded that "it is said that Godot himself, as well as turns of phrase and characters from the play, have since become a permanent part of the private language, the institutional mythology of San Quentin." In 1961, one member of that convict audience, Rick Cluchey, helped form a group that produced seven productions of Beckett's plays for San Quentin audiences from 1961 to 1964. Cluchey later earned his release from San Quentin and had a distinguished career acting on stage and in films, especially as an interpreter of Beckett roles.

CRITICAL OVERVIEW

After nearly a half-century, Beckett's *Waiting for Godot* remains one of the most important, respected, and powerful plays in the history of world theatre. Given its radically innovative style and great degree of difficulty, it is no surprise that audiences and critics have generally reacted to it in extremes—either of love or hate, admiration or disgust. Its original director, Roger Blin, recalled in an article in *Theater* that the reaction to the first production in January, 1953, in a small Paris theatre was "a sensation actually: wild applause broke out from some in the audience, others sat in baffled silence, fisticuffs were exchanged by pros and cons; most critics demolished play and production but a handful wrote prophetically."

Among those who wrote prophetically was the play's first reviewer, a relatively unknown critic named Sylvain Zegel, who proclaimed in a review in *Liberation* that the production was "an event which will be spoken of for a long time, and will be remembered years later." With amazing prescience, Zegel simply asserted that this first-time playwright "deserves comparison with the greatest." A more famous French critic at the time, Jacques Lemarchand, added an awareness of the play's dark humor, observing in *Figaro Litteraire* that *Waiting for Godot* "is also a funny play— sometimes very funny. The second night I was there the laughter was natural and unforced.'' He added that this humor ''in no way diminished'' the play's profound emotional intensity. Internationally acclaimed playwright Jean Anouilh (On-wee) was also one of *Waiting for Godot*'s early commentators and in *Arts Spectacles* simply proclaimed it ''a masterpiece.'' As James Knowlson summarized it in his *Damned to Fame: The Life of Samuel Beckett*, the play's ''success was assured when it became controversial.'' The critical and popular enthusiasm, though not universal, was widespread, and the production ran for four-hundred performances before moving to a larger theatre in Paris.

This process whereby ambivalence to the play ultimately evolved into popular and critical success was repeated when the play moved to London in August of 1955 for its first production using Beckett's English translation. Opening in a small ''fringe'' theatre (London's version of Off Broadway), ''the play created an instant furore,'' according to Alan Simpson, writing in 1962, and quoted in Ruby Cohn's 1987 compilation, *Waiting for Godot: A Casebook*. Simpson added that ''[a]lmost without exception, the popular press dismissed it as obscure nonsense and pretentious rubbish. However, it was enthusiastically championed by Harold Hobson and Kenneth Tynan'' (two of the most influential drama critics in London) and the play once again became controversial and thereby successful, eventually moving to a West End theatre (London's Broadway) and a long run. In February of 1956 an unsigned review in the London *Times Literary Supplement* by distinguished author G.S. Fraser asserted that the play was clearly a Christian morality play. This essay led to weeks of spirited exchange in the *Times* with some critics countering that the play was anti-Christian, others that it was Existentialist, and others that it was something else altogether. Characteristically, Beckett was mystified by the controversy, saying, according to Knowlson, ''why people have to complicate a thing so simple I can't make out.''

The first American production of the play, on the other hand, was quite uncomplicated; it was an unmitigated disaster. In January of 1956, director Alan Schneider opened what was to be a three-week preview run of the play in Coral Gables, Florida, near Miami, with popular comic actors and personalities Bert Lahr and Tom Ewell in the lead roles. As Schneider recounted (as quoted in Ruby Cohn's 1967 compilation, *Casebook on Waiting for Godot*), the production was a ''spectacular flop. The opening night audience in Miami, at best not too sophisticated or attuned to this type of material and at worst totally misled by advertising billing the play as 'the laugh sensation of two continents,' walked out in droves. And the so-called reviewers not only could not make heads or tails of the play but accused us of pulling some sort of hoax on them.'' The production did not even finish the three week preview run, but months later the production did move to Broadway, with a new director and cast (retaining only Bert Lahr as Estragon). In New York, producer Michael Myerberg took a new tack on pre-production publicity, this time asking in his advertisements for an audience of ''seventy thousand intellectuals.'' This time the production was a success, though still drawing divided opinions from critics and audience. The show ran for over 100 performances and sold almost 3,000 copies of the play in the theatre lobby.

There have been so many important productions of *Waiting for Godot* in our century that it is difficult to even list, much less summarize, them. An all-black production of the play on Broadway ran for only five performances late in 1956, with Earle Hyman as Lucky. There was a West Berlin production early in 1975 that Beckett himself directed. In a production in 1976 in Cape Town, South Africa, waiting for Godot seemed to suggest waiting for the end of apartheid. In 1984 there was a San Quentin Drama Workshop production involving Rick Cluchey, former inmate of San Quentin and audience member of the famous 1957 San Quentin production of the play. In 1988 Beckett went to court in an attempt to stop an all-female Dutch production, believing as he did that the characters in *Waiting for Godot* were distinctively male (Beckett and his lawyers lost in court). Also in 1988 there was a production at Lincoln Center in New York City, in which Estragon and Vladimir were played by well-known contemporary comedians Robin Williams and Steve Martin.

According to Martin Esslin in his *The Theatre of the Absurd*, *Waiting for Godot* had been seen by over a million people within five years after its first production in Paris and by the late 1960s had been translated into more than twenty languages and performed all over the world. Audiences coming to it without an awareness of its nature or history are perhaps still baffled by it, but the play can no longer be dismissed as it was by *Daily News* contributor John Chapman, one of its first New York critics, who, as quoted by the *New Republic*'s Eric Bentley, called *Waiting for Godot* ''merely a stunt.''

CRITICISM

Terry Niehuis

Niehuis is an associate professor of English at Western Carolina University. His essay discusses how Waiting for Godot *can best be understood in musical terms such as repeating themes and motifs.*

Waiting for Godot has been and may always be a difficult work to read or view. However, much of the difficulty that readers and audiences have had with the play seems to have come from false expectations. If audiences come to a production expecting a traditional theatre experience featuring a clear plot, realistic characters, and conventional dialogue, they are doomed to frustration and may not be able to adjust and simply experience what the play does have to offer.

The traditional play tells a story and the movement of a story is usually in a more-or-less forward line from beginning to end. The movement in Beckett's play, however, is more like a circle. The play has a beginning, but the beginning seems somewhat arbitrary because what happened before the beginning does not seem to be important. The play has an end, but the end seems to recall the beginning and create a sense of circularity rather than the traditional sense of closure that conventional stories generally provide. So Beckett's play could perhaps be described as ''all middle.'' This, of course, reinforces the Absurdist or Existentialist idea of human life as having no clear purpose or direction, of life being an interminable waiting for a sense of purpose or closure that is not likely to ever arrive. Seen clearly, life seems to these thinkers as something we simply do while we are waiting to die, and the illusions human beings create to give their lives a sense of teleology or purpose will not finally sustain the thoroughly reflective twentieth-century human being.

In a way, these Existentialist ideas in *Waiting for Godot* are encapsulated in the first image and line of the play. As the lights rise on the stage, the audience sees Estragon in a bleak landscape, sitting on a low mound, struggling to remove his boot. He tries, gives up, rests exhausted, tries again, gives up again, repeats the process, and finally says, ''nothing to be done.'' That, in a sense, is the whole play in a nutshell. In an indifferent universe, human beings struggle with the simplest of activities, are tempted to give up, but can do nothing to alter their fate except persist. It can be said, as Hugh Kenner

did in his *A Reader's Guide to Samuel Beckett,* that the rest of the play simply repeats this observation: ''insofar as the play has a 'message,''' said Kenner, ''that is more or less what it is: 'Nothing to be done.' There is no dilly-dallying; it is delivered in the first moments, with the first spoken words, as though to get the didactic part out of the way.'' The rest of the play could be seen as a set of ''variations'' on this theme, much as a jazz or classical musical composition announces a theme or motif and then enlarges upon that theme, modifying it and adding additional themes and motifs until the composition has succeeded in fully presenting its mood, tone, or idea. In the opening moments of *Waiting for Godot* this kind of musical quality is most obvious when Vladimir finally repeats Estragon's opening line, saying himself, ''Nothing to be done.'' At the end of the second page of the script and then near the end of the third, Vladimir's repetition of this opening line echoes like a musical refrain and establishes the main idea of Beckett's play.

To adjust the expectations one brings to the reading or viewing of *Waiting for Godot* it may be useful to think of the play as something like a musical composition. Linda Ben-Zvi explained in her *Samuel Beckett* that Beckett ''bemoaned the fact that his characters could not be portrayed as musical sounds—a simultaneity of sounds played at one time: 'how nice that would be, linear, a lovely Phythagorean chant-chant solo of cause and effect.''' Ben-Zvi went on to observe that ''the theatre, while it still may not explain characters, can do what prose cannot: present the 'chain-chant' directly to audiences who are free to react without the necessity of explanation, who can apprehend life being presented.'' In his *The Theatre of the Absurd* Martin Esslin quoted Herbert Blau, the director of the 1957 San Quentin production, who attempted to prepare the convict audience for the play by comparing it ''to a piece of jazz music 'to which one must listen for whatever one may find in it.''' Peter Hall, the director for the first London production, reported in an interview on the BBC's *Third Programme* that neither he nor his actors really understood the play but that he ''was immediately struck by the enormous humanity and universality of the subject, and also by the extraordinary rhythms of the writing, and it was these rhythms and almost musical flexibility of the lyricism which communicated itself to me and which I tried to pass on to the actors.'' And in a famous letter (quoted in Steven Connor's *Waiting for Godot and Endgame: Samuel Beckett*) to director Alan Schneider, who

WHAT DO I READ NEXT?

- Beckett's *Endgame* (1957) features a more antagonistic pair of men in an even drearier situation, while Beckett's *Happy Days* (1961) demonstrates his focus on women and *Come and Go* (1966) represents how "minimalistic" Beckett would eventually become in his drama.

- Joseph Heller's *Catch 22* (1961) is a famous dark comedy in novel form that deals with the absurdity of the military in World War II.

- Tom Stoppard's *Rosencrantz and Guildenstern Are Dead* (1966) is often seen as a play that consciously imitates Beckett's *Waiting for Godot.*

- Eugene Ionesco's *The Bald Soprano* (1950), *The Lesson* (1951), and *The Chairs* (1952) all epito-

mize the Theatre of the Absurd and provide interesting similarities and contrasts with Beckett's *Waiting for Godot.*

- Jean-Paul Sartre's *No Exit* (1944) shows how Existentialist ideas can be presented in a more traditional dramatic form.

- Albert Camus's *The Myth of Sisyphus* (1942; English translation 1955) was an enormously influential philosophical essay that posed the essential question for the Existentialists—what do human beings do if they reject suicide as a response to a meaningless universe. Camus's *The Stranger* (1942; English translation 1946) is a classic Existentialist novel.

---

was preparing a production of *Endgame,* Beckett wrote: "my work is a matter of fundamental sounds (no joke intended) made as fully as possible, and I accept responsibility for nothing else. If people want to have headaches among the overtones, let them. And provide their own aspirin."

Thinking of the play in terms of a jazz or classical musical composition can solve a number of the problems readers and audiences traditionally have with *Waiting for Godot.* The play's apparent "meandering" quality is accounted for, as well as its obvious repetition and circularity. The quick, stichomythic exchanges between Vladimir and Estragon, as well as their abrupt shifts in topics become as important for their sound and rhythm as they do for their sense, full as they are of crescendos and diminuendos. The numerous pauses and silences also become crucial as they contribute to the dialogue's rhythm. Like a "quartet" the play is a series of voices, all different but all eventually complementary, elaborate variations on the theme of "nothing to be done." Beckett's primary concerns are with mood and tone, using rhythms in language and numerous examples of repetition to create something very much like melody.

Even Lucky's monologue, which exists as the play's greatest frustration when one is expecting traditional "sense" in dialogue, becomes more meaningful when one hears the "sound" of it. When we first see Lucky, he is a pathetic figure sagging under a tremendous load of baggage, tethered by a cruel rope to a whip-wielding figure still offstage. Working silently, like an automaton, Lucky is disgustingly abused but still subservient to a Pozzo who is obviously inflated and unworthy of Lucky's devotion. When Lucky weeps at the mention of his being sold at the fair, he is a moving symbol of human misery, but when he kicks the solicitous Estragon we feel his anger and wonder at the apparent inappropriateness of his response. All of our complex feelings about this figure are gathering momentum, just as perhaps his are, and these feelings find their most powerful expression in the culminating moment of Lucky's monologue. The monologue is breathless, one long shouted sentence without punctuation, as if to express in his heroic effort to "think" all of his suffering, degradation, and yet determination to survive. In the theatre it can be a moment of transcendence, not so much because of what the words "mean" (there are brief flashes of "sense") but because of how the words

---

"sound." James Knowlson recounted in his *Damned to Fame: The Life of Samuel Beckett* that in the 1984 San Quentin Drama Workshop production of the play, "a small, bald-headed actor named J. Pat Miller" played Lucky at a number of performances and "built the speech into so overwhelming and searing a performance that Beckett, hearing him for the first time, sat totally transfixed, tears welling up in his eyes. After the rehearsal, he told Miller that he was the best Lucky he had ever seen."

As another example of how essentially musical the play is, consider the way sound communicates the difference between Pozzo's two appearances in the play. In the first act Pozzo is mostly volume and bluster as he attempts to dominate everyone around him. In the second act, he is a small voice simply crying "help" repeatedly. From his entrance and fall where he lies helpless on the ground, Pozzo cries "help" or "pity" eleven times while the foreground sound is of Vladimir and Estragon debating what to do. Pozzo is thus like a recurrent sound from the percussion section until he offers to pay Vladimir and Estragon to help him up. As Vladimir attempts to help Pozzo up, Vladimir is dragged down and then joins in the refrain of "help" until all three of them are on the ground. Obviously comic, the scene also generates an enormously effective pathos. At one point Pozzo and Vladimir cry "help" in successive lines as Estragon threatens to leave, with the richness of the theatrical experience lying mostly in the different way those two calls for help sound.

Beckett was a poet in the theatre, more interested in the evocative quality of his words than their declarative quality. Declarative language is easier to understand but evaporates very quickly. In simple, declarative language we can say that Shakespeare's Hamlet is a sensitive young man who is so hurt by his father's death and his mother's hasty remarriage that he contemplates suicide in his famous "to be or not to be" speech. But the lasting value and pleasure of that speech lies not in the mere identification of its declarative meaning. Its lasting power lies in the elusive but evocative quality of its images, diction, and rhythms. In all of his art, Beckett sought to emphasize the evocative quality of his language by reducing the appeal of its declarative aspects. Thus, *Waiting for Godot* purposely frustrates the audience's dependence on declarative language in order to force it to pay more attention to the dialogue's evocative quality. Thus, in the simplest of exchanges we can find great poetry. For example, Vladimir gives Estragon a

carrot in Act I and while Estragon chews on it Vladimir asks, "How's the carrot?" Estragon replies simply, "It's a carrot," and Vladimir adds, "So much the better, so much the better. [Pause.] What was it you wanted to know?" Here there are rhythms and tones in the dialogue that not only mirror the sense of the lines but can even stand in for them. The rising tone of Vladimir's question, so full of hope, is countered by the gently falling tones of Estragon's response. Hope and expectation fall back to the earth in simple fact. Life is what it is. Nothing more and nothing less. And the repetition of Vladimir's "so much the better" is as crucial as the phrase itself, as is the pause that follows. "What was it you wanted to know?" is the sound of "resuming" after recognizing that there is "nothing to be done."

Source: Terry Niehuis, in an essay for *Drama for Students,* Gale, 1997.

Ronald Hayman

In this excerpt from his book, Hayman speculates on the symbolism of Waiting for Godot*'s stasis of characters and action, concluding that, despite the play's more opaque moments, it is nonetheless an entertaining work.*

The action of most plays can be summed up in a few sentences, but not the action of *Godot.* Vivian Mercier's summary of the plot is: 'Nothing happens, twice.' But how can we describe the nothing that happens? *The act of waiting is itself a contradictory combination of doing nothing and doing something.* Vladimir and Estragon don't actually do anything and they are agreed right from the beginning that there's nothing they can do. 'Nothing to be done' is the play's opening line and although Estragon is talking about his boot, which he's trying to take off, Vladimir's answer immediately makes the line we've just heard into a general pronouncement about their situation in life:

> I'm beginning to come round to that opinion. All my life I've tried to put it from me, saying, Vladimir, be reasonable, you haven't yet tried everything. And I resumed the struggle.

But now that he has tried everything, or thinks he has, at least everything he's capable of trying, there's nothing left to do except wait for Godot. Which is the same as doing nothing, except that if you're waiting, you aren't free to go. Estragon keeps forgetting that and wanting to go, and each time Vladimir has to stop him. They have the same exchange of lines each time, like a refrain:

Let's go.
We can't.
Why not?
We're waiting for Godot.
Ah!

They wait for Godot both days that we see them and they're going to come back to wait for him again the next day, and no doubt the day after that and we can be family sure they were waiting for him on the previous day and the day before that and the day before that. Godot will never come but they'll never be sure that he's not coming because there will always seem to be some reason for hoping that he'll come tomorrow. And there'll always be the possibility that he came today and that they failed to recognize him. Perhaps Pozzo was Godot. It's even been suggested (by Norman Mailer in *Advertisements for Myself*) that Lucky was Godot. But in any case Vladimir and Estragon are trapped. There's nothing to force them to stay but there's no incentive to make them go. The only way out is death and the only relief is night. They keep talking about suicide but they're incapable of taking any action or even of really wanting to. So in effect waiting for Godot is waiting for your life to be over, waiting for night to fall, waiting for the play to end.

The tensions of the normal play are constructed around the interaction of the characters and the ignorance of the audience about what's going to happen next. In *Waiting for Godot* they soon get to know that nothing is going to happen next and that there's no chance of any development of character through relationships. The characters are not characters in this sense. There are many passages where it couldn't matter less who says which line:

ESTRAGON: They talk about their lives.
VLADIMIR: To have lived is not enough
    for them.
ESTRAGON: They have to talk about it.
VLADIMIR: To be dead is not enough for them.
ESTRAGON: It is not sufficient.
(*Silence.*)
VLADIMIR: They make a noise like feathers.
ESTRAGON: Like leaves.
VLADIMIR: Like ashes.
ESTRAGON: Like leaves.

But although it's not a play in the conventional sense, it's very much a play in the literal sense of the word 'play'. Having nothing to do with their time, Vladimir and Estragon are rather like children who have time to play games and have to play games to pass the time. 'What shall we do now?' is in effect what they're always saying to each other and some of their improvisations are very much like what children might think of to do. They play a game of

being Pozzo and Lucky, they play at being very polite to each other, at abusing each other, at making it up, and they stagger about on one leg trying to look like trees. The audience is involved most directly when they look out in horror at the auditorium, but in fact the audience is involved in the game all the way through because Beckett is playing around with the fact of having actors on a stage playing parts, and playing around with the idea of a play. Instead of working to keep the audience guessing about what's going to happen next, he manages to give the impression of having written the play without himself knowing how he was going to go on. We feel that it's not only Vladimir and Estragon but also Beckett himself welcoming Pozzo and Lucky's second entrance as providing a diversion just at the right moment. There is an air of improvisation about the writing, and though the final script is one that wouldn't allow any improvisation from the actors — it calls for great precision in performance — it has an engaging resemblance to the patter of a well-read conjurer. The tricks are simple ones but the rapid changes of conversational gear are masterly. Anything that appears so spontaneous must have been well rehearsed. And for Beckett, of course, the rehearsal was *Mercier and Camier*.

But what about the tricks? The most important trick in the style and structure of *Waiting for Godot* is the old music-hall trick of protracted delay. No question can be answered and no action can be taken without a maximum of interlocution, incomprehension and argument. You never go straight to a point if you can possibly miss it, evade it, or start a long discussion about a short cut. Vladimir and Estragon ask Pozzo why Lucky doesn't put down the bags. Pozzo is delighted at having a question to answer but it takes two pages of digression, repetition, incomprehension, cross-purpose dialogue and farcical preparations like spraying his throat before he actually answers it. Then a few minutes later, he wants to sit down, but he doesn't want to sit down until someone has asked him to sit, so Estragon offers to ask him, he agrees, Estragon asks him, he refuses, pauses, and in an aside asks Estragon to ask him again, he asks him again and finally he sits.

There is also a great deal of vaudeville business with hats and boots and prat-falls. The bowler-hats that all four characters wear belong to the tradition of Chaplin and Laurel and Hardy. Vladimir has a comic walk and a comic disability that makes him rush off to pee in the wings each time he's made to laugh, and Lucky has elaborate comic business with all the things he has to carry, dropping them, picking them up and putting them down. Although there's very little action, there's an enormous number of actions which the actors have to perform, and in which they're instructed meticulously by stage directions:

> (*Lucky weeps.*)
> ESTRAGON: He's crying.
> POZZO: Old dogs have more dignity.
> (*He proffers his handkerchief to Estragon.*)
> Comfort him, since you pity him.
> (*Estragon hesitates.*)
> Come on.
> (*Estragon takes the handkerchief.*)
> Wipe away his tears, he'll feel less forsaken.
> (*Estragon hesitates.*)
> VLADIMIR: Here, give it to me, I'll do it.
> (*Estragon refuses to give the handkerchief. Childish gestures.*)
> POZZO: Make haste, before he stops.
> (*Estragon approaches Lucky and makes to wipe his eyes. Lucky kicks him violently in the shins. Estragon drops the handkerchief recoils, staggers about the stage howling with pain.*)
> Hanky!
> (*Lucky puts down bag and basket, picks up the handkerchief gives it to Pozzo, goes back to his place, picks up bag and basket.*)

Another important trick is the way Beckett uses interruption. Almost everything in the play gets interrupted—Lucky's big speech, Estragon's story about the Englishman in the brothel, and Vladimir interrupts his own song about dogs digging a dog a tomb. But it's a song that circles back on itself, so, as with Lucky's speech, we welcome the interruption because we feel that otherwise it would have gone on for ever.

All in all, though, the play's brisk rhythm depends less on the frequent interruptions than on the shortness of the speeches. There are very few long speeches and these are judiciously placed at the points where they are most useful as a variation on the basic staccato. The average length of the speeches in *Waiting for Godot* must be less than in any other play that's ever been written. Together with the rapid changes of topic, this builds up an impression of great speed. If Vladimir and Estragon are doing nothing, at least they're doing it fast. . . .

With all the provocative gaps that there are in *Waiting for Godot* between the matter and the manner, between the half-statements and the half-meanings, it invites so much comment that it's easy to leave the most important point of all relatively unstressed—that it's consistently so very funny. In production, of course, there's a danger of getting bogged down in portentousness and letting the

THE SCRIPT PROVIDES THE POSSIBILITY OF AN EVENING IN THE THEATRE WHICH IS NEVER LESS THAN ENTERTAINING AND OFTEN VERY MUCH MORE"

effervescence go out of the dialogue if the pace is too slow. But the script provides the possibility of an evening in the theatre which is never less than entertaining and often very much more.

Source: Ronald Hayman, in his *Contemporary Playwrights: Samuel Beckett,* Heinemann Educational Books, 1968, pp. 4–8, 21.

Murray Schumach

A drama critic for the New York Times, *Schumach examines* Waiting for Godot's *character motivation in this article, drawing on the perceptions of the actors who appeared in the play's original Broadway run.*

Now that *Waiting for Godot,* a two-act tract with four men, one boy and countless interpretations, has been repatriated to Europe as part of the United States drama program at the Brussels World's Fair, an international signal has gone out to extol or deride the most controversial play since World War II, of which its author, Samuel Beckett, said: "I didn't choose to write a play. It just happened that way."

Other things that have happened since the play's stormy Paris debut in 1952—called by Jean Anouilh "as important as the premiere of Pirandello in 1923"—include a ban against any stories or advertising of the show in Spain; near-cancellation in the Netherlands averted by the furious resistance of the cast; successful runs in almost every important city of Europe. And on sophisticated Broadway, where it arrived in 1956, it created one of the most extraordinary phenomena in American show business. For, after the final curtain on many nights, the audience remained and, joined by interested literary figures and laymen, debated the play's meaning and merit. In these debates clergymen were sometimes pitted against each other on whether *Godot* was religious or atheistic. Its continued viability is proved by

NO. THERE IS NO GODOT"

twenty productions of *Godot* given this year in as many states.

On the surface there is little in this plotless drama to rouse the multitudes. It seems little more than a tale about two derelicts who wait vainly, on a bleak set that features a gnarled tree, for a Mr. Godot to appear and lessen their misery. While they wait, they hold long conversations, generally in short sentences, about their physical, mental and spiritual troubles. Their anxiety is diverted and intensified by the antics of a bully and his slave, and by a boy who twice brings them the message: "Mr. Godot told me to tell you he won't come this evening, but surely tomorrow."

Occasionally the pace of *Godot* is changed by comic turns, done by the two derelicts, that range from old-fashioned pratfalls to kicks. The longest speech in the play, a stream-of-consciousness outpouring, is delivered by the slave, who is otherwise mute.

That the force of arguments about *Godot* has not waned appreciably was shown earlier this month at its latest New York revival by the San Francisco Actor's Workshop, which has since taken the play to Brussels. At many of the performances spectators were asked to write comments on *Godot*. At least one-quarter of the 200-odd returns were unfavorable, another third bewildered or undecided, and the rest favorable. Those for *Godot* used such adjectives as stimulating, provoking, enlightening, superb, excellent, magnificent, poetic. Ranged against *Godot* were senseless, boring, vulgar, sacrilegious, hideous, repulsive, decadent. And even some who liked the play thought it unwise to send it to Brussels to represent the nation's regional theatre—the theatre outside New York City.

Almost as interesting as the reasons for argument about *Godot* are the lures that bring crowds to see it. Many undoubtedly come because they love the theatre and the play has caused a stir. Others are intellectuals who are curious about a play that is said to have a deeper meaning than that in most dramas. Finally, there are those who are drawn by a sort of egghead snobbery.

Godot has been much easier to blame or praise than to explain. One difficulty for its defendants is that the play's Irish-born author, who created the work in French, has not helped them in the few comments he has made about *Godot*. Thus, when a publisher wrote to him asking for his explanation of the play's symbols, he replied: "As far as I know, there are none. Of course, I am open to correction." And when Sir Ralph Richardson, the British star, asked him if Godot represented God, he replied: "If by Godot I had meant God, I would have said God, not Godot."

Thornton Wilder, leader of the proGodotians who scrutinize the play's sixty-one pages with the fiery reverence of cabala students, calls the play "a picture of total nihilism" and a "very admirable work." But, adds Mr. Wilder whose Pulitzer-prize-winning *The Skin of Our Teeth* also caused a furor, "I don't try to work out detailed symbolism. I don't think you're supposed to." Michael Myerberg, who first produced the play in this country, says: "It very much reflects the hopelessness and dead end we've run into. What he's trying to say is: 'All we have is ourselves—each other—and we may as well make the best of it.'"

Bert Lahr, who was in the original Broadway production as Estragon, the derelict who does not know why he's waiting, originally did not know what the play meant. Now he has some unusual interpretations.

"The play," he says, "is very complex and has many analyses. But mine is as good as the rest. The two men are practically one—one is the animal side, the other the mental. I was the animal. So far as Pozzo and Lucky [master and slave] are concerned, we have to remember that Beckett was a disciple of Joyce and that Joyce hated England. Beckett meant Pozzo to be England, and Lucky to be Ireland."

Mr. Lahr recalls vividly the post-performance seminars: "I remember one night a lady jumped out of her seat screaming: 'What's the difference? What's the difference? We were entertained, weren't we!'" Then there was a woman who came to his dressing room one night. The actor held out his hand to greet her, but all she did was to say: "Oh, Mr. Lahr —" and run off crying.

"No, I haven't read anything by Beckett since that play," says Lahr. "I'm not that erudite."

E. G. Marshall, whose performance as the other derelict, Vladimir, was as memorable as Mr. Lahr's, attended only one after-theatre symposium. "Then

I ran like a frightened deer. I listened to them and thought: 'My God. Is that what the play means?' Every time a mouth opened, out came a different interpretation. That's no good for an actor.''

In reaching his own interpretation, Mr. Marshall went through a process somewhat different from Mr. Lahr's. ''The first time I read the play I thought it was wonderful. That was about a couple of years before I was in it. Then I saw it in London. It was a hit there. But I thought: 'What the hell did I ever see in that play? It's so boring. It's probably nice to read, but it won't play.'

''Then Mike Myerberg asked me to be in it here. I went through an evolutionary process. At first we actors used to have violent arguments about what the play meant. And then we'd have violent agreements. Eventually, I saw it in black-and-white terms, I was the intellectual in the play. The play, we agreed, was a positive play, not negative, not pessimistic. As I saw it, with my blood and skin and eyes, the philosophy is: 'No matter what—atom bombs, hydrogen bombs, anything—life goes on. You can kill yourself, but you can't kill life.'

''I don't know if it's a great play. But it is a real theatre piece. Not something that has to be molded and hacked to fit in a theatre. The theatre today is too flaccid, too passive, too dull. It is good to have it stirred up by a play like this. I think *Waiting for Godot* will remain in the theatre and will mean something to succeeding casts and to succeeding audiences.''

Members of the San Francisco troupe have a variety of ideas about the play. One calls it ''a play of despair in which a man is seeking salvation, frustrated in finding it, and incapable of coping with waiting.'' Another says: ''This is a fairly modern state of mind, existential, in which man tries to remove despair and find some strength.'' A third recalls: ''At first I thought it trite. Then I realized that Beckett is a tremendous humanitarian. He does not condemn humanity at any time. He asks mankind to look at itself.'' A fourth sees Lucky, the slave, as ''the sensitive artist in modern society.''

Those who admire the play for its beauty cite the following speech by Vladimir, when he is urging Estragon to help the fallen Pozzo, the bully:

''Let us do something while we have the chance! It is not every day that we are needed. Others would meet the case equally well, if not better. To all mankind they were addressed, those cries for help

still ringing in our ears! But at this place, at this moment of time, all mankind is us, whether we like it or not. Let us make the most of it, before it is too late! Let us represent worthily for once the foul brood to which a cruel fate consigned us! What do you say? (*Estragon says nothing.*) It is true that when with folded arms we weigh the pros and cons we are no less a credit to our species. The tiger bounds to the help of his congeners without the least reflection, or else he slinks away into the depths of the thickets. But that is not the question. And we are blessed in this, that we happen to know the answer. Yes, in this immense confusion one thing is clear. We are waiting for Godot to come.''

Those who see Beckett as a satiric sage cite the following: ''There's man all over for you, blaming on his boots the faults of his feet.'' Or: ''We always find something *** to give us the impression we exist.'' Or: ''The tears of the world are a constant quantity. For each one who begins to weep somewhere else another stops. The same is true of the laugh. Let us not then speak ill of our generation, it is not any unhappier than its predecessors. Let us not speak well of it either. Let us not speak of it at all. It is true the population has increased.''

Despite its triumphs in Paris, where it was called *En Attendant Godot,* and London, *Waiting for Godot* had to wait for production in the United States and very nearly died on the doorstep. When Myerberg first saw the script, he dismissed it as impossible to produce. Six months later, in London, he changed his mind, while watching a performance. At first he tried it in Miami. It failed dismally. One estimate is that more than half the opening-night audience failed to return after the intermission. But Myerberg, a stubborn man and a gambler, assembled the cast of Lahr, Marshall, Kurt Kasznar and Alvin Epstein, with Herbert Berghof as director.

With considerable showmanship, he brought it to Broadway, preceding its opening on April 8, 1956, with an advertisement in this paper which reads: ''This is a play for the thoughtful and discriminating theatregoer. We are, therefore, offering it for a limited engagement of only four weeks. I respectfully suggest that those who come to the theatre for casual entertainment do not buy a ticket to this attraction.''

The show extended its run to twice the original four weeks. Author Beckett, in one of his rare comments, wrote to the producer: ''It is gratifying to learn that the bulk of your audiences was made up of young people. This was also the case in Paris,

London and throughout Germany. I must, after all, be less dead than I thought.''

Though Beckett might be gratified that the San Francisco troupe doing his play in Brussels is also young, he may not think as much of the reason that prompted the company to choose his play. It happened to be the least costly play in the troupe's repertory and the State Department was footing no bill for transportation. The San Francisco company, however, has learned to make ends meet during its trying existence since it was formed in 1952. Nearly all of its ninety-two members—only ten have gone abroad —have to support themselves with other work. Productions are usually presented only on week-ends.

Mr. Beckett, too, has faced some tough times. Born in 1906, a graduate of Trinity College, Dublin, where he later took his M. A. and lectured in French, he began wandering around Europe in 1932, settling finally in Paris. He remained in France during World War II, but moved to the Unoccupied Zone. During 1945–46 he was a storekeeper and interpreter with the Irish Red Cross in bombarded Normandy. Before he wrote *En Attendant Godot,* he did a collection of short stories, *More Pricks Than Kicks,* a collection of poems, *Echo's Bones: a* trilogy of novels—*Molloy, Malone Meurt* and *L'Inuomable.* Since *Godot* he has been represented in the theatre by *Endgame,* a play that has not notably increased his following.

Since Beckett is curious about what the young think of *Godot,* the 8 year-old who plays the part of the boy with the San Francisco troupe was asked his interpretation of the play. He replied:

''Two men are waiting for Godot. They want to hang themselves. Lucky and Pozzo come in, Lucky is the slave and Pozzo is the master. Then I come in. I give them a message. Then I go off. So next day they still want to hang themselves. Pozzo is blind. I come in with the same message.''

''What do you think,'' the boy was asked, ''happens to the two men afterward?''

''I think,'' he replied, after a short pause, ''that at the way, way, way end, they hang themselves.''

''Do you think,'' the boy was asked, ''there is a Godot?''

''No. There is no Godot,'' he replied, then picked up his toy battleship and wandered off.

Source: Murray Schumach, ''Why They Wait for Godot'' in the *New York Times Magazine,* September 21, 1958, pp. 36, 38, 41.

FURTHER READING

Bloom, Harold, editor. *Samuel Beckett's ''Waiting for Godot,''* Chelsea House, 1987.
Part of the Modern Critical Interpretations Series, this collection of modern critical commentary is designed for the college undergraduate.

Fletcher, John and Beryl S. *A Student's Guide to the Plays of Samuel Beckett,* Second Edition, Faber and Faber, 1985.
Most valuable to the student because the book's section on *Waiting for Godot* includes notes explaining especially important or difficult details in the text of the play.

Gussow, Mel. *Conversations with and about Beckett,* Grove Press, 1996.
A collection of transcriptions and interviews, some involving Beckett—who generally refused to talk about himself and his work in public—others involving his artistic collaborators.

Schlueter, June, and Brater, Enoch. *Approaches to Teaching Beckett's ''Waiting for Godot,''* MLA, 1991.
A rich and varied collection of teachers' approaches to teaching the play, valuable for students as well.

Worth, Katharine. *''Waiting for Godot'' and ''Happy Days'': Text and Performance,* Macmillan, 1990.
Focusing on the play as a text for theatrical production, this book is aimed specifically at the senior high school and college undergraduate reader, discussing both traditional views of the play and its continued relevance.

SOURCES

Anouilh, Jean. Review in *Arts Spectacles,* February 27-March 5, 1953, p. 1.

Bentley, Eric. Review in *New Republic,* May 14, 1956, pp. 20-1.

Ben-Zvi, Linda. *Samuel Beckett,* Twayne, 1986.

Blin, Roger. ''Blin on Beckett,'' *Theater,* Fall, 1978, pp. 90-2.

Cohn, Ruby, editor. *Casebook on ''Waiting for Godot,''* Grove, 1967.

Cohn, Ruby, editor. *''Waiting for Godot'': A Casebook,* Macmillan, 1987.

Conner, Steven, editor. *"Waiting for Godot" and "Endgame": Samuel Beckett,* St. Martin's, 1992.

Esslin, Martin. "The Absurdity of the Absurd" and "Samuel Beckett: The Search for the Self," in his *The Theatre of the Absurd,* revised edition, Doubleday, 1969, pp. 1-65.

Hall, Peter. Extract from an interview on *Third Programme,* British Broadcasting Company (BBC), April 14, 1961. Reprinted in *"Waiting for Godot": A Casebook,* edited by Ruby Cohn, pp. 30-1, Macmillan, 1987.

Kenner, Hugh. *A Reader's Guide to Samuel Beckett,* Syracuse University Press, 1996.

Knowlson, James. *Damned to Fame: The Life of Samuel Beckett,* Simon & Schuster, 1996.

Lemarchand, Jacques. Review in *Figaro Litteraire,* January 17, 1953, p. 10.

Zegel, Sylvain. Review in *Liberation,* January 7, 1953.

Wedding Band

ALICE CHILDRESS

1966

Although Alice Childress wrote *Wedding Band* (the full title of which is *Wedding Band: A Love/Hate Story in Black and White*) in the early 1960s, the play was not performed professionally until 1966. There was interest in producing the play on Broadway, but because of its controversial subject matter the play remained largely unknown to audiences. Finally in 1972 *Wedding Band* was produced in New York for the first time. Subsequently, a New York Shakespeare Festival production of the play, based on Childress's screenplay, was broadcast by ABC in 1973; however, several ABC affiliates refused to carry the television production. The play examines the enduring nature of love between a white man and a black woman in 1918 South Carolina. *Wedding Band* confronts racism, but Childress reveals that racism is not only directed at blacks, but is also displayed by blacks. In the play, whites, Asians, and Jews are also victims of racism. Childress's depiction of an interracial love affair broke long-standing taboos on stage and television. While white critics argued that Herman should have been stronger and more determined to break away from southern racism, black critics maintained that Childress should have focused her writing on a black couple. Childress's characters are not idealized human beings; they are the imperfect men and women of a real world. Rather than present audiences with a model for racial harmony, Childress exposes the reality of life for black and white Americans as she explores the frailty of a humanity so entrenched in maintaining rules and social lines that it forgets that there are lives at stake.

AUTHOR BIOGRAPHY

Alice Childress was born October 12, 1920, in Charleston, South Carolina. Childress, who dropped out of high school after two years, was raised in Harlem in New York City by her grandmother, Eliza Campbell. Campbell had only an elementary school education, but she was an accomplished storyteller and likely instilled in Childress an early interest in telling stories. Although her formal education ended early, Childress continued to educate herself during hours spent reading at the public library. She became interested in acting after hearing an actress recite Shakespeare and joined the American Negro Theatre (ANT) in Harlem when she was twenty years old. Childress was an actress and director with ANT for eleven years and appeared in some of their biggest hits, including *A Midsummer-Night's Dream, Natural Man,* and *Anna Lucasta.*

Childress wrote her first play, *Florence,* in 1949. This one-act play explored racial issues and was well received by critics and audiences. *Florence* examined the prejudices of both white and black characters and established the direction many of Childress's subsequent plays would take. She followed this early success with another play, *Just A Little Simple,* an adaptation of the Langston Hughes's novel, *Simple Speaks His Mind.* Childress's third play, written in 1952, *Gold Through The Trees,* became the first play by a black woman to be professionally produced on the American stage. Childress's next play, *Trouble in Mind,* focused on a topic she knew well, the difficulties black women faced as actresses. The play was very successful, and Childress became the first woman to win the *Village Voice* Obie Award (for the best original Off-Broadway play of the 1955-1956 season). A revised edition of this play was published in *Black Theatre: A Twentieth-Century Collection of the Work of Its Best Playwrights.* Childress next composed *Wedding Band* and *Wine in the Wilderness;* the latter was written for public television in 1969 and was the first play broadcast by WGBS Boston as part of a series "On Being Black." This was followed by a one-act play in 1969, *String,* an adaptation of the Guy de Maupassant story "A

Alice Childress

Piece of String." Another one-act play, *Mojo: A Black Love Story,* followed in 1970.

Childress continued to write plays, including two for children, *When the Rattlesnake Sounds* (1975) and *Let's hear it For the Queen* (1976). Childress also wrote several books; the first, 1986's *Like One of the Family: Conversations from a Domestic's Life,* was based on conversations with black domestic workers. She also wrote several novels for young adults, including *A Hero Ain't Nothin' But A Sandwich* (1973), *A Short Walk* (1979), *Rainbow Jordan* (1981), and *Those Other People* (1989).

Although Childress never attended college, she was much in demand as a lecturer and speaker at colleges. She was married twice and had a daughter from her first marriage. Childress died of cancer on August 14, 1994.

PLOT SUMMARY

Wedding Band depicts a tragedy involving an interracial affair. The action takes place over a period of three days near the end of World War I. The setting is 1918 South Carolina where state law prevents interracial marriage. Julia is a black woman in love with a white man, Herman. They would like to escape the south and move to the north where they would be free to marry, but Herman is not free to leave, since he must repay money borrowed from his mother when he purchased his bakery. As the play opens, Julia and Herman are celebrating ten years together. Faced with the disapproval of her neighbors, Julia has been forced to move several times; it is clear that she is lonely and discouraged. While the law poses the very real threat of arrest and criminal punishment for any interracial couple who marry or live together, the condemnation of Julia's black neighbors is just as damaging and helps to reveal that racism is not only directed toward blacks but also toward whites.

In Act I, the audience is introduced to Julia's neighbors. Her landlady, Fanny, is a pretentious black woman who is revealed to be superficial and hypocritical. The other women who rent from Fanny, Lula, and Mattie, have been victimized by brutal husbands and have experienced personal tragedy. And it is clear that all of the women in this play have struggled against economic oppression and social injustice. In this first act, Julia's new neighbors ply her with questions about her personal life. To satisfy their curiosity, Julia tells them that she has been in love with a man for ten years but that she cannot marry him because he is white. Her neighbors cannot understand why Julia would choose a white man with no money and their disapproval is clear as they walk away from her. Next, Herman appears with a boxed wedding cake and a ring to celebrate their tenth common-law anniversary. The ring is mounted on a chain so that Julia might wear it, since they both realize that she cannot wear the gift as a wedding ring. Herman gives Julia enough money to buy a ticket to New York, and she makes plans to leave in two days. Herman states that he can repay his debts and join her in a year; in the interim, Julia can stay with her cousin. Herman and Julia begin to make plans for their wedding, but Act I ends with Herman becoming ill.

As Act II opens, Herman has influenza and has collapsed at Julia's home. The landlady refuses to call a doctor for fear of legal action directed against her for sheltering this couple; the landlady also fears that social disrepute will be aimed against everyone present, especially herself. Instead, Herman's sister and mother are sent for but Herman's mother will not move him until she has the protection of darkness. Like the landlady, Herman's mother is more interested in keeping up appearances than in saving

Herman's life. Years of racial hatred explode in the room as Julia and Herman's mother shout racial insults at each other. Finally, Herman is taken away amid many accusations and much rancor.

The last scene opens with Julia dressed in her wedding dress. She seems artificially excited and there is evidence that she has been drinking wine. Julia is surrounded by her neighbors, and it is revealed that her neighbor Mattie is not legally married, since South Carolina does not permit divorce. Although her first husband had beaten and deserted her, Mattie cannot be free of him so that she can marry the father of her child and the man with whom she has lived for eleven years. At this moment Herman arrives with two tickets to New York, but Julia is unable to forget the confrontation of the previous day or a lifetime of racial hatred, and so she gives the tickets and her wedding band to Mattie and her child. As Herman and Julia talk they remember the years of love and closeness, and they finally resolve the tensions that separated them. Herman is ill, however, and dying. Julia locks Herman's mother out of her house, and the play ends with Herman dying in his lover's arms.

CHARACTERS

Annabelle

Annabelle is Herman's sister and is in her thirties. She is evidently very tall and is happy to have finally found a man who is taller than she. She wants to marry Walter, but he is a common sailor, not an officer, and so not socially acceptable as a husband according to her mother. Annabelle wants Herman to break off from Julia and marry a white woman who can help care for their mother; she sees this as the only way she will ever be freed from her mother and able to marry Walter. Because she is German, Annabelle has been discriminated against and so places a sign in a window of her home proclaiming that her family is American. Annabelle is a war-time volunteer at the Naval hospital, but when Herman falls sick she is of little help; like her mother, she is also opposed to calling a doctor and wants to wait for the protection of darkness before moving Herman out of the black neighborhood.

Julia Augustine

Julia is a thirty-five year old black seamstress with an eighth grade education. She is lonely,

Julia and Herman's mother confront each other in a scene from a 1989 Milwaukee production

isolated, and ashamed that she is not respectably married. She is in love with Herman even though he has no money and is uneducated. She is a social outcast, not really a member of her own black race and certainly not welcomed by whites. She is showing the strain of ten years of social disapproval and isolation. She tries to free Mattie by giving her the tickets and the wedding band. For Julia, all white people are the enemy except for Herman.

Bell man

Bell man is a thirty year old white peddler who extends credit to his black female customers, and is owed money by most women in the neighborhood. He asks Julia for sex and offers to give her stockings in return.

Frieda

See Thelma

Lula Green

Like Julia and Mattie, Lula has also suffered economically and personally. Her husband chased women, abused her, and then died. Her young son

died when he wandered in front of a train and was struck. Lula adopted Nelson from an orphanage after these deaths; she now channels all of her energy into caring for her adopted son and worries about him excessively. She tries to shelter Nelson from anyone she thinks might do him harm, even apologizing to bell man to protect her son from the peddler's anger. Lula makes paper flowers to earn extra money.

Nelson Green

Nelson is the adopted adult son of Lula. He is home on leave from the army and due to report back in a couple of days. He is filled with bravado but is really scared and intimidated. He recognizes that, as a black man, he has no real future. Should he survive his time at war, he will return to the same lack of opportunity, the same segregation, and the same hostility he has left; he will not even allow himself to hope that he might come back to something different. Nelson is so cowed by the system and his environment that even when a pail of dirty water is dumped on his head he reacts with apologies and is unable to assert himself. Nelson proposes to the woman he is courting, but she declines his proposal because, as she tells him, he has nothing to offer her.

MEDIA ADAPTATIONS

- *Wedding Band* was adapted for television by the American Broadcasting Company in 1973. Childress wrote the screenplay for the ABC production.

Herman

Herman is a forty year old uneducated man, who is slightly graying. He is a poor but hardworking baker, is genuinely compassionate, and is trapped in South Carolina by the loan he received from his mother when he purchased the bakery. Herman seems to be the only character who does not see people in terms of race; he treats Julia and her black neighbors the same as he would treat any person of any color. Herman is caught between his mother's disapproval of Julia and his love for Julia. In one of the play's climactic scenes both women engage in a shouting match as Herman is dying from influenza.

Fannie Johnson

Fannie is Julia's landlady. Fannie wants to "represent her race in an *approved* manner." She is a nosy woman, full of pride, and pretends to belong to a better social class as a property owner. She fears a quarantine, social condemnation, and legal difficulties if a doctor is called for Herman. Fannie ingratiates herself to Herman's mother because each sees the other for she is, namely a pretentious social climber and hypocrite. Fannie propositions Nelson to live with her as a "business manager."

Mattie

Mattie is a very poor black woman with all the economic problems of a single mother. Her common-law husband, October, is away at sea in the merchant marines. She has a great deal of dignity and struggles to earn extra money making candy and babysitting a white child, Princess. She was deserted by her first husband who beat her, but she cannot divorce him because divorce is not legal in South Carolina. She has been with October for eleven years and they have a daughter. When Mattie tries to claim her husband's merchant marine benefits, she is told their marriage is not valid. Julia frees Mattie when she gives her the two tickets to New York and her wedding band.

Princess

Princess is the eight year old white child who Mattie babysits, and who serves as a playmate for Teeta.

Teeta

Teeta is Mattie's eight year old daughter. As the play opens, Teeta is weeping because she has lost a quarter. Her desperate search for the lost money illustrates how scarce cash is for Mattie and reveals the poverty of her life.

Thelma

Herman's mother is a fifty-seven year old white woman who is bitter, miserable, and without love. She calls herself Thelma, but her real name is Frieda, a German name that she conceals out of fear of discrimination. Frieda is intolerant and would rather her son Herman die then be with Julia. Herman's job as a baker is a source of embarrassment for his mother as is Annabelle's romance with a common sailor; yet, Frieda is a sharecropper's daughter who pretends to belong to a higher social class. She reveals that she was not happy being married to a common man and that five of the seven children she bore were stillborn. She has loaned Herman $3,000 to buy his bakery, and this unpaid debt keeps him in South Carolina. Frieda believes in a racist ideology and is a supporter of the Ku Klux Klan. She so hates the black woman her son loves and is so repulsed by their relationship that she refuses to call a doctor for him. As she waits for the cover of darkness to move him from Julia's house, Frieda accuses Julia of stealing money from Herman's wallet. The women's shouting escalates into a horrific verbal battle of racial insults so intense that both Julia and Frieda seem to forget Herman's illness.

THEMES

Julia, a black woman, is in love with Herman, who is white. The play takes place over a period of three

TOPICS FOR FURTHER STUDY

- Study miscegenation laws in the south and discuss their purpose and effectiveness in keeping blacks and whites separate.

- Investigate the role of black men serving in the U.S. military during World War I. Pay special attention to the role of segregation within the military ranks.

- In *Wedding Band* Herman buys two tickets to New York, but cannot use them because blacks and whites must be separated on the boat. Research segregation laws and the effect they had on public transportation, paying special attention

to when the laws were enacted and for what purpose.

- *Wedding Band* demonstrates that the issue of single motherhood is not a new problem; Childress argues in an interview that laws enacted after the Civil War almost guaranteed that black women would be raising their children as single parents. Study the origins of this problem beginning with the laws enacted after the Civil War that gave black women the sole responsibility for supporting their children.

---

days when Herman's illness forces the main characters to deal with issues that have shaped their lives for ten years.

Alienation and Loneliness

Alienation and loneliness are important themes in *Wedding Band,* because they accurately describe the reality of Julia's life. Because of her love for a white man, Julia is alienated from her own race. She is not accepted by black society and rejected by her own white culture, and she has been forced to move several times by prying neighbors who disapprove of her interracial love affair with Herman. Because marriage and cohabitation between blacks and whites is forbidden by South Carolina law, Julia must isolate herself or risk being prosecuted and punished by legal authorities.

Human Rights

Human Rights is an important issue, since the major conflict in *Wedding Band* is the result of social and racial injustice. Julia and Herman do not have the same rights under the law as a white couple or a black couple. Because their love crosses color lines, they confront the intolerance of society, which is represented by unjust laws. It is the desire to keep races separate that lies at the heart of laws that forbid interracial marriage. *Wedding Band* presents

a convincing argument for the rights of all people to love one another and live together as equals.

Custom and Tradition

Julia and Herman represent a new order in the American south during the twentieth century. They are confronting a tradition of separation of the races with their love for one another. Social custom dictates that Julia should love and marry a black man. Even the law reinforces that custom, but in this play Julia attempts to establish the right to change custom and tradition.

Freedom

The inability to act on personal choice emphasizes the importance of freedom in *Wedding Band.* Julia and Herman lack the basic freedom to love and marry; laws circumvent that freedom, and consequently, this white man and black woman are forbidden personal choice in terms of whom they will love and marry.

Friendship

Julia's quickness in giving money to Mattie and in helping her read the letter from October illustrate how friendship is a theme in *Wedding Band.* It is Julia's need for friends that led her to move back into the city. Her isolation in the country, while providing her with an element of protection from the law, resulted in a loneliness so profound that she was forced into risking social ostracism and legal consequences if her relationship with Herman was revealed. The theme of friendship is also important in a second way; it is the friendship of the women in this play—Julia, Mattie, and Lula—that forms a bond against the poverty and racism that permeates their lives.

Limitations and Opportunities

All of the characters in *Wedding Band* are limited by their location and by time in which they live. Julia lacks the opportunity to marry the man of her choice because the law sets limits on who can and who cannot marry. Herman cannot free himself from his mother and marry the woman he loves because he is limited by the terms of a loan he needs to repay. And although she has been abused and deserted by her first husband, Mattie cannot divorce legally. Her opportunity to marry her partner of eleven years and the father of her child is denied by law, and poverty limits her ability to move and thus seek the divorce she needs. Nelson is limited by the social conditions of the period which require him with to risk his life in the defense of his country but which deny him protection from the racism of his countrymen.

Prejudice and Tolerance

Prejudice and tolerance are important themes in *Wedding Band* because it is the community's intolerance and society's racism that keep Julia and Herman from marrying and from seeking medical attention for the dying Herman. And while it clear that Herman's mother is prejudiced against black people, it is also clear that the black characters in *Wedding Band* are suspicious of the white characters, particularly of Herman. Additionally, Julia's isolation from the community is the result of prejudice and intolerance. She lives alone, moves frequently, and has no friends because the world in which she lives has declared that whites and blacks cannot marry. The law that forbids their union serves to illustrate the depth of social intolerance and prejudice that characterized the south earlier in this century. There is even a prejudice within both white and black society based on class. Fannie sees herself as a step above her tenants because she is a property owner, and Herman's mother is opposed to her daughter's marriage to a ''common sailor.'' Both Fannie and Herman's mother illustrate that subtle nuances of prejudice can be just as oppressive

as the more obvious racial prejudices that create tension in this play.

Race and Racism

Race and racism serves as the most prominent theme of *Wedding Band*. It is racism that leads to Herman's death and to ten long years of denied love. Racism lies at the center of a law that prevents blacks and whites from inter-marrying. *Wedding Band* examines how legal authority and social custom serve as a force to maintain racism within society. There are also examples of other types of racism in the play. The characters are intolerant of Jews, Germans, and of one another. The actions and words of the characters reveal that racism is more than white oppression of blacks; prejudice can also be found in black Americans' distrust of white Americans.

STYLE

Wedding Band is a two act play with prose dialogue, stage directions, and no interior dialogue. The two acts are also subdivided into scenes. There are no soliloquies, and thus, the thoughts of the characters and any action off stage must be explained by the actors. The actors address one another in *Wedding Band* and not the audience.

Structure

Wedding Band is a two act play. The exposition and complication are combined in the first act when the audience learns of the love between Julia and Herman and the issues that prevent their marriage. The climax occurs in the second act when Herman's mother confronts the two lovers. The catastrophe also occurs in this act when Julia and Herman are reconciled.

Conflict

The conflict is the issue to be resolved in the play. It usually occurs between two characters, but it can also occur between a character and society. Conflict serves to create tension in a plot, and indeed, it is often the motivating force that drive a plot. In *Wedding Band* , there is a clear conflict between Julia's love for Herman and the expectations of a society that forbids and even punishes the love between black and white partners. There is also conflict between Herman and his mother who disapproves of her son's love for Julia. And finally,

Julia's isolation from her own race also represents the conflict between the expectations of black society and Julia's choice in loving a white man.

Empathy

Empathy is a sense of a shared experience and can include emotional and physical feelings with someone or something other than oneself. Empathy, an involuntary projection of ourselves, is different from sympathy, which denotes a feeling for someone, rather than an understanding of his or her situation. For example, Mattie and Lula can sympathize with Julia who loves a man who cannot offer her marriage and protection, but they empathize when they reveal that they share the same experience, despite the fact that Julia is involved in an interracial relationship.

Setting

The time, place, and culture in which the action of the play takes place is called the setting. The elements of setting may include geographic location, physical or mental environments, prevailing cultural attitudes, or the historical time in which the action takes place. The location for *Wedding Band* is South Carolina in 1918. The action occurs over a period of three days near the end of the war. The women characters live in poverty, which is depicted by the circumstances of their homes.

HISTORICAL CONTEXT

Racism and Racial Intolerance

In 1966, Alice Childress addressed the lack of freedom that defined the lives of black Americans. In an essay published in *Freedomways,* Childress noted that immigrants arriving in the United States have more freedoms than African Americans: "We know that most alien visitors are guaranteed rights and courtesies not extended to at least one-fifth of American citizens." Childress argued that the story of the black woman has not been told by Hollywood or the popular press. It was the need to tell this story that motivated Childress's writing. In the 1960s blacks were still denied equality in education and in the right to vote. Neighborhoods, towns, and cities were segregated, and black Americans who wished to marry white Americans had to be able to pass as whites or face the punishment of laws that regulated marriage between the two races. Childress noted that children born to mixed couples were required to

be registered as such at birth, and so a child's very existence provided the means to imprison his or her parents. Childress reminded her audience that the lives of black people were still controlled by a legal system dominated by white society. This was the reality of the world in which Childress composed *Wedding Band* in the early 1960s.

Although the action of *Wedding Band* takes place in 1918, the topic of interracial marriage was still so controversial in 1966 that Childress's play proved difficult to produce. It was not until 1973 that the play was performed in New York. Yet even then the controversial content of *Wedding Band* resulted in the refusal of several ABC affiliates to broadcast the production. Childress stated in the *Negro Digest* in 1967 that her play serves as a reminder that, for black women, the world of 1918 had changed little by 1966. That producers were so reluctant to produce *Wedding Band* and so sensitive to public opinion that the play languished for seven years before its New York debut lends credence to Childress's statement.

Miscegenation Law

The inspiration for *Wedding Band* was, in part, the miscegenation law that forbid the marriage or cohabitation of two individuals of different races. Yet even though interracial marriage was forbidden by law in the south, Julia could not have escaped segregation by fleeing to the north. In spite of the fact that her marriage to Herman would have been sanctioned legally in the north, social pressures and racism would still have served to ostracize Julia from the community. In fact, in 1966 laws forbidding interracial marriages were still on the books and being enforced in South Carolina.

Role of Women

After the end of the Civil War and the abolishment of slavery, laws were passed in southern states proclaiming that all children born to black women were the responsibility of the mothers only. The purpose of this law was to provide protection for slave owners from black women who might seek support for their children fathered by white slave owners. The result was that black women were abandoned to raise their children alone without any assistance from either black or white fathers. In the years following the war, women were free to find a black man willing to marry them and assume responsibility for their children; however, most African American men were in no position to support a family, having no access to education or well-

COMPARE
&
CONTRAST

- **1918:** Private Alvin York leads an attack on a German machine gun nest that kills 25 of the enemy. He captures 132 prisoners and 35 machine guns, is promoted to sergeant, and is awarded the Congressional Medal of Honor. York was drafted in spite of his status as a conscientious objector.

  1966: International Days of Protest in many world cities criticize U.S. policy in Vietnam.

  Today: Twenty-two years after the end of the Vietnam war, the Vietnam Veteran's Memorial in Washington D.C. has become the most popular tourist attraction in the city.

- **1918:** A resolution providing for a U.S. Women's Suffrage Amendment to the Constitution passes in the House of Representatives, but the Senate rejects the measure for the third time.

  1966: Governor Wallace signs a bill forbidding Alabama's public schools to comply with the Office of Education's desegregation guidelines.

  Today: Oprah Winfrey, an African American television personality and actress, is one of the highest paid performers and richest women in the United States. She is one of many African Americans who have been able to succeed, despite the fact that racism remains a prevalent American societal problem.

- **1918:** Nearly twenty-five percent of all Americans fall ill from the Spanish Influenza; 500,000 die, including 19,000 in New York. Coffin supplies are exhausted in Baltimore and Washington.

  1966: Inadequate health care and poor nutrition among expectant mothers in low income groups are responsible for an infant mortality rate in the U.S. that exceeds that of Britain and Sweden.

  Today: Health care continues to be a problem for the nation's poor who have little access to health insurance. New welfare reform laws have further eroded the ability of the poor to seek medical attention and thus the U.S. continues to have the highest infant mortality rate of first world countries.

- **1918:** Al Jolson sings "My Mammy" at the Winter Garden Theatre in the opening of the production of *Sinbad.*

  1966: The television drama *Star Trek* has its debut on NBC with a cast that included a black woman in a role of the communications officer. Nichelle Nichols provides young black women with one of the few positive role models in television.

  Today: The movie *Rosewood* opens in theatres with a story of racism and the destruction of a small town in post-World War I Florida.

---

paying jobs. With laws designed to keep the African Americans separate from white society, access to parks, neighborhoods, education, and even drinking fountains ensured the subordination of blacks. Consequently, the first fifty years after the end of the civil war saw a series of laws enacted that served only to enslave African Americans with invisible chains forged out of prejudice and hatred. This lack of opportunity and the devastating poverty that ensued is dramatically illustrated in the opening scene of *Wedding Band,* in which the loss of a quarter represents the loss of significant income for Mattie. It is further depicted when Nelson's marriage offer is rejected because he has no future. Although he will risk his life defending his country as a soldier, he will return to South Carolina after the war and once again assume the position of subservience that has defined his behavior. His mother, Lula, asks Julia to reassure Nelson that he will return to a different world, one in which he will have opportunity and equality, but both Julia and Nelson recognize that his future after World War I is as limited as it was before the war. In short, he had no future and no opportunity in the American south.

CRITICAL OVERVIEW

Wedding Band was largely ignored by critics and producers when it was written. Producers shied away from such controversial topics as interracial marriage and the miscegenation laws still in effect in many southern states. There was a rehearsed reading in 1963 and the play was optioned for Broadway by producers but after changing hands several times was not produced. The first production was at the University of Michigan in 1966 and received positive reviews. But it was not until late 1972 that *Wedding Band* was finally produced in New York before a larger audience. ABC finally presented a production of the play for television audiences in 1973; however, several ABC affiliates in the South banned the showing. In an article in *Melus,* Rosemary Curb reported that there is no clear explanation for why the play was ignored by American producers, since no producer told Childress directly that the subject was too controversial. However, Curb related that Childress herself thinks that the content was simply unpopular and speculated that there was little interest in the story of a middle-aged black woman.

When *Wedding Band* was first produced in New York in 1972, Childress was set to direct. *Southern Quarterly* contributor Polly Holliday asserted that Childress was quick to respond to the actors' concerns and suggestions and that Childress's rewriting always ''enhanced the suggestion'' of the actors. Holliday also observed that ''the rewriting was always done with artistry, incorporating all her knowledge of form, rhythm and picturesque speech. She was, to my mind, a complete professional.'' However, as the play neared opening night there were problems, and Childress was dismissed as director; Joseph Papp, the director of the New York Shakespeare Festival, took over. Still, much of Childress's direction was retained and the show opened to good reviews.

Wedding Band opened off-Broadway to slightly mixed reviews. While the critics were largely enthusiastic and applauded it as a play about black America that is not a ''black play,'' it was also described as a story that could have been taken from a women's magazine. In an essay in *Modern American Drama: The Female Canon,* Catherine Wiley noted that denying that the play is a ''black play'' reassures a potential audience that the play will not be of interest to only a black audience and assumes that white audiences would not be interested in seeing a play about black Americans. Of the review that assigned the play's content to the genre of ''women's magazines,'' Wiley declared that the reviewer assumed that men would have no interest in a subject that focuses on issues of home and hearth. Wiley noted that the fact that none of the critics expressed any shock at the theme of miscegenation was because the New York production occurred six years after the initial Michigan performance, implying that the lack of interest in this play was a reaction to the play's content, although no reviewer would say so in print.

Both black and white critics of the play offered different reactions to *Wedding Band.* Some black reviewers criticized Childress for not having Julia reject Herman, and they argued that Childress should have depicted a black couple's struggle and not focused on the problems of interracial love. And several white critics argued that Herman should have been a stronger individual with the power to reject his mother and a willingness to move North to be with the woman he loved so very much. However, it has also been noted that both black and white critics ignore the fact that Childress is portraying the real world that people experience and not the idealized world of positive models. In *Wedding Band* Childress is suggesting that despite poverty, racism, and social ostracism, loving relationships can survive.

In an interview with Shirley Jordan in her *Broken Silences: Interviews with Black and Women Writers,* Childress was asked if she had felt pressured by a publisher, editor, or audience to portray a particular kind of character or theme, particularly with respect to women's and racial issues. Childress's responded:

> Oh you get pressure. Everyone gets pressure and if you ignore it or pay it no mind, they squirm loose from you or try to get it changed themselves or interfere with it in some way or let you alone. It's not so much that they disagree with you. The commercial world is very smart. They know the place from whence rejection will come. If you show your work to that place where finance will be provided—they know what they're doing. Discrimination, racism, prejudice is not what is called a loose cannon. It's a well-organized thing. They'll say 'Don't you think maybe you can do without this?' But what is your main point. You think, 'I'll give in on this and give in on that and save this one to go straight on down the middle to the heart of my subject.' That's the one they'll find on page 52. Never think they're so dumb they don't see

it. We share that with sisters of any race—and some brothers too.

It is clear from the lengthy efforts to get *Wedding Band* produced that Childress was not willing to compromise her integrity to popular culture. The reviews of the critics and the decision by certain ABC affiliates did not result in a play that ignored the reality of miscegenation; rather, the play depicts the realities of racism.

CRITICISM

Sheri Metzger

Metzger is an adjunct professor at Embry-Riddle University. In this essay she examines some of the ways in which American society discriminates against African Americans—particularly black women. She also discusses the manner in which Childress's play deals with these issues.

Alice Childress noted in a 1966 essay in *Freedomways* that America extends basic rights and opportunities to foreign visitors and to immigrants that are not offered to black Americans. She reminded her readers that visitors may "travel, without restriction, reside in hotels, eat at restaurants and enter public and private places closed to Americans who have built up the country under bondage and defended it under a limited and restricted liberty." This is the injustice that Childress illuminates in her play *Wedding Band*. Childress maintained in a 1993 interview with Shirley Jordan in *Broken Silences: Interviews with Black and Women Writers* that Americans who say they know nothing about racism are failing to look beyond the obvious. When Fanny Johnson says "Don't make it hard for me with your attitude. Whites like me. When I walk down the street, they say 'There she goes'—Fanny Johnson, representing her people in an *approved* manner," what is really happening is that Fanny is as trapped by the system as the poorest black single mother. Fanny is judged as a black person who is trying to better herself according to white society's criteria, but Childress is saying that Fanny should be establishing her strength as a black woman and not as a black woman trying to be white or trying to please whites. The nuances are subtle, but are crucial to understanding the relationship between *Wedding Band* and racism, for it is through the actions and words of the play's primary characters that the audience is forced to recognize and acknowledge the injustice of a system that denies opportunity to African Americans. This is especially evident in the actions of Nelson; he is so cowed by a racist system and so afraid of its consequences that he cannot protest when a bucket of water is dumped on him. He cannot protest when the woman he is seeing rejects him because he has no future; he can only acknowledge the truth of her opinion. Childress's play makes clear that Nelson is at greater risk from his white neighbors than he is from enemy fire during war. The tragedy of *Wedding Band* is that so little has changed for blacks between the time of the play's setting in 1918 and its initial production in 1966. It is this illumination of racism and its legacy that demonstrates the play's importance in the literary canon.

But *Wedding Band* does have an important message to be heard. And, according to Catherine Wiley in her essay in *Modern American Drama: the Female Canon,* the play presents a directive to white feminists that sexism cannot be separated from racism. Human rights are the greater issue of the play, not women's rights. Wiley argued for the inclusion of Childress's play in the literary canon because it functions as a "history lesson pointed at white women to remind them and us, in 1966 or now, that our vision of sisterly equality has always left some sisters out." Wiley maintained that white women need to read the texts of black women in the same way that white men have been forced to read the texts of white women: "Rather than seeing myself reflected in their work, I want to understand why my difference makes these plays a challenge to read." Childress does not separate the issue of women's rights from human rights; for her the two are inexorably bound. In *Wedding Band,* Julia's problems are not only the miscegenation laws; rather, her isolation from the black community, especially the community of women, lies at the heart of the play. But for white women who early saw a link between women's rights and the abolishment of segregation, the focus has shifted to women's rights as a primary concern. Wiley argued that white women need authors like Childress included in the literary canon because she reminds us all that women's rights and human rights cannot be separated. When Julia's love for Herman makes her vulnerable to the advances of the white peddler, she is reduced to being just another black woman who prefers a white man. "This scene," Wiley declared, "points to the inseparability of racism and sexism, an issue that cannot be isolated from the historical relationship of the civil rights and women's liberation movements. The fallacy of *sisterhood* as the

WHAT DO I READ NEXT?

- *Florence* (1949), Alice Childress's first play, focuses on two women waiting in a train station. While Mama's interactions with the other characters serve to reveal the nature of racial prejudice, the play also examines basic assumptions regarding the public's treatment of women and the elderly.

- *Wine in the Wilderness* (1969), also by Alice Childress, examines what it means to be a black American in a segregated and racist society. The play examines several of the issues touched upon in *Wedding Band*, including single motherhood and the lack of opportunity faced by black men.

- *A Raisin in the Sun* (1959) by Lorraine Hansberry also explores segregation, racism, and the lack of economic opportunities that beset black Americans. The integration of white neighborhoods by minority families is still an important issue nearly forty years after this play was first produced.

- Toni Morrison's novel *The Bluest Eye* (1970) examines what it means to grow up black and

female in America. Morrison explores how white standards of beauty affect young black girls, and she looks at the nature of the relationship between black and white women.

- Maya Angelou's autobiography, *I Know Why the Caged Bird Sings* (1970), details her childhood in rural Arkansas. Readers are forced to confront racism and segregation as the author confronts these realities, but they are also exposed to the importance of family in shaping the black experience.

- *In Search of Our Mothers' Gardens* (1974) by Alice Walker is an autobiographical essay that argues for the importance of matrilineage in the growth of a young black girl.

- *The Color Purple* (1982), also by Alice Walker, is a fictional look at the effects of segregation and racism on blacks. The novel and the 1985 film adaptation celebrate the strength of black women.

---

word was used in the women's liberation movement of the 1960s lay in its assumption that oppression was universal.'' But black women face oppression on two fronts: they are discriminated against both as women and as African Americans. *Wedding Band* is important because it exposes both these problems and illustrates that Julia's need extends beyond her love for Herman. Consequently, the play is not only about Julia's love for a white man, it is also about her love for and her need to be loved by black women.

Wedding Band is also about survival, especially the survival of women. Although Herman dies at the play's conclusion, it is clear that Julia is strong enough to survive. Victims' ability to survive, according to Rosemary Curb in her article in *Melus*, is a result of the racism that permeates their lives. The prejudices of society surround Julia; her neighbors are intolerant of Germans, Jews, Chinese, whites,

and certain blacks. In this play, Childress constructs both black and white characters who are petty and narrow-minded. But their behavior arises from their fear, and it is clear that both blacks and whites have much to fear. Herman's mother fears being exposed as German at a time when Germans are feared and ostracized; she also fears the loss of the slight social status she has acquired. Her daughter, Annabelle, fears she will lose her one chance at happiness, and so her prejudice toward Julia is more a function of her desire to escape, which she feels can only occur if Herman marries a white woman. Fanny fears losing the respect that being a property owner has bestowed upon her. And while Lula fears losing her adopted son to the violence of war and racism, Mattie fears losing the name and protection of a man. But the fear is greater for black women who have little protection from injustice, violence, or white society. Still, in spite of the poverty that threatens to envelop their lives, these women manage to earn a meager existence and they endure. The audience knows that it will be difficult, but these black women will survive. Their words and actions belie the prejudices that surround them, but as Curb remarked, ''if an all-pervasive racism has conditioned the women to be suspicious of white cordiality, it has also toughened them with the stamina necessary for survival.'' In asserting that *Wedding Band* belongs in the literary canon, Curb says of the play: ''Although all of Childress's published work deserves to be read, *Wedding Band* is her finest and most serious piece of literature and deserves comparison with the most celebrated American tragedies. Like Childress's other plays, it features an ordinary black woman past her prime. What we have here is that Julia's soul-searching in the midst of her moral dilemmas takes place on stage; her confusion is fully dramatized. The problems which face Julia are complicated by a convergence of historical and political dilemmas with which a woman of her education and conditioning is ill prepared to cope. That she and the other flawed women in *Wedding Band* survive is tenuous but believable.'' It is this depiction of real people and real problems that makes *Wedding Band* an important resource for understanding twentieth-century racism.

But *Wedding Band* is more than a play about racism. In her *Southern Quarterly* essay, Gayle Austin maintained that what Childress did in all her plays was to ''break down the binary opposition so prevalent in western society—black/white, male/female, north/south, artist/critic—with their implications that one is superior to the other.'' (Binary oppositions are the tendency to see issues as pairs of good and bad or simply as opposites inclusive of other ideas.) Instead, by viewing characters and situations that are innately flawed, Childress's audience is forced to acknowledge that there are no clear answers, no simple right or wrong. Herman's mother is not an evil woman simply because she is willing to sacrifice her son's life if it means preserving the sanctity of her position. Rather she is revealed as weak and unhappy (note that she has lost five children to stillbirth, endured an oppressive marriage, and a childhood of poverty as a sharecropper's daughter). Although cast in the role of villain, her fear and self-loathing declare her more victim than villain. And Childress has made it clear that Herman and Julia do not fit the pattern of romantic lovers found elsewhere in literature; they are not like Romeo and Juliet. They are a middle-aged, uneducated couple who lack the strength and

ability to escape the confines of the south. But as Herman's mother reminds them, there is no escape in the north. The north may be more integrated than the south, but racism, segregation, and the lack of an economic future will follow them if they try to escape. Consequently, as Austin noted, there is no clear delineation in Childress's play. The characters and the situations are more complex than the stereotypes of binary opposition would permit.

Source: Sheri Metzger, in an essay for *Drama for Students,* Gale, 1997.

Catherine Wiley

In the following excerpt, Wiley discusses both racial and feminist issues as they pertain to Wedding Band.

In the first act of *Wedding Band,* a scene of reading and performance occurs that lies at the center of a feminist interpretation of the play. Mattie, a black woman who makes her living selling candy and caring for a little white girl, has received a letter from her husband in the Merchant Marine and needs a translator for it. Her new neighbor, Julia, the educated outsider trying to fit into working-class surroundings, reads the sentimental sailor's letter aloud. After her performance, in which the women listening have actively participated, Mattie tells Julia that, in addition to his love, her husband gives her what is more important, his *name and protection.* These two standards of conventional love are denied Julia because her lover of ten years is white; and even Mattie learns that because she never divorced her first husband, she is not now legally married and cannot receive marital war benefits. Neither woman enjoys a man's name or his protection, in part because the chivalry implied in such privilege was unattainable for blacks in the Jim Crow society of 1918 South Carolina. The women in *Wedding Band* learn to depend on themselves and each other rather than on absent men, a self-reliance born painfully through self-acceptance.

Wedding Band received mixed reviews when it opened off-Broadway in 1972. It was described both as the ''play about black life in America that isn't a 'black' play''(Martin Gottfried in *Women's Wear Daily,* October 10, 1972) and too much ''like a story wrenched from the pages of what used to be known as a magazine for women''(Douglas Walt in *New York Daily News,* November 27, 1972). Interesting for their racist and sexist connotations, these comments betray the reviewers' uncritical assumptions about who constitutes a theater audience. The play doesn't look "black" because its integrationist subtext surfaces only occasionally and its political urgency is dressed safely in realistic period costume. New York theater patrons of 1972 applauding the drama as entertainment alone could assure themselves that the play's World War I setting depicted a reality long past. The first reviewer assumes that a "black" play, one that speaks primarily to a black audience, is implicitly alien and uninteresting to a white audience. Representations of so-called minority lives told from a minority point of view cannot interest the rest of us, if we are white. Likewise, the pages of a women's magazine would bore us if we were men, because they focus on the small, private issues of home and heart. And although none of the liberal reviewers profess any shock over the play's important theme of miscegenation, no New York producers would touch *Wedding Band* until 1972, six years after it was written and first performed, attesting to the subject's unpopularity.

My reading of the play argues that its subject is less interracial heterosexual relations than the relations between black women and between black women and white women in World War I—era South Carolina. That said, I must add that I perceive a certain danger in trying to read feminist rather than racial politics into Alice Childress's play. White feminists must take care not to offer our own invaluable "name and protection" to black women writers who do not need them. For a feminist criticism that is not limited to the privileged location of many of its practitioners, it is crucial that white feminists read the work of black women, especially those like Childress who have been all but ignored in academic theater. We might read in the same spirit of canon disruption inspiring the informal creation of a women's literary counter-canon, recognizing that in the same way white women writers were denied membership in the old canon on the basis of "greatness," we may be guilty of blocking black women writers for the same reason. The value of a literary text cannot be defined out of context. White readers should try to decentralize our historically majority context—to see ourselves, for once, in the margins with respect to the Afro-American women's literary tradition. I recognize with dismay the truth of Hortense J. Spillers's statement: "When we say 'feminist' with an adjective in front of it, we mean, of course, white women, who, as a category of social and cultural agents, fully occupy the territory of feminism." But does including Afro-American women writers in the canon ... imitate a

> SISTERHOOD, ESPECIALLY FROM THE POINT OF VIEW OF WHITE WOMEN LEARNING TO UNDERSTAND BLACK WOMEN, BEGINS WITH LISTENING, NOT TO WHAT ONE WANTS TO HEAR BUT TO WHAT IS BEING SAID"

colonizing gesture? Am I offering the protection of the canon to Alice Childress, protection on the canon's (and for now, white women's) terms? Instead of attempting to answer these questions now, I can only say that I am beginning to learn to read black women's plays in the same way many feminists ask men to read women's texts. Rather than seeing myself reflected in their work, I want to understand why my difference makes these plays a challenge to read. . . .

Set chronologically midway between the poles of Reconstruction and civil rights, *Wedding Band* describes an era when lynching presented one answer to demands for equality in the south, while Harlem flowered as a mecca for black culture in the north. In the 1960s, white women and black men's sexual relations generated tension in the black community, but miscegenation as the white master's rape of his slave retains deeper historical ramifications for black women. Childress's drama, subtitled "a love/hate story in black and white," takes place on the tenth anniversary of Julia and her white lover in the small backyard tenement to which Julia has moved after being evicted from countless other houses. Determined to get along with her nosy but well-meaning neighbors, Julia seems to have won a guarded acceptance until her lover, Herman, visits her. He has brought her a gold wedding band on a chain, and they plan to buy tickets on the Clyde Line to New York, where Julia will proudly and legally bear Herman's name. But Herman succumbs to the influenza epidemic, and in the second act he lies in Julia's bed waiting for his mother and sister to take him to a white doctor. Julia's landlady has refused to help because it is illegal for Herman to be in Julia's house, and she cannot appear to sanction Julia's immoral behavior. Herman's mother sides with the landlady in preserving respectability even at the cost of her son's life, and she will not carry him to the doctor until it grows dark enough to hide him. In the last scene, Herman returns to Julia with the boat tickets, which she refuses to take because his mother has convinced her that blacks and whites can never live together. Finally she appears to relent so that Herman can die believing that Julia, even without him, will go north.

The secondary characters, however, more than the two lovers, underscore the drama's didactic politics. They are types, but not stereotypes, and their separate dilemmas and personalities describe the injustices blacks have endured in the south. The landlady, Fanny, the neighbors Mattie and Lula, Lula's adopted son, Nelson, and the abusive white traveling salesman give the stage community a historical idiosyncrasy missing from Julia and Herman's relationship. Fanny has proudly joined the middle-class by acquiring property and exploiting her tenants (in 1918 a relatively new possibility for black women) in the name of racial uplift. As homeworkers, Mattie and Lula exist bound to a variety of semi-skilled, low-paying jobs to feed their children. Nelson, as a soldier in the newly desegregated United States army, assumes that when the war is over he will be given the rights of a full citizen, even in South Carolina. He is a forerunner of the militant youth who would later provide the impatient voice to the nascent civil rights movement of the late 1940s, and whose dreams of integration would be realized only partially in the 1960s.

These characters who inhabit Miss Fanny's backward tenement underscore the vexed issue of difference as explored by the feminist scholars cited above. Julia's problem throughout the play is less her white lover than her reluctance to see herself as a member of the black community. Although a mostly white theater audience would see her as a different sort of heroine because of race, her black neighbors perceive her as different from them for issues more complex than skin color. She assumes that her racial transgression with Herman will make her unwelcome among the women she wishes to confide in, but her aloofness from their day-to-day interests also serves as a protective shield. In this, Julia is similar to Lutie Johnson in Ann Petry's *The Street,* written in 1946. Both characters are ostensibly defined by their unequal relations with men, but their potential for salvation lies in the larger community that depends on the stability of its women. Lutie Johnson is so determined to move off "the street" in Harlem she thinks is pulling her down that

she refuses to join the community Harlem offers her, a community that in some ways defies the white society keeping it poor. Neither poor nor uneducated, Julia finds herself defying the black community by asserting her right to love a white man, but his self-assertion is, in a larger sense, a more dangerous defiance of the white community. She wants her love story to be one of individual commitment and sacrifice, but it is that only in part. Julia's refinement in manners, education, and financial independence, which are middle-class, traditionally white attributes, make her and Herman available to each other. But theirs is, as the subtitle insists, a "love/hate" story, in which interracial love cannot be divorced from centuries of racial hate. . . .

The urgency of integration as a method of combatting such engrained hatred marks Julia's turning point in the play. After Herman and his family are gone, she must face her own difficult reintegration into the community of Fanny's backyard. As the women prepare to escort Nelson to his proud participation in the soldiers' parade, the air of festivity inspires Lula and Julia to perform an impromptu strut dance to the music of Jenkin's Colored Orphan Band. They discover a small common space in the mutual performance of a "*Carolina folk dance passed on from some dimly-remembered African beginning.*" Later, to send Nelson on his way, Lula begs Julia to give him a farewell speech telling him "how life's gon' be better when he gets back . . . Make up what *should* be true," whether Julia believes in her performance or not. Julia makes a speech proclaiming the abolition of the "no-colored" signs after the war and the new lives of respect awaiting Nelson and October after their return home. Although the stage directions do not specify this, according to reviews of the play, she addresses these words directly to the audience. Edith Oliver, writing for the *New Yorker,* called the speech "dreadful . . . like something out of a bad Russian movie," in part because by addressing the audience Julia moves the issue of racism north of the Mason-Dixon line. Breaking the fourth wall or realism brings the drama out of its historical context of 1918 into the present and makes Julia's words about integration harder for a northern audience to ignore.

At the end of the play, Julia gives her wedding band and boat tickets to Mattie and her daughter, finally admitting that "You and Teeta are my people . . . my family." But the gesture is compromised by its implication that the only choice for Afro-Americans is to leave their homes in the

South. It was still illegal for blacks and whites to marry in South Carolina in 1966, but, despite the laws, by that time blacks had already begun to reclaim their homes. As Alice Walker argues in her essay "Choosing to Stay at Home," one thing Martin Luther King gave his people was the possibility of returning to the South they or their parents or grandparents had left. The civil rights movement recreated the South as a site of militant resistance, resistance enacted equally by black women and men. Set in South Carolina and staged in Michigan and New York, *Wedding Band* provides a site of resistance like the political movement from which it grew. Julia's decision to stay at home, to keep her own name, makes the spectator witness to her new-found ability to celebrate, as she says, her "own black self."

Despite her helplessness regarding her mother, Annabelle, the literal "white sister" in the play, is a character who, like Julia and Nelson, embodies hope for the future in the South. Like the audience, she witnesses Julia's articulation of her newly-won independence. Julia's curtain speech with Herman dying in her arms escapes sentimentality only through the staging of Annabelle's mute participation in it. Julia and Herman remain inside Julia's house, after she simply but irrevocably bars Annabelle, Herman's mother, and Fanny from entering. Everyone leaves the stage except for Annabelle, who moves toward the house, listening to Julia's words to her brother. Without entering the house, to which the black woman has denied her access, she hears the other woman's words and so manages to share silently the loss of Herman without translating it into white terms. As Julia comforts Herman by describing their pretend journey north on the Clyde Line Boat together, she says, "We're takin' off, ridin' the waves so smooth and easy . . . There now . . . on our way. . . ." Julia and Herman are not on their way, but perhaps Julia and Annabelle will someday be on *their* way to mutual respect. I can only read these words as a directive to the audience of college students at the University of Michigan in 1966, empassioned with the growing fervor of the anti-war and women's liberation movements and prepared in their innocence to change the world. They cannot do it, *Wedding Band* gently but firmly insists, as gently and firmly as Julia closes her door on the other women, without a renewed commitment to civil rights for all people in the United States, in the South as well as in the North. Sisterhood, especially from the point of view of white women learning to understand black women, begins

> ALICE CHILDRESS' *WEDDING BAND* HAS AN AUTHENTICITY WHICH, WHATEVER ITS FAULTS, MAKES IT COMPELLING BOTH AS SCRIPT AND PERFORMANCE"

with listening, not to what one wants to hear but to what is being said.

Source: Catherine Wiley, "Whose Name, Whose Protection: Reading Alice Childress's *Wedding Band*" in *Modern American Drama: The Female Canon*, edited by June Schlueter, Associated University Presses, 1990, pp. 184–85, 187–89, 194–96.

Harold Clurman

In this review of The Wedding Band, *Clurman states that despite minor flaws, Childress's work offers trenchant realism and qualifies as a significant piece of theatre.*

Clurman is highly regarded as a director, author, and longtime drama critic for the Nation. *He was an important contributor to the development of the modern American theater as a cofounder of the Innovative Group Theater, which served as an arena for the works of new playwrights and as an experimental workshop for actors. Along with Lee Strasberg, he is credited with bringing the technique known as "method acting" to the fore in American film and theatre.*

Alice Childress' *Wedding Band* has an authenticity which, whatever its faults, makes it compelling both as script and performance. The locale is some place near Charleston, S.C., during the last days of World War I. The play tells of a frustrated love; one that has endured for ten years between a black woman, Julia Augustine, and Herman, a white man who is a baker of humble means. They have not been able to marry because such mixed unions were illegal at the time. They both hope to escape the trap of their existence by going North, but poverty prevents them.

The play's basic theme emerges from the portrayal not only of the bigoted opposition of Herman's family, with its vile Klan spirit, but just as saliently in the suspicion and fear with which the blacks confront the two lovers. Herman, on the verge of death during the influenza epidemic which raged at the time, proves his deep attachment to Julia by buying her a ticket to New York even as he lies helpless, still in the grip of his wretched family. She on the other hand, though convinced of his love and freedom from racial bias, despairs of overcoming the barriers between them.

There is an honest pathos in the telling of this simple story, and some humorous and touching thumbnail sketches reveal knowledge and understanding of the people dealt with. The fact that black and white interrelationships have somewhat changed since 1918 does not make the play less relevant to the present. Constitutional amendments and laws do not immediately alter people's emotions; the divisions and tensions which *Wedding Band* dramatizes still exist to a far more painful extent than most of us are willing to admit.

Evidence of this was furnished at the last preview of the play. A black man attempted to heckle the performance. What apparently provoked the outburst was his refusal to accept the sentimentality he found in the treatment of a close tie between a black and a white. He would not countenance it: he felt it an indignity, indeed an insult to the black race.

James Broderick as Herman conveys the character's inner rectitude and hurt with utmost simplicity and truthfulness. He really *listens* to his acting partners, something which cannot be said of many actors of greater acclaim. Ruby Dee too is affecting in her commitment to the man who has shown her deep regard and tenderness as well as in her tormented revulsion from him as part of the community which has victimized her people. Everyone in the cast is right. Special commendation should be accorded to Jean Davis as Herman's mother—a stupefied racist who would be totally abhorrent were it not for the reality of pain with which the actress endows the character. Polly Holliday, as Herman's maiden sister, shows considerable delicacy in communicating the wound of

doubt within the girl's narrowness. Apart from the various players' individual abilities, commendation for the general excellence of the acting must go to the Charleston-born author in conjunction with Joseph Papp.

Source: Harold Clurman, in a review of *The Wedding Band* in the *Nation,* November 13, 1972 , pp. 475–76.

FURTHER READING

Bloom, Harold, editor. *Modern Black American Poets and Dramatists,* Chelsea House, 1995, pp. 51-63.
Bloom assembles excerpts of critical discussions and reviews of Childress's work.

Brown-Guillory, Elizabeth. ''Black Women Playwrights: Exorcising Myths'' in *Phylon,* Vol. 48, no. 3, Fall, 1987, pp. 229-39.
A critical comparison of Alice Childress, Lorraine Hansberry, and Ntozake Shange, three black women playwrights.

SOURCES

Austin, Gayle. ''Black Woman Playwright as Feminist Critic'' in *Southern Quarterly,* Vol. 25, no. 3, Spring, 1987, pp. 53-62.

Childress, Alice. ''The Negro Woman in Literature'' in *Freedomways,* Vol. 6, no.1, Winter, 1966. pp. 14-19.

Curb, Rosemary. ''An Unfashionable Tragedy of American Racism: Alice Childress's *Wedding Band*'' in *Melus,* Vol. 7, no. 4, 1980, pp. 57-68.

Holliday, Polly. ''I Remember Alice Childress'' in *Southern Quarterly,* Vol. 25, no. 3, Spring, 1987, pp. 63-5.

Jordan, Shirley, editor. *Broken Silences: Interviews with Black and Women Writers,* Rutgers University Press, 1993, pp. 28-37.

Wiley, Catherine. ''Whose Name, Whose Protection: Reading Alice Childress's *Wedding Band*'' in *Modern American Drama: The Female Canon,* edited by June Schlueter, Fairleigh Dickinson University Press, 1990, pp. 184-97.

The Zoo Story

EDWARD ALBEE
1959

When Edward Albee wrote *The Zoo Story* in 1958, it was the first play that he wrote as an adult and only the second play that he wrote in his lifetime. His only other play was a sex farce that he wrote at the age of twelve. After being passed from friend to friend, *The Zoo Story* traveled from New York to Florence, Italy, to Zurich, Switzerland, to Frankfurt, Germany and was finally produced for the first time in Berlin, Germany. It opened on September 28, 1959, at the Schiller Theatre Werkstatt. After much critical praise in Germany, it was less than three months before *The Zoo Story* finally opened in New York. It debuted off-Broadway at the Provincetown Playhouse on January 14, 1960, and instantly had a strong impact on critics and audiences alike. The vast majority of the reviews were positive and many hoped for a revitalized theatre because of it. A few critics, however, dismissed the play because of its absurd content and seemed confused as to what Albee was trying to say with it.

The story, in simplest terms, is about how a man who is consumed with loneliness starts up a conversation with another man on a bench in Central Park and eventually forces him to participate in an act of violence. According to Matthew Roudane, who quoted a 1974 interview with Albee his *Understanding Edward Albee,* the playwright maintained that he got the idea for *The Zoo Story* while working for Western Union: ''I was always delivering telegrams to people in rooming houses. I met [the models for] all those people in the play in rooming

houses. Jerry, the hero, is still around.'' Combining both realistic and absurd elements, Albee has constructed a short but multi-leveled play dealing with issues of human isolation, loneliness, class differences, and the dangers of inaction within American society. He focuses on the need for people to acknowledge and understand each other's differences. After garnering its initial critical praise, *The Zoo Story* went on to win the *Village Voice* Obie Award for best play and ran for a total of 582 performances. *The Zoo Story* continues to be a favorite with university and small theatre companies and persists in shocking and profoundly affecting its audiences.

AUTHOR BIOGRAPHY

Edward Albee was born on March 12, 1928, in Washington, DC, where he was given the name Edward Franklin Albee III by Reed and Francis Albee, who adopted him from his natural birth parents. Reed and Francis Albee were the heirs to the multi-million dollar fortune of American theater manager Edward Franklin Albee I. Albee attended several private and military schools, and during this education he began writing poetry and attending the theatre. Albee was twelve when he attempted to write his first play, a three-act sex farce; he soon turned back to poetry and even attempted to write novels as a teen. He studied at Trinity College in Connecticut from 1946 until 1947 and then decided to take the trust fund his grandmother had left him and move to New York City's Greenwich Village. Albee was able to live off of this fund by supplementing it with small odd jobs, thus allowing him to focus on his writing career.

While in his twenties, Edward Albee had some limited success as an author of poetry and fiction, but he was still unable to make a living off of his writing and, therefore, continued to work small jobs to supplement his income, including working as a messenger for Western Union from 1955 until 1958. It was while working as a telegram messenger that Albee came up with the idea for *The Zoo Story,* when he encountered real life counterparts for Jerry and the other residents of the boarding house that he describes in the play.

At the age of thirty, Albee quit his job at Western Union and wrote *The Zoo Story* (1958), his first significant play. Inspired by the works of Samuel Beckett, Bertolt Brecht, Jean Genet, and Tennessee Williams, Albee wrote *The Zoo Story* in three short weeks. After being passed around from colleague to colleague, it was finally produced at the Schiller Theater Werstatt in Berlin, Germany, opening there on September 28, 1959. *The Zoo Story* won the Berlin Festival Award in 1959 and eventually found its way back to the U.S. where it opened off-Broadway at the Provincetown Playhouse in New York on January 14, 1960. While there, *The Zoo Story* shared the bill with *Krapp's Last Tape,* which was written by Samuel Beckett, one of Albee's greatest influences.

The Zoo Story went on to win the *Village Voice* Obie Award for best play in 1960, but it was not until after four more one-act plays that Albee wrote his most controversial and critically acclaimed play. *Who's Afraid of Virginia Woolf?* opened on Broadway a the Billy Rose Theatre on October 13, 1962, and went on to win the Tony Award for best play. Followed by controversy wherever it played, *Who's Afraid of Virginia Woolf?* forced critics and audiences to react, both positively and negatively, and assured Albee's place in American theatre history. Admired and detested for its bleakness and negativity, *Who's Afraid of Virginia Woolf?* was a critical and financial success and was eventually made into a film with Elizabeth Taylor and Richard Burton in 1966.

Edward Albee went on to win the Pulitzer Prize three times, for *A Delicate Balance* (1966), for *Seascape* (1975), and for *Three Tall Women* (1994). Albee continues to be one of the most acclaimed and controversial playwrights in the United States, and he has continued to use the commercial success of his more famous works in order to pursue theatrical experimentation, despite sometimes scathing reviews and commercial failure. Mingling absurdity with acute realism in his early works off-Broadway during the 1960s, Albee has paved the way and inspired such contemporary playwrights as David Mamet and Sam Shepard, while continuing to experiment with and challenge theatrical form.

PLOT SUMMARY

Edward Albee's *The Zoo Story* is a long one act play in which ''nothing happens'' except conversation— until the violent ending. Shorn of much of the richness of Albee's utterly arresting language, and his astonishing nuances of psychological attack and retreat, the play can be described as follows:

A man named Peter, a complacent publishing executive of middle age and upper-middle income, is comfortably reading a book on his favorite bench in New York's Central Park on a sunny afternoon. Along comes Jerry, an aggressive, seedy, erratic loner. Jerry announces that he has been to the (Central Park) Zoo and eventually gets Peter, who clearly would rather be left alone, to put down his book and actually enter into a conversation. With pushy questions, Jerry learns that Peter lives on the fashionable East Side of the Park (they are near Fifth Avenue and 74th Street), that the firm for which he works publishes textbooks, and that his household is female-dominated: one wife, two daughters, two cats, and two parakeets. Jerry easily guesses that Peter would rather have a dog than cats and that he wishes he had a son. More perceptively, Jerry guesses that there will be no more children, and that that decision was made by Peter's wife. Ruefully, Peter admits the truth of these guesses.

The subjects of the Zoo and Jerry's visit to it come up several times, at one of which Jerry says mysteriously, "You'll read about it in the papers tomorrow, if you don't see it on your TV tonight." The play never completely clarifies this remark. Some critic think, because of statements Jerry makes about the animals, that he may have released some from their cages, while others think Jerry is talking about a death which has not yet happened, which might be headlined "Murder Near Central Park Zoo."

The focus now turns to Jerry, who tells Peter that he walked all the way up Fifth Avenue from Washington Square to the Zoo, a trip of over fifty blocks. Adding Washington Square to Jerry's appearance and behavior, Peter assumes that Jerry lives in Greenwich Village, which in 1960, the year the play was first produced, was the principal "bohemian" section of Manhattan. Jerry says no, that he lives across the Park on the (then slum-ridden) West Side, and took the subway downtown for the express purpose of walking back up Fifth Avenue. No reason is given for this but Jerry "explains" it in one of the most quoted sentences of the play: "sometimes a person has to go a very long distance out of his way to come back a short distance correctly." It is possible that Jerry saw his trip up Fifth Avenue, which gradually improves from the addicts and prostitutes of Washington Square to such bastions of prosperity as the famous Plaza Hotel, as a symbolic journey through the American class system to the source of his problem—not millionaire's row but the affluent, indifferent upper middle class.

Edward Albee

Without any prompting from Peter, Jerry describes his living arrangements: a tiny room in a rooming house, with a very short list of possessions; some clothes, a can-opener and hotplate, eating utensils, empty picture frames, a few books, a deck of pornographic playing cards, an old typewriter, and a box with many unanswered "Please!" letters and "When?" letters. Jerry's building is like something out of Dante's *Inferno,* with several different kinds of suffering on each floor, including a woman Jerry has never seen who cries all the time, a black "queen" who plucks his eyebrows "with Buddhist concentration" and hogs the bathroom, and a disgusting landlady whom Jerry describes vividly. Jerry also reveals the loss of both parents—his mother to whoring and drinking and his father to drinking and an encounter with "a somewhat moving city omnibus"—events that seem to have had little emotional effect on him. Jerry's love life is also discussed: an early and very intense homosexual infatuation and, at present, one-night stands with nameless women whom he never sees again.

It is clear in this section of the play that Jerry is trying to make Peter understand something about loneliness and suffering—not so much Jerry's own pain, which he treats cynically, but the pain of the people in his building, the Zoo animals isolated in their cages, and more generally the societal dregs that Peter is more comfortable not having to think about. Peter is repelled by Jerry's information but not moved except to exasperation and discomfort. Desperate to communicate with Peter or at least to teach him something about the difficulties of communication, Jerry comes up with ''The Story of Jerry and the Dog.'' It is a long, disgusting, and eventually pathetic tale of his attempt to find some kind of communication, or at least relationship, with the vile landlady's vile dog (the hound who guards the entrance to Jerry's particular hell). Jerry fails to reach the dog, though he goes from trying to kill it with kindness to just plain trying to kill it; the two finally achieve mutual indifference, and Jerry gains free entry to the building without being attacked, ''if that much further loss can be said to be gain.''

Jerry also fails to reach Peter, who is bewildered but not moved by this story and who prepares to leave his now-disturbed sanctuary for his comfortable home. Desperately grasping at one last chance, Jerry tickles Peter, then punches him on the arm and pushes him to the ground. He challenges Peter to fight for ''his'' bench, but Peter will not. Jerry produces a knife, which he throws on the ground between them. He grabs Peter, slapping and taunting him (''fight for your manhood, you pathetic little vegetable'') until Peter, at last enraged, picks up the knife. Even then, as Albee points out, ''Peter holds the knife with a firm arm, but far in front of him, not to attack, but to defend.'' Jerry says, ''So be it,'' and ''With a rush he charges Peter and impales himself on the knife.''

Peter is paralyzed. Jerry *thanks* Peter and hurries him away for his own safety, reminding Peter to take his book from ''your bench . . . my bench, rather.'' Peter runs off, crying ''Oh, my God!'' Jerry echoes these words with ''a combination of scornful mimicry and supplication,'' and dies.

Portions of Albee's dialogue and stage directions have been included in this summary in an attempt to indicate the huge importance of Albee's incisive use of language and psychology in the play. The play resides, in fact, not in the physical actions of the plot (except the killing at the end) but in the acuteness (not to mention the shocking quality) of the language, in the range of kinds of aggression shown by Jerry—from insult and assault to the subtlest of insinuations—and even in the symbolism which becomes more apparent near the end of the action.

CHARACTERS

Jerry

Jerry, the antagonist in *The Zoo Story,* confronts Peter while he is reading a book in Central Park and coerces him into partaking in an act of violence. Albee gives the following description of Jerry: ''A man in his late thirties, not poorly dressed, but carelessly. What was once a trim and lightly muscled body has begun to go to fat; and while he is no longer handsome, it is evident that he once was.'' In contrast to Peter, Jerry lives in a four-story brownstone roominghouse on the Upper West Side of Manhattan, between Columbus Avenue and Central Park West. During the 1950s, this was a much poorer neighborhood than the East 70s, where Peter lives. Jerry is single and lives in one small room that is actually half a room separated from the other half by beaverboard.

Throughout the course of the play, Jerry tells Peter only what he wants Peter to know, and does not like to be asked questions or be judged. He makes a point of telling Peter very personal details of his life, like how his parents both died when he was a child and how he was a homosexual for a week and a half when he was fifteen and now only sees prostitutes. Peter finds Jerry's stories disturbing but fascinating and it is only when they get very strange that Peter begins to question Jerry's intentions. Jerry uses all of his resources including his storytelling ability, his humor, and finally his violent aggression to make sure that Peter does not leave until he gets what he wants from him. In the end, Jerry resorts to physically attacking Peter so that Peter has to defend himself. Jerry sets it up so that he is able to impale himself on his own knife, while Peter holds it out in self-defense. In the end, Jerry uses Peter to get what he has planned to get from him all along.

Peter

Peter is the protagonist in *The Zoo Story* who after coming to Central Park to spend some time alone on his favorite bench to read a book on a Sunday afternoon, has his life forever changed by Jerry, who confronts him. Albee describes Peter as: ''A man in his early forties, neither fat nor gaunt, neither handsome nor homely.'' Peter lives on Seventy-fourth Street between Lexington and Third Avenues, which was a rather wealthy neighborhood in Manhattan during the late 1950s. He is married, has two daughters, cats, and two parakeets. He holds an executive position at a small publishing house that publishes textbooks. These details about Peter's life all come out of the dialogue that he has with Jerry, and although at first they seem to be trivial facts, they serve an important function in establishing the two different worlds in which Peter and Jerry live.

When Jerry first confronts Peter at the beginning of the play, Peter is reluctant to have a conversation with Jerry and is obviously annoyed by him. However, Jerry's manner and the way he talks intrigues Peter and it is this intrigue that allows Jerry to pull him into his world. The beginning of the conversation seems to be controlled more by Peter, because Jerry must use different tactics to keep Peter interested and to recover when he offends him. However, it is Jerry's vivid descriptions of his life that mesmerize Peter and allow Jerry to gain control over the situation. By the end of the play, Peter has unwillingly allowed Jerry to use him as a pawn in Jerry's plan to end his own life. In the end, Jerry leaves Peter with an experience that will haunt him for the rest of his life. Although he is more educated and has had more social and economic advantages than Jerry, Peter is the weaker and more naive of the two men.

Jerry and Peter begin the struggle that will result in Jerry impaling himself on a knife Peter is holding

THEMES

The Zoo Story by Edward Albee details what happens when one character enters the life of another character and quickly changes it forever. In the play, Jerry confronts Peter while he sits quietly reading on a bench in Central Park; through a quick series of events, Jerry forces Peter into helping him kill himself. Layered throughout this short one-act play are three overriding themes: absurdity versus reality, alienation and loneliness, and wealth and poverty.

Absurdity and Reality

The first theme of *The Zoo Story* has to do with absurdity and reality. During the beginning of the play, Jerry initiates the conversation with Peter and carefully chooses topics with which Peter will be familiar, such as family and career. However, Jerry soon begins to insert strange comments and questions into what is on the surface a conversation between two strangers trying to get to know each other. This is apparent during the moment when Jerry, assuming that Peter does not like his daughters' cats, asks if Peter's birds are diseased. Peter says that he does not believe so and Jerry replies:

"That's too bad. If they did you could set them loose in the house and the cats could eat them and die, maybe." These unreasonable and ridiculous, or absurd, moments in the play begin to shake Peter's sense of reality and place. However, Jerry is quick to counter these moments with genuinely pleasant, benign comments and interesting stories to keep Peter engaged. Throughout the play, as Jerry's stories continue, he is careful to control the conversation and manipulate Peter. By the end of the play, Jerry has managed to alter Peter's perception of reality to such an extent that Peter becomes involved in a physical fight over what he believes to be "his" park bench and in an act of self-defense helps Jerry kill himself. The reality of what has transpired then strikes Peter full force, and he runs off howling "Oh my God!"

Alienation and Loneliness

The theme of alienation and loneliness, which in *The Zoo Story* is presented as being representative of the human condition as a whole, is largely what motivates Jerry to do the things that he does. From the beginning of the play, when Jerry enters Peter's world, it is obvious that Jerry lacks simple

MEDIA ADAPTATIONS

- Albee's *Who's Afraid of Virginia Woolf?* was adapted and filmed by Warner Bros., starring Richard Burton, Elizabeth Taylor, George Segal, and Sandy Dennis. The film was released in 1966.

social skills. Jerry's first words are not, "Hello, may I sit down," but rather: "I've been to the zoo. I said, I've been to the zoo. MISTER, I'VE BEEN TO THE ZOO!" Through Jerry's stories, Peter learns that Jerry lost his parents at the age of ten and then went to live with his aunt, who died on the afternoon of his high school graduation. Jerry also makes very explicit comments about the boarding house he lives in and the other inhabitants there who act as a sort of family to Jerry, even though he does not really even know them. He even includes them in his prayers at night. Albee establishes Jerry's alienation from the rest of the world rather quickly and then continues to fill in the whole picture of his life for the audience. It is the pain that comes with this loneliness that forces Jerry to kill himself with Peter's help at the end of the play. Jerry finally finds solace after he has been stabbed and he tells Peter: "I came unto you and you have comforted me. Dear Peter."

Wealth and Poverty

The final major theme of *The Zoo Story* is wealth and poverty, and the illusions that are created between the social and economic classes. This theme is closely related to alienation and loneliness because Albee establishes the societal pressures of class as the cause of Jerry's suffering. The issue of class is brought up early in the play when Jerry is asking Peter about his family and his job, and then asks: "Say, what's the dividing line between upper-middle-middle class and lower-upper-middle class?" Obviously, Jerry belongs to neither of these classes, and by his own admission is simply being condescending. However, the illusions that Jerry has about Peter's life are very close to the truth, whereas to Peter Jerry's life is completely foreign.

Critics have argued that Albee is condemning the wealthy classes for their false sense of security and their lack of knowledge or understanding of how the other half lives. This point of view seems to be very clear by the end of the play when Jerry has succeeded in bringing Peter down to a basic animal-like level of behavior. It is at this point that their classes become irrelevant and their similarities are seen as the truth. Whether wealthy or poor, the desire for contact and love from others is equally strong. *The Zoo Story* shows what can happen when this need is not fulfilled.

STYLE

Structure

The Zoo Story by Edward Albee is rather simple in structure. It is set in New York's Central Park on Sunday afternoon in the summer. The staging for the play, therefore, consists of two park benches with foliage, trees, and sky behind them. The place never changes and the action of the play unfolds in a linear manner, from beginning to end, in front of the audience. Everything happens in the present, which gives the play its immediacy and makes the events that unfold even more shocking. As an audience member, watching the play makes one feel as if one is witnessing a crime and is directly involved; this sense of involvement is achieved through the structure of the play.

Style

What makes *The Zoo Story* dense and difficult to define is the style in which it is written. It does not fit into the purely realistic nor the totally absurd genres that were both popular in 1958 when Albee wrote the play. The Theatre of the Absurd was a movement that dominated the French stage after World War II, and was characterized by radical theatrical innovations. Playwrights in this genre used practically incomprehensible plots and extremely long pauses in order to violate conservative audiences' expectations of what theatre should be. Albee took this absurd style and combined it with acute realism in order to comment on American society in the 1950s. With *The Zoo Story,* Albee points to French playwright Eugene Ionesco's idea that human life is both fundamentally absurd and terrifying; therefore, communication through language is equally absurd. Albee is also drawing from existential philosophy in *The Zoo Story.* Existentialism is concerned with the nature and perception of human existence, and often deals with the idea that the basic human condition is one of suffering and loneliness. Jerry and his position in American society are clearly examples of this point of view. Another literary style which began emerging around the time that *The Zoo Story* was written is postmodernism. Postmodernists continued to apply the fundamentals of modernism, including alienation and existentialism, but went a step further by rejecting traditional forms. Therefore, they prefer the anti-novel over the novel and, as in *The Zoo Story,* the anti-hero over the hero. Although Albee does not belong solely in the realistic, absurdist, existential or postmodern literary genres, it is evident that all of these movements had an impact on *The Zoo Story* and Albee as a playwright.

Literary Devices

Albee used various literary devices in *The Zoo Story.* The first device is the anti-hero. An anti-hero, like a hero, is the central character of the play but lacks heroic qualities such as courage, physical prowess, and integrity. Anti-heroes usually distrust conventional values and, like Jerry, they often accept and celebrate their position as social outcasts. Along with the anti-hero, Albee uses satire and black humor in *The Zoo Story.* Satire employs humor to comment negatively on human nature and social institutions, while black humor places grotesque elements along side of humorous elements in order to shock the reader and evoke laughter in the face of difficulty and disorder. Albee uses both of these devices in *The Zoo Story* to comment on the way different social classes choose to view and ignore each other in American society; specifically, he highlights the way that in which members of the upper classes deal with members of the lower ones. This is illustrated with the character of Peter, who Albee uses as an example by having Jerry methodically bring him down to an animalistic level in order to show that he is just like everyone else. Another device that Albee uses in *The Zoo Story* is allegory. Allegory involves the use of characters, representing things or abstract ideas, to convey a message. Jerry's story about his landlady's dog could be seen as an allegory for his own inability to relate to others. In the end, Jerry says that he and the dog harbor "sadness, suspicion and indifference" for each other, which is similar to the relationships that Jerry has with other people. Some critics have argued that *The Zoo Story* is an allegory for Christian redemption. Jerry, as the Christ-like figure, martyrs himself to demonstrate the need for and meaningfulness of communication. This Christian

TOPICS FOR FURTHER STUDY

- Edward Albee was a child adopted by rich parents. Describe his attitude towards his upbringing from reading or seeing his one-act play *The American Dream.* In what ways does his upbringing evidence itself in *The Zoo Story?*

- Research the concept of Theatre of the Absurd. Does *The Zoo Story* belong under that heading? Why or why not?

- Compare *The American Dream* point-by-point with Eugene Ionesco's absurdist play *The Bald Soprano.* How are the two plays alike? How are they different?

- Why do you think it was important to Jerry to make Peter realize the misery that exists beneath everyday life? What was Jerry trying to achieve?

allegory viewpoint is also evident in some of the dialogue, such as when Jerry sighs and says "So be it!" just before impaling himself on the knife Peter is holding. This can be viewed as a reference to Jesus Christ's words as he dies on the cross: "Father, into your hands I commend my spirit." Although the manner in which Albee employs literary devices in *The Zoo Story* is subject to critical interpretation, all of the devices are readily apparent and are used to create a compelling drama.

HISTORICAL CONTEXT

Social Climate in the 1950s

The 1950s in the U.S. are viewed by many people as a period of prosperity for American society as a whole. Socially, many catch phrases were being used at this time, like "standard of living" and "cost of living," which implied that life in America could be measured based on personal income and material goods. After experiencing the Great Depression in the 1930s and World War II a decade later, the U.S. was eager to embrace the

COMPARE
&
CONTRAST

- **1950s:** The television set came into prominence in the American household. By 1957, a total of 35 million U.S. families had a television in their homes.

  Today: Almost all American families, rich and poor, have at least one television set and with the emergence of cable television, the amount of channels available is well over 100. The television is now an integral part of American society.

- **1950s:** Conservative family values dominated American society, with so-called "typical" nuclear families like Peter's in *The Zoo Story* viewed as ideal. Early television shows, such as *Father Knows Best,* that depicted such "ideal" families were extremely popular.

  Today: Families are depicted in a much more realistic light on television today, on shows like *Roseanne.* The nuclear family is no longer viewed as the "ideal" and most Americans consider

themselves to have moderate values. Nevertheless, a very vocal conservative Christian movement is leading the fight to return to the idealized view of the family that was popular in the 1950s.

- **1950s:** Consumer confidence and general prosperity within middle- and upper-class American society soared. However, this prosperity failed to carry over from white males to the Americans in lower classes, women, and ethnic minorities, who continued to earn less money and endure more job discrimination than white males.

  Today: The U.S. economy is steady, but after some economic hard times, consumer confidence is far lower than during the 1950s. White males still continue to make more money than women and minorities, but the gap is slowly closing. Many women and members of minority groups have been able to secure employment in powerful, high ranking professions.

---

notion that it had come into its own and, consequently, consumer confidence soared. Household appliances and automobiles became available to more people than ever before and the television became a prominent factor in the daily lives of Americans during the late 1950s. In 1947, a mere 14,000 families owned television sets; ten years later that figure grew to 35 million families. In theory, the television brought people closer together and allowed communication to reach new heights. However, many critics maintain that the way Albee mentions television in *The Zoo Story* and the fact that Peter has difficulty carrying on anything but empty conversation reflect on how disconnected society has become.

Political Climate in the 1950s

Politically, the U.S. was dominated by conservative values during the 1950s. One of the most extreme examples of this conservative tide was the effort led by Senator Joseph McCarthy to harass and

prosecute individuals suspected to have ties with the Communist Party. This anti-Communist sentiment in America turned into a frenzy because of the ruthless and random nature of the McCarthy's witch hunts. Eventually, Americans began to react against the absurdity of these trials, although many were afraid that they themselves would be targeted. Three other factors also played a major role in worrying conservatives: the emergence of rock music, movies that were becoming more and more explicit, and especially, the publishing of Kinsey Reports in 1948 and 1953. Alfred Kinsey, a zoologist, traveled all over the U.S. to interview over 16,000 men and women about their sexual histories. The details that were revealed, especially those concerning premarital sex and homosexuality, shocked the nation. Critics objected to the fact that the researchers failed to pass moral judgment on the data that they collected. Jerry, in *The Zoo Story,* epitomizes the thirty-seven percent of males in the Kinsey Report who reported that they had had a homosexual experience between adolescence and old age. He is also very eager to share the details of his homosexual experiences as a fifteen year old, which clearly makes Peter uncomfortable.

Cultural Climate in the 1950s

The cultural climate in the late 1950s included the beginnings of a backlash against conservative social and political views. Artists who lived outside the mainstream or who were dissatisfied within it began to comment boldly on this fact in their work. The Beat Generation were members of an artistic movement that centered in New York City and San Francisco during this time who protested against conservative values. Film audiences also began to idolize the tough guy at odds with "the establishment," such as those played by Marlon Brando and, most famously, James Dean in *Rebel without A Cause* (1956). The Theatre of the Absurd was a radical movement making an impact on world drama, which dominated the French stage after 1950. Absurdist playwrights sought to violate conservative audiences' expectations of what theatre should be by using incomprehensible plots, stark settings, and unusually long pauses. Playwrights such as Eugene Ionesco believed that life is terrifying because it is fundamentally absurd. Edward Albee used these absurd elements in a realistic mode with *The Zoo Story,* thus causing some confusion among critics and audiences in terms of how to label the play.

CRITICAL OVERVIEW

The Zoo Story, Edward Albee's first play, premiered on September 28, 1959, at the Schiller Theatre Werkstatt in West Berlin, Germany. While there, it received much praise from critics including Friedrich Luft who, as quoted in *Critical Essays on Edward Albee,* called it a "shudder-causing drama of superintelligent style." Riding high on the praise it received in Germany, *The Zoo Story* finally made its way back to New York where it debuted off-Broadway at the Provincetown Theatre on January 14, 1960. What made this debut even more exciting for Albee was the fact that he was sharing the bill with *Krapp's Last Tape,* a one-act play written by Samuel Beckett, one of Albee's idols.

Most New York critics declared *The Zoo Story* to be a very exciting play and viewed it as the beginning of a revitalized New York theatre scene. Henry Hewes in the *Saturday Review* claimed: "[Edward Albee] has written an extraordinary first play." However, a few critics expressed confusion over *The Zoo Story,* such as Tom Driver from *Christian Century* who wrote: "It is more than a little melodramatic, and the only sense I could draw from it is the conviction that one shouldn't talk to strangers in Central Park." Others simply dismissed the play, such as Robert Brustein, who in an article in the *New Republic* labeled the play beat generation "claptrap." The positive reviews outweighed the negative, however, and *The Zoo Story* ran for a total of 582 performances, which is remarkable for a first play. It also went on to win the *Village Voice* Obie Award for best play in 1960.

Whether or not people liked *The Zoo Story,* they felt compelled to discuss it, largely because of the sensational aspects of the play and the fact that people were confused about whether the play was absurd or realistic. Eventually, most people concluded that it was a mixture of the two styles, but critics remained divided over the play's message. Many critics have argued that *The Zoo Story* is a social commentary on the effects that loneliness can have on an individual in American society. George Wellwarth, in *The Theater of Protest and Paradox,* claimed that *The Zoo Story* "is about the maddening effect that the enforced loneliness of the human condition has on the person who is cursed (for in our society it undoubtedly is a curse) with the infinite capacity for love." Other critics viewed the play as a religious allegory, such as Rose A. Zimbardo who asserted in *Twentieth Century Literature* that the images that Albee uses are "traditional Christian symbols which ... retain their original significance." John Ditsky expressed a similar viewpoint in *The Onstage Christ: Studies in the Persistence of a Theme,* declaring that "*The Zoo Story* rests upon a foundation of Christ-references, and indeed derives its peculiar structure from Jesus' favourite teaching device, the parable." Other critics have described *The Zoo Story* as a ritual confrontation with death, a morality play, a homosexual play, and an absurd play. However, in an essay in *Edward Albee: An Interview and Essays,* Mary C. Anderson maintained that *The Zoo Story* can be "explained as a sociopolitical tract, a pessimistic analysis of human alienation, a modern Christian allegory of salvation, and an example of absurdist and nihilist theater." She concluded that the play "has managed to absorb these perspectives without exhausting its many levels of meaning."

The overall opinion of *The Zoo Story* from most critics is that it is an exciting and risky first play from a playwright who has gone on to win numerous awards for his works. After much early success, Albee went on to garner both high praise and censure for his work that followed *The Zoo Story* and *Who's Afraid Of Virginia Woolf?*. He has continued to explore and experiment with both the form and content of theatre, which is a risky venture, especially in the commercial arena. What continues to make Albee so fascinating for many critics and theatergoers is the fact that, as C.W.E. Bigsby noted in *Edward Albee: A Collection of Critical Essays*, "Albee has remained at heart a product of Off-Broadway, claiming the same freedom to experiment and, indeed, fail, which is the special strength of that theatre." It is his penchant for experimentation that has caused Albee to be, as Bigsby contended, one of those "few playwrights" who continue to be "frequently and mischievously misunderstood, misrepresented, overpraised, denigrated and precipitately dismissed." Critical opinion has had little effect on albee as a playwright, for he has continued to write and have his plays produced on and off Broadway.

CRITICISM

Stephen Coy

Coy is an esteemed authority on drama who has contributed to numerous publications. His essay praises the power of Albee's dialogue and the class dischord that it illustrates. Coy also addresses the religious imagery in Albee's play.

There is very little action in Edward Albee's *The Zoo Story*: two men meet, they exchange information, and one dies at the hand of the other. But to a framework of action which any writer might have imagined, Albee brings a master's sense of the ways in which, psychologically, some people are able to dominate and manipulate others, and a frankness and grotesqueness of language which are startling even now, almost forty years after the play's premiere.

Albee opens with an impressive display. Peter, the quiet, insular, middle-class publisher, is reading a book on "his" bench in New York's Central Park. Along comes Jerry, who (as we will see) is not out for a stroll but urgently looking for someone with whom to talk. He spies Peter, approaches him, and begins the elaborate process of getting Peter (who

wants only to be left alone) to put down his book and surrender to Jerry's desire to talk. This opening section of the play is too long to quote here, and in any case should be read through or better still seen onstage, but it is a marvel of resourcefulness.

Jerry announces that he has been to the Zoo, and when that produces no response he yells it. Peter barely responds even to this, so Jerry changes tactics and begins to ask Peter questions about where they are in the Park and in what direction he has (therefore) been walking. Peter fills his pipe as a way of trying to ignore Jerry, who, seeing this, uses it as a way of accusing Peter of a kind of cowardice: "Well, boy; you're not going to get lung cancer, are you?" Peter does not rise to the bait, so Jerry becomes more aggressive and more graphic: "No, sir. What you'll probably get is cancer of the mouth, and then you'll have to wear one of those things Freud wore after they took one whole side of his jaw away. What do they call those things?"

Poor dim Peter, college-educated but not street-smart, can't stop himself from showing that he knows the word: prosthesis—Jerry seizes on this in a way that shows that he himself knows the word, and sarcastically asks Peter if he is a doctor. When Peter says no, he read about prosthetics in *Time* magazine, Jerry responds that "*Time* magazine is not for blockheads." This line is generally delivered sarcastically, so that it both patronizes Peter and shows the audience that Jerry thinks himself superior to most of middle-class America. Finally, Jerry bullies Peter into giving him his full attention by inflicting what is sometimes called "liberal guilt:"

JERRY: Do you mind if we talk?

PETER: (Obviously minding.) Why . . . no, no.

JERRY: Yes you do; you do.

PETER: (Puts his book down . . . smiling.) No, really; I don't mind.

JERRY: Yes you do.

PETER: (Finally decided.) No; I don't mind at all, really.

At this point the first section, or movement, of the play comes to an end. Many critics have pointed out that *The Zoo Story* is a play about the difficulty of communication. But that is a common problem offstage or on and only rises to dramatic urgency when there is something urgent to be communicated. Now that Jerry has finally succeeded in capturing Peter's full attention, the question is: what message has Jerry brought with him from the Zoo that he is so avid to communicate, even (or particularly) to a total stranger?

Avid or not, Jerry suddenly seems in no hurry. He returns to the subject of the Zoo, hinting that "it" (what "it" might be is not explained) will be on TV tonight or in the newspapers tomorrow. He begins to ask Peter about himself and his family, eliciting pieces of personal information. When Jerry guesses that Peter and his wife are not going to have any more children, Peter asks how he could possibly know that. Jerry responds: "The way you cross your legs, perhaps; something in the voice. . . . Is it your wife?" A subtle game is afoot here: Jerry earlier attacked Peter's manhood by implying it was somehow cowardly to smoke a pipe rather than cigarettes, and now, with his remarks about the legs and the voice, he seems to imply effeminacy or perhaps even suppressed homosexuality (a line of thought to which he will return later). In any case, he ends the line with a different kind of attack on Peter's manhood, implying that the dominant voice in the no-children decision, and the household, is that of Peter's wife, whose name is never given. When Peter tacitly admits this, Jerry actually shows a moment of compassion before briskly moving on: "Well, now; what else?"

During this second section of the play, in which the men exchange information about their lives, Albee avoids the dullness which often attends exposition by two means: frequent allusions to the Zoo and tantalizing hints about what may have happened there (we learn that Jerry was depressed by the way the bars separated the animals from each other and from the people but not if he actually did anything about it); and a combination of startling information and aggressive behavior that keeps Jerry firmly in our minds (and Peter's) as a figure of instability and menace.

Jerry tells Peter about his hellish rooming-house, the serio-comic loss of his parents, his first real sexual experience (while admitting it was homosexual, he gets in another dig at Peter's masculinity: "But that was the jazz of a very special hotel, wasn't it?"), and his landlady, "a fat, ugly, mean, stupid, unwashed, misanthropic, cheap, drunken bag of garbage." But the landlady, despite being one of the most arresting offstage presences in American drama, is only the prelude to what might be called the third movement of the play.

It is called "The Story of Jerry and the Dog," and it must be seen or read in its entirety, as no description could come within miles of doing it justice. It tells of Jerry's attempt to "get through to" the disgusting landlady's even more disgusting

WHAT DO I READ NEXT?

- It is essential that anyone wanting to understand Edward Albee read his 1962 play *Who's Afraid of Virginia Woolf?*

- Whether as relevant to Albee or not, everyone interested in modern drama should read Martin Esslin's 1961 text *The Theatre of the Absurd.*

- Those interested in Albee as an adapter of other people's work (and what might draw him to that work) would enjoy *The Ballad of the Sad Cafe,* which he adapted from Carson McCullers's novel and *Malcolm,* adapted from the work by James Purdy.

- After years of obscurity and what some took to be decline, Albee suddenly returned to prominence (and major awards) with the play *Three Tall Women,* produced on Broadway in 1994.

- What was it about America in the 1960's that made Albee call it "this slipping land of ours"? Two places to look for answers are in books and articles about President Dwight D. Eisenhower's administration and in a book called *On the Road* by Jack Kerouac.

dog, which attacked him whenever it caught him leaving or entering the building. Albee makes sure that we understand that Jerry's past attempt to reach the dog is parallel to his present attempt to reach Peter: he has Jerry try several ways to get through to the dog, from killing him with kindness to just plain killing him, just as he tried several different ways to get through to Peter.

The playwright has Jerry, who has so far disgusted Peter but not aroused his sympathy, say, "it's just that if you can't deal with people, you have to make a start somewhere. WITH ANIMALS! Don't you see?" Of his final truce with the dog, a sad indifference, Jerry says, "I have learned that neither kindness nor cruelty, by themselves . . . create any effect beyond themselves; and I have learned that the two combined, together . . . are the teaching emotion." This lesson Jerry learned from his experience is of great thematic importance in the play, where every step forward in communication, large or small, is accomplished with a combination of kindness and cruelty.

Next comes the final section of the play. Of Jerry's story, Peter says, in fact he yells, "I DON'T UNDERSTAND!", but Jerry doesn't believe him and neither do most critics. They think he does indeed understand that Jerry is trying to tell him something about the pain, the loneliness, and the hideous suffering of those parts of society not normally encountered or even acknowledged by Peter's middle class; and they think that Peter's real feelings are more clearly seen in a subsequent line: "I DON'T WANT TO HEAR ANY MORE." Peter prepares to leave, they say, because "his" space has been invaded not only by an unwelcome person but by unwelcome information, both of which threaten the comfortable ignorance of his life.

Jerry is at first angered by Peter's refusal to comprehend, then apparently resigned to it. But he is not ready to quit. He taunts Peter, punches him and pushes him to the ground, challenging him to fight for his bench. Peter refuses, fearing he will be harmed. Jerry pulls out an ugly looking knife (a switchblade, wicked-looking and illegal in New York, is used as a prop by most productions) and throws it on the ground between them. Peter cowers back. Jerry tells Peter to pick up the knife but Peter won't. Jerry grabs Peter and says the following, slapping Peter each time he utters the word "fight": "You fight, you miserable bastard; fight for that bench; fight for your parakeets; fight for your cats, fight for your two daughters; fight for your life; fight for your manhood, you pathetic little vegetable. You couldn't even get your wife with a male child."

Angered at last beyond caution, Peter snatches up the knife, even now holding it defensively. Jerry sighs heavily, says, "So be it," and rushes at Peter, impaling himself on the knife and giving himself, deliberately, a mortal wound. The words Jerry says as he is dying are most important: "Thank you, Peter. . . . Thank you very much. Oh, Peter, I was afraid I'd drive you away. . . . Peter . . . thank you. I came unto you and you have comforted me. Dear Peter." Jerry then sends Peter on his way, making sure he takes his book with him, but asserting that the bench (and, by implication, some part of Peter which will never be the same) belongs to him, to Jerry.

Many critics have pointed out that the Biblical language in this reference to Peter, together with other such language in the play (regarding the dog, Jerry says, "AND IT CAME TO PASS THAT THE BEAST WAS DEATHLY ILL."), and with the number of times God is called on from the stabbing to the end of the play, suggests Christian symbolism: Jesus (Jerry, a distantly similar name) dies for the suffering of mankind but not before he has passed on his gospel to his disciple Peter. This seems a reasonable inference, since playwrights choose their words, Albee more carefully than most. Whether the implication of Christianity expands or narrows the impact of the play is highly debatable, but the language is there—not by accident—and it should not be ignored.

The Zoo Story can best be understood (especially by actors, who are trained to play intentions but not mysteries or ambiguities) by starting off with a single, basic assumption. Jerry, lonely, unstable, and desperate, made a life decision at the Zoo—or perhaps even at home before he went to the Zoo "correctly." He would leave the Zoo and walk "northerly" in the Park until the first human being he spotted. He would strike up a conversation with that person, by whatever means it took, and then make the best effort of his life to teach that person what Jerry already knew about the sufferings of mankind, especially the sufferings others prefer not to notice. He would force that person to understand, or, to make a cliche literal, die trying. Jerry's suicide is thus the last logical item on the list of "whatever it takes" to take from Peter his ignorance, his indifference, and his complacency. Peter may never wander preaching in the wilderness, but he will never again draw breath without the burden of the knowledge that Jerry has conveyed to him. That much of the torch, at least, has been passed.

Source: Stephen Coy, in an essay for *Drama for Students,* Gale, 1997.

Carolyn E. Johnson

In this essay, Johnson heartily endorses Albee's play, citing numerous elements that merit extensive study in the classroom.

Johnson is a critic and educational administrator.

Edward Albee emerges as one of the most controversial and, consequently, one of the most read contemporary playwrights. He does not write of human emotions and relationships in statements of fact that we like to hear. He uses abstract symbols and ideas to portray unidentifiable fears, subtle truths, intangible illusions, and the unattainable standards imposed upon society. Albee is difficult to understand because he does *not* discuss anything concrete. Facts are sensible. Abstracts are disturbing. To write about the mystical secrets of life without presenting any kind of solution exasperates the reader. But this may be Albee's intent. He once said that if after a play the audience is concerned only about finding their cars, the play failed. Therefore, Albee bares the souls of his characters— his audience. He suggests the idiosyncrasies and failings of man and his sociality. And in doing so he often uses the outcast, the distorted man, the pervert.

This is what is shocking and terrifying. And this is one reason why many English teachers refuse to approach his plays in the classroom. Not only is he frustrating to interpret, but he also unveils some very eccentric exponents in society. They are not the type that provoke comfortable discussion. But in my opinion this is not reason enough to shelve Albee. He remains our most colorful coeval dramatist and as such belongs in a modern, progressive curriculum. He refuses to be ignored by the theater. Likewise, we cannot ignore him. Albee depicts some general human weaknesses that are argumentative and provide stimulating discussion for students. . . .

The Zoo Story might be used for student study, because human contact and communication are lacking among young people. It is about a wandering homosexual who, unable to adjust to his own world and hating the conventional world, latches onto a stranger sitting on a park bench and tricks this typical father of parakeets and cats into killing him. Here again Albee resorts to violence. A closer analysis of this play may bring out some ideas for classroom use.

Three human defects exemplified are lack of communication, alienation from society, and mediocrity. Jerry approaches Peter, sitting on a park bench where he has been coming the last four years, and says, "Do you mind if we talk?" And Peter, "obviously minding," replies that he does not mind. Immediately we see that people really do not communicate. They do not say what they actually mean or are thinking. Peter becomes "bewildered by the seeming lack of communication." And Jerry, who feels the need to make contact with someone— anyone—says, "I don't talk to many people— except to say like: give me a beer, or where's the

> "EDWARD ALBEE SHOULD BE A PART OF EVERY AMERICAN LITERATURE COURSE"

john, or what time does the feature go on, or keep your hands to yourself, buddy. . . ." How trite and nondescript we are! Very seldom does one human being fully and completely *talk* with someone, talk with him in such a way as to know what really makes him tick. This is true also about young people. Their music is loud so they do not have to converse; they go to movies so they can look rather than talk; they watch TV rather than visit; even their cars make so much noise it is not necessary to think or talk.

Jerry felt the need. "But every once in a while I like to talk to somebody, really *talk;* like to get to know somebody, know all about him." And so Jerry begins asking questions but does not "really carry on a conversation." The experiences he relates about the dog only indicate the distance one will go to satisfy a need, to make contact. "A person has to have some way of dealing with SOMETHING." "People. With an idea; a concept. And where better, where ever better in this humiliating excuse for a jail, where better to communicate one single, simple-minded idea than in an entrance hall?" The unimportance of the place of communication becomes evident. But what *is* important is that one must communicate; and the entrance hall, even with a dog in an entrance hall, would be a start.

It is at this point in the play that Albee again makes us aware of his theory of the necessity of violence for contact. Jerry says in talking about his dog, "I have learned that neither kindness nor cruelty by themselves, independent of each other, creates any effect beyond themselves." The two of them together are the motivating device. And then the beautiful and desperate lines, "We neither love nor hurt because we not try to reach each other." We are so terribly misunderstood. We cannot understand love. How is love to be interpreted? By whom? This aspect of the play right here could trigger a very healthy discussion among students. And again at the end of the short play Jerry cries in desperation, "Don't you have any idea, not even the slightest, what other people *need?*.'' People need to be needed, and they need someone to need. They must have someone whom they make contact, with whom they can talk and be understood. If people do not make contact with someone, they resort to various perversions trying to find something with which to identify.

This point brings us to another human defect. The reader is made aware of Jerry's alienation and aloneness when he describes his apartment and points out the two picture frames that are empty. ''I don't see why they need any explanation at all. Isn't it clear? I don't have pictures of anyone to put in them.'' And his more complete isolation from the square world is quite obvious when he says, ''I was a h-o-m-o-s-e-x-u-a-l.'' Thus, when Jerry relates his experiences with the dog, we have a sense not only of his failure to communicate but also of his reaction to people. ''. . . Animals are indifferent to me . . . like people.'' People are trapped in their own little worlds like animals in a zoo, and everyone is ''. . . separated by bars from everyone else.'' Some do not seem to mind their cage, because they accept this poor excuse for living and find a certain amount of satisfaction in things—parakeets, cats, a park bench.

This, then, brings us to the third human failing, that of mediocrity. Peter is the ''ordinary,'' life-size. He is married and has a family of girls, parakeets, and cats. He has an ordinary job and can talk about ordinary things. When Peter becomes perturbed at the thought of losing his bench, he says, ''I've come here for years; I have hours of great pleasure, great satisfaction, right here. And that's important to a man. I'm a responsible person, and I'm a GROWN-UP. This is my bench, and you have no right to take it away from me.'' He has found comfort and security in the everyday things that do not need explaining, so much so that he cannot bear the thought of losing one. Jerry sees him as he really is: ''You are a vegetable. . . .'' He further taunts him, bringing out more of his simpleness and sameness, ''. . .You've told me about your home, and your family, and *your own* little zoo. You have everything, and now you want this bench.'' Throughout the play there are indications and prevailing overtones of being trapped. At the very end of the play as Jerry dies, he says, ''. . . Your parakeets are making the dinner . . . the cats . . . are setting the table . . . .'' How very absurd! To be subjected and tied to these menial, dull, unstimulating tasks and responsibilities that we make for ourselves. The sad truth is that these things might be bearable if at the same time we could communicate.

This is the prevailing theme of *The Zoo Story*—communication. It is obvious at once, and with a little guidance and prodding students can recognize quite readily the handicaps and limitation of man and his society as seen in this play. The results of a study of this play are encouraging, as is the idea that attacking a contemporary play on contemporary society is contemporary education.

Now, whether or not Albee deserves to enter the classroom depends upon whether or not the educators—the English educators—are willing to admit him. I firmly believe our students must be taught literature written during their time. And Edward Albee should be a part of every American literature course!

Source: Carolyn E. Johnson, ''In Defense of Albee'' in *English Journal,* Vol. 57, no. 1, January, 1968, pp. 21–23, 29.

FURTHER READING

Anderson, Mary C., editor. *Edward Albee: An Interview and Essays,* Syracuse University Press, 1983.
    A good resource for Albee's thoughts on the dramatic process. Also contains a number of essays that discuss the themes present in *The Zoo Story*.

Bigsby, C. W. E., editor. *Edward Albee: A Collection of Critical Essays,* Prentice-Hall, 1975.
    A good critical overview of Albee's career up until 1974. Contains a number of perceptive essays on *The Zoo Story*.

Ditsky, John. ''Albee's Parabolic Christ: *The Zoo Story*'' in his *The Onstage Christ: Studies in the Persistence of a Theme,* [London], 1980.
    Ditksy's book examines religious imagery in various dramas. He details the parallels to the story of Christ that are evident in Albee's play.

Nilan, Mary M. ''Albee's *The Zoo Story:* Alienated Man and the Nature of Love'' in *Modern Drama,* Vol. 16, 1973.
    An essay that details Jerry's isolation from mainstream society and his failures at forming meaningful relationships.

Woods, Linda L. "Isolation and the Barrier of Language in *The Zoo Story* in *Research Studies,* Vol. 36, 1968.
    A good examination of Jerry's alienation from middle class society and problems that he faces communicating with members of that group—Peter in particular.

SOURCES

Anderson, Mary C. "Ritual and Initiation in 'The Zoo Story,'" in *Edward Albee: An Interview and Essays,* pp. 93-108, Syracuse University Press, 1983.

Brustein, Robert. "Krapp and a Little Claptrap," in *New Republic,* February 22, 1960, pp. 21-2.

Ditsky, John. *The Onstage Christ: Studies in the Persistence of a Theme,* Vision Press, 1980, 188 p.

Driver, Tom. "Drama: Bucketful of Dregs," in *Christian Century,* February 17, 1960, pp. 193-94.

Hewes, Henry. "Benchmanship," in *Saturday Review,* February 16, 1960, p. 32.

Luft, Friedrich. Review in *Critical Essays on Edward Albee,* edited by Philip C. Kolin and J. Madison Davis, p. 41, Hall, 1986.

Roudane, Matthew C. *Understanding Edward Albee,* p. 27, University of South Carolina Press, 1987.

Wellwarth, George. *The Theater of Protest and Paradox: Development in the Avant-Garde Drama,* New York University Press, 1964.

Zimbardo, Rose A. "Symbolism and Naturalism in Edward Albee's 'The Zoo Story,'" in *Twentieth Century Literature,* Vol. 8, 1962, pp. 10-17.

Glossary of Literary Terms

A

Abstract Used as a noun, the term refers to a short summary or outline of a longer work. As an adjective applied to writing or literary works, abstract refers to words or phrases that name things not knowable through the five senses.

Absurd, Theater of the See *Theater of the Absurd*

Absurdism See *Theater of the Absurd*

Act A major section of a play. Acts are divided into varying numbers of shorter scenes. From ancient times to the nineteenth century plays were generally constructed of five acts, but modern works typically consist of one, two, or three acts.

Acto A one-act Chicano theater piece developed out of collective improvisation.

Aestheticism A literary and artistic movement of the nineteenth century. Followers of the movement believed that art should not be mixed with social, political, or moral teaching. The statement "art for art's sake" is a good summary of aestheticism. The movement had its roots in France, but it gained widespread importance in England in the last half of the nineteenth century, where it helped change the Victorian practice of including moral lessons in literature.

Age of Johnson The period in English literature between 1750 and 1798, named after the most prominent literary figure of the age, Samuel John-

son. Works written during this time are noted for their emphasis on "sensibility," or emotional quality. These works formed a transition between the rational works of the Age of Reason, or Neoclassical period, and the emphasis on individual feelings and responses of the Romantic period.

Age of Reason See *Neoclassicism*

Age of Sensibility See *Age of Johnson*

Alexandrine Meter See *Meter*

Allegory A narrative technique in which characters representing things or abstract ideas are used to convey a message or teach a lesson. Allegory is typically used to teach moral, ethical, or religious lessons but is sometimes used for satiric or political purposes.

Allusion A reference to a familiar literary or historical person or event, used to make an idea more easily understood.

Amerind Literature: The writing and oral traditions of Native Americans. Native American literature was originally passed on by word of mouth, so it consisted largely of stories and events that were easily memorized. Amerind prose is often rhythmic like poetry because it was recited to the beat of a ceremonial drum.

Analogy A comparison of two things made to explain something unfamiliar through its similarities to something familiar, or to prove one point based on the acceptedness of another. Similes and metaphors are types of analogies.

Angry Young Men A group of British writers of the 1950s whose work expressed bitterness and disillusionment with society. Common to their work is an anti-hero who rebels against a corrupt social order and strives for personal integrity.

Antagonist The major character in a narrative or drama who works against the hero or protagonist.

Anthropomorphism The presentation of animals or objects in human shape or with human characteristics. The term is derived from the Greek word for "human form."

Anti-hero A central character in a work of literature who lacks traditional heroic qualities such as courage, physical prowess, and fortitude. Anti-heros typically distrust conventional values and are unable to commit themselves to any ideals. They generally feel helpless in a world over which they have no control. Anti-heroes usually accept, and often celebrate, their positions as social outcasts.

Antimasque See *Masque*

Antithesis The antithesis of something is its direct opposite. In literature, the use of antithesis as a figure of speech results in two statements that show a contrast through the balancing of two opposite ideas. Technically, it is the second portion of the statement that is defined as the "antithesis"; the first portion is the "thesis."

Apocrypha Writings tentatively attributed to an author but not proven or universally accepted to be their works. The term was originally applied to certain books of the Bible that were not considered inspired and so were not included in the "sacred canon."

Apollonian and Dionysian The two impulses believed to guide authors of dramatic tragedy. The Apollonian impulse is named after Apollo, the Greek god of light and beauty and the symbol of intellectual order. The Dionysian impulse is named after Dionysus, the Greek god of wine and the symbol of the unrestrained forces of nature. The Apollonian impulse is to create a rational, harmonious world, while the Dionysian is to express the irrational forces of personality.

Apostrophe A statement, question, or request addressed to an inanimate object or concept or to a nonexistent or absent person.

Archetype The word archetype is commonly used to describe an original pattern or model from which all other things of the same kind are made. This term was introduced to literary criticism from the psychology of Carl Jung. It expresses Jung's theory that behind every person's "unconscious," or repressed memories of the past, lies the "collective unconscious" of the human race: memories of the countless typical experiences of our ancestors. These memories are said to prompt illogical associations that trigger powerful emotions in the reader. Often, the emotional process is primitive, even primordial. Archetypes are the literary images that grow out of the "collective unconscious." They appear in literature as incidents and plots that repeat basic patterns of life. They may also appear as stereotyped characters.

Argument The argument of a work is the author's subject matter or principal idea.

Aristotelian Criticism Specifically, the method of evaluating and analyzing tragedy formulated by the Greek philosopher Aristotle in his *Poetics*. More generally, the term indicates any form of criticism that follows Aristotle's views. Aristotelian criticism focuses on the form and logical structure of a work, apart from its historical or social context, in contrast to "Platonic Criticism," which stresses the usefulness of art.

Art for Art's Sake See *Aestheticism*

Aside A comment made by a stage performer that is intended to be heard by the audience but supposedly not by other characters.

Audience The people for whom a piece of literature is written. Authors usually write with a certain audience in mind, for example, children, members of a religious or ethnic group, or colleagues in a professional field. The term "audience" also applies to the people who gather to see or hear any performance, including plays, poetry readings, speeches, and concerts.

Avant-garde A French term meaning "vanguard." It is used in literary criticism to describe new writing that rejects traditional approaches to literature in favor of innovations in style or content.

B

Ballad A short poem that tells a simple story and has a repeated refrain. Ballads were originally intended to be sung. Early ballads, known as folk ballads, were passed down through generations, so their authors are often unknown. Later ballads composed by known authors are called literary ballads.

Baroque A term used in literary criticism to describe literature that is complex or ornate in style or diction. Baroque works typically express tension, anxiety, and violent emotion. The term ''Baroque Age'' designates a period in Western European literature beginning in the late sixteenth century and ending about one hundred years later. Works of this period often mirror the qualities of works more generally associated with the label ''baroque'' and sometimes feature elaborate conceits.

Baroque Age See *Baroque*

Baroque Period See *Baroque*

Beat Generation See *Beat Movement*

Beat Movement A period featuring a group of American poets and novelists of the 1950s and 1960s—including Jack Kerouac, Allen Ginsberg, Gregory Corso, William S. Burroughs, and Lawrence Ferlinghetti—who rejected established social and literary values. Using such techniques as stream of consciousness writing and jazz-influenced free verse and focusing on unusual or abnormal states of mind—generated by religious ecstasy or the use of drugs—the Beat writers aimed to create works that were unconventional in both form and subject matter.

Black Aesthetic Movement A period of artistic and literary development among African Americans in the 1960s and early 1970s. This was the first major African-American artistic movement since the Harlem Renaissance and was closely paralleled by the civil rights and black power movements. The black aesthetic writers attempted to produce works of art that would be meaningful to the black masses. Key figures in black aesthetics included one of its founders, poet and playwright Amiri Baraka, formerly known as LeRoi Jones; poet and essayist Haki R. Madhubuti, formerly Don L. Lee; poet and playwright Sonia Sanchez; and dramatist Ed Bullins.

Black Arts Movement See *Black Aesthetic Movement*

Black Comedy See *Black Humor*

Black Humor Writing that places grotesque elements side by side with humorous ones in an attempt to shock the reader, forcing him or her to laugh at the horrifying reality of a disordered world.

Blank Verse Loosely, any unrhymed poetry, but more generally, unrhymed iambic pentameter verse (composed of lines of five two-syllable feet with the first syllable accented, the second unaccented). Blank verse has been used by poets since the Renaissance for its flexibility and its graceful, dignified tone.

Bloomsbury Group A group of English writers, artists, and intellectuals who held informal artistic and philosophical discussions in Bloomsbury, a district of London, from around 1907 to the early 1930s. The Bloomsbury Group held no uniform philosophical beliefs but did commonly express an aversion to moral prudery and a desire for greater social tolerance.

Bon Mot A French term meaning ''good word.'' A *bon mot* is a witty remark or clever observation.

Breath Verse See *Projective Verse*

Burlesque Any literary work that uses exaggeration to make its subject appear ridiculous, either by treating a trivial subject with profound seriousness or by treating a dignified subject frivolously. The word ''burlesque'' may also be used as an adjective, as in ''burlesque show,'' to mean ''striptease act.''

C

Cadence The natural rhythm of language caused by the alternation of accented and unaccented syllables. Much modern poetry—notably free verse—deliberately manipulates cadence to create complex rhythmic effects.

Caesura A pause in a line of poetry, usually occurring near the middle. It typically corresponds to a break in the natural rhythm or sense of the line but is sometimes shifted to create special meanings or rhythmic effects.

Canzone A short Italian or Provencal lyric poem, commonly about love and often set to music. The *canzone* has no set form but typically contains five or six stanzas made up of seven to twenty lines of eleven syllables each. A shorter, five- to ten-line ''envoy,'' or concluding stanza, completes the poem.

Carpe Diem A Latin term meaning ''seize the day.'' This is a traditional theme of poetry, especially lyrics. A *carpe diem* poem advises the reader or the person it addresses to live for today and enjoy the pleasures of the moment.

Catharsis The release or purging of unwanted emotions— specifically fear and pity—brought about by exposure to art. The term was first used by the Greek philosopher Aristotle in his *Poetics* to refer to the desired effect of tragedy on spectators.

Celtic Renaissance A period of Irish literary and cultural history at the end of the nineteenth century. Followers of the movement aimed to create a romantic vision of Celtic myth and legend. The most significant works of the Celtic Renaissance typically present a dreamy, unreal world, usually in reaction against the reality of contemporary problems.

Celtic Twilight See *Celtic Renaissance*

Character Broadly speaking, a person in a literary work. The actions of characters are what constitute the plot of a story, novel, or poem. There are numerous types of characters, ranging from simple, stereotypical figures to intricate, multifaceted ones. In the techniques of anthropomorphism and personification, animals—and even places or things—can assume aspects of character. "Characterization" is the process by which an author creates vivid, believable characters in a work of art. This may be done in a variety of ways, including (1) direct description of the character by the narrator; (2) the direct presentation of the speech, thoughts, or actions of the character; and (3) the responses of other characters to the character. The term "character" also refers to a form originated by the ancient Greek writer Theophrastus that later became popular in the seventeenth and eighteenth centuries. It is a short essay or sketch of a person who prominently displays a specific attribute or quality, such as miserliness or ambition.

Characterization See *Character*

Chorus In ancient Greek drama, a group of actors who commented on and interpreted the unfolding action on the stage. Initially the chorus was a major component of the presentation, but over time it became less significant, with its numbers reduced and its role eventually limited to commentary between acts. By the sixteenth century the chorus—if employed at all— was typically a single person who provided a prologue and an epilogue and occasionally appeared between acts to introduce or underscore an important event.

Chronicle A record of events presented in chronological order. Although the scope and level of detail provided varies greatly among the chronicles surviving from ancient times, some, such as the *Anglo-Saxon Chronicle,* feature vivid descriptions and a lively recounting of events. During the Elizabethan Age, many dramas— appropriately called "chronicle plays"—were based on material from chronicles.

Classical In its strictest definition in literary criticism, classicism refers to works of ancient Greek or Roman literature. The term may also be used to describe a literary work of recognized importance (a "classic") from any time period or literature that exhibits the traits of classicism.

Classicism A term used in literary criticism to describe critical doctrines that have their roots in ancient Greek and Roman literature, philosophy, and art. Works associated with classicism typically exhibit restraint on the part of the author, unity of design and purpose, clarity, simplicity, logical organization, and respect for tradition.

Climax The turning point in a narrative, the moment when the conflict is at its most intense. Typically, the structure of stories, novels, and plays is one of rising action, in which tension builds to the climax, followed by falling action, in which tension lessens as the story moves to its conclusion.

Colloquialism A word, phrase, or form of pronunciation that is acceptable in casual conversation but not in formal, written communication. It is considered more acceptable than slang.

Comedy One of two major types of drama, the other being tragedy. Its aim is to amuse, and it typically ends happily. Comedy assumes many forms, such as farce and burlesque, and uses a variety of techniques, from parody to satire. In a restricted sense the term comedy refers only to dramatic presentations, but in general usage it is commonly applied to nondramatic works as well.

Comedy of Manners A play about the manners and conventions of an aristocratic, highly sophisticated society. The characters are usually types rather than individualized personalities, and plot is less important than atmosphere. Such plays were an important aspect of late seventeenth-century English comedy. The comedy of manners was revived in the eighteenth century by Oliver Goldsmith and Richard Brinsley Sheridan, enjoyed a second revival in the late nineteenth century, and has endured into the twentieth century.

Comic Relief The use of humor to lighten the mood of a serious or tragic story, especially in plays. The technique is very common in Elizabethan works, and can be an integral part of the plot or simply a brief event designed to break the tension of the scene.

Commedia dell'arte An Italian term meaning "the comedy of guilds" or "the comedy of professional actors." This form of dramatic comedy was popular in Italy during the sixteenth century. Actors were assigned stock roles (such as Pulcinella, the stupid servant, or Pantalone, the old merchant) and given a basic plot to follow, but all dialogue was improvised. The roles were rigidly typed and the plots were formulaic, usually revolving around young lovers who thwarted their elders and attained wealth and happiness. A rigid convention of the *commedia dell'arte* is the periodic intrusion of Harlequin, who interrupts the play with low buffoonery.

Complaint A lyric poem, popular in the Renaissance, in which the speaker expresses sorrow about his or her condition. Typically, the speaker's sadness is caused by an unresponsive lover, but some complaints cite other sources of unhappiness, such as poverty or fate.

Conceit A clever and fanciful metaphor, usually expressed through elaborate and extended comparison, that presents a striking parallel between two seemingly dissimilar things—for example, elaborately comparing a beautiful woman to an object like a garden or the sun. The conceit was a popular device throughout the Elizabethan Age and Baroque Age and was the principal technique of the seventeenth-century English metaphysical poets. This usage of the word conceit is unrelated to the best-known definition of conceit as an arrogant attitude or behavior.

Concrete Concrete is the opposite of abstract, and refers to a thing that actually exists or a description that allows the reader to experience an object or concept with the senses.

Concrete Poetry Poetry in which visual elements play a large part in the poetic effect. Punctuation marks, letters, or words are arranged on a page to form a visual design: a cross, for example, or a bumblebee.

Confessional Poetry A form of poetry in which the poet reveals very personal, intimate, sometimes shocking information about himself or herself.

Conflict The conflict in a work of fiction is the issue to be resolved in the story. It usually occurs between two characters, the protagonist and the antagonist, or between the protagonist and society or the protagonist and himself or herself.

Connotation The impression that a word gives beyond its defined meaning. Connotations may be universally understood or may be significant only to a certain group.

Consonance Consonance occurs in poetry when words appearing at the ends of two or more verses have similar final consonant sounds but have final vowel sounds that differ, as with ''stuff'' and ''off.''

Convention Any widely accepted literary device, style, or form.

Corrido A Mexican ballad.

Couplet Two lines of poetry with the same rhyme and meter, often expressing a complete and self-contained thought. .

Criticism The systematic study and evaluation of literary works, usually based on a specific method or set of principles. An important part of literary studies since ancient times, the practice of criticism has given rise to numerous theories, methods, and ''schools,'' sometimes producing conflicting, even contradictory, interpretations of literature in general as well as of individual works. Even such basic issues as what constitutes a poem or a novel have been the subject of much criticism over the centuries.

D

Dactyl See *Foot*

Dadaism A protest movement in art and literature founded by Tristan Tzara in 1916. Followers of the movement expressed their outrage at the destruction brought about by World War I by revolting against numerous forms of social convention. The Dadaists presented works marked by calculated madness and flamboyant nonsense. They stressed total freedom of expression, commonly through primitive displays of emotion and illogical, often senseless, poetry. The movement ended shortly after the war, when it was replaced by surrealism.

Decadent See *Decadents*

Decadents The followers of a nineteenth-century literary movement that had its beginnings in French aestheticism. Decadent literature displays a fascination with perverse and morbid states; a search for novelty and sensation—the ''new thrill''; a preoccupation with mysticism; and a belief in the senselessness of human existence. The movement is closely associated with the doctrine Art for Art's Sake. The term ''decadence'' is sometimes used to denote a decline in the quality of art or literature following a period of greatness.

Deconstruction A method of literary criticism developed by Jacques Derrida and characterized by multiple conflicting interpretations of a given work. Deconstructionists consider the impact of the language of a work and suggest that the true meaning of the work is not necessarily the meaning that the author intended.

Deduction The process of reaching a conclusion through reasoning from general premises to a specific premise.

Denotation The definition of a word, apart from the impressions or feelings it creates in the reader.

Denouement A French word meaning "the unknotting." In literary criticism, it denotes the resolution of conflict in fiction or drama. The *denouement* follows the climax and provides an outcome to the primary plot situation as well as an explanation of secondary plot complications. The *denouement* often involves a character's recognition of his or her state of mind or moral condition.

Description Descriptive writing is intended to allow a reader to picture the scene or setting in which the action of a story takes place. The form this description takes often evokes an intended emotional response—a dark, spooky graveyard will evoke fear, and a peaceful, sunny meadow will evoke calmness.

Detective Story A narrative about the solution of a mystery or the identification of a criminal. The conventions of the detective story include the detective's scrupulous use of logic in solving the mystery; incompetent or ineffectual police; a suspect who appears guilty at first but is later proved innocent; and the detective's friend or confidant—often the narrator—whose slowness in interpreting clues emphasizes by contrast the detective's brilliance.

Deus ex machina A Latin term meaning "god out of a machine." In Greek drama, a god was often lowered onto the stage by a mechanism of some kind to rescue the hero or untangle the plot. By extension, the term refers to any artificial device or coincidence used to bring about a convenient and simple solution to a plot. This is a common device in melodramas and includes such fortunate circumstances as the sudden receipt of a legacy to save the family farm or a last-minute stay of execution. The *deus ex machina* invariably rewards the virtuous and punishes evildoers.

Dialogue In its widest sense, dialogue is simply conversation between people in a literary work; in its most restricted sense, it refers specifically to the speech of characters in a drama. As a specific literary genre, a "dialogue" is a composition in which characters debate an issue or idea.

Diction The selection and arrangement of words in a literary work. Either or both may vary depending on the desired effect. There are four general types of diction: "formal," used in scholarly or lofty writing; "informal," used in relaxed but educated conversation; "colloquial," used in everyday speech; and "slang," containing newly coined words and other terms not accepted in formal usage.

Didactic A term used to describe works of literature that aim to teach some moral, religious, political, or practical lesson. Although didactic elements are often found in artistically pleasing works, the term "didactic" usually refers to literature in which the message is more important than the form. The term may also be used to criticize a work that the critic finds "overly didactic," that is, heavy-handed in its delivery of a lesson.

Dimeter See *Meter*

Dionysian See *Apollonian and Dionysian*

Discordia concours A Latin phrase meaning "discord in harmony." The term was coined by the eighteenth-century English writer Samuel Johnson to describe "a combination of dissimilar images or discovery of occult resemblances in things apparently unlike." Johnson created the expression by reversing a phrase by the Latin poet Horace.

Dissonance A combination of harsh or jarring sounds, especially in poetry. Although such combinations may be accidental, poets sometimes intentionally make them to achieve particular effects. Dissonance is also sometimes used to refer to close but not identical rhymes. When this is the case, the word functions as a synonym for consonance.

Doppelganger A literary technique by which a character is duplicated (usually in the form of an alter ego, though sometimes as a ghostly counterpart) or divided into two distinct, usually opposite personalities. The use of this character device is widespread in nineteenth- and twentieth- century literature, and indicates a growing awareness among authors that the "self" is really a composite of many "selves."

Double Entendre A corruption of a French phrase meaning "double meaning." The term is used to indicate a word or phrase that is deliberately ambiguous, especially when one of the meanings is risque or improper.

Double, The See *Doppelganger*

Draft Any preliminary version of a written work. An author may write dozens of drafts which are revised to form the final work, or he or she may write only one, with few or no revisions.

Drama In its widest sense, a drama is any work designed to be presented by actors on a stage. Similarly, "drama" denotes a broad literary genre that includes a variety of forms, from pageant and spectacle to tragedy and comedy, as well as countless types and subtypes. More commonly in modern usage, however, a drama is a work that treats serious subjects and themes but does not aim at the grandeur of tragedy. This use of the term originated with the eighteenth-century French writer Denis Diderot, who used the word *drame* to designate his plays about middle- class life; thus "drama" typically features characters of a less exalted stature than those of tragedy.

Dramatic Irony Occurs when the audience of a play or the reader of a work of literature knows something that a character in the work itself does not know. The irony is in the contrast between the intended meaning of the statements or actions of a character and the additional information understood by the audience.

Dramatic Monologue See *Monologue*

Dramatic Poetry Any lyric work that employs elements of drama such as dialogue, conflict, or characterization, but excluding works that are intended for stage presentation.

Dramatis Personae The characters in a work of literature, particularly a drama.

Dream Allegory See *Dream Vision*

Dream Vision A literary convention, chiefly of the Middle Ages. In a dream vision a story is presented as a literal dream of the narrator. This device was commonly used to teach moral and religious lessons.

Dystopia An imaginary place in a work of fiction where the characters lead dehumanized, fearful lives.

E

Eclogue In classical literature, a poem featuring rural themes and structured as a dialogue among shepherds. Eclogues often took specific poetic forms, such as elegies or love poems. Some were written as the soliloquy of a shepherd. In later centuries, "eclogue" came to refer to any poem that was in the pastoral tradition or that had a dialogue or monologue structure.

Edwardian Describes cultural conventions identified with the period of the reign of Edward VII of England (1901-1910). Writers of the Edwardian Age typically displayed a strong reaction against the propriety and conservatism of the Victorian Age. Their work often exhibits distrust of authority in religion, politics, and art and expresses strong doubts about the soundness of conventional values.

Edwardian Age See *Edwardian*

Electra Complex A daughter's amorous obsession with her father.

Elegy A lyric poem that laments the death of a person or the eventual death of all people. In a conventional elegy, set in a classical world, the poet and subject are spoken of as shepherds. In modern criticism, the word elegy is often used to refer to a poem that is melancholy or mournfully contemplative.

Elizabethan Age A period of great economic growth, religious controversy, and nationalism closely associated with the reign of Elizabeth I of England (1558-1603). The Elizabethan Age is considered a part of the general renaissance—that is, the flowering of arts and literature—that took place in Europe during the fourteenth through sixteenth centuries. The era is considered the golden age of English literature. The most important dramas in English and a great deal of lyric poetry were produced during this period, and modern English criticism began around this time.

Elizabethan Drama English comic and tragic plays produced during the Renaissance, or more narrowly, those plays written during the last years of and few years after Queen Elizabeth's reign. William Shakespeare is considered an Elizabethan dramatist in the broader sense, although most of his work was produced during the reign of James I.

Empathy A sense of shared experience, including emotional and physical feelings, with someone or something other than oneself. Empathy is often used to describe the response of a reader to a literary character.

English Sonnet See *Sonnet*

Enjambment The running over of the sense and structure of a line of verse or a couplet into the following verse or couplet.

Enlightenment, The An eighteenth-century philosophical movement. It began in France but had a wide impact throughout Europe and America. Thinkers of the Enlightenment valued reason and believed that both the individual and society could achieve a state of perfection. Corresponding to this essentially humanist vision was a resistance to religious authority.

Epic A long narrative poem about the adventures of a hero of great historic or legendary importance. The setting is vast and the action is often given cosmic significance through the intervention of supernatural forces such as gods, angels, or demons. Epics are typically written in a classical style of grand simplicity with elaborate metaphors and allusions that enhance the symbolic importance of a hero's adventures.

Epic Simile See *Homeric Simile*

Epic Theater A theory of theatrical presentation developed by twentieth-century German playwright Bertolt Brecht. Brecht created a type of drama that the audience could view with complete detachment. He used what he termed ''alienation effects'' to create an emotional distance between the audience and the action on stage. Among these effects are: short, self-contained scenes that keep the play from building to a cathartic climax; songs that comment on the action; and techniques of acting that prevent the actor from developing an emotional identity with his role.

Epigram A saying that makes the speaker's point quickly and concisely.

Epilogue A concluding statement or section of a literary work. In dramas, particularly those of the seventeenth and eighteenth centuries, the epilogue is a closing speech, often in verse, delivered by an actor at the end of a play and spoken directly to the audience.

Epiphany A sudden revelation of truth inspired by a seemingly trivial incident.

Episode An incident that forms part of a story and is significantly related to it. Episodes may be either self-contained narratives or events that depend on a larger context for their sense and importance.

Episodic Plot See *Plot*

Epitaph An inscription on a tomb or tombstone, or a verse written on the occasion of a person's death. Epitaphs may be serious or humorous.

Epithalamion A song or poem written to honor and commemorate a marriage ceremony.

Epithalamium See *Epithalamion*

Epithet A word or phrase, often disparaging or abusive, that expresses a character trait of someone or something.

Exempla See *Exemplum*

Exemplum A tale with a moral message. This form of literary sermonizing flourished during the Middle Ages, when *exempla* appeared in collections known as ''example-books.''

Existentialism A predominantly twentieth-century philosophy concerned with the nature and perception of human existence. There are two major strains of existentialist thought: atheistic and Christian. Followers of atheistic existentialism believe that the individual is alone in a godless universe and that the basic human condition is one of suffering and loneliness. Nevertheless, because there are no fixed values, individuals can create their own characters—indeed, they can shape themselves—through the exercise of free will. The atheistic strain culminates in and is popularly associated with the works of Jean-Paul Sartre. The Christian existentialists, on the other hand, believe that only in God may people find freedom from life's anguish. The two strains hold certain beliefs in common: that existence cannot be fully understood or described through empirical effort; that anguish is a universal element of life; that individuals must bear responsibility for their actions; and that there is no common standard of behavior or perception for religious and ethical matters.

Expatriates See *Expatriatism*

Expatriatism The practice of leaving one's country to live for an extended period in another country.

Exposition Writing intended to explain the nature of an idea, thing, or theme. Expository writing is often combined with description, narration, or argument. In dramatic writing, the exposition is the introductory material which presents the characters, setting, and tone of the play.

Expressionism An indistinct literary term, originally used to describe an early twentieth-century school of German painting. The term applies to almost any mode of unconventional, highly subjective writing that distorts reality in some way.

Extended Monologue See *Monologue*

F

Fable A prose or verse narrative intended to convey a moral. Animals or inanimate objects with human characteristics often serve as characters in fables.

Fairy Tales Short narratives featuring mythical beings such as fairies, elves, and sprites. These tales originally belonged to the folklore of a particular nation or region, such as those collected in Germany by Jacob and Wilhelm Grimm.

Falling Action See *Denouement*

Fantasy A literary form related to mythology and folklore. Fantasy literature is typically set in nonexistent realms and features supernatural beings.

Farce A type of comedy characterized by broad humor, outlandish incidents, and often vulgar subject matter.

Feet See *Foot*

Feminine Rhyme See *Rhyme*

Femme fatale A French phrase with the literal translation ''fatal woman.'' A *femme fatale* is a sensuous, alluring woman who often leads men into danger or trouble.

Fiction Any story that is the product of imagination rather than a documentation of fact. characters and events in such narratives may be based in real life but their ultimate form and configuration is a creation of the author.

Figurative Language A technique in writing in which the author temporarily interrupts the order, construction, or meaning of the writing for a particular effect. This interruption takes the form of one or more figures of speech such as hyperbole, irony, or simile. Figurative language is the opposite of literal language, in which every word is truthful, accurate, and free of exaggeration or embellishment.

Figures of Speech Writing that differs from customary conventions for construction, meaning, order, or significance for the purpose of a special meaning or effect. There are two major types of figures of speech: rhetorical figures, which do not make changes in the meaning of the words, and tropes, which do.

Fin de siecle A French term meaning ''end of the century.'' The term is used to denote the last decade of the nineteenth century, a transition period when writers and other artists abandoned old conventions and looked for new techniques and objectives.

First Person See *Point of View*

Flashback A device used in literature to present action that occurred before the beginning of the story. Flashbacks are often introduced as the dreams or recollections of one or more characters.

Foil A character in a work of literature whose physical or psychological qualities contrast strongly with, and therefore highlight, the corresponding qualities of another character.

Folk Ballad See *Ballad*

Folklore Traditions and myths preserved in a culture or group of people. Typically, these are passed on by word of mouth in various forms—such as legends, songs, and proverbs— or preserved in customs and ceremonies. This term was first used by W. J. Thoms in 1846.

Folktale A story originating in oral tradition. Folktales fall into a variety of categories, including legends, ghost stories, fairy tales, fables, and anecdotes based on historical figures and events.

Foot The smallest unit of rhythm in a line of poetry. In English-language poetry, a foot is typically one accented syllable combined with one or two unaccented syllables.

Foreshadowing A device used in literature to create expectation or to set up an explanation of later developments.

Form The pattern or construction of a work which identifies its genre and distinguishes it from other genres.

Formalism In literary criticism, the belief that literature should follow prescribed rules of construction, such as those that govern the sonnet form.

Fourteener Meter See *Meter*

Free Verse Poetry that lacks regular metrical and rhyme patterns but that tries to capture the cadences of everyday speech. The form allows a poet to exploit a variety of rhythmical effects within a single poem.

Futurism A flamboyant literary and artistic movement that developed in France, Italy, and Russia from 1908 through the 1920s. Futurist theater and poetry abandoned traditional literary forms. In their place, followers of the movement attempted to achieve total freedom of expression through bizarre imagery and deformed or newly invented words. The Futurists were self-consciously modern artists who attempted to incorporate the appearances and sounds of modern life into their work.

G

Genre A category of literary work. In critical theory, genre may refer to both the content of a given work—tragedy, comedy, pastoral—and to its form, such as poetry, novel, or drama.

Genteel Tradition A term coined by critic George Santayana to describe the literary practice of certain late nineteenth- century American writers, especially New Englanders. Followers of the Genteel Tradition emphasized conventionality in social, religious, moral, and literary standards.

Gilded Age A period in American history during the 1870s characterized by political corruption and materialism. A number of important novels of social and political criticism were written during this time.

Gothic See *Gothicism*

Gothicism In literary criticism, works characterized by a taste for the medieval or morbidly attractive. A gothic novel prominently features elements of horror, the supernatural, gloom, and violence: clanking chains, terror, charnel houses, ghosts, medieval castles, and mysteriously slamming doors. The term "gothic novel" is also applied to novels that lack elements of the traditional Gothic setting but that create a similar atmosphere of terror or dread.

Gothic Novel See *Gothicism*

Great Chain of Being The belief that all things and creatures in nature are organized in a hierarchy from inanimate objects at the bottom to God at the top. This system of belief was popular in the seventeenth and eighteenth centuries.

Grotesque In literary criticism, the subject matter of a work or a style of expression characterized by exaggeration, deformity, freakishness, and disorder. The grotesque often includes an element of comic absurdity.

H

Haiku The shortest form of Japanese poetry, constructed in three lines of five, seven, and five syllables respectively. The message of a *haiku* poem usually centers on some aspect of spirituality and provokes an emotional response in the reader.

Half Rhyme See *Consonance*

Hamartia In tragedy, the event or act that leads to the hero's or heroine's downfall. This term is often incorrectly used as a synonym for tragic flaw.

Harlem Renaissance The Harlem Renaissance of the 1920s is generally considered the first significant movement of black writers and artists in the United States. During this period, new and established black writers published more fiction and poetry than ever before, the first influential black literary journals were established, and black authors and artists received their first widespread recognition and serious critical appraisal. Among the major writers associated with this period are Claude McKay, Jean Toomer, Countee Cullen, Langston Hughes, Arna Bontemps, Nella Larsen, and Zora Neale Hurston.

Harlequin A stock character of the *commedia dell'arte* who occasionally interrupted the action with silly antics.

Hellenism Imitation of ancient Greek thought or styles. Also, an approach to life that focuses on the growth and development of the intellect. "Hellenism" is sometimes used to refer to the belief that reason can be applied to examine all human experience.

Heptameter See *Meter*

Hero/Heroine The principal sympathetic character (male or female) in a literary work. Heroes and heroines typically exhibit admirable traits: idealism, courage, and integrity, for example.

Heroic Couplet A rhyming couplet written in iambic pentameter (a verse with five iambic feet).

Heroic Line The meter and length of a line of verse in epic or heroic poetry. This varies by language and time period.

Heroine See *Hero/Heroine*

Hexameter See *Meter*

Historical Criticism The study of a work based on its impact on the world of the time period in which it was written.

Hokku See *Haiku*

Holocaust See *Holocaust Literature*

Holocaust Literature Literature influenced by or written about the Holocaust of World War II. Such literature includes true stories of survival in concentration camps, escape, and life after the war, as well as fictional works and poetry.

Homeric Simile An elaborate, detailed comparison written as a simile many lines in length.

Horatian Satire See *Satire*

Humanism A philosophy that places faith in the dignity of humankind and rejects the medieval perception of the individual as a weak, fallen creature. ''Humanists'' typically believe in the perfectibility of human nature and view reason and education as the means to that end.

Humors Mentions of the humors refer to the ancient Greek theory that a person's health and personality were determined by the balance of four basic fluids in the body: blood, phlegm, yellow bile, and black bile. A dominance of any fluid would cause extremes in behavior. An excess of blood created a sanguine person who was joyful, aggressive, and passionate; a phlegmatic person was shy, fearful, and sluggish; too much yellow bile led to a choleric temperament characterized by impatience, anger, bitterness, and stubbornness; and excessive black bile created melancholy, a state of laziness, gluttony, and lack of motivation.

Humours See *Humors*

Hyperbole In literary criticism, deliberate exaggeration used to achieve an effect.

I

Iamb See *Foot*

Idiom A word construction or verbal expression closely associated with a given language.

Image A concrete representation of an object or sensory experience. Typically, such a representation helps evoke the feelings associated with the object or experience itself. Images are either ''literal'' or ''figurative.'' Literal images are especially concrete and involve little or no extension of the obvious meaning of the words used to express them. Figurative images do not follow the literal meaning of the words exactly. Images in literature are usually visual, but the term ''image'' can also refer to the representation of any sensory experience.

Imagery The array of images in a literary work. Also, figurative language.

Imagism An English and American poetry movement that flourished between 1908 and 1917. The Imagists used precise, clearly presented images in their works. They also used common, everyday speech and aimed for conciseness, concrete imagery, and the creation of new rhythms.

In medias res A Latin term meaning ''in the middle of things.'' It refers to the technique of beginning a story at its midpoint and then using various flashback devices to reveal previous action.

Induction The process of reaching a conclusion by reasoning from specific premises to form a general premise. Also, an introductory portion of a work of literature, especially a play.

Intentional Fallacy The belief that judgments of a literary work based solely on an author's stated or implied intentions are false and misleading. Critics who believe in the concept of the intentional fallacy typically argue that the work itself is sufficient matter for interpretation, even though they may concede that an author's statement of purpose can be useful.

Interior Monologue A narrative technique in which characters' thoughts are revealed in a way that appears to be uncontrolled by the author. The interior monologue typically aims to reveal the inner self of a character. It portrays emotional experiences as they occur at both a conscious and unconscious level. images are often used to represent sensations or emotions.

Internal Rhyme Rhyme that occurs within a single line of verse.

Irish Literary Renaissance A late nineteenth- and early twentieth-century movement in Irish literature. Members of the movement aimed to reduce the influence of British culture in Ireland and create an Irish national literature.

Irony In literary criticism, the effect of language in which the intended meaning is the opposite of what is stated.

Italian Sonnet See *Sonnet*

J

Jacobean Age The period of the reign of James I of England (1603-1625). The early literature of this period reflected the worldview of the Elizabethan

Age, but a darker, more cynical attitude steadily grew in the art and literature of the Jacobean Age. This was an important time for English drama and poetry.

Jargon Language that is used or understood only by a select group of people. Jargon may refer to terminology used in a certain profession, such as computer jargon, or it may refer to any nonsensical language that is not understood by most people.

Juvenalian Satire See *Satire*

K

Knickerbocker Group A somewhat indistinct group of New York writers of the first half of the nineteenth century. Members of the group were linked only by location and a common theme: New York life.

L

Lais See *Lay*

Lay A song or simple narrative poem. The form originated in medieval France. Early French *lais* were often based on the Celtic legends and other tales sung by Breton minstrels—thus the name of the ''Breton lay.'' In fourteenth-century England, the term ''lay'' was used to describe short narratives written in imitation of the Breton lays.

Leitmotiv See *Motif*

Literal Language An author uses literal language when he or she writes without exaggerating or embellishing the subject matter and without any tools of figurative language.

Literary Ballad See *Ballad*

Literature Literature is broadly defined as any written or spoken material, but the term most often refers to creative works.

Lost Generation A term first used by Gertrude Stein to describe the post-World War I generation of American writers: men and women haunted by a sense of betrayal and emptiness brought about by the destructiveness of the war.

Lyric Poetry A poem expressing the subjective feelings and personal emotions of the poet. Such poetry is melodic, since it was originally accompanied by a lyre in recitals. Most Western poetry in the twentieth century may be classified as lyrical.

M

Mannerism Exaggerated, artificial adherence to a literary manner or style. Also, a popular style of the visual arts of late sixteenth-century Europe that was marked by elongation of the human form and by intentional spatial distortion. Literary works that are self-consciously high-toned and artistic are often said to be ''mannered.''

Masculine Rhyme See *Rhyme*

Masque A lavish and elaborate form of entertainment, often performed in royal courts, that emphasizes song, dance, and costumery. The Renaissance form of the masque grew out of the spectacles of masked figures common in medieval England and Europe. The masque reached its peak of popularity and development in seventeenth-century England, during the reigns of James I and, especially, of Charles I. Ben Jonson, the most significant masque writer, also created the ''antimasque,'' which incorporates elements of humor and the grotesque into the traditional masque and achieved greater dramatic quality.

Measure The foot, verse, or time sequence used in a literary work, especially a poem. Measure is often used somewhat incorrectly as a synonym for meter.

Melodrama A play in which the typical plot is a conflict between characters who personify extreme good and evil. Melodramas usually end happily and emphasize sensationalism. Other literary forms that use the same techniques are often labeled ''melodramatic.'' The term was formerly used to describe a combination of drama and music; as such, it was synonymous with ''opera.''

Metaphor A figure of speech that expresses an idea through the image of another object. Metaphors suggest the essence of the first object by identifying it with certain qualities of the second object.

Metaphysical Conceit See *Conceit*

Metaphysical Poetry The body of poetry produced by a group of seventeenth-century English writers called the ''Metaphysical Poets.'' The group includes John Donne and Andrew Marvell. The Metaphysical Poets made use of everyday speech, intellectual analysis, and unique imagery. They aimed to portray the ordinary conflicts and contradictions of life. Their poems often took the form of an argument, and many of them emphasize physical and religious love as well as the fleeting nature of life. Elaborate conceits are typical in metaphysical poetry.

Metaphysical Poets See *Metaphysical Poetry*

Meter In literary criticism, the repetition of sound patterns that creates a rhythm in poetry. The patterns are based on the number of syllables and the presence and absence of accents. The unit of rhythm in a line is called a foot. Types of meter are classified according to the number of feet in a line. These are the standard English lines: Monometer, one foot; Dimeter, two feet; Trimeter, three feet; Tetrameter, four feet; Pentameter, five feet; Hexameter, six feet (also called the Alexandrine); Heptameter, seven feet (also called the "Fourteener" when the feet are iambic).

Mise en scene The costumes, scenery, and other properties of a drama.

Modernism Modern literary practices. Also, the principles of a literary school that lasted from roughly the beginning of the twentieth century until the end of World War II. Modernism is defined by its rejection of the literary conventions of the nineteenth century and by its opposition to conventional morality, taste, traditions, and economic values.

Monologue A composition, written or oral, by a single individual. More specifically, a speech given by a single individual in a drama or other public entertainment. It has no set length, although it is usually several or more lines long.

Monometer See *Meter*

Mood The prevailing emotions of a work or of the author in his or her creation of the work. The mood of a work is not always what might be expected based on its subject matter.

Motif A theme, character type, image, metaphor, or other verbal element that recurs throughout a single work of literature or occurs in a number of different works over a period of time.

Motiv See *Motif*

Muckrakers An early twentieth-century group of American writers. Typically, their works exposed the wrongdoings of big business and government in the United States.

Muses Nine Greek mythological goddesses, the daughters of Zeus and Mnemosyne (Memory). Each muse patronized a specific area of the liberal arts and sciences. Calliope presided over epic poetry, Clio over history, Erato over love poetry, Euterpe over music or lyric poetry, Melpomene over tragedy, Polyhymnia over hymns to the gods, Terpsichore over dance, Thalia over comedy, and Urania over astronomy. Poets and writers traditionally made appeals to the Muses for inspiration in their work.

Mystery See *Suspense*

Myth An anonymous tale emerging from the traditional beliefs of a culture or social unit. Myths use supernatural explanations for natural phenomena. They may also explain cosmic issues like creation and death. Collections of myths, known as mythologies, are common to all cultures and nations, but the best-known myths belong to the Norse, Roman, and Greek mythologies.

N

Narration The telling of a series of events, real or invented. A narration may be either a simple narrative, in which the events are recounted chronologically, or a narrative with a plot, in which the account is given in a style reflecting the author's artistic concept of the story. Narration is sometimes used as a synonym for "storyline."

Narrative A verse or prose accounting of an event or sequence of events, real or invented. The term is also used as an adjective in the sense "method of narration." For example, in literary criticism, the expression "narrative technique" usually refers to the way the author structures and presents his or her story.

Narrative Poetry A nondramatic poem in which the author tells a story. Such poems may be of any length or level of complexity.

Narrator The teller of a story. The narrator may be the author or a character in the story through whom the author speaks.

Naturalism A literary movement of the late nineteenth and early twentieth centuries. The movement's major theorist, French novelist Emile Zola, envisioned a type of fiction that would examine human life with the objectivity of scientific inquiry. The Naturalists typically viewed human beings as either the products of "biological determinism," ruled by hereditary instincts and engaged in an endless struggle for survival, or as the products of "socioeconomic determinism," ruled by social and economic forces beyond their control. In their works, the Naturalists generally ignored the highest levels of society and focused on degradation: poverty, alcoholism, prostitution, insanity, and disease.

Negritude A literary movement based on the concept of a shared cultural bond on the part of black Africans, wherever they may be in the world. It traces its origins to the former French colonies of Africa and the Caribbean. Negritude poets, novelists, and essayists generally stress four points in their writings: One, black alienation from traditional African culture can lead to feelings of inferiority. Two, European colonialism and Western education should be resisted. Three, black Africans should seek to affirm and define their own identity. Four, African culture can and should be reclaimed. Many Negritude writers also claim that blacks can make unique contributions to the world, based on a heightened appreciation of nature, rhythm, and human emotions—aspects of life they say are not so highly valued in the materialistic and rationalistic West.

Negro Renaissance See *Harlem Renaissance*

Neoclassical Period See *Neoclassicism*

Neoclassicism In literary criticism, this term refers to the revival of the attitudes and styles of expression of classical literature. It is generally used to describe a period in European history beginning in the late seventeenth century and lasting until about 1800. In its purest form, Neoclassicism marked a return to order, proportion, restraint, logic, accuracy, and decorum. In England, where Neoclassicism perhaps was most popular, it reflected the influence of seventeenth- century French writers, especially dramatists. Neoclassical writers typically reacted against the intensity and enthusiasm of the Renaissance period. They wrote works that appealed to the intellect, using elevated language and classical literary forms such as satire and the ode. Neoclassical works were often governed by the classical goal of instruction.

Neoclassicists See *Neoclassicism*

New Criticism A movement in literary criticism, dating from the late 1920s, that stressed close textual analysis in the interpretation of works of literature. The New Critics saw little merit in historical and biographical analysis. Rather, they aimed to examine the text alone, free from the question of how external events—biographical or otherwise—may have helped shape it.

New Negro Movement See *Harlem Renaissance*

Noble Savage The idea that primitive man is noble and good but becomes evil and corrupted as he becomes civilized. The concept of the noble savage originated in the Renaissance period but is more closely identified with such later writers as Jean-Jacques Rousseau and Aphra Behn.

O

Objective Correlative An outward set of objects, a situation, or a chain of events corresponding to an inward experience and evoking this experience in the reader. The term frequently appears in modern criticism in discussions of authors' intended effects on the emotional responses of readers.

Objectivity A quality in writing characterized by the absence of the author's opinion or feeling about the subject matter. Objectivity is an important factor in criticism.

Occasional Verse poetry written on the occasion of a significant historical or personal event. *Vers de societe* is sometimes called occasional verse although it is of a less serious nature.

Octave A poem or stanza composed of eight lines. The term octave most often represents the first eight lines of a Petrarchan sonnet.

Ode Name given to an extended lyric poem characterized by exalted emotion and dignified style. An ode usually concerns a single, serious theme. Most odes, but not all, are addressed to an object or individual. Odes are distinguished from other lyric poetic forms by their complex rhythmic and stanzaic patterns.

Oedipus Complex A son's amorous obsession with his mother. The phrase is derived from the story of the ancient Theban hero Oedipus, who unknowingly killed his father and married his mother.

Omniscience See *Point of View*

Onomatopoeia The use of words whose sounds express or suggest their meaning. In its simplest sense, onomatopoeia may be represented by words that mimic the sounds they denote such as ''hiss'' or ''meow.'' At a more subtle level, the pattern and rhythm of sounds and rhymes of a line or poem may be onomatopoeic.

Opera A type of stage performance, usually a drama, in which the dialogue is sung.

Operetta A usually romantic comic opera.

Oral Tradition See *Oral Transmission*

Oral Transmission A process by which songs, ballads, folklore, and other material are transmitted by word of mouth. The tradition of oral transmission predates the written record systems of literate society. Oral transmission preserves material sometimes over generations, although often with variations. Memory plays a large part in the recitation and preservation of orally transmitted material.

Oration Formal speaking intended to motivate the listeners to some action or feeling. Such public speaking was much more common before the development of timely printed communication such as newspapers.

Ottava Rima An eight-line stanza of poetry composed in iambic pentameter (a five-foot line in which each foot consists of an unaccented syllable followed by an accented syllable), following the abababcc rhyme scheme.

Oxymoron A phrase combining two contradictory terms. Oxymorons may be intentional or unintentional.

P

Pantheism The idea that all things are both a manifestation or revelation of God and a part of God at the same time. Pantheism was a common attitude in the early societies of Egypt, India, and Greece—the term derives from the Greek *pan* meaning "all" and *theos* meaning "deity." It later became a significant part of the Christian faith.

Parable A story intended to teach a moral lesson or answer an ethical question.

Paradox A statement that appears illogical or contradictory at first, but may actually point to an underlying truth.

Parallelism A method of comparison of two ideas in which each is developed in the same grammatical structure.

Parnassianism A mid nineteenth-century movement in French literature. Followers of the movement stressed adherence to well-defined artistic forms as a reaction against the often chaotic expression of the artist's ego that dominated the work of the Romantics. The Parnassians also rejected the moral, ethical, and social themes exhibited in the works of French Romantics such as Victor Hugo. The aesthetic doctrines of the Parnassians strongly influenced the later symbolist and decadent movements.

Parody In literary criticism, this term refers to an imitation of a serious literary work or the signature style of a particular author in a ridiculous manner.

A typical parody adopts the style of the original and applies it to an inappropriate subject for humorous effect. Parody is a form of satire and could be considered the literary equivalent of a caricature or cartoon.

Pastoral A term derived from the Latin word "pastor," meaning shepherd. A pastoral is a literary composition on a rural theme. The conventions of the pastoral were originated by the third-century Greek poet Theocritus, who wrote about the experiences, love affairs, and pastimes of Sicilian shepherds. In a pastoral, characters and language of a courtly nature are often placed in a simple setting. The term pastoral is also used to classify dramas, elegies, and lyrics that exhibit the use of country settings and shepherd characters.

Pastorela The Spanish name for the shepherds play, a folk drama reenacted during the Christmas season.

Pathetic Fallacy A term coined by English critic John Ruskin to identify writing that falsely endows nonhuman things with human intentions and feelings, such as "angry clouds" and "sad trees."

Pelado Literally the "skinned one" or shirtless one, he was the stock underdog, sharp-witted picaresque character of Mexican vaudeville and tent shows.

Pen Name See *Pseudonym*

Pentameter See *Meter*

Persona A Latin term meaning "mask." *Personae* are the characters in a fictional work of literature. The *persona* generally functions as a mask through which the author tells a story in a voice other than his or her own. A *persona* is usually either a character in a story who acts as a narrator or an "implied author," a voice created by the author to act as the narrator for himself or herself.

Personae See *Persona*

Personal Point of View See *Point of View*

Personification A figure of speech that gives human qualities to abstract ideas, animals, and inanimate objects.

Petrarchan Sonnet See *Sonnet*

Phenomenology A method of literary criticism based on the belief that things have no existence outside of human consciousness or awareness. Proponents of this theory believe that art is a process that takes place in the mind of the observer as he or she contemplates an object rather than a quality of the object itself.

Picaresque Novel Episodic fiction depicting the adventures of a roguish central character (''picaro'' is Spanish for ''rogue''). The picaresque hero is commonly a low-born but clever individual who wanders into and out of various affairs of love, danger, and farcical intrigue. These involvements may take place at all social levels and typically present a humorous and wide-ranging satire of a given society.

Plagiarism Claiming another person's written material as one's own. Plagiarism can take the form of direct, word-for- word copying or the theft of the substance or idea of the work.

Platonic Criticism A form of criticism that stresses an artistic work's usefulness as an agent of social engineering rather than any quality or value of the work itself.

Platonism The embracing of the doctrines of the philosopher Plato, popular among the poets of the Renaissance and the Romantic period. Platonism is more flexible than Aristotelian Criticism and places more emphasis on the supernatural and unknown aspects of life.

Play See *Drama*

Plot In literary criticism, this term refers to the pattern of events in a narrative or drama. In its simplest sense, the plot guides the author in composing the work and helps the reader follow the work. Typically, plots exhibit causality and unity and have a beginning, a middle, and an end. Sometimes, however, a plot may consist of a series of disconnected events, in which case it is known as an ''episodic plot.''

Poem In its broadest sense, a composition utilizing rhyme, meter, concrete detail, and expressive language to create a literary experience with emotional and aesthetic appeal.

Poet An author who writes poetry or verse. The term is also used to refer to an artist or writer who has an exceptional gift for expression, imagination, and energy in the making of art in any form.

Poetic Fallacy See *Pathetic Fallacy*

Poetic Justice An outcome in a literary work, not necessarily a poem, in which the good are rewarded and the evil are punished, especially in ways that particularly fit their virtues or crimes.

Poetic License Distortions of fact and literary convention made by a writer—not always a poet—for the sake of the effect gained. Poetic license is closely related to the concept of ''artistic freedom.''

Poetics This term has two closely related meanings. It denotes (1) an aesthetic theory in literary criticism about the essence of poetry or (2) rules prescribing the proper methods, content, style, or diction of poetry. The term poetics may also refer to theories about literature in general, not just poetry.

Poetry In its broadest sense, writing that aims to present ideas and evoke an emotional experience in the reader through the use of meter, imagery, connotative and concrete words, and a carefully constructed structure based on rhythmic patterns. Poetry typically relies on words and expressions that have several layers of meaning. It also makes use of the effects of regular rhythm on the ear and may make a strong appeal to the senses through the use of imagery.

Point of View The narrative perspective from which a literary work is presented to the reader. There are four traditional points of view. The ''third person omniscient'' gives the reader a ''godlike'' perspective, unrestricted by time or place, from which to see actions and look into the minds of characters. This allows the author to comment openly on characters and events in the work. The ''third person'' point of view presents the events of the story from outside of any single character's perception, much like the omniscient point of view, but the reader must understand the action as it takes place and without any special insight into characters' minds or motivations. The ''first person'' or ''personal'' point of view relates events as they are perceived by a single character. The main character ''tells'' the story and may offer opinions about the action and characters which differ from those of the author. Much less common than omniscient, third person, and first person is the ''second person'' point of view, wherein the author tells the story as if it is happening to the reader.

Polemic A work in which the author takes a stand on a controversial subject, such as abortion or religion. Such works are often extremely argumentative or provocative.

Pornography Writing intended to provoke feelings of lust in the reader. Such works are often condemned by critics and teachers, but those which can be shown to have literary value are viewed less harshly.

Post-Aesthetic Movement An artistic response made by African Americans to the black aesthetic movement of the 1960s and early '70s. Writers since that time have adopted a somewhat different tone in their work, with less emphasis placed on the disparity between black and white in the United States. In the words of post-aesthetic authors such as Toni Morrison, John Edgar Wideman, and Kristin Hunter, African Americans are portrayed as looking inward for answers to their own questions, rather than always looking to the outside world.

Postmodernism Writing from the 1960s forward characterized by experimentation and continuing to apply some of the fundamentals of modernism, which included existentialism and alienation. Postmodernists have gone a step further in the rejection of tradition begun with the modernists by also rejecting traditional forms, preferring the anti-novel over the novel and the anti-hero over the hero.

Pre-Raphaelites A circle of writers and artists in mid nineteenth-century England. Valuing the pre-Renaissance artistic qualities of religious symbolism, lavish pictorialism, and natural sensuousness, the Pre-Raphaelites cultivated a sense of mystery and melancholy that influenced later writers associated with the Symbolist and Decadent movements.

Primitivism The belief that primitive peoples were nobler and less flawed than civilized peoples because they had not been subjected to the tainting influence of society.

Projective Verse A form of free verse in which the poet's breathing pattern determines the lines of the poem. Poets who advocate projective verse are against all formal structures in writing, including meter and form.

Prologue An introductory section of a literary work. It often contains information establishing the situation of the characters or presents information about the setting, time period, or action. In drama, the prologue is spoken by a chorus or by one of the principal characters.

Prose A literary medium that attempts to mirror the language of everyday speech. It is distinguished from poetry by its use of unmetered, unrhymed language consisting of logically related sentences. Prose is usually grouped into paragraphs that form a cohesive whole such as an essay or a novel.

Prosopopoeia See *Personification*

Protagonist The central character of a story who serves as a focus for its themes and incidents and as the principal rationale for its development. The protagonist is sometimes referred to in discussions of modern literature as the hero or anti-hero.

Protest Fiction Protest fiction has as its primary purpose the protesting of some social injustice, such as racism or discrimination.

Proverb A brief, sage saying that expresses a truth about life in a striking manner.

Pseudonym A name assumed by a writer, most often intended to prevent his or her identification as the author of a work. Two or more authors may work together under one pseudonym, or an author may use a different name for each genre he or she publishes in. Some publishing companies maintain "house pseudonyms," under which any number of authors may write installations in a series. Some authors also choose a pseudonym over their real names the way an actor may use a stage name.

Pun A play on words that have similar sounds but different meanings.

Pure Poetry poetry written without instructional intent or moral purpose that aims only to please a reader by its imagery or musical flow. The term pure poetry is used as the antonym of the term "didacticism."

Q

Quatrain A four-line stanza of a poem or an entire poem consisting of four lines.

R

Raisonneur A character in a drama who functions as a spokesperson for the dramatist's views. The *raisonneur* typically observes the play without becoming central to its action.

Realism A nineteenth-century European literary movement that sought to portray familiar characters, situations, and settings in a realistic manner. This was done primarily by using an objective narrative point of view and through the buildup of accurate detail. The standard for success of any realistic work depends on how faithfully it transfers common experience into fictional forms. The realistic method may be altered or extended, as in stream of consciousness writing, to record highly subjective experience.

Refrain A phrase repeated at intervals throughout a poem. A refrain may appear at the end of each stanza or at less regular intervals. It may be altered slightly at each appearance.

Renaissance The period in European history that marked the end of the Middle Ages. It began in Italy in the late fourteenth century. In broad terms, it is usually seen as spanning the fourteenth, fifteenth, and sixteenth centuries, although it did not reach Great Britain, for example, until the 1480s or so. The Renaissance saw an awakening in almost every sphere of human activity, especially science, philosophy, and the arts. The period is best defined by the emergence of a general philosophy that emphasized the importance of the intellect, the individual, and world affairs. It contrasts strongly with the medieval worldview, characterized by the dominant concerns of faith, the social collective, and spiritual salvation.

Repartee Conversation featuring snappy retorts and witticisms.

Resolution The portion of a story following the climax, in which the conflict is resolved.

Restoration See *Restoration Age*

Restoration Age A period in English literature beginning with the crowning of Charles II in 1660 and running to about 1700. The era, which was characterized by a reaction against Puritanism, was the first great age of the comedy of manners. The finest literature of the era is typically witty and urbane, and often lewd.

Revenge Tragedy A dramatic form popular during the Elizabethan Age, in which the protagonist, directed by the ghost of his murdered father or son, inflicts retaliation upon a powerful villain. Notable features of the revenge tragedy include violence, bizarre criminal acts, intrigue, insanity, a hesitant protagonist, and the use of soliloquy.

Revista The Spanish term for a vaudeville musical revue.

Rhetoric In literary criticism, this term denotes the art of ethical persuasion. In its strictest sense, rhetoric adheres to various principles developed since classical times for arranging facts and ideas in a clear, persuasive, appealing manner. The term is also used to refer to effective prose in general and theories of or methods for composing effective prose.

Rhetorical Question A question intended to provoke thought, but not an expressed answer, in the reader. It is most commonly used in oratory and other persuasive genres.

Rhyme When used as a noun in literary criticism, this term generally refers to a poem in which words sound identical or very similar and appear in parallel positions in two or more lines. Rhymes are classified into different types according to where they fall in a line or stanza or according to the degree of similarity they exhibit in their spellings and sounds. Some major types of rhyme are ''masculine'' rhyme, ''feminine'' rhyme, and ''triple'' rhyme. In a masculine rhyme, the rhyming sound falls in a single accented syllable, as with ''heat'' and ''eat.'' Feminine rhyme is a rhyme of two syllables, one stressed and one unstressed, as with ''merry'' and ''tarry.'' Triple rhyme matches the sound of the accented syllable and the two unaccented syllables that follow: ''narrative'' and ''declarative.''

Rhyme Royal A stanza of seven lines composed in iambic pentameter and rhymed *ababbcc.* The name is said to be a tribute to King James I of Scotland, who made much use of the form in his poetry.

Rhyme Scheme See *Rhyme*

Rhythm A regular pattern of sound, time intervals, or events occurring in writing, most often and most discernably in poetry. Regular, reliable rhythm is known to be soothing to humans, while interrupted, unpredictable, or rapidly changing rhythm is disturbing. These effects are known to authors, who use them to produce a desired reaction in the reader.

Rising Action The part of a drama where the plot becomes increasingly complicated. Rising action leads up to the climax, or turning point, of a drama.

Rococo A style of European architecture that flourished in the eighteenth century, especially in France. The most notable features of *rococo* are its extensive use of ornamentation and its themes of lightness, gaiety, and intimacy. In literary criticism, the term is often used disparagingly to refer to a decadent or over-ornamental style.

Roman a clef A French phrase meaning ''novel with a key.'' It refers to a narrative in which real persons are portrayed under fictitious names.

Romance A broad term, usually denoting a narrative with exotic, exaggerated, often idealized characters, scenes, and themes.

Romantic Age See *Romanticism*

Romanticism This term has two widely accepted meanings. In historical criticism, it refers to a

European intellectual and artistic movement of the late eighteenth and early nineteenth centuries that sought greater freedom of personal expression than that allowed by the strict rules of literary form and logic of the eighteenth-century neoclassicists. The Romantics preferred emotional and imaginative expression to rational analysis. They considered the individual to be at the center of all experience and so placed him or her at the center of their art. The Romantics believed that the creative imagination reveals nobler truths—unique feelings and attitudes—than those that could be discovered by logic or by scientific examination. Both the natural world and the state of childhood were important sources for revelations of "eternal truths." "Romanticism" is also used as a general term to refer to a type of sensibility found in all periods of literary history and usually considered to be in opposition to the principles of classicism. In this sense, Romanticism signifies any work or philosophy in which the exotic or dreamlike figure strongly, or that is devoted to individualistic expression, self-analysis, or a pursuit of a higher realm of knowledge than can be discovered by human reason.

Romantics See *Romanticism*

Russian Symbolism A Russian poetic movement, derived from French symbolism, that flourished between 1894 and 1910. While some Russian Symbolists continued in the French tradition, stressing aestheticism and the importance of suggestion above didactic intent, others saw their craft as a form of mystical worship, and themselves as mediators between the supernatural and the mundane.

S

Satire A work that uses ridicule, humor, and wit to criticize and provoke change in human nature and institutions. There are two major types of satire: "formal" or "direct" satire speaks directly to the reader or to a character in the work; "indirect" satire relies upon the ridiculous behavior of its characters to make its point. Formal satire is further divided into two manners: the "Horatian," which ridicules gently, and the "Juvenalian," which derides its subjects harshly and bitterly.

Scansion The analysis or "scanning" of a poem to determine its meter and often its rhyme scheme. The most common system of scansion uses accents (slanted lines drawn above syllables) to show stressed syllables, breves (curved lines drawn above sylla-

bles) to show unstressed syllables, and vertical lines to separate each foot.

Scene A subdivision of an act of a drama, consisting of continuous action taking place at a single time and in a single location. The beginnings and endings of scenes may be indicated by clearing the stage of actors and props or by the entrances and exits of important characters.

Science Fiction A type of narrative about or based upon real or imagined scientific theories and technology. Science fiction is often peopled with alien creatures and set on other planets or in different dimensions.

Second Person See *Point of View*

Semiotics The study of how literary forms and conventions affect the meaning of language.

Sestet Any six-line poem or stanza.

Setting The time, place, and culture in which the action of a narrative takes place. The elements of setting may include geographic location, characters' physical and mental environments, prevailing cultural attitudes, or the historical time in which the action takes place.

Shakespearean Sonnet See *Sonnet*

Signifying Monkey A popular trickster figure in black folklore, with hundreds of tales about this character documented since the 19th century.

Simile A comparison, usually using "like" or "as", of two essentially dissimilar things, as in "coffee as cold as ice" or "He sounded like a broken record."

Slang A type of informal verbal communication that is generally unacceptable for formal writing. Slang words and phrases are often colorful exaggerations used to emphasize the speaker's point; they may also be shortened versions of an often-used word or phrase.

Slant Rhyme See *Consonance*

Slave Narrative Autobiographical accounts of American slave life as told by escaped slaves. These works first appeared during the abolition movement of the 1830s through the 1850s.

Social Realism See *Socialist Realism*

Socialist Realism The Socialist Realism school of literary theory was proposed by Maxim Gorky and established as a dogma by the first Soviet Congress of Writers. It demanded adherence to a communist worldview in works of literature. Its doctrines required an objective viewpoint comprehensible to the working classes and themes of social struggle featuring strong proletarian heroes.

Soliloquy A monologue in a drama used to give the audience information and to develop the speaker's character. It is typically a projection of the speaker's innermost thoughts. Usually delivered while the speaker is alone on stage, a soliloquy is intended to present an illusion of unspoken reflection.

Sonnet A fourteen-line poem, usually composed in iambic pentameter, employing one of several rhyme schemes. There are three major types of sonnets, upon which all other variations of the form are based: the ''Petrarchan'' or ''Italian'' sonnet, the ''Shakespearean'' or ''English'' sonnet, and the ''Spenserian'' sonnet. A Petrarchan sonnet consists of an octave rhymed *abbaabba* and a ''sestet'' rhymed either *cdecde, cdccdc,* or *cdedce.* The octave poses a question or problem, relates a narrative, or puts forth a proposition; the sestet presents a solution to the problem, comments upon the narrative, or applies the proposition put forth in the octave. The Shakespearean sonnet is divided into three quatrains and a couplet rhymed *abab cdcd efef gg.* The couplet provides an epigrammatic comment on the narrative or problem put forth in the quatrains. The Spenserian sonnet uses three quatrains and a couplet like the Shakespearean, but links their three rhyme schemes in this way: *abab bcbc cdcd ee.* The Spenserian sonnet develops its theme in two parts like the Petrarchan, its final six lines resolving a problem, analyzing a narrative, or applying a proposition put forth in its first eight lines.

Spenserian Sonnet See *Sonnet*

Spenserian Stanza A nine-line stanza having eight verses in iambic pentameter, its ninth verse in iambic hexameter, and the rhyme scheme ababbcbcc.

Spondee In poetry meter, a foot consisting of two long or stressed syllables occurring together. This form is quite rare in English verse, and is usually composed of two monosyllabic words.

Sprung Rhythm Versification using a specific number of accented syllables per line but disregarding the number of unaccented syllables that fall in each line, producing an irregular rhythm in the poem.

Stanza A subdivision of a poem consisting of lines grouped together, often in recurring patterns of rhyme, line length, and meter. Stanzas may also serve as units of thought in a poem much like paragraphs in prose.

Stereotype A stereotype was originally the name for a duplication made during the printing process; this led to its modern definition as a person or thing that is (or is assumed to be) the same as all others of its type.

Stream of Consciousness A narrative technique for rendering the inward experience of a character. This technique is designed to give the impression of an ever-changing series of thoughts, emotions, images, and memories in the spontaneous and seemingly illogical order that they occur in life.

Structuralism A twentieth-century movement in literary criticism that examines how literary texts arrive at their meanings, rather than the meanings themselves. There are two major types of structuralist analysis: one examines the way patterns of linguistic structures unify a specific text and emphasize certain elements of that text, and the other interprets the way literary forms and conventions affect the meaning of language itself.

Structure The form taken by a piece of literature. The structure may be made obvious for ease of understanding, as in nonfiction works, or may obscured for artistic purposes, as in some poetry or seemingly ''unstructured'' prose.

Sturm und Drang A German term meaning ''storm and stress.'' It refers to a German literary movement of the 1770s and 1780s that reacted against the order and rationalism of the enlightenment, focusing instead on the intense experience of extraordinary individuals.

Style A writer's distinctive manner of arranging words to suit his or her ideas and purpose in writing. The unique imprint of the author's personality upon his or her writing, style is the product of an author's way of arranging ideas and his or her use of diction, different sentence structures, rhythm, figures of speech, rhetorical principles, and other elements of composition.

Subject The person, event, or theme at the center of a work of literature. A work may have one or more subjects of each type, with shorter works tending to have fewer and longer works tending to have more.

Subjectivity Writing that expresses the author's personal feelings about his subject, and which may or may not include factual information about the subject.

Subplot A secondary story in a narrative. A subplot may serve as a motivating or complicating force for the main plot of the work, or it may provide emphasis for, or relief from, the main plot.

Surrealism A term introduced to criticism by Guillaume Apollinaire and later adopted by Andre Breton. It refers to a French literary and artistic movement founded in the 1920s. The Surrealists sought to express unconscious thoughts and feelings in their works. The best-known technique used for achieving this aim was automatic writing—transcriptions of spontaneous outpourings from the unconscious. The Surrealists proposed to unify the contrary levels of conscious and unconscious, dream and reality, objectivity and subjectivity into a new level of "super-realism."

Suspense A literary device in which the author maintains the audience's attention through the build-up of events, the outcome of which will soon be revealed.

Syllogism A method of presenting a logical argument. In its most basic form, the syllogism consists of a major premise, a minor premise, and a conclusion.

Symbol Something that suggests or stands for something else without losing its original identity. In literature, symbols combine their literal meaning with the suggestion of an abstract concept. Literary symbols are of two types: those that carry complex associations of meaning no matter what their contexts, and those that derive their suggestive meaning from their functions in specific literary works.

Symbolism This term has two widely accepted meanings. In historical criticism, it denotes an early modernist literary movement initiated in France during the nineteenth century that reacted against the prevailing standards of realism. Writers in this movement aimed to evoke, indirectly and symbolically, an order of being beyond the material world of the five senses. Poetic expression of personal emotion figured strongly in the movement, typically by means of a private set of symbols uniquely identifiable with the individual poet. The principal aim of the Symbolists was to express in words the highly complex feelings that grew out of everyday contact with the world. In a broader sense, the term "symbolism" refers to the use of one object to represent another.

Symbolist See *Symbolism*

Symbolist Movement See *Symbolism*

Sympathetic Fallacy See *Affective Fallacy*

T

Tale A story told by a narrator with a simple plot and little character development. Tales are usually relatively short and often carry a simple message.

Tall Tale A humorous tale told in a straightforward, credible tone but relating absolutely impossible events or feats of the characters. Such tales were commonly told of frontier adventures during the settlement of the west in the United States.

Tanka A form of Japanese poetry similar to *haiku*. A *tanka* is five lines long, with the lines containing five, seven, five, seven, and seven syllables respectively.

Teatro Grottesco See *Theater of the Grotesque*

Terza Rima A three-line stanza form in poetry in which the rhymes are made on the last word of each line in the following manner: the first and third lines of the first stanza, then the second line of the first stanza and the first and third lines of the second stanza, and so on with the middle line of any stanza rhyming with the first and third lines of the following stanza.

Tetrameter See *Meter*

Textual Criticism A branch of literary criticism that seeks to establish the authoritative text of a literary work. Textual critics typically compare all known manuscripts or printings of a single work in order to assess the meanings of differences and revisions. This procedure allows them to arrive at a definitive version that (supposedly) corresponds to the author's original intention.

Theater of Cruelty Term used to denote a group of theatrical techniques designed to eliminate the psychological and emotional distance between actors and audience. This concept, introduced in the 1930s in France, was intended to inspire a more intense theatrical experience than conventional theater allowed. The "cruelty" of this dramatic theory signified not sadism but heightened actor/audience involvement in the dramatic event.

Theater of the Absurd A post-World War II dramatic trend characterized by radical theatrical innovations. In works influenced by the Theater of the absurd, nontraditional, sometimes grotesque characterizations, plots, and stage sets reveal a meaningless universe in which human values are irrelevant. Existentialist themes of estrangement, absurdity, and futility link many of the works of this movement.

Theater of the Grotesque An Italian theatrical movement characterized by plays written around the ironic and macabre aspects of daily life in the World War I era.

Theme The main point of a work of literature. The term is used interchangeably with thesis.

Thesis A thesis is both an essay and the point argued in the essay. Thesis novels and thesis plays share the quality of containing a thesis which is supported through the action of the story.

Thesis Play See *Thesis*

Three Unities See *Unities*

Tone The author's attitude toward his or her audience may be deduced from the tone of the work. A formal tone may create distance or convey politeness, while an informal tone may encourage a friendly, intimate, or intrusive feeling in the reader. The author's attitude toward his or her subject matter may also be deduced from the tone of the words he or she uses in discussing it.

Tragedy A drama in prose or poetry about a noble, courageous hero of excellent character who, because of some tragic character flaw or *hamartia*, brings ruin upon him- or herself. Tragedy treats its subjects in a dignified and serious manner, using poetic language to help evoke pity and fear and bring about catharsis, a purging of these emotions. The tragic form was practiced extensively by the ancient Greeks. In the Middle Ages, when classical works were virtually unknown, tragedy came to denote any works about the fall of persons from exalted to low conditions due to any reason: fate, vice, weakness, etc. According to the classical definition of tragedy, such works present the ''pathetic''—that which evokes pity—rather than the tragic. The classical form of tragedy was revived in the sixteenth century; it flourished especially on the Elizabethan stage. In modern times, dramatists have attempted to adapt the form to the needs of modern society by drawing their heroes from the ranks of ordinary men and women and defining the nobility of these heroes in terms of spirit rather than exalted social standing.

Tragedy of Blood See *Revenge Tragedy*

Tragic Flaw In a tragedy, the quality within the hero or heroine which leads to his or her downfall.

Transcendentalism An American philosophical and religious movement, based in New England from around 1835 until the Civil War. Transcendentalism was a form of American romanticism that had its roots abroad in the works of Thomas Carlyle, Samuel Coleridge, and Johann Wolfgang von Goethe. The Transcendentalists stressed the importance of intuition and subjective experience in communication with God. They rejected religious dogma and texts in favor of mysticism and scientific naturalism. They pursued truths that lie beyond the ''colorless'' realms perceived by reason and the senses and were active social reformers in public education, women's rights, and the abolition of slavery.

Trickster A character or figure common in Native American and African literature who uses his ingenuity to defeat enemies and escape difficult situations. Tricksters are most often animals, such as the spider, hare, or coyote, although they may take the form of humans as well.

Trimeter See *Meter*

Triple Rhyme See *Rhyme*

Trochee See *Foot*

U

Understatement See *Irony*

Unities Strict rules of dramatic structure, formulated by Italian and French critics of the Renaissance and based loosely on the principles of drama discussed by Aristotle in his *Poetics*. Foremost among these rules were the three unities of action, time, and place that compelled a dramatist to: (1) construct a single plot with a beginning, middle, and end that details the causal relationships of action and character; (2) restrict the action to the events of a single day; and (3) limit the scene to a single place or city. The unities were observed faithfully by continental European writers until the Romantic Age, but they were never regularly observed in English drama. Modern dramatists are typically more concerned with a unity of impression or emotional effect than with any of the classical unities.

Urban Realism A branch of realist writing that attempts to accurately reflect the often harsh facts of modern urban existence.

Utopia A fictional perfect place, such as ''paradise'' or ''heaven.''

Utopian See *Utopia*

Utopianism See *Utopia*

V

Verisimilitude Literally, the appearance of truth. In literary criticism, the term refers to aspects of a work of literature that seem true to the reader.

Vers de societe See *Occasional Verse*

Vers libre See *Free Verse*

Verse A line of metered language, a line of a poem, or any work written in verse.

Versification The writing of verse. Versification may also refer to the meter, rhyme, and other mechanical components of a poem.

Victorian Refers broadly to the reign of Queen Victoria of England (1837-1901) and to anything with qualities typical of that era. For example, the qualities of smug narrowmindedness, bourgeois materialism, faith in social progress, and priggish morality are often considered Victorian. This stereotype is contradicted by such dramatic intellectual developments as the theories of Charles Darwin, Karl Marx, and Sigmund Freud (which stirred strong debates in England) and the critical attitudes of serious Victorian writers like Charles Dickens and George Eliot. In literature, the Victorian Period was the great age of the English novel, and the latter part of the era saw the rise of movements such as decadence and symbolism.

Victorian Age See *Victorian*

Victorian Period See *Victorian*

W

Weltanschauung A German term referring to a person's worldview or philosophy.

Weltschmerz A German term meaning "world pain." It describes a sense of anguish about the nature of existence, usually associated with a melancholy, pessimistic attitude.

Z

Zarzuela A type of Spanish operetta.

Zeitgeist A German term meaning "spirit of the time." It refers to the moral and intellectual trends of a given era.

Cumulative Author/Title Index

Marlowe, Christopher
    Doctor Faustus: V1
Medea (Euripides): V1
Miller, Arthur
    Death of a Salesman: V1
The Miracle Worker (Gibson): V2
The Mousetrap (Christie): V2

N

'night, Mother (Norman): V2
Norman, Marsha
    'night, Mother: V2

O

The Odd Couple (Simon): V2
Oedipus Rex (Sophocles): V1
O'Neill, Eugene
    Long Day's Journey into Night:
    V2
Our Town (Wilder): V1

P

Pygmalion (Shaw): V1

R

A Raisin in the Sun (Hansberry): V2

The Rez Sisters (Highway): V2
Rodgers, Richard
    The King and I: V1
Rosencrantz and Guildenstern Are
    Dead (Stoppard): V2
Rostand, Edmond
    Cyrano de Bergerac: V1

S

Shange, Ntozake
    for colored girls who have
    considered suicide/when the
    rainbow is enuf: V2
Shaw, George Bernard
    Pygmalion: V1
She Stoops to Conquer (Goldsmith):
    V1
Simon, Neil
    The Odd Couple: V2
Smith, Anna Deavere
    Twilight: Los Angeles, 1992: V2
Sophocles
    Antigone: V1
    Oedipus Rex: V1
Stoppard, Tom
    Rosencrantz and Guildenstern Are
    Dead: V2
A Streetcar Named Desire
    (Williams): V1

T

Twilight: Los Angeles, 1992 (Smith):
    V2

V

Vidal, Gore
    Visit to a Small Planet: V2
Visit to a Small Planet (Vidal): V2

W

Waiting for Godot (Beckett): V2
Wedding Band (Childress): V2
Wilder, Thornton
    Our Town: V1
Williams, Tennessee
    The Glass Menagerie: V1
    A Streetcar Named Desire: V1

Y

You Can't Take It with You
    (Kaufman and Hart): V1

Z

The Zoo Story (Albee): V2

Nationality/Ethnicity Index

Norwegian

Russian

Subject/Theme Index

Remorse and Regret
    Long Day's Journey into Night:
        71-72, 75-76
Revenge
    The Mousetrap: 130, 134-135
Roman Catholicism
    Long Day's Journey into Night:
        70, 74, 77, 79, 87
    A Man for All Seasons:
        90, 95-99

S

Sanity and Insanity
    The Mousetrap: 134
Satire
    Visit to a Small Planet: 254-255,
        260-261, 264-266
Science and Technology
    Inherit the Wind: 54-56, 59-63
    A Raisin in the Sun: 189-190
Search for Self
    Long Day's Journey into Night:
        75
Self-confidence
    A Raisin in the Sun: 192-193
Setting
    Long Day's Journey into Night:
        76, 79
    The Miracle Worker: 111, 117
    The Mousetrap: 135, 137
    'night, Mother: 153
    Wedding Band: 291, 297
Sex
    Visit to a Small Planet: 260
Sex and Sexuality
    *for colored girls who have
        considered suicide/when the
        rainbow is enuf:* 23, 28, 30
    The Zoo Story: 307, 314
Sex Roles
    A Raisin in the Sun: 187
Sexism
    Glengarry Glen Ross: 44
Sickness
    Long Day's Journey into Night:
        70, 74, 76-77

Sin
    Long Day's Journey into Night:
        77, 81
    A Man for All Seasons:
        95, 97-98
    Twilight: Los Angeles, 1992:
        242-245
Soul
    A Man for All Seasons: 88,
        90, 94-95
Space Exploration and Study
    Visit to a Small Planet: 254-257,
        262-263
Spiritual Leaders
    Inherit the Wind: 55-56, 59
    A Man for All Seasons: 88,
        90, 95-99
Storms and Weather Conditions
    Long Day's Journey into Night:
        76-77
    The Mousetrap: 134-137
    Twilight: Los Angeles, 1992: 237,
        244-245
Structure
    *for colored girls who have
        considered suicide/when the
        rainbow is enuf:* 31
    Glengarry Glen Ross: 40, 44
    The Miracle Worker: 119-120
    'night, Mother: 153
    The Zoo Story: 312, 315
Success and Failure
    Glengarry Glen Ross: 44
    'night, Mother: 151
Suicide
    Crimes of the Heart: 3-4
    'night, Mother: 146-148,
        151-157
Supernatural
    The Rez Sisters: 204
Suspense
    The Mousetrap: 135, 137

T

Time and Change
    Inherit the Wind: 54-57, 60-62

The Miracle Worker: 115-116
Tone
    Waiting for Godot: 281-283

U

Uncertainty
    *Rosencrantz and Guildenstern Are
        Dead:* 225-227

V

Victim and Victimization
    Twilight: Los Angeles, 1992: 243
Violence and Cruelty
    Crimes of the Heart: 8

W

War, the Military, and Soldier Life
    Crimes of the Heart: 10
    *for colored girls who have
        considered suicide/when the
        rainbow is enuf:* 21, 28
    Inherit the Wind: 56, 58, 61-63
    The Mousetrap: 136-137
    The Odd Couple: 171-173
    *Rosencrantz and Guildenstern Are
        Dead:* 223
    Twilight: Los Angeles, 1992: 235-
        236, 244-245
    Visit to a Small Planet: 255-266
    Waiting for Godot: 277-278
    Wedding Band: 297-299
Wealth
    The Zoo Story: 309, 311-314
Wealth and Poverty
    Long Day's Journey into Night:
        75
    The Zoo Story: 312
Wildlife
    Inherit the Wind: 55, 61